STUDIES IN EVANGELICAL HISTORY AND THOUGHT

A Fragile Unity

Anti-Ritualism and the Division of Anglican
Evangelicalism in the Nineteenth Century

STUDIES IN EVANGELICAL HISTORY AND THOUGHT

A Fragile Unity

Anti-Ritualism and the Division of Anglican Evangelicalism in the Nineteenth Century

James C. Whisenant

Foreword by
Dale A. Johnson

Copyright © James C. Whisenant 2003

First published 2003 by Paternoster

Paternoster is an imprint of Authentic Media,
PO Box 6326, Bletchley, Milton Keynes, MK1 9GG

authenticmedia.co.uk

The right of James C. Whisenant to be identified as the Author of this Work has been asserted by him in accordance with Copyright, Designs and Patents Act 1988.

All rights reserved. No part of this publication may be reproduced, stored in a retrieval system, or transmitted in any form or by any means, electric, mechanical, photocopying, recording or otherwise, without the prior permission of the publisher or a license permitting restricted copying. In the U.K. such licenses are issued by the Copyright Licensing Agency, Barnard's Inn, 86 Fetter Lane, London, EC4A 1EN

British Library Cataloguing in Publication Data
A catalogue record for this book is available from the British Library

ISBN 978-1-84227-105-6

Typeset by Susan Carlson Wood, Pasadena, CA, U.S.A.
Printed and bound by Lightning Source

STUDIES IN EVANGELICAL HISTORY AND THOUGHT

Series Preface

The Evangelical movement has been marked by its union of four emphases: on the Bible, on the cross of Christ, on conversion as the entry to the Christian life and on the responsibility of the believer to be active. The present series is designed to publish scholarly studies of any aspect of this movement in Britain or overseas. Its volumes include social analysis as well as exploration of Evangelical ideas. The books in the series consider aspects of the movement shaped by the Evangelical Revival of the eighteenth century, when the impetus to mission began to turn the popular Protestantism of the British Isles and North America into a global phenomenon. The series aims to reap some of the rich harvest of academic research about those who, over the centuries, have believed that they had a gospel to tell to the nations.

Series Editors

David Bebbington, Professor of History, University of Stirling, Stirling, Scotland, UK

John H.Y. Briggs, Senior Research Fellow in Ecclesiastical History and Director of the Centre for Baptist History and Heritage, Regent's Park College, Oxford, UK

Timothy Larsen, Associate Professor of Theology, Wheaton College, Illinois, USA

Mark A. Noll, McManis Professor of Christian Thought, Wheaton College, Wheaton, Illinois, USA

Ian M. Randall, Deputy Principal and Lecturer in Church History and Spirituality, Spurgeon's College, London, UK, and a Senior Research Fellow, International Baptist Theological Seminary, Prague, Czech Republic

Contents

Foreword xiii
Preface xv

Chapter 1
Introduction 1
    Historical Background 2
    Secondary Literature 4
    Focus and Sources of this Study 6
    Outline of the Work 7

Chapter 2
Anti-Ritualism at Mid-Century 16
    The First Ritualist Controversies 17
    The Gorham Case 20
    Papal Aggression 23
    Evening Mission Services 25
    St. George's-in-the-East 27
    Auricular Confession 30
    The Growth of Divisions 33
    Evangelical Unity 37

Chapter 3
The Growth of Partisanship in the 1860s 78
    An Interlude in the Ritualist Controversy:
        The Threat of Rationalism 79
    The Church Association and the Growth of
        Anti-Ritualist Sentiment 81
    The Beginning of Ritualist Prosecutions and
        Episcopal Moderation 85
    Early Opposition to Litigation 88
    The Ritual Commission 90
    The Growing Opposition to Ritualism 92
    A New Rationalist Threat and Party Divisions 95

Chapter 4
The Early Prosecutions: Results and Reactions 129
    The Mackonochie Case 131
    The Purchas Case 135
    The Problem of Compliance 136
    Episcopal Influence and Authority 139
    The Spreading Influence of Ritualism 143
    Questioning Litigation and Evangelical Party Unity 149

Chapter 5
Anti-Ritualism and Evangelical Church Relations 182
    Evangelical Perspectives on Convocation 183
    Church Congresses 187
    Diocesan Synods 195
    Special Mission Services 197
    Anti-Ritualism and the Moderate Section of the
        High Church Party 202

Chapter 6
**The Public Worship Regulation Act:
Context and Reactions** 231
    The Bennett Judgment and Its Impact 232
    The Limits of Episcopal Authority 236
    The Public Worship Regulation Act of 1874 237
    Reactions to the Public Worship Regulation Act 240
    The Ridsdale Judgment 245

Chapter 7
The Impact of the Early Imprisonments 281
    The First Ritualist in Prison: Arthur Tooth 282
    Questioning the Future of the Church Association 284
    The Imprisonment of Dale and Enraght 287
    Episcopal Influence and Opinion 289
    The Five Deans' Memorial 296
    The Growing Division among Evangelicals over
        Litigation 299

Contents

Chapter 8
The Decline of the Anti-Ritualist Movement..........................337
    Evangelical Reactions to the Growing Influence of
        Ritualism 338
    The Case of Sidney Green and Its Repercussions 343
    The Mackonochie Case Revisited................................349
    The Moderation of Evangelical Opinions.......................352
    The Ecclesiastical Courts Commission...........................357
    The Last Ritualist in Prison: James Bell Cox.....................359

Chapter 9
The End of Litigation 404
    The Continuation of Partisan Tensions.............................405
    The Prosecution of Bishop King and Evangelical
        Divisions..410
    The Protestant Churchmen's Alliance...............................414
    The Lincoln Judgment and the Appeal............................417
    The Judicial Committee Verdict and Evangelical
        Reactions 422

Chapter 10
The Division of the Evangelical Party 460
    Challenges to the Policy and Position of the
        Church Association..460
    A New Direction for the Evangelical Party.......................465
    Conclusion..469

Chapter 11
Appendices 483
A. Protest of the Clergy of the Diocese of London (1867).....483
B. Ritualist Remonstrance to the Purchas Judgment
    (1871)..484
C. Letter of the Evangelical Union For Church Reform
    (1874)..484
D. Report of the Committee of the Upper House of
    Convocation On the Revival of Diocesan Synods
    (1867)..485

E. Protest of Ritual Innovations in Missions Services (1874) 486
F. Questions Submitted by the Council of the Church Association to Its Local Branches Regarding Its Future Policy (1873) 486
G. Memorial to the Bishops Urging the Suppression of the Ritualists (1873) 487
H. Clerical Memorial on Eucharistic Vestments and the Eastward Position (1875) 488
I. Memorial of the Church Association to the Upper House of Convocation On Eucharistic Vestments and the Eastward Position (1875) 488
J. Five Deans' Memorial to the Archbishop of Canterbury (1881) 490
K. Evangelical Counter-Memorial to the Five Deans (1881) 491
L. The Church Association: Its Past Action and Future Policy (1880) 492
M. Response of the Upper House of Convocation to a Memorial Adopted by the Lower House Regarding the Imprisonment of Rev. S. F. Green (1881) 505
N. Memorial of the Church Association Protesting the Report of the Royal Commission on Ecclesiastical Courts (1884) 506
O. Private Circular On the Church Missionary Society (1888) 507
P. Church Association Memorial Protesting the St. Paul's Reredos (1888) 508
Q. Church Association Advertisement: 'Special Appeal for Funds' 509
R. Protest Declaration of the Church Association (1889) 511
S. Resolution of the Protestant Churchmen's Alliance (1889) 512
T. Advertisement Declaring the Objects of the Protestant Churchmen's Alliance (1889) 513

U. Church Association Protest Regarding the Judgment
of the Judicial Committee of the Privy Council in
the Lincoln Case (1892) 514
V. Advertisement of the Church Association (1892) 514

Bibliography 517
    Primary Sources 517
    Secondary Sources 521

Index of Persons and Subjects 525

Foreword

In the work that has appeared in the last generation on nineteenth-century Anglican Evangelicalism, the great majority has focused on the first half, where its emergence as a definable party within the Church of England, its engagement with issues of social reform, and its remarkable range of clergy and lay leadership have been prominent topics of investigation. This has been set against the generally dismissive judgments of an earlier generation of scholarship, which tended to see Evangelicalism in terms of its more moralistic tone. More recently, a number of scholars have turned to twentieth-century developments within the party, as much for advocacy purposes as for exploring the reasons behind its renewed vitality and popular appeal. The period that has received the least attention is the half-century or more after the emergence of the Oxford Movement and the activity called ritualism that developed from those beginnings. It is that period and those issues that James C. Whisenant explores here.

The story of the conflicts, debates, and litigation within the Church of England over such issues as clergy vestments and liturgical observance, representing over time the declining influence of the Evangelical party in the second half of the nineteenth century, is not an especially uplifting saga. But besides the balance that this investigation offers in relation to the numerous studies of ritualism that focus on the advocates and ignore the opponents, Whisenant offers insights into the several groups within Evangelicalism and the shifting strategies of its opposition to the increasingly militant ritualist party. With a special focus on the periodical literature, he is able to uncover the multiple threads of the debate within the Church of England and the country at large over ritualism. Equally significant is that he puts these many threads into a framework that enables a reader to emerge with genuine understanding of the issues, the effect of the conflict on the Evangelical party, and the import of all of it on the Church of England.

Surely this side is equally as important as the more stirring beginnings, especially as it offers a better perspective on the contentious nineteenth century. Whisenant's study thus fills a notable lacuna in the literature in two respects, and by doing so it will enable other scholars to pursue further dimensions of the Evangelical world.

Dale A. Johnson
Vanderbilt University
May 2002

PREFACE

I owe a debt of gratitude to many people for their assistance and support in the successful completion of this work. Professor Dale A. Johnson has been an understanding advisor throughout the course of my doctoral studies and an insightful critic. The final product has been immeasurably improved by his sage advice. The other members of my dissertation committee have also provided a great deal of guidance and help. I would also like to thank the Graduate School at Vanderbilt University which provided monetary assistance in the form of a Dissertation Enhancement Award which enabled me to travel to England for research. Portions of the research presented here were published earlier in *Anglican and Episcopal History* (December 2001). The Historical Society of the Episcopal Church has graciously given their permission to reprint that work here. I would be remiss to omit my gratitude to my wife and children for their continued support and patience when hours of research and writing took time away from more important matters.

By way of dedication, I would like to thank Gary B. McGee, John R. Fitzmier, and Dale A. Johnson. They are three wonderful teachers who have greatly influenced the course of my studies. My work has been greatly enriched for having had the opportunity to study under them, and I count their friendship a blessing. Whatever substance or merit is to be found in my work owes much to their influence, and I gratefully dedicate this volume to them.

CHAPTER 1

Introduction

The purpose of this study is to describe the activities of the anti-Ritualists in the second half of the nineteenth century, and to evaluate the results and influence of their movement, focusing particularly on the involvement of Evangelicals and the impact that the movement had both on the party itself and on its place in the Church of England.[1] The central thesis of the work, in tracing the rise, progress and decline of anti-Ritualism, will be to suggest that it became an all-consuming passion for many Evangelicals; what became of the Evangelical party in the second half of the nineteenth century cannot be explained without reference to the events it precipitated and the bitter feelings it engendered, and the fragmentation of the fragile Evangelical unity is best understood as its most important result.

Evangelicals were by no means alone in their reaction to the ceremonial innovations introduced by the Ritualists. Many others within the Church of England were similarly disturbed by the activities and opinions of the extreme High Church section, but their responses were generally less strident and defensive. Evangelical anti-Ritualism, in contrast, was characterized by an increasingly reactionary and partisan rhetoric. The identification of their cause with Evangelicalism in general could not fail to have negative consequences for the party as the century wore on. The bitter tone of the anti-Ritualist movement ultimately weakened the influence of Evangelicals in the church and in society as a whole. In an era of popular support for the expansion of both religious and political toleration, anti-Ritualism came to be viewed as a relic of the intolerant past. Finally, the campaign resulted in the internal division of the loosely gathered Evangelical alliance. Moderates, no doubt influenced by their contemporaries, sought to move their party toward the center and argued that the real threat to the Christian faith came from its rational and secular critics. Conservatives, however, were unwilling to concede anything to the spirit of the age and were determined to maintain their stridently anti-Ritualist position at all costs. The result was a division that would continue for decades to come and further undermine the already diminished influence of the Evangelical party.

Historical Background

Unlike other more focused movements that arose in response to specific events or developed a characteristic theology around a central theme, as was the case with the Oxford Movement, Evangelicalism developed during the eighteenth century without a specific unifying program and often with a good deal of internal debate among its principal proponents. Arguments could become quite heated, as seen for example in disputes that arose with regard to the degree of one's churchmanship or the importance of Calvinist presuppositions. There was certainly a central core of doctrinal beliefs held in common by all orthodox Protestants, along with the particular emphasis on the necessity of a conversion experience that distinguished Evangelicals as a narrower group within that body, but there was little sense of a unified movement during the early years of development – no central organizations, no established leadership, and no party publications. The early Evangelicals were held together chiefly by their shared spiritual experiences and the opposition they faced from the ecclesiastical hierarchy.

By the early nineteenth century, Evangelicals had gained a degree of cohesion with the rise of the Clapham Sect, a loosely gathered group of moral and social reformers who came to be identified chiefly with the crusade against slavery. William Wilberforce provided Evangelicalism with an attractive voice and personality, and various societies were formed to pursue goals that were widely supported.[2] With the formation of such organizations and the establishment of the first substantial Evangelical periodical, the *Christian Observer* (established in 1802), one can begin to speak of an Evangelical alliance or 'party' in some sense. These voluntary party organizations gave the movement a sense of unity previously unknown. It is probably no accident that the early Evangelicals, filled with a sense of mission and having to pursue their goals against the established opposition of the ecclesiastical hierarchy, were particularly attractive to later historians; Wilberforce and the others of his era are the only Evangelicals who have been the subject of sustained scholarly attention.

What Wilberforce and the other early crusading Evangelicals could not provide for the movement, however, was a continuing sense of party unity. With the passing of the earlier generation, the movement seems to have lost both the leadership and the sense of common goals that held it together.³ It also lost a large number of adherents among the next generation to the Tractarians at Oxford. This shift was later interpreted as a sign of fundamental intellectual deficiencies within Evangelicalism, as well as an indication that the movement was already on the wane before the middle years of the nineteenth century.⁴ Whether or not the Evangelical party was in a state of decline so early in the nineteenth century, it certainly lost to the Oxford Movement many who might otherwise have become its intellectual leaders, including W. E. Gladstone, Henry Manning, and William Wilberforce's own sons.⁵

That movement, characterized by its *Tracts for the Times*, which were sponsored by Keble, Pusey, Newman, and their disciples, began as a defense of the church's spiritual autonomy in response to a perceived threat from reforms that it feared the government was going to impose. It developed, however, into a much broader call for the revival of catholic doctrinal emphases and liturgical practices. In the process it also reinvigorated the High Church party and spurred the development of an Evangelical reaction. Many Protestants, including a number of bishops, were troubled by the direction taken by the Tractarians, but Evangelicals were particularly disturbed.⁶ The Oxford disciples elaborated a doctrine of the church that emphasized the role of the clergy – the parish priests stood as mediators between God and the laity, and the bishops constituted the very foundation of the church. Evangelicals countered by emphasizing the Reformation doctrine of the priesthood of all believers. Further, they placed little value on the office of the bishop, particularly since it was a position held by few of their own. The Tractarians also emphasized the importance of the church as the dispenser of the sacraments through which God imparted grace to all. Evangelicals, however, were more likely to view the church as a voluntary association of believers who had each received grace individually during their own conversion experiences.

Historically, the distinctive sections within the Church of England, often characterized as High, Low, and Broad, were allowed a wide degree of latitude so long as they did not appear to pose a radical threat to either the church's doctrinal or liturgical traditions.⁷ The bishops, in reality, had little effective means of curbing excesses among the clergy that fell short of heresy, and in practice, they often avoided any interference that might give the appearance of taking sides in a partisan dispute. But increasingly, ecclesiastical combatants began to question the legitimacy of their opponents' position within the church. Their contrasting theological perspectives, combined with the growth of partisan machinery, set the stage for the development of the controversy over Ritualism in the second half of the century. Evangelicals, who had suffered at the hands of a number of bishops in the early years of their movement, initially had few allies in high ecclesiastical positions. They were drawn together by the continuing enmity they faced from High Church critics such as Bishop Philpotts of Exeter, who condemned as heresy the low view of baptismal regeneration espoused by the Evangelical George Gorham. Still, the party lacked an organization that could serve as a unifying center, and neither Lord Shaftesbury, who came to prominence as a social reformer, nor J. B. Sumner, who became Archbishop of Canterbury in 1848, took upon themselves the role of party leader.[8] Throughout the years of controversy to come, Evangelicals would frequently lament the divisions within their party while often expressing the fear that their opponents were more unified and better organized.

Anti-Catholicism had been a potent force in English history since the Reformation, and its resurgence in the nineteenth century only encouraged the development of partisan feelings. Protestants feared for the establishment in the years following Roman Catholic emancipation in 1829, and many were disturbed by the apparently Romeward tendencies of the Oxford Movement. The origins of anti-Ritualism can be traced to the long-established tradition of anti-Catholicism that Evangelicals shared with most other Protestants.[9] As the successors of the Oxford Movement, the Ritualists elaborated the theological and liturgical implications of that movement in ways that could never have been imagined by its original proponents and were widely believed to be undermining the Protestant foundation of the Anglican church. Their opponents believed they were attempting to undo the Reformation and to return the Church of England to a Roman conception of the Mass. That perception was the fundamental motivation for the anti-Ritualist movement, and it was shared by most Protestants. Over the course of the second half of the century, however, the Evangelical party was increasingly divided over the controversial methods and strident tone adopted by the more conservative section, with the final result being the division of the party and a general decline in its influence.

Secondary Literature

The rise of Evangelicalism, the work of William Wilberforce and the Clapham Sect, and, to a lesser degree, the life and work of Anthony Ashley Cooper, the Seventh Earl of Shaftesbury have all been well covered by historians. Very little, however, has been written on the state of the movement in the second half of the nineteenth century.

Introduction

Several factors might account for this relative dearth of historical interest. First, no significant leaders emerged during the latter part of the century who were able to galvanize party support or were imminently compelling figures, and it has generally been assumed by historians that Evangelicalism was by then a movement in decline. Perhaps the most prominent figure in the party and one whose voice was most likely to gain widespread support, was J. C. Ryle, who published hundreds of widely read tracts and became the first Bishop of Liverpool in 1880. Ryle has attracted some interest among Evangelical historians, but neither he nor the other Evangelical bishops of the period have been the focus of the concentrated study they deserve. A second factor might be the failure of Evangelicals to produce any works of creative brilliance or lasting significance, despite the fact that the second half of the century was a time of great theological development, as scholars attempted to come to terms with the rise of new critical methods and the implications of scientific discoveries. In contrast, many of the most prominent thinkers and church leaders of the age came out of the High Church tradition, and their work has continued to attract attention. Finally, and largely as a consequence of their role in the Ritualist controversy, the Evangelical party, at least in terms of popular perception, suffered from a largely negative reputation during the second half of the nineteenth century. Although Evangelicals were concerned with other causes, and their many societies continued to pursue varied evangelistic and social interests, anti-Ritualism became the principal focus and that on which their reputation was established. For better or for worse, Evangelicalism came largely to be identified with a message of protest and opposition.

There have been several studies of the Ritualist movement and the controversy that grew around it, but none has explored the role of Evangelicals in any substance or considered the impact the controversy had on their party.[10] And there have been no significant studies that focus particularly either on the role and motivation of Evangelical anti-Ritualism or on the results that followed from it. Several older surveys of nineteenth-century Evangelicalism are frequently cited in the literature, but they are largely uncritical studies written from within the movement, and they tend to focus on the more positive aspects of the party while downplaying the place of the Ritualist controversy.[11] Two more recent surveys of Evangelicalism are somewhat useful and deal with the movement more critically, but they also have distinct limitations and deal with issues involved in the Ritualist controversy only briefly.[12] Other works have indicated a renewed interest in nineteenth-century Evangelicalism in recent years, and several excellent monographs have been published, but none have focused particularly on the period at hand or the theme of this dissertation.[13]

Focus and Sources of this Study

This study will examine the efforts and concerns of the anti-Ritualist movement from the relatively unreported perspective of the Evangelical party. Details of various events such as conflicts in churches, court proceedings, legislation, and protests presented to the bishops and Parliament will be recounted insofar as it is necessary to present readers with a coherent narrative. The central emphasis, however, will be to focus on the role played by the Evangelicals and to consider what impact the controversy ultimately had within the party. It will be suggested here that, for all of their other work in missionary and social endeavors, concern over the spread of Ritualism came to dominate the interest of Evangelicals (certainly in public perception if not in reality), and division over the goals and methods that guided the anti-Ritualist effort were largely responsible for the fragmentation of the Evangelical party itself.

Evidence of the all-important nature of the controversy can be seen throughout the pages of the *Record* as one follows the story of the Evangelical party through the latter half of the nineteenth century. The *Record* was a weekly paper of Evangelical opinion begun in 1828, and it became the dominant journalistic voice of the party.[14] It also established itself as the advocate of a controversial and partisan Evangelicalism.[15] In the paper's editorial columns and news reports, one can follow the development of anti-Ritualism, the appeals made first to the episcopacy and then to the legislature and the courts, the growth of moderate opposition to the use of litigation after it resulted in the imprisonment of several Ritualist clergy, and, finally, the impact of the controversy on the unity of the Evangelical party. In addition to the opinions expressed by the editors of the paper itself, one can also find there detailed reports of speeches given by prominent Evangelicals at the meetings of party organizations and accounts of the episcopal charges given by the bishops to the clergy of their dioceses. Perhaps at least as important are the correspondence pages in which various letters appeared (many of which, unfortunately, followed the custom of the day and were published anonymously or over a pseudonym) either supporting or debating the editorial stance adopted by the paper itself, or arguing points made by other correspondents, or simply commenting on the state of affairs in the party or the church. The *Record* then serves as the primary source of material for this study, valuable for the expression

Introduction 7

of its own influential opinions, but equally important as the single best conduit of the broad spectrum of views within the Evangelical party on every issue of the day.

The *Times* of London is also an important source, both for the details of the major events of the controversy (including comprehensive summaries of the arguments presented in the various prosecutions and of the debates in Parliament and Convocation) and for a largely non-partisan editorial perspective to which the opinions of the *Record* can be compared. Although the *Times* was no friend of the Evangelical party and was often critical, it is worth noting that for many years it supported the anti-Ritualist movement in its editorial columns. Other journals of the period are also a useful source of further information and opinions representing all the parties in the Church. Periodicals such as the *Quarterly Review*, the *Contemporary Review*, the *Edinburgh Review* and the *Nineteenth Century*, among others, although generally secular in nature, published substantial articles showing a great breadth of theological and historical knowledge covering various aspects of the controversy. Finally, the mid-nineteenth century was a great age of pamphlet literature, and partisans on all sides of the debate published them by the hundreds. In their pamphlets, the protagonists could expand and elaborate upon the arguments found in newspaper articles and letters, while still responding to their opponents and critics, or the perceived crises of the day, more quickly than if they attempted to publish a book (and much more cheaply as well). Through these sources, one can trace the growth of the Ritualist controversy and the simultaneous shattering of a precarious Evangelical unity.

Outline of the Work

The first chapter describes the context of the development of the Ritualist controversy, looking particularly at early disturbances about the middle of the century and the growth of partisan divisions within the Church of England. Seen together with the seemingly resurgent threat from Roman Catholicism in 1850 and the challenge to Evangelical doctrine issued by Bishop Philpotts in the Gorham case, the rise of Ritualism appeared to Evangelicals to be yet another threat to the Protestant foundation of the national church. In this early stage of the controversy, however, neither side had yet developed into a party in the truest sense of the word, and disturbances, although sometimes violent, were largely seen as scattered incidents of a local nature. The second chapter traces the development of party organizations during the 1860s, with the consequent hardening of partisan divisions. In 1860, the Ritualists united under the banner of the English Church Union, and in 1865 their Evangelical opponents formed the Church Association. It became evident during the decade that the controversy had escalated beyond isolated parishes and threatened to divide the Church of England. The troubles could no longer be overlooked by ecclesiastical and political leaders, and the issues were considered first in the Convocation of Canterbury and then by a royal commission, but neither was able to arrive at any satisfactory settlement. Evidence of the growing chasm between the two parties can be seen in how they reacted to crises involving perceived threats to orthodoxy at the beginning and end of the decade. When *Essays and Reviews* was published in 1860, Evangelicals and their High Church opponents were able to set aside their differences for a time in order to face the threat of a common challenge. By the end of the decade, however, the two sides were hopelessly divided. When Frederick Temple was elevated to the episcopacy by Prime Minister Gladstone, most Evangelicals refused to even consider the possibility of a united protest. While acknowledging their common interests in this particular matter, Evangelical leaders refused to consider joining a committee headed by E. B. Pusey, lest they be viewed as sanctioning by association the validity of High Church teaching.

The third chapter deals with the early prosecutions brought by the anti-Ritualists. They first appealed to the courts in order to clarify the interpretation of the rubrics ordering the church's services, arguing that the Ritualists' innovations stood outside the legitimate limits imposed by those guidelines. The first two prominent cases involved A. H. Mackonochie and John Purchas. It was assumed by the anti-Ritualists that once the courts had ruled on the disputed points, the bishops would enforce the decisions and the Ritualists would comply. Events soon proved, however, that the rulings were ineffective. The Ritualists, following the example of Purchas, were unwilling to submit to the judgments of what they argued was a secular judiciary, and the bishops were largely unwilling to take decisive action that might appear to favor one party over the other. By the early 1870s it was evident that a few test cases would not suffice to halt the innovations. In addition, the use of prosecution served to escalate partisan feelings and further divide the groups involved. By then, Evangelicals had also begun to raise two new concerns – first, they were worried that the influence of the Ritualists was actually spreading and gaining popular support; and second, they were increasingly concerned about the unity of their own party, with some beginning to express the view that the Church Association, by its very nature a defensive and polemical organization, could not unite the Evangelical party.

Introduction

The fourth chapter deals with the impact of the anti-Ritualist movement on Evangelical church relations, particularly as seen in their interaction with those from other parties in the organized meetings that were developed shortly after mid-century. It was evident in their varying reactions to the renewal of Convocation, the rise of church congresses and diocesan synods, and also mission services to reach the urban masses, that a rift was developing between moderate and conservative Evangelicals. In each of those areas, moderates sensed that they needed to be involved in the broader life of the church if they were to have a positive influence and defend Evangelical interests. In contrast, conservatives viewed such involvement in an entirely negative light. It was argued that participation would only lend credence to their opponents' claim to a legitimate place in the church and would ultimately water down the distinctive Evangelical message. Over the course of the 1860s and 1870s, the moderates established their view, and it generally became the dominant one, but it also widened the fractures in the party.

The fifth chapter covers the high-water mark of the anti-Ritualist campaign in the mid-1870s. The Church Association's next significant appeal to the courts moved the controversy to the level of doctrine, charging William Bennett with heresy regarding his view of the Lord's presence in the sacramental elements. Bennett was acquitted, but the case served to gather opposition to the Ritualists and led to a general outcry against their unwillingness to be bound either by judicial rulings or episcopal admonitions. The result was the passage of the Public Worship Regulation Act in 1874. Anti-Ritualists believed that if the process were simplified and more Ritualists could be brought before the courts, their resolve would be worn down. It was evident during this period that even moderates within the High Church party were disturbed by the more extreme positions being adopted by the Ritualists, and there were some calls for a coalition movement. The High Church moderates, however, were opposed to litigation and urged Evangelicals to pursue less divisive methods. Ultimately, the two sides could never overcome their differences, but one effect was to cause moderate Evangelicals to reconsider their party's use of prosecution. The period ended with the first prosecution under the Public Worship Regulation Act in 1876. Charles Ridsdale was convicted of using ceremonies previously condemned by the courts, but he repudiated the authority of the court and refused to be bound by its ruling. Ridsdale was finally convinced to submit through the personal intercession of Archbishop Tait, but his example established the pattern for the next stage of the controversy.

The next two chapters deal with the Ritualist prosecutions that ended in imprisonment and the decline of the anti-Ritualist movement. The sixth chapter covers the first three cases. Arthur Tooth was the first to be imprisoned for contempt of court in 1877. He spent only a month in jail, however, before his conviction was overturned on a technicality. His case, however, had little effect on the anti-Ritualist movement. They continued to believe it was the best means for halting the activities of their opponents, and even the secular press argued that Tooth alone was responsible for his fate. At the same time, however, it was evident that the influence of the Ritualists was spreading and some of their moderate innovations were being adopted even in Evangelical parishes. A few moderates expressed their opposition to further prosecution, but the leaders of the Church Association refused to reconsider their goals or policies. The imprisonment of Tooth also raised questions concerning the power of the episcopacy. While the ability of the bishops to restrain the Ritualists remained in doubt, they were increasingly opposed to further appeals to the courts and began to exercise their authority to veto proceedings. In 1880, T. P. Dale and R. W. Enraght were both imprisoned for several months. Their cases did a great deal of damage to the anti-Ritualist movement and further divided the Evangelical party. The *Record* continued to lend its editorial weight to the Church Association, but acknowledged that there was growing concern about further prosecution. The paper also published letters from two prominent Evangelicals, Francis Close and Samuel Garrett, who were sharply critical of the proceedings.

The seventh chapter covers the final imprisonments. The imprisonment of Sydney Green, which lasted for a year and a half in 1881-82, largely sealed the fate of the anti-Ritualist campaign. Thereafter, the bishops were almost entirely opposed to litigation that might end in imprisonment and vetoed most of the cases. At least as troubling, for moderates, was the decision of the Church Association to impound Green's household goods to pay the court costs. That decision finally turned the *Record*, with all of its editorial influence, against the movement. The Green case also led to the appointment of a royal commission to consider the ecclesiastical courts. They reached a non-partisan conclusion in their report, but the divided state of the church gave Parliament little encouragement to act. The final Ritualist to be imprisoned was James Bell Cox of Liverpool, who was briefly jailed in 1887. Permission to proceed with that case was given by the Evangelical bishop, J. C. Ryle, who was strongly opposed to the episcopal veto as a matter of principle and refused intervene. But neither he nor most Evangelicals had any sympathy for the case, and it had little impact other than to further alienate the conservative section.

The final chapter brings the controversial history of anti-Ritualist litigation to a close. There were two final cases involving the erection of an ornamental reredos in St. Paul's Cathedral and the Church Association's prosecution of Edward King, the Bishop of Lincoln. The power of the veto was upheld in the St. Paul's case, when Bishop Temple refused to allow the proceedings to go forward even though they were not directed against any particular clergy but simply challenged the right of the Dean and Chapter to make changes in the cathedral. The case had a secondary importance in that it brought to the surface a long standing debate over the Church Missionary Society. That organization held a service in the cathedral shortly after the reredos was erected, and conservatives charged its leaders with a compromise of fundamental principles. The dispute served to illustrate the depth of the divisions within the party. The final case was the prosecution of Bishop King in 1889. The case was heard by Archbishop Benson, who ruled almost entirely in King's favor and overturned several previous decisions handed down by the Judicial Committee of the Privy Council. Throughout the proceedings the *Record* protested that the conservative section conducting the litigation represented the interests of only that small minority which supported the Church Association, but the damage to the party's reputation was already done.

The impact of the anti-Ritualist movement on the Evangelical party can be seen throughout the second half of the nineteenth century, and it played a significant part in the declining influence of the party. Its impact can be seen in the failure, despite repeated efforts, to found an organization capable of gathering the support of a majority of Evangelicals. It can also be traced in divisions between conservatives and moderates with regard to Evangelical participation in mixed church meetings at which their opponents were present, such as church congresses and diocesan conferences, both of which became increasingly important in the life of the church during the second half of the century. Moderates finally rejected the methods and the tone of the anti-Ritualists, arguing that Evangelicals needed to return to the positive interests of the early movement and turn away from their preoccupation with bitter, partisan controversy – but not before the anti-Ritualist movement had divided their party and left it with little influence in the church.

Notes

1 Since this study will be restricted to the movement within the Church of England, the terms 'Evangelical' and 'Evangelical party,' unless otherwise noted, will be limited to those within the Anglican communion. In keeping with the usage of the nineteenth century, labels indicating a party affiliation within the Church of England (e.g., Evangelical, Ritualist, High Church, etc.) will be capitalized.

2 The most important and widely supported societies were those with evangelistic aims. The two most prominent throughout the nineteenth century were the Church Missionary Society (established in 1799) and the British and Foreign Bible Society (established in 1804).

3 In his study of Anglican leaders, David Edwards suggested that Lord Shaftesbury was 'the most prominent Evangelical statesman at a time when there was no major Evangelical thinker, with the result that the leadership of that party's many organizations largely devolved on him while the leadership of the party's intellectual life went by default.' David L. Edwards, *Leaders of the Church of England: 1828-1944* (Oxford: Oxford University Press, 1971), p. 133.

4 That view was widely established by W. E. Gladstone in his 1879 essay, 'The Evangelical Movement: Its Parentage, Progress, and Issue,' *British Quarterly Review* 70 (1879): 1-14. Gladstone had himself been raised in an Evangelical home but came under the influence of the Oxford Movement. His thesis was adopted and elaborated upon by later historians; cf. George W. E. Russell, *A Short History of the Evangelical Movement* (London: A. R. Mowbray & Co., 1915), pp. 90-95; and Yngve Brilioth, in *Three Lectures on Evangelicalism and the Oxford Movement* (London: Oxford University Press, 1934).

The idea of a decline in the Evangelical movement, however, predated Gladstone's work. As early as 1843, the *Record*, an Evangelical paper that was establishing itself as the popular voice of the party, felt compelled to address the subject in an editorial. The paper suggested that the Tractarians over-estimated their own influence and mistakenly assumed that they were drawing the brightest of the younger generation into their circles. The *Record* noted that the notion was 'warmly entertained in many quarters.' The paper continued, 'Thus a noted Archdeacon of the London diocese, observed a short time since, that "at least the Tractarians have done *one* good thing – they have broken up the evangelical party"'... A London newspaper in the same interest, describes Mr. M'Neile as "a leader of a small and *rapidly decreasing* party".' (Their italics.) In contrast, the paper suggested that Evangelicals had, in fact, made great advances. Cited as evidence was the multiplication of Evangelical clergy in the metropolitan areas, as well as the growing circulation of the *Record* itself. It had grown from only about 1,000 subscribers in the early 1830s to 3,274 in 1843, and its circulation was now comparable to that of other evening papers. The *Standard* had 3,333 subscribers, and the *Globe* had 3,154. *Record*, 30 March 1843.

5 The stories of the Wilberforce children and Henry Manning, their move-

Introduction 13

ment away from Evangelicalism and their eventual separation over Catholicism, is poignantly recounted in David Newsome, *The Wilberforces and Henry Manning* (Cambridge: Harvard University Press, 1966).

6 Peter Toon has described the development of Evangelical theology in reaction to the catholic elements of the Oxford Movement in *Evangelical Theology, 1833-1856: A Response to Tractarianism* (Atlanta: John Knox Press, 1979).

7 The inclusion of Evangelicals under the heading of Low Church did not occur until well into the nineteenth century, and often the appelation was used by their critics in a pejorative sense, since the Low Church section was traditionally accused of spiritual apathy. The classic study of church parties in the middle of the nineteenth century is W. J. Conybeare, 'Church Parties,' in *Essays Ecclesiastical and Social*, reprinted, with additions, from the *Edinburgh Review* (London: Longman, Brown, Green, and Longman, 1855).

8 In his somewhat devotional history of the Evangelical party, H. C. G. Moule divided the century into three periods. He dealt with the second (roughly the late 1830s to the early 1880s) as 'the times of Shaftesbury,' suggesting that he was the dominant figure of the period. Interestingly, Moule scarcely mentioned Archbishop Sumner. H. C. G. Moule, *The Evangelical School in the Church of England* (London: James Nisbet & Co., 1901), pp. 36-50.

9 There is a large body of literature dealing with the general subject of anti-Catholicism in Victorian England. The best work on nineteenth-century Evangelical anti-Catholicism in particular is John Wolffe, *The Protestant Crusade in Great Britain: 1829-1860* (Oxford: Oxford University Press, 1991).

10 Nigel Yates wrote a brief but significant pamphlet on the relationship of Ritualism to the Oxford Movement; cf., *The Oxford Movement and Anglican Ritualism* (London: The Historical Association, 1983). James Bentley has surveyed and explained the political and legislative side of the controversy, and in doing so, dealt with Evangelical involvement in applying political pressure and influencing Parliament in his work, *Ritualism and Politics in Victorian Britain* (Oxford: Oxford University Press, 1978). Peter T. Marsh studied the place of Archbishop Tait and his response to the controversy in his book *The Victorian Church in Decline: Archbishop Tait and the Church of England, 1868-1882* (London: Routledge & Kegan Paul, 1969). The most recent study, and the most comprehensive work on the Ritualist movement, is John Shelton Reed, *Glorious Battle: The Cultural Politics of Victorian Anglo-Catholicism* (Nashville: Vanderbilt University Press, 1996). Most surveys of the Victorian church deal with the Ritualist controversy to some degree, but in terms of their treatment of the Evangelical party's involvement, all suffer in varying degrees, from the limitations of space or the biases of the respective authors. Owen Chadwick's two-volume work is by far the best survey available. He was generally fair in his treatment of Evangelicals, but his interests clearly lay with the High Church tradition. Cf. Owen Chadwick, *The Victorian Church: Parts One (3rd ed.) and Two (2nd ed.)* (London: A. & C. Black, 1971-72). Of other surveys, Desmond Bowen devoted a relatively large amount of space to Ritualism but was quite unsympathetic in his treatment of Evangelicals; *The Idea of the Victorian Church* (Montreal: McGill University Press, 1968).

11 G. R. Balleine, *A History of the Evangelical Party in the Church of England*, 3rd

ed., with an Appendix covering 1900-1950, by G. W. Bromiley (London: Church Book Room Press, 1951); Leonard Elliott-Binns, *The Evangelical Movement in the English Church* (Garden City: Doubleday, Doran & Co., 1928); Moule, *Evangelical School in the Church of England*; and George W. E. Russell, *A Short History of the Evangelical Movement* (London: A. R. Mowbray & Co., 1915). Interestingly, these works as well, because they tended to focus on great personalities and leaders, covered the early years of the Evangelical movement much more thoroughly than the second half of the nineteenth century. And in general, they tended to look for an Evangelical organization or movement on which to focus during that period, such as the Church Missionary Society or the Church Pastoral-Aid Society.

12 D. W. Bebbington, *Evangelicalism in Modern Britain: A History from the 1730s to the 1980s* (London: Unwin Hyman, 1989) is an excellent study of both Anglican and Nonconformist Evangelicalism. It is the best recent work, but because Bebbington covered the broader scope of the whole movement, he was unable to devote much space to Anglicans in general or anti-Ritualism in particular. Kenneth Hylson-Smith, *Evangelicals in the Church of England: 1734-1984* (Edinburgh: T. & T. Clark, 1988) is a less useful study. For the eighteenth and nineteenth centuries, much of Hylson-Smith's research is derived from secondary materials, mostly the works cited in the previous footnote.

13 John Wolffe's previously cited study of anti-Catholicism deals most nearly with the issues considered here, but his work stopped shortly after mid-century and did not attempt to cover the Ritualist controversy. That was also the case with Peter Toon's work on the response of Evangelicals to the Oxford Movement. Other recent works are Boyd Hilton, *The Age of Atonement: The Influence of Evangelicalism on Social and Economic Thought: 1795-1865* (Oxford: Oxford University Press, 1988); and Donald M. Lewis, *Lighten Their Darkness: The Evangelical Mission to Working-Class London, 1828-1860* (Westport: Greenwood Press, 1986).

14 The paper struggled for several years, but came into its own under the editorial guidance of the conservative and opinionated Alexander Haldane. He later became the primary owner and directed the paper for the next half-century. In 1882, with Haldane in failing health and no longer actively involved, the paper was transformed into a weekly (issued each Friday) of greater substance (up to twenty-four pages per issue from the eight it maintained when it was issued on Mondays, Wednesdays & Fridays). About the same time, it also adopted a much more moderate tone. For a general survey of the paper's history, cf. Josef L. Altholz, 'Alexander Haldane, the *Record*, and Religious Journalism,' *Victorian Periodicals Review* 20 (1987): 23-31.

15 In 1846, William Gresley wrote that it was 'the organ of the Evangelical party, and that by which a great part of the mischief which they do is effected. The Evangelicals, as a body, are responsible for what appears in the columns of that paper.... It is, in truth, the embodiment of the Evangelical party-spirit.' W. Gresley, *The Real Danger of the Church of England* (London: James Burns, 1846), p. 57.

In an 1868 article on church parties, the Broad Church moderate, E. H.

Plumptre, suggested that the Evangelical party had been 'singularly unfortunate in its representative organ in the press.' The *Record*, said Plumptre, was characterized chiefly by its lack of 'candour, manliness, and generosity... It has exaggerated whatever of narrowness and prejudice it found within the ranks of the party, and stirred them to a perpetual policy of suspicion and alarm.' E. H. Plumptre, 'Church Parties: Past, Present, and Future,' *Contemporary Review* 7 (1868): 331.

CHAPTER 2

Anti-Ritualism at Mid-Century

Disputes over the ritual and worship of the Church of England first arose in London in the early 1840s. Initially, only a few minor innovations were involved, and those were recommended by two bishops, first Blomfield in London and later Phillpots in Exeter. Neither could have foreseen the vehement and long-term consequences their support for the changes would provoke.[1] The clash of opponents with deeply held beliefs over seemingly insignificant alterations might have been dealt with peacefully during the early years of the debate. At the time, the successors to the Tractarians were only beginning to work out the ceremonial implications of their particular view of the catholic nature of the church, and Evangelicals were a loosely knit body with little sense of unity. The Protestant sensibilities of the latter were offended by the general direction of the Tractarian alterations, but neither side had yet developed into a full-fledged party or had a great deal at stake in the controversy. Circumstances and events, however, would combine to prevent either an early or an easy resolution. The Gorham case and 'papal aggression' exacerbated party divisions at mid-century and drove the two sides further apart. In the years that followed, continuing innovations, and particularly the reintroduction of auricular confession among some of the more extreme Tractarians, would further alienate the Protestants and set the parties on their respective paths of development. As points of conflict multiplied and ill-will grew, the issues involved became increasingly complicated, and resolution of the conflict became more difficult. The decades following saw the growth of partisan activities and rhetoric, with a corresponding escalation of the controversy, although nothing to come could match the explosive events during the summer of 1859, when riots broke out over ritual innovations introduced in the London parish of St. George's-in-the-East. Both the tone of the debate and the central issues were settled on during the 1840s and 50s, when Tractarians and Evangelicals first clashed and began to develop as church parties. Eventually, however, Evangelicals would discover that a party unity established in controversy was hard to maintain.

The First Ritualist Controversies

Disturbances over the alteration of liturgical observance and ceremonial dress first arose in London in 1842.[2] They were provoked by Bishop Blomfield who, in his annual charge to the clergy, decried the laxity among some clergy both in doctrine and in rubrical obedience. In doing so, he cited with approval the Tractarian emphasis on baptismal regeneration and 'a stricter discipline.' He acknowledged that in some cases they had gone too far, but he was equally disturbed by those critics who saw only the negative and 'overlooked the good that had been effected by these divines.'[3] With regard to the rubrics, Blomfield defended services on saints' days and lesser festivals, as well as the more frequent celebration of communion. He also acknowledged the support of ancient tradition, dating to Clement of Alexandria and Tertullian, for the practice of the priest facing eastward during the Eucharist.[4] And while disapproving of ornamental flowers on the altar, he was willing to permit candles provided that they were not burning 'except when the church is lighted up for evening service.'[5] Finally, Blomfield suggested that the priest should ascend to the pulpit directly from the altar without discarding his surplice.[6]

With his encouragement of these changes, Blomfield sought to raise the level of liturgical worship in London churches and rejected the concerns of those who suggested that the changes hinted at popery.[7] The Evangelical protest, however, finally forced Blomfield to acknowledge the controversy created by his decision. At confirmation proceedings in May 1843, he met with the London clergy and 'emphatically' criticized the Tractarians. In recommending some of their ceremonial innovations, Blomfield affirmed that he had only intended to prevent any occasion for reproach regarding 'laxity or departure from the Church's directions.'[8] The bishop also expressed his surprise that his charge had raised such great concern. Nevertheless, he reaffirmed his position and gave it the force of an injunction requiring clerical observance.[9] Within a week, however, the bishop issued a circular letter reversing his decision and leaving any changes to the discretion of the individual clergy. According to the *Record*, this change came after he met with the Evangelical clergy in the parish of Islington and after the *Quarterly Review*'s sharp criticism of the ritual innovations.[10]

The controversy continued for some months, however, and numerous memorials were drawn up by congregations disturbed by either the innovations or the perceived threat thereof. In Evangelical parishes, the memorialists reaffirmed their support for the traditional ceremony.[11] Elsewhere, resolutions were drawn up to protest changes made by clergy acting on the discretion given them by the bishop. One example was the parishes of Shoreditch and Ware, where the laity voiced their disapproval in the summer of 1843.[12] In early 1844, similar disputes were reported in the parishes of Great Ilford and East Farleigh.[13] It is difficult to ascertain, from the reports in the press, whether or not the memorialists represented the majority opinion in their respective parishes. The articles often reported that the entire congregation was in an uproar and that memorials had been unanimously adopted by the parishioners, but the clergy involved took a rather different view. In the case of Ware, Bishop Blomfield evidently believed that the complainants did not represent the majority opinion of the congregation. And the vicar at Great Ilford said in a meeting that he had informed Bishop Blomfield 'that the opposition to the credence-table proceeded from a "faction",' and that its removal 'was not generally desired by the communicants.'[14] Still, it was evident that there was substantial lay opposition to most alterations to the familiar service.

Henry Phillpotts, Bishop of Exeter, was the next to take up the question of the rubrics. Charges were brought by some of the parishioners of Helston against their curate, Walter Blunt, on a number of issues, but chiefly regarding his adoption of the surplice in the pulpit.[15] Phillpotts had little patience for the parishioners' concerns and supported Blunt in his strict adherence to the rubrics; in November 1844, he issued a pastoral letter requiring the surplice of all the clergy in the diocese of Exeter.[16] Phillpotts, however, had underestimated the fervor of the opposition to liturgical innovation and was unprepared for the reactions, which were even more vehement than had been the case in London.[17] By late November, Phillpotts was advising his clergy to be cautious and patient with their church members as they renewed their obedience to the rubric. Still, he thought the uproar over the use of the surplice irrational and required full compliance, believing that the only way to overcome the partisan feelings associated with its use was to require it of all the clergy.[18] Numerous protests and memorials were circulated, and by the end of December, the uproar forced Phillpotts to retract his demands. He still hoped to put an end to diversity in the services of the church, but for the time being he was willing to leave compliance to the discretion of the clergy.[19]

The controversy continued into the following year with more than 1,850 church members signing a memorial to the Mayor of Exeter in which they requested that he call a meeting for the purpose of petitioning the queen concerning the innovations. The *Times* reported on the uproar and lent its support to the memorialists, whom it believed were 'all members of the Church, and all of a credible station in society.' The paper concluded that the meeting was a clear demonstration of the broad popular opposition to the 'inauspicious novelties' being introduced into the worship service.[20] Archbishop Howley later addressed the issue in a letter to 'the Clergy and Laity of his Province.' Taking a middle ground, he refused to question the motives of either of the parties. But unlike Phillpotts, he did not ridicule those who strongly opposed the innovations.[21] Howley affirmed the need for uniformity in the services of the church but did not think it worth the price of lasting division; he was therefore willing to allow for varying degrees of ritual in different congregations until some satisfactory compromise could be obtained.[22] Nevertheless, peace was not easily found. The clergy of St. Sidwell's, Exeter, continued in the use of the surplice in the pulpit and there followed a series of riots that continued through January 1845. Phillpotts initially refused to intervene but was finally goaded to respond by Edward Woolmer, the mayor of the city, who convinced the bishop to request that the curate return to the black gown.[23]

During the course of the dispute in Exeter, the *Record* was pleased to note that the *Times* had, for once, not given its complete support to the Tractarians and their disciples. In November, John Walter, the publisher, printed his correspondence concerning what he thought was the illegal introduction of a weekly offertory at his parish church.[24] Both Blomfield and Phillpotts had recommended that the offertory portion of the service, which had for some time been used only on communion Sundays, should be included each week. The change does not seem to have been clearly connected with other innovations more closely related to the central doctrines of the Tractarians, but it was introduced along with them during a period of heated debate, and it was widely attacked.[25] The *Record* took note of Walter's fruitless appeal to the Bishop of Oxford, and expressed the hope that he would reconsider his paper's editorial position in light of 'this practical acquaintance with the fruits of Tractarianism.'[26]

This first period of controversy over ritual innovation aroused sufficient public concern to bring about the demise of the Cambridge Camden Society. The society had been established in 1839, for the study of ecclesiastical art, but its emphasis on medieval architecture as a supplement to the revival of earlier forms of ritual elicited Evangelical protests and undesired attention.[27] As early as 1843, the *Record* was frequently criticizing the society and took great pleasure in noting that several bishops had withdrawn their support.[28] The controversy expanded when the society undertook the restoration of

St. Sepulchre's in Cambridge. In February 1844, the non-resident incumbent, R. R. Faulkner, solicited funds through advertisements in the Cambridge papers for the completion of the project, noting that he had been compelled to withdraw his sanction of the Camden Society's renovation of that church, as a result of their having 'introduced a stone altar without his knowledge or consent; and having also, in addition, put in a credence, *in open and direct opposition to his will, and in defiance of him.*'[29] Francis Close, the influential Evangelical incumbent of Holy Trinity, Cheltenham, later attacked the society from his pulpit with a sermon entitled 'The Restoration of Churches is the Restoration of Popery.'[30] He suggested that the Cambridge group was teaching the same false doctrine as the Oxford Tractarians 'in a still more plausible and attractive form, namely, under the plea of reviving church architecture.' The popery that had been taught 'analytically' at Oxford was now being promulgated 'artistically' at Cambridge.[31] To emphasize the outward forms of ritual and architecture in worship, said Close, was simply to fall back on the superstitious and idolatrous forms of medieval popery. The Camden Society sought to restore to their original condition churches built during the middle ages, and for Close, it necessarily followed 'that the *restoration of churches is the restoration of Popery.*'[32]

Faulkner had a great deal of public support for his position, including the editorial page of the *Times*.[33] According to the *Times*, the Protestant laity of the country had little sympathy for the extreme section of the High Church party, and it was only natural that the laity should express a 'wholesome alarm' at the perceived Romeward trend of the changes being made.[34] The article went on to accuse the Camden Society of disingenuous 'doubledealing' in its arrangements with Faulkner. He had been promised by the society that all changes would be subject to his approval; but having been assured that the communion table could be replaced if necessary, he later discovered that it had been destroyed by the society after the stone altar was installed.[35] Finally, the president of the Camden Society attended a vestry meeting at the church where he 'stimulated the parishioners to go to law to oppose the removal of the offensive additions, and even volunteered to pay the expenses of the lawsuit.'[36] The churchwardens, who supported the changes, sued Faulkner, and the consistory court decided in their favor. But after losing the initial decision, Faulkner won the case on appeal and the 'offensive medieval furniture' was removed.[37]

The Gorham Case

The contentious issues and atmosphere surrounding the Gorham case formed an important part of the context of the growing tensions between the Evangelical and High Church parties, and the case brought to a boil the long-simmering debate over the Anglican understanding of baptismal grace.[38] At the center of the controversy was George C. Gorham, whose view of baptism had raised suspicions even in the early years of his career (in 1811, Bishop Dampier of Ely had threatened not to ordain him). Nevertheless, in January 1846, Bishop Phillpotts of Exeter, a vehement anti-Evangelical, instituted him in the parish of St. Just-in-Penwith, Cornwall. Phillpotts shortly had cause to rebuke Gorham, however, when the new vicar advertised in the *Ecclesiastical Gazette* for a curate who was 'free from Tractarian error.'[39] When Gorham was presented by the Crown with the living of Brampford Speke in November 1847, he was told he would have to sit for a theological examination regarding his views on baptismal regeneration before a new license would be granted.[40] In fact, he was grilled with 149 questions, covering about 52 hours over eight days in December 1847 and March 1848.[41] On the 11th of March, Phillpotts ruled that Gorham's doctrine was unsound and refused to install him in the new parish. In his public protest, Gorham sought to expand the issue beyond Evangelical concerns about infant baptism and argued that the bishop had overstepped his disciplinary authority, an innovation which, if allowed to stand, would limit traditional clerical liberties.[42] Evangelicals were never a majority among the English clergy, and they did not often enjoy widespread support for their causes, but in this case they were joined by many moderate and Broad Church clergy who were anti-Tractarian or feared the narrowing of doctrinal positions (especially following the controversy over the appointment of Bishop Hampden in 1847-48).[43]

Gorham appealed to the Court of Arches of Canterbury.[44] In the intervening months, before the decision was handed down, both archbishops indicated that they were opposed to a narrow interpretation of baptismal regeneration.[45] Thomas Musgrave, the Archbishop of York, issued his annual charge to the clergy in July 1849, and indicated that the English Reformers had never intended to make only one view of baptismal regeneration the authoritative position of the Church of England.[46] In fact, said Musgrave, they had wisely avoided too precise a definition of the doctrine, excluding only 'the *ex opere operato* doctrine of the Church of Rome.' Their language was adopted largely from Martin Bucer, and, as was the case in his theology, 'the words were intended to express only the feelings of hope and charity. That our service is open to another mode of interpretation is, no doubt, understandable. And probably it was intended to be so by those who drew it up. But one can hardly deny that those who interpret it in the hypothetical sense approach the nearest to the mind of the Reformers.'[47] At the end of July, J. B. Sumner, the Archbishop of Canterbury, indicated his support for the Evangelical position when he preferred William Goode to the Rectory of All Hallows the Great, London.[48] Goode was the most prominent Evangelical theologian of the day and would shortly publish an extensive work on the doctrine of baptism in which he meticulously traced the historical background of the Anglican formularies and detailed the case against the doctrine of baptismal regeneration.[49]

On 2 August 1849, Sir Herbert Jenner Rust, the Dean of the Court of Arches ruled that baptismal regeneration was, in fact, the authoritative doctrine of the Church of England, and that Bishop Phillpotts had acted legally in refusing to license Gorham.[50] Gorham then appealed to the Judicial Committee of the Privy Council.[51] That court consisted of seven lay judges, with the two archbishops and Bishop Blomfield of London being asked to sit as assessors. The case created no small stir in the church. It became a rallying point for Evangelicals and helped to create a greater sense of common party interest, as the whole controversy was widely viewed as an attempt by the extreme High Church party to exclude them from the Church of England.[52] For the Tractarians, the case went beyond the basic question of Gorham's orthodoxy; of equal importance was the issue of whether or not a secular court should be able to overturn the decision of a church court involving a matter of doctrine.[53] On 8 March 1850, the Judicial Committee reversed the judgment handed down by the Arches Court, with only one of the lay judges and Bishop Blomfield dissenting.[54] The judges' ruling took a unique approach and, to a certain degree, attempted to avoid further complications by skirting the issue of a secular court ruling on church doctrine. Their reversal of the earlier decision was based not on the interpretation of doctrine but on the breadth of opinion that had been allowed historically in the Anglican church: 'In the examination of this case we have not relied upon the doctrinal opinions of any of the eminent writers by whose piety, learning and ability the Church of England has been distinguished; but it appears that opinions, which we cannot in any important particular distinguish from those entertained by Mr. Gorham, have been propounded and maintained, without censure or reproach, by many eminent and illustrious prelates and divines who have adorned the Church from the time when the Articles were first established.'[55]

The Judicial Committee's ruling elicited a wave of vehement protests from the High Church party.[56] A 'meeting of the clergy and laity' was held in July to discuss the situation, and a petition was circulated condemning the decision and calling on Queen Victoria to allow the church a measure of spiritual self-determination through the revival of Convocation.[57] A petition with 2700 signatures was presented to the Archbishop of Canterbury by the Metropolitan Church Union, asking him to refrain from instituting Gorham. Archbishop Sumner replied that there were no grounds for him legally to overrule the Judicial Committee in that way.[58] Bishop Phillpotts of Exeter also published a pamphlet in which he repudiated the decision, reiterated his refusal to institute to Gorham, and came close to accusing the Archbishop of Canterbury of heresy.[59] The outcome of the case ultimately led to a wave of secessions to Rome; many of the extreme Tractarians were unable to tolerate the Evangelical view of baptism and even less willing to accept its legitimization by what they believed was a secular court.[60]

Papal Aggression

With the 'Papal Aggression' of 1850, the position of the Evangelical party in relation to their High Church opponents was suddenly reversed, and the Tractarians were forced to defend their position in the church, as they were widely blamed for having at least indirectly inspired the papal encroachment.[61] Ironically, it was Bishop Blomfield who heightened public concerns in his charge to the clergy of London. Having precipitated the first conflicts over ritual with his support of ceremonial changes introduced by High Church clergy, Blomfield reversed his position and accused the Tractarians of having encouraged the adoption of Roman forms of worship.[62] He was willing to allow that the innovators were adopting what they thought were the best means for 'retaining in our communion persons of warm imaginations and weak judgment,' but he concluded that despite their intent, their methods had been an utter failure and had led many to secede to Rome. If some few had been kept in the Anglican church by these means, many more had been lost.[63]

Lord Russell saw in the controversy the opportunity for political gain and penned his famous letter to the Bishop of Durham in November 1850. Referring to Blomfield's charge, he concluded that it was the innovators within the Anglican church who posed the gravest threat to England: 'What, then, is the danger to be apprehended from a foreign prince of no great power, compared to the danger within the gates from the unworthy sons of the Church of England herself?'[64] On the 5th of December, Lord Shaftesbury presided over an 'immense meeting of lay members of the Church of England,' at the Freemasons' Tavern in London. Shaftesbury complained about the audacity of the Roman hierarchy but reserved his strongest language, like Russell, for those within the Church of England who sought to undermine its Protestantism from within. A memorial was proposed by the participants invoking 'Her Majesty's aid to suppress the various Romish innovations recently introduced, in some quarters, into the services of the Established Church.'[65] In the turmoil surrounding the Gorham controversy, the onus had been largely on the Evangelical party, as it was forced to defend its doctrine and to justify its place in the Church of England. But with the challenge from Rome, in the form of the revived Roman Catholic hierarchy in England, the burden of defense fell on the High Church position. Both the Gorham decision and the reaction to papal aggression were important for the development of Evangelical self-consciousness, and tended as well to harden the partisan divisions in the church.[66]

In the context of the heightened spirit of anti-Catholicism, the continuing controversy surrounding ritual innovation compelled the episcopacy to address the situation. In 1851, the two archbishops and twenty-two bishops issued a pastoral letter in an effort to restore a degree of calm without alienating either of the parties involved.[67] The bishops called on those who had disturbed the uniformity of worship, 'whether by excess or defect,' to exercise a degree of self-restraint and to consider the feelings of their congregation and the church as a whole before introducing any innovations that might offend. Above all, they encouraged the clergy to heed the advice of their diocesan pastors when disputes arose.[68] In only one case did the bishops voice their distinct opposition to the innovators – they utterly repudiated the notion that the liturgy of the Church of England could or should be returned to a pre-Reformation state.[69] The Anglican church, concluded the bishops, had rejected the corruptions of Rome, without breaking with the tradition of the 'ancient Catholic Church,' and had established 'one uniform ritual, according to which her public services should be conducted.'[70]

The *Quarterly Review* thought the document was almost 'synodal' in its character, given the unanimity of the episcopacy that stood behind it, but suggested that it was 'at least ten years too late,' having been issued only after the controversy had 'grown desperate.'[71] Unlike the bishops, the writer was quite willing to affix blame for the controversy – it lay almost entirely with the innovators who misconstrued the basis of the Anglican system and desired to return the national church to pre-Reformation ceremonies despite three hundred years of tradition and custom.[72] Clearly, by mid-century, Evangelicals were only one segment of the popular opposition to the movement for ritual innovation. Ultimately, however, neither the bishops' memorial nor the broad public support for the opposition movement would convince the innovators to moderate their activities.[73] And although the Evangelical party would temporarily gain a greater degree of influence, opposition to the High Church party did not necessarily translate into a corresponding sympathy for partisan Evangelical interests.

Evening Mission Services

In 1855, Lord Shaftesbury introduced legislation to abolish the limitations of the Conventicle Acts of 1664 and 1670, and allow for Anglican services in unconsecrated buildings. The Religious Worship Bill was intended to enable Evangelicals to imitate the successful evening services held by Nonconformists.[74] The bill was strongly opposed by the Bishop of Oxford and members of the High Church party, and more mildly criticized by several other bishops who feared it would threaten the autonomy of parish clergy. The bill's supporters, however, suggested that the real threat to the church lay not in perceived challenges to the parish system but elsewhere:

> A vast population growing up in ignorance of the first principles of Christianity, – an Episcopal Bench that seems potent to obstruct good measures, impotent to check bad ones, that strains at rubrical and canonical gnats, but swallows semi-Popish camels, – a constant disposition in high quarters to check and stop and persecute all active Evangelical clergymen but to let alone every one that is idle, – a rigid adherence to forms, precedents, traditions, usages of bygone days, – an almost judicial blindness to the palpable wants of the people, – these, these are the perils of the Church of England.[75]

In general, the bill had strong support, and with changes suggested by Archbishop Sumner, it successfully made its way through Parliament.[76]

During the winter of 1857, special evening services were scheduled in several Evangelical parishes to reach the disaffected working classes who avoided traditional church services.[77] In March, the *Record* noted that evening services had been held at Bristol, Birmingham, and Ipswich, and the paper called for other Evangelical parishes to follow their lead.[78] In May, similar services were held in Islington as well as in the Tractarian parish of St. George's-in-the-East at the Wellclose-Square Chapel.[79] Other than in Bristol, however, these services were all held in parish churches.[80] In the summer of 1857, London Evangelicals took the innovative step of holding a series of twelve Sunday evening services at Exeter Hall. An advertisement announced that the services were held 'under the sanction of the Right Rev. the Lord Bishop of London, and of the Incumbent of the district.' The services were scheduled for 6:30 p.m. and intended for the working classes. The announcement expressed the hope 'that the regular attendants at churches and chapels will not occupy the room intended for others.'[81] Bishop Henry Villiers of Carlisle preached at the first service, which was attended by over three thousand, the majority of whom appeared to come from the working classes, with 'many in clothing which would probably deter them from appearing in a church or chapel.'[82] The services consisted of the litany, three hymns, and an evangelistic address.[83] Many Evangelical leaders lent their aid, and the hall was crowded each Sunday evening.

Encouraged by the results, the committee planned another series for November 1857. In spite of the apparent success of the meetings and the continuing support of Bishop Tait, however, A. G. Edouart, Vicar of St. Michael's, Burleigh Street, in whose parish Exeter Hall was located, exercised his right to prohibit their renewal.[84] Tait tried to dissuade Edouart, but he refused to yield, and the services were thereafter taken over by Nonconformist ministers.[85] Shaftesbury introduced an amendment to his original bill that would allow an ordained minister to conduct services in any parishes of more than 2,000 persons, without the incumbent having the power to inhibit the services unless his protest was countersigned by the bishop. The amendment, however, attracted strong opposition, and Shaftesbury was forced to withdraw it.[86]

Following the model adopted by a growing number of Evangelical parishes, Sunday evening services soon became a fixture throughout the metropolis. On 3 January 1858, the first in a series of evening services was held in the nave of Westminster Abbey, and a degree of partisan jealousy could be seen in the *Record*'s complaint that the meetings attracted at least as many of the curious upper class as they did the intended working class audience.[87] Growing party divisions were also evident when some Evangelicals refused to support mission services that included any degree of cooperation with the Tractarians. The tensions were made further evident when a series of services were begun in four London parishes under the auspices of the London Diocesan Home Mission. The services were held at St. Pancras; St. Mary's, Whitechapel; St. Barnabas, Kensington; and St. Giles-in-the-Fields. Handbills were circulated throughout the city advertising the services and listing the scheduled preachers, which were to include High Church clergy, such as W. F. Hook and Bishop Wilberforce, as well as several well-known Evangelicals. The council of the Diocesan Home Mission included a number of influential Evangelicals, and the slate of preachers was evenly drawn from the various parties of the church, but Evangelical support for the evening service program was clearly divided.[88] Despite the great need to reach the working classes and the clearly evangelistic nature of the services, the *Record* opposed the plan – it published a number of critical letters and editorialized against Evangelicals making common cause with those who had 'orchestrated' the end of the Exeter Hall services. Taking a parting shot at the Westminster Abbey services, the paper concluded, 'They may get a crowd into the nave of the cathedral, drawn by the music and lights and novelty; but mixed courses of sermons to the working classes by men of known and distinctly opposite religious opinions, in our parish churches, will not succeed at all. God cannot and will not bless them.'[89]

A new series of evening services at Westminster Abbey were announced in the spring of 1858 (with meetings for the overflow crowd to be held at St. Margaret's, Westminster).[90] Once again, the slate of preachers was to include both High Church and Evangelical clergy, and the inclusion of F. D. Maurice, whose orthodoxy had been questioned, created additional concern for conservative Evangelicals. In large part, it was feared that the association of Evangelicals with those of other parties would necessitate a degree of compromise in their preaching.[91] In this series of services, the preachers involved were two of the most prominent in Evangelical circles, Hugh McNeile of Liverpool, and the Bishop of Carlisle, Henry Villiers. The *Record* apparently received some criticism for the tone of its attack, although no critical letters were printed; on the 10th of May, it published another editorial in which it denied any 'intention of making a personal attack on the Bishop of Carlisle and Dr. McNeile,' and affirmed that both were worthy of 'unfeigned and affectionate respect.' Rather, it concluded that they must not have known who the other preachers were going to be when they accepted the opportunity to preach at Westminster. But the paper could not ignore the opportunity to issue another warning as well and declared that it would not hesitate to criticize those who knowingly participated in programs that appeared to sanction an association with 'the error of Sacramentarians and Neologians.'[92]

St. George's-in-the-East

In the summer of 1859, a series of riots disrupted the parish of St. George's-in-the-East, one of the strongholds of the Tractarian clergy in London.[93] The troubles began when the vestry, which controlled an endowment for the appointment of afternoon lecturers, elected an Evangelical, Hugh Allen, of St. Jude's, Whitechapel.[94] When Allen came to speak on the afternoon of May 26th, he was met by a supportive though somewhat boisterous crowd of over three thousand. According to the *Record*, 'The demonstration was what it was intended to be, a public demonstration of the ratepayers against the Tractarian innovations and practices of the Rector [Bryan King] and his Curates.'[95] Over the course of the summer, the situation steadily worsened. King attempted to prohibit the lectures, and Bishop Tait suspended them in June as the disturbances grew more violent, but his intervention did little to calm the situation. The *Record* reported on the June 7th service:

> the inhabitants... continue to manifest their aversion to the Tractarian practices in the Church. On Sunday afternoon there could not have been less than 1,800 persons within the church. In a few moments the Rev. Bryan King, the Rector, appeared with a train of nearly thirty choristers, and proceeded along the aisle of the church, amid an indescribable scene of hooting, hissing, and confusion. On reaching the communion-table, which was decorated, as usual, with crosses, candlesticks, and flowers, he commenced the Litany, the choristers intoning the responses, upon which the audience began shouting, hissing, and stamping their feet, so as completely to drown out their voices. The Rector persisted for some time, but at length seemed convinced that it was useless to proceed. A strong body of police was in attendance. There was another demonstration during the evening service.[96]

Throughout the summer, the services were continually disrupted, and the violence seemed to escalate with each passing Sunday.[97]

When Allen was allowed to resume his lectures in August, the rioters targeted the afternoon service following his lecture. In response to complaints from the vestry regarding Frederick G. Lee, who had conducted services during the month of September, Bishop Tait suggested that both sides were responsible for 'the miserable controversy' into which the parish had fallen.[98] He expressed his great disgust at the "desecration" of the services by 'disorderly persons,' and required the churchwardens to be present at all services 'and to exercise the powers inherent in their office for the suppression of disorder.' But he also made it clear that he had little sympathy for the innovations. With regard to the use of eucharistic vestments, he wrote:

> It is well known that I have announced my determination of putting a stop to such follies when I can do so by my summary juris-

diction over those who are placed more immediately under my personal control; and such jurisdiction I have already exercised at St. George's; and I hereby require the churchwardens to give me immediate information if any clergyman so officiates in the church as to give reasonable offense by this childish mimicry of antiquated garments, as by so dressing himself up that he may resemble as much as possible a Roman Catholic priest.[99]

Tait noted that F. G. Lee had 'no leave to minister in my diocese' and that he had been ordered 'to desist from so officiating till he obtains my formal authority.'[100] The bishop noted, however, that his authority was somewhat limited in the matter, he could do little other than to prohibit the use of illegal vestments and to require the churchwardens to maintain the peace. The parish system gave a great deal of independence to incumbents, and the bishop had little discretion for direct intervention. Nevertheless, Tait offered to mediate between the two sides in the controversy, if they would both agree to binding arbitration. The churchwardens immediately accepted his offer, but King refused.

The *Record* was, by then, beginning to recognize that the rioting did little to raise public support for the Evangelical cause among those concerned by any threat of social unrest (particularly the middle and upper classes). Early in the controversy the disturbances were viewed as an expression of popular Protestant opposition to the innovations. But it soon became clear that the riots were little more than a mob expression of common anti-Catholic prejudices. The paper recognized that the disruption of worship could only bring discredit to the Evangelical party and limit the effectiveness of their own, more respectable protest. But it continued to blame the clergy of St. George's for the popular reaction.[101] In late September, Bishop Tait took the extreme measure of closing the church, if only to gain a measure of peace for a time.[102] By mid-October, King had agreed to arbitration, but only on the two original matters of dispute – the time of the afternoon lecture (which had been shifted to early afternoon to make it less convenient) and the use of eucharistic vestments.[103]

In November, Tait ruled that the afternoon lecture was to be returned to its original time and reiterated his ban of the vestments. The parish church was formally reopened with a choral service attended by a large congregation and occasionally interrupted 'by hisses, stamping of feet, and the slamming of pew doors.' In his sermon, King spoke of the desecration of the church as 'a sin of sacrilege' and accused outsiders of coming in to disturb his parish. He also expressed his great regret that 'so few had raised up their hands in support of the doctrines of the Church to which they adhered.'[104] King's tone, however, did little to calm the situation, and the riots continued.[105] The press reported that the services on the 13th of November were the worst ever.[106] The crowd was made up almost entirely of men and boys, a fact that would seem to verify King's assessment that the rioters had little connection to the parish congregation. By this time it was apparent that the rioters were little more than a lower-class mob giving expression to popular anti-Catholic sentiment in their free time on Sundays; the continuation of the uproar at the parish church became for a time their preferred form of amusement.[107]

In December, the riots finally began to subside. About four hundred attended the morning service on December 4th, and some forty police were present to maintain the peace. The churchwardens also prevented the mob from gathering in the chancel, the location from which most of the disturbances had arisen.[108] Finally, it was announced that the lecturer, Hugh Allen, had been presented by the Lord Chancellor to the rectory of St. George's, Southwark, and it appeared that he would be unable to hold the lectureship at St. George's-in-the-East in combination with his new appointment.[109] With the focal point of the mob's anti-Catholic activities thus removed, the disturbances gradually died out, much to the relief of all. By this point, the riots had little to do with the Evangelical campaign against ritual innovations, and the appearance of social unrest did more to damage that movement than it did to help. Evangelicals were keen to make use of a popular Protestantism that could turn the tide of public support in their favor, but they had little interest in and could gain little good from disturbances that seemed to run out of control and appeared to threaten the stability of the national church. The disruptions were briefly renewed in early 1860, and the *Times* wrote of the services on the 29th of January, 'everything which had previously occurred sinks into insignificance when compared with the terrible scene which was witnessed there last night.'[110] The rioting continued for some weeks but was finally halted when Parliament passed a bill for the prosecution of those who disrupted services and King was convinced to take a leave of absence.[111]

Auricular Confession

During the course of the controversy, those concerned to defend the Protestant foundation of the national church were increasingly disturbed by the renewed use of auricular confession. Other than innovations involving ceremonial, which were disturbing precisely because they involved the public worship of the church, the private practice of confession was the most disturbing element of the High Church revival.[112] Evangelicals were already protesting the practice by the early 1850s.[113] But the controversy attracted broader public interest in the summer of 1858, when Frederick Baring, an Evangelical minister, brought charges against Alfred Poole, a curate in the High Church parish of St. Barnabas, Pimlico. Baring presented Bishop Tait of London with a detailed report of his correspondence with three women who had gone to Poole for confession and described their experiences for Baring.[114] In June 1858, Baring presented his evidence to a public meeting at St. James's Hall, attended by about fifty peers and two hundred members of Parliament (admission was restricted to gentlemen due to the allegedly graphic nature of the material discussed).[115] After interviewing Poole regarding the charges, Tait suspended him. In July, the *Times* published, at the request of the Churchwardens of St. Barnabas, the correspondence exchanged between the two. Tait said he was unimpressed with Baring's evidence; but having heard Poole's own admission regarding his ministry, he claimed the practice was "likely to cause scandal and injury to the Church."[116] Poole appealed to Archbishop Sumner, but he replied that he firmly supported Tait's decision.[117]

A letter (signed 'Paterfamilias') published in the *Times* during the heat of the controversy, touched on the two spheres that were perceived to be most directly endangered by the confessional – the nation's Protestantism and the sanctity of the family. The writer put one question to the innovators: Were the clergy of St. Barnabas encouraging the practice of habitual confession? He continued:

> The Roman Catholic clergy openly insist upon it as a sacrament necessary to salvation. Mr. Liddell and his curates may possibly consider it their duty to do so too; but surely they cannot consider it right that there should exist any doubt as to their practice.
>
> If Mr. Liddell will answer this question briefly and clearly – as I am sure he must feel it ought to be answered – his parishioners will then know in what position they, their wives, and their daughters stand towards him and his curates.
>
> In saying this, I do not mean to insinuate in the most remote degree anything against the morality of the curates of St. Paul's and St. Barnabas – who are, I have no doubt, excellent and laborious members of the clergy; but I do say that every Protestant who feels strongly against the practices of the Confessional has a right to know whether the women of his family are taught, as a sacred duty, to confess privily their weaknesses, their frailties, and their faults to young unmarried yet marriageable men.[118]

Robert Liddell, under whose charge Poole had served, denied that confession was necessary to salvation or that it was even encouraged by the clergy of the parish. But he also justified its use in some cases, as allowed for by the Visitation service prescribed in the Book of Common Prayer, and affirmed its continuing value.[119]

Auricular confession was abhorrent to both Evangelicals and other moderate Anglicans on two counts. First, it was the most offensive evidence of an effort to reestablish a sacramental view of the priest's office; similar in nature to a more elaborate eucharistic ritual, only more secretive and therefore more threatening than visible innovations.[120] Both were condemned as an attempt to elevate the priest to the role of a sacrificial mediator between God and the congregation, the central tenet of the Roman church that had been rejected by the Protestant reformers.[121] Ultimately, the entire controversy turned on the Ritualists' claim that a sacerdotal view of the priesthood could be legitimately deduced from the church's articles and formularies, and the rejection of that claim by their opponents.[122] The *Record* noted that many critics attributed the renewal of confession to a licentious curiosity among the High Church clergy, but, in its own view, the more serious threat was the subversion of the Protestant church. In an editorial, the paper traced the development of the sacramental system, arguing that it was the invention of a powerful priesthood bent on controlling the lives of the laity:

> The institution of the ordinance of confession – including penance and absolution – was the master stroke of the whole Sacramental scheme, and that on which its power has mainly rested for the accomplishment of its corrupt ends; for it is obvious that those who have been induced to confide to a priest their most secret sinful thoughts and deeds must feel themselves completely in his power, and the priest thus becomes the depository of every personal and family secret. The tremendous use that a clever and artful Priesthood can make of such a power may easily be conceived, and has been fully demonstrated in the history of the Papacy; for it is chiefly by the awful power of the confessional that this great apostasy has succeeded in establishing and maintaining her spiritual, domestic, and political domination for so many ages over the greatest portion of Christendom.[123]

The second argument made against the confessional, and that not by Evangelicals alone, was alluded to in many of the earlier citations. It was widely assumed that the priests took advantage of their influence on "weak-minded and emotional" women and children who could be easily manipulated once secreted within the confes-

Anti-Ritualism at Mid-Century 33

sional closet.[124] Given the structure of Victorian society, the priest serving as private confessor appeared to threaten the place of the husband as the head of his household. A decade later, an essayist in the *Quarterly Review* complained that while 'vestments and ceremonies' offended religious feelings, 'the practice of confession' was a threat to 'our domestic peace.' He cited with approval a speaker at the Wolverhampton Church Congress who warned 'that the priestly idea leads to the establishment of another master in every household, by every hearth, in the place of the husband and the father.' The author suggested that 'the great mass of the English people would be forever alienated from the Church, if they found the priest extracting from their wives their most secret thoughts, from their sons what they dared not tell their fathers, and from their daughters what they would blush to confess to their mothers.'[125] The supporters of confession were seen as a threat to the English family, the Protestant church, and the very stability of the nation. And the practice would remain a source of constant friction between Ritualists and Protestants through the rest of the century.

The Growth of Divisions

Two events during the 1850s illustrate the increasingly vitriolic and divisive nature of the controversy. As the rhetoric intensified, it served to exacerbate partisan divisions within the church, but it also created tensions within Evangelicalism as well. Some moderates were uncomfortable with the whole tenor of Protestant polemic; but when they questioned the tactics and tone, they themselves became targets as well. In 1854-55, during the Crimean War, Florence Nightingale and her nurses were repeatedly attacked in the columns of the *Record*. The paper cited the case of one clergyman, known to be of 'uncompromising Protestant principle,' who had warned his congregation not to send their money to support the work of 'Romish or semi-Romish hands.' The pastor replied to a letter written to one of his parishioners by Elizabeth Herbert, who was responding to one of his earlier attacks on the nurses.[126] The anonymous clergyman replied, with some vehemence:

> If I wanted any further testimony beyond that supplied by Mr. Sidney Herbert himself of the nature of Miss Nightingale's religious opinions, this letter of his wife's would furnish it. The endorsement of that lady by two such Anglo-Catholic Dissenters as Mr. and Mrs. Sidney Herbert, is quite conclusive of the character of her creed, notwithstanding Mrs. Herbert's extraordinary assurance that she is 'what is called rather Low Church.' I have always un-

derstood her to be an Anglican Papist, and everything that has appeared in the public journals, of different shades of ecclesiastical politics, has confirmed this impression....

I am not surprised at the 'indignant' tone of Mrs. Herbert's letter. The Anglicans have been very much annoyed at the exposure of their pretty little plot, and, if I may adopt one of their own words, 'conspirators' do not usually like the light to be let in upon their plans and operations. It is my full conviction that a Jesuit conspiracy is in active operation for the subjugation of England and the ruin of her Church.[127]

According to the *Record*, the 'the restoration of the conventual system' was part of the Tractarian scheme 'for the subversion of our Protestant faith.' Part of the conspiracy, the paper suggested, was the employment of 'unconscious agents persons distinguished for philanthropy and benevolence, such as Miss Nightingale.'[128]

In February 1855, the Rev. J. H. Gurney gave a lecture to the Christian Young Men's Association at Exeter Hall. The title of his lecture was 'God's Heroes and the World's Heroes,' and among the former, he gave a high place to Florence Nightingale. He suggested that she was 'a gifted and holy woman' who had been unfairly 'assailed in print by self-styled religious men, as not being perfect in her theology.' When criticized by conservatives, Gurney defended her again in a letter to the *Record*:

Truly, religious partisanship has done much already to make wits merry and infidels more bold. Men of sagacious and candid minds have marveled to see the spirit of Christianity so imperfectly reflected, so often contradicted, in the periodical literature which many serious-minded people love best. But the last exhibition, I think, is the worst; and for myself, while I deplore the bigotry, I wonder at the hardihood, which, in the face of the English nation, could make Florence Nightingale the mark for hostile criticism, while the walls of Scutari resound with blessings on her name.[129]

The *Record* was quick to defend itself. While reciting its opposition to the nursing scheme, the paper claimed to have the highest regard for Miss Nightingale herself. In the strictest terms the paper might not have criticized her personally, but it had clearly implied that Nightingale was at best an unconscious accomplice, and it published letters from correspondents (without editorial comment) who said or implied much worse. But Gurney's critique apparently stung, and the attacks on Nightingale quickly subsided. For several issues in February and March, however, Gurney himself became the target.[130]

A second instance illustrating the growing partisan divisions was centered around Bishop Wilberforce, who had long been a favorite target of the *Record* and its correspondents, and was widely viewed as the second strongest supporter of the Tractarians on the episcopal bench (only Bishop Phillpotts of Exeter was more reviled on this account).[131] In 1858, charges of ornamental and ritual innovation were made against his diocesan training school, Cuddesdon College, first in an article published in the *Quarterly Review* and later in a circular letter issued by C. P. Golightly, of Oriel College, Oxford.[132] Wilberforce appointed three archdeacons to investigate. They largely exonerated the bishop and the college, but the bishop's Evangelical opponents remained unconvinced.[133] The Principal, Rev. A. Pott, later resigned, after he had accepted a country living for his health, and Vice-Principal Liddon was induced to offer his resignation early the next year, after Wilberforce realized just how far apart the two were with regard to their respective views of the Eucharist.[134]

Shortly after the controversy concerning Cuddesdon College, an anonymous pamphlet was published entitled *Facts and Documents showing the Alarming State of the Diocese of Oxford, by a Senior Clergyman of the Diocese*. The pamphlet detailed numerous romish innovations that the author suggested Wilberforce had approved – these included auricular confession, altar crosses, processions with crosses, stone altars, eucharistic wafers, wine and water mixed in the chalice, bowing to the elements, praying for the dead, and sisterhoods. Over one hundred clergy from Oxford had seceded to Rome since the beginning of the Oxford Movement, and conservative Evangelicals were convinced that many more still remained within the Anglican church who were actually Romanists. It was suggested that High Church extremists remained within the Church of England merely to assimilate 'its services to those of that apostate Church to which they really belong..., many of the clergy under the episcopal care of Dr. Wilberforce have little more title to the name of Protestant than Dr. Wiseman himself has.'[135]

The publication of the pamphlet and the ensuing controversy elicited a response from three archdeacons and twenty-three rural deans, who signed a memorial supporting the bishop and denying the allegations. In his response to the memorial, Wilberforce defended his administration:

> With the wide margin left in our Church to the individual action of her clergy it must often happen that a Bishop may see in the ministrations of really good men, who are neither secret Romanizers nor secret Puritans, variations (sometimes in excess and sometimes in defect) from what he in his own judgment considers to be the

proper line of ritual observance among us. In the generality of such cases it would be injudicious as well as unkind in the Bishop, until he had tried all other means, publicly to stigmatize the clergyman with his disapprobation; and consequently, though the Bishop may be employing his best efforts to repress such variations quietly and without violence to the feelings of the clergy concerned, he is exposed to being misrepresented by those who seek occasion against him, as approving and encouraging that which he altogether disapproves, and is in the wisest way removing from his diocese.[136]

A remonstrance to the memorial was issued in March, signed by two rural deans and over one hundred clergy of the diocese who affirmed the concerns raised in the pamphlet.[137] The *Record*, for its part, continued its caustic campaign against Wilberforce and responded to the bishop's defense with sarcasm.[138] The paper was concerned by the seemingly genuine esteem in which the bishop was held and warned its readers not to be 'restrained by any feelings of false delicacy' toward the bishop or to be lulled to sleep by his words. It was clear, said the paper, that 'the spirit of superstition is at work in their diocese; let them manfully resist it; – if it has been known to lurk beneath "the wings of an angel of light," it comes within the limits of possibility that it might hide itself beneath episcopal robes.'[139]

In May, one of the original remonstrants, while still worried about the Romeward trend of innovations allowed in the diocese, complained about the tone adopted by the Evangelical controversialists:

In common with many others who signed that address, I am most anxious that this controversy may be conducted without infringing the law of Christian charity, by indulging in personal abuse, or by impugning the motives of those who act on different principles to ourselves. I believe I shall find a responsive echo in the hearts of many of the anti-Tractarian party, when I say that I have read with painful feelings bitter invectives, unjust insinuations against, and unworthy motives imputed to, the Bishop of Oxford, as if he acted with secret desire of Romanizing our Church, but concealing that intention by an open avowal of pure Evangelical principles. Surely we ought long to hesitate before we admit the truth of such charges against any one, still more against a Bishop of our Church. My own private opinion is, of course, worthless to the public at large; and yet I am confident, not only that I speak the honest truth, but that ninety-nine out of a hundred of the clergy will concur with me when I affirm that a more earnest, sincere Christian does not exist than the Bishop of Oxford....

The controversy may surely be conducted on far higher and more Christian ground than on personalities. We are contending against principles and against a system which we confidently believe are sapping the fundamental truths of our Reformed religion. To support our position we can point (as our witnesses) to all the clergy and laity who since this movement [began] have seceded to the Church of Rome. We can appeal to the various publications now issuing from the press, embodying the most pernicious doctrines of that Church, and published by the Tractarian party (e.g., works printed at Mr. Painter's, Strand). We can appeal to the opinions of the Roman Catholics themselves to prove the Roman tendency of this movement; but we may and ought to yield to our opponents that which we claim for ourselves – sincerity of motives and a conscientious conviction of the purity of the principles on which they act; whilst we cannot but lament the apparent infatuation by which their judgments are blinded....

As I am not ashamed of my name any more than I am of my principles, I shall not attempt to conceal myself under an anonymous signature, but beg to subscribe myself

Your obedient servant, H. W. Lloyd[140]

The *Record*, in its response to the letter, pled innocence and claimed it was unable to discern Lloyd's intent. It defended both its own editorials and the correspondence published on the subject as having maintained the highest degree of civility in spirit: 'With Bishop Wilberforce as a man we have nothing to do; to God, not to us, he stands or falls. It is with the Bishop and his official acts alone that we have dealt.' In the paper's view, the attacks had all been purely impersonal and directed only towards the misguided principles of Wilberforce's Tractarian position.[141] But for all of the paper's protest, Lloyd's letter clearly touched a sore point and apparently resonated with a number of moderate Evangelicals. For the rest of 1859, Wilberforce's name disappeared from the pages of the *Record*, and the rising tide of Romanism that threatened to engulf the diocese of Oxford was not mentioned again.[142]

Evangelical Unity

It was evident throughout the 1850s, that Evangelicals were concerned by the lack of unity in their nascent party. Dating back to the turn of the century, they had been unable to gain a voice for their missionary concerns in the two most prominent church societies (the Society for the Propagation of the Gospel and the Society for Promoting Christian Knowledge). As a result, they formed voluntary societies of their own to pursue their particular goals and concerns. The Church Missionary Society (hereafter abbreviated CMS), the British and Foreign Bible Society, and the Church Pastoral-Aid Society (hereafter abbreviated CP-AS) were perhaps the most influential, but the number of Evangelical associations quickly proliferated as new groups were organized to address numerous issue and concerns. The May meetings at Exeter Hall became the focal point of the Evangelical calendar; by mid-century, the numbers had outgrown their accommodations, and the schedule stretched from mid-April to mid-June.[143]

With the proliferation of associations and societies, however, came a certain diffusion of interests. If Evangelicalism represented a body of Anglicans who shared a common core of beliefs about God, humanity, redemption, and the church, it nevertheless remained a rather fragmented group lacking a leader, central organization, or mindset strong enough to bind the whole together as a cohesive party. Faced with the growing challenge of an increasingly united body of devoted and highly motivated Anglo-Catholics, however, Evangelicals were concerned to present a unified opposition. But at the same time, their own methods and polemical tone belied the difficulties involved in such an undertaking – a jealously guarded independence (the right of private judgment was usually identified, with little concern for historical context, as a cornerstone of the Reformation) and a certain rhetorical edge that could quickly be turned against friends as well as foes. The tone adopted by the *Record* often gave public expression to that fact. On one occasion, while reciting the necessary qualities for any society that hoped to unify the party, the paper sharply criticized the Evangelical Alliance. That body, it concluded, could never unite the party because it did not 'contemplate political action,' and, it was feared, did not adopt a narrow enough line with regard to 'the admission of Tractarians within its ranks.'[144] The charge drew a quick reply from J. P. Dobson, Secretary of the Alliance, who said he was unaware of any Tractarian members and doubted that they would sign the doctrinal statement required for membership. Concerning the tone of the article, Dobson wrote, 'I must be pardoned if I add my deep regret that the *Record*, in its zeal against certain measures taken by other parties, which it does not approve, should have permitted itself gratuitously to make statements so calculated to injure the Evangelical Alliance.'[145]

Dobson touched upon a central point in his reply – it was evident that the concern of many Evangelicals for the unity of the party was largely related to their opposition to the growing threat from the extreme section of the High Church party. Following a meeting of the Evangelical clergy of Yorkshire, in 1857, the *Record* emphasized the need for a central organization capable of disseminating information and forming a unified body of opinion in the face of the Tractarian threat:

> Some centre of communication in each diocese or county is a *desideratum*, through which information can be conveyed at once to such of the Evangelical clergy as can be depended upon, who in their turn can enlist the co-operation of the laity around them. We are no advocates for needless excitement or unnecessary agitation. But we do desire with all our hearts to see the clergy who are not ashamed of the name of Evangelical, drawn more closely together. We are sure there is a broad and scriptural basis on which they might meet and act unitedly when occasion requires. There is a united phalanx against us. The opponents of Evangelical truth display a self-denying earnestness in the maintenance and spread of their own views which fairly puts to the blush the isolated and spasmodic efforts of the Evangelical clergy.... Next to the Divine blessing the secret of success in a good cause is, mutual confidence based upon the knowledge of each other, and a cordial interest in the one common object. In the absence of these elements, the Evangelical clergy must be little more than an assemblage of units, instead of a well-ordered and unified body, ready and willing to act together on behalf of the faith, and in the advancement of the Redeemer's kingdom.[146]

The article assumed, of course, that all true Evangelicals would readily agree on the common objects of the party, who their common enemies were, and what were the appropriate methods to be adopted in the campaign against them. In fact, however, party unity remained a rather elusive goal; and in spite of a broad current of both theological and popular opposition to ritual innovation, the success of that movement, over the course of the latter half of the nineteenth century, tended to exacerbate the divisions within Evangelicalism itself as well as those between the parties in the Church of England.

Still, in spite of deep-seated internal divisions, and in spite of the movement's inability to enlist broad public support for its own causes (regardless of the broad strand of anti-Catholicism and popular opposition to the activities of the ritual innovators), the Evangelical party was thriving at mid-century. In 1843, an anonymous archdeacon proclaimed that one positive result of the Oxford Movement was that it had 'broken up the Evangelical party.'[147] He seemed, however, to be giving voice to his own partisan desires rather than expressing the facts. Three years later, William Gresley, a Tractarian who thought the Evangelical party posed a grave threat to the Church of England, expressed his concern about the movement's rapid growth. He feared that if the advance of 'the Puritan party' continued unchecked, would 'ere long have established such an influence as to defy control.... At present, as it appears to me, the evil is just manageable; but let it proceed much farther unchecked, and it will have become too firmly established to be rooted out.'[148] Gresley's interpretation of events proved to be the more accurate of the two. In fact, the Evangelical party became more influential as opposition to the ritual innovations grew, especially after 1850.[149]

In his famous essay on church parties, published in 1855, W. J. Conybeare suggested that the Evangelical party, 'that which is termed Low Church by its adversaries,' had been the most influential in recent years.[150] By his count, there were roughly the same number of moderates in both the High and Low Church parties, but the extreme type of the High Church (the 'Tractarians') probably only numbered about 1,000, while the extreme type of the Low Church (the 'Recordites') was closer to 2,500.[151] Evangelicals, however, were far less likely to be found in influential church offices – among the episcopacy, he identified thirteen from the High Church, ten from the Broad Church, and only five from the Low Church.[152] The correction of this one-sided representation in the higher offices of the church was to become an area of significant change in the coming decades and would prove to be a further point of contention between the two parties. Conybeare rejected the notion, however, which had been suggested already by its opponents, that the Evangelical party was 'effete.' But he did conclude that its influence was on the wane, and its impact 'less that it was in the last generation.'[153] Influence, however, is difficult to quantify and measure. If the Evangelical party was less of a spiritual force at mid-century, it nevertheless remained a significant factor in the years of controversy that would follow as it sought to counter the advances of that group which it believed was undermining the Protestant character of the national church.

The events of mid-century conspired to aggravate the controversy over the church's ritual (which for both Evangelicals and Ritualists was a battle over the very nature of the church) and to intensify the divisions that would harden party lines during the following decade. The Gorham case and the events surrounding the perceived "papal aggression" set the tone for Protestants who were convinced that their reformed Church of England was under siege. The battles over St. George's-in-the-East and the renewed use of auricular confession only strengthened their resolve, but they also motivated the successors of the Tractarians to gather their own forces in self-defense. During the 1860s, that movement established its own identity apart from the Oxford Movement. The Ritualists formed a new party organization and became increasingly militant in advocating their innovative ritual as the only valid expression of the catholic nature of the church. In response, Evangelicals began to gather their forces, drawing together those who were determined to defend the Protestantism of the English church. The rhetoric became increasingly partisan and the controversy grew as each group developed its own organizations and pursued its own vision of the church. As Conybeare suggested in his essay, 'A common hate is the cement to consolidate a party.'[154] He could not have imagined the degree to which the following decades would prove the truth of his words. Still, as was indicated already by a few voices of moderation during the 1850s, a unity formed in response to a common opponent during a time of controversy was difficult to maintain. And Evangelicals in particular, during the decades to come, would continue to find that controversy and debate could breed divisions within as well as without.

Notes

1 Looking back in 1876, an anonymous essayist in the *Quarterly Review* expressed regret that the controversy involved worship. 'Public worship,' the author wrote, 'is the one area that ought to be kept free from innovation and controversy. We can disagree about theology and sermons, but at worship, the Church of England ought to be united in spite of differences.... Proverbial as is the *odium theologicum*, the passions roused by outward forms are more intense and move a far greater mass, and naturally so, for these things appeal to the senses and the multitude. The riots and outrages which marked the long Iconoclast disputes in the Greek Church give a warning the more impressive from some premonitory signs of the disorders provoked by Ritualism among ourselves.' Anonymous, 'Church Innovations,' *Quarterly Review* 141 (1876): 527-28.

   A. P. Stanley, the prominent Broad Church Dean of Westminster, cited an unnamed 'great divine' who had noted that it was 'the peculiar blot of factions or parties in the Church of England' to have argued over the dress of the clergy on three occasions: when Bishop Hooper of the Reformation era refused to wear a square cap, in the controversy between Archbishop Laud and the Puritans, and in the current controversy which he dated to the Exeter riots of the 1840s. No such controversy of minimal doctrinal import, concluded Stanley, had ever distracted the churches of the continent. Arthur P. Stanley, *Christian Institutions: Essays on Ecclesiastical Subjects*, fourth ed. (London: John Murray, 1884), pp. 209-10.

2 The best comprehensive study of Ritualism is John Shelton Reed, *Glorious Battle*. In the first two chapters Reed covered the rise of the Oxford Move-

ment and the transition from Tractarianism to Ritualism, noting that the two movements were quite distinct. He suggested that the earliest innovations, which provoked no response, could be dated to the late 1830s; cf. pp. 26-28.

3   C. J. Blomfield, *A Charge Delivered to the Clergy of the Diocese of London, at the Visitation in October 1842*, cited in the *Times*, 12 Oct. 1842; cf. Chadwick, *Victorian Church*, Part One, p. 215. With regard to Blomfield's general view of churchmanship as well as his relations with Tractarians during the events of this period, cf. P. J. Welch, 'Bishop Blomfield and the Development of Tractarianism in London,' *Church Quarterly Review* 155 (1954): 332-44.
4   Cited in the *Record*, 13 Oct. 1842.
5   They were 'forbidden by the Injunction of King Edward VI in 1549; but they were in use when the first Liturgy of that monarch received the authority of Parliament, and therefore seem to be sanctioned by the rubric in our present Common Prayer-book.' They had also been maintained throughout the years in cathedrals and in the royal and college chapels. Ibid.
6   Except in the cathedrals, the surplice had for many years been worn only during the communion service, while the sermon was preached in a black gown. Blomfield thought the gown had probably first been worn 'by lecturers who preached when no part of the communion service was read.' But following the innovation of the Tractarians, he thought the clergy should proceed to the pulpit in their surplice. He did, however, allow for the use of the black gown for the evening sermon. Ibid.

According to an essayist in the *Quarterly Review*, the different robes were already signs of party rivalry – the white surplice being identified as a 'rag of Popery,' and the black gown being a 'badge of Calvinism.' The reviewer suggested that the distinction of preaching in the gown and ministering in the surplice dated back to the Reformation, with the gown signifying the personal act of preaching while the surplice emphasized the 'sacred character of the divine office.' With the exception of cathedrals and colleges, however, preaching in a surplice was elsewhere 'wholly unsanctioned by the rubrics.' Anonymous, 'Rubrics and Ritual of the Church of England,' *Quarterly Review* 72 (1843): pp. 261-64.

Shortly after Blomfield's adoption of the change, Richard Mant, Bishop of Down and Connor, published a work for his clergy in which he took the same position. Mant noted that in some parishes, the clergy would withdraw to the vestry prior to the sermon and change from the surplice into a black gown. Repudiating that tradition, he wrote: 'Neither at this time, nor at any other time of the service should the minister separate and absent himself from his congregation.' In Mant's view, the church 'neither enjoins, sanctions, nor permits, nor recognizes, a change of dress; but sends him straight, not to the vestry, but to the Pulpit. Nor does she know any thing of a black gown for her officiating ministers. To some minds indeed any change of dress is an innovation, savoring of Rome: the particular change, of Geneva. At all events, neither the one, nor the other, is acknowledged by the Anglican Church.' Richard Mant, *Horae Liturgicae: Containing, Liturgical Discrepancy; Its Extent, Evil, and Remedy... and Liturgical Harmony; Its Obligations, Means, and Security against Error...* (New York: Stanford & Swords,

1847), p. 77. In a note to the British edition, first published in 1845, Mant said that he had been made aware of Bishop Blomfield's moderation of his position only after the book had gone to press. With reference to the use of the black gown, he reaffirmed that he could find no authority for its use and therefore could not approve of it. But he was willing, for the sake of peace, to concede the point. Ibid., p. xv.

7   The *Times* interpreted Blomfield's charge as a response to the contrary opinion expressed by Bishop Pepys of Worcester: 'We ought not to be deterred from *what some persons may term an over-scrupulous observance* of the rules and customs which our own Church has actually prescribed or sanctioned, by a dread of being thought too careful about the externals of religion. If we are not to go beyond the ritual, at least we ought not to fall short of it, or to make our public services more jaded and inexpressive than she intended.... An honest endeavour to carry out the Church's mind in every part of divine worship ought not to be stigmatized as Popish or superstitious. *If it be singular the singularity is to be cured, not by one person desisting from it, but by all taking it up.*' *Times*, 19 Oct. 1842 (their italics).

In his survey of Evangelicalism, G. R. Balleine suggested that there was little strenuous opposition to the changes at that time. The correspondence in the *Record* during the period, however, indicated sharp divisions in the party; some were willing to comply, but there was also strong vocal opposition. Balleine, *Evangelical Party*, pp. 174-75.

The *Record*, in an October editorial, criticized Blomfield's charge, but thought the ritual issue insignificant compared to the doctrinal concerns. In the months that followed, concern largely focused on Blomfield's support of baptismal regeneration; but there was growing concern over ritual innovation. A brief article in the *Record* in January, indicated that compliance was widespread. It noted that 'a large number of the metropolitan clergy' were now preaching in the surplice, including the Evangelical Rev. Spry at St. Marylebone. One letter fairly represented those who were opposed to the changes and disturbed that some Evangelicals were willing to comply: 'It is true, that it matters but little whether a clergyman preaches in a gown or surplice, provided he preaches the Gospel without 'reserve;' but as giving place to these men, the change which has taken place in so many churches in the diocese of London is most deeply to be lamented; and it is much to be regretted that clergymen, eminent for their piety, have thus far with their diocesan made common cause with the enemies of our Church.' The writer warned that familiarity with 'ceremonial religion' would lead the laity 'to prefer, as the Tractarians do, the Church of Rome to the Church of England.... Their doctrines are the dogmas of Romanism; and their ceremonies, so far as they can possibly practice them, with their candles and candlesticks, their crosses, and turnings and bowings, are the ceremonies of Romanism; and that such men *within* our Protestant Church should receive any degree of praise from our Bishops, or any countenance from ministers of sound judgment and *enlightened piety*, is a fearful sign of the times.' Letter (signed "Luther") to the *Record*, 5 Jan. 1843 (their italics).

8   *Record*, 15 May 1843. The *Quarterly Review* questioned the validity of Blomfield's argument. The author professed a willingness to cooperate with a

stricter adherence to the rubrics but expressed the fear that the innovations were actually 'laying the foundation of new and more extensive deviations from that practical uniformity which the Church of England has so long, and we will say, so happily enjoyed.' Anon., 'Rubrics and Ritual,' *Quarterly Review*, p. 247.

9   The *Record* suggested that many clergy had been waiting for such an injunction before giving their compliance, but they could now explain to their congregations that the changes were necessary. The paper still opposed the changes but noted that 'had the order been given in 1823 instead of 1843, it probably would scarcely have caused a single hour's sensation.' *Record*, 15 May 1843.

10 *Record*, 24 May and 15 June 1843; cf. Chadwick, *Victorian Church, Part One*, p. 216. Looking back on the episcopacy of Blomfield, the *Quarterly Review* blamed him for lacking the foresight necessary to have averted the controversy. 'Even if it were clear that he rightly interpreted the rubric when he laid it down, that the surplice should be worn in morning prayer alike in the pulpit and at the altar, yet we are sure that the attempt of a single bishop to lay down such a rule for the present practice of his diocese argued small previous consideration and little comprehensive discernment of the signs of the times. He himself believed, and his biographer still thinks, that the Charge was at first well received, and that all that it advised might have been adopted but that... Islington thundered. But the Bishop's miscalculation lay in this that he did not from the first perceive that Islington was sure to thunder. Accordingly, when the storm broke out he was helpless.' Anonymous, 'The Church of England and Her Bishops,' *Quarterly Review* 114 (1863): 573.

Samuel Garratt defended Blomfield in a letter when the *Record* later blamed him for having started the Ritualist controversy: 'With a single exception the Islington clergy had resolved to obey him if he insisted on the changes being made. But while he expressed his opinions in favour of preaching in the surplice, because he considered it, which the clergy of Islington did not, the legal dress of a preacher, he yielded the point, and recommended delay in this and all other changes, when he learned what their effect would be in breaking up the congregations.' In Garratt's view, Blomfield was a strong Protestant who had no interest in furthering the Catholic movement. 'His real object in attempting to obtain uniformity,' concluded Garratt, 'whatever that of some of his advisers may have been, was the very opposite to what you say.... His policy was mistaken, but it was the mistake of a most honest and conscientious man.' Letter to the *Record*, 10 Jan. 1881.

11 A memorial to the clergy in the Evangelical parish of Islington was signed by 2,835 church members. They cited the 1841 charge of Archbishop Howley (which would seem to indicate that innovations were occurring at least a year prior to Blomfield's charge), in which he rejected the 'introduction of novelties,' even if they were merely the revival of old forms which had fallen into disuse. The memorial continued: 'We cannot but view with apprehension and alarm the prospect of "the introduction of novelties," and believing that such changes would actually paralyze those efforts which

have so long and so happily distinguished this parish; that they would disturb the harmony prevailing between you and your congregations; lead to separation, and thereby weaken the influence of the Church of England; we respectfully but earnestly entreat you to refrain from making any alteration in the mode of conducting the public services of the Church, which has prevailed for more than a century.' Daniel Wilson drew up the clerical response to the memorial and reaffirmed their Evangelical tradition. Acknowledging that Bishop Blomfield had given them the liberty 'to adhere to our usual mode of conducting the services of the Church.' Cited in the *Record*, 22 June 1843.

12 Memorials drawn up by the parishioners of Shoreditch and Ware were reprinted in the *Record*, 26 June and 20 July 1843. The churchwardens of Ware received little sympathy from Blomfield, who evidently believed, despite their reassurances, that they represented only a small minority of the parish. Finally, his secretary wrote that the Bishop would have no further correspondence with them since they had published their letters in the *Record* prior to the conclusion of the matter. Thereafter, the churchwardens appealed to Archbishop Howley for help, but he refused to intervene. The vestry then adopted two resolutions complaining of the vicar's uncompromising attitude in forcing the innovations on the parish and suggesting that 'the congregation should quit the church immediately after the Nicene Creed.' Both resolutions were passed unanimously. *Record*, 17 August and 18 September 1843. The dispute continued into 1844. The *Record* published letters in which the vicar, Henry Coddington, and the churchwardens traded accusations. Coddington referred to it as 'an unhallowed warfare' which had been carried on 'by a party of laymen impatient of control, against the Bishop of the diocese and the clergy of the parish.' *Record*, 25 March and 7 April 1844.

The *Times* later published correspondence in which the churchwardens raised further concerns. The bishop, however, once again sided with the vicar. The *Times* sided with the churchwardens in an editorial and concluded, 'It appears to us that both the Bishop of London and the Vicar of Ware are without excuse.' *Times*, 13 Nov. 1844.

13 *Record*, 1 Jan. and 8 March 1844. At East Farleigh, the innovations were introduced by Henry Wilberforce, one of the sons of William Wilberforce, the prominent Evangelical anti-slavery crusader.

14 Ibid. Bishop Blomfield requested that the churchwardens leave the new credence table in the church unless otherwise directed by him. The credence table was a 'side table on which the bread and wine is placed until the Offertory sentences have been read.' The *Record* expressed its opposition on the grounds that its use broke with 'universal' practice, in which the elements were placed on the communion table (they would not refer to it as an 'altar') by attendants before the service. The Ritualists now sought to change the furniture and procedure: 'Every clergyman is to place the bread and wine on the table himself; and the object of this is to introduce the idea of an offering, or oblation to God, of the elements which are to 'become the very body and blood of Christ our Saviour.' The paper thought it lamentable that Blomfield would allow such an innovation and not recognize it for

what it was – the introduction of Popery. *Record*, 11 Jan. 1844.

15 Phillpotts appointed a commission to investigate the charges which included Blunt's refusal of the Lord's Supper and burial rites to parishioners who had been baptized in Dissenting chapels, as well as his adoption of the surplice and a few other minor changes in the service. A complete report of the commission's proceedings was published in the *Times*, 15 and 16 Nov. 1844.

16 Mr. Hill, the churchwarden, told the commission that he would not have objected to the surplice 'except that it had become the badge of a party.' Phillpotts responded, 'This, I am aware, is a very common cry. But I cannot forbear from saying, that if any of the clergy deserve to be called a party, in an invidious sense of the phrase, they who agree in violating the law of the Church ought to be so designated, not they who observe it.... There is one way, and one only, in which all appearances of party and division among the clergy, in this respect, may be avoided. I mean by all of them complying with the easy requisition of the Church, that they wear one and the same garb, during the whole of the Communion service, including the sermon, which, I repeat, is only a part of that service.' The final report of the commission along with Phillpott's complete judgment was published in the *Times*, 19 Nov. 1844. Cf. Reed, *Glorious Battle*, pp. 35-37; and Balleine, *Evangelical Party*, pp. 175-76.

17 One correspondent in the *Record* admitted that most of the issues involved were rather insignificant. 'The only thing that adds importance to them, is the suspicion, which is generally entertained, that they are connected with other things of a more serious consequence; and this suspicion, under the present circumstances, is by no means groundless. And it is most strange that the Bishop regards it as unreasonable, when it is well known, that the Tractarians, some of whom have actually apostatized, began in this way, commenced their career by reviving obsolete rituals, and made so much of them as to lose sight wholly of the fundamental doctrines of the Reformation.' Letter to the *Record*, 28 Nov. 1844.

While acknowledging that most of the changes were relatively harmless, the *Quarterly Review* was also concerned about the cumulative effect. When considered altogether, the changes seemed 'to confer on the table the character of a *sacrificial altar*' and to create 'a superstitious reverence of the elements which the Church of England has never sanctioned.' The writer was especially disturbed by the adoption of the eastward position. The other changes might be considered insignificant, but that alteration appeared to threaten the fundamental idea of 'common prayer.' It was 'a most blamable misconception' of the priest's function, and, whatever the original intent, it was 'a most dangerous recurrence to Romanist – nay, Pagan practices.' Anon. 'Rubrics and Rituals,' *Quarterly Review*, pp. 266-67, 276-77 (their italics).

18 Henry Phillpotts, *Letter to the Clergy of the Diocese of Exeter on the Observance of the Rubric in the Book of Common Prayer*; cited in the *Record*, 5 Dec. 1844.

The *Record* complained that the clergy had surrendered too easily: 'What chiefly mortifies us so far in this business is the universal timidity of the parochial clergy of the city of Exeter: it is stated that every one of them, without exception, assumed the surplice in the pulpit last Sunday! This on the mandate of their Bishop, probably illegal, which so far from considering "godly," some of them viewed as "ungodly," and which accordingly it was morally and religiously impossible they could obey with a "glad mind".' *Record*, 12 Dec. 1844. It was somewhat ironic that the paper should have written in such terms of the clergy's right to judge episcopal admonitions in such a manner and obey only those they considered 'godly.' The argument was quite similar to that used by the Ritualists later to justify their own disobedience.

19 *Record*, 30 Dec. 1844. Phillpotts suggested 'that in using your own discretion in this particular, you will so use it as shall least expose you to the reproach of cherishing party spirit. Wherever, therefore, the surplice is now used without offense, there I hope it will be continued in use.' Phillpotts, *Letter to the Clergy of the Diocese of Exeter*; cited in Ibid.

20 The paper hoped the 'influential meeting' would indicate to Phillpotts that he had 'entered upon an undertaking which, on calm reflection, as well as by general acclamation, has been condemned, and that he errs grievously if he still supposes that anything short of entire concession will appease the popular irritation which he has so inconsiderately roused into action.' The article reproduced the memorial as well as the petition to the queen that was drawn up and unanimously adopted at the meeting. *Times*, 3 Jan. 1845.

21 In fairness to them we must allow, that this dislike of alterations in the manner of worship to which they have been accustomed from their infancy, proceeding, as it does, from attachment to the ordinances of the Church, ought not to be visited with unkindly censure; and we can hardly be surprised at any change being regarded with suspicion when so many attempts have been made to introduce innovations which are really objectionable.' Cited in the *Record*, 16 Jan. 1845.

22 Ibid. In this regard, Howley's final conclusion was similar to that of Phillpotts, but more moderate in tone. Tractarians were unimpressed with the letter. In 1846, William Gresley illustrated an interesting anomaly in the extreme High Church position – while attempting to elevate the authority of the bishops, the ritual innovators were rarely willing to submit to any authority that favored their opponents. Gresley repudiated the archbishop's authority, in this instance, and claimed that only Convocation could authorize the alteration of the rubrics. He went on to accuse Howley of virtually establishing 'the very principle of Nonconformity" in the church by giving congregations "a license to depart from the prescribed ritual.' In this, Gresley concluded, he was giving the vestry ultimate control over the ritual of each parish – a power that ought to preside with the diocesan. W. Gresley, *The Real Danger of the Church of England* (London: James Burns, 1846), pp. 13-14.

Francis Close noted the irony of Gresley's attacks on the episcopacy. The extreme section of the High Church, while elevating the episcopacy in principle to an 'almost apostolic' status, frequently criticized and condemned any bishop that 'opposed their peculiar opinions.' Francis Close, *An Apology for the Evangelical Party* (London: J. Hatchard & Son, 1846), pp. 7-8. Interestingly, the Ritualists would later turn the archbishop's logic on its head to support their innovations, and they were then accused by their critics of importing congregationalism into the Church of England.

23 Woolmer wrote to Phillpotts, 'After the morning service in St. Sidwell's, Mr. Courtenay was met at the church-yard-gate by a large mob of persons, and upwards of 600 followed him with occasional hisses and groans till he had reached his residence on Southernhay. In the afternoon, notwithstanding pouring rain, more than 2,000 persons assembled in the same disorderly way, and with increased violence desecrated the Sabbath.... In the evening, Dr. Coleridge, who preached at St. Sidwell's in his surplice, was also assailed by a formidable mob on his quitting the church.

'I felt it to be my duty, with the concurrence of the magistrates who have assisted me, to give your Lordship this information; and respectfully to inquire if your Lordship can recommend any measures to prevent the cause of such disorderly assemblies.' Correspondence reprinted in the *Record*, 3 Feb. 1845. Phillpotts denied any responsibility for the riots, but he agreed to ask Courtenay not to preach in his surplice. Ibid. Cf. Chadwick, *Victorian Church, Part One*, pp. 219-20.

24 *Times*, 12 Nov. 1844.

25 Whether or not it had doctrinal significance, the introduction of the weekly offertory was quickly taken up as another innovation over which the two sides were divided along party lines. In his pamphlet accusing Evangelicals of being the real threat to the church, William Gresley included it in his list of 'church principles' which had been opposed by the 'Puritan party.' He bemoaned the fact that the Bishop of Exeter had not been supported by the rest of the episcopacy on this issue. Gresley, *Real Danger of the Church of England*, pp. 11-12.

In response to Gresley, Francis Close argued that 'vital doctrines' were involved in the ceremonial innovations, however slight they might seem. The conflict involved 'the essentials of Protestant truth and Papal error,' and Evangelicals were determined 'to resist the one and cling to the other.' Close, *Evangelical Party*, pp. 15-18.

26 *Record*, 18 Nov. 1844. Looking back from 1881, Samuel Garratt observed that Ritualism aroused much more alarm than had the Oxford Movement simply because it touched on the familiar and the traditional in the worship service. 'Men, neither thoughtful nor religious, united with those who saw its spiritual danger, in denouncing it, and numbers, utterly indifferent to what was preached, were indignant at finding alterations in the accustomed order of their churches.' Samuel Garratt, *What Shall We Do? Or, True Evangelical Policy* (London: William Hunt & Co., 1881), p. 11.

William Gresley accused Evangelicals of allying with "the spirit of the world" in order to combat the High Church movement. 'They have to thank the *Times* and *Quarterly Review* for their successful opposition to their Bishops... unquestionably this union with the powers of the world gives them a formidable influence.... They have acquired a sort of favour and popularity with the worldly and irreligious, which they did not before possess, as opponents of an encroaching priesthood, and defenders of the nation from ecclesiastical tyranny.' Gresley blamed the episcopacy for allowing the Evangelical party to gain sufficient power to threaten the church. The bishops, said Gresley, were men of both the church and the world; and they had been too willing to sacrifice the truth of the gospel for the sake of conciliation in the eyes of the world. In his opinion, the only resolution would be for the episcopacy to stop ordaining Evangelicals. Gresley, *Real Danger of the Church of England*, p. 30, pp. 54-60.

27 The most thorough study of the Camden Society is James F. White, *The Cambridge Movement* (Cambridge: Cambridge University Press, 1962). White, however, dealt with the controversy surrounding St. Sepulchre's only briefly and omitted a number of the details that cast the Camden Society in a bad light; cf. pp. 136-38. Nigel Yates noted the role played by the society in the developing interest in a more ceremonial ritual. Yates, *Oxford Movement*, pp. 15-16.

James Bentley more thoroughly considered the intermediary role played by the Camden Society in the transformation of Tractarianism into Ritualism. Bentley, *Ritualism and Politics*, pp. 25-27. That point has been similarly emphasized by John Shelton Reed, who suggested that it was but a small step from 'ornamenting the church' to 'ornamenting the ministers and choir,' and then on to 'ornamenting the service.' Reed, *Glorious Battle*, p. 30.

A general survey of Victorian church architecture can be found in Horton Davies, *Worship and Theology in England, vol. 4: From Newman to Martineau, 1850-1900* (Princeton: Princeton University Press, 1962), pp. 42-64.

28 Cf. the *Record*, January through March, 1843.

29 The paper reported that Faulkner needed about three hundred pounds to complete the task, while 'the Camden Society has expended *thousands* in toys, painted windows, and other needless ornaments.' In contrast to other cases, here it was the incumbent defending Protestant principles, 'while the churchwardens, having been employed and flattered by the Cambden Society, reply to their pastor's letter in a most vehement epistle.' *Record*, 26 Feb. 1844 (their italics).

30 Close's sermon was the culmination of an ongoing pamphlet war he had carried on with a number of the supporters of the Camden Society. The pamphlets were summarized by White, *Cambridge Movement*, pp. 139-44. For a survey of Close's ministry, written largely from a negative and somewhat anti-Evangelical perspective, cf. Geoffrey Berwick, 'Close of Cheltenham: Parish Pope, Parts One and Two,' *Theology* 39 (1939): 193-201, 276-85.

31 Close reprinted his sermon with a new introduction in 1881. Over the course of years his mind was unchanged, and he thought events had proved him right. Nevertheless, the work of 'superstition' had continued to spread far and wide. 'There are few churches which have been faithfully restored to their original features which do not abound with Popish imagery; the dead walls corresponding with the dead forms of worship which in too many instances harmonize with the architectural superstition.' Francis Close, *The Restoration of Churches is the Restoration of Popery* (London: Newman & Co., 1881 reprint), pp. 3-4, 6.

In a review of the new edition, the *Record* noted that Close had received several congratulatory responses from bishops who were not identified with the Evangelical party. Bishop Copleston, of Llandaff, wrote, 'Your sermon contains the best exposure I have yet seen of that insidious Cambridge Camden Society, whose designs I have long suspected, and which I rejoice to see thus exhibited in their true character.' Correspondence cited in the *Record*, 13 April 1881.

Many Evangelicals shared Close's view of church architecture. In 1875, G. T. Fox complained of the growing interest in church restoration. 'The religion of the day is not to be measured by the zeal displayed for church building, a considerable portion of which must be traced up to the aestheticism and fashion of the age, and is compatible with great ignorance of Gospel truth, great worldliness, and general irreligiousness of character, whilst it is still more frequently connected with the development of that sensuous, unspiritual, superstitious creed, which is in closest alliance with that of Rome.' Letter to the *Record*, 1 Nov. 1875.

From a considerably more moderate Evangelical position, James Colley took a rather different view in 1869. He wrote, 'Forty years ago the revival of ecclesiastical architecture was looked upon, as Choral Services are now, with great suspicion, and loud was the outcry that it was leading us headlong to Popery; whereas the revolution has turned out to be a mere matter of taste; new Churches everywhere, and even dissenting meeting-houses, being now frequently erected after the most approved mediaeval models.' James Colley, *Evangelical Churchmanship: True Churchmanship* (London: William MacIntosh, 1869), p. 9.

32   Ibid., pp. 15-16 (his italics).
33   Cf. Faulkner's advertisement in the *Record*, 2 Jan. 1845, in which he thanked all those who gave him monetary support to finish the church and to pay his legal expenses. He gave a detailed version of the events at the church and accused the president of the Cambden Society of having worked to influence the churchwardens against him, even to the point of offering to pay their legal expenses if they would take the case to court. He noted that several bishops had sent money to assist him. The *Times* reported that Faulkner had received 'letters of support and encouragement from persons of rank and distinction, expressing in the strongest terms their approval of his conduct in oppostion to the stone altar and credence table.' They quoted from the letter sent by the Bishop of Llandaff, who also enclosed five pounds to assist Faulkner. *Times*, 1 Jan. 1845.
34   *Times*, Jan. 1, 1845.
35   'This was not what is called courteous in the ordinary intercourse of society. Something there is due to every one in his station, and to a clergyman, certainly, in altering or beautifying his church, one might have supposed constant reference would have been made in every instance where a doubt existed as to his acquiescence. But no; the Camden Society is above such condescension, and omits the compliment which even railway companies feel themselves bound to pay.' Ibid.
36   The *Times* noted that even the Bishop of Exeter, 'himself the object of distrust, in consequence of his countenancing rubrical alterations distasteful to the laity, has shown his dislike to their principles by withdrawing his name from their list of members.' Ibid.
37   The society disbanded a short time later; cf. Chadwick, *Victorian Church, Part One*, p. 221.

38 In 1846, even before the controversy over Gorham had begun, William Gresley suggested that Evangelical theology had no place the Church of England. In his view, the fundamental issue was the doctrine of baptismal regeneration, and Evangelicals were heretics who were eroding the foundation of the church. Gresley, *Real Danger of the Church of England*, pp. 15-28. Francis Close responded to Gresley's charges and summarized the traditional Evangelical position that attempted to reconcile a belief in the necessity of conversion with the doctrine of infant baptism. Close, *Evangelical Party*, pp. 15-17.

39 Cf. Gorham's detailed summary of his conflicts with Phillpotts and the examination in his letter in the *Record*, 17 April 1848. According to Balleine, Phillpotts began a campaign against Evangelicals shortly after the failure of his attempt to institute the surplice; 'licenses were refused to Evangelical curates; licenses were withdrawn from proprietary chapels; the clergy were forbidden to admit into their pulpits deputations from the Evangelical societies.' Balleine, *Evangelical Party*, p. 176. On 12 Jan. 1843, the *Record* noted that Phillpotts had recently revoked the licenses of two clergy; one for his views on baptismal regeneration (Rev. Beale at Tavistock) and one for his attacks on Puseyism (Rev. Babb at Turnchapel). For a detailed summary of the Gorham case, cf. Chadwick, *Victorian Church, Part One*, pp. 250-71.

40 Bowen, *Idea of the Victorian Church*, p.96. According to Bowen, Bishop Phillpotts was not well-liked in his diocese and 'had a reputation for nepotism, time-serving and pluralism.' He was also combative and was involved in over fifty lawsuits during his episcopate. He was similarly portrayed by Chadwick, *Victorian Church, Part One*, pp. 217-18.

41 'In the course of it, 149 questions were proposed to me, on the single subject of *baptismal efficacy*, the Bishop making a constant effort to impose on me *his* interpretation of the Articles and Formularies, while I maintained my ground of a sincere "subscription" to the Articles, in their plain sense, as the *standard* of the doctrines of the Church; and of an honest "assent" to the Formularies, interpreted in conformity with that *standard*.' *Record*, 17 April 1848 (their italics).

There has been only one thorough study of the Gorham case, J. C. S. Nias, *Gorham and the Bishop of Exeter* (London: SPCK, 1951). Nias gave extensive accounts and analyses of the original examination, the court cases, Bishop Phillpotts' letter to Archbishop Sumner and some of the tracts published in the wake of the final decision. He has also provided a comprehensive bibliography on the subject. He did not, however, devote much space to the impact of the controversy.

For a brief look at the Gorham case a century later, written from the perspective of a twentieth-century Evangelical, cf. J. R. S. Taylor, 'Gorham on Infant Baptism,' *Churchman*, New Series 66 (1952): pp. 141-47. Taylor surveyed both the strong and weak points of Gorham's defense before Phillpotts.

42 'If, in my case, this precedent be established, a Tractarian Bishop (or one who, in any other respects, un-episcopally acts as the influential leader of a reckless party,) will be able to exclude from his diocese, not only stipendiary and perpetual Curates whose views he dislikes (as the Bishop of Exe-

ter does, and, it is said, can do, without appeal, in the existing state of the law), but to prevent any clergyman being appointed to Benefices therein, whatever be their age, station, or qualifications, whose religious sentiments are opposed to the Diocesan's peculiar standard and private views.' Letter to the *Record*, 17 April 1848.

43 Chadwick, *Victorian Church, Part One*, p. 256. According to Chadwick, Gorham's supporters numbered many 'for whom the name of Phillpotts was anathema.'

44 An account of the presentations made before the Arches Court can be found in the *Record*, 1 and 15 March 1849.

45 Gorham in his personal views was perhaps not entirely representative of Evangelicalism as a whole, but he did reflect the widespread rejection of baptismal regeneration as commonly held by the High Church. All honest clergy must have held some form of the doctrine since the baptismal service included the concluding words, 'This child is regenerate.' The question then became how that regeneration was to be interpreted. For many Evangelicals, it involved what came to be called a 'charitable hypothesis.' The blessings gained for the infant through baptism were believed to be conditional on a later act of personal acceptance. Thus the infant could be proclaimed regenerate and be accepted into the church, but final proof of the efficacy of grace would be postponed until the child matured and took up the faith in a personal way. Cf. Balleine, *Evangelical Party*, pp. 177-78.

46 'That all the baptized should be spiritually regenerate was in their view utterly impossible; and therefore they could not intend, in the formularies they drew up, to require or to express such a belief, unless we unfairly attribute to them that shameless effrontery, that gross and scandalous dishonesty, which to the reproach of our times, has been openly avowed by some, that men may teach what they do not believe, and that they may believe what is contrary to their teaching. With the knowledge of this *historical fact* before us, we cannot insist on it as a *ruled doctrine* of our Church that all baptized children are, as such, spiritually regenerate. For such was not the doctrine of our Reformers themselves. Nor is such doctrine laid down in the Thirty-Nine Articles.' Cited in the *Record*, 12 July 1849 (their italics).

47 The question, in the archbishop's opinion, had to be left open and differing opinions had to be considered with charity. In what seems to have been a pointed reference to Bishop Phillpotts of Exeter, he concluded, 'It is not a Christian part to cast stones at every one who on abstruse and intricate questions does not see exactly with our eyes, and in ignorance of the truth of history, to deal out anathemas.' Ibid.

48 *Record*, 30 July 1849. Comparatively little has been written on Archbishop Sumner. According to Nigel Scotland, he has been overlooked both as a Churchman and an Evangelical leader because, apparently out of a sense of modesty, he left behind no personal collected papers. Scotland argued that Sumner's episcopate was characterized by a non-partisan and moderate spirit that had a great calming effect on the church. Nigel Scotland, 'John Bird Sumner in Parliament,' *Anvil* 7 (1990), pp. 141-53.

49 William Goode, *The Doctrine of the Church of England as to the Effects of Baptism in the Case of Infants* (London: Hatchard & Sons, 1849).

50 The *Record*, gave an extensive report of the judgment, which was so long that it took four hours to read in court, on 6 August 1849. It reprinted the entire judgment from a published pamphlet on 22 October 1849.

51 For a detailed account of the arguments presented before the court, cf. the *Record*, 13, 17, and 20 December 1849. In 1862, the paper returned to the subject in a review of J. B. Mozeley's *A Review of the Baptismal Controversy*. The paper reported that it was William Goode who urged Gorham to appeal the judgment and helped in his defense, despite the fact that many Evangelicals, including Archbishop Sumner, wanted him to withdraw from the controversy and not appeal to the Privy Council (apparently fearing that another negative decision would invalidate the Evangelical position). *Record*, 12 Nov. 1862.

52 When Samuel Garratt reviewed the rise of the Ritualist movement, some thirty years after the Gorham decision, he still considered it an important turning point. He viewed it as the attempt of a Tractarian bishop to drive the whole Evangelical body out of the Church of England. Had Phillpotts been successful, the traditional Evangelical view of regeneration would have been unlawful. Garratt also thought the Gorham case was the real beginning of the program of prosecution in the Ritualist controversy, and one that was not begun by the Evangelical party. Nevertheless, he thought Evangelicals were badly served by following the example. 'The result in that case, both in its failure, and still more in the impetus which the attempt at crushing it gave to the Evangelical cause, ought to have prevented the leaders of that cause from imitating the bad tactics of their opponents.' Garratt, *What Shall We Do?*, p. 8, 13.

53 The *Record* accused the Tractarians of disingenuousness on this point. It cited articles by both William J. E. Bennett and Henry Wilberforce in which they rejected the right of the Judicial Committee to hear the case. They argued that the Arches Court was a spiritual one, since its justice was appointed by the Archbishop of Canterbury, and the appeal to a purely secular court should not have been allowed. The *Record* noted that some years prior, the same arguments were being used against the Arches Court when it had ruled against the legality of stone altars, which were favored by the High Church party. But now that the court had sided with them, it had suddenly become a 'spiritual' court and was fit to hear ecclesiastical appeals. The paper also asked how it could be a more spiritual court when its judge was a lay lawyer appointed by the archbishop, while the Judicial Committee included, in this instance, both archbishops as well as the Bishop of London. *Record*, 4 March 1850.

A. O. J. Cockshut, in an interesting study of controversies involving authority in the nineteenth-century Anglican church, devoted a chapter to the Gorham case. He interpreted it along the lines set down by Gorham's High Church opponents, who viewed it as a conflict over the limits of the state's ultimate right to intervene in spiritual matters. The great question was, wrote Cockshut, 'Is the Church of England a church, that is, an autonomous spiritual body dispensing doctrine and law, or is it a body dependent on the State, and destined always to alter its message in accordance with the changing pressures of national policy or popular opinion?' A. O. J.

Cockshut, *Anglican Attitudes* (London: Collins, 1959), p. 41. Gorham's view of what was involved in the case was substantially different, and he, along with most Evangelicals, would have fervently denied any intention of altering the fundamental message of the Gospel.

54 The ruling was reprinted in the *Record*, 11 March 1850. Bishop Blomfield explained his decision later that year in his charge; cf. C. J. Blomfield, *A Charge of the Bishop of London to the Clergy of his Diocese... on the occasion of his Sixth Visitation, November 1850*, cited in the *Record*, 4 Nov. 1850. For a sense of the importance of the case for Evangelicals of the day, cf. Eugene Stock, *The History of the Church Missionary Society: Its Environment, its Men, and its Work*, vol. 2 (London: Church Missionary Society, 1899), pp. 4-6.

55 The judgment cited numerous Anglican divines, including Jewell, Hooker, Usher, Taylor, Whitgift, Pearson, Carlton and Prideaux. Without arguing for the truth of their doctrine, it had to be allowed that the Articles and formularies of the church had left a great deal of liberty for seemingly contradictory positions. The ruling continued: 'The case not requiring it, we have abstained from expressing any opinion of our own upon the theological correctness or error of the doctrine of Mr. Gorham, which was discussed before us at such great length and with so much learning. His Honour the Vice-Chancellor Knight Bruce dissents from the opinion we have formed, but all the other members of the Judicial Committee who were present are unanimously agreed in opinion – that the doctrine held by Mr. Gorham is not contrary or repugnant to the declared doctrine of the Church of England as by law established; and that Mr. Gorham ought not by reason of the doctrine held by him to have been refused admission to the vicarage of Brampford Speke.' Cited in the *Record*, 11 March 1850.

C. S. Bird later criticized the calls for a renewal of Convocation, which came following the Gorham decision, on this ground. The Judicial Committee's decision had 'no intention whatever of deciding the truth of any doctrine, or restraining the liberty of any man's opinions, provided he will not take away the same liberty from his neighbour. The sentence has left the doctrine what it found it.' The ruling, Bird continued, had 'proceeded on the plain historical ground, that Mr. Gorham had but used a freedom, which the Church of England had silently granted to all her children since the Reformation, and which some of the most illustrious had used. Nevertheless, these men insist on having the power to take that freedom away. In demanding this power from Convocation, they would necessarily assail the Reformers and their successors, the fathers of our Church.' C. S. Bird, *The Dangers Attending an Immediate Revival of Convocation, detailed in a Letter to the Rev. G. Hutton, Rector of Gate Burton* (London: T. Hatchard, 1852), pp. 8-9, and p. 20.

According to Donald Lewis, the Gorham controversy accomplished two things. First, it made Evangelicals more keenly aware of their Reformation heritage and thus 'served to underline their points of divergence from Catholic and Tractarian teaching.' Second, it confirmed in Evangelicals the assurance of their place in the Church of England. In Lewis's thesis, this new confidence allowed Evangelicals to cooperate more freely with Dissent and to be less concerned with what their High Church critics thought.

Lewis, *Lighten Their Darkness*, p. 186.

56 A list of nine resolutions were widely circulated by some of the leaders of the movement, in which they outlined their case against the judgment on doctrinal and ecclesiastical grounds. In general, they argued that Gorham's doctrine was heretical and that its adoption would divide the Anglican church from the rest of Christendom. They concluded by calling on the episcopacy to reaffirm the High Church view of baptismal regeneration. The statement was signed by H. E. Manning, Robert J. Wilberforce, Thomas Thorp, W. H. Mill, E. B. Pusey, John Keble, W. Dodworth, William J. E. Bennett, Henry W. Wilberforce, Richard Cavendish, Edward Badeley and James R. Hope. Cf. the *Record*, 21 March 1850.

George A. Denison published two strongly worded protests challenging the validity of the court's decision and the orthodoxy of all those involved in it, from the judges to the archbishop to the queen. The *Times* published his protests but responded critically: 'A misguided clergyman, whose fanaticism may serve to protect him from the ecclesiastical censures and legal penalties to which his violent language and illegal conduct undoubtedly expose him, has been moved by the irritation caused by the decision of the Privy Council on the case of Mr. Gorham to protest with a ridiculous solemnity against the legal constitution of the Church to which he professes to belong. We had anticipated, as our readers may remember, some opposition of this sort to the moral effect of the late judgment; but we had hardly anticipated that any beneficed clergyman of the Church of England would have presumed so far on the indulgence of his diocesan or the indifference of the public as to declare his open resistance to every authority which he is bound to obey. Mr. George Anthony Denison, Vicar of East Brent, has delivered himself of the burden which this judgment seems to have cast upon his uneasy conscience, but he has violated the statutes of the realm, he has violated the canons of the Church, he has broken his oath of canonical obedience to the Articles of that Church, and he has been wanting in his duty to the undoubted supremacy of the Crown.' *Times*, 15 March 1850.

57 Cited in the *Record*, 25 July 1850. According to the *Record*, the meeting was attended by about 800-900 clergy ('mostly young') and about 300-400 laity. But the paper thought it an important sign that there were few dignitaries in attendance – only the Bishop of Bath and Wells and four archdeacons.

58 'Mr. Gorham's case having been brought before the legitimate tribunal, and solemnly deliberated upon, the sentence of the Court was pronounced to the effect that there was no just impediment to his institution.

'Your address proposes that I should assume to myself the authority of reversing this sentence of the Court; should refuse to do what the law requires of me; and should deny to Mr. Gorham a right to which, after a legal trial and examination, he is declared to be entitled.' Cited in the *Record*, 12 August 1850.

59 The *Record* reprinted the conclusion of Phillpotts' pamphlet: 'Meanwhile, I have one most painful duty to perform. I have to protest not only against the judgment pronounced in the recent case, but also against the regular consequences of that judgment. I have to protest against your Grace doing what you will be speedily called to do, either in person or by some other

exercising your authority. I have to protest, and I do hereby solemnly protest, before the Church of England, before the Holy Catholic Church, before Him who is the Divine Head, against your giving mission to exercise cure of souls, within my diocese, to him who proclaims himself to hold the heresies which Mr. Gorham holds. I protest that any one who gives mission to him till he retracts is a favourer and supporter of heresies. I protest, in conclusion, that I cannot without sin – and by God's grace will not – hold communion with him, be he who he may, who shall so abuse the high commission which he bears.' Henry Phillpotts, *A Letter to the Archbishop of Canterbury. By the Bishop of Exeter*, cited in the *Record*, 25 March 1850.

Phillpotts questioned in court the right of the archbishop to intervene in his diocese, but that decision went against him as well, and Gorham was finally installed in his parish in August 1850. The rulings, however, did little to alter Phillpotts' opinion of his own episcopal power. The *Record* continued to report on his activities, and in 1855, published the correspondence of John Hatchard, Vicar of St. Andrew's, Plymouth, who attempted to hire an Evangelical curate. Phillpotts examined the curate, James Turner, who had been ordained for over seven years, and rejected him because of his deficient view of infant baptism. *Record*, 21 June 1855.

60 Among them were several of the young leaders of the movement, including Henry Manning, Robert and Henry Wilberforce and James Hope-Scott. For an extended survey of the reactions to the decision of the Judicial Committee, cf. Chadwick, *Victorian Church*, Part One, pp. 261-71. For a detailed study of the painful processes they went through in their separation from the Anglican Church and family ties, cf. David Newsome, *The Wilberforces and Henry Manning* (Cambridge: Harvard University Press, 1966).

To the credit of the Evangelicals, there was a great deal of talk about secession following the decision of the Court of Arches, but almost all of the correspondence in the *Record* was opposed to it. In the months leading up the hearing before the Judicial Committee, almost all of the writers argued that the proper course was to stay in the Church of England, even if the final decision went against them. On 8 October 1849, the *Record* also took that position in an editorial.

Over half a century later, the Gorham decision still bothered Anglo-Catholics. In his survey of the Anglo-Catholic revival, W. J. S. Simpson thought it was easy to sympathize with the extreme reaction the judgment evoked from the High Church clergy. After the lapse of some years, however, he confidently proclaimed that "the Privy Council Decision on Baptismal Regeneration is practically as if it had never been." W. J. Sparrow Simpson, *The History of the Anglo-Catholic Revival from 1845* (London: George Allen & Unwin, 1932), p. 51. Regardless of the argument over the validity of a secular court attempting to determine the boundaries of the church's formularies, Simpson suggested that their decisions ultimately had little importance. In the Gorham case, 'a priest pronounced heretical by the Ecclesiastical Court was allowed to contradict the Church's formularies on Baptism,' but the Anglo-Catholics continued, in Simpson's opinion, to proclaim the true doctrine of the Anglican Church. Ibid., p. 64.

61 The name 'papal aggression' was popularly given to the reconstitution of

the Roman Catholic hierarchy in England in 1850. The announcement was made by Cardinal Wiseman in a somewhat inflammatory pastoral letter, entitled 'From out of the Flaminian Gate,' that resulted in a wave of new anti-Catholic protests. For the general context of the English reactions to the papal brief, cf. Walter Ralls, 'The Papal Aggression of 1850: A Study in Victorian Anti-Catholicism,' *Church History* 43 (1974): 242-56; and D. G. Paz, 'Popular Anti-Catholicism in England, 1850-1851,' *Albion* 11 (1979): 331-59. The anti-Catholic political activities during this period have been well-summarized by E. R. Norman, *Anti-Catholicism in Victorian England* (New York: Barnes & Noble, 1968). On papal aggression, cf. pp. 57-75.

The rivalry between Tractarians and Evangelicals did not begin at mid-century with the Gorham case and papal aggression. It had been building since the later years of the Oxford Movement and the early 1840s, and anti-Catholic feelings were especially roused by the Maynooth Grant in 1845. But events at mid-century gave new focus to the controversy. Regarding this period G. I. T. Machin wrote, 'Tractarians, on the other hand, were regarded as a Romanizing group within the Church, and were if possible more disliked than Rome itself.... For the rest of the nineteenth century the Tractarian and Evangelical movements pulled the Church of England in opposite directions, the broad churchmen pulling it in a third.' G. I. T. Machin, *Politics and the Churches in Great Britain, 1832-1868* (Oxford: Oxford University Press, 1977), p. 91.

62 The *Times*, in an editorial, pointed out that Blomfield ought to share in the blame. The paper suggested that in condemning those who had aided the progression, 'the Bishop of London may not have called to mind the ceremonies in which he himself consented to take a part at the consecration of St. Barnabas, Pimlico; but it is a matter of general regret that he did not avail himself of that occasion to restore that and other churches of his diocese to the simplicity which their character and purpose seemed peculiarly to demand.' Still, the paper supported the tone of the bishop's charge, which, it said, 'partakes of the nature of a political event.' In general, it thought the reaction to papal aggression indicated the strength of English religious convictions, however crudely they might be expressed. *Times*, 4 Nov. 1850.

63 Blomfield continued: 'A taste has been excited in them for forms and observances, which has stimulated without satisfying their appetites; and they may have naturally sought for its fuller gratification in the Church of Rome. They have been led step by step to the very verge of the precipice, and then to the surprise and disappointment of their guides, have fallen over.' With regard to doctrine, he complained of a growing devotion to Mary, the attribution of 'a propitiatory virtue' to the Eucharist, prayers for the dead, the renewal of auricular confession, the use of crucifixes and a revival of the sacrament of penance. Concerning ritual changes, he said, 'These innovations have, in some instances, been carried to such a length as to render the Church Service almost *histrionic*. I really cannot characterize by any gentler term the continual changes of posture, the frequent genuflexions, the crossings, the peculiarities of dress, and some of the decorations of churches, to which I allude. They are, after all, a gross imitation of the Ro-

man ceremonial.' Cited in the *Times*, 4 Nov. 1850 (their italics).

64 Lord John Russell, *Letter to the Bishop of Durham* (4 Nov. 1850), cited in the *Times*, 7 Nov. 1850.

Robert Klaus wrote, 'The papal aggression, rather than uniting the Church of England against the foreign intruder, pushed it to the brink of "wide open schism".' Robert J. Klaus, *The Pope, the Protestants and the Irish: Papal Aggression and Anti-Catholics in Mid-Nineteenth Century England* (New York: Garland Publishing, 1987), pp. 145-6. Klaus, however, thought the attempt to turn anti-Catholic sentiment against the Tractarians was rather disingenuous. 'For some, like Russell and the Evangelical Party of the Church of England, the hierarchy was a kind of windfall to be turned to account and worked for a profit.' Ibid., p. 236.

On the political and social context of Russell's letter and his general dislike for the Tractarians, cf. G. I. T. Machin, *Politics and the Churches in Great Britain, 1832-1868*, (Oxford: Oxford University Press, 1977), pp. 209-17; and John Nikol, 'The Oxford Movement in Decline: Lord John Russell and the Tractarians, 1846-1852,' *Historical Magazine of the Protestant Episcopal Church* 43 (1974): 341-57. On the Evangelical view of Roman Catholicism as a threat to the Protestantism and security both of the church and the nation, cf. John Wolffe, 'Evangelicalism in mid-nineteenth-century England,' in *Patriotism: The Making and Unmaking of British National Identity*, vol. 1, ed. Raphael Samuel (London: Routledge, 1989), pp. 188-200.

65 For a summary of Shaftesbury's speech, cf. Edwin Hodder, *The Life and Work of the Seventh Earl of Shaftesbury, K.G.*, Popular Ed., (London: Cassell & Co., 1890), pp. 431-34.

The memorial touched on papal aggression, but the bulk of the address dealt with ritual innovation in the Church of England. The memorialists complained 'that the Court of Rome would never have attempted such an act of aggression had not encouragement been held out to that encroaching power by many of the clergy of our own Church, who have for several years past shown a desire to assimilate the doctrines and services of the Church of England to those of the Roman communion. While we would cheerfully contend for the principles of the Reformation against all open enemies, we have to lament that our most dangerous foes are those of our own household; and hence we feel that it is to little purpose to repel the aggressions of the foreigner, unless those principles and practices which have tempted him to such aggressions be publicly and universally repudiated.

'We... humbly entreat your Majesty, in the exercise of your Royal prerogative to direct the attention of the primates and bishops of the Church to the necessity of using all fit and lawful means to purify it from the infection of false doctrine; and, as respects external and visible observances, in which many novelties have been introduced, to take care that measures may be promptly adopted for the repression of all such practices.'

The memorial went on to charge that the innovations all tended to highlight the 'sacramental system' and separate the priest from the laity. Viewed separately, the alterations might appear insignificant, but when considered altogether, they tended to undermine the Protestantism of the national church. A lengthy account of the meeting along with the entire memorial was published in the *Times*, 6 Dec. 1850.

66 G. W. E. Russell thought the Evangelical reaction to papal aggression was the turning point in their controversy with the High Church. From that time their oppsition grew and the 'bitterness increased tenfold.' He suggested that the negative transformation was what turned the Evangelical movement into the Low Church party. Russell, *Evangelical Movement*, p. 104.

Owen Chadwick suggested that the events of 1850 made the English more conscious of their Protestantism. Cf. Chadwick, *Victorian Church*, Part One, p. 303. He thought the papal aggression was a boon to the Evangelical party which went on to reach the height of its influence in the following decade. 'Five or six years after Dr. Wiseman was made a cardinal, in part because Dr. Wiseman was made a cardinal, the Evangelicals attained the summit of their influence in the Church of England.... The Evangelicals were never triumphant. But there was an epoch when they were powerful; the epoch after 1855, while the memory of papal aggression still rankled, while Sumner was still Archbishop of Canterbury, while Lord Palmerston presided over the cabinet, and while Shaftesbury the noble head of evangelical laymen was stepson-in-law to the prime minister.' Ibid., p. 440.

Donald Lewis similarly thought this period was the height of Evangelical influence, but he traced it to the Gorham decision rather than papal aggression. The conclusion of the Gorham case gave Evangelicals a new sense of self-confidence regarding their place in the Church of England. Evangelical clergy, during this period, were particularly influential in London, and they felt free to work in conjunction with like-minded Dissenters to achieve their common goals. Lewis, *Lighten Their Darkness*, pp. 231-2.

67 Only four bishops did not sign the letter: Bagot (Bath and Wells), Hampden (Hereford), Lee (Manchester) and Phillpotts (Exeter). The full document was reproduced in Anonymous, 'Rubric Versus Usage,' *Quarterly Review* 89 (1851): 204-208.

In his history of the CMS, Eugene Stock noted that some supporters of the society wanted it to issue its own protest against the Ritualists. The general committee, however, refused to do so. Whatever their own personal sympathies, they noted that the CMS, as a foreign missions organization, had always avoided any 'direct part in controversial movements at home.' That position would later draw criticism from conservative Evangelicals. Stock, *Church Missionary Society*, vol. 2, pp. 8-9.

68 Anon., 'Rubric Versus Usage,' *Quarterly Review*, p. 205.

69 The bishops rejected the argument of the Ritualists that 'whatever form or usage existed in the Church before its reformation may now be freely introduced and observed, unless there can be alleged against it the distinct letter of some formal prohibition.' Ibid., pp. 205-6.

70 Ibid., p. 206.

71 Ibid., p. 207.

72 Ibid., p. 215.

73 There were a few voices of reason during the period. Robert Aitken, in a visitation sermon to the diocese of Exeter, argued for the necessity of maintaining both the Evangelical and High Church positions within the Church of England. Aitken thought either group, left without the moderat-

ing influence of the other, tended to move toward an exaggerated position – Evangelicalism drifted into antinomianism and the High Church moved into cold formalism. He concluded that it was 'God's good providence,' that the Anglican church should have come to possess 'a Catholic liturgy and evangelical articles of faith.' Robert Aitken, *Truth Against Truth; or, the Battle of the Covenants* (London: W. M. Pardon, 1851), p. vi. Aitken was influential during the course of the century among those who had sympathies for both positions, several of whom became leaders of the diocesan missions movement which combined elements of Tractarianism with evangelistic preaching. His son, W. H. Hay Aitken, became one of the most prominent mission preachers.

74 The Conventicle Acts prohibited the assembly of more than twenty people for religious worship outside buildings of the established church (with the Toleration Act of 1689, the privilege was extended to include licensed Dissenting chapels).

Shaftesbury viewed the existing law as the chief impediment to reaching the masses 'who were absolutely without the pale of Christianity.' Bishop Wilberforce took the lead in opposing the bill, arguing that it would destroy the parochial system and allow clergy to cross parish boundaries. According to him, the episcopacy was unanimous in its opposition. The first vote in the House of Lords was 31 in favor, and 30 opposed. *Times*, 13 June 1855. In an editorial supporting the bill, the *Record* noted the irony of the Bishop of Oxford's opposition, since his own father, William Wilberforce, had frequently broken the law and held large religious gatherings at his home. *Record*, 14 June 1855.

A detailed account of the opposition to the bill can be found in Shaftesbury's biography. Lord Derby offered an alternate bill on behalf of the High Church party, but it was withdrawn in the face of strong opposition. Thereafter, support gathered for Shaftesbury's bill. Hodder, *Life of Shaftesbury*, pp. 511-15.

75 Anonymous Letter to the *Record*, 21 June 1855.

76 The *Times* lent its editorial weight in favor of the bill, but disliked the style of its Evangelical supporters. It was worried that many zealous Anglicans were forced out of the church by the current state of the law, even if they wanted to be loyal. There were others who simply defied the law, 'who preach and pray themselves in public, upon all manner of pretenses, of course innocent enough, but who are taught rather to plume themselves on the notion that they are defying the law. That evidently is Lord Shaftesbury's tone. He is rather pleased than otherwise at the thought that he and his legionaries of the City Mission and other similar societies are so many religious Arabs, pitching their tents anywhere, and despising the orthodox dwellers in consecrated walls. Such a feeling is very natural under the circumstances, though rather too braggart for our taste.' *Times*, 18 June 1855.

77 The *Record* feared that the working classes stood 'in suspicious isolation alike from the Church of England and from the Dissenting bodies of the land.... We have long entertained great doubts whether the resources of the Church in this direction have been properly applied. New churches have been built and opened, but the services have been confined to the old paro-

chial routine. The Church has stood far too stiffly and exclusively on her old recognized habits; and the rigidity of modern efforts for the extension of the Gospel stands in curious contrast with the pliant adaptability which marked the early ages of primitive Christianity.' *Record*, 26 Jan. 1857.

On the evangelistic interests of the period, cf. Eugene Stock, *The English Church in the Nineteenth Century* (London: Longman's Green & Co., 1910), pp. 54-55. James Bentley suggested that Shaftesbury's bill and the growth of the evening services movement was part of the Evangelical response to the 1851 census; they were appalled by its findings and began to search for ways to reach the unchurched masses. Bentley, *Ritualism and Politics*, pp. 9-10.

78 *Record*, March 2, 1857. According to J. C. Ryle, the first mission services were those held for six evenings in the parish of St. Martin's, Birmingham, with himself, Hugh M'Neile, and J. C. Miller preaching. J. C. Ryle, *No Uncertain Sound: Charges and Addresses* (Edinburgh: The Banner of Truth Trust, 1978), p. 154.

79 The services in St. George's were widely attended by 'many of the metropolitan clergy known for their love of high ritual observance.' *Record*, 6 May 1857.

80 A correspondent described the Bristol services, which were held on Thursday evenings from Jan. 22nd to March 19th, in school rooms throughout the city. The services were well-attended and were scheduled to begin again the following November. Anonymous Letter to the *Record*, 27 May 1857.

81 Advertisement in the *Record*, 15 May 1857. According to the *Times*, the use of a secular building for worship and preaching was traceable to C. H. Spurgeon, who attracted large crowds to the music hall at the Surrey Zoological Gardens. Shaftesbury helped organize a Special Services Committee that planned the Evangelical services. Unlike Spurgeon, however, who guaranteed the best seats for those who purchased tickets, the Evangelical meetings were open to all with no admission being charged. Exeter Hall was considered the best location for the meetings since it was easily accessible to the working classes. *Times*, 8 June 1857. Cf. Chadwick, *Victorian Church, Part One*, p. 525.

For a description of Exeter Hall and its use by the Evangelicals, especially for their 'May Meetings,' which were the annual meetings of the various Evangelical societies (both Anglican and nondenomi-national) held each year in April, May and June, cf. Leonard W. Cowie, 'Exeter Hall,' *History Today* 18 (1968), p. 390-97.

82 *Record*, 25 May 1857. After the first three services, however, the *Times* was unconvinced that the working classes formed a large proportion of the congregation. 'Judging from their general appearance, the great majority of the men who sought admission were in the position of decent clerks or small tradesmen.' The report did note with interest, however, that the congregation was predominately male, in contrast to the usual audience at the Exeter Hall May meetings. *Times*, 8 June 1857.

After the first service, Lord Dungannon challenged the legality and appropriateness of the meetings in the House of Lords, suggesting that they would 'introduce a sort of Spurgeonism into the Church of England.' Bishop Tait responded, 'Not only do I consider these meetings to be strictly legal but in the highest degree expedient. (Hear, hear.) I believe, from my heart, that there are thousands upon thousands of people in this metropolis and other large towns, of whose condition your Lordships are pained to hear, who have not entered a place of worship for many years. I believe that some such persons were present at the Meeting to which the Noble Lord has alluded, and I fondly trust they were not brought there without receiving benefit. (Hear, hear.)' Cited in the *Record*, 29 May 1857.

The *Times* criticized Dungannon in an editorial. He questioned the propriety of a bishop appearing on such a stage, to which the *Times* sarcastically asked where exactly a bishop ought to preach if he desired to reach those outside the church? 'One would think that the presence of that important and necessary element in the work of conversion – the sinner – was a great preliminary advantage, which was worth a slight sacrifice to form. But no, thinks Lord Dungannon, better to preach to ecclesiastical stone walls than to Exeter-hall souls....

'We must frankly, – for our own part, say that we like numbers in these cases; we like to see people brought together; we like masses.... We had rather, for association's sake, see it in the nave of St. Paul's than in Exeter-hall, but we had rather see it in Exeter-hall than nowhere.' *Times*, 1 June 1857.

83 The *Times* gave a thorough report of the third service in the series held on the 7th of June. It described the crowd present as well as the details of the service and a summary of the sermon preached by Capel Molyneux. The 'simple and practical sermon' lasted for about an hour, 'and the congregation listened throughout with earnest and almost breathless attention.' *Times*, 8 June 1857.

84 In a letter to Bishop Tait, Edouart wrote, 'In thus protesting against public preaching within my parish by strange clergymen, and in an unconsecrated building, I am only upholding the parochial system which for many centuries has been maintained inviolable throughout England, and am setting my face against a proceeding altogether irregular, and which, if permitted, would prove thoroughly subversive of all discipline and order in the Church.' Edouart allowed that he had given his reluctant consent to the earlier services but only on an experimental basis. He concluded, without any further elaboration, 'that experiment so utterly failed that I now feel doubly called upon to interpose the veto which I possess.' Correspondence cited in the *Record*, 13 Nov. 1857.

On Tait's position in the controversy, cf. Randall Thomas Davidson and William Benham, *Life of Archibald Campbell Tait, Archbishop of Canterbury*, vol. 1 (London: Macmillan & Co., 1891), pp. 255-59. According to the *Edinburgh Review*, Tait was convinced that the church had to adapt to meet the challenges of urban centers, and unlike his predecessor, Bishop Blomfield, he was willing to support new endeavors. Anonymous, 'The Life of Archbishop Tait,' *Edinburgh Review* 174 (1891): 478-49. Similarly, cf. Anonymous, 'Archbishop Tait and the Primacy,' *Quarterly Review* 155 (1883): 12-13. Bishop Tait, in this regard, was much more kindly disposed toward Evangelicals than had been his predecessor, Bishop Blomfield. Tait was particularly concerned with reaching the unchurched masses and was willing to support almost any methods that might be useful in this regard. Cf. Lewis, *Lighten Their Darkness*, p. 254.

85 The *Record* noted the irony of Edouart's opposition – the immediate effect of his veto was to prevent his own diocesan from presiding over a service in his parish and to throw it open to the influence of Nonconformist preachers. *Record*, 18 Nov. 1857.

The *Quarterly Review* wrote favorably of the Exeter Hall services. 'The recent experiment of giving services in Exeter Hall was viewed with jealousy by Churchmen who could not reconcile themselves to the idea of a service in any but a consecrated building. But the object was to obtain a hearing for the Gospel-message from those who never could be induced to enter the doors of a church; and there is strong reason for believing that they, on their part, felt how much the Church was sacrificing of her conventional proprieties – how much she was going out of her way to seek them.' The article noted that there were many problems with the parochial system in overcrowded urban parishes and suggested that a degree of flexibility was needed. The writer also challenged Edouart's claim that the meetings were unsuccessful. While acknowledging that different interpretations could be put on the facts, it was clear 'the Hall, which contains upwards of five thousand persons, was overflowing. That a great mass of the working classes were present is undeniable, and of the many well dressed men who were seen amongst them, it is by no means certain (we wish it were) that even the majority were members of regular congregations. Contrary to the usual statistics of church attendance the men greatly outnumbered the women. We wish the reverend incumbent had paused to calculate how small a percentage of persons seriously affected among the vast multitude assembled would constitute a great success.' Anonymous, 'Church Extension,' *Quarterly Review* 103 (1858): 167-69.

The *Times* thought it difficult to assess the lasting impact of the meetings and concluded that most of the congregations probably did not consist of the working classes as intended. Nevertheless, the paper strongly supported any attempt to reach the masses and thought it was 'perfectly monstrous to say that a mere individual should have such a power as this – that a simple private clergyman should of his own paltry whim or scruple be enabled to thwart the public designs of a Bishop for his diocese, and suppress a powerful and a large and well-considered means of spiritual benefit.' The paper suggested that the law enabling a parish priest to veto the meetings should be abolished immediately. *Times*, 10 Nov. 1857.

86 The text of Shaftesbury's amendment can be found in John C. Miller, *Special Services in the Church of England: A Letter to the Rt. Hon. the Earl of Shaftesbury* (London: Thomas Hatchard, 1858), p. 4. Miller was the leading Evangelical clergyman in Birmingham and had been involved in a number of the special services throughout the country, but he was troubled by certain aspects of the amendment. He worried that it gave too much power to the diocesan and threatened the traditional freedom of the parochial clergy. He feared, for instance, that it could have been used by High Church clergy to invade Evangelical parishes (pp. 8-9). He went on to offer several limitations that might prevent abuses of the amendment or expansion of

episcopal authority.

His tract indicated that Shaftesbury's amendment did not find much support among the clergy, who feared encroachment upon their traditional sovereignty in their parish. This was true even in his own party, and Shaftesbury complained that the clerical reaction was indicative of 'an immense amount of sacerdotalism, even among the Evangelical clergy.' Hodder, *Life of Shaftesbury*, p. 543-44.

The *Quarterly Review* supported Shaftesbury's measure but noted that it was hastily worded and would require polishing. But, the reviewer continued, whatever its defects the remedy could not be as 'dangerous to the Church as the actual state of the law, which gives to one man the power, if he chooses to incur the awful responsibility of exerting it, to stop all her efforts to christianize a whole district.' Anon., 'Church Extension,' *Quarterly Review*, p. 171.

In August 1858, Edouart complained to Tait that Anglican clergy were involved in new services at Exeter Hall, apparently attempting to elude his veto by discarding the litany (the services were scheduled to include only hymns, extempore prayer and a sermon). Having obtained legal counsel, however. he decided not to pursue the matter but reiterated his opposition to the irregularities.

Bishop Tait's reply indicated that he had little sympathy for Edouart's position and clearly favored all attempts to reach the working classes of the city, whether or not they followed traditional forms: 'Allow me to say that I think you have come to a wise determination in resolving not to move further in the question of the Exeter Hall services. You are aware that I have all along been of the opinion that it is only in a technical sense that a great building like Exeter Hall, intended for the use of London generally, could be held, in its character of a place of public meeting, to be included in the parish of St. Michael's, Burleigh-street, and therefore subject to you. I have never been able to look upon the services there as likely to interfere with your parochial arrangements; and therefore it is, as you will understand, that I the more readily concur in the opinion of your friends, that you can in no way be held responsible for these services, and need have no apprehension lest you be compromised by ceasing to take any further steps against them. You may, with a perfectly safe conscience, leave the decision of the question, as to the propriety of the clergy of the diocese taking part in these services, in other hands; and if any such dangers to the Church as you seem to apprehend should arise from these services, no one can have any right to blame you....

'With respect to these Exeter Hall services you are, I think, right in coming now to the conclusion that on me must devolve the responsibility, if zealous efforts, on the part of my clergy, to enable the Church to do missionary work in the midst of our overwhelming population be allowed to interfere with sound doctrine or the due discipline of the Church.' Correspondence cited in the *Record*, 2 and 6 Aug. 1858.

87 *Record*, Jan. 4, 1858. In contrast, by the end of the century, Eugene Stock wrote with much admiration of Bishop Tait and the effectiveness of the new cathedral services he encouraged. Cf. Stock, *Church Missionary Society, vol. 2*,

pp. 28-29.
88   An advertisement for subscriptions to the London Diocesan Home Mission quoted from its charter and listed its council members. It was described as a society under the direction of the Bishop of London, 'instituted for the purpose of aiding the parochial clergy in the reclaiming of those large masses of persons of both sexes, whom a regular parochial system cannot at present reach. It proposes to employ ordained Missionaries, men specially suited for the work, to seek out, preach to, and visit, that large class, which to all intents and purposes is living without God in the world.' Evangelicals on the council included Lord Shaftesbury, Lord Ebury, J. Gurney Hoare, W. W. Champneys, J. H. Gurney, and Daniel Wilson. *Record*, 4 Feb. 1858.

The *Record* responded negatively when the mission announced the formation of a college where unmarried missioners could live together in community. When the Mission College of St. Paul was established, the paper immediately called on all Protestants to withhold their support. *Record*, 12 April 1858. A letter from a correspondent the next year illustrated the sort of innuendo and rumor that became a staple of the partisan warfare: 'Can you or any of your readers tell me who the present Principal of St. Paul's Mission College, Dean-street, Soho, is? Is he or is he not a "Tractarian?" If the rumours about him be correct, I very much doubt if he be "the right man in the right place." All who appear to know anything about the College and its Principal look upon it with great suspicion. What can the Bishop of London be thinking of to appoint a semi-Romanist as the Principal of a Mission College in Soho? I have heard from good authority that the Reverend Gentleman is strongly in favour of habitual auricular confession, and that ladies visit him frequently at the College as their Father Confessor. One thing is certain, that "Sisters" and Mothers Superior are closeted with him for hours together, and strict orders are given that they are not to be disturbed.' Letter (signed 'A Protestant') to the *Record*, 14 Jan. 1859.

89   *Record*, 4, 6, and 18 Jan. 1858. The paper was similarly critical when St. Paul's Cathedral was opened for evening services in Nov. 1858. There were about 2,500 people in attendance and over 10,000 had to be turned away, but the *Record* doubted the usefulness of cathedral services as a missionary endeavour. They were beautiful and many might be drawn for the 'show,' but they were ill-suited for presenting the gospel to the working classes. *Record*, 29 Nov. 1858.

90   *Record*, 28 April 1858. The *Record*, quickly attacked the Diocesan Home Mission when the services were announced, but in this case, the paper was too quick with its criticism. In the edition of April 30th, it printed a letter from Edward Parry, the secretary of the London Diocesan Home Mission, in which he stated that the mission was in no way connected to the Westminster Abbey services.

91   *Record*, 28 April 1858.

92   *Record*, 10 May 1858. By 1861, however, the perspective of the paper had changed. It took a positive view of a meeting convened by Lord Shaftesbury and the Bishop of London to describe for the nobility the great effects of the theatre services and the Diocesan Home Mission and to seek their financial

support. By then, the paper approved of the work of the mission. *Record*, 17 July 1861.

93 The controversy began in late 1858. In December, the *Times* published a letter in which Bishop Tait reiterated the substance of a meeting (necessitated by the complaints of the churchwardens) between himself and Bryan King. At the meeting, Tait raised the issue of green stoles worn by King and his assistant, and forbade 'these (you must excuse me for calling them) foolish vestments.' He concluded the letter with an admonition against further innovations: 'And now allow me, my dear Sir, to conclude by repeating, what I endeavoured to express to you at the close of our interview, how gladly I would endeavour to strengthen your hands if you could bring yourself to alter your course. I do beg you to give up the matters complained of, which are, I believe, a grievous impediment to your usefulness.' A duplicate of the letter was sent to the churchwardens at St. George's, and they forwarded it to the *Times*, with Tait's permission. It was clear from the events of the following year that King ignored Tait's warning. *Times*, 20 Dec. 1858. On Tait's role in the controversy, including some of his correspondence with those involved, cf. Davidson and Benham, *Life of Tait*, vol. 1, pp. 228-49.

John Shelton Reed dated the beginning of the Ritualist movement to the St. George's riots. In addition to all of the ritual elements being present, the events served to gather High Church support and led to the development of the English Church Union. Reed, *Glorious Battle*, pp. 57-59. He also suggested, however, that the riots had as much to do with King's personality as with his Ritualist innovations. He was, said the *Times* in a private report, 'as remarkable for his extreme pride and hauteur,' as he was 'notorious for want of propriety and discretion in the administration of the duties appertaining to his public function.' Cited in Ibid., pp. 168-69.

94 *Record*, 23 May 1859.

95 Some of the parish clergy refused to allow Allen to robe in the vestry and prevented him for a time from climbing to the pulpit, but he was vocally supported by the crowd. *Record*, 27 May 1859.

96 *Record*, 8 June 1859.

97 On the 9th of August, there was an altercation between some of the 'surpliced choristers and men standing in the lobby, as the former processed out of the church. There was much pushing and shoving, accompanied by cries of 'Turn out the Puseyites' and 'Go to Rome.' *Record*, 10 Aug. 1859. Two weeks later, the paper reported on a hearing concerning disturbances 'in which a Capt. Savage Hall (an adherent of Mr. King's) used his umbrella rather freely on a Mr. Rosin. He offered to apologize, and at the end of the examination the case was dismissed.' The magistrate said that 'it did appear there was no doubt that the rector's service was unpopular; and there was no doubt that the party opposed to the rector made all the disturbance, and conducted themselves in a very improper manner; but there was no justification for Capt. Hall striking a blow.' *Record*, 22 Aug. 1859.

98 After the disruption of the services on the 4th of September, Lee complained to the *Times* about the mob and defended his own moderate ritual. Letter to the *Times*, 6 Sept. 1859. The churchwarden, W. J. Thompson, immediately responded with a letter contradicting a number of the details

supplied by Lee, and suggesting that those present were only partly to blame. Another correspondent responded to Lee's letter. He wrote, 'The rev. gentleman has the remedy in his own hands, and he can cause a cessation of the disturbances at our parish church immediately by performing the services in a similar manner to those of the surrounding churches, and by delivering the sermon in a black gown. If the rev. gentleman will pursue this course next Sunday, he may be assured he will be free from any interruption.' Letters (signed 'An Old Inhabitant of St. George's') to the *Times*, 7 Sept. 1859.

99 The bishop went on to note that he had engaged King in several previous conversations and believed that 'common sense' would eventually prevail in the parish. He preferred not to enter into an uncertain course of legal prosecution which might only make matters worse and bring contempt upon the church. But he confessed that he would allow others, if necessary, to prosecute the rector for his use of offensive vestments. Correspondence cited in the *Times*, 8 Sept. 1859.

100 Ibid. For a time, A. H. Mackonochie, who would later become a prominent figure in the Ritualist controversy, was licensed to serve in the parish.

101 Having criticized the rioters, the paper continued, 'We must denounce with even greater energy the conduct of the Rector and his curates, for the simple reason that they ought to know better. Let them say what they will, the present position of matters at St. George's is clearly traceable to them.' *Record*, 9 Sept. 1859.

102 Tait's letter to the vestry read: 'I deem it necessary to close the parish church of St. George's-in-the-East for a time. This letter is to be your warrant for so closing it. I trust that arrangements will soon be made for enabling it to be reopened. The rector will, in the meanwhile, as is usual in such cases, provide for the due celebration of marriages, &c.' Correspondence cited in the *Times*, 23 Sept. 1859.

The *Times* followed the announcement with a withering editorial condemnation of the clergy involved. King had, the paper thought, brought the mob on himself by driving away his parishioners. 'The Rector was left without his natural parochial guard, and the enemy attacked him in that defenseless state. The discontent of the respectable gives scope to the passions of the vulgar.... The fabric of ritualism goes on rising and rising, adding stone to stone, filling up this space, pointing this corner, balancing here, and finishing off there, till, just as the coping stone is put to it, down it falls with a crash. The keen ritualist imagination cannot check itself, simple defect is destruction to it, and just to stop short of the vortex is the same as to have done nothing.... So Mr. Bryan King has advanced from the old original parson and clerk to choristers in surplices, from choristers in surplices to an ornamented chancel, from ornamented chancel to tapestry, from tapestry to something else, till intonation, service in chancel, candles on altar, back to congregation, being all in succession gained, it only remained to add the final consummating ornament of the priest – the cope. But now the congregation, that had been passive hitherto, thinking things were going a little too far, but not prepared to make open resistance, loudly complained; their open disaffection has let in the mob, and the result is that Mr. Bryan King's church is shut up.' The paper went on to suggest that King should use the time during which his church was closed to reflect on his responsibility for the peace and well-being of his parish. *Times*, 24 Sept. 1859.

103 Correspondence cited in the *Times*, 14 Oct. 1859.

104 In opening the service, King proclaimed that it had been 'at his own special request, having been put in trust for the sanctity of that place, that the Bishop closed the church.' In allowing that the eucharistic vestments would no longer be worn, King said that 'they must worship God in that holy sacrifice in the garb of humiliation.' He also announced that the Eucharist would no longer be celebrated during the Sunday services, but only on Tuesday and Thursday mornings. *Times*, 7 Nov. 1859.

105 The *Times* was extremely critical of his sermon on the reopening of the church: 'The public is so willing to give a clergyman and a man of education credit for good sense, that though Mr. Bryan King has not hitherto been remarkable for that quality, they were inclined to think that he had at length seen the folly of outraging the feelings of his parishioners and innovating on the customs of the Church.' But, the paper continued, King was in no mood for compromise: 'On a day of reconciliation, when the church had been opened for the first time after so long a period of disturbance, it became the officiating minister, himself the chief cause of what had happened, to speak words of kindness and moderation. But Mr. Bryan King was in no humour to deal kindly with those who differed from him. The loss of his green stoles seemed to have embittered him more than the return of peace and charity comforted him. He had no word of regret that the ceremonial which he thought decent should have dissatisfied others; he had no warning for his congregation that these things were of little moment in themselves, and should not be allowed to bring discord into the House of God. No; everything proceeded from the malice of his enemies; without any fault of his they had committed "the sin of sacrilege."... All this had the effect which might be expected. Rioting recommenced, and those who came with the desire for reconciliation were unable to restrain the temper of the mob.' *Times*, 8 Nov. 1859.

106 The evening service, conducted by A. H. Mackonochie, was heavily attended 'by partisans on both sides, who scowled at each other with a hatred which only religious party zeal could have inflamed, and shouted or sang, according to the side on which they were, the responses in an opposition chorus with hideous profanity. To hear the Lord's Prayer and some of the sublimest aspirations of the Liturgy, chanted on the one hand and shouted on the other, by contending factions bent on tiring each other down, mingled at intervals with ill-restrained laughter, coughing, and jeering, was an outrage on all public decency and decorum, and a scandalous desecration of a place of worship which requires to be felt and witnessed to be fully understood. There were features in the spectacle verging on the ludicrous. For example, a man sat on the pulpit stairs, close behind Mr. Mackonochie, who conducted the service, and bawled out the responses at the very top of his voice into the rev. gentleman's ear throughout the whole of the prayers. A policeman several times gently attempted to moderate his ardour, but he paid not the slightest heed to the admonition and continued shouting as

hard as before, without moving a muscle of his face.' The paper noted that it was the first time 'in this or any other civilized country' that policemen were stationed within a church to try to maintain the peace during the services. They were not, however, very effective. It appeared that they were hesitant to act with any force. 'The truth would seem to be that they appreciated the delicacy of their novel position so completely and evinced so much temper and forbearance on the occasion as almost to expose them to the momentary suspicion of winking at, if not countenancing, the surrounding excitement which at times and for a moment broke out into open uproar.' *Times*, 14 Nov. 1859.

107 In an editorial, the *Times* noted that most of those present were foreign to the parish and missed their Sunday amusement while the church was closed. The stationmaster at Shadwell had to direct large numbers every Sunday afternoon who 'asked him the way to the "Puseyite Church." Brompton, Hackney, Clapham, and twenty other places supplied the combatant congregation of St. George's, and for miles round London every other row of houses sent its champion to fight St. George. The saint changed places with the dragon, and the tables were fairly turned upon him. A good weekly row is a godsend to a great many spirited fellows who feel the *ennui* of ordinary life and the oppression of the forms of society, and sigh internally for variety and collision, great crashes and convulsions.' *Times*, 24 Sept. 1859.

108 The paper continued, 'Not that there was no irreverent behaviour on the part of many of the congregation at all the services, always excepting that of the afternoon lecturer; but much less remarkable than at any time heretofore since the disturbances first commenced.' *Times*, 5 Dec. 1859.

109 *Times*, 9 Dec. 1859.

110 At the evening service, there was a crowd of about 3,000, of whom the paper thought at least one-third were boys. For half an hour prior to the service they were virtually in control of the church, and the appearance of the rector brought them to a frenzy. 'People jumped on to their seats, pew-doors were violently slammed and loud shouts of execration proceeded from every part of the church.' In opposition to the choristers, the responses were shouted by the crowd, with many indulging 'in responses which are not in the Prayer-book, and which were nothing short of blasphemous mockery.' King was continually shouted down during the sermon, and as he left with the choristers, the altar became the focus of attack. 'A considerable amount of church furniture has been destroyed, the cushions in the galleries were torn up and thrown into the body of the church, Bibles and Prayer-books flew about in all directions, and many of the altar decorations have been injured.' *Times*, 30 Jan. 1860.

111 The law to prevent church rioting was passed in July. It provided for a fine of up to five pounds or imprisonment for up to two months; cf. *Record*, 9 July 1860. In the July 20th issue, the paper reported on the first conviction under the new law and noted that it appeared King would retire for a year to allow for calm and for the recovery of his health. In November, after a meeting with the vestry, the Bishop of London issued a monition for the removal of all the offensive decorations that had been put up by King. This

change led King's replacement to resign, since he felt it breached the original agreement with the rector. Thereafter, the Bishop appointed an Evangelical to the parish, and the riots ended. *Record*, 26 Nov. 1860, and 7 Jan. 1861.

112 According to James Bentley, it 'aroused greater opposition' than any of the other innovations of ceremonial or ornament that were introduced by the Ritualists. Bentley, *Ritualism and Politics*, pp. 31-33.

The practice of confession remained a concern for Evangelicals throughout the remainder of the century. In addressing the clergy at the 1896 Liverpool Diocesan Conference, Bishop Ryle dealt at length with the subject and reiterated many of the complaints made throughout the second half of the century. Ryle, *No Uncertain Sound*, pp. 329-31.

113 Lord Shaftesbury presided over a meeting, called by the Protestant Defence Committee in November 1852, to protest the introduction of the confessional by Rev. G. R. Prynne, an incumbent near Plymouth, who adopted the practice with the girls at an orphanage in his parish. Hodder, *Life of Shaftesbury*, p. 464.

114 *Record*, 11 June 1858. On Tait's view of the controversy, cf. Davidson and Benham, *Life of Tait*, vol. 1, pp. 223-28.

115 In describing the evidence, the *Record* inserted a parenthetical addition, 'Here followed in the original document some detailed questions, so grossly indecent and revolting, that it is impossible for us to print them. They created a great sensation in the meeting.' *Record*, 14 June 1858. The *Times* reported that Poole reportedly asked the women about their sexual contacts prior to marriage. But it also broke off the narrative with a similar note regarding the 'grossly indecent' nature of the questions asked. The paper also attacked Poole and the growing use of confession on its editorial page. *Times*, 12 June 1858. Poole denied the charges a few days later, and noted that Tait had not considered Baring's accusations in suspending him. Letter to the *Times*, 15 June 1858.

116 Tait continued, 'I feel especially that this questioning of females on the subject of violations of the Seventh Commandment is of dangerous tendency, and I am convinced, generally, that the sort of systematic admission of your people to confession and absolution, which you have allowed to be your practice, ought not to take place.' The churchwardens supported Poole, and in their letter to Bishop Tait of July 3rd, argued that he had dealt unfairly and too harshly with Poole. Correspondence cited in the *Times*, 12 July 1858.

117 *Times*, 15 July 1858. The archbishop refused to hear the case, but the next year he was forced to do so on appeal by Poole. He once again supported the decision of Bishop Tait. The judgment was reprinted in the *Times*, 24 March 1859. The *Record* thought the decision an important one and praised the *Times* for maintaining its opposition to the confessional throughout the controversy. It was indeed a scandal, wrote the paper, that clergy should promote 'the doctrine of Auricular Confession as if it were accordant with the doctrines of the Church of England; and that the clergy of Knightsbridge should, under cover of such a misinterpretation, invite the young women of Belgravia to meet them within locked doors, and submit to im-

modest questions as preparation to absolution and admission to the Lord's Table. Our contemporary the *Times* deserves all credit for the powerful manner in which it has written on this subject.' *Record*, 25 March 1859.

118 Letter to the *Times*, 16 June 1858.

119 'That this is the doctrine of the Church of England set forth in our Book of Common Prayer, whether it be popular or unpopular just now, we have no more doubt than we have of our own existence. If we are wrong, let us be proved so by the Church's law; if we are right, let honest men give us credit for telling the truth, even though they differ from us.' *Times*, 18 June 1858.

Opponents, however, were unconvinced by Liddell's arguments. 'Paterfamilias' rejected the appeal to the Visitation Office, which made allowance for confession in exceptional cases when visiting the sick. He argued that the formulary could not possibly be construed as justifying the use of habitual confession. Letter to the *Times*, 21 June 1858.

The *Times* reiterated its own strong opposition to confession in recounting a similar dispute in Oxford during the summer of 1858. The paper criticized Bishop Wilberforce, who sided with the curate in the controversy and suggested that the revival of the confessional was an affront to the Protestant sensibilities of the nation. *Times*, 18 and 21 Aug. 1858.

In a private letter to Wilberforce, W. F. Hook, who was a highly regarded leader of High Church moderates, indicated his strong opposition to the Ritualists and the revival of confession. Hook, who had been through his own controversy earlier in Leeds, suggested that 'the time had come, or was near at hand, when all sound Churchmen must go over to Lord Shaftesbury and his associates, in order to make common cause against these traitors.... It will be a bitter pill for me to swallow, but I am prepared to swallow it.' Wilberforce refused to consider that option. 'Our struggle with such men as Lord Shaftesbury is for our *existence* as a *Church*, their denial is the denial of the fundamental principle of the Church Catholic.' He acknowledged that he too was disgusted by 'the nauseous Romanizing peculiarities' of the Ritualists with their extreme view of confession. But, he told Hook, 'we must not give up the doctrine of the power of the keys because ridiculous men make themselves ridiculous or provoking with them.' A. R. Ashwell and Reginald G. Wilberforce, *Life of the Right Reverend Samuel Wilberforce, D.D.*, vol. 2 (London: John Murray, 1880-82), pp. 393-94 (his italics).

120 Francis Close would later argue that Protestantism was endangered less by the elaborate ceremonial of the 'noisy Ritualists' than by 'the secret poison infused at the confessional.' Francis Close, *Auricular Confession and Priestly Absolution, Three Sermons* (London: Hatchard & Sons, 1873), p. 45.

121 In a sermon first published in *Knots Untied* (1877), J. C. Ryle summarized the Evangelical position: '"Search the Scriptures."' Mark what a conspicuous absence there is in the New Testament of what may be called the Sacramental system, and the whole circle of Ritualistic theology.... Find, if you can, a single text in which the New Testament ministers are called sacrificing priests, – or the Lord's Supper is called a sacrifice, – or private confession to ministers is recommended and practiced.... You may find your authority for Ritualism in garbled quotations from the Fathers, – in long extracts from monkish, mystical, or Popish writers; but you certainly will not find it in the

Bible.' Reprinted in J. C. Ryle, *Warnings to the Churches* (Edinburgh: The Banner of Truth Trust, 1967), p. 79.

A century later, the fundamental division over the nature of the priesthood still separates Evangelicals from Anglo-Catholics, although with much less animosity and vituperation than in the nineteenth century. In a recent work discussing the ordination of women, R. T. France, a prominent Evangelical biblical scholar, inserted the following footnote in the opening pages of his book: 'While "priest" has been the term most used in the discussion, and is the term used in the official formularies of the Church of England, many evangelicals prefer to use the term "presbyter" (from which 'priest' is etymologically derived) so as to avoid the more sacerdotal associations with which the more catholic members of the church invest the term "priest". While this usage is generally intelligible (if surprising to those used to the traditional term) within the Church of England, it can cause confusion in discussion with members of other churches which use "elder" (presbyter) to denote officers other than ordained ministers.... I shall stick to the term "priest", as the accepted terminology, while sharing the misgivings of other evangelicals as to the implications it is sometimes made to carry.' R. T. France, *Women in the Church's Ministry* (Grand Rapids: William B. Eerdmans Publishing Co., 1997), p. 9.

122 The fundamental theological and liturgical differences were well summarized on both sides in an 1893 exchange in the *Contemporary Review* between the moderate Evangelical, F. W. Farrar, and the Ritualist, W. J. Knox Little. The first article in the series was Farrar's 'Sacerdotalism,' *Contemporary Review* 62 (1892): 48-58. He followed that piece the next year with 'Undoing the Work of the Reformation,' *Contemporary Review* 64 (1893): 60-73. Knox Little took exception with Farrar's analysis and criticism, and he responded in 'Archdeacon Farrar and the "Ritualists",' *Contemporary Review* 64 (1893): 182-97. Farrar then reiterated his position in 'The Principles of the Reformation,' *Contemporary Review* 64 (1893): 351-61. The fundamental issue, in Farrar's view, was the idea of a sacerdotal ministry. He began by citing Bishop Lightfoot's influential study on the Christian ministry. Lightfoot wrote, 'The kingdom of Christ has no sacerdotal system. It interposes no sacrificial tribe or class between God and man.' On that point, Farrar insisted, the Protestant Church of England could make no compromise. Cited in Farrar, 'Sacerdotalism' *Contemporary Review*, p. 51.

123 *Record*, 23 August 1858.

124 Cf. Bentley, *Ritualism and Politics*, pp. 30-32. G. Best has suggested that there was no social fear quite as strong 'as that felt by dominant males for an idealized womankind.' The idealized Victorian woman was perceived to be 'intellectually weak, pliable, submissive: eager – fatally too eager – to do what was right, and anxious to be instructed in it.' G. F. A. Best, 'Popular Protestantism in Victorian Britain,' in *Ideas and Institutions of Victorian Britain*, ed. Robert Robson (New York: Barnes & Noble, 1967), pp. 134-35. Cf. Reed, *Glorious Battle*, pp. 195-201.

125 Anonymous, 'Private Confession in the Church of England,' *Quarterly Review* 124 (1868), pp. 86, 115-16. W. F. Taylor, in a lecture for the Church Association, complained that the confessional engendered a view of the

clergy that was 'unChristian and unEnglish.' The 'sacredness of the home' was invaded by the priest in secrecy, and, Taylor concluded, 'I am no longer the master of my own home.' W. F. Taylor, 'Ritualism, the Enemy of Domestic Peace, Doctrinal Purity, Social Progress, and National Independence,' in *Church Association Lectures, 1869* (London: Hatchards, 1869), pp. 63-64.

A writer in *Fraser's Magazine* similarly complained, 'We have to do with a system which is aggressive and organized, which will not let us alone; which addresses itself, not to "the adult males," not to the trained understanding, but to hysteria, to imagination, to fear, to nervousness, to emotional weakness, to the identical qualities which yield on the other side to mesmerism. The husband and father is no longer the ruler of his house and family; a spiritual director whom he regards himself as a contemptible quack, steals into his wife's confidence, penetrates into his secrets, stands between him and his children.' Anonymous, 'Recent Movements in the Church of England,' *Fraser's Magazine* 74 (1866): 291. The writer went on to warn that further toleration of the Ritualists would inevitably drive men away from the church.

126 Herbert wrote, in part, 'It is melancholy to think that in Christian England no one can undertake anything without these most uncharitable and sectarian attacks; and, had you not told me so, I could scarcely believe that a clergyman of the Established Church could have been the mouthpiece of such slander. Miss Nightingale is a member of the Established Church, and what is called rather Low Church; but ever since she went to Scutari her religious opinions and character have been assailed on all points.' Correspondence cited in the *Record*, 8 Jan. 1855. Her husband, Sidney Herbert, of the Home Office, and Henry Manning (who had converted to Roman Catholicism following the Gorham decision) were accused of having masterminded the plan.

127 Correspondence cited in the *Record*, 8 Jan. 1855.

128 *Record*, 18 Jan. 1855.

129 Letter to the *Record*, 1 Feb. 1855.

130 By 1861, the paper took a more generous view of Nightingale. 'We have a peculiar pleasure in paying a tribute to Miss Nightingale, because we do not think that all her great services in the Crimea were sufficiently acknowledged. The difficulties which she had to encounter are even yet but partially known, – difficulties arising not exclusively from the jealousies of red-tapeism, and of those who adhere rigidly to routine, but difficulties arising from the intrigues and the opposition of those who were bent on converting an errand of mercy into one of Popish proselytism. It must ever be spoken to the honour of Miss Nightingale, that from the first she resisted the attempt to enlist her in the Popish crusade.' *Record*, 18 Oct. 1861.

A decade after the original dispute, the *Record* was still bothered by the controversy. In Dec. 1866, Henry Alford, the Dean of Canterbury, gave a YMCA lecture at Exeter Hall in which he criticized the religious press. He had served under Gurney in the 1850s and brought up the incident as an illustration of the spirit in which the 'party papers' conducted themselves. The *Record* was critical of Alford's lecture and gave a lengthy recounting of their version of the events. *Record*, 17 Dec. 1866.

131 His family heritage was seldom mentioned by Wilberforce's Evangelical critics, but his emergence as a High Church leader probably formed the basis of their intense distrust. In his exchange of letters with C. P. Golightly, he once wrote, 'You do not suppose that I am so blind as not to see perfectly that I might have headed the Evangelical body and been seated by them at Lambeth.' Ashwell, *Life of Wilberforce*, vol. 2, p. 360.

In late 1853 and early 1854, Wilberforce exchanged a series of private letters with Alexander Haldane, the editor of the *Record*, complaining of his treatment in the pages of the paper. When the editor complained that he could not understand what Wilberforce meant by the paper's 'unworthy hostility,' Wilberforce responded with several pages of detailed accounts and noted that Archbishop Sumner had personally told him that the conduct of the paper, with regard to him and another High Church bishop, was 'execrable.' Above all, Wilberforce complained of the divisive nature of the tone adopted by the paper, 'But, sir, that of which I complain above all is, your unceasing efforts to divide my own clergy of all schools allowed within our Church – whom I desire to unite, quicken and help in their ministerial work – in habitually striving to render these men suspicious of their brethren and their Bishop.... It is as to the lawfulness by Gospel rules of your conduct, in thus habitually trying to widen the breach between the different sections of Churchmen, and to lead them to distrust and hate one another, that above all I would beg you to examine both yourself and your words.' Haldane responded with a letter accusing Wilberforce, as a result of his belief in baptismal regeneration, of being a papist. He wrote, 'We firmly believe that whoever believes in that doctrine is a Papist in reality, whatever he be in name, and that the salvation of his soul is thereby jeopardized.' Wilberforce answered the charge in his concluding letter, 'I did not blame you because by fair arguments you opposed my views but, because to oppose my views you habitually calumniated my character, perverted my motives and misrepresented my actions.' Ibid., pp. 218-23.

132 Wilberforce and Golightly exchanged a series of private letters on the issue during the fall of 1857. In them, the bishop reiterated his opposition to all things Roman, both in doctrine and in ceremony. He noted the differences between himself and H. P. Liddon, the Vice-Principal of the college. He believed, however, that Liddon was a man of great piety who would lead his students away from any Roman tendencies if given the chance and dealt with moderately. After several cordial letters, it was clear that Golightly viewed Wilberforce's preference for private episcopal influence as a policy of no action at all and proceeded to broadcast the issue publicly. Cf. Ashwell, *Life of Wilberforce*, vol. 2, pp. 359-62.

Evangelicals were not alone in their concerns. The *Quarterly Review* opposed the separate education of clergy and laity, suggesting that theological colleges tended to promote 'a sectarian spirit' and 'formalism.' The review, however, was disinclined to blame Wilberforce. Rather, it suggested, that all institutions tended 'to go further than was intended in the line of the impulsion first given, whatever that may be.' The writer was also concerned that 'rival colleges' would be established by the other parties leading only to 'sectarian bigotry' and the perpetuation of 'our unhappy divisions.' Anon., 'Church Extension,' *Quarterly Review*, p. 162.

The feeling was a general one during the period. Peter Marsh wrote that Archbishop Tait 'shared the old Protestant suspicion of secluded institutions.' Tait favored training colleges only if they were opened in connection with the universities, and thus later gave his blessing to the Evangelical Wycliffe and Ridley Halls that were established respectively at Oxford and Cambridge. Marsh, *Victorian Church in Decline*, p. 88. In 1876, Bishop Magee of Peterborough similarly complained that the "darkened side chapels of theological colleges" worked great mischief in the church. He feared that they gave rise to the 'rapid growth of young, hot-headed, and ignorant sacerdotalism, to be followed ultimately by skeptical reaction.' John Cotter MacDonnell, *The Life and Correspondence of William Connor Magee*, vol. 2 (London: Isbister & Co., 1896), pp. 60-61.

Brian Heeney related the development of theological colleges to the growing professionalization of the clergy – it was suggested that their unique position required a unique education. In particular, the High Church party tended to focus on this aspect of ministerial education and developed the first diocesan colleges. As a result, they were viewed with suspicion by Evangelicals as training grounds for popery. Brian Heeney, *A Different Kind of Gentlemen: Parish Clergy as Professional Men in Early and Mid-Century Victorian England* (Hamden: Archon Books, 1976), pp. 100-03.

133 The committee concluded that the ornamentation was excessive but not illegal. They did, however, suggest that the excesses tended 'to strengthen the already existing prejudices against these institutions, and also to impress the minds of the students too deeply with a disproportionate regard for the mere accessories of public worship.' Nevertheless, they did not believe there was any reason to impute to the lavish ornamentation 'any party meaning.' Report cited in the *Record*, 24 Feb. 1858. The paper was unimpressed by the findings and continued its editorial campaign against the college in the next issue. *Record*, 26 Feb. 1858. In the issue of April 3rd, the paper published a ditty that played on the names of those involved, the college president (Pott) and his Evangelical accuser (C. P. Golightly):

"Mr. T. to his neighbour:-
Go-lightly when you make a charge
　Against an erring brother;
Nor with the bigot's pen enlarge
　The failings of another.

'Tis true, in Cuddesdon's priestly home,
　Hard is the student's lot;
But still, he is not sent to Rome;
　He simply 'goes to Pott.'

"His neighbour's reply: –
Golightly! – on in faith and truth
　With zeal sustained by knowledge,
And still to Oxford's pious youth

Protest 'gainst Cuddesdon College.

For, from 'report' of what is past,
    The proof is surely got,
That he will get to Rome at last,
    Who first has 'gone to Pott'."

In a letter to Pott, following the publication of the report, Wilberforce asked that he and Liddon consider the suggestions and do what they could to minimize any partisan spirit among their students. He concluded, 'I do not expect you to satisfy Mr. Golightly. The habits of his mind make him quite unable to form an unbiased judgment on any matter which appeals to his inveterate prejudices. I doubt whether any Diocesan College would satisfy him. I am sure that none could which simply embodied in its conduct the full teaching and practice of the Church of England.' Ashwell, *Life of Wilberforce*, vol. 2, p. 362.

134 Cf. Ibid., pp. 366-73.
135 *Record*, 28 Feb. 1859.
136 The memorial and correspondence were reprinted in the *Record*, 11 March 1859. The paper suggested that the memorialists owed their positions to the bishop and so had a vested interest in supporting him in the controversy.
137 Reprinted in the *Record*, 30 March 1859. Another clerical address, which responded to the remonstrants and reaffirmed the support for the bishop, was signed by over 470 clergy. *Record*, 15 April 1859.
138 'If the Bishop of Oxford really has not Popish tendencies, if his simple mind honestly cherishes Protestant truth, then we must endeavour to trace his proceedings to some more occult, refined, and artistic principle in his soul! To the picturesque, the sentimental, the sublime, which lead him to delight so much in pomp and ceremony, and outward show!' *Record*, 6 April 1859.
139 Ibid.
140 Letter to the *Record*, 25 May 1859.
141 Ibid.
142 Cuddesdon College, however, was to remain a divisive issue over the years, and it was often criticized as a training ground for Ritualists. Controversy over the tendencies of the school erupted again two decades later, with C. P. Golightly once again at the center. He published a pamphlet, *On the Romanizing Tendency of the Teaching at Cuddesdon Theological College*, and E. A. Knox, who was then a Fellow and Tutor at Merton College, attempted to bring it before the Oxford Diocesan Conference in 1878. Bishop Mackarness, however, ruled the motion out of order; cf. E. A. Knox, *An Address Respecting Cuddesdon College, Intended to Have Been Delivered at the Oxford Diocesan Conference, 1878* (London: Simpkin, Marshall, & Co., 1878). For several months, almost every issue of the *Record* contained correspondence on the controversy regarding the influence of Ritualists at the school, the facts cited in Golightly's pamphlet, or the treatment of Knox at the hands of the bishop; cf. *Record*, 11, 14, and 25 Oct. and 1 Nov. 1878.
143 In 1859, when the *Record* published its schedule of meetings and speakers, there were some fifty-six societies represented (both Anglican and interdenominational). Among the more important, in addition to the CMS, the

Bible Society, and the CP-AS, were the London City Mission, the Evangelical Alliance, the Protestant Reformation Society, the Protestant Alliance, the Religious Tract Society, the National Temperance Society, the Lord's Day Observance Society, and the Sunday School Union. *Record*, 20 April 1859.

144 *Record*, 15 March 1855.
145 Letter to the *Record*, 19 March 1855.
146 *Record*, 26 Oct. 1857.
147 A London paper also described it as 'a small and rapidly decreasing party.' But the *Record* argued that there had been substantial growth during recent years. The paper cited the growing number of Evangelical preachers in the metropolitan areas and also pointed to its own circulation. It had expanded from about 1,000 subscribers during the early 1830s to 3,274 in 1843. *Record*, 30 March 1843.
148 Gresley, *Real Danger of the Church of England*, pp. 28-9. The Evangelical party, by then, had the support of some of the popular press against the extreme High Church section, especially the *Times* and the *Quarterly Review*. Through them, said Gresley, Evangelicals gained 'a sort of favour and popularity with the worldly and irreligious, which they did not before possess, as opponents of an encroaching priesthood, and defenders of the nation from ecclesiastical tyranny.' This alliance with worldly powers had damaged the religious character of Evangelicalism,' wrote Gresley, but it was also responsible for increasing 'its political or rather social power. And in this respect it is becoming more and more identified with the Puritanism of two centuries back.' Ibid., pp. 30-31.

According to Gresley, the party was now made up of 'multitudes of well-meaning persons, especially females, in the middle classes, and others of imperfect education, who were vehement partisans of the Evangelical clergy, and under their teaching become bitter opponents and denouncers of this vital and primary doctrine [baptismal regeneration] of the English Church, supposing all the while that they are excellent Church-people.' Ibid., p. 61.
149 According to Owen Chadwick, the Evangelicals, while far from ever achieving dominance, did obtain a certain degree of power during the decade of the 1850s, 'while the memory of papal aggression still rankled, while Sumner was still the Archbishop of Canterbury, while Palmerston presided over the cabinet, and while Shaftesbury the noble head of evangelical laymen was stepson-in-law to the prime minister.' Chadwick, *Victorian Church, Part One*, p. 440.
150 Conybeare, 'Church Parties,' in *Essays Ecclesiastical and Social*, p. 60.
151 Conybeare thought there were about 3,300 moderates in the Low Church party and about 3,500 in the High Church. Ibid., p. 158.
152 Ibid., pp. 158-59.
153 Ibid., p. 73.
154 The Broad Church found it more difficult, thought Conybeare, to unite in true party fashion; unlike the extreme wings of the other two parties, for whom it was easier 'to raise an army for the assault of Rome, or for a crusade against Geneva.' Ibid., p. 150.

CHAPTER 3

The Growth of Partisanship in the 1860s

An anonymous writer in 1859 complained that the campaign to undermine the Protestant foundation of the Church of England had entered a new phase by the end of the 1850s. The 'romanizing movement,' which began with the Tractarians and their introduction of foreign doctrines into the Anglican church, now belonged to their successors who emphasized instead 'Romish practices and observances.' Their ceremonial innovations, it was claimed, were intended to acclimate 'the public mind, especially of the young, to the externals of the Romish system, in the hope that the doctrine would then follow of itself.'[1] Whether or not the writer fairly assessed the intent of the Ritualists, he was at least correct in suggesting that the controversy had moved beyond its original boundaries. The 1860s saw the development of party organizations with a corresponding growth of the partisan rhetoric and a hardening of the divisions that separated the groups within the Church of England.[2] The Ritualists were the first to unite, gathering under the banner of the English Church Union (hereafter abbreviated ECU) in 1859.[3] In 1860, they attempted to prosecute Evangelicals who were holding mission services in theatres that had been rented in several of the poorer sections of London, but no incumbents in the respective parishes could be found who were willing to initiate the charges.[4] Several years later, Evangelical anti-Ritualists formed the Church Association (hereafter abbreviated CA). By the middle of the decade, and particularly after the anti-Ritualists appealed to the courts, there was a dramatic increase in partisan activity. Numerous petitions and memorials were circulated by those on both sides of the controversy, and Evangelicals were not alone in their protests against the Ritualists. There was a growing desire for some authoritative intervention, but the bishops were hesitant to act lest they exacerbate existing tensions or be accused of partisan sympathies. During the course of the 1860s, the disputed elements of ritual were considered first by Convocation and then by a government commission. But little came from either of their deliberations, and by the end of the decade, the two sides were more firmly entrenched than ever in their opposing positions. And anti-Ritualist Evangelicals, except for a few hesitant moderates, were convinced that litigation offered the best prospect of bringing the matter to a close.

There was some concern, however, that the actual intent of the law was ambiguous. In May 1860, Lord Shaftesbury offered the first of many anti-Ritualist bills into the House of Lords, 'An Act for the Further Regulation of the Rites, Ceremonies, and Ornaments used in the Churches or by the Ministers of the United Church of England and Ireland.' The bill would have given authority to the Queen in Council (assisted by the Archbishops of Canterbury, York, Armagh, and Dublin) to order the rites, ceremonies and ornaments used by Anglican clergy. It also provided for the punishment of those who refused to comply – first with an admonition, next with suspension for a period not to exceed twelve months, and finally the recalcitrant would be deprived of 'all ecclesiastical promotions and dignities.' The *Record* thought the bill moderate in both tone and content but was nevertheless certain it would be opposed by the 'Romanizing party.' The paper took the opportunity to warn the bishops that the patience of the Protestant laity had worn thin. But the bill gained little support.[5] For a time, however, the interest of Shaftesbury and other Evangelicals was diverted by the publication of *Essays and Reviews*.

An Interlude in the Ritualist Controversy: The Threat of Rationalism

During the 1850s, Evangelicals had only occasionally expressed any concern regarding the growth of new critical methods in biblical and theological studies. With the publication of *Essays and Reviews* in 1860, and Bishop Colenso's work on the Pentateuch in 1862, the threat of skepticism became the dominant focus for several years, and the *Record* devoted much of its attention to the rationalists.[6] Many Evangelicals expressed the view that the Ritualists and the rationalists shared a common heritage as 'antagonists of truth' and were more dangerous than any external foes because they were both working to subvert the church from within.[7] Charles Girdlestone, in a pamphlet written to his parish upon his retirement, suggested that both undermined the authority of Scripture. The rationalists made 'natural reason' the ultimate test of truth, while the Ritualists elevated the importance of the traditions and offices of the church. But both, he thought, arrived at a similar result.[8]

Evangelicals were not alone in their opposition to the rise of critical theology as popularized in England by the writers of *Essays and*

Reviews and Bishop Colenso.⁹ The bishops were almost unanimous in their criticism and many moderate journals adopted a similar view.¹⁰ Faced with the threat of a common foe that seemed determined to undermine the very foundations of the faith, many moderate Evangelicals were willing, for a time, to set aside their deep-seated distrust of those within the High Church and join forces. For a few brief years, and for the only time in the second half of the century, the inherent conservatism of the two traditions became more important than their other theological differences and a degree of cooperation was possible. The change was evident in April 1863, when the *Record* adopted a conciliatory tone toward Bishop Wilberforce, who had often been the subject of strident criticism in the paper.¹¹

The unlikely alliance between the two parties was further strengthened when the Judicial Committee of the Privy Council reversed a lower court decision against two of the authors of the *Essays and Reviews*. In a letter to the *Record*, the Tractarian leader, E. B. Pusey called for a united memorial repudiating the ideas represented by the essayists.¹² Pusey's initiative was warmly welcomed by most Evangelicals and strongly endorsed by the *Record*. The paper expressed some concern that the reaction to the Judicial Committee's decision might lead to renewed support for the revival of Convocation and, in a return to the High Church refrain from the years of the Gorham controversy, to an attack on the validity of the Judicial Committee as a lay court of appeal. But it praised the framers of the Oxford Declaration for having exhibited great wisdom and restraint in mentioning neither the judgment itself nor other controverted issues that would only divide the supporters of the memorial.¹³ With a committee comprised of influential members from both the High Church and Evangelical parties (E. B. Pusey and G. A. Denison were the Tractarian members, and J. C. Miller and W. R. Fremantle were the Evangelical representatives), the Oxford Declaration was drawn up and circulated for clerical signatures:

> We, the undersigned presbyters and deacons in holy orders of the Church of England and Ireland, hold it to be our bounden duty to the Church of England and Ireland, and to the souls of men, to declare our firm belief that the Church of England and Ireland, in common with the whole Catholic Church, maintains, without reserve or qualification, the inspiration and Divine authority of the whole Canonical Scriptures as not only containing but being the Word of God; and further teaches, in the words of our Blessed Lord, that the 'punishment' of the 'cursed' equally with the 'life' of the 'righteous' is everlasting.¹⁴

A few Evangelicals, however, questioned the wisdom of forming common cause with the High Church party. Critics of the plan argued that the protest against rationalism could be better maintained by a distinctively Evangelical voice, particularly in light of the fact that the High Church party was reacting to the same court and in much the same terms as they had done following the Gorham decision.[15] The leading opponent was William Goode, the most prominent Evangelical theologian of the day, who argued that the declaration, in questioning of the authority of the queen's court, was, in effect, a rebellion against the royal supremacy.[16] But support for the cause was broadly based, and the *Record* lent its editorial weight to the combined effort.[17] In the end, the Oxford Declaration gained substantial support and stood out as the single instance in the second half of the nineteenth century when the two parties were able to overcome their fundamental differences.[18] By the time the protest was presented to the Archbishop of Canterbury in May 1864, 11,000 signatures had been gathered, representing well over half the clergy.[19] Ultimately, however, the combined protest had little effect, and any hope for future cooperation between the two parties soon passed. By the fall of 1864, concern over the rationalist threat began to fade, and the Ritualists once again became the central target of Evangelical polemics.[20]

The Church Association and the Growth of Anti-Ritualist Sentiment

After a lull in the controversy with the Ritualists for several years, old rivalries soon took precedence again. Evangelicals often argued that the rationalist movement was simply a reaction to the growth of Sacerdotalism and the former would lose its motive force when the latter was properly suppressed.[21] The rationalists might have been considered less of a threat because they drew few away from the Evangelical faith. If anything, they desired above all, to make Christianity attractive to those who had already left the church (Schleiermacher's 'cultured despisers'). In this regard, the Ritualists were a more immediate challenge to the Evangelical party because they were both drawing on a common but limited pool of devout and theologically conservative believers. By the mid-1860s, Evangelicals were largely convinced that the Ritualists posed the more direct threat to the Church of England. It was widely believed that they were united in their desire to undermine the Protestant foundation of the church, and warnings were often addressed to young Evangelical clergy advising against cooperation or assimilation. In reality, only a few churches had adopted the more extreme ceremonial forms, but the movement's influence could be seen in the growing numbers of churches that adopted moderate innovations – evident particularly in the new emphasis on choirs and the role of music in worship.[22]

Concern was often raised during this period regarding the need for an Evangelical organization that might present a united front against their opponents.[23] With the intention of forming a means of organized response to the Ritualist ECU, an advertisement in the press in early 1866 announced the organization of the 'Church Association to uphold the Principles of the Reformation in the United Church of England and Ireland.' While disavowing any partisan motivation, the group claimed its goal was 'to repress, by legislative and other measures, the Romanizing movement which is now assuming such alarming proportions in the Church of England, especially as regards her ceremonial.'[24] The CA was concerned initially to solidify the different strands of the anti-Ritualist movement as well as to raise support for an immediate Parliamentary response. But it was recognized that Parliament was reluctant to address religious questions 'except under the pressure of public opinion.' The association's supporters, such as J. C. Ryle, therefore urged a 'voluntary union of all Protestant Churchmen' that could apply the necessary pressure on the legislature. The laity of the nation, he trusted, would rally to the cause once they were made aware of the nature of the threat.[25] The theme became a common one throughout the years of controversy. Anti-Ritualists often proclaimed the Protestant sensibilities of the English laity and announced with assurance that they would join the battle as soon as they realized the danger to the church and nation. In the later years of the century, however, it took on the tone of a lament, with true supporters bemoaning the lack of commitment found among the nominally Protestant majority.

A second advertisement appeared in March 1866, explaining the motivation for the association and listing its objectives:

> Its object is to defend the Church. A revision of the Liturgy forms no part of its plan. That question it does not entertain. Its aim is to stop the Romanising practices within the Church, and this it seeks to do –
>
> 1. By publishing information, holding public meetings, presenting memorials, etc.
>
> 2. By pressing for an authoritative disapproval and suppression of all ceremonies, vestments, and ornaments which depart from

the practice of the Church as sanctioned by three centuries of usage.

3. By endeavouring to obtain – if necessary, through the appointment of a Royal Commission or otherwise, such power for the rulers of the Church, and so clear a declaration of the law of the Church, as shall prevent the continuance of practices which, being borrowed from Rome, corrupt the integrity and endanger the safety of the Reformed Church of England.[26]

It soon became clear, however, that obtaining legislative intervention would be no simple task. Consequently, the focus quickly shifted to judicial action as the most effective means of obtaining a timely end to the innovations. Within a year, the association added a fourth object reflecting that goal. A later version of the advertisement carried the addition: 'By assisting aggrieved parishioners to obtain protection from practices which drive them from their parish church by assimilating its worship to that of the Church of Rome.'[27]

From the very beginning, the CA had a difficult time attracting members outside the Evangelical party. There were, however, many non-partisan moderates who were also disturbed by the Ritualists' activities and desired to raise opposition both among the general public and the ecclesiastical authorities. At the opening of the new session of Parliament and Convocation in 1866, a large number of the London clergy presented a memorial to the Archbishop of Canterbury complaining of the alterations being introduced into the church's worship,

> which, by their diversity, and by their deviation from law or from long-established usage, are disturbing the peace and impairing the efficiency of the Church, and are disquieting the minds of many devout members of our Communion.
>
> Without venturing to suggest any remedy for the evils of which we complain, we earnestly pray your Grace to devise such measures, in concert with your Suffragans, as may be best calculated to repress such of the practices referred to as are illegal, and to secure that measure of uniformity in the celebration of Divine Service which is involved in the idea of a National Church.[28]

The memorial was signed by one archdeacon, 6 canons residentiary, 14 rural deans, and 481 clergy. In presenting the memorial to the archbishop, Archdeacon Christopher Wordsworth denied that the memorialists were motivated by any 'feelings of party spirit.' They only desired, he said, to protest 'against the encroachments of that private spirit which is not content with those rites and ceremonies that are prescribed by law, and are sanctioned by long usage in the Church of England.'²⁹ In receiving the petition, Archbishop Longley acknowledged the necessity of determining exactly what the law allowed, indicating perhaps that he thought litigation on the matter was inevitable, and to a certain degree, necessary. Only after they were certain of the state of the law could the bishops determine how they ought to proceed.³⁰

Later that year, the CA presented memorials to both archbishops, expressing their concerns regarding the innovations. Without stipulating any specific measures, they requested that the archbishops 'adopt such measures as will effectively put a stop to innovations upon the customary ceremonial.' Archbishop Longley, in receiving the memorial, attempted to maintain a strictly non-partisan position, but he indicated that the entire episcopacy shared their concern over the innovations.³¹ In response to the anti-Ritualist protests and Bishop Tait's intimation in Parliament that many of the bishops were ready to support legislation to enforce conformity, the ECU mounted its own campaign to oppose legislation. On the 3rd of February, the Ritualists presented their own memorials to the Archbishop of Canterbury, signed respectively by 3,021 clergy and 37,077 laity. They argued against any alteration of the rubrics that might limit their interpretation of the ceremonies allowed.³²

The many petitions being circulated gave evidence of a growing public concern, and a committee of the High-Church dominated Lower House of Convocation took up the subject during the summer of 1866. With regard to the innovations, it offered its guarded approval of three. It approved the use of eucharistic vestments, which were largely modeled after those used in the Roman Catholic Church and becoming increasingly elaborate. It concluded that altar candles were not without precedence even though they had fallen into disuse since the Reformation (except in the cathedrals and college chapels). And, finally, while rejecting the censing of the clergy, it considered the use of incense acceptable if approved by the respective diocesan. In an effort to maintain a middle ground, however, the committee expressed its opposition to three other innovations. The elevation of the sacramental elements was forbidden since it implied an adoration of Christ's presence therein. On similar grounds, the committee discouraged the presence of non-communicants during the celebration of Holy Communion. And the use of wafer bread, while not condemned, was not to be encouraged. The committee concluded by noting that the clergy owed their 'dutiful acquiescence' to the bishops as well as a 'discreet and charitable consideration' of the desires of their congregations. Finally, it expressed its opposition to legal proceedings as likely only to aggravate existing divisions.[33] The *Record* thought the report was a weak attempt at compromise; it was entirely unsatisfied by the committee's 'impotent conclusion that those who dislike "a high ceremonial" should not be compelled to have it, and those who like it should not be compelled to go without it.'[34]

The Beginning of Ritualist Prosecutions and Episcopal Moderation

Initially, the CA intended only to offer legal assistance and financial support to those who undertook the prosecution of Ritualists on their own; but as the controversy grew, it began to take a more active and controversial role.[35] The early lawsuits were brought in order to determine the exact limits of legal ritual within the Church of England, with the expectation that the Ritualists would either comply with the judgments of a competent court or else secede.[36] G. R. Balleine suggested that the disputes were complicated, in part, by the anomalies of the English Reformation.[37] The partisans were further divided by their differing presuppositions. The traditional view assumed 'that every medieval ceremony was abolished except those explicitly or implicitly enjoined in the Prayer Book. On the other hand, the Ritualists maintained that any rite was lawful, unless it was specifically forbidden.'[38] Evangelicals, on occasion, were willing to admit that some ambiguities remained in the liturgy. But for the most part they were certain that theirs was a Protestant church and that the Ritualists were united in a conscious attempt to undo the Reformation through the imposition of Roman Catholic rites and ceremonies that embodied beliefs entirely inconsistent with the formularies of the Anglican church.[39]

The long and tortured path of anti-Ritualist litigation began, ironically enough, in the diocese of Exeter. Bishop Phillpotts, who was himself no friend of the Evangelical party, agreed to allow proceedings against the Incumbent of East Teignmouth, T. B. Simpson.[40] In August 1866, the CA announced the creation of a 'Defence Fund' to offer financial support for the prosecution of Ritualist clergy. The organization thought it imperative that those who were willing to undertake legal proceedings should be assisted with their court costs and provided with competent counsel. That feeling was reinforced when it became evident that Simpson would be assisted in his defense by the ECU. At this early stage of the controversy, most Evangelicals supported the prosecution of Simpson. If a few moderates opposed the idea of litigation, in principle, they remained a largely silent minority.[41] The *Record* wrote, 'We have at length the question fairly raised before our courts, whether a clergyman of the Church of

England may of his own will alter our services, introduce into our Church portions of the Romish ritual, and in defiance of law, reintroduce the Romish mass. No question can be more important or more practical; on the settlement of this, the purity and the safety of our Church depend.'[42] The paper also suggested, perhaps with too much optimism, that many of the bishops desired a judicial clarification of the law. Before they would exercise their own authority to suppress the innovations or attempt to bring a bill before Parliament, they desired 'to have the questions raised by this case thoroughly sifted through a legal investigation, and ruled by the sentence of the courts of law.'[43] Anti-Ritualists expected that a definitive judgment in the East Teignmouth case would force the hands of both the bishops and the Ritualists.[44]

The bishops, for their part, had for some time maintained a policy of moderation, generally desiring to avoid charges of partisanship and hoping that the movement could simply be contained until the more extreme voices on either side of the debate faded. They had also to consider the interests of each particular parish. In some cases the congregations were enthusiastic in their support of a more elaborate service, a point the anti-Ritualists refused to concede, recognizing the legitimacy only of the claims of those 'aggrieved parishioners' who protested the innovations.[45] Nevertheless, it was clear that some of the bishops were beginning to lose their patience with the innovations. Bishop Tait of London, while questioning the usefulness of litigation in his 1866 charge to the clergy, was forceful in his condemnation:

> Beginning with the use of lighted candles during the daylight at the administration of the Holy Communion, some men have gone on to incense, to the distinctive Roman habits and to prostrations, which, if they mean anything, speak of an idolatrous worship of the consecrated elements. I feel confident that all good members of the Church of England will pause before they encourage this downward course. If the introduction of these things which I have specified, by individual clergymen on their own responsibility, be not contrary to the letter of our laws, it is certainly contrary to their spirit, as well as to the authorised practice of the Church ever since the Reformation.[46]

Tait did not believe a judicial decision would be finally conclusive or that a majority of the Ritualists could be persuaded to accept it, but many of the laity were disturbed by the innovations. 'If these practices are persisted in,' he said, 'it must be settled, even though the settlement be incomplete, by some controlling authority, judicial or legislative, how far the liberty of altering the outward form of worship thus boldly claimed is to be allowed or stopped.'[47] The bishop's concerns were indeed warranted, and the conclusion to the trial proved to be neither as quick nor as decisive as Evangelicals had hoped. Delayed by a long series of legal manuverings, the East Teignmouth case was finally combined with the case brought against A. H. Mackonochie of St. Alban's, and it was not resolved until the two cases were heard together over a year later.

Anti-Ritualists often criticized the episcopacy's policy of moderation, complaining that their tolerant attitude was responsible for both the audacity of the Ritualists and the resulting public outcry.[48] In October 1866, the *Times* similarly complained that the bishops had tolerated the innovations for far too long. The paper believed that public opinion would eventually turn against the extremes of the movement and there was some hope the 'folly might have been left to cure itself.' But, the writer concluded, the 'deliberate and systematic perversion' of the doctrines and services of the church had grown desperate, and it was the duty of the bishops to take a stand.[49] For several weeks, the paper also published letters from 'S.G.O.' (Lord Sydney Godolphin Osborne), who sharply criticized Bishop Hamilton of Salisbury for his tacit support of Ritualist clergy in his diocese.[50] The *Times* followed up this correspondence with another editorial calling Hamilton and the Ritualists to account. The paper challenged the innovators to consider their position as clergy in the national church. The Ritualist might be quite sincere, 'but if he deliberately sets himself against the religious beliefs or the moral sentiment of the nation, of which he is bound to inform himself, he fails in his allegiance to the institution which he has contracted to support, and which can only live as long as it is the religious representation of the nation.'[51] The editorial concluded by challenging Bishop Hamilton to consider the cost of his actions and the divisions created in the church by the innovations. It was increasingly evident, thought the *Times*, that many, particularly among the middle classes, were being driven from the established church.[52] Whereas Evangelicals generally relied on religious arguments regarding the anti-Protestant nature of the Ritualist movement, the *Times* and the quarterly journals often relied on arguments of a rather more erastian and secular tone.

It was clear, by the late 1860s, that anti-Ritualism was not a movement unique to the Evangelical party. In early 1867, a strongly worded memorial, addressed to the Bishop of London, was signed by 423 clergy of the diocese.[53] The same year the *Quarterly Review* published its first substantial article on the movement – a sharply critical review of several prominent Ritualist publications.[54] It reiterated the point that the innovators, 'a small knot of men, unknown except for their extravagances,' were disturbing the long-established traditions of the church. Still more troublesome for the reviewer, however, was the attitude found in their writings and actions: 'Although as yet they ask only for a place among us, they show plainly that nothing less than a triumph over all other parties could satisfy them; and even already they denounce "liberty of conscience and the emancipation of the intellect" as an intolerable offence against the truth.'[55]

Early Opposition to Litigation

From the earliest stages of the controversy Evangelicals were divided regarding the best means of dealing with the Ritualists, and some preferred the legislative route as being less likely to create further strife.[56] At the Islington Clerical Conference in January 1867, there was discussion of the need for a more positive organization that might garner the support of a greater number of Evangelicals than the CA. There were also rumors of a resolution disavowing litigation and advocating 'a declarative Act of Parliament' as a more positive response to the Ritualists. It was reported that Culling Hanbury, a leading figure among the Evangelical laity, was heading a newly formed committee that hoped to organize a more broadly based anti-Ritualist program than that of the CA – one that might attract the support of non-Evangelicals.[57] This was the first of several largely unsuccessful attempts to gain High Church support for the anti-Ritualist campaign which was largely dominated by Evangelicals. From time to time during the years to follow, a few prominent High Church moderates criticized the Ritualists, but the hoped for union remained an elusive goal.

The *Record* was decidedly cool toward the idea of another organization and suggested that a great public meeting of the laity could have already been organized by the CA had it not been for all the distractions created by those seeking an alternative. It also lent its editorial weight to the appeal to the courts. The paper was willing to allow that legislation would be better than litigation if there was any indication that Parliament could be convinced to act quickly, but it saw no evidence to support that view.[58] Given the circumstances, it was suggested that Evangelicals should put aside their differences and unite under the banner of the CA in pursuing the path of prosecution already begun.[59]

The debates over how best to proceed against the Ritualists led to the expression of renewed concerns regarding the divisions among Evangelicals. At the annual meeting of the CA in 1867, the chairman of the council, J. C. Colquhoun, took great pains to put his group forward as the best hope for party unity. He gave some indication of the tensions dividing the party when he noted the state of discussions regarding the merger of the many clerical and lay organizations throughout the country with the CA. Those bodies had largely responded negatively and insisted on the maintenance of their independence. Nevertheless, he believed there was room for some sort of affiliation that could draw such groups to affiliate with the CA and enable Evangelicals to develop a united plan of response to the Ritualists. Colquhoun suggested the formation of a committee consisting of the secretaries of the clerical and lay associations, meeting in London in conjunction with the CA.[60] Once again, the *Record* supported the CA, but the organization found little sympathy for its plan outside its own adherents. Although most Evangelicals favored some plan for the suppression of Ritualism, and the CA had the support of many for its program of litigation for a number of years, it never truly represented a definitive majority of the Evangelical party to the degree that the ECU served that function for the Ritualists.[61]

While the debate over litigation continued, Lord Shaftesbury introduced his 'Clerical Vestments Bill' for the regulation of clerical dress in 1867. He indicated in his speech to the House of Lords that his bill was purposely limited to the issue of 'sacrificial vestments' for two reasons: 'first, because those vestments have offended the country in an unusual degree; and, secondly, because there is some ambiguity in the law on the subject.'[62] Shaftesbury's bill proposed to clarify the ambiguous wording of the law 'without touching the rubric or the Canons.' In effect, it would have given 'force of law' to the Fifty-eighth Canon which had regulated usage since being enacted by Convocation in 1603.[63] The Ritualists commonly argued that the rubric, while requiring the surplice, did not explicitly forbid eucharistic vestments. Shaftesbury's legislation would have clarified that limitation. But even that relatively moderate alteration gained little episcopal support, an indication of just how reticent the bishops were to adopt a position that might be interpreted as favoring one party over another or as allowing the erastian intervention of Parliament through a bill proposed by the laity.[64] In March 1867, Lord Derby intimated that the Queen was ready to grant a royal commission to investigate the disputed elements of ritual, but Shaftesbury refused to withdraw his bill. Anti-Ritualists feared that the commission would only delay action for several more years and allow the Ritualists to strengthen their position.[65] Ultimately, the bill was defeated by a vote of 61 to 46, before its second reading, but Shaftesbury thought it had been a success in terms of forcing the episcopacy to consider the issue.[66] In the following years, Shaftesbury brought a number of other unsuccessful measures, most of which attempted to reform the ecclesiastical legal system in order to make prosecution of the Ritualists less expensive.[67]

The Ritual Commission

With the evident concern of a large portion of the general public over the growth of Ritualism and the escalation of the controversy on all sides, it was probably inevitable that the government should finally have to intervene. Lord Derby initially indicated that he believed the Ritual Commission should deal with all the disputed questions involved in the Ritualist controversy, but a majority of the episcopacy desired to limit the sphere of inquiry so as not to open the discussion to include the revision of the Book of Common Prayer. When the members of the commission were announced in June 1867, however, the reaction was decidedly negative, and Evangelicals thought there was little hope for an unbiased result. Of the 29 members appointed, the *Record* counted 16 whom it considered to be either extreme Ritualists or High Church, and it suggested that Bishop Wilberforce had been allowed to manipulate the process.[68] Since most of the other members were moderate non-partisans, anti-Ritualists feared they would support a report that gave toleration to a broad range of innovations. The Archbishop of York, William Thomson, and the Bishop of Durham, Charles Baring, were asked to serve and might have exercised a moderating influence, but both declined upon learning of the other appointments to the commission.[69] The only Evangelical members were Lord Portman and Henry Venn, who was the lone Evangelical clerical representative. It was rumored that Venn had only been included 'at the last moment, when it was noticed that there was not one of the Evangelical school amongst all Mr. Walpole's nominees.' And for all of the esteem in which Venn was held in Evangelical circles (he had long been the Honorary Secretary the CMS), the paper worried that his age and health would leave him incapable of exercising much influence.[70]

After sitting for some twenty sessions and hearing eighteen witnesses from both sides of the controversy, the commission released the first of four reports in August 1867. The report limited itself to the use of sacramental vestments, and despite its somewhat vague conclusions, its general opposition was more definite than Evangelicals had expected. The conclusion read:

> We find that while these vestments are regarded by some witnesses as symbolical of doctrine, and by others as a distinctive

vesture whereby they desire to do honour to the Holy Communion as the highest act of Christian worship, they are by none regarded as essential, and they give grave offense to many.

We are of opinion that it is expedient to restrain in the public services of the United Church of England and Ireland all variations in respect of vesture from that which has long been the established usage of the said United Church, and we think that this may be best secured by providing aggrieved parishioners with an easy and effectual process for complaint and redress.

We are not yet prepared to recommend to your Majesty the best mode of giving effect to these conclusions, with a view at once to secure the objects proposed and to promote the peace of the Church; but we have thought it our duty in a matter to which great interest is attached not to delay the communication to your Majesty of the results at which we have already arrived.[71]

The report was signed by all 29 commissioners, with three prominent Ritualists expressing some reservations.[72] Still, the commissioners, not wanting to give a decisive victory to one partisan section, left the question much as they had found it without offering any solutions to the controversy.[73]

It was almost a year before the second report of the Ritual Commission was completed. It extended the earlier condemnation of eucharistic vestments to include the use of altar lights and incense as well.[74] The commission concluded by suggesting that the usages of the past three centuries should be definitive for the church and that the laity had a right to appeal to the bishops when innovations were introduced.[75] The commissioners hedged their conclusions by affirming that they did not intend to place partisan restrictions on the traditional liberties enjoyed by the clergy of the Church of England. But, they concluded, 'this large comprehension seems to us to render it most desirable that in the celebration of the Church's rites there shall be introduced no novel features which are welcome only to some, but are offensive to others.'[76] Even this general affirmation of the traditional ceremonies of the church, however, was unable to obtain unanimous approval, and it was signed by only 23 of 29 of the commissioners, with several attaching their reservations.[77] The *Times*, while dissatisfied with the degree of division, thought it a satisfactory report.[78] The *Record*, however, found it a vaguely worded document, which, given the general nature of its conclusions and the lack of unanimity among the commissioners, would do little either to satisfy the anti-Ritualists or to resolve the ongoing crisis.[79] Given the level of division among the commissioners, even over a report that was intent on offending no one and proposed no specific resolutions, it was little wonder that their work would have a negligible impact.

Following the second report, Evangelicals seem to have lost interest in the commission along with any hope that it might be instrumental in halting the innovations.[80] The commission then broadened its field of study, and it was over a year before another report appeared (on suggested alterations to the lectionary readings). When Gladstone added two more High Church members to the commission as replacements, the *Record* suggested that all hope had been lost for a balanced result.[81] As the months dragged on, the paper occasionally took note of the commission's work, usually with a degree of sarcasm, but it expected little practical result from any further resolutions.[82] In general, Evangelical support was renewed for the litigation sponsored by the CA and the legislative efforts of Lord Shaftesbury. The third report, which was not issued until January 1870, dealt with proposals for new lectionary readings.[83] The *Record* was convinced that the commission was now thoroughly dominated by its High Church members who believed procrastination was the best policy regarding the Ritualists.[84]

The fourth and final report was issued in September 1870. It acknowledged that most of the rubrics had been left unconsidered, but a few alterations were proposed 'to explain and amend rubrics so as to secure general uniformity of practice in those matters which may be deemed essential.' No suggestions were made for any legal or legislative changes, however, and the commission left unaltered the 'Ornaments Rubric,' the ambiguity of which allowed for the variant reading upon which the Ritualist innovations were based.[85] Even the *Times*, which had taken a positive view of the commission's earlier work, was quite critical of the final report.[86] The *Record* suggested that the commission 'had been for a long time virtually defunct.' It had held few meetings, with the extended illness of the Archbishop of Canterbury, and had largely issued its final report as a formality.[87] Any impact the report might have had was further limited by the evident lack of unity among the commissioners – numerous protests were attached registering various degrees of dissent, and three refused to sign it altogether.[88] Ultimately, the *Record* thought the report would only hinder future legislation with 'its multiplied absurdities and its attempt to revoke the decisions promulgated in previous reports.'[89]

The Growing Opposition to Ritualism

While there was no authoritative intervention forthcoming from either the government or the ecclesiastical hierarchy, it was evident that Evangelicals were not alone in their view that some concrete response to the Ritualists was required.[90] In February 1868, the Bishop of London offered a resolution in the Upper House of Convocation:

> That this House viewing with anxious concern the increasing diversity of practice in regard to Ritual observances, as causing disquiet and contention, and perceiving with deep regret that the Resolutions adopted at the Convocations of Canterbury and York have failed to secure unity, deems it expedient for the peace of the Church – 1. That the limits of Ritual observance should not be left to the uncontrolled discretion of individual clergymen, and ought, therefore, to be defined by lawful authority. 2. That some easy and inexpensive process ought to be provided whereby the liberties of the officiating clergy and their parishioners might be protected, and the evils of unrestricted license might be checked.[91]

In presenting the resolution, Bishop Tait lamented the fact that the Ritualist clergy refused to be guided by the episcopacy, either individually or in joint counsel, but seemed intent on pursuing their own interests. He affirmed that he had always tried to give the clergy of his diocese the greatest amount of freedom, but he feared 'that in this particular matter liberty had now degenerated into license.'[92] Tait's speech indicated that at least some of the bishops had begun to consider the possibility that a judicial solution to the controversy might be the only hope for a timely resolution. The ensuing debate, however, indicated the degree of division that existed, and an alternate resolution was adopted that was somewhat more general and innocuous.[93]

Henry Alford gave voice to the growing concern of many nonpartisan moderates when he expressed his concern over the Ritualists' attempt to dominate a meeting of the Society for Promoting Christian Knowledge in December 1868. In describing the events, Alford characterized the party in terms quite similar to those used by their Evangelical opponents. The Ritualists, he wrote, were bound together by a 'compact organization and unvarying uniformity;' they were 'a party burning with zeal for a definite object, unscrupulous as to the means of attaining it, complete and ready in organization.' Since the society meetings were held in London, where the greatest concentration of Ritualists was to be found, they were able to exercise 'an exaggerated importance' beyond the true measure of their limited numbers.[94] Alford, was particularly disturbed that High Church moderates had shown an 'unaccountable sympathy' for 'the innovating and disloyal,' and he believed it was necessary for them to work together with Evangelicals if the Ritualists were to be held in check:

> Thinking themselves perhaps to stand too deeply committed to certain principles still enunciated by these latter [the Ritualists], – or finding themselves driven to extremes by the wicked slanders of the worthless secular organs of Evangelicalism, they have become accustomed to dissimulate the danger impending, and to look more kindly upon those who are cutting away the ground from under them, than upon their Evangelical brethren, who are doing their best to maintain it.[95]

In Alford's view, such cooperation among anti-Ritualists would be possible only if Evangelicals were willing to moderate the tone of their polemics. He suggested that they needed to learn to appreciate without suspicion those coming out of the High Church tradition who described the truth in language dissimilar to their own. Probably referring to the *Record*, he suggested that Evangelicals disavow 'the weapons of private defamation and slander by which they are contented to suffer their ostensible organs to undermine the work of the Church.'[96] Second, he believed Evangelicals needed to take a more active role in the organizations and life of the church. Their absence, in fact, only gave further ground to the influence of their opponents.[97] In the years to follow, Alford's criticisms were often repeated by moderates within the Evangelical party who were equally disturbed by the tone that characterized the debate.

With the bishops divided and either unable or unwilling to take any effective steps to deal with the Ritualists that might appear to unfairly favor their opponents, and the Ritual Commission similarly unable to recommend a compromise plan of action, Lord Shaftesbury once again took the initiative in the House of Lords. In May 1868, he questioned the government's intention of acting on the commission's early reports and received the reply that no response would be considered until its work was complete. Shaftesbury argued that the first two reports were 'ripe for legislation.' He went on to warn the government that the subject was 'no trifling matter' and that further delays would have a negative impact among both educated and working class citizens with regard to their loyalty to the national church.[98] A month later, Shaftesbury submitted a bill for the 'Uniformity of Public Worship' that resembled the legislation he had offered prior to the formation of the Ritual Commission. The new bill, however, went further and attempted to enact the recommendations of the commission's first two reports by regulating the use of the surplice and forbidding the use lighted candles and incense.[99] In July, it was soundly defeated in a vote that indicated there was little episcopal support for a legislative solution (or at least for one stringent enough to satisfy the anti-Ritualists).[100]

During the parliamentary campaign that summer, the CA mounted its first extensive effort to make Ritualism a political issue.[101] The association took out advertisements calling on 'the electors of the nation' to question candidates on the subject and to make their answer a decisive factor in the voting. Thirty years of 'Romish innovations,' the advertisement proclaimed, were 'a scandal to an Established Church and an outrage to a Protestant nation.' The innovators had steadfastly refused to heed the admonitions of the episcopacy, the judgments of the courts, or the recommendations of the Ritual Commission; 'it is time that Parliament should interfere, to declare what the law is, and to make it effectual, and to give the parishioners an easy remedy by which these practices may be stopped.'[102] At the CA's autumn conference, J. C. Ryle suggested that the Ritual Commission's inconclusive results and the delay in action only gave the Ritualists time to expand their influence and to establish their position. Furthermore, neither the bishops nor Convocation had shown any inclination to act. The time had come, thought Ryle, for a 'reasonable, fair, and moderate Bill,' and it was the House of Commons that had always protected 'the liberties of the people.' He urged the Protestant electors to vote for members who promised to support an anti-Ritualist bill.[103] The campaign had little impact on the election, but it continued the process by which both ecclesiastical and political leaders were made aware of the growing public dissatisfaction with Ritualism and brought under increasing pressure to find some effective means of resolving the controversy.

A New Rationalist Threat and Party Divisions

The Evangelical reaction toward the threat of rationalism at the end of the 1860s gave some indication of the degree to which the growth of anti-Ritualism had widened the divisions within the Church of England. Many Evangelicals, after years of conflict, were simply unable to overcome their deep-seated distrust of the High Church party. The hardening of party lines can be illustrated by comparing the Evangelical response in 1869, to their reaction under similar circumstances at the beginning of the decade. When the issue of rationalism was raised anew, Evangelicals had little interest in allying with the High Church party, despite sharing with them a concern to defend the conservative view of Scripture.

The problem of rationalism resurfaced with the case of Charles Voysey, Vicar of Healaugh. Following the publication of his book

The Sling and the Stone, Voysey was accused of heresy by the Archbishop of York, William Thomson.[104] At the CA's annual meeting that year, Edward Garbett proposed that the objectives of the organization ought to be expanded to include opposition to the rationalists as well as the Ritualists. Toward that end, he suggested that the organization's name should be shortened to delete all references to Ritualism; with the broader emphasis, he hoped it could be simply known as the English Church Association in contrast to the ECU.[105] Garbett's proposal was rejected after a heated discussion; while all affirmed their opposition to rationalism, most of the members thought their anti-Ritualist program should remain the association's priority. However much they feared the rationalists, it was clear that many Evangelicals still viewed the Ritualists as the primary threat to the church.

The Voysey case led to an exchange of letters between J. C. Colquhoun, chairman of the CA's council, and C. L. Wood, President of the ECU. Wood proposed that the two groups each raise £500 to assist the archbishop with the financial burden of the case. Colquhoun, however, refused even such mutually beneficial cooperation:

> I am bound at once to express my own opinion that, as the Church Union has been actively engaged in promoting the errors and perversions of our Reformed Church, which the Church Association was instituted to resist, any idea of co-operation between two Societies having such opposite objects seems to me inadmissible.
>
> And when I bear in mind the remark of the Bishop of St. David's, that 'no Churchman who does not desire the subversion of our Reformed Church and its final absorption into the Church of Rome, can too deeply distrust or too strenuously oppose the proceedings of the English Church Union,' you will not be surprised that, with every feeling of sincere personal respect for yourself, I should decline, as a loyal Churchman, any association with the body over which I regret to see that you preside.[106]

Wood forwarded the correspondence to Archbishop Thomson with an expression of his regret that the CA was unwilling to work together with the ECU. He thought it a great tragedy and suggested that a common cause might have helped soften the differences that so often divided the two parties. Wood then offered the archbishop the £500 that the ECU proposed to raise on its own. Interestingly, Thomson also refused the ECU's offer; he replied that he could not accept their aid given 'the course adopted towards me in my office by the Church Union Society now for some years, and by members of it who claim to represent it and are not disavowed.'[107] In June 1869, the archbishop formally prohibited Voysey from ministering. In December, the Chancery Court of York ruled that Voysey had in fact expressed views that were incompatible with the doctrines affirmed by the Church of England.[108] In February 1871, the final ruling against Voysey was handed down by the Judicial Committee of the Privy Council, and after refusing to recant, he was deprived.[109]

The reaction to Voysey, however, was a relatively minor affair compared to the controversy that arose when Gladstone nominated Frederick Temple to become the Bishop of Exeter in 1869. One of the contributors to *Essays and Reviews*, Temple's nomination was immediately opposed by High Church and Evangelical alike. The *Record* began a campaign against the appointment, and the editor of *John Bull* wrote to commend the paper for its strong stand. He suggested that a united effort would be the most potent means of protest: 'It affords an opportunity, too, for moderate Churchmen, who believe in the inspiration of Holy Scripture, to combine as one man.... May I suggest that if representative Churchmen, such as Lord Shaftesbury and Dr. Pusey, would head a Committee in London, the moral force would be irresistible?'[110] The *Record* thought the elevation of Temple was a threat to all who worshipped the trinity, acknowledged 'one faith, one Lord, one baptism,' and believed in the inspiration of Holy Scripture. But while recognizing the need for 'one harmonious organization' to coordinate the efforts and protests, it still questioned 'whether it may be thought best that Dr. Pusey and his friends should move in one column, and that the Evangelical clergy shall move n another.'[111]

John Bull shortly announced an organizational meeting and intimated that Lord Shaftesbury and Dr. Pusey had agreed to act in union and lead the committee.[112] Shaftesbury had, in fact, been in contact with Pusey, but he denied having consented to act 'in unison' or 'to sit on a Committee.' As a result of his earlier experiences during the controversy over *Essays and Reviews*, Shaftesbury took the position that the two parties should 'in perfect harmony, act separately, rather than conjointly, to attain their common end.' He also noted that, as a result of the earlier article, he had received several anonymous letters of rebuke for his presumed association with Pusey; and while refusing to serve on a common committee, he responded to his accusers by defending Pusey's honor.[113] The meeting was attended by a number of Evangelicals but not by Shaftesbury. Pusey moved that 'notwithstanding Lord Shaftesbury's letter,' a resolution should be adopted asking him to serve. The resolution was passed unanimously, and Dr. Pusey was elected vice-chairman. A number of other prominent Evangelicals were also elected to the committee, and while no well-known Ritualists were asked to serve, almost all of the Evangelicals declined to participate.[114] Ultimately, the independent protests accomplished little. The CA sent a memorial to Gladstone, but the decision was by then certain, and the protest carried little weight.[115]

The 1860s saw a decisive escalation of partisan activities in response to the growth of Ritualism. An important step was taken when associations were formed to galvanize party support on both sides. Thereafter, the rhetoric became increasingly heated, and the party faithful were organized to gather public support for their respective concerns. The anti-Ritualist campaign, however, was increasingly supported by moderates who were put off by the more extreme innovations even though they had little or no connection to the Evangelical party. No doubt it was the growth of this general tide of opposition that finally convinced the government to take up the issue in special committee. But while the Ritual Commission and most of the bishops (both individually and together in the Upper House of Convocation) agreed that the more extreme innovations were clearly departures from the long-standing usage of the church, probably illegal, and certainly offensive to a large majority of the laity, neither body was willing or able to take the decisive steps necessary to resolve the crisis. The government would not intervene without the almost unanimous support of the episcopacy, and the bishops seemed intent on not making the controversy worse or appearing to take sides. They were willing on occasion to condemn some of the innovations but not sufficiently disturbed to take action against the innovators.

On several occasions, Lord Shaftesbury sought to force a response by introducing bills in the House of Lords – either to establish limits on the innovations or to simplify the litigation process and thereby make it easier for aggrieved parishioners to challenge in court any clergy who made undesired alterations to their worship. While a few moderate Evangelicals questioned the wisdom of pursuing the Ritualists in the courts, prosecution seemed to offer the only reasonable hope for bringing a timely conclusion to the controversy. The end of the decade saw the beginning of the anti-Ritualist lawsuits. Ultimately, they were unsuccessful in obtaining the desired results – the innovations would only expand over the course of the coming years, and the rulings emanating from the judicial bench, as also the admonitions issuing from the bishops, failed to find a responsive audience. During the 1860s, partisan animosities had only grown sharper as was evident when the two sides, by the end of the decade, could not even agree on a common means for opposing the rationalism that challenged their mutually held beliefs. Events of the coming years, however, would only further separate them, and ultimately, the spirit of controversy would threaten to dissolve the fragile unity of the Evangelical party itself.[116]

Notes

1   Anonymous, *Facts and Documents Showing the Alarming State of the Diocese of Oxford*, by a Senior Clergyman of the Diocese (London: Wertheim, Mackintosh & Hunt, 1859), p. 8.

Along with Bishop Blomfield, Bishop Mant attempted to require the surplice in the pulpit in the 1840s. But at the same time, Mant rejected other innovations that had been excluded during the Reformation. In listing some of these 'objectionable rites,' Mant mentioned most of the alterations that would become central to the Ritualists. He concluded, 'If not altogether in exact form, yet in spirit, a disposition has appeared in recent times for reverting to some at least of these. On all such questions the Church should be our guide. Some of these ceremonial observances she has rejected as being repugnant to the word of God: some as obscuring God's glory: some as giving occasion for vanity and many superstitions. But in any case our obedience to her is due: and what she has repudiated you may be assured that you ought not to adopt.' Richard Mant, *Horae Liturgicae*, pp. 184-85.

A essayist in the *Quarterly Review*, surveying the development of Ritualism, noted how the movement had expanded far beyond anything conceivable at the time of the Oxford Movement or even during the 1840s and early 50s: 'The Ritualists (as they delight to style themselves), while they acknowledge a connection with the "Tractarians" and the "Ecclesiologists" of an older time, look back on those fellow-labourers in the "great Catholic Revival" as mere babes in knowledge.' Anonymous, 'Ultra-Ritualism,' *Quarterly Review* 122 (1867): 163.

James Bentley made the point in his study of Ritualism: 'The limited ritual of the early Tractarians no longer sufficed the innovators. Many of them were now clearly imitating the Church of Rome, and the more intelligent admitted this.' Bentley, *Ritualism and Politics*, p. 28.

Anti-Ritualists, while recognizing that the Ritualists went far beyond the initial limits of the Oxford Movement, discerned a continuity of fundamental principles and held the Tractarians responsible for the Romeward tendencies of their successors. The connection was evident in Walter Walsh's work which condemned the whole as a Romanist conspiracy. While devoting the bulk of his work to the Ritualists, Walsh titled it *The Secret History of the Oxford Movement* (London: Swan Sonnenschein & Co., 1897).

2   Stephen Neill suggested that Anglican Evangelicals were never a party in the truest sense of the word. 'They have always been obstinate individualists – this is their strength, and in part also their weakness. They formed voluntary societies, but the vigorous assertion of their own independence has always, and fortunately, made impossible the formation of a unified party organization.' Stephen Neill, *Anglicanism*, 4th ed., (London: Mowbray & Co., 1977), pp. 190-91. In contrast, he thought the High Church, from the

time of the Oxford Movement, was a party. It had an established center, a central organ of opinion (the *Tracts for the Times*) and 'acknowledged leaders.' Ibid., p. 255.

3   M. A. Crowther surveyed the rise of numerous local unions of High Church clergy during the late 1840s, largely in response to the perceived threat of state interference, such as in the Gorham Judgment and the Hampden appointment. Later, those independent bodies combined to form the ECU. She also dealt with the rise of a variety of organizations in the same chapter, titled 'Church Defence.' She suggested that the ECU, the Church Association, the revival of Convocation, and the annual Church Congresses begun in the early 1860s were all concerned, from varying perspectives, with the defense of the church. Cf. M. A. Crowther, *Church Embattled: Religious Controversy in Mid-Victorian England* (Hamden: Archon Books, 1970), pp. 186-218.

On the rise of the ECU, particularly in reaction to the St. George's-in-the-East riots, and the role it played in unifying the Ritualist movement, cf. Reed, *Glorious Battle*, pp. 85-86.

4   Some twenty years later, when the Ritualists protested that they were being persecuted and that the ECU was a purely defensive organization, an anonymous correspondent cited evidence to the contrary. The first annual report of the ECU, he noted, mentioned 'an unsuccessful attempt to prosecute Evangelical clergymen, for preaching in London theatres, in company with Dissenting ministers; and that the only thing which prevented the Union, as such, bringing these Evangelical clergymen before the Courts was the want of – tell it not in Buckingham-street! – an "aggrieved" parson, willing to promote the office of a judge! But let the Report speak for itself. It says: – "Your Committee have next to report that the attention of the Society has been directed to the great scandal which has been given by certain clergymen of the Church of England, consorting with Dissenting preachers, in the use of the theatres for public worship, in London and elsewhere. An opinion upon the legality of such proceedings has been obtained from Dr. Phillimore, by the Society, and published in the newspapers; but the difficulty of 'promoting the office of judge' in the Ecclesiastical Courts against offenders is very great; and, indeed, it cannot be promoted at all, except at the instance of the incumbent of the parish in which the theatre is situated. It does not, therefore, appear to your Committee that there is any hope of putting down this profane and degrading practice by an appeal to law".' Letter (signed 'Boanerges') to the *Record*, 7 Nov. 1881. According to Balleine, the ECU also attempted to prosecute Samuel Waldegrave, the Evangelical Bishop of Carlisle, for heresy. Balleine, *Evangelical Party*, pp. 181, 195-96.

In January 1860, the special services to reach the working classes were moved to the even more secular venues of theatres in the city. The plan was conceived by several men connected with the London City Mission, including Lord Shaftesbury. The first services were held in five theatres and led by both Anglican and Nonconformist clergy. By February, the number had grown to seven, and attendance each Sunday evening was averaging over 20,000. For a description of the meetings and Shaftesbury's involvement, cf. Hodder, *Life of Shaftesbury*, pp. 563-66. There was some debate even among Evangelicals concerning the appropriateness of such meetings, but a majority seemed to favor them. One skeptic, Rev. John Courtenay, attended one of the services and was convinced of their usefulness; it was apparent to him that the services attracted the lower classes who rarely attended regular church services. He also noted that the services avoided using the litany or other elements of the Book of Common Prayer in order to avoid legal concerns. Letter to the *Record*, 6 Jan. 1860.

A decade later, the *Record* summarized the success of the annual winter services: 'There were eight theatres open every Sunday evening, at which there were two hundred and eight services, attended by over two hundred and sixty-seven thousand persons. At the Standard, the largest theatre in London, and in one of the poorest districts, the average number of the congregation was two thousand; and, when it is remembered that those who attend the theatre services are mostly the poorest of the poor, who seldom or never think of attending any regular place of worship, the vast amount of good done is plainly apparent.' *Record*, 20 Oct. 1869.

A number of histories suggest that the ECU was formed as a defensive body. Horton Davies, for example, wrote that it was organized 'to provide legal support for the prosecuted ritualistic priests.' Davies, *Worship and Theology in England, vol. 4*, p. 115. In fact, however, it was not entirely defensive in nature. Such portrayals appear to be a case of reading earlier events in light of the later history of the controversy.

5   'If under these circumstances, the bishops manifest any unwillingness to act, and hamper instead of supporting those who propose reasonable and temperate measures for arresting the evil, they cannot be surprised if others occupy the post which they have deserted, and take the matter in hand in a way less agreeable to them. We should have no such scenes as those which have occurred at St. George's-in-the-East if the people had seen a serious intention on the part of the authorities of the Church to provide a remedy for the Romish follies that have been introduced there.' *Record*, 11 May 1860. The bill was intended as a temporary measure, a means of securing peace in the church until a more lasting solution could be worked out.

6   In an 1861 editorial, the paper interpreted the rise of rationalism as a reaction to Tractarianism. The Rationalists were reacting to 'superstitious religionism' of the Oxford Movement, and 'we are got to the opposite pole of theological error, and have to do with a party who are not content with disencumbering the Gospel of the swaddling-bands that Puseyism has wrapped around it, but are assiduously seeking to divest it of all its Divine power and authority.' *Record*, 17 April 1861.

In his article on the history of the *Record*, Josef Altholz noted that Edward Garbett had joined the paper as a co-editor (along with Alexander Haldane, who was also the managing proprietor) in 1854. Altholz suggested that Garbett's influence was evident in the shift of emphasis during this period, since he was particularly concerned about the growth of rationalism and somewhat more moderate concerning Evangelical relations with the High Church. Altholz, 'Alexander Haldane,' *Victorian Periodicals Review*, pp. 26-28.

7   *Record*, 12 Sept. 1860. The common thread between Ritualism and rational-

ism became a common theme for Evangelicals. In 1864, even as Evangelicals were uniting with some of the High Church party to oppose the rationalists, Bishop Bickersteth of Ripon suggested that both groups sought to attain ascendance in the church – the Ritualists argued for the exaltation of authority and the rationalists for the exaltation of the intellect; the former claimed absolute authority for the church and the latter for reason. 'The extravagant claim on the footing of authority which has been set up by the one has prepared the way for the extravagant exaltation of reason, as independent of authority, by the other.... But in each case the real root of the evil is to be found in the want of due reverence for the supreme authority of Scripture as a Divine revelation.' Cited in the *Record*, 4 May 1864.

The connection between the two movements became a common one. Bishop Magee suggested that Oxford was largely divided between 'pietistic Ritualists' and 'anti-clerical and anti-Christian materialists.' He continued, 'What a change from the days when Newman and his school absorbed the intellect of Oxford! And yet a change which they have largely helped to effect. I always looked for this reaction of skepticism against overstrained authority in religion.' MacDonnell, *Life of Magee, vol. 2*, p. 148.

8   He concluded, 'Between believing too little, and believing too much, there is a middle course, alone meet for our adoption, – to believe in the Bible as it is, neither taking from it, nor adding to it, but receiving just all of it, and no more; and this amounts to professing Gospel Christianity.' Charles Girdlestone, *Gospel Christianity; or, the Religion of the Bible Compared with Sceptical Theology and Papal Superstition* (London: William Hunt & Co.), 1866.

9   Of the two, the *Record* thought the writers of the *Essays* presented the much greater danger to the church. The paper thought Colenso's work was 'eminently foolish' and would have raised little concern had he not been a colonial bishop. The *Essays* were more critical both for their content and for the positions held by their authors; 'far more deeply do we feel the danger which threatens our own Universities, and through them the high places in our Church.' *Record*, 11 March 1863.

For a general survey of the rationalist controversy, cf. Owen Chadwick, *Victorian Church, Part Two: 1860-1901*, 2nd ed. (London: A. & C. Black, 1972), pp. 75-85

10 In 1863, almost the entire episcopacy issued a statement calling on Colenso, in effect, to resign. They affirmed the entire Scriptures to be the Word of God and charged Colenso with no longer believing that which he had 'voluntarily professed to believe" at his ordination regarding "all the Canonical Scriptures of the Old and New Testament.' The bishops asked him to reconsider his ordination vow when it was apparent he could 'no longer discharge its duties or use the formularies to which you have subscribed.' Cited in the *Record*, 2 March 1863. Only three bishops did not sign the letter, and two of them later gave it their whole-hearted support. The Bishop of Peterborough was ill when it was signed, and Bishop Hampden of Hereford, whose own orthodoxy had once been questioned, affirmed the letter but said that it was 'not as condemnatory as I could have wished it to have been.' *Record*, 4 March 1863.

The *Record* was especially pleased to note the critical article on the *Essays* published in the *Quarterly Review*. Given the scholarly reputation of that journal, the paper thought the article would be quite damaging to the reputation of the authors. *Record*, 23 Jan. 1861.

11 The paper claimed its disputes with Wilberforce had never been personal and affirmed that it was pleased to have the opportunity to acknowledge the 'service which the Right Rev. Prelate has rendered to the cause of truth' by prohibiting Colenso from presiding anywhere in the diocese of Oxford. *Record*, 6 April 1863. Bishop Wilberforce's declaration read, in part, 'It seems to me, and to the great majority of my brethren, to be our plain duty to guard our own dioceses from the ministry of one who is, in our judgment, disqualified for the exercise of any spiritual function in the Church of England. I therefore forbid his being suffered to minister in the Word and Sacraments within my diocese.' Cited in the *Record*, 30 March 1863.

12 Pusey began his letter: 'I have long anticipated the coming of a time when the pressure of the common enemy of unbelief would draw closer into one band all who love our Lord as their Redeemer and their God, and the Bible as being the very Word of God. The recent, miserable, soul-destroying judgment surely requires one united action on the part of every clergyman and lay member of the Church to repudiate it.' Letter to the *Record*, 19 Feb. 1864.

Lord Shaftesbury responded with a letter to Pusey expressing a similar perspective. The struggle, he wrote, was over the doctrine of atonement and the very heart of the Gospel. 'For God's sake let all who love our blessed Lord and His perfect Word be of one heart, one mind, one action on this great issue, and show that despite our wanderings, our doubts, our contentions, we may yet be one in Him.' Hodder, *Life of Shaftesbury*, p. 593.

13 *Record*, 29 Feb. 1864; cf. the editorial opposing the idea of turning the decision into a case for altering the final court of appeal, *Record*, 9 March 1864.

14 Cited in the *Times*, 2 March 1864.

15 Henry Venn, the moderate secretary of the CMS, was opposed to joint action, believing that Evangelical differences with the extreme section of the High Church party were at least as great as their opposition to the Broad Church. Cf. Stock, *Church Missionary Society, vol. 2*, p. 342.

The *Record*, however, was hopeful that the campaign against the rationalists might exercise a moderating influence on the High Church section and lead to 'the reunion to the one fold of all those who love the Lord Jesus.' The paper allowed, however, that Evangelicals could never ally with those who had given themselves over to 'the figments of Popery.' *Record*, 4 March 1864.

16 Goode was especially concerned about the continuing High Church attacks on the Judicial Committee of the Privy Council given his close connection to Gorham. *Record*, 14 March 1864. The *Record* rejected the premise of Goode's argument on the grounds that the declaration never specifically mentioned the judgment and only affirmed what the signers believed to be the doctrine of the church. Goode's position was also taken up by E. A. Litton, another influential theologian who refused to sign the document. Litton was also troubled by the ambiguity of the language adopted by the commission in the effort to obtain the approval of both Evangelicals and Tractarians. *Record*, 21 March 1864.

17 'If, indeed, the Evangelical party were asked to enter upon a course of intricate and continued action in combination with those from whom they are separated by important doctrinal questions, we should feel differently. But it appears to us that much needless suspicion and jealousy have been aroused by the combination of names on the Oxford Committee. We honour the feeling in which the distrust originates, but we deprecate its application to the present case. The invitation to sign the declaration does not emanate from the Tractarian party, but from a combination of parties. In entering on this combination Dr. Pusey and his associates have given, in our judgment, a satisfactory pledge for their good faith and honesty of purpose.' *Record*, 11 March 1864.

18 The *Quarterly Review* thought the declaration awkward 'in form, construction, and language,' but remarkable for the unanimity of support it gathered. 'Never, we believe, was there so wide-spread a concord amidst what have been supposed to be absolutely irreconcilable sections of thought and action in the Established Church. Names which, even in the placid stillness of the printer's type, almost start at their unwonted contiguity, appear united in common action, founded on common religious convictions.' Anonymous, 'The Privy Council Judgment,' *Quarterly Review* 115 (1864): 539.

19 In a preliminary report, W. R. Fremantle noted that it had been signed by 10,500 out of about 19,000 clergy. *Record*, 6 April 1864. By the time it went to the printers, that number had grown to over 11,000. *Record*, 18 April and 13 May 1864.

The *Quarterly Review* complained that the bishops had not done enough to unite High Church and Evangelical conservatives. Looking back over the development of critical theology that culminated in *Essays and Reviews* the essayist wrote, 'If those who were risking all for Catholic faith and observance; if those who held as their one spiritual inheritance a belief that the apprehension of the doctrine of the Atonement and of the Spirit's influences lay at the root of all individual life in God; if, lastly, those who received passively, but held firmly, the old Anglican teaching, leaning neither to the individualism of the last, nor to the objective yearnings of the first class; if these three could have been brought to act really together, where might not now the Church of England be?' Anon., 'Church of England and Her Bishops,' *Quarterly Review*, pp. 572-73.

20 By October, the *Record* had returned to the offensive. While noting Pusey's role in the protest and reaffirming the utmost respect for him personally, the paper complained about those associated with him. 'We believe that, so far as concerns himself, he holds so large a portion of fundamental truth as in a great measure to neutralize, in his own case, the evil tendencies of his erroneous system. But it is impossible to shut our eyes to the mischief of the Romanizing tendencies which, under the shelter of his name, have been pushed into notice, and which have, in fact, been the precursors and the aids of that reactionary infidelity which has sprung up at Oxford.' *Record*, 3 Oct. 1864.

In the later months of 1864, the *Record* began to devote an increasing amount of space to Ritualist churches and the innovations introduced into their worship services. These reports had appeared frequently in the paper during the earlier years of the controversy but had largely disappeared from its columns for several years while Evangelicals combined with the High Church against the feared onset of skepticism.

An anonymous writer in *Fraser's Magazine* suggested the *Essays and Reviews* case was partially responsible for the expansion of the Ritualists' activities. The judgment indicated the degree of toleration allowed by the law, and 'a number of clergy, then inclining to the Church of Rome, discovered that without abandoning a single tenet of the Romish doctrines they might remain where they were, and make the language of the reformed Prayer Book suit the purpose of the mass.' Anon., 'Recent Movements,' *Fraser's Magazine*, p. 285.

21 John Richardson complained in a lecture for the CA, 'Men bid us turn against modern scepticism. We hate it, we fear it; but modern scepticism is the bitter fruit of our modern superstition.' John Richardson, 'Ritualism, Too Late and Too Soon; Too Little and Too Much; Too Narrow and Too Wide,' in *Church Association Lectures, 1869* (London: Hatchards, 1869), p. 45.

Charles Girdlestone thought the rationalists and the Ritualists both undermined the authority of Scripture, but he doubted that the 'thinly-veiled Infidelity' of the former would ever attract many disciples. He seemed to imply that intellectual theologians generally had little impact on the average church members and was far more concerned by 'the other form of unbelief now canvassing for proselytes, that which doubts the sufficiency of the Scriptures to make wise unto salvation, that is to say, the Papal Superstition.' Girdlestone, *Gospel Christianity*, p. 10.

There were a few Evangelicals who took the opposite view. One anonymous writer, after several years of the anti-Ritualist campaign, argued that the rationalists posed a greater threat. 'I am strongly inclined to think that, misled by the noise and clamour of the one, and the stealthy advance of the other, we have given our chief attention to the smaller evil, and only some leisure scraps of time and thought to the greater. I shall much regret it if the tendency of my remarks shall appear to extenuate or diminish the danger arising from Ritualism, but I cannot conceal my belief that the perils of Rationalism (against which we are doing nothing) are of a far more deadly kind.' Letter (signed 'Observer') to the *Record*, 1 Jan. 1868.

22 The *Pall Mall Gazette* tabulated figures given in the second edition of *Mackeson's Guide to the Churches of London and its Suburbs*. The report gave information on the ritual used in 553 churches that lay within twelve miles of the general post office:

Vestments	12	
Incense	6	
Fully Choral Services	94	(of these, 84 had surpliced choirs)
Partly Choral Services	66	
Gregorian Music	39	
Services on Saints' Days	169	
Daily Services	90	

Adding together the figures on choral services, the paper concluded that one quarter of the churches in London were chanting the psalms, and one third were holding services on Saints' Days, both of which were changes first introduced by Ritualists. But the figures on vestments and incense indicated just how few churches were controlled by the extreme section. Cited in the *Record*, 1 Feb. 1867.

In an 1869 pamphlet, James Colley suggested that musical innovations were a matter of taste best left to the discretion of each minister and congregation. 'In many localities choral services are very general, with, in some places, surpliced choristers. In other parts of the country these things are deemed objectionable, and spoken of as "High Church" – a term almost synonymous with papistical; whereas, after all, these (like the architecture of our Churches) are mere matters of taste, than which nothing can be more fluctuating.' He thought that, in general, Evangelical churches were improving in their use of music. They were aware 'that although truth changes not, public taste does vary in the course of time, and services that satisfied our forefathers, and were considered attractive in a season of religious listlessness, have ceased to be so in this more musical age.' Colley, *Evangelical Churchmanship*, pp. 8-9.

Harding Girdlestone suggested that Evangelicals opposed only those innovations that implied doctrinal affirmations that tended toward Romanism. Evangelicals could not support innovations that were 'more or less imbued with semi-Romanism,' but he did not believe that opposition to the Ritualists should not be allowed to degenerate into 'slovenliness or indifference' regarding church architecture, ornaments, music, or similar innovations. W. Harding Girdlestone, *The Romanizing Tendency of Ultra-Ritualism* (London: Rivingtons, 1867), pp. 70-79.

An essayist in the *Edinburgh Review* took a moderate view and suggested that many of the innovations owed their origins to a 'vast wave of antiquarian, artistic, architectural, romantic sentiment' that was evident all over Europe. The Ritualists, while claiming that they were responsible for the adoption of the alterations, were in fact, simply a part of a 'great secular movement.' The reviewer thought aesthetic innovations were of little real concern; much more disturbing, he suggested, was the contempt with which the Ritualists treated those in authority over them and their own congregations. Anonymous, 'Ritualism,' *Edinburgh Review* 125 (1867): 441-49.

23 Charles Stirling, who later seceded from the church following the Lincoln judgment, proclaimed, 'We need, Sir, the formation without delay of a "Church of England Evangelical Alliance" which shall present a firm front to the hosts that are gathering against us. At present, the Evangelical body in our Church are like a rope of sand. They are scattered and unorganized, while our opponents are working, as they have ever done, in concert, and proving every day the value of combined action.' Letter to the *Record*, 2 Dec. 1864.

24 The advertisement continued: 'During the last Session of Parliament the Bishop of London, in reply to the Marquis of Westmeath, expressed his readiness, and that of the Bishops in general, to co-operate in such legisla-

tion as will directly meet the case.

'"The English Church Union," and the numerous Romanizing organizations which exist throughout the kingdom, are now engaged in getting up petitions, and bring influence to bear upon the Bishops against any interference with their proceedings.

'It is obvious that if Churchmen do nothing to support the proposed legislation the Romanizing system will go on extending, until it is at length allowed to settle in the Church with lamentable results.

'Experience has shown that, as the case now stands, legal proceedings, tedious and expensive, are not sufficient to put a stop to innovation. The evil can be easily and directly met by a declaratory Act of Parliament. The sympathies of all true Churchmen will go with a movement which is preservative of the customary ceremonial and worship of our Church.

'If some such measure be not carried into effect the consequence will be ruinous. The Church, notwithstanding our Acts of Uniformity, will become a Babel, 'a city of confusion,' and at last fall to pieces, to the triumph of Rome. The Romanizers are at work. Petitions are being got up everywhere against any interference with Romanizing ritualism, and the *Church Review* states that thousands of names have been obtained."'

The advertisement went on to list the members of the Executive Committee, Vice-Presidents and Honorary Local Secretaries. It noted that 'the Bishops, for obvious reasons, have not been invited to join. As the Association has only just been formed, it is daily augmenting its lists of Vice-Presidents and Committees.' The advertisement ran in the *Times* and the *Record*, 10 Jan. 1866.

According to Elliott-Binns and Charles Bury, the Church Association was formed in 1865, but the January 1866 reference was the first public notice of the organization in the *Record*. Elliott-Binns, *Evangelical Movement*, p. 58. Bury suggested that the CA was formed in direct response the activities of the ECU. It became evident, said Bury, 'that the loyal members of the Church should combine for the defence of its Protestant character.' Charles A. Bury, *The Church Association* (London: William Macintosh, 1873), pp. 9, 19. According to Eugene Stock, the early supporters of the CA hoped to organize it along non-partisan lines, and for that reason, Lord Shaftesbury was not appointed president. Stock, *English Church*, p. 75.

William Magee, then the Dean of Cork, was asked to become a vice-president but refused. In a letter to John MacDonnell, he suggested that the organization's objects were of 'the vaguest and most expansive kind, "to uphold the Reformation generally" by pamphlets, speeches, meetings. This may mean anything, and in the hands of the promoters of the movement would certainly mean a great deal more than you or I would endorse.' He concluded, with regard to ecclesiastical controversies, that 'associations for party ends in the Church do, in the long run, more harm than good, even when the party is in the right.' MacDonnell, *Life of Magee, vol. 1*, pp. 118-19.

25 J. C. Ryle suggested that they could not wait for the bishops, who were 'hampered by the necessities of their position as pastors of a comprehensive church, and naturally shrink from the very appearance of taking side with a party.' Neither, he thought, were the clergy likely to speak out on their

own. The burden, then, rested on the laity who must 'speak out in the press and in the House of Commons like men.' J. C. Ryle, 'Archbishop Laud and His Times,' in *Church Association Lectures, 1869* (London: Hatchards, 1869), pp. 169-70.

26   *Record*, 19 March 1866. The moderate J. C. Miller gave one of the early set of lectures sponsored by the CA. In describing the organization's aims, he made no mention of prosecution: 'We are aiming, in the first place, at the enlightenment of public opinion. We are endeavouring to show what is the doctrine of the Church of England, and what is going on under the false teaching of men who are still ministering at her altars. And we hope, under God's blessing, that when public opinion is stirred, our Bishops will come forward, and that they will take some such active and decisive measures, as that either this evil will be checked, or that those who are determined to beard the Bishops, and defy authority, and outrage public opinion, shall be compelled to leave the Communion of the Church.' John C. Miller, 'The Confessional,' in *Church Association Lectures* (London: Hatchards, 1967), p. 30.

27   *Record*, 14 Jan. 1867. In an 1875 letter to Bishop Fraser of Manchester, responding to the accusation that the CA was merely 'an instrument of party' and 'a persecuting association,' T. R. Andrews, the chairman of the council, recounted the organization's rise: 'The founders of the Church Association (which has been formed since the English Church Union) did not at first contemplate legal proceedings at all. Their object was simply by means of the press and platform, to enlighten the public mind, and thus counteract the spread of Romanizing principles in our Church. When, however, gross cases of this character were brought before the Archbishop of Canterbury and other Bishops, they declared their inability to deal with them till the law had been ascertained; inasmuch as the innovators solemnly declared their belief that all they had introduced was sanctioned by the laws ecclesiastical....

'It was under these circumstances that it became necessary for some public body to undertake the duty of bringing the subject before the Courts of Law, as the Bishops declined the responsibility.' Correspondence cited in the *Record*, 4 Jan. 1875.

Charles Bury, however, suggested that the appeal to the courts was implicit from the beginning. According to Bury, the bishops were largely opposed to the Ritualists but did not believe prosecution would be effective. In the first place, the precise meaning of the formularies was viewed as uncertain, and it was by no means clear that the decisions handed down would be favorable. In the second, the costs were prohibitive given the existing legal system. 'The straight-forward course,' thought Bury, 'seemed to be to ascertain whether these innovations were or were not illegal by bringing them to the test of the law; and if the existing laws should prove to be so complicated or confused as to be insufficient for the repression of the evil, then to go to Parliament for a reform of the law.' An association was necessary since 'no bishop or private individual could be reasonably expected to provide funds so large as were required to carry cases through the different courts.' Bury, *Church Association*, pp. 8-9.

Eugene Stock reported that there was much 'painful difference of opinion' during the first two years regarding the future action of the CA. Thereafter, however, the organization settled on its policy of aggressive opposition to the Ritualists which quickly led to the appeal to the courts. Stock, *Church Missionary Society*, vol. 2, pp. 348-49.

28 'Memorial of the London Clergy' reprinted in the *Times*, 2 Feb. 1866.
29 According to Eugene Stock, the memorial was sponsored by the CA, and Wordsworth's participation was indicative of the movement's early appeal to anti-Ritualists outside the Evangelical party. Stock, *English Church*, p. 75. Wordsworth, who was himself a moderate High Churchman, echoed a criticism of the Ritualists frequently voiced by Evangelicals. While claiming to reverence the catholic church, the Ritualists were acting out of 'a private spirit' that destroyed all 'reverence for authority' and elevated their own interests above those of either the episcopacy or the church. *Record*, 2 Feb. 1866.

Harding Girdlestone similarly complained that the Ritualists were 'acting on the principles of the Congregationalists or Independents,' altering the services in their parish however they desired 'without reference to higher constitutional authorities' or their position as members of an established church with an Act of Uniformity. What, he asked, had become of 'that respect for good order, that reverence for the sacred office of the Bishop, that loyalty to the vow of Canonical obedience which used to be so characteristic of the Church of England?' Girdlestone, *Ultra-Ritualism*, pp. 68-69.

30 *Times*, 2 Feb. 1866. The *Times* doubted the wisdom of either an appeal to the courts or the establishment of a royal commission to consider the revision of the Prayer-book (Lord Ebury had recently presented a memorial to Lord Russell in that regard). Sounding an almost prophetic warning, the editorialist wrote, 'It is scarcely possible to doubt that many of the obnoxious practices are positively illegal. But for this force [the law] to be exerted to any effect each particular abuse must be challenged in turn, and each case must be carried from Court to Court. The struggle would be endless, and would keep up an incessant excitement. A new law would seem to be the only remedy, and this, as we have shown, is out of the question.'

The *Times* thought the excitement aroused by the Ritualists was out of all proportion to their number. They had little real influence and the paper thought the common sense of the English laity would prevent further expansion. It also suggested, citing Wordsworth's participation in the memorial deputation, that the Ritualists were without the support of the 'true leaders' of the High Church party. 'In short,' the paper concluded, 'if the Protestantism of the Church of England is endangered by albs, tunicles, dalmatics, copes, incense, thurifers, acolytes, and such like frippery, it will certainly not be maintained by all the Royal Commissions that ever were issued. It is, indeed, a melancholy spectacle to those who wish well to the Church to see her clergy thus excited at such child's play as these Ritualistic practices. In Tractarianism, and even in the recent Rationalistic controversy, questions were at issue not unworthy of discussion by thoughtful men, but one is tempted to think that the clergy must have lost all sense of the dignity and importance of their office before they could allow their attention to be absorbed by these childish questions of dress and ceremonial. At all events, we trust nothing will be done to encourage the Ritualists in fancying themselves of any importance. This is just one of those follies which are best left to run their course and die a natural death.' *Times*, 5 Feb. 1866.

31 The Canterbury memorial was signed by 2,499 clergy and 3,010 churchwardens, and the York memorial was signed by 2,124 clergy and 2,610 churchwardens.

Archbishop Longley responded, 'My Lords and Gentlemen, I have already expressed on a recent occasion, and I hope with sufficient distinctness, my strong disapproval of the introduction in several places of novel vestments, incense, and other Romish observances, into the services of our Church. In that disapproval a very large number of the Bishops of the United Church of England and Ireland have signified their concurrence.... It is strongly felt that these innovations are but a mimicry of the Church of Rome, and involve, in some instances, the adoption of her erroneous teaching. It will be my duty to pursue such a course as I may deem most effectual for the discouragement and suppression of them.' He went on, however, to note that portions of the address given in presenting the memorial gave him cause for concern regarding the Evangelical view of the Lord's Supper; he affirmed that the Church of England did, in fact, confess the real presence of Christ in the Eucharist, although that belief was to be distinguished from a carnal presence. Cited in the *Record*, 22 June 1866

32 'We... respectfully object to any alteration being made in the Book of Common Prayer respecting the "ornaments of the Church and the ministers thereof;" and the mode and manner of performing Divine service 'according to the use of the Church of England.' *Times*, 5 Feb. 1866. Like their opponents, the Ritualists denied that they were acting from any 'party spirit.' It was, they said, a movement of self-defense in response to those who sought to alter 'the rubrical law of the Church' from their own interests, even though they themselves often broke it. H. G. Liddell, like many of the Ritualists, argued that they 'desired only to maintain for themselves that freedom for which others called so loudly; they desired freedom, not to break, but to obey the law.' Cited in the *Record*, 5 Feb. 1866.

33 Report of the Committee on Ritual cited in the *Times*, 27 June 1866. The Upper House of Convocation later unanimously approved a resolution concerning ritual innovation that similarly relied on the influence of the episcopacy. It concluded, 'Our judgment is that no alterations from long sanctioned and usual ritual ought to be made in our churches, until the sanction of the Bishop of the diocese has been obtained thereto.' Cited in Davidson, *Life of Tait*, vol. 1, p. 406.

The *Quarterly Review* was astonished that the committee could conclude that most of the innovations were 'free from any intentional tendency to Romanism.' The writer thought 'the imitation of Romanism in its externals' in the innovations was obvious. Anon., 'Ultra-Ritualism,' *Quarterly Review*, p. 199.

The *Edinburgh Review* took a more moderate perspective but thought that all such declarations were 'too vague to be of any real significance.' It was much more optimistic, however, about the personal declarations made by individual bishops in their dioceses, and suggested that the Archbishop

Longley, Bishop Tait of London, and Bishop Thirlwall of St. David's had recently set good examples for the other bishops to follow by clearly indicating their dissatisfaction with the movement's extremes. Anon., 'Ritualism,' *Edinburgh Review*, pp. 466-67.

34 *Record*, 27 June 1866.
35 When it was later announced that a CA 'Defence Fund' had been formed to assist those bringing lawsuits against Ritualist clergy, the *Record* noted that the association itself would not be originating any prosecutions. All that the organization proposed was to have funds ready to assist 'when a judicious and legitimate prosecution originates with *local parties*.' *Record*, 22 Aug. 1866 (their italics). As the role of the CA expanded, that boundary was soon crossed. The distinction was not lost on the Ritualists who thereafter accused the organization of persecution.
36 Elliott-Binns, *Evangelical Movement*, p. 58.
37 'The rubrics had been framed at different dates for different types of services; sometimes they seemed to conflict with one another; sometimes they seemed inconsistent with the Canons and other documents of authority; and lawyers of the greatest eminence gave contradictory opinions.' Balleine, *Evangelical Party*, p. 182.
38 Ibid. Owen Chadwick wrote of the controversy, 'The Protestant tradition of the country ran deep in the people's mind. Any innovation of usage was suspect. The epidemical difficulty of this whole controversy consisted in the formularies of the Church of England being broader and more comprehensive than a lot of laymen wanted them to be.' Chadwick, *Victorian Church*, Part Two, p. 319.

One anonymous writer suggested that the Ritualists' audacity was related to their sacerdotal principles. 'The ordinary priest having power to perform the high sacerdotal act of making and offering up his Creator, is *a fortiori* competent for all minor offices, and if his superiors are silent his natural rights revert to him. He may receive vows, hear confessions, absolve sinners, anoint the sick, conjure holy water, prescribe penances, invent and arrange rituals. His functions are limited only by his power, and his power far exceeds the ability of his imagination, broken-winged as it is by Protestant training, to conceive.' Anon., 'Recent Movements,' *Fraser's Magazine*, p. 290.
39 For many years Lord Ebury headed the Prayer-Book Revision Society which found a degree of support and held its meetings every year in the spring in conjunction with the other Evangelical societies at Exeter Hall. The society, however, was never able to make much progress, and when the CA was formed, it specifically excluded the idea of revision. For most anti-Ritualists, the admission of ambiguities in the Book of Common Prayer and the formularies, would have been to concede a decisive point to their opponents. Charles Girdlestone summarized the arguments for liturgical revision. He suggested, for instance, that the language of the baptismal service did in fact imply, however mistakenly, that all baptized infants were regenerated. He also admitted that there were 'definite though slight traces of Romish phraseology, and of ascetic, sacerdotal, and sacramental superstition, which have long been lurking in the formularies of our church.'

Charles Girdlestone, *An Appeal to Evangelical Churchmen in Behalf of Liturgical Revision* (London: William Hunt & Co., 1864), pp. 8-9. Cf. Bentley, *Ritualism and Politics*, pp. 36-37.

For several examples of Ritualist clergy and their motivation for introducing ceremonies in their new parishes, along with the results following, cf. W. N. Yates, '"The Only True Friend;" Ritualist Concepts of Priestly Vocation,' in *Religious Motivation: Biographical and Sociological Problems for the Church Historian*, Studies in Church History, vol. 15, ed. Derek Baker (Oxford: Basil Blackwell, 1978), pp. 407-15.

40 The five charges were lighted altar candles, mixing the eucharistic wine with water, elevating the bread and the wine, placing the alms on a stool next to the communion table, and omitting the word "all" from the closing benediction. *Record*, 11 and 16 July 1866.

The first case of ritual litigation actually occurred in 1854. R. Liddell of St. Barnabas, Pimlico, was charged with several innovations involving the altar, crosses, candles, and a credence table. He was found guilty in the Court of Arches, but the decision was reversed by the Judicial Committee of the Privy Council. The case came before the formation of partisan organizations, however, and involved little of the animosity that characterized later cases. The case also came before the Ritualists had rejected the authority of the final court of appeal, a fact that would later be turned against them by their opponents. Cf. Davidson, *Life of Tait*, vol. 1, pp. 216-19.

41 In a pamphlet published in 1881, Samuel Garratt denounced the appeal to the courts and claimed he had opposed it from the beginning. But, he said, the few who had foretold the failure of prosecution 'were disregarded, and looked on as half-hearted Protestants.' Garratt, *What Shall We Do?*, p. 12.

42 *Record*, 22 Aug. 1866. According to Owen Chadwick, this program was supported for the first ten years or so even by 'devout and high-minded Evangelicals' who believed it was the only way to determine the exact interpretation of existing law. Owen Chadwick, *Victorian Church, Part Two*, p. 319.

A writer in *Fraser's Magazine* took a Broad Church perspective. While supporting as wide a degree of toleration as possible, he affirmed the rule of law and a decidedly erastian view of the of the State's role. The Church of England, he wrote, 'is maintained by the State for the benefit of the nation, as providing them with better spiritual food than they would be likely to provide for themselves. Its doctrines are under the control of the judge, and, in the midst of considerable latitude, the laity are entitled to expect its ministers to be guided by its general traditions, and to maintain, at all events, the distinctive principles which were established at the Reformation.' Anon., 'Recent Movements,' *Fraser's Magazine*, p. 284.

43 *Record*, 22 Aug. 1866. This view of the episcopal interest in the case said more about what the *Record* thought it should be than the reality of the situation. In his visitation charge to the clergy, delivered in December 1866, Bishop Tait of London indicated that, however decisive the judgment might be, it would probably not be viewed as binding by the Ritualists. 'It seems difficult to see how the Courts, if they preclude certain vestments or overt acts of adoration, can restrain the posture, gestures, look, manner, and tone

of voice of any one who, being resolved, without regard to authority, to make himself as like a Roman Catholic priest as possible, may accomplish his object by a series of Protean changes which no law can bind.' Tait similarly doubted that the authority of Convocation or Parliament would be recognized by those 'who are not loyal to their bishops and their Church.' Ultimately, he believed that the best 'arguments to use with them are not to threaten penalties and endeavour to overwhelm by force (for in this sense all Church of England men are Protestants, being jealous, and rightly, of preserving their individual liberty), but to reason, to remonstrate, to appeal to their consciences and to the love they bear their Church.' Cited in the *Times*, 4 Dec. 1866. The *Record* complained that Tait's proposal was simply a continuation of the episcopacy's policy of inaction and compromise. *Record*, 3 Dec. 1866.

44 The *Record* expected that almost all points would be decided against the Ritualists and believed that most of them would submit to an authoritative decision, although a few might secede to Rome. The paper believed it would be a crushing blow to the unity of the 'anti-Reformation party.' But it was willing to concede that a few points might be lost. 'In such a case our advice to the Evangelical party would be frankly to accept the decision and act upon it, if, as we assume, it were satisfactory in all its main points, and only distasteful on some minor details.' *Record*, 19 Oct. 1866.

45 Cf. Reed, *Glorious Battle*, pp. 75-76. The *Edinburgh Review* stressed the need for comprehensiveness in the national church and, during the early years of the controversy, allowed that the Ritualists ought to be tolerated to a large degree. Congregations that were satisfied with the ceremonial adopted by their clergy should be allowed a large measure of self-determination. Anon., 'Amendment of the Anglican Rubric,' *Edinburgh Review*, p. 503.

46 Cited in the *Record*, 3 Dec. 1866.

47 Ibid. It was reported in *Fraser's Magazine* in 1866, that Tait had consulted with lawyers who had discouraged him from attempting 'forcible repression' of the Ritualists. The writer thought that the 'folly' would soon exhaust itself and would expire more quickly if left alone. But, he continued, 'we cannot but think that there is a limit to forbearance.' Anon., 'Recent Movements,' *Fraser's Magazine*, p. 291.

The *Quarterly Review*, in a survey of Tait's career, noted that he had a reputation for tolerance and had long opposed the use of prosecution, of either the Ritualists or the Rationalists. In his charge for 1862, he had suggested that it was the wise tradition of the English church to try more peaceable means in most cases, seeking 'to overcome the danger of heresy by the manifestation of superior learning and acuteness and a truer Christian spirit, than to prop up truth by the terrors of the law.' Anonymous, 'Archbishop Tait and the Primacy,' *Quarterly Review* 155 (1883): 19.

48 The *Record* frequently blamed the episcopacy for allowing the controversy to get out of hand, and in an editorial in January 1866, suggested that Evangelicals needed to unite under an umbrella organization in order to bring their influence to bear on the situation (thus implicitly supporting the CA which was then being formed). The paper noted, however, that even when the bishops had tried to exercise their authority, they had only met with re-

sentment or been 'contemptuously defied.' *Record*, 17 Jan. 1866.
49 'Though the evil might in time thus cure itself, we cannot help asking what is the use of Bishops if they cannot at least make some attempt to put a legal prohibition on these obnoxious practices and doctrines? It is their express business to protect the public against notoriously unlawful teaching, and we have some right to complain if we are so entirely left to take care of ourselves.' *Times*, 19 Oct. 1866.
50 In particular, he criticized the Ritualist view of the priesthood and the idea that the clergy served as mediators between God and the laity. He concluded, 'The millineristic proclivities and Roman Catholic doctrines of these men have been so condoned by the long sufferance of the Bishops, so connived at, if not encouraged, by some of them, that there seems no reason to doubt that to expect any serious resentment against this treachery to the principles of our Church, any vigorous attempt at its suppression on the part of the Bench, is vain.' *Times*, 10 Nov. 1866.
51 The paper suggested that the clergy who desired to alter the 'doctrine, practice, or ceremony' of the established church were bound by duty to ask themselves if their innovations had a realistic chance of being accepted. They might even legitimately attempt to gain public support for their cause. 'But if, after sufficient trial has been made, there is such a plain and unmistakable repugnance as to prove to a reasonable man that the innovation will not be accepted, the clergyman is bound to give it up. If his conscience forbids him to do that, he should no longer minister in the national Church.' *Times*, 13 Nov. 1866.

An anonymous essayist in the *Edinburgh Review* came to a similar conclusion when the Ritual Commission published its first report in 1867: 'The Report before us supplies a new and crowning proof that they have had to deal not only here and there with unwilling congregations, but everywhere with an unwilling church and an unwilling nation. This is a fact which has now been established by every conceivable method.... Surely if capitulation or surrender is often a duty morally incumbent on the bravest soldiers, we have a right to look for a generous submission from Christians and from churchmen, when submission means deference to legitimate authority and to the still higher law of charity, at the sacrifice only of personal tastes, and when resistance would mean internecine warfare, ending of necessity in the expulsion or secession of the recalcitrant few.' Anonymous, 'Amendment of the Anglican Rubric,' *Edinburgh Review*, 126 (1867): 501.
52 *Times*, 13 Nov. 1866.
53 The 'Protest of the Clergy of the Diocese of London,' in contrast to earlier memorials, was both more condemnatory in its language regarding the Ritualists and more demanding in its appeal for action than had been the case with the earlier memorials. Reprinted in the *Record*, 4 Feb. 1867; cf. Appendix A.
54 With regard to Rev. Thomas W. Perry, one of the prominent apologists for the movement who was frequently cited as a leading authority by other Ritualists, the reviewer wrote, 'It is, no doubt, a great thing to be at the head of one's department, whatever that department may be; but Mr. Perry's success is a convincing proof that the highest eminence may be attained in

the line of ecclesiastical furniture and dresses with a wonderfully small amount of knowledge and an utter want of common sense.' The reviewer identified eight key innovations being introduced by the Ritualists: ancient vestments, lights on the altar, incense, the mixed chalice, the eastward position, wafer bread, elevation of the consecrated elements, and non-participating presence of 'the faithful' at 'spiritual communion' in which they adored the elements without partaking of them. These were described in some detail along with the arguments used by Ritualists to support them. Anonymous, 'Ultra-Ritualism,' *Quarterly Review*, pp. 167, 184-99.

Fraser's Magazine published its first significant critique of the Ritualists the year before, an essay condemning the principles set forward in two collections: *Essays on the Church and the World*, edited by Rev. Orby Shipley, and *Directorium Anglicanum*, edited by Rev. F. G. Lee. Cf. Anon., 'Recent Movements,' *Fraser's Magazine*, pp. 277-96.

55 Ibid., p. 209. The *Edinburgh Review* similarly suggested that the 'sacerdotal pretensions' of the Ritualists implied an attitude of intolerance; 'the determination not merely to have their own way, but to allow no contrary practice or opinion to exist beside them, is one of the fixed characteristics of the High Church party.' The writer suggested that the tendency had appeared throughout the history of that party but was taken to an extreme by the Ritualists. Anon., 'Ritualism,' *Edinburgh Review*, pp. 457-58.

56 In an 1869 lecture for the CA, J. C. Ryle noted that some urged a delay in legal action, arguing that many of the Ritualists acted with great sincerity and zeal. Ryle, however, supported the CA and its program of prosecution. Archbishop Laud, he said, had also been 'zealous, and earnest, and well-meaning,' and he had nearly ruined the church. He concluded that if the Ritualists were not resisted, the days of the Church of England were numbered. Ryle, 'Archbishop Laud,' *Church Association Lectures*, p. 170.

57 *Record*, 23 and 25 Jan. 1867. According to the paper, the committee considered six possibilities: a public meeting of the laity in London, legal prosecutions, the call for a Royal Commission, a declarative Act of Parliament, a memorial to Queen Victoria, and a petition to parliament. *Record*, 25 Jan. 1867.

58 'We revert for a moment to the rumoured resolution of the Islington Committee which deprecates legal prosecutions, and advocates a Declaratory Act of Parliament. If Acts of Parliament could be as easily passed as solicited, we should applaud the wisdom which dictated this resolve. But is it probable that Parliament will proceed to legislate on such a subject, after litigation has commenced, before the state of the law is ascertained? For our own parts, we confess that the idea seems altogether preposterous, so far as concerns either the House of Lords or the House of Commons, in the approaching busy season. If, then, Parliament is likely to do nothing at present, is it wise to throw cold water on those endeavouring to establish the illegality of the Ritualistic proceedings?' Ibid.

59 'The action of the Church Association was proceeding under wise counsel with every promise of success, when the delusive meteor of a great and united gathering of High Churchmen with Evangelicals, and the more secular with the more religious portion of the laity, arrested, or at least sus-

pended its proceedings. We are still sanguine enough to hope that the great Evangelical body will be enabled to agree upon a course of proceeding by which, under God's blessing, the plague may be stayed.' *Record*, 4 Feb. 1867.

The paper was also concerned that Lord Shaftesbury had been omitted from the leadership of the committee because of his partisan reputation. *Record*, 28 Jan. 1867. By mid-February, the paper was reporting that the divisions had been largely resolved. Hanbury had only desired a broader coalition of anti-Ritualists (both Evangelical and High Church), and he affirmed that the committee had no desire to displace Shaftesbury, but only sought a leader who was less identified with any one party. While pursuing a separate route, the paper affirmed that committee leaders such as Hanbury and J. C. Miller were also 'lending their aid to the Church Association, and sanctioning its objects, if not entirely uniting to its policy.' *Record*, 15 Feb. 1867.

In March 1867, an Address from the Council of the CA described the priorities of its program: '1st. To ascertain and vindicate the law of the Church by a prosecution for practices considered illegal. 2d. To strengthen the law of the Church by an enactment directed against the most obnoxious practices of Ritualism. 3d. To enlarge the power of the Bishops, and give them discretionary jurisdiction to regulate the performance of public worship. 4th. To refer the whole question to a Royal Commission.' Cited in the *Record*, 27 March 1867.

60 On perhaps the most delicate matter, Colquhoun suggested that a percentage of the funds collected by those groups should be sent to support the parent organization. Report in the *Record*, 10 May 1867.

61 In addition to differences of opinion over the best means of proceeding against the Ritualists, some Evangelicals opposed the idea of making the CA the central body simply because it was a defensive organization. J. B. Whiting, the Honorary Secretary of the Northern Home Counties Clerical and Lay Association, thought the various clerical and lay societies ought to unite under an independent central committee. In that way, they could continue their own particular work without overstepping the boundaries of other organizations. The CMS would remain the central Evangelical missionary body, and the CA would still be the primary defensive organization. Letter to the *Record*, 8 Nov. 1867.

J. C. Ryle supported the case for the CA at the Islington Clerical Conference in January 1868. He bemoaned the fact that the Evangelical party was 'a rope of sand.' They all believed the same doctrines and supported the same the societies, but that was the limit of their union. They lacked a common principle or union to achieve their goals and oppose their enemies. Ryle, *We Must Unite*, pp. 5-6. Ryle believed the CA could best fill the need. It might have made mistakes in the beginning and begun 'too much as a negative Anti-Ritualistic Society, and not sufficiently as a positive Protestant and Evangelical Society,' but Ryle believed it was now pursuing a broader and more positive direction and was the best hope for Evangelical union. Ibid., p. 24.

The moderate Anthony W. Thorold, who later became the Bishop of Rochester, took a rather different view. He noted that the Evangelical party had no central organization 'precisely corresponding to the English Church Union,' and he, for one, was quite glad about it. Citing Ryle's Islington address, he wrote, 'If he means that we want drilling for party warfare, as electors are drilled in the United States for political purposes, I regret to differ from him, but differ from him I do. Two or three Church Unions inside us would soon do the work of wild horses, and tear poor Mother Church into a hundred sects.' Thorold was quite content to leave matters in the hands of groups such as the Evangelical clerical conferences, which met regionally for discussion and spiritual encouragement. Anthony W. Thorold, 'The Evangelical Clergy of 1868,' *Contemporary Review* 8 (1868): 575-76.

62 Shaftesbury thought the other controverted issues were well-defined by the law and needed only enforcement: 'With respect to candles, incense, and other matters of that description, I believe the law is not doubtful, and we can redress the abuses by prosecutions in the courts of law; but, with respect to sacrificial vestments, there is a doubt.' Cited in the *Times*, 12 March 1867. Cf. Hodder, *Life of Shaftesbury*, pp. 625-27.

63 Shaftesbury's bill required the wearing of the surplice and allowed only the addition of academic hoods for university graduates or a "decent tippet of black." Any other "clerical vestments or ornaments" were expressly forbidden. The entire bill was reprinted in the *Record*, 13 March 1867.

The bill was later amended to make the academic hood optional rather than mandatory and to allow for a 'black silk scarf' that was in common use. The *Record* reaffirmed its support for the bill. It might entirely suppress the Ritualists, but by 'stripping the Ritualistic priests of their histrionic robes, and compelling them to conform to the simple usages of our Reformed Church, a heavy blow is struck at the sacrificial system of these sacerdotal innovations.' *Record*, 8 April 1867.

64 Bishop Tait supported Shaftesbury's measure, but the High Church bishops were entirely opposed. According to Peter Marsh, it was widely thought that the elimination of the Ritualists 'with an evangelical, legislative axe' would have threatened 'High Churchmen generally.' Marsh, *Victorian Church in Decline*, p. 119.

Bishop Wilberforce expressed his outrage at the bill in a letter to Gladstone. He thought it just the sort of idea for Shaftesbury's 'cramped, puritanical, persecuting mind.' At a meeting called by Archbishop Tait, prior to the Parliamentary debate, Wilberforce was disturbed to learn that 'the whole phalanx of Archbishop and Bishops from the north, and all the puritan Bishops, were hot for it.' He described his part in the debate to Gladstone: 'I set before them at length the ignominy of the course; its shameless party spirit; the suicide of the English episcopate being dragged at the tail of Shaftesbury; and I so far with difficulty succeeded that the Bishops in league with Shaftesbury said that if the Archbishop would undertake to legislate, they would persuade Shaftesbury to wait.' Ashwell, *Life of Wilberforce, vol. 3*, p. 206.

65 Archbishop Longley announced in the House of Lords that the bishops had been considering a bill of their own in response to Shaftesbury's measure, but that they had decided to abandon it 'in consequence of the probability of a Royal Commission being issued on the subject.' *Times*, 27 March 1867.

Shaftesbury was determined, however, to persist with his bill. *Times*, 29 March 1867.

66 Cf. Hodder, *Life of Shaftesbury*, p. 626-27. Edward Vaughan, who generally favored granting the Ritualists as much toleration as possible, suggested in the *Contemporary Review* that Shaftesbury's bill was as moderate as any that might be expected. He thought the very appointment of the commission necessitated some resulting legislation. 'And if there must be legislation, to interpret, if not to alter the present law, the direction which it ought to take can scarcely be doubtful. It is best that it should obtain legislative sanction for that construction of the present law which has in its support the express language of the 58th Canon, and (with the very fewest and most doubtful exceptions) the universal practice of our parish Churches, from the time of the Advertisements under Elizabeth, up to and since the final revision of the Prayer Book, in 1662.... Those whose aim in Church matters is to keep things as they are, and, when this cannot be, to change as little as possible, have reason to regret that the opponents of Lord Shaftesbury's Bill succeeded in their attempt to avert one small change by evoking a spirit for which, when raised, work of far greater import must be and has been found.' Edward T. Vaughan, 'The Commission on Ritualism,' *Contemporary Review* 6 (1867): 70-71.

67 Cf. S. C. Carpenter, *Church and People, 1789-1889: A History of the Church of England from William Wilberforce to 'Lux Mundi,'* vol. 2 (London: SPCK, 1959), p. 228.

68 Lord Derby turned the selection process over to Spencer Walpole, his former Home Secretary, who was a close associate of Wilberforce. Among the Ritualists, the *Record* numbered Bishops Wilberforce and Ellicott, Sir Robert Phillimore, who was Wilberforce's chancellor and a defense lawyer in several of the Ritualist cases, and several other clergy and laity. The Archbishop of Canterbury was among the five members the paper listed as High Church. *Record*, 10 June 1867.

The *Times* also viewed the commission with skepticism. And while it was somewhat less strident in its criticism, the editorialist noted the High Church dominance: 'We find at least seven names which must be assigned without hesitation to the High Church party, and as many would say, to the most advanced section of that party. We observe, on the other hand, but one name which is associated, in a like degree, with the Evangelical party, and but two or three others, at the most, which it could accept as representative of its own principles. Among the High Church spokesmen are several learned, dexterous, and eminent controversialists, deeply committed to Ritualism, and most zealous in its support. Among their twenty-two colleagues there are few capable of contending with them in argument, and fewer still prepared to demand as much on the one side as they would demand on the other. Since there is an irresistible gravitation towards compromise in all conferences of this kind, we cannot shut our eyes to the probable consequence. The tendency will be to settle each disputed point on a basis favourable to Ritualism, and to deviate in that direction from the *via media* of long-established usage in the English Church. Such a verdict may be right, or it may be wrong, in law and reason, but if it be delivered by a jury suspected of having been placed it will be worthless or worse than worthless, for the purpose of allaying agitation.' *Times*, 15 June 1867.

69 The *Quarterly Review* reported that the Archbishop of York declined to serve, at least in part, because there were not an equivalent number of anti-Ritualists appointed to the commission to counter-balance the High Church influence. Anonymous, 'Ultra-Ritualists,' *Quarterly Review* 126 (1869), p. 135.

In the House of Lords, Archbishop Thomson acknowledged that he objected to the constitution of the commission, believing that 'there was too great a preponderance of interested persons.' But he also thought that there might be a conflict of interest involved in his participation since he also sat on the Judicial Committee. Ethel H. Thomson, *Life and Letters of William Thomson, Archbishop of York* (London: John Lane, 1919), p. 181.

Shaftesbury also refused to serve on the commission but for rather different reasons. Recognizing his own partisan reputation, he suggested that his presence would be widely criticized by some in the High Church party and 'would deprive the Commission, in their eyes at least, of the character of entire impartiality, should the decisions be of an adverse nature.' He concluded that all with prominent and decided opinions, such as himself and Wilberforce, ought to leave the matter in other hands in order to demonstrate a sense of 'fair play between contending parties.' Hodder, *Life of Shaftesbury*, p. 627.

70 *Record*, 10 June 1867. The *Morning Advertiser* also noted Venn's age and fragility. Against the weakened Venn, Walpole had put on the commission two of the leading Ritualists of the day, including Rev. T. W. Perry of Brighton, who was 'active, intrepid, and full of the questions, and the great writer of the Ritualistic party. Is it supposed that when the country wishes to set aside Romish Ritualism, a gentleman should be placed on the judgment-seat who is the leader and captain of the offenders?' The article also noted that no one from the House of Commons was included who had ever supported the Protestant cause, although two were included who had been its vehement opponents. Cited in the *Record*, June 12, 1867. On Venn's participation, cf. Stock, *Church Missionary Society*, vol. 2, pp. 654-56.

71 First Report of the Royal Commission on Ritual, cited in the *Times*, 29 Aug. 1867. The *Times* thought it was an excellent and fair report: 'The claims of the Ritualists, in short, have been most maturely considered under every possible advantage, and the result is, as we see this morning, that they are decisively rejected.' *Times*, 29 Aug. 1867. The paper later gave an extensive survey of the report and the arguments presented by the Ritualists before the commission; cf. *Times*, 10 Sept. 1867.

The *Edinburgh Review* took a similar view. It thought the report 'a decisive verdict' against the Ritualists: 'Its conclusions rest on grounds of morality and expediency, and as such they are decisive. And if the public will see in this Report the expression of their own unalterable convictions, we also trust that the Ritualists will feel that it is a judgment to which they are bound to defer. They cannot but feel that they have been treated by the Commissioners with the utmost consideration and tenderness. Their case has been tried before a tribunal, supposed by public opinion to be decidedly prepossessed in their favour, and undeniably containing several pronounced friends and even some pledged advocates of their views. Yet even this tribunal has pronounced against them.' Anon., 'Amendment of the Anglican Rubric,' *Edinburgh Review*, pp. 500-01.

For a brief survey of the work of the contents of the committee's reports and their general impact in the church, cf. G. J. Cuming, *A History of Anglican Liturgy* (London: Macmillan & Co., 1969), pp. 197-202.

72 Robert Phillimore and A. J. Beresford Hope signed on the stipulation that it did not 'exclude the consideration of cases in which the authority of the Bishop and the rights of the parishioners and congregations are carefully guarded,' apparently intending that vestments ought to be allowed in those cases where there were no protests. T. W. Perry was concerned to limit narrowly the definition of 'aggrieved parishioners.' *Times*, 30 Aug. 1867.

73 Bishop Wilberforce's biographer later confirmed, with no regret, the suspicions of the commission's critics. He wrote that, immediately on beginning their work, several of the commissioners formed their own smaller group including Wilberforce, Lord Beauchamp, Dean Goodwin (later Bishop of Carlisle), Canon Gregory, Sir R. Phillimore, J. G. Hubbard, A. J. Beresford Hope and T. W. Perry. 'This committee, although less than a third of the whole body, was enabled, by showing a united front, to really guide the Commission, and to virtually settle the Report.' The committee largely controlled the content of the first report and was able to moderate its tone by using the word 'restrain' with regard to the vestments, rather than 'abolish' or 'prohibit' which had been preferred by other commissioners. Ashwell, *Life of Wilberforce, vol. 3*, p. 214.

The *Record* complained that the only tangible result was the delay of Lord Shaftesbury's Vestments Bill (the report was released after Parliament had adjourned). *Record*, 2 Sept. 1867. *Punch* issued its own satirical version of the report:

'Your Majesty's faithful Commissioners, appointed to inquire into Ritualistic Practices, have the honour to inform Your Majesty that they have not done so.

'For reasons with which they need not trouble Your Majesty, they abstained from making any reports at all until Parliament had dispersed. They may, however, just mention, that they considered it would not tend to the peace of the Church to have disagreeable Parliamentary debates on the subjects in question.

'They now beg to state that they have asked several persons what they thought of the new Vestments, and that the Commissioners have arrived at the important discovery that there are different opinions on the topic.

'They are strongly of opinion that it is Expedient not to give offence.

'They therefore unhesitatingly say, that where persons are aggrieved by the ritualistic Vestments, those persons should be enabled to obtain redress.

'The name of Mr. Walpole, subscribed to this report, will be a sufficient guarantee to Your Majesty that no uncalled-for joke is meant in the last word of the preceding paragraph.

'The Commissioners are quite unable to offer the slightest hint as to the means whereby such redress should be obtained, but they beg to disclaim in the strongest manner the idea that the Bishops of the Church ought to be troubled to inquire into the doings of clergymen. If parishioners are aggrieved, they should take action themselves, if able to afford it.

'The Commissioners need not add, that where a minister can induce his flock to assent to Vestments, or any other novelty, interference would be objectionable, inasmuch as no principle is involved in Church matters, and, as has been said, the question is one of Expediency.

'They conclude by expressing to Your Majesty their conviction of the great value of the Commission, and of the satisfaction with which all good persons will hail this conclusion of an important controversy."

Cited in the *Record*, 9 Sept. 1867.

74 The *Times* thought the conclusion was decisive: 'The Ritualists, it is known, have consistently maintained that the disuse introduced at the Reformation, though general, was not universal. They have now had the opportunity of collecting all possible evidence in their favour, and in the judgment of a most impartial tribunal they have failed to adduce a single satisfactory instance. For the future there will be no room for doubt that these ceremonies are a return to distinctly Roman Catholic practices, and the opposition they have encountered is abundantly justified.... There is a limit to everything, and it is generally felt that in these innovations the Ritualists have passed all reasonable limits. The three observances in question are distinctly Papistical, they are destitute of the shadow of a precedent, and they give grave and general offence. There is ample reason for prohibiting them by special interference, and we rejoice that so decided a Report should have received so general an assent.' *Times*, 5 May 1868.

75 Their conclusions read: 'First, that whensoever it shall be found necessary that order be taken concerning the same, the usage of the Church of England and Ireland as above stated to have prevailed for the last 300 years shall be deemed to be the rule of the Church in respect of vestments, lights, and incense; and secondly, that parishioners may make formal application to the Bishop *in camera*, and the Bishop on such application shall be bound to inquire into the matter of the complaint; and if it shall thereby appear that there has been a variation from established usage by the introduction of vestments, lights, or incense in the public services of the Church, he shall take order forthwith for the discontinuance of such variation, and be enabled to enforce the same summarily.' Second Report of the Royal Commission on Ritual, cited in the *Record*, 4 May 1868. The commissioners' recommendations, much to the dissatisfaction of the Ritualists, left intact the existing process of appeal from the ecclesiastical Court of Arches to the secular Judicial Committee of the Privy Council.

76 Ibid.

77 Reservations were expressed by Bishop Wilberforce, Dean Goodwin, A. P. Stanley and John Coleridge. The six who refused to sign were all Ritualists. *Times*, 5 May 1868. Wilberforce tried to propose a minority report but it was disallowed. The four then signed the majority document with reservations. A. P. Stanley and John Coleridge added a footnote. They affirmed that there had always been two distinct parties in the church and that toleration must be allowed for both, 'as far as is consistent with general uniformity in such

matter as may be deemed essential. Within such limits a variety and elasticity of outward observance appears to us to be desirable.' Lights and incense were not, they thought, doctrinal issues, and even those who used them could not agree upon their meaning. They ought then to be allowed wherever they gave no offense. Cited in the *Record*, 6 May 1868.

78 *Times*, 5 May 1868.
79 *Record*, 4 May 1868.
80 J. C. Ryle thought united Evangelical action was necessary to compel the authorities to act. 'The Royal Commission, like the Indian elephants, is as likely to trample on one side as the other, and at most can only report.' Ryle, *We Must Unite*, p. 18.
81 The paper continued, 'Before the appointment of Lord Carnarvon and the Bishop of Chester its Resolutions had just been sufficient to delude the country and arrest vigorous legislation. It is well known that on the part of the sacerdotal party it is deemed the wisest policy to keep all things in doubt and confusion; to discourage any decided efforts to expel from the Church Romanizing doctrines, Romanizing practices, or Romanizing teachers; to leave the ecclesiastical laws and ecclesiastical courts in the chaos of uncertainty and to strive to build up, by means of Pan-Anglican, Diocesan, or Provincial Synods, a new spiritual Babel of sacerdotal empire, on the model of the Romish Babylon which is now tottering to its fall.' *Record*, 19 Feb. 1869.
82 A brief note was inserted in the paper in July, when rumors were beginning to surface concerning the lectionary changes to be recommended: 'The Ritual Commission still exists, and occasionally meets in the Jerusalem Chamber, but all interest in its tedious, dilatory, and inefficacious proceedings has long since evaporated. We may, however, expect a Report at the end of the third session on the Lectionary and some other minor points.' *Record*, 28 July 1869.
83 *Times*, 27 Jan. 1870.
84 *Record*, 28 Jan. 1870. In contrast, the *Times* took a positive view of the third report and thought the consideration of the lectionary an important part of its work. In general, it thought the commission had done good work and was perhaps a portent of things to come, such as the amendment of the Prayer-book. *Times*, 20 Jan. 1870.
85 Edward Cutts later wrote, 'The Ritual Commission, issued in 1867, to deal with these vexed questions by suggesting new legislation upon them, found the subject so complicated and difficult, and perhaps found the subject so unripe yet for legislation, that it left the matter exactly as it found it.' Edward L. Cutts, *Dictionary of the Church of England* (London: Society for Promoting Christian Knowledge, [1887?]), p. 517.
86 The *Times* wrote, 'We presume that some one, on behalf of Her Majesty, will have to take into consideration the recommendations of the Commissioners, and we hope he will be able to discover what the recommendations are. It is in this respect the most extraordinary document it has ever been our misfortune to endeavour to comprehend.... We greatly regret the collapse of an undertaking which at one time promised to render substantial service to the cause of order in the Church. Indeed, the good work done by former Re-

ports of the Commissioners is practically undone in the present Report.' Having left the 'Ornaments Rubric' without alteration or elaboration, the commissioners 'have left practically untouched the chief evil they were expected to remedy.' *Times*, 13 Sept. 1870.
87 The commission's final report, concluded the paper, was 'a most remarkable document; and viewed as the consummation of one astute Prelate's [Wilberforce] method of strangling legislation adverse to Romanizing innovations, it is in its way a masterpiece of strategy.' *Record*, 19 Sept. 1870.
88 Sir John Coleridge withdrew in protest. Sir Robert Phillimore and the Earl of Carnarvon felt their differences were too great to allow them to sign the document in good conscience. *Record*, 16 Sept. 1870. The *Times* wrote, 'The Report itself consists of half a page. The expressions of dissent from the Report occupy no less than 21 pages. All the Commissioners dissent once. Sixteen of them protest twice. Three of them protest three times..., and Mr. Perry breaks out into as many as eight pages of elaborate dissent from even the most minute recommendations of his fellow Commissioners.... It is evident that, after long consultation, the Commissioners have agreed to differ.' *Times*, 13 Sept. 1870.

Henry Venn, the lone Evangelical clerical representative, protested: 'I humbly express my regret that the Commission has left several rubrics ambiguous, which have been of late years perversely made use of to introduce practices repudiated at the Reformation; especially that the rubric on ornaments has not been altered so as to express distinctly the rule and principle laid down in our first two Reports; also that the Black Letter saints' days have been retained in the Calendar; also that the position of the minister while consecrating the elements in the Lord's Supper is not clearly defined; and that a rubric in the Visitation of the Sick is retained which is alleged as giving a general sanction for auricular confession and absolution.' Cited in the *Record*, 19 Sept. 1870.
89 Ibid.
90 Edward Vaughan, while generally favoring a policy of toleration, expressed the view that some of the innovations were stretching the patience of the general public. 'If those who lead the Ritualistic movement go on to shock public feeling a little more violently, – above all, if they invade the parish churches of our large towns, frequented by the middle classes, whose prejudices are so strong against all which can be called Roman Catholic, or of our villages, where the instinctive feeling of all classes is, on the whole, in the same direction; they will provoke a reaction which may force Parliament into measures of coercion in themselves most undesirable.' Vaughan, 'Commission on Ritualism,' *Contemporary Review*, pp. 68-69.

The *Times* took a similar point of view in an editorial following the first report of the commission. While recognizing that 'tastes for ritual vary, and toleration is necessary,' the paper thought the innovators had exceeded the boundaries of fair play. If the 'excesses of the Ritualists' were confined to a few churches in the cities, 'we might view them with tolerance,' the innovators often forced their ceremonial on the smaller parishes, where the congregation had no alternative places of worship. 'We believe these practices, if persevered in, would alienate a large proportion of the middle class from

the Church of England. Men of education and refinement are apt to underrate the Protestant or Puritan feeling of the English people.' *Times*, 20 Aug. 1867.
91   Cited in the *Times*, 19 Feb. 1868.
92   In spite of episcopal admonishments, resolutions of Convocation, and the reports of the Ritual Commission, the Ritualists continued in their practices. Tait came to the conclusion that they intended 'to get into the most advanced post, so as to make it the more difficult for the authorities to dislodge them when the time for action came.' Ibid.

The *Edinburgh Review*, while suggesting that the threat from the Ritualists' innovations was greatly exaggerated, thought the real danger of the movement lay in the presence within the national church of clergy who 'fly in the face of constituted authorities or of their congregations.... It has been reserved for those by whom the bishops are professedly regarded as the successors of the Apostles, as the one evidence of a true Church, to treat them with a contempt and a defiance which in no other profession of men would be tolerated from inferiors to superiors. No Dissenter, no Presbyterian, has ever lavished on the episcopal order fouler language than that which is weekly poured forth by the organs of the Ritualist party against those whom they theoretically regard as the oracles of the Christian Church.' Anon., 'Ritualism,' *Edinburgh Review*, pp. 448-49.
93   Interestingly, the compromise resolution was offered by the elderly Evangelical Bishop of Winchester, Charles Sumner: 'That the limits of Ritual observance cannot be left to the unrestrained discretion of individual clergymen, and ought therefore to be defined by rightful authority, and that, therefore, means should be provided for enforcing a due observance of the rule already laid down at the end of the rubric concerning the service of the Church for duly interpreting all diversities taken from common usage, and, if necessary, with a view of removing ambiguities considered to exist in the law at present.' Only one bishop voted against the resolution. Cited in the *Times*, 20 Feb. 1868.
94   Henry Alford, 'The Next Step,' *Contemporary Review* 10 (1869): pp. 3-9. John Shelton Reed referred to the moderates, including many from the High Church tradition, as 'the party of Common sense.' In general, they were less strident than were their Evangelical counterparts, and more likely to view the Ritualist movement as a passing fancy or an object of amusing ridicule. Often, however, the expressions of opposition in the popular press were mixed, said Reed, 'with stronger doses of contempt.' Reed, *Glorious Battle*, p. 230.
95   Alford, 'Next Step,' *Contemporary Review*, pp. 6-7. A writer in *Fraser's Magazine* suggested that the Ritualists were concerned to prevent any alliance of the moderate section of the High Church party with the Evangelicals; 'the old-fashioned High Churchmen have been frightened from their traditional standing-ground, and have united with the Evangelicals to crush the Liberals. If Ritualism can establish itself in a legal position, the more extravagant its developments the more it will act as a solvent to the mischievous combination.' Anon., 'Recent Developments,' *Fraser's Magazine*, p. 293.
96   He concluded, 'Let the published opinions, let the patent conduct, of indi-

viduals be visited with fair criticism in the spirit of courtesy and Christian allowance; let every approach of false doctrine be the subject of vigilant warning; but let Christian charity, and not diabolical malice, be the medium through which such notices are conveyed.' Ibid., p. 7.

Writing from a moderate Broad Church position, E. H. Plumptre was similarly critical of the *Record*. He thought the Evangelical party had been 'singularly unfortunate in its representative organ.' Appealing largely to 'passions and prejudices,' the paper had been 'conspicuous chiefly for its absence of candour, manliness, and generosity.... It has exaggerated whatever of narrowness and prejudice it found within the ranks of its party, and stirred them to a perpetual policy of suspicion and alarm. It has done all it could to keep open and to widen the gap between Evangelical and other schools.' Plumptre, 'Church Parties,' *Contemporary Review*, p. 331.

97 Ibid., pp. 7-8.
98 *Times*, 16 May 1868; cf. *Record*, 18 May 1868.
99 *Record*, 26 June 1868.
100 Shaftesbury had little hope for the bill but felt compelled to bring some measure before the house. He believed the bishops all opposed him and were concerned more for their own patronage and dignity. But, he concluded, he could at least 'exhibit the evils' that required reform. Having done that, he recorded in his journal his intention to never again 'touch so hopeless, so thankless, so fruitless a work, as the reform of Church abominations.' Hodder, *Life of Shaftesbury*, p. 635.

In the course of the debate, Archbishop Tait indicated his support, in principle, for some such legislation but objected to its source. He said, 'Now, my lords, if the Government of the day were to introduce a Bill, and if the voice of the Church were heard as well as the voice of Parliament, I should concur in such a measure. (Hear, hear.) But my great objection to this Bill is that, if passed, it would be simply an act of the Legislature without any reference to the feelings, views, or opinions of the Church – an act which, might, perhaps, override the opinions of the clergy. For my own part, I have always been desirous to put effectual restraints on these ritualistic practices, but I wish to do so in such a way as to avoid producing a convulsion in the Church. Now I firmly believe that if a private individual were to bring in a Bill and if that Bill were carried without any reference to the clergy, it would effectually lead to disruption. (Hear, hear.)' *Times*, 10 July 1868.

101 It was the first time Ritualism was made a political issue, but Evangelicals had a long history of attempting to use the political process for party goals. They campaigned against pro-Catholic measures, and during the 1840s, in particular, had opposed the Maynooth Grant. Cf. Machin, *Politics and the Churches, 1832-1868*, pp. 71-72.
102 The advertisement continued, 'We ask you then to put the following questions to the candidates who seek your votes: – 1st. Will you support a Bill in the next Parliament to put down the Ritualistic practices condemned by the Royal Commissioners? 2nd. Will you support a Bill for the reform of the Ecclesiastical Courts?' Advertisement in the *Times*, 13 Aug. 1868.

In commenting on the growth of interest in the controversy, a writer in the *Quarterly Review* took note of the campaign, 'Such has been the excitement on the subject that candidates at the late election are said to have been frequently questioned about it during their canvass, and have found themselves obliged to clear themselves on the hustings from the imputation of ultra-Ritualistic opinions.' Anonymous, 'Ultra-Ritualists,' *Quarterly Review* 126 (1869), p. 135.

103 Cited in the *Record*, 7 Oct. 1868.
104 The history of the case and the correspondence between Archbishop Thomson and Voysey can be found in chapter seven of Thomson's biography. Voysey had attracted criticism for a number of years before prosecution was finally undertaken. Thomson, *Life of Thomson*, pp. 212-32. For a general survey of the controversy, cf. the chapter on Voysey in Crowther, *Church Embattled*, pp. 127-37.
105 Garbett thought that broadening the objectives 'would vindicate the Association from the painful, though untrue imputation, that it had been moved by love of party rather than love of truth, and that whilst prosecuting Mr. Bennett on the one side, it had done nothing to stop the rationalistic flood on the other.' The full name was 'Church Association, to uphold the Principles and Order of the United Church of England and Ireland, and to counteract the efforts now being made to assimilate her services to those of the Church of Rome.' Garbett suggested the name should stop after Ireland. *Record*, 14 May 1869.
106 Correspondence reprinted in the *Record*, 2 June 1869.
107 Correspondence cited in Thomson, *Life of Thomson*, pp. 223-24. C. L. Wood, who later became the Second Viscount Halifax, became the president of the ECU in 1868. According to Nigel Yates, he was 'the unofficial leader' of the High Church party following the death of E. B. Pusey in 1882. Yates, *Oxford Movement*, p. 40.
108 The *Times* summarized Chancellor Harcourt's view of Voysey's theology: 'Mr. Voysey had grafted some German metaphysics on the heresy of Arius, or the theology of the neo-Platonians, and it might be inferred from some passages in his defence that he did not intend, in the views he had promulgated, to assail the Articles.... It was decided, however, by the Court that, as he had acted deliberately in the matter, it must be assumed that he had done that with the purpose which his language had in fact effected, and that it was immaterial whether he had intended to impugn the Articles if he had done so in effect.' Cited in the *Times*, 3 Dec. 1869.
109 The judgment of the Privy Council was reprinted in the *Times*, 13 February 1871.
110 Letter to the *Record*, 13 Oct. 1869.
111 *Record*, 15 Oct. 1869.
112 *Record*, 18 Oct. 1869.
113 'I have said before, and I say again, that I shall ever be willing to join with him in whatever I am conscientiously of opinion can subserve the cause of Christ. These gentlemen or ladies, as the case may be, seem to think that there is no danger to the Church or to religion, but from Tractarian excesses. I presume to differ from that learned person on many doctrines of vital importance; but I will always maintain that the able, pious, and sincere author

of the Lectures on the Book of Daniel is entitled to the respect and admiration of every believer in God's Word.' Letter to the *Record*, Oct. 20, 1869. Curiously, Shaftesbury's biographer reported that he took the presidency of the committee, with Pusey serving as vice-president. Cf. Hodder, *Life of Shaftesbury*, p. 639.

Peter Marsh believed there was much less lay interest in the controversy over the Temple appointment than had been the case with *Essays and Reviews*. He suggested that Shaftesbury overcame his differences with Pusey to oppose the nomination, but, 'to Shaftesbury's chagrin, his fellow Evangelicals gave him much less support now than on the previous occasion.' Marsh, *Victorian Church in Decline*, p. 149. On this point, Marsh seems to have been in error. Shaftesbury was criticized by other Evangelicals who, falsely as it turned out, believed he had agreed to serve with Pusey on the committee.

114 The *Times*, in an editorial on the 22nd of October, still assumed that Lord Shaftesbury would be chairing the committee. He replied that he was neither serving as chairman nor participating on the committee. He wrote, without further elaboration, 'Feeling very strongly on the subject of the appointment of Dr. Temple, I was prepared, acting separately for a common end, to advise my friends to do the same as Dr. Pusey's friends, and present a remonstrance to the Prime Minister.' Letter to the *Times*, 23 Oct. 1869.

Daniel Wilson responded, 'I strongly object to the appointment of Dr. Temple, but I am not prepared to act on a committee composed of gentlemen who differ so widely in matters which I consider essential to the welfare of our beloved Church.' *Record*, 22 Oct. 1869. Other Evangelicals, were even more critical of their High Church allies. Hugh M'Neile, in refusing to participate, wrote that he had lost all confidence in the sincerity of Pusey, and 'considered him more really dangerous to the best interests of our reformed Church than two Dr. Temples.' In his view, they represented two cups of poison. Dr. Temple's cup was at least labeled as such, whereas that of Dr. Pusey was labeled 'syrup' and 'dishonestly conceals its deadly drug, enticing the unwary by a honeyed edge.' Letter to the *Times*, 26 Oct. 1869.

G. A. Denison, a well-known Ritualist, sent a letter to the *Record* expressing his regret that the Evangelicals could not put aside their differences in this great cause. 'I cannot understand why differences, however great, in the interpretation of the Bible, touching the application of the One Sacrifice to the bodies and souls of men, are to prevent our uniting as one man to maintain, at this juncture, the genuineness and authenticity, the integrity and authority, of the Bible itself.' Denison looked back to the protest over the publication of *Essays and Reviews* and suggested that it had been beneficial in that they had been able to put aside party divisions for the greater good of the church. If anything, he believed the threat to the church was now even greater, and he concluded, 'Is there to be no union between us even here – no common testimony even to the Word of God?' Letter to the *Record*, 8 Nov. 1869.

115 The memorial claimed to have the support of the seven thousand members of the CA, 'who regard with anxiety and alarm the adoption and teaching by a considerable body of the clergy of that Church, of Romish and Ration-

alistic opinion, which are alike calculated to undermine the authority of Holy Scripture as the sole rule of faith and practice for Christian men, and to subvert the doctrine and worship of the Church established at the Reformation.' Cited in the *Record*, 27 Oct. 1869.

Shaftesbury thought the protest would only damage the Evangelical party; it was 'rash, violent, undignified, and abortive,' and did 'irreparable mischief.' It indicated the weakness and disunity of the party and left Gladstone stronger than ever. He had no need to fear them in the future, thought Shaftesbury, 'they stand simply naked, weak, and beneath consideration.' He also complained that the criticism he received from Evangelicals as a result of his support for Pusey was an indication of the 'utter intolerance' of the conservatives. Hodder, *Life of Shaftesbury*, p. 639.

116 Writing at the end of the century, Eugene Stock noted an important negative consequence of the anti-Ritualist interests of the period. There was a severe decline of support for the CMS from the early 1860s to the early 1870s, with a corresponding decline in the society's budget and effectiveness. Stock suggested that the CMS did well just to survive during that period when many Evangelicals were more concerned with theological disputes at home than with evangelism and foreign missions. Stock, *Church Missionary Society, vol. 2*, pp. 337-38, 353-54.

CHAPTER 4

The Early Prosecutions: Results and Reactions

A. H. Mackonochie and John Purchas were the first two prominent Ritualists to face prosecution, and in many ways their cases established the parameters and tone for the years of controversy to follow. Between the two cases, most of the important ceremonial innovations were considered by the courts and judged illegal, and the responses of Mackonochie and Purchas established the pattern that would be emulated by many Ritualists thereafter. Mackonochie skirted episcopal and judicial admonitions as best he could and was repeatedly returned to the courts for controverting at least the spirit of the law if not the letter. Purchas took the next step and simply refused to comply. Together they raised the basic issue of compliance which was central to the debate for years to come and ultimately the stumbling block on which the anti-Ritualist campaign of litigation would fall. But when the prosecutions were first begun, it was simply inconceivable that clergy of the established church might refuse to obey the rubrics as interpreted by the appropriate courts. It was equally unimaginable that they would refuse to be bound by the admonitions of their bishops. It was assumed by those involved that a few conclusive verdicts would suffice to settle the controversy. As the first two prosecutions proved, however, the Ritualists refused to bend. Far from conceding anything, they were determined to challenge the traditionally recognized voices of authority (both ecclesiastical and secular) in defense of their beliefs.

It was evident that most of the bishops opposed the more extreme Ritualist practices. They desired both to maintain the uniformity of the church's worship and to reaffirm the respectable ideal (expected, above all, of the clergy) of an English nation of law-abiding citizens. Many, however, motivated largely by genuine concerns for the unity of the church, were hesitant to intervene. They had also, unlike the Evangelical controversialists, to consider the broader implications of their policies and to balance the desires of the parish against the literal demands of the law. While anti-Ritualists demanded an absolute enforcement of the law regardless of popular opinion, many bishops refused to proceed in cases where the parishioners appeared to support the innovations. Finally, the bishops recognized that in most cases their legitimate authority was decidedly less comprehensive than commonly believed. The anti-Ritualists, frustrated by the failure of the lawsuits, often criticized the bishops either for preventing the cases from being heard or for failing to enforce the judgments rendered. Viewed from their perspective, the episcopacy's attempt to maintain a balanced and non-partisan perspective could only be condemned. At best, their refusal to enforce the law demonstrated a lack of courage and commitment; at worst, it was interpreted as tacit support for the Ritualists and their Romanizing tendencies.

During this period, Evangelicals began to express concern regarding the spreading influence of the Ritualists. The Purchas judgment seemed to imply that the surplice was the proper attire for the clergy in the pulpit. Many Evangelicals continued to wear their academic gowns, but a growing number adopted the surplice as recommended by several of the bishops. Still more disturbing, however, was the evidence of the movement's subtle influence, characterized particularly by a growing emphasis on the musical elements of the service and the widespread adoption of the High Church hymnal, *Hymns Ancient and Modern*. They could not dismiss the aesthetic interests of the age and the growing popularity of its expression in the worship service, even in Evangelical parishes. But many conservatives feared that a greater emphasis on music, the appearance of a surpliced choir, or the adoption of a new hymnal represented only the leading edge of a more extreme Ritualist threat. Elder statesmen of the Evangelical party often warned the younger clergy that compromise on seemingly minor points frequently led to other innovations of a more insidious nature.

Still, the early prosecutions were not without a broad degree of support, even outside the Evangelical party. Nor were they without effect. Even though the Mackonochie and Purchas cases did not succeed in halting the innovations, they did serve to clarify the law regarding the legitimate interpretation of the church's rubrics and formularies, and they clearly defined those practices that were illegal. But the judgments of the courts could never succeed where the admonitions of bishops had failed. And from the very beginning, the appeal to the courts led to charges of persecution. A majority of Evangelicals would continue to support litigation for several years to come, but by the early 1870s, significant voices were already questioning the wisdom of clerical prosecutions.

The differences expressed regarding the future conduct of the controversy gave evidence of the internal stress created by the anti-

Ritualist movement. Even the *Record*, which supported the use of litigation as a matter of policy, suspected that the Church Association, by its very nature as a polemical organization, could never unite the party. The validity of that fear was illustrated by the failure of the Clerical and Lay Union, established as a branch of the CA in 1871. Evangelicalism proved to be an exceedingly diverse movement, and the controversial tone adopted by the leaders of the anti-Ritualist movement had little appeal to those of a more moderate nature. If the establishment of party organizations early in the 1860s had set the course for an expansion of the conflict between Evangelicals and Ritualists, the use of prosecution as a means of halting the innovations made the breach irreparable. But it also set the stage for a growing division within the Evangelical party between the extreme anti-Ritualists and those drawn to a more moderate and less contentious position.

The Mackonochie Case

The first significant test case concerning Ritualist innovations came to the Court of Arches from the diocese of London. Charges were brought in April 1867 against A. H. Mackonochie, Incumbent of St. Alban's, Holborn, which was perhaps the most advanced Ritualist parish in the city.[1] In an 1866 editorial, the *Times* described the 'High Service' held there on special Sundays, which it thought was 'sufficient to startle even the most tolerant of ordinary Churchmen.' The paper wrote:

> Priests, as they delight to call themselves, in defiance of the most judicious of English divines, are conspicuous in dresses unknown to the English eye for three hundred years. Three of these personages, bedizened with green and gold and yellow, and covered with black stripes and crosses, stand with their backs to the congregation on the elevated steps at the east end of the church. The altar is overladen with gorgeous ornament and illuminated at noonday with two great lighted candles. Pyramids of tapers, such as are seen in Roman Catholic churches, are placed at each side; the chancel is emblazoned with tinsel banners, and the white surplices of the choristers are the only things in the gaudy spectacle which could remind one of the customary ritual of the English Church. Here, across an atmosphere which is faint with the odours of incense, the green and gilded priests are dimly discerned performing unintelligible manoeuvres, bowing and bending and turning and crossing from side to side, until the recitation of the words of the service becomes the smallest part of their function. Two white

dressed attendants carry a silver censer, from which the fumes of the incense are incessantly tossed, now over the altar, now over the book from which the Gospel is read, and now into the faces of all the performers in the chancel. A fine organ and excellent singing, in which, where it is allowed, the congregation join with impressive effect, supply the only legitimate elements of the ceremonial, and the performance culminates in a series of flexions and genuflexions which can only be fitly described as the Elevation of the Host.[2]

Mackonochie was brought before the court on four counts: the elevation and adoration of the holy elements in the sacramental blessing; placing lighted candles on the communion table; the use of incense; and mixing water with the wine in the chalice.[3]

The proceedings quickly took a strange turn when Archbishop Longley named Dr. Robert Phillimore to be the new Dean of the Court of Arches. The appointment was an unusual one in that Phillimore was himself involved in the controversy; in addition to being the Chancellor for the Bishop of Oxford and having been named to serve on the Ritual Commission, he was also Mackonochie's defense attorney. The *Record* immediately protested that he should not be allowed to preside over the case when it came to trial.[4] Phillimore was initially inclined to step aside, but he later decided to hear the St. Alban's and the East Teignmouth cases together and to preside over the court himself.[5] When he handed down his decision in March 1868, anti-Ritualists were surprised by the verdict. He ruled in favor of 'his late clients' only with regard to the use of lighted candles on the altar, and reluctantly found the other practices illegal. In an apparent attempt to blunt the force of the ruling, however, Phillimore declined to rule against Mackonochie in the matter of costs, which meant that he did not have to pay the legal fees of the prosecuting attorney as well as his own.[6]

John Martin, who brought the case against Mackonochie, quickly notified Bishop Tait that he intended to appeal to the Judicial Committee of the Privy Council.[7] That court condemned Mackonochie's innovations on all counts and ordered him to pay costs for both the lower court and the appeal. The *Record* thought the ruling undermined the very foundation of the Ritualist movement.[8] The CA was equally pleased with the decision and expressed its hope that such a definitive court ruling would quickly bring the innovations to a halt.[9] In one of his last acts as Bishop of London, Tait suggested in a letter to Mackonochie that the time had come for the Ritualists to heed the admonitions of the bishops.[10]

The Ritualists were understandably disconcerted by the ruling and searched for some positive aspect to the judgment. They fixed on the issue of the surplice in the pulpit, which had not been under consideration by the court, and argued that since its use had not been condemned it might therefore be considered mandatory. J. C. Miller, a prominent Evangelical leader in Birmingham, suggested that if the Ritualists exceeded the limits imposed by the rubrics, Evangelicals were often guilty of failing to fulfill them completely. In Miller's view, it would involve 'no surrender of principle' for Evangelicals to render 'a literal and close obedience to the rubrics,' even if that meant compromise for the sake of 'unity and order' on minor matters such as the surplice.[11] The *Quarterly Review*, a non-partisan journal that had been sharply critical of the Ritualists, described Miller as 'an eminent Evangelical clergyman' and expressed the hope that 'advice so evidently reasonable from a man so highly respected' would not go without effect.[12] Miller, however, drew a storm of criticism from other Evangelicals with his letter. In general, it was argued that nothing ought to be conceded to the Ritualists that was not required either by bishop or judge.[13]

One of Miller's most strident critics was the equally prominent J. C. Ryle. Unlike Miller, Ryle thought Evangelicals should maintain their position and give no ground to the Ritualists. More disturbing for him, however, was the perception created by Miller that Evangelicals might not have been fully complying with the rubrics. He suggested that there was a 'vagueness' to Miller's language that might lead some to assume falsely that the Evangelical clergy were 'a lawless class' similar to the Ritualists in their deviations from the rubrics. That, claimed Ryle, was an errant view.[14] It was rather significant that Miller's letter counseling a policy of moderation should have drawn such fire. The vehement reaction presented an image of a somewhat insecure party in spite of the fact that the court had largely vindicated its view of the rubrics. The level of rhetoric indicated that the Ritualists' criticisms had touched a sore point, and despite Ryle's argument to the contrary, the reaction to Miller was a clear sign that many feared for the Evangelical position; the Ritualists might have gone too far but a nagging doubt remained that at least some Evangelical parishes were susceptible to the charge of being less than fully compliant with the intent of the rubrics.

It soon became evident that the anti-Ritualist victory in the Mackonochie case was largely symbolic. The Ritualists mostly refused to modify their services, and there was nothing like an abdication of their basic principles regarding the sacramental nature of the church's worship service. The *Record* gave almost weekly reports in its Monday editions describing how the literal interpretation of the law was circumvented by the Ritualist clergy in the previous day's services.[15] In June 1869, the CA presented memorials to the archbishops reiterating the Mackonochie judgment and asking that the episcopacy enforce 'obedience to the law' as interpreted by the court.[16] Both noted the great English tradition of obedience to the law and expressed their hope that the clergy would abide by the rulings of the court. Archbishop Thomson of York responded:

> Where the law has pronounced any rite or practice to be illegal it would be the plain duty of a bishop in any case which might be brought to his notice to use all the means in his power to secure that the rite or practice is discontinued. I do not believe that there will be much need to resort to further legal proceedings for this purpose. Some persons who stand committed to some novel practices may for a time endeavour to evade or disobey a legal decision against them, but in the end a respect for law which has so great a power over us will prevail. In the mean time, however, as long as the law fails to produce that effect, there may be cases which require the vigilance of a bishop and even a resort to legal proceedings. I have every reason to think that the bishops of the Northern province will do their duty in this respect. (Hear, hear.)[17]

Events, however, would prove the archbishop's optimism unfounded.[18]

As it became evident that a single court ruling would not be sufficient to bring the innovations to an end, the anti-Ritualists became increasingly concerned with the state of the ecclesiastical courts. Under existing law, suits could only be brought with the approval of the diocesan. Furthermore, defendants were able to exercise a number of appeals that could extend the process indefinitely and make the cost of litigation prohibitive. In February 1869, Lord Shaftesbury introduced a bill for the reform of the ecclesiastical courts. The legislation, largely prepared by the legal counsel of the CA, was clearly written with the prosecution of the Ritualists in mind. It also attempted to reform several aspects of episcopal patronage, but its main intent was to simplify the judicial process for ecclesiastical cases. If passed, the bill would have sharply curtailed the power of the bishops and given the laity the right to bring cases without episcopal approval (a right that had been unintentionally suppressed by the Church Discipline Act of 1840), if three 'aggrieved parishioners' agreed to the proceedings. It would also have created a new provincial court that could transfer significant cases directly to the Privy Council, thus reducing the time and expense of the appeals process.[19]

The bishops were opposed to many of the reforms contained in Shaftesbury's bill and quickly introduced an alternative measure.[20] Their version excluded the elements aimed at reducing episcopal influence. It also brought the diocesan courts more completely under their jurisdiction, with the chancellors serving as assessors rather than judges. The *Record* was unimpressed with the bishops' bill, particularly with regard to the limits it imposed on right of the laity to institute legal proceedings, and concluded that it was another 'lamentable attempt to stave off a substantial reform.'[21] With time running out on the parliamentary session, both bills were sent to a select committee and effectively tabled. Recognizing the likely result, the *Record* expressed its hope that Shaftesbury's proposal had at least laid the groundwork for significant reform.[22]

The Purchas Case

The next significant prosecution brought by the CA involved John Purchas, Perpetual Curate of St. James's Chapel, Brighton. Purchas had been at the center of the Ritualist controversy for a number of years before he was brought to trial.[23] By 1868, St. James's Chapel was widely known for its elaborate ceremony, and anti-Ritualists had often complained about the services performed there. When disturbed parishioners protested in a memorial to Bishop Gilbert of Chichester, he replied that 'ritualistic' did not begin to describe the character of the services conducted by Purchas.[24] He thought them extreme and 'irreverent violations of the rubrics and doctrine' of the Anglican church and concluded that there was no need for a commission. If any church members were prepared to bring the proper charges, he would immediately send the case to the Court of Arches.[25]

The case was delayed by various legal proceedings for over a year, but it was finally heard by Sir Robert Phillimore in the Court of Arches in February 1870. As in the Mackonochie case, the judgment went almost entirely against Purchas. It reiterated several of the earlier rulings and extended them to include other less significant innovations.[26] Phillimore, however, ruled in favor of Purchas on several points, and the *Record* accused him of 'blind partisanship' in siding with the Ritualists wherever he was not bound by the earlier decisions of the Privy Council. The most damaging point of the decision, for the anti-Ritualists, concerned the use of vestments. He decided in favor of the use of eucharistic vestments and suggested that the surplice was the only appropriate attire for the minister in the pulpit.[27]

The ruling created a degree of consternation among the Evangelical clergy, most of whom still wore a black academic robe in the pulpit and viewed the surplice as a party badge of the Ritualists. As in the prior case, Evangelicals were divided both in regard to the exact meaning of the ruling and concerning whether the wisest policy might not be simply to concede this point to their opponents and adopt the surplice. According to the *Record*, the issue of the surplice had not been a part of the case, and Phillimore's ruling only indicated his lack of 'a well-balanced judicial mind.'[28] The position of the paper clearly reflected the view of a majority of Evangelicals, but there were some who thought it ought not to be contested any longer.[29] The CA immediately appealed the objectionable sections of the judgment, and the Judicial Committee delivered its ruling in February 1871. It included a detailed examination of the Elizabethan rubrics to substantiate its conclusions concerning the legality of the disputed practices.[30] The court vindicated the anti-Ritualist position when it overturned the Court of Arches on almost every point. The judges rejected the wearing of eucharistic vestments, the mixed chalice, wafer bread, and the eastward position.[31] Only in reference to the use of holy water and the wearing of a biretta did the judges rule in favor of Purchas, finding that the charges were not proved by the evidence. Evangelicals thought the judgment a crushing defeat for the Ritualist movement, and they were not alone in that view.[32] The *Times* similarly hoped that it would bring an end to the controversy.[33] But their optimism proved to be short-lived.

The Problem of Compliance

The Mackonochie and Purchas judgments raised a basic issue previously unconsidered by the anti-Ritualists – What if their opponents refused to obey the courts? At a large meeting of Ritualist clergy following the Mackonochie judgment, the issue of compliance with the court's ruling was hotly debated. W. J. E. Bennett, who was himself the subject of prosecution, favored a program of passive disobedience and issued a declaration repudiating the authority of the Privy Council.[34] A resolution was ultimately passed that protested the judgment but suggested that submission would follow.[35] The Ritualists would return often to this fundamental argument – the Judicial Committee of the Privy Council, as a final court of appeal, was a civil court and could hold no legitimate jurisdiction in matters involving the doctrine and worship of the church. According to Bennett, Ritualist priests felt 'bound to continue as heretofore, in our several churches, those rites, ceremonies, and usages of the Primitive Church which have been condemned by a Court purely secular, and contrary to the English Constitution.'[36]

The issue of compliance with legal judgments and the appropriate form of punishment for those who refused it would further aggravate the controversy in the years to come.[37] The anti-Ritualists and bishops were unprepared for the noncompliance of the Ritualists. At the time, it was simply inconceivable that clergy of the national church would withhold their obedience to the courts. In response to Ritualist claims of an erastian intrusion of the state, their opponents argued that it was simply a matter of the clergy fulfilling the responsibilities imposed on an established church. Having accepted the obligations of their ordination oaths, the anti-Ritualists claimed that the clergy had no right thereafter to claim that they owed their obedience only to a higher authority.[38] The issue was further complicated by the largely unreformed legal system that provided neither a simple means of response nor satisfactory penalties for those guilty of contumacy. The Ritualists had already achieved a degree of notoriety for their unwillingness to heed the pleadings of bishops or the recommendations of committees. But neither their opponents nor the ecclesiastical authorities were prepared for the challenge issued by Mackonochie and Purchas when they refused to comply with the monitions of the Judicial Committee.[39]

A. H. Mackonochie returned to court on charges of noncompliance in 1869. He was acquitted on most of the charges, but the judges made it clear that they were unimpressed with his concept of obedience. The *Record* believed the ruling was only 'a formal acquittal' and suggested that the language conveyed 'a strong moral rebuke' of the Ritualists.[40] Mackonochie was again before the court in 1870 and was found guilty of contempt of court.[41] The judges concluded that Mackonochie had deliberately set out to determine how far he could maintain the ceremonies prohibited by their earlier monition without actually breaking the law:

> Mr. Mackonochie must be reminded that the right of the Church of England to ordain ceremonies was asserted by the 34th article of religion, to which he had given his assent, and that none of the ceremonies and practices which he observed were prescribed by the Church. In his attempt to satisfy his conscience and shelter himself behind a strictly literal obedience, Mr. Mackonochie has been a second time foiled. On the former occasion their Lordships, did not think it necessary to do more than to mark their disapprobation of Mr. Mackonochie's course by directing him to pay costs. Upon this repetition of his offence, however, their Lordship's felt they ought to proceed further.[42]

Mackonochie was suspended from office for three months and ordered to pay the court costs.[43]

Mackonochie defended himself in an eloquent letter to the *Record*, which was published in two parts in December 1870. In the first half, he denied the paper's charges that he was guilty of 'jesuitical casuistry' in his attempt to evade the intent of the law while staying within its letter.[44] In the second half, Mackonochie presented his basic convictions regarding the Eucharist and his view of the controversy.[45] Based on his beliefs, he asked, what was he to do when presented with the current situation? He could not leave the church he believed in, but neither could he simply acquiesce to the judgments. He believed they were mistaken and imposed by a court with no valid authority in matters of faith. Having detailed his attempts at a limited concurrence, he concluded, 'as a matter of course I believed my Lord to be there, and must show Him some reverence. The very principles of my duty to God obliged me to save as much for his honour as I could; and thus forbade me to obey to a hair's breadth beyond the mere letter of that which seemed to me to assail his honour.'

In conclusion, he drew a striking parallel between his situation and that of the early Evangelicals, who had been hounded and persecuted by the ecclesiastical authorities: 'Let me ask you, Sir, who drove Wesley from the Church of England? The bishops and the upper middle classes in Church and State. In fact, the "Chief Priests with the Scribes and Pharisees" Who tried to drive the early Evangelicals from the Church? The same "Chief Priests with the Scribes and Pharisees." Who are now trying to drive from the Church those who are fruits of the labour of Wesley, and the old Evangelicals? The same "Chief Priests with the Scribes and Pharisees".'[46] Having drawn that parallel, he ended his letter by suggesting the two parties, in fact, shared a common view of the ministry. They both believed the 'sacred ministry' was a gift from God that could not be touched by the Queen and her courts. 'We differ as to what it is, but the essence of the ministerial life we both believe to be God's alone.' On that basis, he believed, even his Evangelical opponents must understand that, while accepting his suspension as 'a legal compulsion,' he refused to be bound by it or to allow it to alter his view of the church and its sacraments.[47] Mackonochie's letter was a strong defense of his position. It probably did little to change the views of those who were adamantly opposed to the Ritualist innovations, but it could not have gone without effect in swaying the opinion of those who had begun to realize that an appeal to the courts could never arrive at a satisfactory conclusion of the controversy.[48]

John Purchas was brought before the Privy Council again in February 1872. In a symbolic act that would be repeated by many Ritualists after him, Purchas indicated his disdain for the process by refusing to appear before the court or even hiring counsel to represent him. The judges quickly found him in contempt of court and suspended him from office for one year. They also placed a sequestration on his 'lay property' to cover the court costs he had refused to pay.[49] Purchas continued to disregard the judgment, and on February 25th, he concluded his evening sermon with an emphatic rejection of the right of either the episcopacy or a secular court to interfere with the traditional freedom of the parish clergy.[50] The Purchas case illustrated a fundamental problem facing the anti-Ritualists – the existing law provided no further recourse, within reasonable limits, by which the Ritualists might be forced into compliance. The CA decided to pursue the case, noting its regret that imprisonment was a possibility. The council suggested that they would urge upon the court some alternative form of punishment.[51] It was evident to anti-Ritualists, at an early stage of the controversy, that the imprisonment of clergy could have a negative effect on the popular support for their cause. The court's final ruling against Purchas, however, had little effect; he died suddenly in October 1872. The funeral sermon by Mackonochie elevated Purchas to the status of a martyr who had been persecuted for the faith.[52] Whether or not he was a martyr, the model of non-compliance he established would have a continuing effect on the controversy.[53]

Episcopal Influence and Authority

The controversy was further complicated by the contrasting views of episcopal authority held by the various parties. Anti-Ritualists believed that the law should be strictly applied and assumed that the bishops had the necessary authority to do so. After the Purchas verdict in the Court of Arches, Bishop Jackson of London sent a letter to the prominent Ritualists in his diocese inviting them to meet with him to discuss its implications.[54] According to the *Times*, the bishop gave notice that he intended to enforce the law regarding those elements of ritual condemned in the Purchas case. The paper noted, however, that the Ritualists were apparently determined 'to resist the Bishop's attempt to suppress the practices in which they are interested, and that a fierce ecclesiastical battle may be expected.'[55] The *Record* took the occasion to stress the bishops' responsibility for the growth of the controversy. It blamed them, with their policy of toleration and inactivity, for the growth of the Ritualist movement and the animosity aroused by the Protestant reaction:

> The apathy of some is alienating the middle classes, and encourages both ultra-Ritualism and ultra-Sacramentarianism. The rest-

less Sacerdotalism of others, such as the Bishop of Lichfield, at Wolverhampton, is fomenting strife between the clergy and laity, about such frivolous questions as the surplice and the black gown.... Had it not been for the expectations of amendment which the successes of the Church Association have inspired, the prospect would be still more gloomy. As it is we yet cling to the hope that our prelates will be aroused to a sense of the danger and adopt measures fitted to meet the crisis.[56]

It was somewhat ironic that the controversy led Evangelicals to urge episcopal intervention. They had long expressed their aversion to the growth of episcopal power, and yet their desire for the bishops' suppression of Ritualism could only serve to elevate their importance and authority in general.

Immediately following the decision of the Judicial Committee in the Purchas case, Bishop Jackson again declared his intention of enforcing the law. The Ritualists defended the eastward position in a remonstrance signed by over 4,500 clergy. The number of signatures would seem to indicate that the generally-worded document appealed to many outside the Ritualist section of the High Church party with its argument for a policy of toleration in the church.[57] Jackson responded that a bishop, as a magistrate, 'was bound both by law and by the obligation of his consecration promise to take cognizance of ecclesiastical offences, if duly brought before him.' The remonstrants, he wrote, were quite mistaken in assuming that the bishops had the power to abstain from acting in the matter. He also admonished the Ritualists not to make the mistake of elevating their own individual judgment to the place of final authority.[58]

The Ritualists continued to disobey the rulings and to challenge further prosecution. When admonished by the bishops, who referred to the authority of the judicial rulings, the Ritualists argued that they were bound by their sacred duty to obey and pay reverence to a higher authority – 'Catholic antiquity' and apostolic tradition.[59] Arthur Tooth, Vicar of St. James's, Hatcham, refused to even meet with his bishop unless issued a formal citation. He claimed that 'the orders of the Catholic church,' which he received at his ordination, committed him to the revival of ancient ritual even if it brought him into conflict with his diocesan. The *Record* rejected both the supposition concerning the primitive nature of the ritual innovations as well as Tooth's understanding of his duty: 'If he has candour enough to read over again the Ordination Service he will find that neither in the commission accepted by him nor in the promises made by him is there the slightest reference to any imaginary Catholicism.... We fully admit that obedience can only be due in things lawful, but we maintain that a readiness to hear what a Bishop has to say, to give it respectful attention and consideration is not only the simplest courtesy, but is the first palpable duty of the obligations which he then undertook.'[60]

Undoubtedly there were a few bishops who sympathized with the interests of the Ritualists and were reluctant to intervene. More likely, those who were criticized by anti-Ritualists for their moderation were simply interested in pursuing a policy that they hoped would maintain the peace in their respective dioceses. Such a program, however, found little support among fervent anti-Ritualists who viewed it as appeasement. In August 1871, several churchwardens in Buckinghamshire published a memorial protesting the ritual innovations of their parish priest. Bishop Mackarness of Oxford, however, refused to be swayed by their arguments. And in contrast to Bishop Jackson, Mackarness believed he was allowed a broad degree of latitude in applying the law; he noted that he had refused to interfere in an earlier case regarding a priest who continued to wear the black gown in the pulpit, and he informed the memorialists that he would not attempt to enforce 'rubrical conformity' in the present case either. He argued his case on several points. First, he did not believe absolute uniformity could be obtained except at great cost to the peace of the church. Second, he was unconvinced that the churchwardens represented a majority of the congregation and did not wish to intervene unless there were clear indications that the parish was generally unhappy with the innovations. And finally, he was convinced that the vicar, Rev. William Norris, was a man of high character, who was widely esteemed. He concluded, 'It would be repugnant to all my notions of a bishop's duty to single out such a clergyman for censure, while the negligent and careless, for such unhappily are to be found, provoke no observation, and incur no attack.'[61]

Evangelicals were outraged that a bishop would claim such broad discretionary powers and simply refuse to uphold the law as interpreted by the courts. As a general principle, they were unwilling to consider the idea that a bishop might allow the desires of the congregation to offset the demand for a literal obedience to the rubrics. Regardless of his reasoning and concern for the general peace of his diocese, Mackarness's inaction was condemned as part of the Ritualist plan to impose their views on the church.[62] Given their argument that the episcopacy had it in their power to halt the innovations if they so desired, it was somewhat disingenuous for anti-Ritualists to argue that the bishops had no corresponding right to choose not to act. But having the perception of the situation that they did, it was little wonder that determined anti-Ritualists were increasingly skeptical of the episcopacy's desire to resolve the controversy, and they came to believe that the appeal to the judiciary remained their best option for halting the innovations. The Public Worship Regulation Act of 1874, however, validated the discretionary powers of the episcopacy, and the use of that power ultimately became the only means for halting the largely ineffective prosecutions.

Other bishops, however, questioned whether the controversy could ever be resolved simply through their intervention and suppression of the Ritualists. The Portsmouth branch of the CA sent a memorial to Archbishop Tait expressing their concerns and their 'indignant sorrow and surprise at the supineness and apathy that have prevailed for so long a period on the part of their ecclesiastical rulers.' Tait responded:

> I am not surprised that many members of the Church of England should feel indignant at practices and doctrines which have in some places sprung up during the last 20 years, having a manifest tendency to assimilate the worship and teaching of our pure, scriptural, and Reformed Church to the system of the Church of Rome. But I cannot in any way agree with you in the belief that this evil is owing to supineness and apathy on the part of the bishops. You must be well aware that the beneficed clergy of the Church of England are not, like priests of some portions of the Church of Rome, dependent for their position on the arbitrary will of their Bishops, nor, like some Dissenting ministers, liable to be removed by a vote of their congregations or the heads of their community. I, for my part, whatever disadvantages may follow from this freedom of the clergy, rejoice that it is secured to them, and that no clergyman of the Church of England can be removed until he has had a fair and open trial before a competent tribunal, in which his violation of the law of the Church has been legally proved.[63]

Tait thought it unjust to attribute blame to those who thought it their duty, 'however much their patience has been tried, always to act according to law, and not to seek some arbitrary mode of crushing those whose opinions they disapprove, when such power is not conferred upon them either by the Church or the law of the land.'[64] The archbishop later touched on the issue in a letter to the bishops of the province of Canterbury discussing the upcoming parliamentary session. That letter helped explain the inactivity of both the bishops and the Ritual Commission. Looking at the subjects that were certain to be considered, Tait noted that 'the most vexed questions' were likely to be settled by the courts of law before they ever made it to the floor of Parliament. That perception, he thought, also explained why the Ritual Commission was determined to wait for the courts' decisions before coming to any conclusions regarding proposed legislation. While offering no opinion on the possibility of legislation, the archbishop concluded that the episcopacy would not have done its duty to the Church and the nation until 'all these questions have been firmly settled.'[65] Tait, like many of the anti-Ritualists, seems to have been overly optimistic in believing that a few court rulings clarifying the legitimate interpretation of the rubrics would be sufficient to bring the matter to a close.

The Spreading Influence of Ritualism

In spite of the early success of the anti-Ritualist movement in the courts, it was evident that the more moderate innovations being introduced were growing in popularity. For example, the surplice in the pulpit was more common, even among Evangelicals, and, as noted earlier, there was a greater emphasis on music and the choir. Several bishops interpreted the Court of Arches' decision in the Purchas case as a definitive judgment in favor of the surplice.[66] In response to a dispute in his diocese, Bishop Fraser of Manchester acknowledged that many of the innovations being introduced by the Ritualists were an 'abomination,' but he also expressed his regret that suspicions were often raised about harmless attempts to beautify the church or its services. Reiterating a line of thought often voiced by the bishops, Fraser suggested that every change ought not to be immediately stigmatized as Ritualism, particularity if it fell within the broad limits of Anglican order and 'carried the congregation along.' He 'did not think it was Christian – he was sure it was not kindly – that a few members in a congregation who might not like it should stand as obstructives in the way of the great majority who did like it, and so raise suspicions of unkindly feeling in a parish when, above all other things, it was desirable that, as members of the Church of England, they should at heart be one.'[67] In this instance, and in many similar cases, the anti-Ritualist protest suffered from the appearance that it represented only the opposition of a small and extreme minority within the parish – those who, in their zeal, could not distinguish the efforts of faithful clergy attempting to beautify the church's worship from those extremists trying to undermine the Protestant foundation of the church.[68]

By 1872, the Bishops of London (Jackson) and Winchester (Wilberforce) had joined the list of those who supported the use of the surplice and recommended it in their annual charges. The *Record* voiced its strong opposition and recounted the history of Bishop Blomfield's ill-fated attempt to require the surplice in the pulpit in the early 1840s, implying that the bishops were simply repeating the mistakes of the past and that vehement protests would soon follow. The paper claimed that several Evangelical clergy, who had been willing to accommodate the desires of their bishops, had 'wisely yielded to the remonstrances' of their congregations and returned to the black gown.[69] But the adoption of the surplice was no longer the controversial issue it had once been. Later that summer, the Bishop of Carlisle also requested that the clergy in his diocese wear the surplice in the pulpit.[70] As the more provocative Ritualists moved on to ever more extreme positions, their more moderate innovations found increasing acceptance throughout the church and were adopted with but slight controversy even in Evangelical parishes.[71] Despite the best efforts of Evangelicals over more than a decade, the influence of the Ritualists had begun to filter down to churches far beyond their immediate circle.[72]

The impact of the Ritualist movement could also be seen in the greater importance given to music in the churches, which, unlike many of the other ceremonial innovations, presented a less overt challenge to Protestants.[73] As early as February 1861, the *Record* published a lengthy letter from Edward Young under the heading 'Liturgical Music and Liturgical Revival.' Young cited biblical illustrations of the power to be found in music and contrasted that perspective with the views of fellow Evangelicals, who from ignorance, indifference or outright opposition, believed that music was unimportant in the church or that it 'was for Papists and not for Protestants.' Throughout the Bible music had been associated with the very highest and best in human nature, and Evangelicals were not being wholly scriptural in their worship if they were not fully incorporating it.[74] He also noted the growing appropriation of music in the services of the church – it was a simple fact of the times. If then it was not contrary to Scripture, and it was popular with the laity, why were Evangelicals not making full use of it? According to Young, there was a clear parallel between the place of music in worship and that of the sermon, which for Evangelicals was the focal point of the service – both were attempts to bring Scripture alive to the people. He concluded, 'If God has indeed endowed music with certain powers, we are sacredly bound to see that the endowment be not abused or neglected.'[75]

For its time, Young's position was a rather surprising admission of the general diffusion of the Ritualist influence. In a later editorial, the *Record* half-heartedly endorsed his effort to promote the increased use of music, but it also felt bound to warn against the dangers of the 'music of Puseyism.'[76] But Young was clearly not the only Evangelical moving in that direction. Another clergyman turned the argument against musical innovation on its head in order to support the adoption of the changes. If the Ritualists attracted the interest of the younger generation, he thought it unwise for Evangelical clergy 'to neglect so attractive an instrumentality as good Church music.' He went so far as to endorse the use of the High Church hymnal, *Hymns Ancient and Modern*, for which he was sternly rebuked by the *Record*.[77] Nevertheless, his central argument went unanswered – the church owed the best to God in its worship, and for Evangelical churches that meant following the lead of the Ritualists.[78] In the months that followed, the *Record* published numerous attacks on the popery promoted by the High Church hymnals, especially *Hymns Ancient and Modern*, but their effort to negate its impact only proved the degree to which conservatives were concerned by its influence in Evangelical churches.[79]

In 1865, Francis Close, Dean of Carlisle and an influential conservative Evangelical, published a pamphlet on the subject. His *Thoughts on the Daily Choral Services in Carlisle Cathedral*, gave expression to his changed views on church music:

> At the risk of being judged egotistical in this matter, I must testify that an attendance upon musical public services daily for nearly ten years has created a new habit in my mind; a decided preference to this mode of worship has been awakened, and unless I am greatly deceived, my conviction is that the comfort thus experienced in Divine worship has been not a little enhanced by the regular cadence, the measured time, the continuous monotone in which our prayers are uttered.[80]

Even though he warned against putting too much emphasis on music in parish churches, Close was strongly criticized by the *Record* which considered the publication of his pamphlet 'a grievous mistake.' His work could not have come at a worse time, thought the paper, for those who were attempting to turn back the Ritualists and 'resisting the progress of choral services as one of the perils of the times.'[81] Close's view was particularly disturbing in that his conservative reputation was well established, and any change in his perspective represented a real threat to the anti-Ritualist movement.

As the Ritualist controversy grew throughout the 1860s and 70s, Evangelicals were forced to admit that the innovations were popular with at least some of the laity. Most often, they attributed their opponents' influence to the emotional appeal the movement held for women and young men who failed to fully appreciate the characteristics of a 'manly' Protestantism.[82] Nor were they alone in this regard. The *Times*, in describing the services at St. Alban's, Holborn, noted the predominance of young men and women in the congregation.[83] In an editorial from 1867, it commented more broadly on those who were attracted to the ceremonial of the Ritualists:

> It is often found that clever, tasteful women of the higher classes have a strong tendency towards an elaborate Ritual. A rather weak kind of young man is a good deal given to the same opinions. Besides these, there are a great number of educated people, rather fastidious and artistic in their natures, who, without much theological bias, like choral services and a richly dressed altar, and think that, as they have to go to church, they may as well go to a place where the service is tastefully conducted.[84]

The *Times* counseled a policy of toleration for moderate Ritualists, especially in the larger cities and endowed chapels, but thought the movement's 'cultured' supporters tended to underestimate 'the Protestant or Puritan feeling of the English people.'[85] More strident anti-Ritualists emphasized the latter point and suggested that the innovators were driving the masses into Dissenting chapels and were a threat to the establishment.[86]

While noting that the use of 'banners, decorations, ceremonies and processions' had a certain natural appeal among the general population, conservative Evangelicals were generally unwilling to admit the argument for even a limited toleration. They often countered that natural instincts and emotions had little place in truly spiritual religion which was distinguished from sacramental superstitions both by its reasonableness and its 'manliness.' It was feared, however, that the younger clergy failed to recognize the nature of the threat.[87] Daniel Wilson, one of the elder statesmen among Evangelical clergy in London, made the case at the Islington Clerical Conference in January 1867: 'An opinion has been expressed in some quarters that a certain amount of outward attraction is necessary in order to draw the people to our churches. That these novelties have in some cases had this effect, I allow, but it admits of grave doubt how far they are legitimate or tend to edification. If the simple preaching of the Gospel with earnestness and power does not fill the church, I should hesitate to adopt other methods.'[88] J. C. Ryle expressed similar sentiments at the Ipswich Clerical and Lay Conference later that year. He warned that 'church decorations, church music and a semi-histrionic mode of going through Church worship' might seem to have some appeal, but they were a threat to spiritual religion and introduced dangerous tendencies into otherwise Protestant parishes. He worried that 'scores of Evangelical clergymen' had introduced such innovations with the best of intentions but 'had ended by going a great deal further than they had intended, disgusting their own believing hearers and rendering themselves miserable.' Ryle concluded, 'Processions, banners, flowers, crosses, music, beautiful vestments, etc., might please children and weak-minded people, but they would never help forward heart conversion or heart sanctification.'[89]

Writing from a moderate Broad Church position, E. H. Plumptre suggested that Evangelical clergy had only themselves to blame for the loss of adherents, particularly among the younger generation. He suggested that Evangelical preaching was bound too much within a small range of traditional doctrine and that their worship was dull and repetitive, relying on the inherited traditions and forms.[90] And moderate anti-Ritualists were realizing as well that some of the innovations were both legitimate and aesthetically pleasing. That position was similarly adopted by the A. W. Thorold, who suggested in an 1868 article, that Evangelicals had no need to fear 'a bright and hearty service.'[91]

The division among moderate and conservative Evangelicals was evident at the Islington Clerical Conference in 1871. Daniel Wilson set a conservative tone for the meeting, expressing his concerns regarding the tendency of the age. Above all, he feared that a tendency to compromise was becoming prevalent among Evangelicals. At the same time, however, he admitted that the spirit of the age had also contributed to the lessening of party divisions in the church, with a consequent growth of piety and a renewed emphasis on outreach. In this, it was clear that the High Church party had been reinvigorated and many believed they were now the most active group in the church.[92] At the same conference, however, J. C. Miller, the newly appointed Canon of Worcester, read a paper on 'Charity in Controversy.' Quite expecting that he would meet with some disapproval, Miller hoped to encourage a more moderate tone in the debate. In his opinion, the time had come for Evangelicals 'to adjust the relative claims of truth and charity, that they might be faithful without bigotry, and charitable without latitudinarianism.'[93]

While denying that he intended to promote an attitude of compromise, Miller proposed several 'rules of charity in religious dispute.' He suggested that in matters of controversy a distinction had to be made between persons and their doctrines, for it was clear that they would later find in heaven some whom they presently suspected of 'grave error.' He also argued that they ought not to impute to others inferences from their doctrines which they themselves denied. Evangelicals had themselves faced critics who accused them of holding a low view of the Lord's Supper simply because they denied the doctrine of real presence. Having suffered thus at the hands of others, said Miller, they ought not engage in similar practices themselves. He disliked the term 'real presence,' but he thought it 'unfair for the Evangelical party to say that all who spoke of the Real Presence held the coarse, material doctrine of Transubstantiation.' He also believed that charity demanded that they distinguish between essentials and non-essentials, not allowing a partisan spirit to condemn too quickly the High Church tradition. He acknowledged that he was increasingly impressed by the zeal and piety of many High Church clergy and thought their hymnals a vast improvement over older works.[94]

Miller concluded by expressing his continuing support for Evangelical convictions and his opposition to compromise; nevertheless, and in rather sharp contrast to the position taken by Wilson, he declared his concern regarding the spirit of the controversy and the impact it had on the younger clergy:

> But I speak out honestly, as you would have me speak, although not sure of universal assent, when I express the conviction which has grown with years, and amid large intercourse with brethren of our school of thought – a conviction which I must express at all hazards of misconception or mistrust, that, while not one whit less tenacious – God forbid! – we must be more charitable, more candid, more large-hearted. We must not exact the so nice pronunciation of our shibboleths; we must not make men offenders for a phrase or an observance; we must recognize more frankly and more ungrudgingly in men of other schools the gifts of God and the grace of God; we must not suppose that God has given to us a monopoly of usefulness and blessing; we must seize, rather than avoid, such occasions of united action as may involve no sacrifice of principle. There is a large body of men rising up in our curacies, among our younger incumbents, and in our colleges, who are preaching, or will preach, substantially evangelical doctrine, but who are repelled by narrowness. And even at such times as we are called, brethren against brethren, to prefer to peace what our strong convictions teach us to be truth, we do well to remember the words of Richard Baxter, 'In essentials, unity; in non-essentials, liberty; in all things, charity.'[95]

Miller was criticized by several respondents, but his was certainly an influential opinion. His expression of concern, at some personal risk to his reputation, also indicated that disenchantment with the current state of the controversy, usually expressed in opposition to the continuation of litigation, was not simply a generational issue.[96]

Questioning Litigation and Evangelical Party Unity

Despite the success of the appeal to the courts, anti-Ritualists recognized almost from the beginning that the prosecutions could also have a negative side effect. As early as December 1867, Archdeacon Denison had described the Ritualists as 'a persecuted party.' The *Record* worried that the Ritualists, despite the facts of the case, would be able to manipulate public opinion in their favor; 'they know that many persons who care but little for the momentous issues which are involved in the controversy between us, will side with them from a chivalrous instinct, if they can but persuade them that they are oppressed.'[97] There were also indications that some Evangelicals, from the early years of the controversy, doubted the wisdom of litigation. In October 1869, J. C. Colquhoun, Chairman of the CA council, addressed a speech to those 'who from conscientious, but, he thought, mistaken scruples, had kept aloof from the Church Association.' They were thoroughly Protestant and opposed to the Ritualists, but they kept their distance because they 'thought the action of the Society savoured of persecution.' Colquhoun argued that the apostle Paul himself would have been satisfied with their program, especially since he had devoted much of his writing to dealing with false teachers. He concluded, 'If men who were appointed to preach the truth of Christ taught rank Popery instead, the Association was not to be charged with persecution because it called them to account.'[98]

J. C. Ryle returned to the subject at an association conference the next year, arguing that it was simply a matter of determining through the courts the precise meaning of the law. In this regard, he was glad to report, the association had been successful in all of its cases.[99] Ryle also responded to the common accusation that Evangelicals were narrow-minded and wanted to exclude from the Church of England those of differing opinions. He was fully willing to allow that there was room in the national church for a variety of schools but maintained that it was never intended to be so broad as to include those 'who preached downright Popery.' If such were excluded, said Ryle, it was 'by their own fault and not by the proceedings of the Church Association.'[100] Even the *Quarterly Review*, at this stage of the controversy, thought the lawsuits served a necessary function. On the whole, the essayist suggested that the best strategy was to leave the Ritualists alone and let them follow their own self-destructive path.[101] But however much it was to be expected that 'in a few years, the Ritualists will probably be scattered by their own doing,' some immediate action was necessary 'for the assurance of the multitudes who are perplexed by distrust and suspicion, for the protection of those who are likely to be misled by the audacious pretensions of the ultra-Ritualists.' On this account, the writer was glad to see the suits undertaken and rejected the charge of persecution, particularly since the Ritualists boasted that the law was on their side, and dared their bishops to take action. He hoped that some who might have been duped by the Ritualist claims would be convinced 'if, in addition to the opinions of bishops and synods, the judgment of those who are authorised to expound the law should decide against them.'[102]

The early anti-Ritualist prosecutions were successful in so far as they achieved two of the desired results: first, the legal limitations to which the rubrics could be stretched were clarified; and second, a number of the innovations were declared to have exceeded those limits. But they were unsuccessful insofar as the Ritualists would not be deterred by the judgments and doubts grew even among those who had initially supported litigation. After Mackonochie and Purchas illustrated the effectiveness of a policy of non-compliance and the difficulties involved in enforcement of the law, some anti-Ritualists questioned whether further prosecutions would be any more successful. That perspective was expressed, from outside the Evangelical party, by the *Quarterly Review* in 1870, only a year after it had published an article in favor of lawsuits. It was evident to the author that little had been accomplished 'for the suppression of the so-called Ritualism by prosecutions directed against such matters as incense, lights, and genuflections.'[103]

The first significant expression of that opinion among Evangelicals came in a letter to the *Record* in July 1870, signed R. B. S. (the prominent Evangelical publisher, Robert B. Seeley, who was a close friend of Alexander Haldane, the owner and editor of the paper).[104] He did not want to deprecate the work of the CA and believed it had been important for the courts to clarify the status of the law, but a nagging doubt remained with regard to the final result:

> Still, however, any person, or any body of men, engaged in a work of this kind, may very reasonably, after a progress of some duration, pause and ask the question, Whither does this course lead us? We thought – we reasonably thought – when we first took this road, that it was the right and the only road. But we have advanced some way, and the prospect begins to extend before us. Let us seriously inquire whether the course we have taken seems likely

to lead to a satisfactory issue, or whether any other path is open to us with, perhaps, larger probabilities of success.[105]

Seeley was particularly convinced by the activities of Mackonochie, who having been convicted by the court, altered his ritual only so far as necessary to maintain a barely literal obedience. The CA had done all it could, but with Ritualists such as Mackonochie, the law was 'inoperative.' He concluded, 'Will any amount of legal proceeding put a stop to High Mass, and "bread-worship," in St. Alban's Church in Holborn? I believe that it will not; and therefore I would ask, that the question should be re-considered, in order to find out, if possible, another and a more advisable way.'[106]

Faced with an united opponent, Evangelicals frequently expressed concerns regarding the unity of their own party during this period. And while there was a growing opposition to further litigation, the CA remained a prominent Evangelical society and was often mentioned when the subject of party unity arose. But many were unwilling to participate in the formation a central organization if the CA was involved. The *Record* wrote in 1869, 'We shall not be suspected, we trust, of any lukewarmness in the cause of the Association or any lack of appreciation of the great service it has already done to the cause of the Church of England; but nevertheless the Association, from its very character and object, is mainly supported by the bolder and more resolute spirits of the party, and many stand aloof from it whom we cannot afford to lose, and who are true brothers in mind and heart.' The paper was convinced that some union must be devised that could gather moderate Evangelicals as well as other anti-Ritualists. In this regard, the best plan would be one that would unite the many clerical and lay associations that already existed around the country.[107]

Following the Islington Clerical Conference in January 1870, a meeting was held at the Terminus Hotel, Cannon-street, 'for the purpose of considering what steps should be taken to unite together Evangelical Churchmen for conference and action.' The meeting drew a number of prominent Evangelical clergy and culminated with the formation of a committee that was charged with the task of developing a plan for unification.[108] It was announced at the CA's annual meeting the next year that a Clerical and Lay Union would be organized as a branch of the association.[109] The *Record* therefore lent its support to the plan drawn up by the provisional committee and the association's council:

> The proposal demands the more attention because the Council of the Association does not stand alone in making it, but is associated

with the representatives of the large and influential Meeting which was called together in Cannon-street at the beginning of last year to deliberate upon the subject. The movement is not therefore exclusively connected with the Association. We believe that a formal scheme has been adopted, based on the clerical and lay associations already existing in different parts of England, and directed to bring them into communication with each other through a central representative Committee. Such a plan will at once leave to the local associations their entire freedom of local action, and yet will call into existence a consultative and executive body.[110]

It concluded that the plan was the best hope for uniting Evangelicals under one banner, and it was worthy of receiving the 'respectful consideration' of the entire party.

The first goal of the new union was to organize the existing associations, of which there were about a dozen, and to assist in the development of new ones.[111] But the union's connection to the CA remained a sore point. The *Record* went out of its way to note that the promoters 'profess to base it on no other and no narrower platform than the Church of England herself, and profess their anxiety to devote the strength of the Union to no party objects, but to the defence of the principles and the maintenance of the integrity of the Church.' According to the paper, the supporters of the union did not desire to establish another new society and would therefore be 'incorporated into the Church Association as a separate and independent branch.' But it was quick to note that the two bodies would only be 'so far united as to secure mutual co-operation,' while maintaining their independence of membership and leadership.[112] Still, suspicions remained, as evidenced by a letter from T. D. Harford Battersby. In his view, opposition arose less from the connection to the CA than from the general principle of a central leadership. It was feared that such a committee might attempt to influence 'matters of opinion' or to 'exercise a certain tyranny over the minds of its members.' More specifically, he was concerned that it would be a London committee, of recent creation, attempting to limit the freedom of long-independent country associations. It was against that idea, he wrote, that 'we undoubtedly felt a certain rebelliousness, as conscious that our Associations were of much older date.' In this regard, he feared that the attempts to fit Evangelicalism into the confines of an organizational structure would put limits on the heart of Evangelical religion which was to be found in its individual spirituality.[113] Harford Battersby concluded that his concerns had been resolved by the organizational meeting, but many others remained unconvinced.

In fact, nothing came of the union, and it never accomplished its goal of uniting moderate and conservative Evangelicals.[114] Many in the party continued to support the efforts of the CA, and only a few dissenting voices were raised as the prosecution of Ritualists continued, but the organization and its affiliates could never attract a broad range of support. The ECU, despite its beginnings, became a largely defensive organization at the center of the Ritualist movement, drawing together those who suffered for a common cause. In contrast, the CA never obtained that position among Evangelicals. To a large degree, its influence within both the party and the church as a whole was hindered by its polemical nature. Almost from the beginning, the methods adopted were controversial and divisive. Whether or not the Ritualists were justified in labelling the CA an organization of persecution, it was evident that a number of moderate Evangelicals and other non-partisans were uncomfortable with the nature and tone of the CA's program. The anti-Ritualist movement ought to have been able to draw upon the support of laity and clergy beyond the bounds of the Evangelical party, but it is clear that the CA kept many away. Although the popular press denounced the Ritualists and admitted, in principle, the usefulness of an appeal to the courts, there was little corresponding sympathy for the programs of the CA. Its membership was drawn entirely from the conservative section of the Evangelical party. For a time, however, it was able to maintain its momentum and its influence, and the anti-Ritualist campaign was widely understood to represent the interests of the Evangelical party in general.

Notes

1   The *Times* wrote of St. Alban's and its reputation, 'For some time past the "Church in Baldwin's-gardens," as St. Alban's is popularly called, has been talked about as one of the ecclesiastical curiosities of London, and many people who have passed their Sunday mornings at the less exceptional places of worship which are satisfactory to their consciences have deemed it venial transgression to visit St. Alban's in the evening for the sake of hearing the music and witnessing those ritualistic splendours which, however sanctioned by ancient usage, seem eccentric at the present day.

   'The fame of St. Alban's is not unmerited, and perhaps there is no church in the capital that will give so clear a notion of the extent to which ritualism can go.' The article went on to describe the architecture and ornamentation of the church as well as the ritual used in the service. *Times*, 27 Aug. 1866.

2   *Times*, 19 Oct. 1866.

3   The *Record* reported that the CA also wanted to bring charges on the use of wafer bread in the eucharistic service, but their lawyer, A. J. Stephens, would not allow the charge as it would have required evidence from the communicants, 'and to this the Learned Counsel declined to resort.' *Record*, 1 April 1867.

Perhaps the best brief summary of the ritual innovations involved in the Mackonochie and Purchas cases, and the decisions of the courts (together with extensive quotations from the judgments) can be found in Cutts, 'The Ritual Judgments,' in *Dictionary of the Church of England*, pp. 518-24.
4   *Record*, 29 July 1867.
5   *Times*, 29 Aug. 1867.
6   Phillimore thought the mixing of water with the eucharistic wine was 'an innocent and primitive custom' and ruled that it would not be illegal if done prior to the service. The judgment was reprinted in full in the *Record*, 20 March 1868. The *Times* thought Phillimore's decision was weighed down with theological intricacies and betrayed 'a certain sympathy' with the Ritualist position. 'On the one point he has decided in their favour his judgment conflicts with an opinion expressed by Dr. Lushington in the St. Barnabas case. In one instance he seems almost to go out of his way to suggest for their benefit what would by most people be considered an evasion of the law.' Ultimately, however, he 'found it his duty to decide against them on three material points.' *Times*, 30 March 1868.
7   Correspondence cited in the *Record*, 13 April 1868. The *Times* expressed its strong support for pursuing the issue in the courts. 'It is melancholy, no doubt, to witness all this litigation, now on mere trivialities, and now on serious points of doctrine; but it is the only satisfactory means of dealing with such a party. They have refused to yield to remonstrance either from the public or from their ecclesiastical superiors, and there is no resource, therefore, for those who are aggrieved by their innovations but to appeal to law. Moreover, no further steps can be satisfactorily taken until we know how the law stands. For our own part, we cannot have a doubt as to the issue if the prosecutions are judiciously conducted. If our Articles will not restrain Romish doctrines and Romish ceremonial, it can only be concluded that all legal restrictions are worthless. The Articles were drawn up for this purpose, and can scarcely fail to fulfill it.... We all stand upon law in public matters, and to abide by it is the only security for peace. We cannot share the horror which is sometimes expressed at ecclesiastical prosecutions, for experience has shown that the final decision of the Judicial Committee, however unwelcome at first, has in the end always allayed theological animosity.' *Times*, 30 March 1868.
8   'The language of the Preface to the Prayer-book which is of Parliamentary authority, shows that all ceremonies not expressly 'retained' are, by necessary implication, "abolished." This is a decision which every intelligent Englishman is able to understand without having recourse to obsolete canons or to Councils; to injunctions or advertisements; or the still more doubtful and misleading traditions of Primitive Christianity.' *Record*, 24 Dec. 1868.
9   The Council of the CA passed a resolution at their first meeting following the judgment: 'The Council desire to record their heartfelt gratitude to Almighty God for the judgment of the Judicial Committee of the Privy Council in the case of Martin v. Mackonochie – and rejoicing that the Law, as thereby clearly defined, restricts the use of ornaments and ceremonies to such as are expressly directed by the Book of Common Prayer, the Council

earnestly trust that this decision will effectually restrain all such practices as have recently disturbed the peace of the Church, and tend to restore in the public mind that confidence which is so essential for its stability.' Cited in the *Record*, 1 Jan. 1869.

10   Tait wrote, 'Probably before you receive formal notification of what is now required of you through the proper officers of the Bishop's or Archbishop's Court I shall have ceased to be your diocesan. But I will take upon myself, as my last act in that capacity, to advise you and all others of the London clergy who may now feel themselves placed in a difficulty by their having conscientiously, though I believe unwisely, thought it their duty hitherto to act against the advice and judgment, I believe I may say, of all the bishops, in introducing novelties of worship, to do now what I am sure all true Church principles must suggest – viz., to take counsel with those directly set over them in the Lord as to the mode in which their services are henceforward to be conducted, in conformity with the ascertained law of the Church.' Tait forwarded a copy of the letter to the *Times*, undoubtedly to declare his position (for both the Ritualists and the general public) as he left London to become the Archbishop of Canterbury. Correspondence cited in the *Times*, 31 Dec. 1868.

11   Miller continued, 'Let us first distinctly ascertain the points in which the Judgment bears on the practice. Where duty is clear, let us not wait for Episcopal monitors to compel us. In points of doubt or diversity of opinion, let us "resort to the Bishop of the Diocese." And throughout, let us not forget that the clergy do not constitute the Church. Our laity must be considered, consulted, and not overridden. If changes are now necessitated, let us explain our position to them, and make it clear that we are not innovating from caprice or from sympathy with Rome, or as symbolizing false doctrine, but only under a sense of duty, and in obedience to law and order.' Letter to the *Record*, 4 Jan. 1869.

For a largely positive but brief survey of Miller's influential ministry, cf. David E. H. Mole, 'John Cale Miller: A Victorian Rector of Birmingham,' *Journal of Ecclesiastical History* 17 (1966): 95-103.

James Colley, in an 1869 pamphlet defending 'Evangelical churchmanship,' took a similarly moderate position. 'Why,' he asked, 'should the surplice be made a point of conscience, and its use in the pulpit be allowed to disturb the peace of any congregation? It is surely a very minor matter, and may be treated (on both sides) as one of indifference.' Colley, *Evangelical Churchmanship*, pp. 7-8.

12   While the journal thought the excesses of the Ritualists were far worse than any supposed failure to comply with the rubrics, it hoped both clergy and laity would 'see the propriety of correcting such defects as may be noticeable in their own ritual practice, however these defects may be palliated by the plea of long-standing usage.' The writer believed the surplice in the pulpit was a minor concession and one that could be adopted without partisan significance. Anon., 'Ultra-Ritualists,' *Quarterly Review*, pp. 169-70.

Several bishops, in an attempt to maintain a non-partisan standing, raised the issue in response to anti-Ritualist protests. E. H. Plumptre, in an 1868 article on church parties, suggested that Evangelicals conveniently ignored the fact that the Ritualists' excesses were no worse than 'their own neglect and non-observance.' He suggested they should work to proclaim in positive terms their own position rather than attempting to suppress their opponents. E. H. Plumptre, 'Church Parties,' *Contemporary Review*, p. 332.

Other bishops, however, were more decidedly critical the Ritualists, particularly as they became more determined in their opposition to both legal decisions and episcopal admonitions. In 1876, the *Edinburgh Review* cited, with approval, Bishop Thirlwall's criticism of Gladstone's use of the argument during the debate over the Public Worship Regulation Act in Parliament. Thirlwall entirely rejected the comparison: 'It is, I think, notorious that the Low party drifted into a departure from the Rubrics from manifold causes, without the slightest consciousness of any doctrinal bearing in their practice. The Tractarian ritualistic party, on the other hand, have introduced innovations avowedly for the sake of their doctrinal significance and with a most distinct and deliberate design, which is no other than that of transforming the character of our Church until it becomes ripe for union with Rome.' Anonymous, 'Connop Thirlwall, Bishop of St. David's,' *Edinburgh Review* 143 (1876): 307.

13 *Record*, 8 Jan. 1869. The *Times* also criticized the Ritualist attempt to twist the implications of the judgment. 'They have been invariably wrong – at least, we know of no exception to the rule – in their opinions of the law, and it could not well be otherwise, since they begin from a totally wrong premise in their conception of the legal constitution of the English Church. That they should have misunderstood the Privy Council is a matter of course. The strange part about the comments on the recent Judgment is that persons who are presumably free from the cardinal errors of this school have not hesitated to accept their version of the determination of the Privy Council as if it were unquestionable.'

The Ritualists made two claims. Since only prostration was prohibited during the eucharistic prayer, they concluded that the eastward position was allowed. And since candles were condemned not as ornaments but as a ceremonial innovation, they argued that the wearing of the surplice in the pulpit, which was ornamental, must be valid. The editorialist suggested that if it ever came before the Judicial Committee, the Ritualists would quickly discover 'that their interpretation of the law of ornaments is as unsound as their speculations on the law of ceremonies.' *Times*, 7 Jan. 1869.

14 'It is my own firm conviction that most English Churchmen are quite satisfied with the way in which the Evangelical clergy observe the rubrics of the Prayer-book, and desire no change. I believe that any attempt to enforce on all clergymen daily services, saints'-day services, preaching in the surplice, consecrating the elements with your back turned on the people, and the like, would give immense offense, and do more harm than good.' Ryle concluded his letter, 'I am for standing firm and awaiting any attack that is made upon us. I would not give way a hair's breadth in the direction of ceremonialism, except under downright compulsion. There has been too much giving way and trimming already.' Letter to the *Record*, 8 Jan. 1869.

15 In January 1869, immediately after the Mackonochie decision, the *Times*

gave detailed reports of several churches in which the illegal ritual was continued. The paper wrote, 'Not withstanding the recent decision of the Privy Council in the St. Alban's case, and the letter of the late Bishop of London to Mr. Mackonochie commenting on it, it will be found that the extreme Ritualistic party are determined, in spite of the expressed law and of Ecclesiastical censure, to act in direct defiance of the highest Court of Appeal, and completely to ignore its judgment.' The paper went on to summarize the sermon of Rev. Upton Richards, of All Saints', Margaret-street, who avowed that the Judicial Committee was 'not recognized or sanctioned by the Church, but which had by a most unjust decree upset the decision of the Church's own tribunal – the Court of Arches.' The judgment, according to Richards, was an attack on the church and the truths it held dear. He concluded, in a sermonic flurry, 'that days of prosecution and persecution were in store, and that some would seal their confession with their blood.' *Times*, 4 Jan. 1869.

16 The memorials were only signed by those present at the CA conference, 87 clergy and 129 laity, but they claimed to represent the feelings of the association's 7,500 members. *Times*, 18 June 1869.

17 Ibid.

18 The reputation of the Ritualists for refusing to obey either the episcopacy or the courts was already established. The *Quarterly Review*, in 1867, had noted their contempt for all authority whenever a decision went against them. In the face of such reversals, they employed all 'their ingenuity in finding out what details of their system may have been overlooked in the condemnation, and what evasive tricks may be practised on the words of the sentence.' Anon., 'Ultra-Ritualism,' *Quarterly Review*, pp. 175-6.

A correspondent in the *Times* thought it would be necessary for the bishops to issue a united declaration on the subject. 'It is notorious that differences of opinion have existed among the Bishops, just as much as among their clergy, and that, while nearly all of them have in their several spheres denounced excesses of ritual with more or less severity, that was considered "Ritualism" in one diocese which in another was regarded as harmless.' The writer suggested that the Ritualists had been able to disrupt the church because of the divisions that existed within the episcopacy; and only an authoritative and united declaration on their part would be able to end the controversy. Letter (signed 'A Berkshire Incumbent') in the *Times*, 6 Jan. 1869.

19 *Record*, 17 Feb. 1869. For a complete reprint of the bill, cf. *Record*, 26 Feb. 1869.

20 On the different perspectives taken by Archbishop Tait and Lord Shaftesbury, cf. Davidson, *Life of Tait*, vol. 2, pp. 112-14.

21 *Record*, 19 March 1869. The *Record* cited an article from the *Daily News*, which noted that 'any three churchmen' could institute charges prior to the Church Discipline Bill. The paper thought it was 'tolerably certain' that the authors of that statute had not intended any change in that regard. It continued: 'We are no admirers of the system of regulating religious and ecclesiastical matters by suits of law; but while this remains part of the system of the Church of England, it is most unfair that the laity should not be able to

resort to it without leave of the Bishop, who may have many reasons for conniving at practices contrary to the law of the Church. The notion that frivolous prosecutions would spring up and multiply under such a state of the law as it is proposed to restore is contrary to reason and experience.' Cited in the *Record*, 23 April 1869.
22 *Record*, 16 April 1869.
23 In 1866, seven of the parish clergy complained to the vicar, H. M. Wagner, about the innovations introduced by Purchas. At that time, Purchas adopted an irenic tone and concluded that his position was a moderate one which he expected would cause no further offense in the parish. Correspondence cited in the *Record*, 31 Oct. 1866.
24 The memorial was signed by 648 members of the parish, including five clergy, the mayor, ex-mayor and twelve magistrates. *Record*, 14 Oct. 1868. The memorial noted that neither the bishop nor Wagner had spoken out publicly against the innovations introduced by Purchas. Wagner replied that he had informed the bishop that the sentiments expressed in the document represented the opinions of 'thousands of Brightonians, lovers of the beautiful and simple services of our Church, and therefore all the more shocked by the revival of obsolete and superstitious practices.' Correspondence cited in the *Times*, 13 Oct. 1868.
25 The bishop believed, however, that the findings of the Ritual Commission made a legislative settlement likely and therefore thought prosecution unwise. He further informed the protesters that he had 'inhibited Mr. Purchas from preaching, administering the Sacraments, or officiating in Divine Service' in the diocese, but that Purchas had maintained he had a legal right to disregard the inhibition. Correspondence cited in the *Times*, 13 Oct. 1868. The *Times* reported that Purchas planned to demonstrate his contempt for his bishop the next Sunday with 'an even more Ritualistic service than before.' The paper continued, 'We are thus afforded, if this intelligence be true, another instance of that insolent disregard of all authority which has from the first characterized the Ritualistic clergy. Their proceedings have been an open defiance alike of Archbishops, of Bishops, of a Royal Commission, of established custom, and even of the older members of the High Church party. Notwithstanding the express injunction of the Prayer-book, they have refused to accept the arbitration of their Diocesans; and, with no better justification than disputed interpretations of obscure rubrics, they have set themselves to carry out their own devices.... Mr. Purchas has now rendered it evident that if he can be inhibited he ought to be; and Church discipline needs to be rendered much more stringent if a Bishop can be thus flouted by the self-willed incumbent of a petty proprietary chapel.' The paper went on to express its regret that the rest of the episcopacy had not acted in a similarly decisive manner: 'A little more vigour such as the Bishop of Chichester now displays might have nipped these mischiefs in the bud... but the Bishops have done nothing more than utter a hesitating disapproval. Let a firmer course be adopted; let the Bishops discountenance the Ritualistic clergy in private and in public, and repress their practices by all the power of their office, and the innovators will at least be led to realize the hopelessness of their attempts.' *Times*, 14 Oct. 1868.

26 Those included crucifixes on the communion table, consecrated candles, processions with banners and crosses, hanging a stuffed dove over the altar on Whitsunday, and the imposition of ashes on foreheads on Ash Wednesday. Judgment of the Court of Arches, cited in the *Times*, 4 Feb. 1870.

Individually, the *Record* thought most of the innovations were rather trivial, but they all combined, to threaten the Protestant nature of Anglican worship. The paper thought the ruling doubly important since it was handed down by a lawyer who had formerly represented the ECU. The paper believed it was 'a great victory, as well as a heavy blow and great discouragement to those innovators, who desire to restore the gorgeous Ritualism of Rome.' *Record*, 4 Feb. 1870.

27 Phillimore ruled that the use of a 'mixed chalice' was legal so long as the water was mixed with the wine in the vestry prior to the service. He also allowed the use of wafer bread. The vestments prescribed, according to Phillimore, were 'for ministers below the order of Bishops, and when officiating in the Communion Service, cope, vestment, or chasuble, surplice, alb, and tunicle; in all other services, the surplice only, except in cathedral churches and colleges the academical hood may be also worn.' Ibid.

28 *Record*, 7 Feb. 1870.

29 An anonymous correspondent protested against remarks made at the annual CA conference and argued that academic robes, since they could also be worn by the laity, did nothing to distinguish the clergy. For that reason, he had worn the surplice for over twenty years, and he did not believe it was still 'a badge of party distinction.' Letter (signed an 'Essex Incumbent') to the *Record*, 25 May 1870.

W. E. Gladstone suggested that the use of the surplice in the pulpit, properly viewed, tended toward Protestantism rather than Romanism. 'Popery,' he wrote, 'would have led to the use of a different and lower garb in preaching, not to the use of the same vestment which was also to be used for the celebration of the Eucharist.' W. E. Gladstone, 'Ritualism and Ritual,' *Contemporary Review* 24 (1874): 670.

30 The complete judgment can be found in the *Times*, 25 Feb. 1871. The use of Eucharistic vestments would remain a fundamental point of contention throughout the controversy. For Evangelicals, the adoption of a particular vestment during the celebration of the Eucharist signified two important sacramental doctrines (the Real Presence and the sacrificial ministry of the priesthood) concerning which they were unwilling to make any compromise. The issue continued to divide the two parties long into the twentieth century. When a canon was proposed to Convocation in 1958, that would allow for the use of eucharistic vestments, Evangelicals immediately protested. M. A. P. Wood, in an article in the *Churchman*, returned to arguments that echoed throughout the nineteenth century. He suggested that Anglo-Catholics owed the church an explanation for their insistence on the distinctive attire. He wrote, 'If vestments are necessary to teach doctrine, what do they teach which is not already taught by the present order of Holy Communion in the Prayer Book, and the usual dress of the minister? Why, then, are vestments so important as to cause so much division in the Church? Those who have introduced them and now desire to legalize them,

must share with those of us who oppose their legalization the responsibility for this conflict, distasteful as it is to all concerned, for none of us enjoys controversy.' M. A. P. Wood, 'The Vestments Canon,' *Churchman* New Series 72 (1958), p. 8.

31 The Judicial Committee left unconsidered the issue of the surplice in the pulpit, and the debate continued among Evangelicals as to whether the earlier decision in the Court of Arches necessitated its use. J. C. Ryle contended that he would never change until ordered to do so by 'competent authority.' Letter to the *Record*, 13 March 1871.

In contrast, John Hawksley, Rector of Clifton, took a more conciliatory position. He suggested that Evangelicals ought to adopt the surplice as a matter of 'Christian charity.' He continued, 'All agree that there can now be no objection to the surplice in itself, and the Evangelical body have obtained such a decided success that they can well afford to make so trifling a sacrifice of personal taste and feeling. Unless, indeed, this concession is made, I fear it will be impossible for the bishops to enforce the recent judgment. It is quite clear that the High Church party and the public in general regard it as excluding the gown.... Such a course, I think I may venture to say, would tend not a little to increase respect for Evangelical religion, and to promote order and discipline in the Church.' Letter to the *Record*, 17 March 1871.

32 The *Record* wrote: 'The blow thus struck at Ritualism itself by this sweeping away of its external emblems is almost incalculably great.... The loss inflicted on the system is so severe that we can scarcely conceive that the judgment can be honestly obeyed and yet Ritualism survive.' *Record*, 27 Feb. 1871.

33 Ritualism, said the *Times*, 'was profoundly repugnant to the general sense of the English people,' and the legalization of its innovations would have driven many to Dissent. The paper thought the High Church party had damaged their position 'by their refusal to condemn and repudiate the extremities to which their doctrines and practices were pushed.' But it believed that the great majority of that party stood in unity with the Reformed spirit of the Church of England and would approve of the judgment. It concluded: 'For our part, we welcome the conclusion of a wearisome controversy. No man of sense and sound piety will be aggrieved by being forbidden to dress himself up in obsolete garments, or to resume mediaeval attitudes in the most solemn Ordinance of Religion.' *Times*, 25 Feb. 1871.

Moderate non-partisans generally took a positive view of the judgment. William Magee, who later became the Bishop of Peterborough and Archbishop of York, thought it delayed the threat of disestablishment for several years. Had the decision gone the other way, he thought it would have resulted in 'a gigantic schism' of Protestants or enforced reform from the House of Commons. He hoped it would lead to the secession of the 'ultra-Ritualists.' But he feared that they would maintain 'a dogged resistance, one by one to be met by a series of law suits, which will wear out English patience at last, and so promote the disestablishment, which is coming fast enough without it.' MacDonnell, *Life of Magee*, p. 266.

34 The protest began, 'We, the undersigned priests and deacons of the English

Church, yielding to none in devoted loyalty to Her Majesty the Queen and the crown of these realms, as in all cases ecclesiastical and civil supreme, are nevertheless constrained, by prior obedience to the Catholic Church of Christ, to repudiate the authority of the Court of the Judicial Committee of the Privy Council, which has lately pronounced a judgment in regard to the rites and ceremonies of the Church.' Cited in the *Record*, 15 Jan. 1869.

While the charges against Bennett were under appeal, the *Times* defended the court's legitimacy in an editorial: 'The Courts are invoked, not for the purpose of pronouncing on abstract points of doctrine or ritual, but for the purpose of protecting English laymen in the enjoyment of their legal privileges. The clergy in this country are invested with certain rights and endowments, in return for which laymen may require from them the performance of certain duties according to certain stipulated conditions. Every Englishman has a right to have Divine worship performed in his parish church according to the Book of Common Prayer, and to hear public instruction according to the doctrines laid down in the Formularies. If the directions of the Book of Common Prayer are violated, or the Formularies are disregarded in preaching, he is aggrieved in one of his public rights He applies, therefore, very fitly to a Court of Law for redress. That is the simple meaning of these prosecutions, and nothing can be more just or more in accordance with common sense.' *Times*, 18 April 1868.

For a thorough discussion of the Judicial Committee of the Privy Council – including its establishment as the final court of appeal in ecclesiastical cases in the 1830s, the constitution of the court, and the rise of Ritualist opposition to it, cf. Marsh, *Victorian Church in Decline*, pp. 119-23.

35 The *Times* published a lengthy report of the meeting and the many resolutions and amendments discussed. *Times*, 13 Jan. 1869. 4,700 clergy signed a remonstrance to the archbishops and bishops questioning the judgment and calling on the episcopacy not to enforce the verdict. In his response, Archbishop Tait rejected their arguments and argued that the bishops had no discretion in the matter. Davidson, *Life of Tait, vol. 2*, pp. 96-100.

36 *Record*, 15 Jan. 1869. The Ritualists equally rejected any episcopal admonitions that appeared to be based on legal judgments. A writer in the *Quarterly Review* described the Ritualist view with a degree of sarcasm, 'It is assumed by the party that the directions or advice of their Bishops must always be contrary to the law; "sometimes," says Dr. Littledale, "the Bishop gets some worthless legal opinion on his side, and the priest, knowing better, treats it as waste paper".... It is clear that the opinions of lawyers are to be regarded only when in accordance with the wishes of the party.' Anon., 'Ultra-Ritualists,' *Quarterly Review*, pp. 154-55.

37 Cf. Balleine, *Evangelical Party*, p. 183. According to Desmond Bowen, the Purchas decision marked a turning point in the controversy; 'From now on those who persisted in such practices were regarded as law-breakers.' Nevertheless, the judgment was 'widely disobeyed... as being without spiritual authority; and the eastward position was maintained even in St. Paul's Cathedral.' Bowen, *Victorian Church*, p. 119.

A. O. J. Cockshut argued that the controversies of the age were exacerbated by the confusion over ecclesiastical authority. The High Church viewed the decisions of the courts in the cases of Gorham and *Essays and Reviews* as mistaken and refused to be bound by them, claiming an erastian intervention of the state. Given the confusion over spiritual and secular authority, and the often contradictory judgments of the courts, he argued that no decisions were final and most were viewed as non-binding. The result was an 'uneasy equilibrium.' The state issued judgments which the opposing clergy refused to obey. The state then largely ignored their disobedience. The ultimate result was the overthrow of the absolute power of the state 'without a revolution' and 'without a change of written principles, because it had come to seem to many people crushing and arbitrary.' Cockshut, *Anglican Attitudes*, pp. 48-49.

38 Aubrey Price, in a lecture for the CA, claimed the Ritualists had no ground for complaint when they were taken before the courts: 'Either observe the rules of the society, which gives you your position and your privileges, or otherwise leave, like an honest man, the society, and seek a home elsewhere. To the Ritualists, then, who charge us with Erastianism, we say, we are not surprised at your anger, but we are not going to be turned from our purpose by your hard words. We mean to hold you to the law, and we shall do this in what we believe to be the best interests of a society, which we conceive to be most useful to the nation as a whole; that is to say, the Established Church.' Aubrey Price, 'The Doctrines of Our Church Positive and Primitive; Ritualism Negative and Novel,' in *Church Association Lectures, 1869* (London: Hatchards, 1869), p. 126.

39 Interestingly, Owen Chadwick argued that the growth of Ritualism came in part from a strong 'historical consciousness' among the clergy concerned 'to find and obey lawful authority.' In Chadwick's view that tradition explained Ritualist concerns, from their interpretation, to fully comply with the rubrics. It does little, however, to account for their abuse of judges and bishops, except that they denied either constituted "lawful" authority whenever they opposed the Ritualists. Cf. Chadwick, *Victorian Church, Part Two*, pp. 315-17.

40 It was ruled that he did not technically disobey since the candles on the altar were extinguished prior to the communion service and the eucharistic elements were not elevated above his head. Only on the issue of prostration did they rule against Mackonochie. The judges emphasized their displeasure, however, by ruling in favor of the prosecution for the entirety of costs. *Record*, 6 Dec. 1869.

The *Quarterly Review* detailed at great length what it believed was 'the spirit of disingenuousness and evasion' to be found throughout the Ritualists' readings of the formularies, in their arguments before the court, and in their attempt to circumvent the rulings delivered against them. Anonymous, 'Ultra-Ritualists,' *Quarterly Review*, pp. 148-56.

41 The case was presented on the basis of affidavits filed from reports made by CA informants who were sent to the church to record the events between December 1869 and February 1870. Judgment of the Judicial Committee of the Privy Council, cited in the *Times*, 26 Nov. 1870.

42 Mackonochie's defense consisted of the argument that he had not raised the elements above his head, and in kneeling before the altar, his knee had not

actually touched the ground. Ibid.
43 *Record*, 25 Nov. 1870.
44 Letter to the *Record*, 7 Dec. 1870. Evangelicals were not alone in taking a dim view of Mackonochie's evasive measures. The *Times* wrote, 'Mr. Mackonochie has finally been condemned for elevating the elements and for prostrating himself before them during the Prayer of Consecration. The reader is aware that these two practices are the outward expression of the most distinctive doctrine of Ritualism; and it is for this reason Mr. Mackonochie has so persistently endeavoured to maintain them. For the sake of them he has descended to a multitude of shifts and evasions which would be dishonourable if they were not evidently fanatical.' *Times*, 29 Nov. 1870.

An essayist in *Fraser's Magazine* was similarly critical: 'To say "The Courts of Law have no right to meddle with me, and I will not give way to them one inch," would be intelligible and honourable. To say, "Though their right is doubtful, I will submit for the sake of peace on any non-essential matters," would be equally intelligible. But to profess to submit, and then to try by every variety of strained interpretation to make the supposed submission nugatory, is a course to which no gentleman would condescend in any other sphere of life. Somehow, in ecclesiastical questions all stratagems become sanctified; yet it is not pleasant to see this sort of sharp practice carried on upon such infinitesimal matters by our modern martyrs to the truth, and to remember that whilst these gentlemen are wrangling over chasubles, the outside world is seriously discussing whether Christianity has really anything to say for itself.' Anonymous, 'Mr. Voysey and Mr. Purchas,' *Fraser's Magazine* New Series, 3 (1871): p. 458.

The Ritualists were widely accused of dishonesty both in their innovations and in the defenses they offered for them as legitimate interpretations of the rubrics; cf. Reed, *Glorious Battle*, pp. 233-35.

45 '1. I believe the doctrine of the Real, Objective, Spiritual, and Heavenly Presence of Our Lord in the Holy Sacrament, as being as true as God is True.

'2. I believe it to be taught by the Church of England, as by all the rest of the Catholic Church from the beginning. I do not see how I could have the Catechism, the service for Holy Communion, or more than all, the Sacramental Articles, without believing it.

'3. I believe that it is the essence, the very life of the Church of England, that she is bound up in the life of her Lord, as being simply the same Church which he founded.' Letter to the *Record*, 12 Dec. 1870.

46 Ibid. The argument became apparently became a common one. In an 1881 essay condemning the Ritualists, the *Quarterly Review* rejected the suggestion that the church would be hurt if they and their supporters were driven to secede. They had already adopted a schismatic position, teaching doctrines that the church had rejected. At any rate, the writer concluded, the church had not driven out the Wesleyans as was commonly argued in support of toleration for the Ritualists. The Methodists had gradually changed their minds regarding the doctrines of the church and had departed on their own. They had, the writer suggested, at least done the honorable thing by leaving a church whose position they could no longer affirm. Anonymous,

'The Ritualists and the Law,' *Quarterly Review* 151 (1881): 211.

47   Ibid. Mackonochie stretched the comparison in order to make his point. In fact, Evangelicals and Ritualists had fundamentally different views of the priesthood. The controversy came, in essence, to focus on the meaning of the sacraments and the role of the clergy. For the Ritualists, he was a 'sacrificing priest' presiding over the eucharistic elements; in contrast, Evangelicals had a much lower view of the clergy as minister, emphasizing preaching as much as the administration of the sacraments. For a thorough view of the differences, cf. Bishop Samuel Waldegrave's charge to the clergy of Carlisle, *The Christian Ministry not Sacerdotal but Evangelistic* (London: W. Hunt & Co., 1867).

   Brian Heeney suggested, in his work on the professionalization of the clergy, that the idea of the clergy participating in a 'consecrated character' had become commonplace by the 1860s. It was shared by both High and Low Church, although each invested it with their own particular interest. Heeney, *Different Kind of Gentlemen*, pp. 11-12.

   With regard to the Ritualists' view of the priesthood, cf. the chapter entitled, 'Appeal to the Clergy,' in Reed, *Glorious Battle*, pp. 128-47. Reed suggested that the Ritualist movement was particularly attractive to younger clergy whose positions were less influential and whose futures were more likely to be threatened by the diminished place of the clergy in society during the second half of the nineteenth century.

48   The *Record* took note of the elaborate ritual used in the Christmas services at St. Alban's and concluded, 'The High Celebration seemed designed to show that the only result of the Church Association's proceedings against the incumbent will be to make St. Alban's more offensive to them than ever.' *Record*, 26 Dec. 1870.

49   *Times*, 8 Feb. 1872. The sequestration had little effect since Purchas had transferred all of his possessions into the names of his wife and children, a policy that other Ritualists were to follow; cf. Bentley, *Ritualism and Politics*, p. 81.

50   'It is stated that I officiate here on the Bishop's licence. That is not the case. His Lordship of course inducted me to the benefice of St. James's. I officiate here simply in virtue of a private Act of Parliament passed on that behalf.... Neither the Bishop nor the Privy Council have any right whatever to interfere with me – that is what I have always resisted – interference in my mode of conducting Divine service. So I shall continue to do, until they provide an Act of Parliament abrogating that, and making another in its stead. I do not suppose that will be the case, for that would be to confiscate my private property. I think you know my views in regard to the Privy Council. I entirely deny the power of a secular court to suspend a priest from his office. They may fine, but they cannot suspend. It is rumoured that this chapel will be closed. It will not be closed under any possible circumstances. The Privy Council may, if they like, imprison me. If they do the services will be carried on entirely (by my friends) and precisely as they are carried on now. And when they liberate me, I will repeat the services in every detail, just as I have done this evening. I will never acknowledge the power of the Privy Council to interfere with my right of conducting the service in any way I

please.' Cited in the *Record*, 26 Feb. 1872.
51 *Record*, 22 March 1872. The case was heard by the Privy Council in July. Purchas again refused to appear, and the judges, after deliberating for a brief time, determined that he should be suspended from both his office and benefice for twelve months. *Times*, 25 July 1872.

    A decade later, an essayist in the *Quarterly Review* suggested that the timidity of the Judicial Committee in the Purchas case was to blame for the escalation of the controversy. 'Finding no precedent for depriving a clergyman for persisting in disobedience (though it was not likely that there should be any, such rebellion being a perfectly new phenomenon), [they] were too timid to make one, and so merely brought themselves into more contempt, from Mr. Purchas at least, by suspending him for a year; which was as little attended to as the previous monition and all subsequent ones have been. That was the true cause of all the later troubles.' Rather than the much maligned Public Worship Regulation Act, the writer suggested that a simple bill enacting a penalty of deprivation for clergy found in contempt would have settled the matter. 'Surely rebellion deserves deprivation as much as heresy.' Anon, 'Ritualists and the Law,' *Quarterly Review*, p. 235.
52 By way of contrast, the *Record* published a sermon delivered by Rev. Paxton Hood in a Nonconformist chapel in Brighton. Hood doubted whether Purchas had been persecuted or could be considered a martyr. He had attempted to introduce rites into the church that were inconsistent with the established ceremony of the Anglican Church and had merely paid the price for his disobedience. Hood continued, 'John Purchas illustrated the magnanimity of private judgment; he was an Episcopalian, but he defied his Bishop; indeed, that is the first item of a Ritualistic creed, defy your Bishop. He was a State Churchman, but he defied the State, and with singular magnanimity broke the seals placed by the State when it interdicted his entrance to his church.' Cited in the *Record*, 4 Nov. 1872.
53 Archbishop Tait returned to the subject in his Visitation Charge of 1872. He rejected the Ritualist supposition that when the cases moved to the final court of appeal they somehow crossed an imaginary line dividing the sacred from the secular. In the post-Reformation era, he argued, the final appeal had always been to the Sovereign of the realm. Tait then turned to those who elevated their own personal judgment above the rulings of either bishop or court. 'I believe there are very few clergymen in this diocese who will differ from my views in this matter, but there may be a few, and we live in an age when a very few persons, by making themselves conspicuous, by talking very loudly, are able very often to make it appear that, though they are but a small minority, they are really a majority, and therefore the mischief that may be done even by a few persons acting in a lawless way, taking upon themselves to interpret where they ought to listen, may very infinitely injure the Church. Therefore I beg that all who are at all tempted to act in this lawless spirit will at once reflect carefully how wrong it is thus to act in a manner in which no humble man placed under authority can ever expect to act. I must beg to ask those clergymen who are in the habit of doing so that they will hereafter discontinue to introduce anything into the services of their churches which has no place in the Prayer-book or the Arti-

cles of the Church, or to decide as to what is the law of the Church of England, as they are not justified in such a course. Do not let it be supposed that I wish that we of the Church of England should be tied up hand and foot in some very narrow formularies.... but the persons to whom I allude are not satisfied with this wide range, but are determined to introduce from foreign communions practices which have no place in the custom or in the law of England.' Visitation Charge of the Archbishop of Canterbury, cited in the *Times*, 4 Oct. 1872.

According to Peter Marsh, the early cases pointed out the fundamental flaw in the policy of attempting to halt the Ritualists through the courts. It was expected that, once the law was clarified by the courts, it would be generally obeyed. But Purchas demonstrated the fallacy of that assumption. And it became evident that the only way to enforce obedience would be 'to prosecute each deviant.' Such action would be expensive, however, both in financial terms and in its impact on public opinion. Marsh, *Victorian Church in Decline*, p. 125.

54 The bishop noted that the decision had implications regarding the duties of both the clergy and the episcopacy, 'unless you have already altered certain ceremonies hitherto in use in your church.' He invited the prominent Ritualists to confer with him at London House; 'I should much prefer the meeting to be private, as a friendly conversation; but if, on consultation with the other clergy invited, you should wish to bring a legal adviser with you, I shall not object, provided that you inform me in good time.' Correspondence cited in the *Record*, 4 April 1870.

55 The paper reported that Bishop Jackson had invited 'the five clergymen in whose churches Ritualism is most fully developed to meet him – viz., the Rev. C. F. Lowder, Vicar of St. Peter's, London Docks; the Rev. John Going, Vicar of St. Paul's, Walworth; the Rev. D. Nihill, Vicar of St. Michael and All Angels, Shoreditch; the Rev. C. J. LeGeyt, Vicar of St. Mathias, Stoke Newington; and the Rev. A. H. Mackonochie, Vicar of St. Alban's, Holborn. Subsequently many other clergymen were invited.' According to the paper, the bishop intended to enforce 'the prohibition of the notices of high celebration of the Holy Eucharist; the ceremonial mixing water with the wine at the Holy Communion; the elevation of the paten and the cup; the ringing of a bell at the time of consecration and elevation; making the sign of a cross when about to mix water with the wine; wearing stoles and dalmatics at the Communion Service; using lighted candles on the Communion table during celebration; the ceremonial use of lighted candles at other times; using incense for censing persons and things; processions round the church with thurifers, incense vessels, crucifixes, and candles; leaving the Holy Table uncovered on Good Friday; blessing of candles, &c. The points which the Bishop proposes to leave untouched for the present are those on which Sir Robert Phillimore decided against the promoter of the suit. They are as follows: – The vases of flowers on the Holy Table, regarding which the Dean of Arches said there was no evidence to prove that they had been used as an additional rite or ceremony; administration of wine and water mixed; standing in front of the Holy Table, with back to the people during the prayer of Consecration; the use of wafer bread; wearing a chasuble at the

Communion Service; wearing tunicles and albs at the Communion Service; wearing a biretta.' *Times*, 4 April 1870.

56   The Purchas judgment especially brought out the ire of the paper, since it appeared Evangelicals might be forced to adopt the surplice while the Ritualists went unpunished. *Record*, 18 May 1870.

57   Reprinted in the *Times*, 13 April 1871; cf. Appendix B. Peter Marsh suggested that many of those who signed the remonstrance apparently had no intention of defying the courts but 'were repelled by the CA's aggressiveness and afraid of the threat the judgment contained to historic High Churchmanship.' Marsh, *Victorian Church in Decline*, pp. 127-8.

58   Jackson's letter was addressed to the Rev. R. Temple West, Incumbent of St. Mary Magdalene, Paddington, but he sent copies to all incumbents in the diocese who had signed the remonstrance. He wrote, 'I may, of course, be in error; but the responsibility of the error (if such it be) rests properly on me, and is one of the inherent burdens of my office. You, if you accept my ruling, are free from all such responsibility, especially if you accept it for duty's sake in opposition to your own judgment, and in spite of your own strong convictions. Such a sacrifice of self – one, perhaps, of the most difficult – is never made without a blessing.

  'But on those who take a different course, even if their judgment on the matter in dispute is right – much more if it should prove to be wrong – there must lie a very heavy responsibility. They must contravene the first principles of episcopacy and indeed of all good government, by limiting their obedience to such rules and guidance as happen to coincide with their own opinions or feelings.' Correspondence cited in the *Times*, 22 May 1871.

  Archbishop Tait took a similar position in a letter to the remonstrants. He wrote, 'Again, I feel myself at a loss quite to understand the request, which upon the supposition, as I apprehend your meaning, that final judgment has been delivered, you make to the Bishops, "that they should abstain from acting upon this decision," being certain that you do not so estimate the Bishop's office as to consider it superior to the law, and that you will at once acknowledge with me that the chief pastors of our Church are of all men the very last who ought to be requested to set to this nation the example of refusing obedience to the highest tribunals.' While adamant that eucharistic vestments had to be abandoned, Tait did attempt to soften the blow of the judgment with regard to the eastward position. And he affirmed that the ruling would not lead to a 'tyrannical interference' with the liberties of the clergy. Correspondence cited in the *Times*, 13 April 1871; cf. Marsh, *Victorian Church in Decline*, p 128.

59   An essayist in the *Quarterly Review* considered this point in an article published in 1874. 'As to any reasoning with the promoters of the system, grounded solely on the recognised laws of the English Church, and the example of her divines of various schools, it has long been obvious that it is totally useless.... For the Book of Common Prayer, and for Anglicanism, as such, they care nothing. By their own avowals, they have quite a different teacher, to which they go for instruction, and to which they appeal as being *in foro conscientiae* immeasurably superior to the English Church, in its claims to obedience. This teacher is a certain phantom, which they call "The

Catholic Church." Not that the true Catholic Church is a phantom. It is only the Catholic Church, as venerated by the Ritualists, which is a phantom. With an audacious eclecticism they pick out from the practices of modern Rome just those portions which fall in with their personal wishes, treating Rome itself as a living institution, that is, as a reality, with the same contemptuous indifference with which they treat the English Church herself. They care as little for the actual laws of one Church as for those of the other.' Anonymous, 'Sacerdotalism, Ancient and Modern,' *Quarterly Review* 136 (1874): 106.

James Bentley suggested that the Ritualists viewed themselves as the true 'representatives of the supernatural, universal, and eternal Catholic Church. Since no human authority could override this Church, whoever opposed their activities was bound to be wrong.' Bentley, *Ritualism and Politics*, p. 24.

60 *Record*, 28 June 1871.
61 Correspondence cited in the *Record*, 11 Aug. 1871. A. P. Stanley, writing from a Broad Church perspective, thought there was little hope for a revision of the rubrics, and in any case, the church had never enforced complete obedience. Consequently he argued that legal sanction ought to be given to widely prevailing practices, so long as they were approved by the bishop. He believed, perhaps somewhat naively, that allowing for variations of practice would put an end to the more extreme innovations and that the episcopal admonitions would thereafter be obeyed. A. P. Stanley, 'How Shall We Deal with the Rubrics?' *Contemporary Review* 23 (1873-74): 492-93.
62 *Record*, 16 Aug. 1871. The paper reported on a similar case in 1873, involving Bishop Goodwin of Carlisle. The churchwardens of the parish of Wetheral, forwarded to the bishop a memorial signed by 165 parishioners protesting innovations made by the rector, W. Blake. These included flowers and decorations, lighted candles and a cross on the altar, use of the eastward position, the chanting of the psalms and a surpliced choir. After corresponding with Blake, the bishop replied that the rector had been able to explain all of the changes except the eastward position. Goodwin replied that he had admonished the rector accordingly. He also suggested that some who had signed the protest might have been led astray by a vocal minority. In any case, he gave his full support to Blake: 'You must bear in mind that while on the one hand rash innovation is to be avoided, and innovation which is false to the Church of England is to be detested, yet on the other it is the clergyman's duty to order Divine Service according to his judgment of what is best, and not to be content with slovenly arrangements which may have satisfied our fathers, if he thinks that improvement is practicable.' Correspondence cited in the *Record*, 30 July 1873.

For fervent anti-Ritualists, any episcopal attempt to arrive at a peaceful settlement of controversy was interpreted as compromise. T. H. Paddon complained that there could never be any 'compromise between believers and unbelievers.' And insofar as that was the policy of the bishops, said Paddon, the laity of the church were 'betrayed' by their leaders and the days of the establishment were numbers. It was the 'miserable policy of compromise and concession' that had allowed the Ritualists to gain power in the church. In Paddon's view, the Evangelical laity should unite with Protestant Dissenters to oppose the Ritualists and save the Reformed heritage of the nation. He also thought they should support lay preaching to limit the further growth of clericalism. T. H. Paddon, *Thoughts for the Christian Laity* (London: William Macintosh, 1873), pp. 19-20.

63 Correspondence cited in the *Times*, 4 Aug. 1870.
64 Ibid.
65 The letter was forwarded to the *Times* for publication by Bishop Jackson. *Times*, 11 Jan. 1871.
66 When parishioners of St. George's, Wolverhampton, complained to Bishop Selwyn of Lichfield regarding the vicar's adoption of the surplice, Selwyn thanked them for their concern but affirmed his belief that its used had been 'fully established by law.' Correspondence cited in the *Record*, 18 Feb. 1870.
67 Cited in the *Record*, 1 June 1870. Bishop Fraser was responding to a dispute in the parish of St. Jems's, Accrington, between Rev. J. Rogers and some of the parishioners. The protesters were opposed to flowers on the communion table, the publication of banns of marriage after the second lesson and the wearing of the surplice in the pulpit. Fraser believed the first was legal but not necessarily expedient, and thought the second a matter of little importance. Regarding the surplice, he expressed his opinion that Phillimore's ruling prescribed the surplice as the only legal attire for the officiating minister. But in such matters, he did not believe it appropriate to alter established custom 'without good reason or against the wishes of the congregation.' *Record*, 8 June 1870.
68 *Fraser's Magazine*, while quite critical of the Ritualists, particularly in regard to their lawlessness, suggested that the movement presented little real threat to Protestants. 'There never was a period at which the claims of sacerdotal authority were more contemptible to the bulk of the English people. The various causes which have led to the efflorescence of the sacerdotal theory in recent times might deserve examination, though their general nature is obvious enough; but whatever the opinions of a certain number of sentimental ladies and weak-minded clergy, this is not a time at which an English clergyman can come forward and say, 'I am a supernaturally authorised ambassador from Heaven, and demand your humble submission,' with much chance of being respected beyond the limits of his own little clique.' Anon., 'Voysey and Purchas,' *Fraser's Magazine*, p. 467.
69 The paper cited the cases of A. W. Thorold, William Cadman and 'other clergy.' *Record*, 22 Jan. 1872. In January 1872, representatives of the Clerical and Lay Union of London sent a resolution protesting the surplice to the archbishops. The resolution, offered by J. C. Ryle, met with some vocal opposition in discussion, but only five participants voted against it. It read, in part: 'That the general adoption of the surplice as the pulpit dress, before the legality of such dress is duly established by law, is highly inexpedient, inasmuch as it is a departure from long-established usage, is contrary to the recommendation of the Ritual Commission, and is not desired by the laity; and furthermore is likely to give grave offence to many congregations and to disturb the peace of the Church.' Cited in the *Record*, 2 Feb. 1872.

70 The division among Evangelicals was evident when Francis Close, Dean of Carlisle and himself a fervent anti-Ritualist, responded to a letter criticizing the bishop's charge. Close thought it a matter of little concern that should be left to the judgment of the individual clergy: 'In one case it may be desirable to use the gown, in another the surplice. The character and disposition of the congregation, and that of the minister personally, may lead to different conclusions; and at all events, I think it unwise to make this a party question, and one upon which we ought to act collectively. The bishop leaves us a considerable margin for difference of opinion and practice in this matter, and we may hamper each other's conscientious liberty by interfering with individual action. ' Letter to the *Record*, 12 July 1872.

71 W. E. Gladstone made the point in an 1874 essay: 'from a view of the modes which have become usual for the celebration of Divine service, in average churches not saddled with a party name, there appears this rather startling fact, that the congregations of the Church of England in general now practise without suspicion, and the Parliament, representing the general feeling out of doors, is disposed to enforce, by the establishment of more stringent procedure, what thirty years ago was denounced, and rather more than denounced, as Ritualism.' Gladstone, 'Ritualism and Ritual,' *Contemporary Review*, p. 671.

72 The spreading influence went far beyond the bounds of the Church of England. In a letter regarding the need for Anglican Evangelicals to unite with like-minded Dissenters, one correspondent wrote, 'I am assured by eminent Dissenters that there is among their people an increasing desire for liturgical worship.' Given this fact and their common theological positions, the author hoped that the way would soon be paved for a comprehension that would enable them to rejoin the established church and strengthen the Evangelical voice. Letter to the *Record*, 11 April 1860.

Gladstone noted of the movement's influence outside the Church of England: 'It has been, when all things are considered, quite as remarkable among Nonconformists and Presbyterians; not because they have as much of it, but because they formerly had none, and because their system appeared to have been devised and adjusted in order to prevent its introduction.... Crosses on the outside of chapels, organs within them, rich painted architecture, that flagrant piece of symbolism, the steeple, windows filled with subjects in stained glass, elaborate chanting, the use of the Lord's Prayer, which is no more than the thin end of the wedge that is to introduce fixed forms, and the partial movements in favour of such forms already developed, are among the signs which, taken altogether, form a group of phenomena evidently referable to some cause far more deep and wide-working than mere servile imitation, or the fashion of the day.... True the distance between these Presbyterian and Nonconforming services, and those of the Church of England, in point of ritual, remains as great, or perhaps greater than, before; but that is because one and the same forward movement has taken possession of both, only the speeds may be different.... In truth, there is a kind of ritual race; all have set their faces the same way, and none like to have their relative backwardness enhanced, while the absolute standing-point is continually moved forward.' Gladstone, 'Ritualism and Ritual,'

Contemporary Review, p. 671-72.
   Gladstone was apparently repeating a claim commonly made by the Ritualists regarding their own influence. Critics, however, had already challenged the argument several years prior to Gladstone's essay. The *Edinburgh Review* suggested that there were two causes. The first was a 'vast wave of antiquarian, artistic, architectural, romantic sentiment' that was sweeping all over Europe and had a permanent and reasonable influence on all denominations. Nonconformists met in 'buildings which their forefathers would have regarded only as the fit shrines of apostasy and idolatry.' The second influence was the Ritualist, but the author argued that it was 'local and temporary' and frequently elevated doctrines and practices that were 'repugnant to the feelings and the sense of the great mass of educated men in civilised Christendom.' The Ritualists were, in fact, only one small part of a 'great secular movement which they seem to deprecate.' Anon., 'Ritualism,' *Edinburgh Review*, pp. 442-43.
   Gladstone's idea was elaborated by Dale Johnson, who took a broader approach and dealt with the influence of the Oxford Movement in general. In one section, however, he concentrated specifically on the Ritualist influence on Nonconformist architecture and worship; cf. Dale A. Johnson, 'The Oxford Movement and English Nonconformity,' *Anglican and Episcopal History* 59 (1990): 83-88.
73 On the impact of the Ritualists through their hymnody, cf. Reed, *Glorious Battle*, pp. 73-74.
74 Letter to the *Record*, 4 Feb. 1861.
75 Ibid. The spreading influence could also be seen in a letter from the pastor of 'a somewhat fashionable congregation,' who wrote for advice. Some of his people desired a choir 'of young ladies' and had petitioned the church wardens to alter the musical arrangements. The pastor wanted to know if he had ultimate authority in such matters. He was willing to yield wherever possible, but was afraid that having once permitted the choir 'we shall have all sorts of newfangled Psalm-tunes and chants introduced which nobody but the self-appointed choir will be able to sing.' Letter to the *Record*, 28 June 1861. Numerous respondents, in the following issues, informed the pastor that he had final authority in how the service was to be conducted, and the church wardens had no control over the matter. This was somewhat ironic given the fact that the early years of the controversy often saw Evangelical church wardens taking positions against the innovations introduced by their Ritualist pastors and doing everything they could to reverse the situation.
76 This beautiful element of worship was 'most miserably perverted,' thought the paper, by the use of singers and instruments that turned the church into a concert hall. The duty of choirs was to lead the congregation and not to perform on their own. The principle of the Tractarians, the paper concluded, seemed to be that nothing ought to be said if it could be sung instead. *Record*, 13 Feb. 1861.
   In 1863, the paper published an anonymous letter that criticized an advertisement for the Lichfield Cathedral choir in which they offered to present 'a full cathedral service' or selections of secular music in parish

churches while the cathedral was closed for cleaning. The correspondent was concerned that such a use of music served only to amuse the congregation and turn them into mere observers. 'In all of this we cannot but see and lament its papal tendency. We are losing in choral services and decorated altars the simplicity and devotion of Protestant worship, and the expectations of the Papists are excited that we shall come over to a Church that can boast of richer music and better performances.' Letter to the *Record*, 12 Aug. 1863.

77 The correspondent argued that there was no excuse for continuing to use 'unsingably bad music' when there was a collection such as *Hymns Ancient and Modern*, 'wherein are found nearly all the old English tunes of any real worth, together with a number of good modern ones.' He acknowledged that some of the lyrics were 'rank Popery,' but nevertheless thought the use of the hymnal had greatly improved the worship at his church. The *Record*, in reply, could not understand how he could justify the use of a hymnal that propagated Romanism. Letter (signed 'A Lancaster Presbyter') in the *Record*, 24 Oct. 1864.

78 He concluded, 'A reformation in the music and singing is greatly needed in the churches of our land where the Gospel is preached. Let us, in this, follow the example of the High Church party, and not refuse to use the attractive power which good music and singing possess.' Ibid.

79 One anonymous correspondent expressed concern that the younger clergy were left puzzled when they saw what was happening in the Evangelical churches. What were they to think when they saw their elders in the ministry 'using *Hymns Ancient and Modern* and having too much congregational music' in their churches, as well as employing curates who were not 'Evangelical to the backbone?' Were the younger clergy to infer from this that Evangelicalism had been 'too uncompromising' or that its 'tone' ought to made less distinct?' Letter (signed 'A Young Clergyman) to the *Record*, 3 Feb. 1865. This letter was rather an anomaly in that Ritualism usually made its greatest inroads among the younger generation and was more stridently resisted by the older.

80 Cited in the *Record*, 27 Sept. 1865.

81 Ibid. The paper also published several letters criticizing Close; cf. *Record*, 4 Oct. 1865.

82 It was widely noted that the High Church revival was chiefly influential among the younger clergy, beginning with the Oxford Movement and continuing with the development of Ritualism. In his 1846 pamphlet, William Gresley proclaimed in a triumphalist tone that the High Church movement was attracting thousands of the clergy, including 'the most zealous and learned, and, what is much to be considered, the youngest.... The rising generation at our Universities is deeply embued with them.' Gresley, *Real Danger of the Church*, p. 4.

One strident anti-Ritualist drew an analogy to the story of Adam and Eve; Satan tempted Eve first, knowing that women had 'the weaker spirit.' And ever since, 'his agents, the workers of priestcraft in every age and country, adopt his tactics, and make women the special subjects of their ambitious designs.' The author was uncertain, however, who tempted whom in most cases. Rather than charging the Ritualists with deception, he suggested that women were often responsible for attempting to decorate the church with flowers, fine millinery and music, and were often able to entice young, inexperienced clergy 'and so get possession of the Church for the exercise of her sensuous proclivities.' The young curate, attempting to satisfy his 'religious yearnings,' was led along a downward path with 'visions of sacerdotal power and importance' that were encouraged by misguided women whose urgings contained 'more romance than reason, and more poetry than prudence.' Anonymous, *Women and Priests* (London: Haughton & Co., [1878?]), pp. 2-4, 14-15.

A writer in the *Contemporary Review* took a similar position, but with the altogether different purpose of suggesting that the Ritualists ought to be allowed a great degree of latitude. The opponents of Ritualism, he suggested, ought not to forget 'how strongly the current is setting at present in favour of a religious system which shall not exclude the help which the love of the beautiful in form, and colour, and music, may give, within its proper sphere, as the handmaid of religious worship. It is certain that where there are any habits at all of hearty religious devotion in the *young men and women* of our day, the preference for musical services and richly decorated churches, and a tone of thought alien from dogmatic Protestantism, is usually very decided. This is the case not only in the upper and middle classes, but increasingly in the lower classes of society also.... And if this be so, it is obvious that it would not be well to alienate the mind of the rising generation from the Church, and probably from religion, – at least in any Protestant form, – by any harsh or violent measures of repression.... A large indulgence should be shown to all which is not unmistakably tainted by the intention to imitate a ritual founded upon and giving expression to a belief which has been solemnly repudiated by the English Church for three centuries past.' Vaughan, 'Commission on Ritual,' *Contemporary Review*, pp. 69-70 (his italics).

For a survey of the attraction the movement held for women, cf. John Shelton Reed's chapter on 'Women and Anglo-Catholicism,' in Reed, *Glorious Battle*, pp. 186-209; on aestheticism and the idea of a 'manly Protestantism,' cf. pp. 216-21.

83 'Although the church is situated in a very poor neighbourhood the congregation is by no means composed of humble persons. Some evidently belong to decidedly fashionable society, while scarcely any are below a very respectable middle class. The spirit of devotion that pervades the whole assembly is remarkable, and foremost, perhaps, among the devotees are young men of 19 or 20 years of age, who seem to have the intricacies of ritualism at their fingers' ends. Yesterday morning the church was completely filled, the male and female portions of the congregation being apparently equal to each other.' *Times*, 27 Aug. 1866.

Malcolm MacColl gave voice to the Ritualist argument in an 1871 essay in which he suggested that the heart was reached through 'the imagination and feelings' rather than by reason. This explained, thought MacColl, the movement's appeal to 'the young and the uneducated.' Malcolm MacColl, 'The Rationale of Ritualism,' *Contemporary Review*, 17 (1871), p. 179.

84 *Times*, 20 Aug. 1867. In an 1874 article defending Ritualism, Gladstone noted that many of its proponents were drawn from the wealthier classes, and he suggested that the movement's appeal was not entirely a matter of spiritual concerns. He made reference to 'the vast amount of new made wealth in the country,' those who expected their churches and services to have a degree of refinement and ornament. 'It is quite possible that no small part of what we call the improvements in fabrics and in worship may be due simply to the demand of the richer man for a more costly article, and thus may represent not the spiritual growth but the materializing tendencies of the age.' W. E. Gladstone, 'Ritualism and Ritual,' *Contemporary Review*, p. 677.

Queen Victoria expressed her dismay in letter to Gladstone, concerning the number of young clergy who were falling under the Ritualist influence. She thought them particularly 'self-willed and defiant.' *The Letters of Queen Victoria*, Second Series, Vol. 2, ed. George E. Buckle (London: John Murray, 1926), p. 302. Victoria was equally opposed to extreme High Church and Evangelical appointments, and favored moderates; cf. Chadwick, *Victorian Church, Part Two*, pp. 335-37.

James Bentley also noted the wealthy background of many of the young Ritualist clergy and suggested that it accounted for some of their audacity. They were mostly Oxford or Cambridge graduates, and many could count on influential family connections. Such a social background accounted, in part, for their self-assurance. Bentley, *Ritualism and Politics*, pp. 23-4. From a different perspective, however, John Shelton Reed suggested that the appeal of the Ritualist movement for young clergy lay in its elevation of the priesthood, particularly at a time when suffered from decreasing influence in secular society. Reed noted, that the Ritualists were mostly younger and held positions that were less financially secure. In general, he found that the members of the CA were older and held higher-paying incumbencies than did members of the ECU. Cf. Reed, *Glorious Battle*, pp. 128-333, and Appendix 2, p. 269.

85 'We believe these practices, if persevered in, would alienate a large proportion of the middle class from the Church of England.... "Society" looks with toleration or sympathy on Ritualism as rather a pretty thing, and on Ritualists as a cultivated class of clericals, who, if they have not much real intellectual power, are, in some cases, men of taste and a certain sort of learning. But "Society" generally takes the wrong view of things, and is, moreover, always powerless to protect any institution which is assailed by the multitude below.' The paper was certain a revolt would soon follow if the extreme Ritualists were allowed to continue. The 'farmers, tradespeople and artisans' would not silently allow their church to be transformed. *Times*, 20 Aug. 1867.

86 W. F. Taylor complained that the Ritualists, with their desires for reunion with Rome, were a threat to the establishment and even to the independence of the nation. If allowed to proceed unchecked, they would sooner or later 'disgust the people of England with the national Church.' Taylor continued, 'I believe that the Church of England is in many places losing the affections of the people.' The English masses would never return

to Rome, and to the degree that the Ritualists succeeded, they would be driven from the church. Taylor, 'Ritualism,' in *Church Association Lectures, 1869*, pp. 77-80.

87   At a CA conference, Edward Auriol suggested that one of their great objects ought to be the prevention among the younger clergy of that vagueness which prevailed concerning the distinctive principles of the Church of England. 'To say, as so many of the younger clergy did, "We belong to no party," was to say, in effect, "We have no distinctive principles".' Cited in the *Record*, 13 Oct. 1869.

The influence of Ritualism can be seen indirectly in evidence gathered by Wesley Balda. In his survey of clergy holding parishes through the Simeon Trust, he noted that there were a number who introduced moderate innovations into their churches. And despite the Evangelical nature of the organization, it took no steps to discipline them or determine the direction of their work. Wesley Balda, '"Simeon's Protestant Papists": A Sampling of Moderate Evangelicals within the Church of England, 1839-1865,' *Fides et Historia* 16 (1983): 58-59.

88   Cited in the *Record*, 18 Jan. 1867. Several years later, the *Record* described Wilson's reputation as 'the character of combining with a large heart a somewhat rigid and unbending theology, and a stiff adherence to Evangelical traditions, which unfriendly critics are apt to describe as narrowness of view.' By 1872, however, the paper thought it detected a broadening of his perspective. *Record*, 19 Jan. 1872.

Wilson's perspective, however, was not unique to Evangelicals. A writer in the *Quarterly Review*, while criticizing the Ritualist claim that their innovations attracted the poor and uneducated to the church, expressed a similar perspective: 'No doubt this is one way to fill a church; but so, as has been truly said, will any sort of eccentricity in the minister; and surely it is a degrading thing to rest our cause on pompous displays in which we might easily be surpassed by paganism.' Anon., 'Ultra-Ritualism,' *Quarterly Review*, p. 204.

Malcolm MacColl claimed that the 'simple worship' of most English churches, and particularly those particularly influenced by 'the Puritanical coldness and baldness,' was largely responsible for driving the poor away from the national church. He continued, 'Give them a bright service – something that interests their eyes and ears, cheerful sights and joyful sounds – something that shall penetrate the crust of their seeming apathy, and touch their feelings; give the poor a worship of this sort, and they will gladly flock back to the churches which now know them not.' MacColl, 'Rationale of Ritualism,' *Contemporary Review*, p. 191.

D. W. Bebbington gave a brief survey, along with some examples, of Ritualist innovations that were being increasingly appropriated by Evangelicals. Interestingly, he cited Daniel Wilson as an example, as Wilson was one who adopted the 8 a.m. communion service. Bebbington, *Evangelicalism in Modern Britain*, pp. 147-49.

Donald Lewis wrote of the Islington Clerical Conference, which had been established in 1828, 'These meetings quickly became an important focal point for many Evangelical clergy and were the closest Evangelical approximation to a national party conference.' They were presided over first by Daniel Wilson, Sr., and after he became Bishop of Calcutta, by his son, Daniel Wilson, Jr. Lewis, *Lighten Their Darkness*, p. 5.

89 Cited in the *Record*, 14 Oct. 1867. Four years later, however, Ryle was willing to give a little more credit to the Ritualists. He noted that they were widely praised for the revival of church music, although he was unwilling to concede the point entirely, suggesting that Evangelicals of the eighteenth century really deserved much of the credit. Nevertheless, he concluded that Evangelicals rarely gave sufficient emphasis to music. 'Be the cause what it may, the singing of Evangelical congregations, as a matter of fact, is often sadly inferior to that of Ritualistic congregations. Unhappily there are scores of churches where you will hear a very good sermon, and very poor, slovenly singing.' Cited in the *Record*, 14 April 1871.

George Henry Sumner took an even more moderate position in response to MacColl's essay defending Ritualism. In Sumner's view, there was no point in debating the fact that ritual was useful in teaching spiritual truths. 'The mind of man,' he wrote, 'is so constituted that for the purposes of intercourse with his Maker there must be a certain amount of Ritualism. In this sense we are all ritualists. It is only a question of degree.' The question was, for Sumner, what doctrines were taught by the ritual in use? 'There must be identity of purpose between the symbol and the institution the purposes of which it is intended to subserve. Here it is that from our point of view Ritualism fails to stand the test applied to it. The vestments, incense, genuflexions, *et hoc genus omne*, are not ends in themselves. They are one and all intended to convey doctrines which anti-Ritualists deem foreign to the spirit of our English Church.' George Henry Sumner, 'The Rationale of Anti-Ritualism,' *Contemporary Review* 17 (1871), pp. 541-42.

90 'Trusting to the continuation of emotions which in their nature cannot continue,' he wrote, 'they have forgotten the importance of associating the thought of worship with joy, beauty, brightness; of enlisting, as far as may be, the willing services of men, women, and children in ministering to its completeness.... And so, in many cases (I gladly acknowledge a marked improvement of late years both as to the architecture of the churches they have built and the choral element of worship), their *cultus* has been heavy, flat, uninviting; and those whom they did not supply with wholesome food have drifted off (I can scarcely blame them) in search of something to satisfy cravings which are in themselves natural and innocent, and cannot safely be neglected.' Plumptre, 'Church Parties,' *Contemporary Review*, pp. 330-31.

91 Thorold continued, 'To confound good music, and even a surpliced choir, with either Romanism or Ritualism is not only foolish, but it is unfair. I would not in the least advise that we should push for anything of this kind; my own personal preference is for the greatest possible simplicity, that is compatible with hearty, solemn, and reverent worship. But let us have liberty in the matter to exercise our own judgment, without thereby compromising ourselves as sound teachers and good Protestants. All I wish to maintain is, that if our congregations want these things, and are ready to pay for them, why should we refuse?' Thorold, 'Evangelical Clergy,' *Contemporary Review*, p. 589.

The *Times* took a similarly conciliatory view, suggesting that minor innovations were often much needed improvements. The paper continued, 'There is no doubt that the general introduction of music and of a more impressive ritual has greatly increased at once the decorousness and the attractiveness of Church services. But there is a total difference between the musical service which was the extreme limit of Anglicanism a few years ago and the recent Ritualistic innovations.' *Times*, 19 Oct. 1866.

92 Wilson was still unwilling to compromise on Ritualist practices, 'I do not hesitate to say that if the devotional services of our Liturgy, and the bold, faithful preaching of the Gospel, do not serve to fill my church, nothing would induce me to sharpen my weapons at the Philistine's forge.' Cited in the *Record*, 20 Jan. 1871.

93 Ibid.

94 Ibid.

95 Ibid. The spirit Miller most feared was evident in an exchange of letters in the *Record* in 1873. C. H. Collette wrote regarding Ritualist innovations in Ventnor, Isle of Wight, where he spent his summer vacation. He claimed that Dissenting chapels were filled with those who had been driven from the parish church. He complained to Bishop Browne of Winchester and threatened to publish the correspondence if the bishop did not take action. When the bishop refused, Collette chastised him in the pages of the popular press. Letter to the *Record*, 27 Oct. 1873. George W. Sheppard wrote to defend the Rector of Holy Trinity, Ventnor: 'The hearty manner in which the congregation join in this portion of the service appears to prove that their taste differs from that of your correspondent; at all events, all is simple and congregational.' More to the point, however, Sheppard protested against the tone of Collette's letter: 'I venture, Sir, to ask whether it is just that a church in which neither vestments, incense, nor lights on the altar are used, and in which the only things savouring of Ritualism (and they are those which we of the opposite party may well borrow therefrom) are the careful observance of the holy-days appointed by our Prayer-book and frequent and well-attended celebrations of the Holy Communion, should be branded in the columns of the *Record* with "Ritualistic heresy"?' Following Sheppard's letter was another from an anonymous writer who criticized the paper for even printing a letter written in the tone used by Collette when addressing a bishop of high character. 'I cannot but feel it must have been through some exceptional failure of editorial supervision that your paper has been made the vehicle of anything like discourtesy.' Letters to the *Record*, 3 Nov. 1873.

96 At the Islington Conference the following year, J. C. Ryle, himself no stranger to controversy and a vocal supporter of the Church Association, spoke on the topic 'Can a greater unity be obtained among zealous and pious Churchmen of different schools of thought?' Ryle took a position similar to Miller's and affirmed that Evangelicals needed to recognize 'the grace of God and love to Christ' in others. Many 'who were wrong in their head were right in their heart.' This necessitated, said Ryle, that they 'cultivate the habit of speaking charitably and courteously of those who disagreed with them.' Like Miller, Ryle realized this might offend some fervent

controversialists, but he believed there was no place for 'the use of uncivil and discourteous language.' In order to develop this new spirit, Ryle suggested they 'should cultivate opportunities of meeting men of other schools on neutral ground' such as those provided by congresses and synods. Unnecessary prejudices, he believed, could best be dispelled by meeting one's opponents face to face. *Record*, 19 Jan. 1872.

According to Eugene Stock, Ryle, Edward Garbett, and Edward Hoare led the moderate section and were increasingly criticized by conservative anti-Ritualists, especially in the pages of the *Rock*, a penny paper of the extreme section. 'The three canons' were repeatedly denounced as traitors of the Evangelical party, and the term Neo-Evangelical was coined as a pejorative term by their opponents. Stock, *Church Missionary Society, vol. 3*, p. 9.

97 The paper thought it an emotional appeal: 'Instead of raising the unmanly cry of persecution, they should rather accept the position as a natural consequence of their course, and be prepared to meet the investigation which they have courted.' *Record*, 4 Dec. 1867.

Evangelicals were not alone in their criticism of the Ritualists in this regard. A writer in the *Quarterly Review* noted that the Ritualists boasted that the law was on their side and dared their opponents to take them before the courts, but he thought their rhetoric disingenuous. 'No doubt this sort of vapouring looks very courageous; but surely even the persons who indulge in it must understand that there is no equality of terms between themselves and those to whom their defiances are thrown out. It costs a ritualist nothing to perform a feat which he knows or suspects to be illegal; but the illegality of it cannot be brought home to him until after long delay and much anxiety, at a frightful cost of money, and at the risk of incurring the odium which is popularly attached to everything that can be represented as persecution.' Anon., 'Ultra-Ritualism,' *Quarterly Review*, p. 181.

Charles Bury, in his defense of the CA, noted that the Ritualists, in defying the admonitions of the episcopacy, had steadfastly maintained the legality of their innovations. How then, he asked, could it be considered persecution when the CA appealed to the courts for a legal interpretation? Bury, *Church Association*, p. 9.

98 Cited in the *Record*, 15 Oct. 1869. In an 1873 pamphlet following the Bennett Judgment, J. Guinness Rogers touched on the subject from a Nonconformist perspective. He noted that Ritualists referred to the CA as the 'Joint-stock Persecution Association Limited.' 'The truth is,' he wrote, 'the Church is either meant to have a restrictive law, or it is not. If it is not, why is there an Act of Uniformity, and why are any excluded? If there is a law, what persecution is there in applying it? A man who should attempt to hold a living and assume the cure of souls without Episcopal orders would be very soon brought under the law, and we do not apprehend there would be any complaints of persecution if he was deprived. Why, then, should indulgence be shown to those who teach a false doctrine, a doctrine subversive of the essential principles of the Church's faith?... Their course is not ours, but then we have no faith in the power of the law for the promotion of spiritual truth. But a State Church is the creation of the law, and we cannot see how its defenders can consistently object to those who seek to assert the author-

ity of the law in it.' J. Guinness Rogers, *The Bennett Judgment and Recent Episcopal Charges* (London: Hodder & Stoughton, 1873), pp. 18-19.

According to Bury, it was the Ritualist paper, the *Church Times*, that referred to the CA as 'The Persecution Society, Ltd.' Bury, in the second chapter of his work, dealt with the 'character' of the CA and refuted the major arguments used to support the charge of persecution. Cf. Bury, *Church Association*, pp. 11-17.

99 Bury, in his history of the CA, which was written in 1873, listed 44 points regarding which the courts had ruled against the Ritualists. These ranged from the more prominent and important points raised during the Mackonochie and Purchas cases, to the more obscure and tangential such as '43. Figure of the Infant Saviour with lilies over the credence-table at Christmas' and '44. Stuffed Dove over the Holy Table on Whitsunday.' Bury, *Church Association*, pp. 20-4.

100 Cited in the *Record*, 25 Feb. 1870. Ryle elsewhere noted that the CA was 'very unpopular' with some. Their opponents considered them 'a narrow-minded, illiberal, and exclusive body,' but Ryle argued they merely desired to establish the proper limits of the church's comprehensiveness. And he maintained that the church 'never intended to include within her pale men who contradict her Articles and teach downright Popery.' Ryle, 'Archbishop Laud,' in *Church Association Lectures*, p. 171.

101 The writer claimed that the Ritualists elevated the role of private judgment in a manner similar to the Nonjurors of an earlier period. The leaders of that party followed their own paths 'until after divisions and subdivisions and bitter disagreements, occasioned by progressive developments of extravagance, Nonjurorism died out in a condition so miserably reduced that its extinction passed unnoticed by the world.' Anon., 'Ultra-Ritualists,' *Quarterly Review*, p. 163.

102 Ibid., pp. 164-65.

103 The Ritualists, handed a decision against their practices, only altered them as much as necessary to avoid a strictly literal disobedience. 'And all the while such a man gives himself the airs of a martyr – a martyr with a turn for legal quibbling.' The only hope for a permanent solution, thought the writer, was to be found in the attitude of the general public; 'in that revulsion of thought which has, we think, already begun. England is in the main, as Dr. Newman has more than once told us, thoroughly Protestant.' Anonymous, 'The Church and the Age,' *Quarterly Review* 129 (1870): 58.

E. H. Plumptre wrote, 'I own, with whatever reluctance, that even when it springs from a natural and noble anxiety to protect the peace of the Church against those who trouble it, I see little prospect of any such measures being successful; that the temper which clamours for them seems to me to be too often that of panic, irritation, unwisdom. It profits but little to drive in the external, eruptive symptoms of disease, while the disease itself remains unhealed.' Further, he doubted whether restrictive legislation would be any more effective. 'It will be difficult for the most accomplished jurist to draw up an anti-Ritualist Act of Parliament through which a Ritualist pleader will be unable to drive his proverbial "coach and six".' Plumptre, 'Church Parties,' *Contemporary Review*, p. 336-37.

The *Edinburgh Review* similarly doubted the wisdom of prosecution: 'For our own part, therefore, we are free to own, while we admit that the spirit of defiant lawlessness in too many instances calls for some strong measure of repression, that we view with little hope or satisfaction the prosecutions with which we're threatened by the Church Association, turning, as they do on rubrics that are obsolete or obscure, and which, even if their meaning were clear, are but a small portion of a code of rules which no one pretends to keep in its entirety.' Anon., 'Connop Thirlwall,' *Edinburgh Review*, p. 308.

104 In the paper's obituary for Seeley in June 1886, it identified him as the correspondent who had often graced its pages under the initials R.B.S. *Record*, 4 June 1886.

105 Letter to the *Record*, 15 July 1870. In his survey of the Ritualist controversy, Owen Chadwick suggested that 'for the first ten or twelve years devout and high-minded evangelicals believed in the policy of taking clergymen to court as the only effective way of determining what was the law of the Church of England.' Cf. Chadwick, *Victorian Church, Part Two*, p. 319. It would appear, however, that support for the CA's program of litigation began to break down long before that, although it perhaps took that long before a majority of Evangelicals became vocal opponents.

In an 1874 essay, R. F. Littledale complained about divisions within the High Church party in contrast to what he believed was the unity of the Evangelicals. He did not believe that all Evangelicals supported prosecution, but, he concluded, 'those who abstain from active share in it, also abstain from all protest or remonstrance publicly made.' Richard F. Littledale, 'Church Parties,' *Contemporary Review* 24 (1874): 313.

106 Letter to the *Record*, 15 July 1870. In a later letter, he offered his suggestions which largely amounted to a moral campaign by example. He suggested that Evangelicals should concentrate on providing the strongest possible contrast to the Ritualists – the Lord's Supper was the focal point, and he believed the Evangelical clergy must begin to reemphasize the Protestant understanding in opposition to the sacramental view. Letter to the *Record*, 27 July 1870.

E. H. Plumptre expressed a similar perspective from a moderate Broad Church position. He suggested that the use of prosecution was an expensive and self-defeating attempt to take advantage of 'popular middle-class antipathy to Ritualism.' He thought Evangelicals would be better served 'to preach, write, in every way proclaim what they believe to be the truth, and to abstain carefully from all such coalitions and prosecutions.' Plumptre, 'Church Parties,' *Contemporary Review*, p. 332.

107 *Record*, 3 Nov. 1869. Stephen Neill suggested that Evangelicals never formed a party because of 'their inveterate habit of biting and devouring one another over microscopic differences of opinion.' They were never able to form a central organization and never had a single organ of opinion. But this did not mean that they were simply extreme individualists. Rather their emphasis on the individual's relation to God found its community expression in the form of 'intense and intimate fellowship,' one of the chief characteristics of which was 'the formation of societies.' Stephen Neill, *Anglicanism*, Fourth Ed. (London: Mowbray & Co., 1977), pp. 237-38.

108 *Record*, 26 Jan. 1870.
109 The CA Council was particularly concerned that the formation of an entirely separate organization would lead to 'misconception and opposition, and would tend in its results rather to create divisions in the Evangelical body, than to produce either union of sentiment or community of action.' The new union's goals were listed in the report:
   'To act as a consultative body to advise on questions affecting the interests of Protestant and Evangelical truth with the Church of England.
   'To establish communication with clerical and lay associations, constituted on like principles, and to encourage the formation of them where they do not at present exist.
   'To suggest to local associations subjects for consideration on which it may be thought important to ascertain the opinion of Evangelical Churchmen, and to take measures to give effect to the prevalent opinion of the body, by an annual aggregate meeting or otherwise.
   'To encourage concerted action for the advancement and progress of spiritual religion.' Report of the CA annual meeting cited in the *Record*, 1 March 1871.
110 It began its editorial, however, by noting again that many still kept their distance, 'men with scrupulous consciences, albeit men of their own principles, and as warmly and sincerely attached to Protestant truth as themselves, have loudly protested against all appeals to the law.' But the paper thought support would be encouraged by the recent judicial decisions. *Record*, 1 March 1871.
111 The regional meetings had a long history of independence, most of them having been formed by mid-century and several of them even prior to that. As separate associations, they seem to have had little interest in surrendering their autonomy to an umbrella organization. Furthermore, they largely met as bodies of spiritual encouragement, discussing topics of pastoral concern rather than theological or partisan disputes. For an interesting local study of the Western District Clerical and Lay Association (founded in 1858), which was drawn from notebook reports kept of its meetings, cf. John Kent, 'Anglican Evangelicalism in the West of England, 1858-1900' in *Protestant Evangelicalism: Britain, Ireland and America, c.1750-c.1950*, Studies in Church History, Subsida, vol. 7, ed. Keith Robbins (Oxford: Basil Blackwell, 1990), pp. 179-200.
112 *Record*, 15 May 1871.
113 Letter to the *Record*, 29 May 1871.
114 Lord Shaftesbury was skeptical of the endeavor from the beginning. In a journal entry from January 1870, he suggested that there were too many sections within the party to establish any true union. 'We have in prospect an "Evangelical Union," which cannot be, in our present state, anything but a union of words and expressions, of wishes and fears, of arguments and plans, without the possibility of union in any one course of action, or, indeed, of any combined and concentrated declaration. People are speaking glibly of Evangelical union, without knowing what an Evangelical is.' Hodder, *Life of Shaftesbury*, p. 527.

CHAPTER 5

Anti-Ritualism and Evangelical Church Relations

Throughout the second half of the nineteenth century, Evangelicals were criticized by their High Church counterparts for lacking a true understanding of the nature of the church. With their emphasis on personal conversion and their interest in numerous voluntary societies, Evangelicals had neither the theoretical incentive nor the time to spare for involvement in the communal life of the national church. They were often disinterested in, and at times blatantly hostile toward that body of mixed believers called the Church of England (at least as it existed outside their parish and party boundaries).[1] The partisan animosities engendered by the Ritualist controversy only further diminished the level of Evangelical interest at a time when there was new impetus for the development of ecclesiastical organizations. The second half of the century was a period of great concern for the leaders of the Church of England. It was evident that secularization posed a grave threat to the church – both in the critical, rationalist approach to religious thought and in the declining influence of the church among the urban masses. In addition, there was great pressure, both in society and government, for church reform. Faced with such concerns, it was little wonder that new forms of organized church meetings were being established. The process began with the revival of Convocation, but given the difficulties involved in any attempt to reform that body's antiquated structure without the direct intervention of Parliament, the focus soon turned to other groups. Annual church congresses were begun in the early 1860s, and they were soon followed by the establishment of diocesan synods. Both provided clergy and laity with an opportunity to meet together to discuss the important concerns facing the church.

Unfortunately, the very meetings required by the needs of the church were threatened by the partisan divisions of the Ritualist controversy. Evangelicals were suspicious of mixed gatherings from the beginning. They viewed any attempt to portray Convocation, congress, or synod as the authoritative voice of the church with great alarm, and they accused the Ritualists of attempting to dominate the meetings of those bodies for their own partisan interests. The separation of Evangelicals from the rest of the church, however, was not the only result of their partisan campaign. It also tended to divide the Evangelical party within itself. Over the course of the 1860s and 70s, moderates came to oppose a policy of isolation. It was increasingly evident that their participation in the life of the national church was necessary, both to present their own views in a positive light and to exercise a moderating influence on the activities of their ecclesiastical opponents.

The irony of the self-defeating tendencies of the extreme anti-Ritualist policy was most evident in relation to their reaction to the organization of special mission services to reach the unchurched London masses. With their focus on evangelism and outreach, the meetings ought to have been of obvious interest to them. But the services were organized by Ritualists, and it was thereafter a difficult task for Evangelicals to justify their cooperation. By the late 1870s, however, a policy of moderation became more widespread, and Evangelicals regularly took part in the meetings of the church and in special missions services – but only after the divisions, both within the church and within their own party, had been further exacerbated and done great damage to their own reputation.

Evangelical Perspectives on Convocation

The campaign for the revival of Convocation in the nineteenth century faced opposition from Evangelicals almost from the beginning. It was especially viewed as a divisive issue after it gained the support of High Church partisans who hoped thereby to obtain a reversal of the Gorham decision. In an earlier and less controversial era, some Evangelicals had supported the idea of empowering Convocation to serve as the Church of England's legislative voice (with Parliament, in an era of reform, being increasingly less willing to fill that role).[2] In reaction to the Oxford Movement, however, Evangelicals viewed the idea of an authoritative Convocation with a great deal of suspicion. And by mid-century, faced with a High Church party apparently intent on gaining a majority in a revived Convocation, Evangelicals were almost unanimously opposed.

C. S. Bird, a prominent Evangelical clergyman, condemned the effort of 'the clerical party' to establish its position beforehand and thus insure its control of the body.[3] Given the tenor of the High Church party polemic, he suspected that 'violent individuals would take the lead' if they were to gain such a platform for their opinions.[4] Bird also feared that conflict with the High Church party over the sacraments in such an arena would only result in a massive secession from the church on one side or the other. In his view, the desperate desire for a renewal of Convocation was a last ditch attempt by the High Church party to 'either retrieve their fortunes in a last battle, or depart from us in a manner which would do them the greatest honour.' In either case, the result would be the division of the church, with irreparable damage done to its reputation with the laity.[5] Bird also made the case that would be reiterated by Evangelical apologists for many years to follow – Convocation, to be truly representative of the church, had to make room for the laity. This point was fundamental to the Evangelical view of the church. 'To exclude them,' argued Bird, 'would be to return to the false and fatal principle, which characterizes the medieval time and the Church of Rome, that the Church, as regards God's promises of illumination, consists of the clergy alone.'[6]

At mid-century, neither J. B. Sumner nor Thomas Musgrave, the Archbishops of Canterbury and York, supported the revival of Convocation.[7] By the late 1850s, however, some Evangelicals had begun to recognize the hazards inherent in a policy of isolation. In May 1859, the *Record* took note of the upcoming elections for proctors from the archdeaconries and called on Evangelicals to exercise their influence in the polls:

> To a considerable extent the Evangelical clergy probably share our objections against the restoration to this assembly of its legislative functions. This should not, however, prevent them from taking part in the forthcoming election, and doing their utmost to secure the return of proctors like-minded with themselves on all the grave questions which at this present time occupy the attention of Churchmen. In many cases, where it has been assumed that the Evangelical clergy were in a minority, a little effort and organization have enabled them to disprove the assumption and to carry the election of their nominees.[8]

While still desiring to avoid any appearance of cooperation with their ecclesiastical opponents, some were beginning to realize that participation in organized church meetings was expedient, if only to prevent the appearance that the upper hand had been gained by 'the party who are studiously labouring to unprotestantize our National Church.' Evangelical proctors were needed, both to limit High Church influence and to 'convince the anxious laity that a healthy Evangelical spirit still pervades the Church of England.'[9]

By the early 1860s, when the more immediate threat appeared to be the growth of rationalism, partisan tensions were somewhat diminished for a time, and there were fewer expressions of concern about Convocation.[10] But conservatives continued to oppose participation. In large part, they objected that Convocation, as then constituted, allowed no place for the participation of the laity; and the Evangelical party drew much of its strength from the middle and upper class laity.[11] And many believed that a bias remained in favor of the clerical party. J. C. Colquhoun published a pamphlet in 1869, criticizing the moderate position and calling for Evangelicals to avoid Convocation, church congresses, and the newly developed diocesan synods. Those in higher offices, he acknowledged, could hardly refuse to participate in such meetings; but he believed the clergy and laity ought to avoid them entirely. With regard to the Lower House of Convocation, Colquhoun argued that it was unrepresentative and ineffective; to participate in its deliberations would only lend a degree of legitimacy to a body dominated by the Ritualists and their High Church allies.[12]

In addition to concerns regarding the representation of the laity, Evangelicals frequently argued that the parish clergy deserved a better representation. J. C. Ryle, one of the moderate leaders who encouraged Evangelical participation in church meetings, argued that it was 'simply preposterous and absurd' to suggest that the Lower House fairly represented the clergy:

> The Lower House of Convocation consists of 145 members. Of these 23 are Deans, 56 are Archdeacons, 24 are Proctors for Cathedral Chapters, and only 42 are Proctors for the parochial clergy! Every one knows that Deans are nominated by the Crown and Archdeacons by the Bishops, and that in neither case have the clergy the slightest voice in the nomination. And yet in the face of these 79 nominees of the Crown and the Bishops, the parochial clergy are only allowed to elect 42 representatives of their own body! Can anything be imagined more contrary to reason and common sense?[13]

If the opinion of Convocation was to carry any weight with Parliament and the nation, reforms were imperative, and, above all, it must be made a truly representative body. In Ryle's view, that required the creation of a place for the laity as well. Nevertheless, Ryle was a strong voice urging Evangelicals not to vacate their responsibility to the church.[14] Evangelical bishops similarly encouraged a broader participation. The Bishop of Norwich, John T. Pelham, urged Evangelicals to participate while reiterating the need for broader representation.[15]

A growing number of Evangelicals, especially those holding prominent appointments, urged participation in Convocation while continuing to campaign for its reform. In an 1868 article, the moderate A. W. Thorold suggested that the party policy with regard to Convocation had been 'suicidal for ourselves and unjust to others.'[16] In 1869, the non-partisan Henry Alford also chided Evangelicals for viewing the church's official meetings with 'contempt.' Their 'scorn,' he suggested, was expressed in their favorite dictum, 'It can enact nothing.' Hoping to bring moderates from the Evangelical and High Church parties together to form a united opposition to the Ritualists, Alford suggested that the policy of abstention had been self-defeating and allowed Convocation to become 'a very powerful engine for the enemy's work.' It was, said Alford, 'a venerable debating society,' and Evangelicals needed to come out of the self-imposed isolation of 'their clerical meetings' and take part in the broader meetings and organizations of the church if they wanted to have a positive influence.[17]

Nor were Evangelicals alone in their concerns regarding the reform of Convocation. In an article published in 1874, following the enactment of the Public Worship Regulation Act, the *Edinburgh Review* challenged the Ritualist claim that Convocation alone had the right to enact reforms involving the church. Convocation had, in the opinion of the writer, never acted except in the best interests of the clerical party. It had always fallen to Parliament to enact reforms for the church, and it was clear from its history that Convocation 'will adhere to the principles to which it has hitherto pledged itself, and will admit of no other changes than those which further the interests of the party which now governs its majority.'[18] A. P. Stanley, writing from a Broad Church position, took a similar view. He suggested that there was little hope that a revision of the rubrics would end the controversy so long as Convocation was involved and unreformed.[19]

The first of several organizations that Evangelicals would form in the largely unsuccessful attempt to create a moderate alternative to the CA, was the Evangelical Union for Church Reform. In announcing its formation, W. R. Fremantle took pains to note that it was 'entirely independent of all other Societies' and desired to appeal to all Protestants who were 'determined to maintain the faith once delivered to the saints from the aggressions and innovations of the present day.' Supporters of the union were convinced that the work must begin with the reform of Convocation, as it was the only body that represented the whole church. According to Fremantle, the organization had the support of Lord Shaftesbury, who had agreed to serve as the chairman of the committee.[20] In February 1874, the new organization sent a letter explaining itself to all Church of England clergy.[21] The *Record* lent its editorial support to the union. It was clear to all, said the paper, that 'some decided action' was necessary to halt the innovations and establish the authority of the legitimate interpretation of the rubrics, but neither the episcopacy nor the CA had been able to accomplish those goals. The paper continued: 'Men are burning to act, but they know not how.... The conclusion appears irresistible that action must begin with reform in the system of the Church, which shall restore her discipline, and open the way for the resolute action of the great body of the laity.'[22] Shortly thereafter, the paper published an editorial urging Evangelicals to take seriously the upcoming election of proctors for the Lower House of Convocation and to return clergy who would pursue a policy of reform.[23] The new union had little success, either in gathering Evangelical support or in accomplishing its goals. But party moderates continued to emphasize the necessity of involvement in the church's deliberative bodies, and the wisdom of their view was gradually accepted.[24]

Church Congresses

As was the case with regard to the question of cooperation with the Ritualists in a revived Convocation, Evangelical opinion was divided as well concerning attendance at church congresses and diocesan synods, meetings first organized in the second half of the century during the early years of the controversy. Evangelicals were largely critical of the early congresses and viewed them with great distrust.[25] The annual meetings, which were begun at Cambridge in 1861, and included both clergy and laity, were criticized by conservatives, who detected a High Church predominance. By joining them, it was suggested that Evangelicals would only lend credence to meetings that were largely an attempt to propagandize on behalf of High Church extremists.[26] A number of Evangelicals participated in the Oxford meetings the following year, but the *Record* remained skeptical. The paper concluded that, regardless of any High Church pretensions, the meetings were little more than voluntary clerical gatherings promoted and dominated by partisan speakers.[27] The correspondence in the paper, however, gave evidence of division among Evangelicals. Opponents suggested that little good could come from meetings where controversial but important subjects had to be avoided because clergy from different sections of the church were gathered together. But at least one correspondent argued that the meetings held much potential for overcoming the divisions within the church and encouraged Evangelical participation at future congresses.[28]

In 1864, conservative Evangelicals attempted to respond by organizing a meeting of their own, claiming that congresses could achieve no lasting result. Drawing on their system of regional lay and clerical meetings, a national meeting was arranged, free from the influence of other parties, where the central issues of the day could be openly discussed.[29] Despite the support of the *Record* and several prominent Evangelicals, however, the plan for the Ipswich meeting ran into trouble when it was scheduled for the same dates as the Bristol Church Congress. When the list of speakers for Bristol was announced, it was clear that a significant number of influential Evangelicals still intended to participate.[30] J. C. Ryle sought to defuse the situation and refuted rumors that the dates had been deliberately chosen in order to conflict with the Bristol Congress. Ryle maintained that the October dates had been selected only after a conflict had arisen with the original schedule. At any rate, he thought those planning to attend the Ipswich meetings would probably not have gone to Bristol anyway.[31] But the conflict continued, and the organizers of the Ipswich Congress were ultimately forced to postpone their meeting until the next year.[32]

There was a stronger Evangelical representation at the congress in Norwich in 1865. An anonymous writer made the case for attendance that would be repeated by other proponents for years to come – church congresses would go on with or without Evangelicals, and the party would be better served by having its views elaborated by competent representatives than by refusing to participate and leaving the floor to their opponents:

> If it be more than ever incumbent upon us in these 'perilous times' to 'contend earnestly for the faith once delivered to the saints,' and to endeavour to avert from our beloved Church that ritualistic incubus which we believe would tend fatally to eat away true spiritual religion, ought we to forego the opportunity afforded us by these Congresses of publicly advancing our views and principles? Ought we to leave the field entirely open to our opponent? Would not the adoption of such a course be mistaken by many for a sign of weakness? If the unanswered arguments of those from whom we differ help to swell their ranks with the weak and wavering, should we be clear of responsibility? We often hear complaints made of the progress of High Church principles, but is not that progress due in a great measure to the too retiring policy of their opponents?
>
> The question, to my mind, is not 'Shall we mix with High Churchmen?' or, 'Have we any prospect of convincing them?' but, 'What is our duty to the Church at large?' Shall we let judgment go against us by default? Is it, after all, impossible to suppose that we can either learn or teach anything by being present at a Congress?
>
> Let, then, the Evangelical clergy of the diocese of Norwich come

forward boldly upon this occasion – let them not seem to the outer world to shut themselves up proudly in a sort of sublime superiority; let them stand up in a spirit of faith, and prayer, and brotherly love, and thus seek to commend the principles so dear to them.[33]

Nevertheless, a vocal group continued to maintain their opposition to any meetings involving Ritualists, and were unwilling to allow that Evangelicals had anything to learn from other parties in the church or any responsibility to participate in general meetings.[34] By the close of the Norwich Congress, however, even the *Record* was willing to allow that the meetings had been more successful than expected. In the paper's view, there was less of a 'party character' and more Evangelicals were included than had previously been the case, a fact it attributed to the influence of the Evangelical bishop of Norwich, J. T. Pelham. The paper still doubted the lasting value of the meetings, but it was willing to allow that a broader participation might have intangible positive effects that ought to be considered.[35]

By the late 1860s, heightened partisan tensions were evident at the annual church congresses and in a growing Evangelical reaction. The York Congress in 1866 was disrupted several times when the Ritualists mounted vocal protests, especially during the speech of Archibald J. Stephens, the ecclesiastical lawyer retained by the CA.[36] But the *Record* refused to allow their behavior to alter its view of the meetings' usefulness and concluded that the congress was a general success.[37] By 1867, the impact of the Mackonochie prosecution was evident. There were few prominent Evangelicals among the speakers at the Wolverhampton Church Congress, and the *Record* suggested that their exclusion had not been from any unwillingness to participate on their own part. In contrast, the paper complained that the Ritualists had been given an important place in the meetings. Still it held out hope for the next congress, which would be held in London, where the Evangelical clergy could not be 'overlooked.'[38]

That article, however, brought a response from John Richardson, Vicar of St. George's, Wolverhampton, who had served on the selection committee. According to Richardson, the committee made repeated attempts to secure Evangelical speakers, only to have their offers 'refused by one person after another.' Far from there being any bias at work, he suggested that Evangelicals had withdrawn because of presence of the Ritualists. Richardson concluded by expressing his regret that their party apologists would not 'come forward, and, accepting the Congress as a fact, do battle for their principles on its platform. The Acting Committee at Wolverhampton showed every disposition to give them an ample and fair opportunity of doing this.'[39] But Evangelical opinion remained divided in the years that followed. In contrast to the early 1860s, there was relatively more support for attendance, but the negative impact of the Ritualist prosecutions, which served to broaden existing party divisions, confirmed conservatives in their opposition to mixed meetings.

In an 1869 pamphlet, J. C. Colquhoun rejected the arguments of Evangelical moderates who supported cooperation. He was particularly disturbed by the revival of Convocation and the rise of the newly instituted diocesan synods, but he was equally opposed to Evangelicals meeting with their ecclesiastical opposites at church congresses. His language illustrated the enmity of the extreme anti-Ritualist opinion:

> But this objection occurs to many: – If they go there, they meet, as Churchmen, men who are, in fact, not members of the Church of England, but schismatics of the Church of Rome. To encounter, as if he were orthodox, a heresiarch like Dr. Pusey (whose avowed object for thirty years has been to unprotestantize and Romanize our Church); or Mr. Bennett, whose heresies are flagrant; or Mr. Lyne; or Ritualists, who are substituting the rites of the Church of Rome for the order of the Church of England, – this is to extend the countenance of Anglican Churchmen to notorious Romanists.[40]

According to Colquhoun, the Protestant laity were deeply disturbed when they saw their pastors associating with Ritualists at such meetings. Given the divided nature of the church, congresses ought to be avoided, he concluded, at least until the Ritualists seceded to Rome.[41]

A significant number of Evangelicals were scheduled to speak at the Liverpool Congress in 1869, but controversy arose over the inclusion of A. H. Mackonochie among the scheduled speakers. J. C. Ryle, who by then supported Evangelical participation, withdrew his name in a letter of protest to the Secretary of the Liverpool Congress:

> I know very well that a Church Congress is a comprehensive assembly of Churchmen just as the Church of England is pre-eminently a comprehensive Church.... If anyone supposed that I wish to narrow this comprehensiveness, and to confine the selection of speakers at a Church Congress to one school of thought, he is greatly mistaken. I trust I am neither unwilling nor afraid to meet Churchmen of any school on any Congress platform.
>
> But I maintain firmly that there are some limits to the compre-

hensiveness of the Church of England. If there are none, she is a Church without a creed and without order. I maintain in like manner that there ought to be some limits to comprehensiveness in the selection of appointed speakers at a Church Congress. And, I say that to select out of the myriads of Churchmen in 1869 a clergyman who was condemned in a very grave ecclesiastical suit in 1868 is to overstep all reasonable limits of comprehensiveness. At any rate, it is an arrangement to which I entirely decline to give any countenance.[42]

But the growing level of commitment among moderates was evident in the fact that few of the other Evangelical participants chose to follow Ryle's example.[43] Ultimately, Ryle and Hugh McNeile were the only prominent Evangelicals to withdraw from the congress.[44] The *Record*'s own reporter also supported Evangelical participation. The church congresses would exercise a great influence over local audiences whether Evangelicals participated or not; so long as they existed, he was convinced there could be little doubt concerning 'the duty of Evangelical men to claim their place and take part in them.'[45]

Despite the general shift in Evangelical opinion concerning participation in the congresses, prominent opponents remained. Francis Close, Dean of Carlisle, continued to express his opposition and thought Evangelical leaders should gather to formulate a united plan of response. He questioned whether any good achieved by their participation had not been neutralized 'by the confident assertions and subtle suggestions of error,' and 'by a seeming fellowship with either Broad Church scepticism, or Ritualistic Romanism.' In an era when the 'tendency of the age' was toward latitude and complacency, Close believed Evangelicals were simply helping to promote the errors of the day by meeting those from other parties. He was willing to support meetings that promoted unity among those with mutual beliefs, but a 'hollow truce with semi-Papists and semi-sceptics' could benefit no one.[46]

J. H. Titcomb of St. Stephen's, South Lambeth, thought Close ought to have known that many of the London clergy had met, following the controversy over Mackonochie's appearance, and a majority of those present were resolved to support Evangelical attendance. While regretting that Close would not join them, Titcomb wanted him to understand what had become the dominant view among moderates:

Towards the end of his letter, the Dean describes himself as 'an old-fashioned Evangelical, with the prejudices of some sixty years and more' about him. But this, however true, proves nothing. One of the highest attributes of age is to recognise the changes of the times, and, though truth never changes, to see that what might very well have suited the wants of the day thirty years ago, will not do now. Nothing can be more damaging to us than a policy of isolation and abstention such as that which the Dean advocates. The younger and more vigorous-minded of the Evangelical clergy are not prepared for it; who, in proportion as they are deserted by their leaders, will feel betrayed. This cannot be true policy. If the time should ever come when we drift into two opposite divisions – the one represented by our elder, and other by our younger clergy – by a large-hearted desire for manly independence – the days of our influence on the Church are numbered. The times we live in require unflinching courage combined with loving charity; let us exhibit them, and we need not fear. On the other hand, let us separate unlovingly from all ranks but our own, and we shall have reason to fear the worst.[47]

Titcomb, in his letter, gave expression to a view that was often hinted at – the shift of opinions that divided the Evangelical party was attributable, at least in part, to a generational divide. The moderates tended to be younger clergy, and the more conservative elder clergy often expressed their concern that the younger generation was particularly susceptible to the influence of the Ritualists. It was clear from Titcomb's letter, however, that a generational shift also meant a shift of leadership; and the younger Evangelicals, while not capitulating their principles, were determined to be fully engaged in the life of the church. Close, in his response to Titcomb, saw the division in other terms, and his argument would be repeated by conservatives for years to come. On the one side, there were those who were willing to make compromises for the sake of peace and unity in the church; on the other, there stood those who thought it necessary, above all else, to maintain their fundamental principles without any accommodation.[48]

In reporting on the Southampton Church Congress in 1870, the *Record* suggested that the influence of the Evangelical party had been evident. In contrast to earlier congresses, the extreme section of the High Church had been unable to dominate.[49] By way of illustrating the change of tone that Evangelical involvement had fostered, the paper reprinted an exchange of letters between the prominent Ritualist G. A. Denison and Francis Morse, who was the secretary for the upcoming Nottingham Church Congress. Denison wrote to inquire whether or not it was true that the organizing committee had passed a resolution excluding those who had been condemned 'by a court of law for alleged ritual or other ecclesiastical offence.' Morse replied that they indeed had, following the example set by the Southampton Congress, which merely excluded them from presenting lectures and not from participation. He also noted that the exclusion referred only to those who had been condemned by the Judicial Committee of the Privy Council. Denison regretfully expressed his decision not to attend the Nottingham Congress.[50] For the *Record*, the decision made by the organizing committee and the opinion expressed by Denison were simply signs that the Ritualists were no longer able to dominate the meetings, either in planning or operation.[51]

For a time in the mid-1870s, particularly as partisan tensions were further increased about the time of the Bennett judgment and the Public Worship Regulation Act, a rather dimmer view prevailed with regard to Evangelical participation.[52] The *Record* even wavered in its support, following the Stoke-on-Trent Congress of 1875, and questioned whether anything of substance was ever accomplished at the meetings. 'Can it with any truth be avowed,' the paper asked, 'that the enlarged acquaintance with what Evangelical men really hold has conciliated more favour from opponents through the medium of these assemblages?' Much was made of 'moderate churchmanship,' but what good was it if all 'the burning questions of the day' had to be avoided for the sake of compromise? Finally, it was feared that, despite the good obtained by an Evangelical message at the meetings, error was promulgated there as much as truth; and 'of those who attend these meetings many are quite as likely to return inoculated with error from which they were previously free as relieved from prejudices under which they had laboured.'[53] By the late 1870s, anti-Ritualists were concerned about the spread of their opponents' influence, and the last point made by the paper soon became the dominant argument against Evangelical participation in church congresses – those who attended became more tolerant of Ritualist error and were less inclined to join in the controversy or to support the CA.

Prior to the Croydon Church Congress of 1877, the debate over Evangelical participation was renewed. During the summer, a furor erupted over *The Priest in Absolution*, a manual instructing clergy in the use of confession, published by the Society of the Holy Cross. The book was discussed in Convocation and widely condemned by the bishops, but the controversy gave new impetus to conservative demands that Evangelicals withdraw from church meetings. W. W. Phelps, in a letter to the *Record*, protested the appearance of Evangelicals on the same platform with Ritualists: 'Let all Evangelical clergymen absent themselves from the compromising gathering, unless Archdeacon Emery and the managing committee assure us that no known and avowed Ritualist, no member of the E.C.U., the C. B. S., the Holy Cross, and other bodies implicated in the Ritualist conspiracy will be allowed to read a paper or to say a word.'[54]

Moderates, however, were by then firmly committed to their policy. Edmund Wickham, in reporting that the Surrey Clerical and Lay Association had unanimously adopted a resolution supporting Evangelical cooperation, rejected Phelps's rationale:

> Mr. Phelps seems to think that such men as Canon Garbett, Canon Ryle, and others of Evangelical views who will take part in the Congress, and we who purpose to support them with our sympathy, will expose ourselves to 'the ridicule and disgust of the country.' Many will think that it is anything but wise for Evangelicals to commit ecclesiastical suicide by declining to take their part in such public demonstrations in the Church as the Croydon Congress.[55]

Part of their policy involved a less antagonistic view of the High Church party in general. Wickham thought it important to distinguish the Ritualists from the historic High Church tradition. The moderates of that party were equally opposed to the Ritualists and needed to know they could count on Evangelical support at the meetings. He concluded, 'Surely we owe a duty to the good and honest High Churchman, as well as to those more immediately of our own school.'[56]

Shortly before the Croydon Congress, a circular was issued by a committee formed to encourage Evangelical participation.[57] A large group of moderates met during the congress to approve a resolution urging party support for attendance at future meetings. One of the principal reasons cited was the enlargement of the permanent consultative committee, which was charged with selecting the topics for discussion and arranging speakers. Evangelicals, both clerical and lay, were well-represented on the committee, and the petitioners suggested that this would result in fairly balanced platforms. Edward Garbett drew applause from the congress audience when he suggested that there was no reason for strife between the Evangelical party and 'the great historical High Church party.' While admitting that there were doctrinal differences of no small importance between them, he acknowledged that the Church of England had always been comprehensive enough to include both.[58] Evangelicals, he said, were concerned only with those who moved beyond the boundaries of legitimate parties in the church; those who either rejected Scripture as the rule of faith or who 'desired to restore the practices and principles of mediaeval Christianity.'[59]

The debate over compromise and assimilation only resulted in increased tensions within the Evangelical party. Moderates were sharply criticized for their attempt to assuage their High Church counterparts. For conservatives, whose perspective of the meetings was dominated by their anti-Ritualist concerns, there could be no compromise with 'moderate sacerdotalism' or 'moderate error.' If the participation in church congresses had produced any synthesis of differing opinions, they charged, it had all been one-sided. 'Has the change,' asked one critic, 'from simple Protestant worship to an elaborate cathedral service drawn recruits from High Churchism to Evangelicalism? Has not the reverse been the case?' If that was the result of the spirit of toleration fostered at church congresses, he suggested that the Ritualists could not have found a more successful means of hindering Evangelicals than by advocating their continued participation.[60] For a time, anti-Ritualists continued to protest Evangelical cooperation, but their arguments carried little weight and increasingly sounded like the reactionary and defensive polemic of an extreme minority.[61] By the late 1870s, the importance of the church congresses was generally recognized and moderates were largely successful in establishing their arguments for the necessity of continued Evangelical involvement.[62] By the mid-1880s, although conservative opposition remained, the debate had largely subsided and the policy of moderates was widely approved.[63]

Diocesan Synods

The subject of diocesan synods had been under discussion for several years prior to their introduction, and Evangelicals were suspicious because the establishment of such meetings had been enthusiastically supported by High Church clergy.[64] In 1867, the Upper House of Convocation discussed their restoration as a means to facilitate the consultation of clergy and laity with their bishop. The committee appointed to study the subject refused to support an authoritative synod but thought the idea of a democratic conference useful.[65] In 1868, Bishop Selwyn of Lichfield, drawing on his experiences as a bishop in New Zealand, announced a synod and asked each parish to send clerical and lay representatives. Evangelicals were divided over the plan. The fears voiced were not unlike those expressed regarding church congresses – they thought it was dangerous to participate in meetings attended by Ritualists and doubted that any good could come from the resulting interchange of ideas, they worried that votes passed on a majority rule might force unwanted innovations on Evangelical parishes against their will, and they feared that synods would exaggerate the authority of the bishop.[66]

Edward Garbett, a moderate Evangelical, focused on the latter of those concerns in a pamphlet published in 1868. He was convinced, despite all good intentions and promises to the contrary, that the implementation of synods was a radical change of church structure that would have a drastic effect on the parish clergy.[67] And in spite of the exclusion of doctrinal subjects, he was concerned that synodal decisions could ultimately threaten the 'free and independent action' of the parish clergy. Garbett was particularly concerned that episcopal authority would be greatly expanded, without the benefit of any checks or balances. On those grounds, he called for the Evangelical clergy to unite as 'a body in their respectful refusal to take any part in the constitution of a Synodical government.'[68] It was somewhat curious, however, that Evangelicals should be opposed to meetings intended to allow the laity an opportunity to express their views on ecclesiastical matters. In that regard, the synods ought to have held a certain appeal for them, in contrast, for example, to Convocation. But their suspicions remained regarding the motives of the bishops and the influence of the Ritualists.[69]

Even at the early stages of the movement, however, there were some who supported an Evangelical presence. One correspondent in the *Record* noted that the bishop had pledged that the synod would not interfere with traditional clerical liberties and that any resolutions passed would not be binding. Withdrawal, the author wrote, would only serve to divide the clergy from their bishop. As with the church congresses, he argued that they had a certain responsibility for 'bearing our testimony and exercising our influence in this great movement.'[70] In an attempt to allay such fears, the participants passed a resolution affirming 'that the Conference shall not assume legislative or judicial functions, nor assume to infringe the liberty secured by law to the clergy.'[71] Still, many remained opposed, and there was almost unanimous support at the annual meeting of the CA in 1869, for a resolution 'condemning the introduction of synods.'[72]

By the early 1870s, however, the number of synodal conferences had grown, and Evangelicals were compelled to admit their importance.[73] In 1870, J. C. Ryle lent his support to the movement. In his opinion, synods had become an established institution whether or not Evangelicals approved of them. He had come to the conclusion that, so long as the meetings were fairly conducted and the laity fully represented, the party would only damage its reputation by staying away:

> Their presence may prevent much mischief. Their absence will certainly not be understood by the bulk of the laity, and will be at-

tributed to sense of weakness and inferiority, or to cowardice. I would not have said this a year ago; but I do not hesitate to say it now.

We live in perilous times. We cannot choose our field of battle, and must be content to act according to circumstances, and accept the position. The sooner all Evangelical Churchmen make up their minds to come out from their seclusion to come forward and fight boldly everywhere for God's truth, the better for the Church of England. We have nothing to be ashamed of in our principles, but we must not be timid in confessing them before men. The laity are far more with us than we think. They abhor the least semblance of priestcraft and semi-Romanism.... It is no pleasant thing to attend either Congresses or Conferences, and meet a huge host of men who hold opinions diametrically contrary to your own. It is not pleasant to feel that the great majority of the clergy present on such occasions are looking at you with cold suspicion and distrust, and regarding you as little better than a heretic, or at least as an ignorant, bad theologian, and a very unsound Churchman! Yet a good conscience ought to make this cross sit lightly on our shoulders. When truth is at stake unpleasant things may sometimes become a positive duty.[74]

The evident change of heart reflected in Ryle's letter, in contrast to some of his earlier perspectives, ought to be noted. It was about the same time that he became a convinced supporter of Evangelical participation in church congresses as well. Ryle was one of the most influential Evangelicals of his day and a strong supporter of the CA. It was consequently a matter of some importance that he took the view that the Evangelical party needed to come out of its seclusion and take its place in the consultations of the church. And increasingly, the position of moderate Evangelicals became dominant in the party.[75]

Special Mission Services

The continuing impact of the anti-Ritualist movement can be traced in the animosity it created between the two largest sections of the church. But equally important, in the long run, was the impetus it gave to the division of the Evangelical party itself. Both aspects can be seen in the Evangelical reaction to the rise of meetings designed to reach the urban masses. They were hesitant to cooperate with High Church clergy when the first series of mission services were scheduled for the fall of 1869. The meetings, which were to be held simultaneously in a number of London churches and designed to reach the working classes, ought to have held great attraction for Evangelicals. But they were largely sponsored by Ritualist clergy, some of whom incorporated non-traditional methods such as those first pioneered by Evangelicals in their theater services.[76] The announcement left the Evangelical clergy in a difficult position – the methods and goals were clearly those they could support, but they were largely unwilling to cooperate in services initiated by High Church clergy.[77]

After the services concluded, the *Record* reported that about seventy churches had participated, mostly drawn from the extreme section of the High Church party, although some others had been drawn in by the evangelistic aim.[78] It thought the meetings were an odd mixture of 'the earnestness of Revival preaching' together with 'the sacerdotal errors of Romanism.'[79] It did not desire to oppose any evangelistic work, but given this mixture of truth and error, the paper would not give the services its editorial support and suggested they were unlikely to have any lasting positive effects.[80] Fearing that their opponents might gain an advantage, Evangelical churches were quick to announce a similar series of services to be held in their own churches during the Advent season.[81]

In a letter addressed to the three bishops who had sanctioned the London meetings (London, Winchester, and Rochester) as well as the Bishop of Oxford who had given his blessing to similar services, J. C. Colquhoun protested the unauthorized innovations that had been introduced into many of the services. The bishops responded politely but, while expressing their disapproval of excessive ritual, concluded that they believed the services had done much good for the city.[82] In October 1870, a meeting of London clergy was held to consider a new series of mission services. A committee had been in communication with the Bishops of London, Winchester, and Rochester, and it was apparent from their reply that the complaints concerning ritual innovations had not been without effect. The bishops agreed to sanction a new series of meetings, but only with several conditions:

> 1. That no religious services shall be used in church other than those which are contained in the Prayer-book, or consist of the very words of Scripture.
>
> 2. That no ritual shall be used in any church in excess of, or in addition to, the ordinary ritual of such church; and in particular, that no unauthorised form be introduced as a renewal of the baptismal vow.
>
> 3. That although every facility should be given for personal and private communication with the clergy to those who are troubled

in conscience, or who require further comfort, counsel, or instruction, the services shall not be made the occasion of recommending the practice of habitual confession to the priest as a duty of the Christian faith.[83]

The *Times* reported that 'a long and somewhat desultory' debate followed the reading of the episcopal conditions. Several High Church representatives protested against the restrictions as 'an infringement of their rights as priests,' while Evangelicals deprecated 'the introduction of confession' into the services. Ultimately, a resolution was passed in favor of holding another series of services, but the question of when to hold the meetings and whether they might not be more effective if divided by sections of the city and held at different times was referred back to the committee.[84] Support for the meetings was somewhat broader among Evangelicals than had previously been the case, but the further services were delayed for several years.

When the new mission services were scheduled for February 1874, some Evangelical opposition remained.[85] Critics were especially concerned about the issue of the confessional, with the services following closely on the Ritualist petition on confession that was presented to Convocation in 1873. It was feared that the Ritualists intended to use the 'after meetings' to advocate the necessity of auricular confession. But in defending Evangelical participation, C. F. S. Money argued that no comparison could be drawn between the two: 'To require confession and to give absolution is entirely different from asking if the sinner has found peace, and pointing him to Christ.... That such services and opportunities may be perverted is only saying what may be said of every ordinance and means of grace. But it would be a grievous mistake to allow the abuse of an instrumentality like this to hinder the right and judicious use of it.'[86]

Most moderates thought participation was imperative, if only to avoid questions regarding Evangelical loyalty to the Church or the possibility of the Ritualists being able to gain the upper hand in public opinion.[87] A. W. Thorold, who later became the Bishop of Rochester, suggested that non-participation indicated a lack of faith on their part.[88] Some drew a parallel between the mission services and the revivals of the late 1850s. Samuel Garratt suggested that the missions were unique insofar as they were prescheduled and utilized planned methods. The revivals, in contrast, had been spontaneous and 'did not come as the result of any special means, but in answer to prayer.... accompanied by the plain and faithful preaching of justification by faith.'[89] But the two were similar, said Garratt, in that both divided the Evangelical party. Like the missions movement, some Evangelicals had reacted negatively to the revivals, disturbed by widespread public criticism and fearing any association with incidents of extreme emotionalism.[90] Despite the concerns regarding emotionalism and cooperation with Ritualists, Garratt argued that the party must support the work at hand:

> To those who have known Revival blessings they [mission services] seem at first distasteful, because there is in them so much of man's arrangements, and because they can be used for the propagation of error as well as for the teaching of truth. But God has blessed them; and if God is pleased with them, it would be very unwise and ungrateful in us to neglect them. But we must be careful when engaged in Mission work to use only those weapons which are in the armoury of God, and not to seem to sanction error.[91]

The missions had the approval of the bishops, and most Evangelicals soon gave their support as well. Prior to the 1874 services, a meeting was held at St. Paul's Cathedral Chapter House, attended by prominent mission preachers, both Evangelical and High Church. The topic of the conference was the use of the after-meeting following the sermon. Although the importance of the after-meeting was reaffirmed by the conference, the published report of the meeting made no mention of Evangelical dissent regarding the topic of confession.[92] Still, conservative fears remained, and a memorial protesting any Ritualist involvement was forwarded to the three bishops sponsoring the mission.[93] The bishops, however, were not inclined to allow a partisan tone to divide the work of the mission. In their reply to the memorial, they noted that it was already too late to alter any of the arrangements and expressed their confidence that the clergy involved, if conducting services in a church, would strictly adhere to the rubrics. Many, they hoped, would come forward to seek repentance and get counsel from the clergy – indeed, that was the whole point of the mission. 'But,' they continued, 'such confession as this – the legitimate and natural outpouring of a heart touched by sense of sin and desirous of restoration – has little in common with, and is not likely, we believe, to lead to, the practice of habitual and "sacramental confession" taught as the remedy for post-baptismal sin on the rule of a holy life.'[94]

When the subject was raised at the fall meeting of the CA in 1876, even the fervent anti-Ritualists were willing to support a limited cooperation so long as it did not involve any direct work alongside High Church clergy.[95] A few moderates present, such as J. B. Clifford, Incumbent of St. Matthew's, Bristol, took a still broader position. He regretted the partisan rhetoric of the anti-Ritualists, and suggested that 'they tended to disturb the holy feeling which ought to exist in contemplating such a work as the coming Mission – a Mission which he had been partly instrumental in originating.'[96] By the 1880s, there was little question of Evangelical participation. In his 1887 charge to the clergy of Liverpool, Bishop Ryle viewed the rise of mission services as one of several signs of the renewed vitality of the church. After thirty years, said Ryle, the meetings were 'approved, patronized, and supported by every school of thought.'[97]

Evangelical opinion was similarly divided over the subject of cooperation in the area of foreign missions. When a day of prayer for Christian missions was announced in December 1872, J. C. Miller suggested that Evangelicals ought to put aside the differences separating them from the other church parties and unite in combined services wherever possible:

> In some cases there may be difficulties arising from the fact that Divine service at the church selected may be celebrated somewhat differently from the manner of others. But surely, on such an occasion, we may, if vital principles be not compromised, 'give and take.'
>
> For example, to put my meaning clearly and practically, the mere fact that, at the church selected, there is more elaborate and florid service, would appear a very insufficient reason for the holding back of any clergyman who has a plainer service in his own church.
>
> Let our hearts be filled with the grandeur and solemnity of the one thought of unity in the cause of Christian Missions, and questions of more or less singing, surpliced choirs, black or white in the pulpit, will sink into their proper proportions.[98]

Miller was sharply criticized by Francis Close, who condemned the advocacy of a broad tolerance as 'a perilous, unwise and unscriptural experiment.' For his part, Close questioned the wisdom of Evangelicals joining in prayer for missions with those holding views fundamentally divergent from their own and argued that any form of cooperation involved a degree of compromise. In concluding, he adopted an isolationist attitude that all too often characterized the conservative outlook: 'I had rather join no one in prayer, and shut myself up in my chamber, and pray alone, than unite in the most solemn exercise of spiritual duty and of a living faith with those from whose religious tenets I recoil; and in whose aspirations I have no interest whatever.'[99] It was, however, a perspective that was losing its hold over a majority of the Evangelical party.

Anti-Ritualism and the Moderate Section of the High Church Party

The moderation of tone adopted by some Evangelicals during the 1870s created the possibility of a broader coalition with moderates from the High Church in opposition to the Ritualists.[100] Part of the growing reaction, particularly as the extreme Ritualists became more resolute in their refusal to acknowledge either the admonitions of bishops or the rulings of judges, came from High Church moderates.[101] While discussing partisan divisions and the hardening of those lines as a result of litigation, Bishop Ellicott, at the Gloucester and Bristol diocesan conference for 1872, affirmed his hope for better relations between the two sections of the church. Many, he thought, had begun to realize that both parties faced a common enemy of far greater threat in the form of 'indifference to distinctive doctrines' and the 'drift toward Socinianism in modern thought.' At the same time toleration was acknowledged as a 'condition of their existence as a national Church.' That meant, in Ellicott's view, that the lawsuits must cease.[102] While acknowledging that the vast majority of Anglicans thought the law ought to be obeyed and that 'the distinctive features of Reformation truth' were the foundation of the Church of England, it was nevertheless clear to 'more calm and moderate minds' that the 'legal proceedings would not insure either obedience or orthodoxy.' He concluded, 'It might be unpalatable to many to own it, still it did seem certain that they were all beginning to be convinced that lawsuits were making an evil, already great, even greater than it was before, and that really all they had safely to rely on was healthy public opinion, and a sound estimate of the heavy responsibilities of waywardness and disobedience.'[103]

In June 1873, the *Record* took note of a pamphlet published by a 'High Churchman of the Old School,' entitled *Quosque? How Far? How Long?* The anonymous author was disturbed by the activities of the Ritualists and thought it important for moderates of all parties to unite in protest. Evangelicals had been widely accused of persecuting their opponents, but he believed they had performed a necessary task. The prosecutions undertaken by the CA were justifiable on two grounds. First, the Ritualists themselves had courted the challenge by claiming that the laws and rubrics were on their side; and second, the bishops had declined to take action so long as the state of the law remained uncertain. It was time, he affirmed, for moderates on both sides to issue a united call for enforcement of the law.[104] In November, J. W. Burgon, Vicar of St. Mary's, Oxford, and the Gresham Reader in Divinity at the university, took a similar position in two sermons. Burgon was particularly concerned by the Ritualist teaching on the real objective presence of Christ in the Eucharist and their advocacy of the confessional.[105] Burgon was convinced that the tendencies of the movement could only end with the assimilation of the doctrine and worship of the Church of England to that of Rome.[106] It was often suggested that the Ritualists had been successful only because the moderates in the High Church party had refused to make public their opposition.[107] The *Record* was hopeful that the example of Burgon and others might result in the formation of a majority coalition sufficiently powerful to compel the bishops to act. In making its case, the paper took on a conciliatory tone, not unlike that adopted by Canon Miller several years earlier:

> Mr. Burgon's two sermons are a symptom of a tendency in this direction and are in that proportion the source of great encouragement. To effect this alliance and to compact it into a working cooperation, is the object to which the most strenuous efforts should now be directed.... No doubt all parties have something to learn and something to forget. The Evangelical on his side has to forget a little of his jealousy, and to learn to appreciate, more candidly than he has hitherto done, the piety and honesty of motive of such men as Mr. Burgon. We do not mean for a moment that Evangelical Churchmen should compromise one jot of their own distinctive principles, or bate in the slightest degree their zeal for the maintenance and extension of God's truth. But we mean that they should recognise more frankly the possibility that men may truly love Christ who do not see things eye to eye with themselves, and should accept them as fellow defenders of the common faith.[108]

In the years that followed, the hope was often expressed, both by Evangelicals and other moderates, that the majority of the High Church party would withdraw their support from the Ritualists. Following the Ridsdale judgment in 1877, the *Quarterly Review* suggested that the Ritualist 'crisis' threatened to undermine the position of the established church. And, the essayist argued, it fell to the 'old historical High Church party' to resolve the matter.[109] But the union failed to materialize, and High Church critics of the Ritualists generally refused to join with Evangelicals or to support their more controversial programs and litigation.[110]

The two parties were, in fact, separated by their fundamentally different views of the church. High Church moderates shared with the Ritualists a common view of the church as a divine society; the body of Christ on earth apart from which there was no salvation. Grace was transmitted through the sacraments which were administered by a priestly mediator. For Evangelicals, however, the church held a decidedly less important position. Salvation came through personal conversion rather than the sacraments, and there was no priestly mediator between God and humanity save Jesus Christ. From their perspective, a sharp distinction had to be maintained between the church as the visible body of Christ and that invisible body made up of believers known only to God. The latter could as easily be gathered in a voluntary society meeting at Exeter Hall as in a church building, and it was the real focal point for Evangelical ecclesiology.[111]

Nevertheless, Evangelicals were concerned with the correlation between the two and were not entirely disinterested in the condition of the visible church. When it came to the organized meetings of that church, however, their level of commitment and understanding of toleration was sharply tested by the presence of Ritualists. The conservative section of the Evangelical party, as a matter of fundamental principle, was unwilling to associate with Ritualists regardless of the setting or the relative importance of the meeting in ecclesiastical terms. Convocation, church congresses, and diocesan synods were immediately suspect on those terms.[112] And the depth of anti-Ritualist sentiment only resulted in sharp divisions within the Evangelical party when moderates began to question the wisdom of a policy of isolation. Throughout the nineteenth century and for years to come, Evangelicals were criticized by High Church historians for the deficiencies in their ecclesiology and their lack of commitment to the church. The former point was debatable, depending upon one's own theological commitments; the latter was simply another reflection of the worsening tensions of the Ritualist controversy.[113] By the mid-1870s, moderates had largely won the day in compelling Evangelicals to recognize the importance of their participation in the life of the church. But the worst was yet to come with regard to the results of the anti-Ritualist crusade.

Notes

1. It could be argued that, for Evangelicals, their voluntary societies became the visible manifestation of the church. Whereas the parish congregation included many who held different and sometimes opposing opinions, Evangelicals could be relatively certain of the doctrinal conformity of those who gathered at Exeter Hall. And for many, the societies and their respective ministries were much more important than the established church. That interest in para-church organizations continues among Evangelicals of the twentieth century.
2. As late as 1835, John Kempthorne the examining chaplain for the Evangelical bishop Henry Ryder, had published a work supporting the renewal of Convocation entitled *The Church's Self-Regulating Principle*; cf., Balleine,

Evangelical Party, p. 213. For a general summary of the movement for the revival of Convocation, cf. Stock, *English Church*, pp. 58-60.

3   Bird, *The Dangers Attending an Immediate Revival of Convocation*, p. 3. In January 1848, the *Record* rejected the idea of granting legislative power to Convocation. The idea, thought the paper, was especially dangerous when there were, within the church and in positions of influence, 'men who dislike and disown the principles upon which our Protestant Church is formed, and give a preference to the idolatrous superstitions of the Romish apostasy.... It would not only be an assemblage of men of principles the most inconsistent and irreconcilable, but of a body, a great part of which would have it, as a specific object, to ruin the Church of which they were professed members, with a view of re-establishing on its ruins a fresh buttress and section of the Church of Rome.' *Record*, 10 Jan. 1848.

4   Bird, *Dangers Attending an Immediate Revival of Convocation*, pp. 12-13. Convocation would become a stage, he thought, for 'a young zealot, or a self-sufficient theorist, or an ambitious mediaevalist.'

5   Ibid., p. 39.

6   Ibid., p. 18. Nor were Evangelicals alone in this concern. Following the controversy over R. D. Hampden's appointment as the Bishop of Hereford in 1847, Broad Church adherents were similarly suspicious of a Convocation that might be dominated by the High Church. According to Owen Chadwick, about half the clergy and most of the laity opposed Convocation. The laity feared a Convocation dominated by the High Church party and 'saw Parliament as the pledge of liberty.' Chadwick, *Victorian Church, Part One*, p. 311. For a brief survey of Evangelical opinion regarding the revival of Convocation in the early 1850s, cf. Toon, *Evangelical Theology, 1833-1856*, pp. 94-96.

7   Nigel Scotland briefly surveyed Archbishop Sumner's addresses in the House of Lords when the bill to revive Convocation was introduced in 1851. Sumner thought its revival would only lead to increased discord in the church, and he feared that the controversial issues would become inflamed to the point that attempts might be made to revise the Book of Common Prayer, to which he was entirely opposed. Nigel Scotland, 'John Bird Sumner,' *Anvil*, pp. 150-51. When it became clear that support was growing, however, Sumner did not attempt to prevent it; cf. Nigel Scotland, *John Bird Sumner, Evangelical Archbishop* (London: Gracewing, 1995), pp. 120-22.

In 1851, an essayist in the *Quarterly Review* expressed doubts concerning the usefulness of a revived Convocation. The episcopacy issued a memorial that year addressing the issues of ritual innovation, but four bishops refused to sign the document. The writer thought the incident illustrated the folly of expecting any unity to come out of a revival of Convocation. 'We are satisfied that the few thinking men who may have hitherto been inclined to adopt the idea that national synods and convocations would insure unity of either doctrine or discipline, will now be convinced that the Houses of Convocation – upper or lower – would probably have no great resemblance to the Temple of Concord.' Anon., 'Rubric Versus Usage,' *Quarterly Review*, p. 210.

At an 1852 meeting called to protest the renewal of auricular confession,

Lord Shaftesbury complained that the revival of Convocation was equally evil; 'I should just as soon think of separating, in Guildhall, Gog and Magog as separating these two things."' Its revival, he feared, would suppress the laity and make them the servants of "a select knot of sacerdotal dignitaries.' Hodder, *Lord Shaftesbury*, p. 464.

8 *Record*, 4 May 1859. On the shift in Evangelical opinion during this period, cf. Stock, *Church Missionary Society*, vol. 2, pp. 10-11.

9 *Record*, 4 May 1859.

10 The *Record* continued, however, to oppose granting Convocation any real legislative power. It suggested that there had been no results of lasting value, but it was at least willing to allow that its own 'unfavourable anticipations' had not been realized. *Record*, 4 Feb. 1863.

11 Owen Chadwick suggested that it was the most clerical age in English history, from 1868 (the abolition of church rates) to 1921 (the parochial church councils measure), and that this fact influenced the degree of lay opposition to Ritualism; cf. Chadwick, *Victorian Church, Part Two*, p. 322.

12 In contrast to England, Colquhoun noted that the laity played an important role in the Anglican Church of Canada, forcing the 'wavering and weak' bishops to maintain their control over the 'noisy section of Ritualists' that existed there. J. C. Colquhoun, *Shall Protestant Churchmen Take Part in Convocation and Diocesan Synods?* (London: Hatchards, 1869), pp. 6-9.

13 Letter to the *Record*, 1 Jan. 1872. Ryle returned to the subject at the Croydon Church Congress. He noted that the House of Commons disliked religious questions and was reluctant to consider legislation involving the church. While rejecting the idea of Convocation ever holding legislative power, he suggested that if reforms were undertaken it might truly become 'the living voice of the Church' that the High Church section desired. He suggested several reforms: (1) the combination of York and Canterbury; (2) an end to 'ex-officio' members such as deans, canons and archdeacons, who were appointed by and represented only the crown and the bishops; (3) the reform of the process for electing proctors for the parish clergy; (4) an equal number of lay representatives; and (5) all should sit in one house with no divisions of upper and lower. J. C. Ryle, *Church and State, a Paper Read at the Croydon Church Congress* (London: William Hunt & Co., 1877), pp. 10-15.

14 Ryle defended his position before conservatives in a lecture at the annual meeting of the CA in 1872: 'Let me, then, express an earnest hope that Evangelical Churchmen will not allow questions like that before us to fall into unsatisfactory hands by not coming forward and taking interest about them.... If we mean to hold our own in the eyes of the country, it will never do to give up such questions as convocations, synods, conferences, congresses, the universities, the press, middle-class schools, the handling of scientific subjects, and the like, to be manipulated by High Churchmen and Broad Churchmen alone....

'In love to Evangelical principles I give place to none. But I never can withhold my opinion that we need "educating" to take more practical and active interest in all that affects the Church of England as an ecclesiastical system. We have kept aloof too long, and allowed other Churchmen to manage all affairs of Church organization pretty much as they please. It is

high time to change our plan. Let us be men of understanding of the age, and not least in this matter of Convocation.' Cited in the *Record*, 10 May 1872.
   Ryle returned to the theme in a speech to the diocese of Liverpool in 1886, by which time he was the bishop and a 'House of Laymen' had been created in Convocation. In order for Convocation to be what it ought, said Ryle, 'the Church of England by representation, the laity needed to be included completely and given a more distinct, authorized, and efficient position... The House of Laymen, no doubt, is a move in the right direction, but it must possess far more power than it does at present if it is to be of much use to the Church.' J. C. Ryle, *The Outlook: An Opening Address at the Liverpool Diocesan Conference, 1886* (London: William Hunt & Co., 1886), p. 29.

15 Pelham wrote, 'Enlarge the franchise, and admit the laity, and there would be a legally constituted body, fully representing the Church, with authority, not to legislate, but to deliberate upon and suggest to the Legislature measures required for the Church's welfare and efficient service; a body, whose voice could not fail to have weight with any Government.' John T. Pelham, *A Charge delivered to the Clergy and Churchwardens of the Diocese of Norwich* (London: Rivingtons, 1872), p. 39.

16 'We have had,' Thorold wrote, 'absolutely no one either to assert our claims, to express our convictions, or to maintain our existence. And how can it be fair to find fault with Convocation, and to accuse it of being nothing but a clerical debating society, when, in the first place, discussion is about the best as well as the only thing it can be busy about at present, and when we ourselves resolutely refuse to do anything to make it better?' Thorold, 'Evangelical Clergy,' *Contemporary Review*, p. 588.

17 Henry Alford, 'Next Step,' *Contemporary Review*, p. 8.

18 Anon., 'Convocation, Parliament and the Prayer Book,' *Edinburgh Review*, p. 460.

19 Stanley thought the Lower House of Convocation was 'so peculiarly constituted as to represent chiefly one current of clerical opinion, often adverse, not merely to the opinion of the educated laity, but also of the clergy themselves....' The High Church bias was evident in the debate over the use of the Athanasian Creed. There was broad clerical support for dropping it, but only twelve (out of almost two hundred) in the Lower House voted for the revision. Stanley concluded, 'Such a wide divergence between the actual feeling of the clergy at large and this body proves that the changes which the general opinion of the Church and the clergy deem necessary, can hardly be expected to pass through an assembly which so very inadequately corresponds to the general sentiment of those whose representatives it is supposed to contain.' A. P. Stanley, 'How Shall We Deal with the Rubrics?' *Contemporary Review* 23 (1873-74), p. 491.

20 Letter to the *Record*, 22 Sept. 1873.

21 Reprinted in the *Record*, 2 Feb. 1874; cf. Appendix C.

22 The paper did not believe there was any need for altering the constitution of Convocation or changing its relationship to the state. 'The mere increase of the number of proctors, a fairer distribution of the franchise, or the admis-

sion of the laity, whether voting in a separate chamber or in the same with their spiritual guides, cannot possibly alter the relation which the Convocations bear towards the State. Nor do we see why it should be assumed that a fairly constituted Convocation should be more aggressive, more ambitious, more useless, than any unfairly constituted one has already proved itself to be.' Ibid.

J. C. Ryle thought it was a great advance when a house of laity was created in the 1880s, although he did not expect much to come of it as long as it remained a merely consultative body with no authority. Nevertheless, it was 'the admission of a great principle, far too long most foolishly ignored, that the laity of a church have a right to be consulted, and ought to have a voice in all its proceedings.' Ryle, *No Uncertain Sound*, p. 157.

The increased activity of the Ritualists late in the century, following the Lincoln judgment, gave new impetus to the movement for lay influence. In 1898, Alfred Barry wrote that the laity often felt a since of 'helplessness' with the appeal to the courts closed to them and the bishops unable or unwilling to impose limitations. It was imperative under the circumstances, he argued, that the laity be given a full voice in the deliberations of the church. Alfred Barry, 'Breach of Church Law: Its Danger and its Remedy,' *Nineteenth Century* 48 (1898): 949.

23 Evangelicals, thought the *Record*, had long thought it useless to get involved in the election process for Convocation, since they were largely outnumbered by the other church parties. The paper, however, was 'most anxious to suggest whether these feelings are really adequate to justify what appears to us to be, not the exercise of a right, but the discharge of a bounden duty which men owe to their Church and their principles.' *Record*, 20 Feb. 1874.

24 Conservatives, however, continued to oppose Evangelical participation. In 1873, T. H. Paddon complained about the moderation of the Evangelical leadership. Convocation, he wrote, was 'a great sham,' but he was still more disturbed that 'the long-loved and long-acknowledged leaders of our Evangelical Body,' were nowhere to be found in opposing its growing influence. Paddon, *Thoughts for the Christian Laity*, p. 17.

Writing at the end of the century, Evangelical historian Eugene Stock thought 'a fair and unprejudiced review' called for the 'frank acknowledgment that [Convocation] has won for itself a position that is respected, and that if it has not effected very much, it has done some good and very little harm.' Stock, *Church Missionary Society, vol. 2*, p. 11.

25 According to M. A. Crowther, the church congresses, along with other organizations and the revival of Convocation, were part of a broader movement of 'church defence.' The congresses were begun, she suggested, in an effort to unite the church in the face of many threatening concerns. Crowther provided a general survey of the first few years of the movement and the attitudes adopted by the various parties in the church. Evangelicals were not alone in their scepticism; for entirely different reasons, many Broad Church clergy also refused to participate. In particular, Crowther cited the opposition of Charles Voysey and Mark Pattison, both of whom thought the meetings merely reinforced the conservative mindset of the

church. Crowther, *Church Embattled*, pp. 198-205.

Eugene Stock thought Evangelical suspicions were largely a continuation of their feelings from the early part of the century, when they were a marginalized minority and were allowed little part in the community life of the church. Consequently, they arranged meetings of their own and were reluctant to alter their habits when the new meetings were organized. Unlike other Evangelical historians, however, Stock correctly noted that some Evangelicals were present from the beginning. Stock, *Church Missionary Society*, vol. 2, pp. 357-59.

26   In his opening address to the Oxford Congress in 1862, Bishop Wilberforce sought to allay such fears, noting that the organizers claimed no authority and did not seek to foster any legislation. The congress merely provided the opportunity, said Wilberforce, 'to discuss in a spirit of friendly questioning some of the great subjects upon which depends the advance of the Church of England in her great work of God.' Cited in the *Times*, 15 July 1862.

27   *Record*, 16 July 1862. The *Record* published an anonymous letter criticizing the 1862 Oxford Congress based on the subjects chosen and the list of speakers provided beforehand. The writer suggested that the organizing committee was dominated by the High Church clergy of Oxford. *Record*, 2 July 1862.

The *Times* was also critical of the meetings but without noting any partisan bias. It complained that a congress was 'an indescribable and incomprehensible thing.' In particular, the paper thought that the church did nothing to increase its influence in society by holding isolated meetings in Oxford. The paper concluded, 'Thousands upon thousands rot into worldliness, harden into selfishness, or shrink up into just nothing at all, for the want of a little companionship, sympathy, and guidance – for the want of social development. For them it is too plain we must go somewhere else than to institutional Christianity, parochial organizations, and Ecclesiastical Congresses.' *Times*, 15 July 1862.

28   W. Robert Morrison, Incumbent of St. James's, Halifax, argued that Evangelical opinions would be given a fair hearing at the meetings and their expression would have a great benefit. He continued, 'Of course some crude things will be said on such occasions, and some objectionable sentiments will be broached, but there will be, on the other hand, those present who can expose the fallacy, and refute or reply to the objectionable matter. I can truly say, that if the inquiries that were entered on at Oxford can at future Congresses be carried on in the same admirable spirit, and with the same temper and mutual courtesy, I augur great good for the Church.' Letter to the *Record*, 28 July 1862.

29   The *Record* strongly supported the plan: 'To speak plainly, we much question the advantage of meetings composed of all shades and sections of opinion in the Church of England.... If doctrinal matters are to be shut out from these conferences we doubt the value of them. If doctrinal matters are admitted at them it seems to us impossible to avoid unseemly collision.' The paper quoted approvingly from the circular announcing the Congress: 'The basis on which the Congress will be held is a common desire to maintain whole and undefiled the distinctive Protestant and Evangelical princi-

ples of the Church of England and to resist the Romish and sceptical tendencies of the present day.' *Record*, 31 Aug. 1864.
30 Papers were to be presented by Hugh McNeile, John C. Miller, G. H. Sumner, Hugh Stowell, E. A. Litton and J. C. Colquhoun (a leading lay Evangelical who later opposed attendance at the meetings). *Record*, 16 Sept. 1864.
31 Letter to the *Record*, 16 Sept., 1864. Interestingly, J. C. Ryle, who later became a strong supporter of an Evangelical presence at church meetings, was one of the organizers of the Ipswich meeting.
32 Ryle again reiterated the view that the dates were not chosen with the intention of conflicting with the Bristol meetings. Letter to the *Record*, 23 Sept. 1864.

The *Record* was sharply critical of the Bristol Congress. It served no useful purpose, said the paper, and gave 'a fresh impulse to the insidious movement which is aiming to introduce monasticism, and to change the character of the Church of England.' *Record*, 21 Nov. 1864.

The *Times* also took a largely negative of the meetings. It was willing to allow that some good could come out of congresses when the topics were limited to pastoral concerns, but the paper thought that a line was often crossed when the discussions went on to political issues. In 1862, for instance, Bishop Wilberforce remarked that they claimed no 'deliberative authority' for the meetings but then went on to urge clerical opposition to the Burials Bill. At Bristol, there were no political issues broached, but the paper thought the discussion of 'the Episcopate and the revival of Synods' indicated 'the purposes to which some would be glad to turn this new engine of agitation.' It was concerned that there was a tendency toward 'the undue predominance of the clerical element,' a tendency 'to wander out of that line of deliberation which leads to agreement, and thence to some useful result, into that which leads inevitably to discord within the Church, and possibly to collision with an external power.' The paper did not want to magnify any divisions between the clergy and laity, but it concluded that it was 'impossible to shut our eyes to the growth of an antagonism, which, if aggravated to a certain point, might be fatal to the Church of England.... The danger is that hot-headed champions of ecclesiastical authority should put forward pretensions calculated to estrange educated minds from the Church.' *Times*, 13 Oct. 1864.
33 Letter (signed 'Clericus') to the *Record*, 3 March 1865. Later, an anonymous vicar in Norwich, who was involved in the planning of the congress, also wrote to encourage broader involvement. In meeting to discuss the program, he said that Evangelical clergy had 'received due consideration through the whole course of the arrangements. We have endeavoured to maintain Christian moderation, and we have met with the same at the hands of others.' Letter to the *Record*, 27 Sept. 1865.
34 Samuel Walker, Incumbent at St. Maryleport, Bristol, and a prominent conservative, strongly opposed participation. Instead of viewing it as a duty to attend church meetings, he believed Evangelicals could only maintain their witness to the truth by standing apart from the other church parties. Rather than meeting on false principles of unity, he held it to be his duty 'to denounce them and their system, no matter what the Church relationship in

which they may stand to me.' Walker was unconvinced that Evangelicals needed to attend to make their voice heard: 'I reply, if that way is not of God, I am content that they should have it all to themselves, and I will walk in God's way, and trust to his guidance and blessing. If I by grace have been led into the right way, I will not exchange it for theirs whatever dangers there are to be avoided or advantages secured.' Letter to the *Record*, 22 March 1865.

35 'Meetings of this kind may be productive of great good, and in the long run of practical effects of the highest value, in assimilating the minds of men to each other, smoothing their mutual differences, producing a more candid mutual appreciation of each other, and awakening an earnest and practical temper.' *Record*, 16 Oct. 1865.

The *Record* seemed to echo the sentiments expressed by the *Times* a few days earlier. The *Times* thought the meetings had been successful in bringing members of the various church parties together only so long as controversial topics were avoided. But, it continued, 'we cannot but be afraid that inherent diversities of thought are rather veiled than removed in such meetings.' The Archbishop of York had suggested that the meetings would go a long way toward resolving partisan disputes, but the *Times* thought his view somewhat 'visionary.' The meetings might smooth differences on minor points, 'but let one of those theological storms arise which shake the convictions of men to their centre, and the apparent harmony will be very roughly disturbed.' But the paper hoped the meetings would at least temper partisan spirits. 'The edge of bitter controversy in the future cannot but be somewhat softened by the memory of a good dinner or of a friendly discussion; and a man must learn, at least, to regard his adversary as an Englishman and a Christian, instead of as a heathen man and a publican.' Still, the paper thought the congresses had limited importance. The real work of the church and clergy was in the world, not meeting together amongst themselves for 'good dinners and pleasant conversation.' *Times*, 5 Oct. 1865.

36 The *Times* gave a detailed account of the controversy surrounding Stephens and strongly criticized the Ritualists, some of whom, it was rumored, had attended the congress for the sole reason of participating in the staged demonstration and walk-out during Stephens's lecture. The Ritualists accused Stephens of belittling the sacraments during his courtroom arguments regarding the mixing of water with the eucharistic wine. He had rejected the supposition that the rubrics could have had this mixture in mind when they spoke of 'wine' and compared it to a mixed drink, 'just as rum and water was no longer rum, but "grog".' The *Times* thought his comparison ill-chosen, but repudiated the notion that he had intended to denigrate the sacrament itself, and took the Ritualists to task for not allowing a gentleman the opportunity to explain his intent. *Times*, 20 Oct. 1866.

37 It was clear, thought the paper, that the Evangelical influence was being felt throughout the church (for example, it cited the positive session on lay readers). The paper also thought the patience of those present left a positive impression, in contrast to the Ritualists' protests. The Evangelicals present, said the paper, 'stood in striking contrast to the fierce rudeness, gross discourtesy, and audacious turbulence of the Ritualistic and Romanizing sec-

tion.... These men have injured themselves to a great extent; and if among one class more than another, amid the dignitaries of the Church. They see that such men are impervious to all appeals to their reason and their candour, and cannot be dealt with save by authority and repression.' *Record*, 24 Oct. 1866.
38 *Record*, 7 Oct. 1867.
39 Letter to the *Record*, 14 Oct. 1867.
40 J. C. Colquhoun, *Protestant Churchmen*, p. 28. Colquhoun's language, especially with regard to Pusey, stood in stark contrast to that used by Shaftesbury during the controversy over Charles Voysey later in the year. While refusing to join the committee formed to oppose Voysey (which included Pusey and others from the High Church), Shaftesbury expressed his great admiration for Pusey's view of the authority of Scripture.
41 Ibid.
42 Correspondence cited in the *Record*, 22 Sept. 1869.
43 They did, however, produce a protest signed by thirty of the clergy of Liverpool. The protest recited the facts of the Mackonochie case and concluded: 'We feel called upon, therefore, to make this protest in order to relieve ourselves from all suspicion of sympathy with the erroneous practices so happily condemned, and also from appearing to countenance the dangerous opinion that disturbers of the Church – after direct condemnation, and without a direct expression of penitence – should yet be treated as if their position entitled them to the same weight and consideration as before.' The *Record*'s own reporter, however, defended the selection committee and noted that Mackonochie's appointment had been twice reconsidered; but most of the members of the committee, who did not support the Ritualists, felt bound by honor to allow the invitation to stand. Cited in the *Record*, 6 Oct. 1869.

When Ryle became the first Bishop of Liverpool, an anonymous 'clerical correspondent' in the *Times* suggested that his change of heart with regard to church congresses came the following year. He suggested that Ryle had moderated his opinions since a 'memorable day' at the 1870 Southampton Church Congress, when 'he walked about with a leading Ritualist.' Since then, he reported, Ryle had 'more and more won the hearts of High Churchmen who have met him at subsequent congresses.' *Times*, 16 April 1880.
44 *Record*, 8 Oct. 1869.
45 He thought the Evangelical presence had forced the Ritualists at the meetings to adopt a more moderate tone. More than at any previous congresses, he concluded, the Liverpool meetings devolved into a conflict between two parties, and it was imperative that Evangelicals be fully represented. *Record*, 18 Oct. 1869.

An anonymous correspondent expressed his regret at the absence of Ryle and McNeile, but suggested that a policy of isolation would only harm the Evangelical party in the long term. While the speakers were mostly convinced partisans, he suggested that many in the audience were uncommitted lay members, and the meetings presented an important platform from which Evangelicals could state their case. Their absence would only abandon the audience to the Ritualists and do great harm 'to the cause of Protestant truth.' Letter to the *Record*, 18 Oct. 1869.

The *Times*, in an editorial, suggested that there was something disconcerting about the conflict of opinions at a meeting of the church, as if it could come to no united view on any matters of importance. It was good that clergy and laity from different sections were at least meeting together, but the paper worried about the spectacle of the disputes being publicly aired: 'It must be confessed that the impression is one rather to distract and confuse than to urge, to unite, or to persuade. If this is not a religious movement, designed to present a fair open front to the world, to reassure the friends of the English Church, and to unite all in the greatest of causes, it has ill-luck in being so like one and failing.' Still, the paper thought the meetings important and expressed its hope for an improvement in the future. *Times*, 16 Oct. 1869.

46 Letter to the *Record*, 18 July 1870. The disruptive York Congress in 1866 was apparently the only congress Close ever attended. Thereafter, he swore never to go to another; cf. Chadwick, *Victorian Church, Part Two*, p. 363.

47 Letter to the *Record*, 27 July 1870.

48 Close responded to Titcomb with a degree of alarm. He was 'startled' by the suggestion that there was a generational split within the party and wrote that such a thought had never occurred to him. Of even greater concern to Close, however, was the spirit of conciliation expressed by Titcomb. Close wrote, 'I confess if I thought that such a spirit were prevalent among us I should be alarmed. He fears separation and "isolation;" I dread amalgamation and hollow alliances with the enemies of God's truth.

'I confess I think Mr. Titcomb is in danger of misplacing his love, and of extending his charity beyond the bounds of truth. He is caught by the specious professions of the Broad Church party, who affect such unbounded fellowship with everybody.' Above all, Close, while not doubting Titcomb's sincerity, desired 'to warn him against insidious, indiscriminating charity, and the danger, especially to young men, of the plausible amenities of those who neither hold nor love the truth.' Letter to the *Record*, 8 Aug. 1870.

49 The paper pronounced the meetings a great success. 'It has been shown that Evangelical men have no reason to shrink from public discussions of this kind, or to retire in a false timidity from the open and candid vindication of their principles. *Record*, 24 Oct. 1870. Following on the focus of Titcomb's letters regarding the commitment of the younger clergy to participation in the church congresses, the *Record* noted a meeting regarding ritual and Christian antiquity at which 'several young and comparatively unknown men came forward and rendered most effective service. The Ritualists were confessedly on the defence all through. Their arguments were ably refuted, and many strong, clear statements of the truth made.' *Record*, 14 Oct. 1870.

50 Correspondence cited in the *Record*, 10 July 1871.

51 When the congress was held, the paper thought a moderate tone prevailed. Evangelicals, it concluded with optimism, appeared to be in ascendance; 'instead of being on the defensive and maintaining a difficult protest against the dominant influence of sacerdotalism, they were strong both in numbers and in influence, and supplied beyond all question the most

popular and effective of the speakers.' *Record*, 16 Oct. 1871.

The next year, the paper reported on the strong Evangelical representation and suggested that they had 'asserted their position with fairness and moderation,' in sharp contrast to the noisy demeanor of the Ritualists. That opinion was reiterated in the report published by the High Church *Guardian*: 'While they [Evangelicals] testified very distinctly their disapprobation of any sentiments that were obnoxious to them, they never refused to hear any speaker on the opposite side, or attempted to put him down by the mere clamour of unreasoning cries. That form of opposition was reserved for a small party of extreme men in the opposite direction, who succeeded on Thursday morning in producing a scene of tumult which was not creditable to a religious meeting composed largely of clergymen.' Cited in the *Record*, 18 Oct. 1872.

52 One strident anti-Ritualist that there was a conspiracy underway. Most of the ecclesiastical offices, claimed T. H. Paddon, were bestowed upon the Ritualists and those who were willing to take a non-controversial position. That moderation, he wrote, was promoted by large gatherings of clergy from all parties, such as church congresses, diocesan conferences, and Convocation. Worse still was the fact that many leaders of the Evangelical party were drifting toward the middle and were afraid to condemn the meetings and their influence. Paddon, *Thoughts for the Christian Laity*, pp. 14-15.

With less vituperation, the moderate non-partisan R. E. Bartlett came to a similar conclusion. He thought Evangelicals had obtained a 'new tone of Churchmanship... partly from a dread of being stigmatised as low Churchmen, partly also from the new life which has been infused into the Church of England, it has of late years been their custom to vie with the opposite party in professing devoted and exclusive allegiance to the Church.' Bartlett worried that Evangelicals would no longer be able to balance the influence of the High Church party. He suggested that they had more in common with Nonconformists and ought to use their influence to draw their natural Protestant allies into the national church. [R.E.B.], 'On the Position of the Evangelical Party in the Church of England,' *Fraser's Magazine* New Series, 17 (1878): 25-26.

53 *Record*, 20 Oct. 1875.
54 Letter to the *Record*, 20 July 1877.
55 Letter to the *Record*, 25 July 1877.
56 Ibid. The Vicar of Pantney (signed 'J. S. B.') suggested that 'the attitude of ceaseless opposition' did more to harm the Evangelical movement in the eyes of the laity than did any supposed compromise by attendance at mixed meetings such as church congresses. He concluded, 'Some of our good brethren, I cannot help feeling, are rather reckless in their opposition, not sufficiently bearing in mind, that while truth is to be held supreme, it may be maintained in a courteous manner, and with the charity that "hopeth all things".' Letter to the *Record*, 10 August 1877.
57 It was signed by the Earl of Harrowby, the Hon. Francis Maude, Mr. H. F. Bowker, Canons Garbett, Hoare and Ryle, and Rev. Dawson Campbell. The circular read: 'The cause of Evangelical truth, and the interests of the national establishment, alike demand that every possible sacrifice of personal

convenience should be made by clergymen and laymen in order to maintain the Protestant character of the Church of England, and to vindicate it from possible misapprehension during the proceedings of Congress. Aware of the convenience of a central meeting place for friends from different parts of the country, rooms have been engaged at the Greyhound Hotel, which will be supplied with newspapers, writing materials, &c., &c., where, we trust, we may have the pleasure of welcoming you. A meeting for the purpose of asking God's blessing on each day's proceedings will be held daily at the Greyhound Hotel at 9 a.m. A luncheon for our friends (ladies welcome) will be provided daily (1.15 p.m.) in the large room of the Greyhound Hotel at 2s. per head.' Cited in the *Record*, 3 Oct. 1877.

58 Garbett rejected the common accusation that Evangelicals were narrow-minded and lacked a strong commitment to the church: 'Evangelical Churchmen are sometimes described, and therefore, I suppose, conceived of, as if in a blind self-confidence in our own private interpretation of the Word of God we rejected the testimony of the primitive ages and the just authority of the Church as the keeper and witness of Holy Writ. Such a description is wholly untrue. I cannot, indeed, contrast the Church with the Word of God, for to me they are one. It is because I believe her teaching to embody the Catholic Faith that I minister within her pale.' Cited in the *Record*, 12 Oct. 1877.

59 Cited in the Times, 11 Oct. 1877.

60 Letter of J. Bennett to the *Record*, 19 Oct. 1877. Garbett replied that his critics ought to have read the whole report of his speech, in particular, the section where he had acknowledged 'great and serious' differences between the two parties. But, he continued, 'I see no reason as yet to qualify my opinion that the relation in which Evangelicals stand towards the historical High Church party and the Protestant Low Church party is, and ought to be, essentially different to the attitude of indignant protest in which they stand towards Rationalistic theologians at one extreme and Romanizing Sacerdotalists at the other.' Letter to the *Record*, 29 Oct. 1877.

J. C. Ryle also spoke at the Croydon Church Congress in a similar vein and was even more harshly criticized. Ryle was encouraged, in this regard, by the Parliamentary debate over the Burial Bill, and he declared that he was ready 'to stand side by side with the High Church party in defence of our churchyards.' Cited in [R.E.B.], 'Evangelical Party,' *Fraser's Magazine*, p. 31. The *Record*, on October 22nd, reprinted a report from the *Ipswich Journal* that summarized Ryle's speech. Samuel Walker complained, 'Now if Canon Ryle said this, or anything like this, then attendance at the Congress and union with the enemies of the truth have acted upon him precisely as some of us said they would do, and his case is calculated, with God's blessing, to act as a more effectual warning to God's people against all such compromises of Christian and Protestant principle than any remonstrance that I or any of the brethren who agree with me could possibly utter.' Walker concluded, somewhat self-righteously, that he could not believe 'that Canon Ryle uttered the language imputed to him,' and that he felt he was doing Ryle 'a service in provoking him in brotherly love to a reply.' Letter to the *Record*, 26 Oct. 1877.

Ryle was provoked to a reply, but with little of Walker's sense of brotherly love. He suggested that Walker ought to have ascertained the facts before writing a public letter. He then gave a more extensive report of his remarks than those cited by the paper. He had suggested that there ought to be toleration for and a degree of cooperation with all who honestly maintained their adherence to the articles and formularies of the Church of England. He refused to concede, however, that any toleration ought to be offered to those who transgressed the accepted boundaries. He continued, with regard to attendance at congresses, 'If anyone thinks that we sanction and endorse other teaching than our own, by going to Congresses, I cannot agree with him. No Resolutions are ever passed at a Congress, and the hearers are left to form their own conclusions after listening to all sides. If anyone thinks that it is our duty to use rough and severe language towards men with whom we differ, and to turn a Congress platform into a bear-garden, I can only say that I disagree with him.... Finally, if Mr. Walker or anyone else supposes that I have gone back from any of the great Evangelical principles which I have now maintained for thirty-five years, because I go to Congresses, I can only tell him that he is utterly, entirely, wholly, and completely mistaken. Let him only read two volumes I have lately published, *Old Paths* and *Knots Untied*, and judge for himself. But I am not able to see that it is my duty to refuse to meet men of other schools than my own, when I can do it without compromise. And when I do meet them, I think it a plain duty to treat them with civility, courtesy, and respect, even when I cannot agree with them.' Letter to the *Record*, 31 Oct. 1877.

61 Perhaps the most amazing argument against Evangelical participation came in 1880. In the course of the year, several prominent Evangelicals had died, including S. A. Walker, J. C. Miller, Edward Auriol, and Henry Wright, the CMS secretary. An anonymous correspondent (signed 'Watchman') suggested that their deaths might be a sign that God had 'a controversy with the Evangelical section of the Church of England. See Isaiah iii.1-4, "Many are weak and sickly among us, and many sleep".' He charged that the party was guilty of combining with those of unsound doctrine at church congresses and concluded, 'God knows I write this with an aching heart. It is laid upon my conscience. I believe the Evangelical party has entered upon the downward path of compromise, and that God is just now giving us a solemn warning as to our position. Shall we give heed to it? Alas! I fear not.' Letter to the *Record*, 20 Aug. 1880.

Benjamin S. Clarke, of Christ Church, Southport, was deeply troubled both by the logic of the argument and by its implications. He wrote, 'The argument amounts to this – Because Mr. Walker and Mr. Auriol have recently died at an age beyond the allotted span of three score years and ten, and because Mr. Wright has been recently drowned while bathing in Coniston, therefore it may be the Lord is manifesting his displeasure with us Evangelicals for attending Congresses, and particularly for taking part in their devotional meetings.

'I confess that this is a kind of argument that grieves me sorely. It reflects on the dead as well as on the living. It reflects on Prebendary Auriol himself, whose judgment has been so much and so justly commended. It was he who took the chair at a meeting held at Croydon three years ago, when it was unanimously agreed, with his entire approval, that it was advisable that Evangelicals should attend Church Congresses. Arguments of this kind, moreover, are like two-edged swords; they cut both ways. I might argue, for instance, that God has been very much pleased with the action of Evangelicals with regard to Church Congresses, and that his approval has been manifested in the raising of Canon Ryle, their acknowledged leader, first to the Deanery of Salisbury and then to the See of Liverpool. But we have no right to argue one way or the other.' Letter to the *Record*, 30 Aug. 1880.

62 In the *Record*'s report on the Newcastle Church Congress in 1881, the paper's reporter returned to the central argument voiced by the opposition: 'I have often heard it said that the effect of Church Congresses upon the Evangelical men who attend them is to make them more churchly, more disposed to fraternize with Ritualists, and less concerned about distinctive Evangelical doctrines. As often as I have heard this I have wondered at the very poor estimate it expresses of the power of our distinctive principles to hold and to control the moral and spiritual intelligence of Evangelical Churchmen. I know it is said we are "a rope of sand," a "bag of marbles," and I know that we do fail of definite organization and of power of prompt rallying for united action on critical occasions; but I do not know, and I will not believe, that the men whose yearly increasing liberalities sustain and whose wise energies direct the mightiest missionary agencies of our times at home and abroad, hold so lightly by their convictions as to be moved from their steadfastness by a bishop's smile, or by the courtesies they may happen to exchange with old college companions of different opinions on doctrine or church ritual.' *Record*, 14 Oct. 1881.

E. H. Bickersteth argued that it was the duty of Evangelicals to breathe spiritual life into the meetings of the church. The Church had to address the needs of the day, and it was 'not by holding aloof from, but holding her own in these gatherings of our brethren, that in my judgment we shall most glorify our Master.' E. H. Bickersteth, *Thoughts for Today, No. 1: Evangelical Churchmanship and Evangelical Eclecticism* (London: Sampson, Low, & Co., 1883), pp. 33-34.

63 Opposition was renewed, however, following the Cardiff Church Congress in 1889. The local committee, which was responsible for the opening worship service, turned it into a 'High Mass' with every conceivable element of ritual included, much to the chagrin of Evangelical participants. In response to an Evangelical protest, the Bishop of Llandaff expressed great regret at the proceedings. Cf. *Record*, 4 and 11 Oct. 1889. In the weeks that followed, conservative Evangelicals used it as an argument against attendance. E. A. Knox suggested that the events indicated just how little Evangelicals had been able to influence the atmosphere of the meetings. If anything, they were being adversely influenced by their association with High Church partisans, and the public were led to suppose that Evangelicals were willing to compromise the purity of the church if only given toleration for their own position. Letter to the *Record*, 25 Oct. 1889.

At a meeting of the Representative Council of the Union of Clerical and

Lay Associations shortly thereafter, Rev. A. Oates, of Christ Church, Ware, read a paper in defense of Evangelical participation. According to the *Record*, it was a convincing argument, and the paper later reprinted it in entirety. Oates suggested that Evangelicals must be organized to make their participation effective, and in that regard, suggested that the Union was the best group to accomplish that goal. Participation was necessary for the good of the party and of the church, and Evangelicals had nothing to fear from meeting with those representing the other sections of the church. He concluded, 'For the truth's sake, for the Church's sake, for the sake of our credit and influence, I appeal to my brethren to unite in concerted effort, as well as in private prayer, for the maintenance of the things we hold dear, and for the promulgation of the truths which we believe to be the life of the Church.' Cited in the *Record*, 24 Jan. 1890.

When Capt. Cobham complained about the service, on behalf of the CA, to Archbishop Benson, he received a sharp rebuke. Benson suggested that those who sought the peace of the church ought to 'detach themselves from factions within.' The rebuke, applicable to the CA and the ECU alike, brought a complaint from Archdeacon Denison, for whom Benson similarly had little sympathy. Cf. Arthur Cristopher Benson, *The Life of Edward White Benson, Sometime Archbishop of Canterbury*, vol. 2 (London: Macmillan & Co., 1899), pp. 287-88.

64 In 1864, the *Times* complained about the partisan activities of the 'clerical party' at the Bristol Church Congress. The paper noted that the extreme views expressed were likely to raise lay opposition to synods in so far as they would apparently be dominated by the clergy. *Times*, 13 Oct. 1864.

According to Eugene Stock, the idea was first promoted by Archdeacon Emery, who organized the first synod in the diocese of Ely, under Bishop Browne, in 1864. Stock, *Church Missionary Society*, vol. 2, p. 361.

65 The report of the committee was reprinted in the *Times*, 8 June 1867; cf. Appendix D. Many of the bishops were opposed to the diocesan synod movement in its early years; cf. Stock, *English Church*, p. 61.

66 Rev. J. N. Worsfold gave voice to the depth of feeling in opposition to attendance. 'I believe that all attempts to vindicate Reformation truth in the Lichfield Synod, whether archdiaconal or diocesan, would meet with the most violent resistance, and that those who attend those gatherings would go under a tacit if not an avowed pledge to be silent....

'I earnestly trust that Evangelical men will not fall into this new snare spread for their feet, and that those who have, to some extent, compromised themselves, may be led to see the true bearing of this movement.' Letter to the *Record*, 17 July 1868.

J. C. Colquhoun, Chairman of the CA council, was particularly concerned by the rise of the diocesan synod movement and feared it would result in great evil. 'Such a scheme is open, through its constitution, to a grave objection. It combines the evils of irresponsible power, of clerical isolation, and of the ultimate estrangement of the laity.' He feared, above all, that it would leave the bishop with practically unlimited power. Colquhoun, *Protestant Churchmen*, p. 10.

67 Garbett, writing in the midst of the debate over Irish disestablishment, was

particularly concerned about the role diocesan synods might take on if the discussion culminated in the disestablishment of the entire Anglican church. How much more influential would the synods then become? He was, however, concerned about the accusation that Evangelicals were only acting out of a 'party spirit' and sought to refute that charge as well as to encourage Evangelical participation in general church meetings. 'We have much to learn from our opponents, and there is something very humiliating in the passive indifference with which Evangelical men keep away from public meetings, compared to the zeal and devotedness with which other sections of the Church flock together on every occasion, in support of their principles and their cause.' Edward Garbett, *Diocesan Synods* (London: William Hunt & Co., 1868), pp. 7, 10.

68 Ibid., pp. 13-16.
69 J. C. Colquhoun was convinced the Evangelical laity would be excluded, and that those chosen to participate would only reflect the views of the diocesan hierarchy. Similarly he suspected that the clerical representatives would be men who were either 'obscure and deferential,' or those who held 'exaggerated views of the priestly office.' Colquhoun, *Protestant Churchmen*, pp. 14-15.
70 Letter (signed 'A Derbyshire Vicar') to the *Record*, 3 June 1868.
71 The 'Derbyshire Vicar' felt the resolution secured all that was necessary for evangelical participation. 'With such a Resolution I maintain that we need not be afraid of joining this movement, we are guilty of no inconsistency in doing so, and if the Evangelical party would only act together in this matter, they might, with the support of the laity, exercise a powerful influence in the affairs of these conferences.' Letter to the *Record* 24 June 1868.
72 *Record*, 12 May 1869.
73 In an 1874 survey of the rise of diocesan synods, Archdeacon Bickersteth counted 13 dioceses out of 21 in the province of Canterbury that had instituted synodical meetings, and 10 of those had taken on a permanent character. He thought they were now greatly valued by all and were 'generally recognised as an important (I may say an essential) part of our Church system.' Letter to the *Record*, 12 Oct. 1874.
74 Letter to the *Record*, 4 May 1870. The next year, Ryle published a pamphlet elaborating his view, *A Churchman's Duty about Diocesan Conferences* (London: William Hunt & Co., 1871). The *Record* summarized the views expressed in the pamphlet and gave it a very favorable review. *Record*, 28 July 1871.

Interestingly, Bishop Magee of Peterborough complained in a letter to a friend that Ryle had instigated a 'determined attempt of ultra-Evangelicals' to undermine his first diocesan conference. MacDonnell, *Life of William Magee, vol. 1*, p. 266.

75 Unlike Ryle, Edward Bickersteth took an even more optimistic perspective and viewed the meetings as being of great usefulness for both clergy and laity. He also thought they were a source of strength and support for the bishops during a trying period. Evidence of their practical importance could be seen in their rapid growth, and he thought it safe to conclude that they would be instituted in every diocese within the space of a few years.

Record, 12 Oct. 1874.

76 For a survey of the 1869 meetings and their domination by the Ritualist clergy, cf. the chapter entitled, 'Anglo-Catholic Revivalism,' in John Kent, *Holding the Fort: Studies in Victorian Revivalism* (London: Epworth Press, 1978), especially pp. 236-71. Kent questioned the thesis of Dieter Voll, who suggested that the Ritualists shared certain affinities with the Evangelical tradition, and, in effect, assimilated its better points. This could be illustrated, argued Voll, by the 'Catholic Evangelicalism' of the prominent missioners such G. H. Wilkinson, George Body and others. Cf. Dieter Voll, *Catholic Evangelicalism* (London: Faith Press, 1963). Kent argued that 'revivalism' was broader than its American and Evangelical strands. He believed that Voll failed to take account of the tradition of mission preaching among Roman Catholics, and argued that the Ritualist missioners were influenced by them rather than by Evangelicals.

In support of Voll's argument, however, one could cite the prominent Ritualist, R. F. Littledale. In an essay on church parties, he cited the example of the services as an indication of the movement's great flexibility and comprehensiveness. It was able to assimilate the better aspects and methods of the Evangelical movement, he claimed, while still maintaining its distinctiveness; cf. Littledale, 'Church Parties,' *Contemporary Review*, pp. 301-02.

J. C. Ryle, looking back in 1892, suggested that the mission services explicitly followed the precedent established by Evangelicals in the evening services held in Birmingham, Ipswich, Islington, and at Exeter Hall. J. C. Ryle, *Facts and Men. Being Pages from English Church History, between 1553 and 1683* (London: William Hunt & Co., 1882), p. xxviii.

77 George Mansfield, Vicar of St. John's, Brixton, wrote to the *Record* asking for counsel from his fellow Evangelical clergy. He noted that the circular announcing the meetings was signed by Canon Gregory and other clergy whom it was 'no libel to designate Ultra High Churchmen, if not Ritualists.' The circular, he wrote, invited cooperation 'in a movement of twelve days' duration "to open our churches, mission-rooms, and school-rooms, daily during this period for services, sermons, classes, prayer meetings (!), and whatever spiritual exercises may be suitable for this one end – the conversion of men's hearts from the love of the world and sin unto the love of God and our Lord Jesus Christ." Nothing can sound better than this. It is a leaf from the Evangelical book.

'But how can I co-operate, even in such a movement as this (which I approve of with all my heart), with men of Tractarian and Ritualistic principles without incurring the risk, as far as I am concerned, of leading the world to suppose that, after all, the differences between the High Church Ritualistic party and men who hold Protestant and Evangelical truth are but small and of no moment? I cannot do this, for I believe that the differences between us touch the very vitals of saving truth.' Letter to the *Record*, 29 Oct. 1869.

78 Later the *Record* cited an article from the *Pall Mall Gazette* in which that paper took a similar view of the meetings: 'The twelve days' services have been, therefore, in plain reality, only an attempt to gain one little step of vantage ground in the progress now making towards Rome under cover of

the general goodwill with which men regard any energetic attempt to rouse the consciences of sinners. And the simple and well-meaning clergymen, of other shades of belief, who have joined in the movement, may say with justice that they were entirely unaware beforehand – though, in our minds, they ought to have suspected – the compromising attitude into which their good intentions were about to lead them' *Record* 29 Nov. 1869.

The *Times* detailed the development of the plan for the meetings by a group of Ritualists the previous summer, in connection with 'the Society of St. John the Evangelist' located in Cowley. In describing the course of the services, it noted, 'At the end of each separate service one of the clergy remains in the schoolroom, the church, or the sacristy, to give spiritual advice to each separate penitent, and, if necessary, to hear his confession. There is no disguise upon the subject, and, be it right or wrong, be it in harmony with the theory of the English Church or not, there can be no doubt in the minds of those who have attended these Mission Services that confession is no longer a moot point or a matter of discussion, but part and parcel of the religious 'revival,' and differing only in a very slight degree from the practice of the Roman Catholic Church.' *Times*, 23 Nov. 1869.

Charles Westerton complained, in a letter to the *Times*, regarding a handbill being circulated to advertise the mission services at St. Paul's, Knightsbridge. After listing an extensive series of services throughout the day, the bill concluded, 'The Mission priests (whose address will be 16, Wilton-crescent, S.W.) will be ready to give spiritual direction and to hear confessions in the church – Rev. W. J. E. Bennett, from 12 to 4, and Rev. Canon Jenkins, from 5 to 8.' Westerton questioned the right of the clergy involved 'to hear confessions,' and asked how the bishops could have given their 'sanction' to such. Letter to the *Times*, 15 Nov. 1869. W. D. Maclagan, Rector of Newington, defended the meetings from a High Church perspective and suggested that it was not necessary for the participants to all agree upon the methods used in their respective parishes. The different parishes, if united in purpose, did not all have to follow the same methods to achieve the intended goal, or to approve of the means used elsewhere. Letter to the *Times*, 16 Nov. 1869.

79 The paper described George Body, an influential mission preacher, as 'a man who delivers thrilling addresses, and stands before the communion-table pointing to the crucifix, and exhorting men to come to Jesus. So far as Christ is truly preached, we wish Godspeed to the message by whomsoever it is delivered, but we are assured, on the most impartial authority, that even the addresses of Mr. Body... [are] indissolubly associated with the fatal error of Rome; and that whilst Christ is preached, it is virtually through the medium of the priest and the absolution obtained after resort to the Confessional.' *Record*, 22 Nov. 1869.

The *Times* reported on the services conducted by Body, comparing his style and effectiveness to that of Wesley and Whitefield. The paper, noting that his preaching had been called 'sensational' in a less than complimentary sense, concluded that it deserved to be held in higher opinion. Cf. *Times*, 19 Nov. 1869.

80 The importance of the meetings in public opinion was clear as the topic was

taken up again a week later. The *Record* responded to an article in the *Saturday Review* which suggested that Evangelicals had done little to reach the working classes and belittled the theater services as ineffective in this regard. *Record*. 29 Nov. 1869.

An Evangelical correspondent later suggested that the mission services were, in fact, a sign of the growing influence of their party. In reporting on the Southampton Church Congress, the writer took note of Body's preaching: 'A stranger hearing for the first time the speeches of Mr. Body would have taken him for a Wesleyan preacher. This must be attributed to the growth of Protestantism, notwithstanding the yearnings after Roman teaching and ceremonial. The advocates of Ritual begin to find that the novelty and attraction of music, incense, colour, and candles will not convert souls, and if they are in earnest for souls, as some of them are, they are compelled to fall back upon the example of our Evangelical fathers, and put in its proper place the ordinance of preaching.' Letter to the *Record*, 24 Oct. 1870.

In contrast, the non-partisan *Quarterly Review* was strongly supportive. The meetings, it reported, had been 'employed with excellent effect in many parishes, under the guidance of clergymen of all parties.' But it was also concerned about the Ritualist impulse; 'if the Act of Uniformity has been something strained in the midst of this varied activity – well, we do not think that any one very much regrets it, so long as it is only strained in the way of earnest work, not of ritual vagaries.' Anon., 'Church and the Age,' *Quarterly Review*, p. 48.

Strangely, the Ritualist, R. F. Littledale, thought the Evangelical press had been bewildered by 'the entire absence of ceremonial display or rubrical observance.' In fact, they found those elements present and strongly condemned them. Littledale, 'Church Parties,' *Contemporary Review*, p. 302.

81 Evening services were scheduled for Islington, South London, Lambeth and Southwark. The Evangelical publisher, Seeley's, printed a special *Guide to the United Evening Services*. The program was to include sermons, prayer meetings and house to house visitation in each parish. *Record*, 29 Nov. 1869.

A letter from A. Rogers of St. Peter's, Bristol, described mission services that were held at twelve churches in Bristol from Feb. 21st to March 1st. The services were held each evening at 8:00 p.m., with a different preacher each night. There was a door to door visitation program and circulars were handed out to invite the working classes to the special meetings. 'Immediately after the service (always a short one) inquirers were requested to retire into the schoolroom, if near, for counsel, advice, personal and more private intercourse, and I know in some cases this seemed to be eminently blessed; but to carry this out, more than one clergyman is required to be present.' In this work, Rogers thought an experienced missioner was especially valuable. Letter to the *Record*, 11 March 1870.

82 Included among these were the use of crucifixes and incense, the elevation of the eucharistic elements, processions with banners and one ceremony in which candles were blessed and lighted for five hundred penitents. Colquhoun described the last event as 'a performance of gross superstition, which, as far as I know, has never before profaned a Protestant Church.'

Correspondence cited in the *Record*, 5 Jan. 1870.
83   Cited in the *Times*, 11 Oct. 1873.
84   Ibid. The opposition to the Ritualists extended to other forms of ecclesiastical cooperation as well. The *Record* noted in November 1870, that a number of Evangelical clergy in Wolverhampton had refused to participate in services at which two new Ritualist churches were consecrated. They sent the Bishop of Lichfield a memorial stating their opposition 'in firm but respectful and courteous terms.' The paper expressed its hope that other clergy would similarly refuse to participate in such mixed services. 'We think that if this course were generally adopted, bishops would be compelled by the force of public opinion to be more cautious in giving personal sanction to sacerdotal extravagances, and would exercise greater vigilance over the character of the services in which they permit themselves to participate.' *Record*, 18 Nov. 1870.
85   The *Times* published a letter from Harry Jones, Rector of St. George's-in-the-East, which had been the scene of anti-Ritualist rioting in the 1850s. In his letter, Jones explained his opposition. Making no mention of Ritualism, he objected to the whole emotional appeal of the special mission services and suggested that they undermined the normal working of the parish. They created, he thought, a 'hot house' pressure that was not conducive 'to the wholesome apprehension of the truth. The contagious strain of reiterated addresses, night after night, in the same church, the stress of fervid hymns, accompanied by the persuasion that they form a part of an impassioned chorus praying for supernatural influence, seems to me ill calculated to kindle or to promote the growth of healthy godliness.' Correspondence cited in the *Times*, 9 Feb. 1874.

In an editorial the next day, the *Times* applauded the courageous stance of Jones. The paper feared that missioners preyed on 'weak and susceptible minds' that could easily end in 'a morbid excitement.' The paper thought numerous clergy probably had similar reservations but did not want to offend their bishop. *Times*, 10 Feb. 1874.

The opposite view was argued in an 1879 pamphlet by J. F. B. Tinling. In his view, parish clergy were usually too busy or unprepared to reach the unchurched masses. Experienced mission preachers and the excitement of evangelistic meetings were no threat to the parish system; rather, thought Tinling, they were simply the best way to reach those who would not otherwise be attracted to the church. J. F. B. Tinling, *The Gospel in the Churches; a Plea for Special Evangelistic Services by the Regular Ministry* (London: Samuel Bagster & Sons, 1879).
86   Letter to the *Record*, 3 Sept. 1873. According to John Kent, despite the opposition of the bishops, the Ritualists did, in fact, continue to use the mission services to inculcate the laity with their particular doctrine of confession. Cf. Kent, *Holding the Fort*, pp. 275-81.
87   The *Record* wrote in an editorial, 'We suggest that the Evangelical clergy as a body should solemnly memorialise the three Bishops, and should represent that they accept the invitation to concur in the Mission, on the assurance that the Bishops will not allow them to be compromised by practices which they believe in their conscience to be contrary both to Scripture and

to the Church. They therefore demand security that their Lordships will not allow the Mission to be perverted to party purposes, or be made the means of extending the abominations of the confessional.... The demand would be so fair and right and just that it would be impossible for the Bishops to refuse it. Thus any extravagances to which the Mission may possibly give occasion will at all events be deprived of all public and official sanction. But if Evangelical men stand aloof they lose the opportunity of making this protest, and throw the whole conduct of the movement hopelessly into the hands of their opponents.' *Record*, 23 June 1873.

88 Thorold concluded, 'If those who are confident that they possess the truth decline, without good reason, such an occasion of publicly proclaiming it, they must run the risk of confessing their loss of influence in the face of an age only too ready to be sceptical as to the power of divine truth of any sort. What is even worse, they may not only convict themselves of an actual want of faith in the power of the Gospel, but they may be playing the very game of the truth's worst enemies, and (without meaning it) be refusing service to Christ.' Anthony W. Thorold, *Parochial Missions* (London: W. Isbister & Co., 1873), pp. 2-3.

89 Letter to the *Record*, 3 Aug. 1873.

90 As was the case with both the earlier revival and the rise of the holiness movement, some Evangelicals distrusted the emotional element present in the mission services, especially in the 'after service,' when those who stayed were exhorted to repent. One observer complained about meetings led by William Hay Aitken, who became one of the most prominent Evangelical mission preachers. The correspondent described the meeting for penitents: 'After the service in the church we went to the prayer-meeting in the schoolroom, anxious to see how it was conducted, and to hear Mr. Aitken further. I confess to the wish that I had not gone. It destroyed all the impressions that the sermon had made. The proceedings were, to my thinking, marked by a sad want of sobriety and reverence. After a hymn and while another man was praying, Aitken began his rounds among the people in the room, asking one and another "Have you found Christ?" "Have you found the peace?" If the answer returned was "Yes," then he would say "Glory be to God!" "Bless God!" If no reply was made, or the answer was "No," then he would kneel down by them, and pray with them, or urge them at once to come to Christ for peace. Nor was he the only one who did this; he had helpers in the room, men and women, who pursued exactly the same course, so that from all parts of the meeting cries of "Glory be to God!" "Bless God!" were heard, or words of entreaty when the sinner who had not found peace was urged to seek it there and then. In some cases where a person would say he had "found Christ," and yet made no demonstration to that effect, the Mission preacher would strike them on the shoulder once or twice, with the question, "Why don't you say, 'Glory be to God'?" And all this time, let it be remembered, the clergyman was on his knees at the table praying loudly and urgently that "souls might be converted now; that God would send down his Spirit now." I had never been at a "Revival" prayer meeting before, and the effect was indescribable; so painful indeed to me and my companion that we got up from our knees,

and left the room as quietly as possible.' Letter (signed C. D. B., Ambleside) to the *Record*, 18 Dec. 1871.

91 Garratt deeply lamented the Evangelical rejection of the revivals and drew a spiritual conclusion: 'Our venerated friend, Mr. Henry Venn, once said to me (and I fully agreed with him then, and agree with him still) that he feared that Ritualism was the permitted scourge upon us for the rejection of that blessing. I do not remember the words, but the thought, and the earnestness with which he expressed it, I can never forget.' Letter to the *Record*, 3 Aug. 1873. H. C. G. Moule similarly regretted the negative reaction of Evangelicals to the revivals; c.f. Moule, *Evangelical School*, pp. 55-59.

92 'The majority of the Conference were in favour of the whole after-meeting being conducted in the church, chiefly on the grounds (1) that an undesirable break was produced by adjourning elsewhere, during which many persons left altogether; (2) that a more solemn and less excited tone usually prevailed; (3) that it was easier to reach individuals for private conversation; and (4) that it was important to associate the special spiritual blessings of the Mission with the house of God. On the other hand, some preferred the schoolroom, where they felt more free. In poorer parishes it was found that persons would come to a schoolroom who would not come to the church.' *Record*, 2 Feb. 1874.

93 Reprinted in the *Record*, 2 Feb. 1874; cf. Appendix E.

94 The bishops allowed that there might be a few who would seek to introduce confession, just as some others might use the services to introduce Nonconformist or lay preachers into the pulpit. But both parties knew that the Bishops 'would never have sanctioned the Mission but in the frank confidence that neither would be attempted; and that the attempt in either case would be an unfair and unworthy advantage impossible to be taken by truthful and religious men while engaged in a great work which, without God's blessing, must be the idlest waste of time and toil.' Cited in the *Times*, 7 Feb. 1874.

A. W. Thorold thought the moderate pastoral letter from the bishops was persuasive and fair: 'it will disarm the prejudices of many hostile judgments, and to those among the clergy, who for so long have been earnestly calling on the bishops to lead them, it gives an excellent opportunity for showing if they are willing to be led.' Thorold, *Parochial Missions*, p. 1.

95 In 1877, the *Record* suggested that Evangelicals, while participating in the missions, ought to avoid any direct cooperation with the Ritualists. While much good could come from the meetings, the danger remained of misleading the laity if there were any appearance of a joint effort. *Record*, 14 Feb. 1877. The paper attempted to downplay divisions within the party and suggested after the 1877 missions, that there was greater unanimity than commonly thought. *Record*, 12 March 1877. Later in the year, however, the paper reiterated its opposition to any direct cooperation. Many Evangelicals, it suggested, gave their support because they felt bound to their bishop. But it was clearly the case that a majority of the missioners were Ritualists who wanted to subvert 'the Protestantism of the Church.' The whole movement had taken on 'the character of a conspiracy,' and missions had become a central focus of the Ritualists in the effort to spread

their teaching. *Record*, 10 Dec. 1877.
96 Clifford complained that it was 'painful' to hear some of the accusations made and suggested that their opposition to the Ritualists ought to take a more positive form. 'He would repeat what their dear friend Mr. Biddulph used to say, "Out-preach them, out-pray them, and out-live them".' Cited in the *Record*, 30 Oct. 1876.

A. S. Page, Vicar of Selsley, Stonehouse, also expressed his concerns about the reactionary attitude of conservative Evangelicals. He refused 'to scout and attack' every mission preacher whose preaching might cause a few 'unstable souls' to be led astray. Many more, he thought, were hurt by 'the apparent want of charity which is seen in these loudly published and warmly defended differences of opinion.' Furthermore, he suggested that many of laity lost respect for the clergy when they saw them entangled in bitter strife. Page continued, 'I am not proposing that Evangelical clergymen should invite Ritualists to come and conduct Missions in their churches, though I always go when invited to preach by my High Church brethren. But I do say that the attitude taken by some Evangelicals during the recent Missions in Manchester, Bristol, and Gloucester was calculated to harm the Evangelical cause.' Page went on to say that two Evangelical churches had shut their doors rather than participate in the mission, but that those who had participated had experienced great blessing. He concluded, 'I would, therefore, urge upon my brethren the duty of inculcating and practising Christian charity, as well as Christian faithfulness. Party spirit and controversy certainly do not tend to increase love and spirituality of mind.' Letter to the *Record*, 28 Feb. 1877.
97 Ryle, *No Uncertain Sound*, p. 154.
98 Letter to the *Record*, 20 Nov. 1872.
99 Letter to the *Record*, 25 Nov. 1872.
100 R. E. Bartlett suggested in an 1878 essay that Evangelicals were misguided in that regard. Writing from a moderate Broad Church perspective, he suggested that the tendencies of the age had moved the Evangelical party closer to the High Church at the cost of their relations with Nonconformists. In his opinion, however, they would be better served to join with their natural allies in opposing the Ritualists, 'not by prosecutions and associations, but by setting before the Christian people of England a more liberal and a less professional type of Christianity.' [R.E.B.], 'Evangelical Party,' *Fraser's Magazine*, p. 30.
101 Bishop Magee of Peterborough addressed the issue in his 1872 charge to the clergy. If a bishop admonished the priest with regard to any extravagances, he was condemned as merely 'the nominee of the Prime Minister,' who had 'neither the learning nor the piety' to command the obedience of 'a truly Catholic priest.' Magee continued, 'Finally, if his bishop, having exhausted every effort of remonstrance, counsel, and even of entreaty, proceeds at last to enforce the law and discipline of the Church of which he is a chief pastor, he is met by an indignant cry of tyranny and persecution, and fierce accusations of attempting to stamp out the liberties of the Catholic priesthood; followed probably, by a denunciation of the hateful union between Church and State.' He noted that in one regard the Ritualists did not tend toward

Romanism – their demands for the individual liberty of the clergy would never be tolerated in that church. MacDonnell, *Life of Magee, vol. 1*, pp. 280-81.

102 Bishop Ellicott believed the lawsuits were responsible for driving a wedge between the two parties. The moderates in the High Church were pushed toward one extreme wing, while those more 'closely associated with Protestant principles' were driven toward the other. Cited in the *Times*, 30 Oct. 1872.

Bishop Magee similarly regretted the effect of the campaign. He acknowledged that there were many 'High Churchmen who, though themselves truly loyal to our Church, throw their shield over those whom I cannot honestly regard as loyal to her.' But neither could he support 'the vulgar, bitter, ignorant Puritanism' that was 'persecuting' the Ritualists. And, he concluded, their policies were self-defeating; 'they are forcing on that alliance between the High Churchmen and the extremist Ritualist which a common danger naturally impels to.' MacDonnell, *Life of Magee, vol. 2*, pp. 56-57.

In 1874, an anonymous writer attempted, following the example of Conybeare's famous essay, to survey the relative strength of the various parties in the church. Writing apparently from a moderate, non-partisan perspective, he suggested that the anti-Ritualist extremists represented only a small percentage of the Evangelical party but had a negative impact that far exceeded their numbers. They were 'a noisy, unrenewed race, full of excitement, party phrases, fancied superiority in doctrinal knowledge, spiritual pride, narrow-mindedness, and uncharitableness.' Rather than achieving their goals, though, they brought 'religious profession into contempt' and had 'undeservedly given a bad name to the Evangelical party.' Anonymous, *Church Parties*, pp. 15-16.

103 Cited in the *Times*, 30 Oct. 1872. Bishop Temple of Exeter expressed his concern in response to an anti-Ritualist memorial (signed by 12,000 clergy and laity) protesting the Ritualist petition on confession presented to Convocation: 'It is to me a cause of very deep regret that some among us should use their position in the Church to teach what the Church does not teach, and to revive practices which the Church has discontinued and discouraged. it is a cause of deep regret that the decisions of the courts should be willfully disregarded, and I find it difficult to understand how any whose position requires them to teach should be insensible to the serious mischief that is sure to be the consequence of such an example of lawlessness. The attempt to introduce the practice of habitual confession is of all these attempts the most to be regretted, and if it succeeded would do the most mischief.' Temple went on, however, to suggest that the movement's influence ought not to be exaggerated. He also thought some of the clergy who adopted innovations were unconscious of their errors and ought not to be unfairly accused of disloyalty. Ultimately, he believed, the Ritualists would only be put down by the exertion of a moral influence: 'Whatever is mistaken in their action will have less chance of long influence, and far less chance of being continued into the next generation of clergy, if we show a hearty and generous appreciation of what is good. The principles of the Reformation

have everything to gain from our practising the most patient and most kindly toleration.' Cited in the *Times*, 5 Jan. 1874.
104 *Record*, 18 June 1873. The pamphlet's author was particularly disturbed by the elaborate Ritualist funeral of Thomas Combe in Oxford; cf. Reed, *Glorious Battle*, pp. 92-93.

For examples of other non-partisan moderates who were increasingly alienated by the more extreme innovations of the Ritualists and their evident disregard for the law; cf. Bentley, *Ritualism and Politics*, pp. 39-40; and Marsh, *Victorian Church in Decline*, pp. 117-18.
105 John W. Burgon, *The Oxford Diocesan Conference; and Romanizing within the Church of England: Two Sermons, Second Ed.* (London: James Parker & Co., 1873), pp. 24-31. Burgon was also disturbed by the whole spirit and development of the movement, with its apparent goal of assimilating the Church of England to Rome. In the preface to his pamphlet he wrote, 'It is very painful to me to be forced into direct antagonism with many persons whom I would fain look upon as friends. But I am forced; and it is they who force me. Theirs is the blame if anything of scandal attaches to the spectacle of "brother going to law with brother, and that before the unbelievers." Their unfaithfulness exceeds all bounds. Their irregularities outrage common decency.' (p. 4.)
106 He wrote: 'I speak of the studious assimilation of our practices, – our vestments, – our terminology, – our very ritual, to the practices, vestments, terminology, ritual of Rome. Even this is not all. Encouraged by their successes, – emboldened by the forbearance of the lay-people, and by the lamentable absence of anything like discipline within the Church, – yes, and above all carried forward by the very necessity of their position (for the logical development of a principle is of the nature of a necessity, be it true or be it false;) – this little handful of disloyal men are already teaching Romish doctrine and inculcating Romish principles by every means in their power. How much further is this to be allowed to proceed? How much longer is this unfaithfulness to go on unrestrained?' Ibid., pp. 14-15.

The subject was also taken up by Bishop Jackson of London in his charge to the clergy for 1875. Jackson noted that the Ritualists had themselves proclaimed their intention of undoing the Reformation and surveyed the numerous points of their teaching at which the doctrine of Rome had been assimilated. He concluded that many innocent innovations had provoked suspicion merely because 'the shadow of the Romanizing movement' had fallen on them. Thus, they were viewed as 'a first step, to be followed by others, away from the principles of the Reformation.' With congregations alarmed over every alteration, Jackson concluded that it would have been good for the church if the great section of High Church moderates 'had marked themselves off distinctly from the innovating and Romanizing party to which, if true to their own principles, they in no wise belong.' Cited in Nevison Loraine, *The Church and Liberties of England* (London: Smith, Elder & Co., 1876), pp. 82-83.
107 The *Record* noted that the Ritualists claimed to have some 2,000 clerical adherents but thought they were a small minority compared to 'the mass of moderate High Churchmen.' The paper recognized that the moderates were

opposed to the tone and methods adopted by the CA, but had little use for their objections. 'Can anyone deny that it has been the sympathy and prejudices of moderate High Churchmen which have swelled the senseless clamour against the Association, and have thus, to an incalculable degree, impeded its influence and destroyed the success of its efforts?' With the support of those such as Burgon, the paper thought, the Ritualists would be easily restrained. *Record*, 14 Nov. 1873.

John Shelton Reed discussed the fundamental doctrinal connections that held together the High Church party in the seventh chapter of his work on Victorian Anglo-Catholicism. For all their differences, the moderates and Ritualists shared certain core beliefs that made it difficult for them to separate. Still, he concluded, 'after the Purchas judgment and especially after the Public Worship Regulation Act of 1874, the breach between the two wings of Anglo-Catholicism threatened to become a chasm.' Reed, *Glorious Battle*, pp. 108-27.

108 *Record*, 14 Nov. 1873. The paper failed to note, for obvious reasons, the preface to Burgon's pamphlet. He began by warning that he had no intention of making common cause with extremists in the anti-Ritualist movement. They could not count him an ally, he wrote, 'If the utmost order in Divine Service, joined in surpassing beauty in the furniture of God's House, is any offence to them at all: if conspicuous zeal, (aye, zeal which may sometimes overleap the limits of a severe discretion,) does not enjoy a large measure of their sympathy. With Clergymen who deny the doctrine of Baptismal Regeneration, – apparently think anything good enough for the House of God, – systematically disregard the Rubrics, – suppress the Athanasian Creed, – I have less sympathy than I have with the Mediaevalists themselves.' Burgon, *Two Sermons*, p. 4.

109 'If, under the cover of her Articles and Formularies, Roman and Medieval doctrines, ceremonies and practices can be systematically practised, then, whether established or not, she ceases to be the Church of the English nation. We greatly fear that, as we have said, these vital issues have now come to a final arbitrament, and it will be our main object in this article to indicate the grounds for such an apprehension. We make the attempt in the hope of inducing that large body of moderate laymen and clergymen who, in this as in all other spheres, are preponderant in English life, to make their influence felt before it be too late.' Anonymous, 'The Ridsdale Judgment and "The Priest in Absolution",' *Quarterly Review* 144 (1877): 244.

In his charge of 1877, Archdeacon Prest suggested that the move was underway and that moderates were beginning to withdraw their umbrella of protection. As a result, the movement was increasingly 'circumscribed within the comparatively narrow limits of its avowed adherents,' and would thus be more easily identifiable and 'more likely, in the course of time, to be repressed.' Cited in the *Record*, 1 Oct. 1877.

110 The non-partisan J. S. Howson, Dean of Chester, feared that moderates of the High Church party, whom he thought were the most numerous section of the church, had allowed the Ritualists to use their association. By their 'passive encouragement,' feared Howson, they had sheltered the Ritualists despite concerns regarding 'their Romeward movement.' J. S. Howson, *Be-*

fore the Table (London: Macmillan & Co., 1875), PP. 154-55; cf. Howson's 'Introduction,' to Loraine, *Church and Liberties of England*, p. xvii.

111 The Evangelical view of the church, particularly as distinguished from the High Church perspective, was well summarized by R. H. Coats, *Types of Evangelical Piety* (Edinburgh: T. & T. Clark, 1912), pp. 78-85. The problem continues for modern Evangelicals. In a 1993 essay, Alister McGrath noted that Evangelicalism was frequently charged with being 'devoid of a distinctively Anglican ecclesiology.' Part of the problem, he suggested, lay in the very nature of Evangelicalism. It had 'no defining or limiting ecclesiology' such as the Anglo-Catholic insistence on apostolic succession, and it could 'accommodate itself to virtually any form of church order.' Nevertheless, McGrath argued that Evangelicals could be loyal and devoted Anglicans. Alister E. McGrath, 'Evangelical Anglicanism: A Contradiction in Terms?' In *Evangelical Anglicans*, ed. R. T. France and A. E. McGrath (London: SPCK, 1993), pp. 13-17.

112 In an 1885 essay, the non-partisan R. E. Bartlett expressed his regrets concerning the self-defeating policy. He suggested that Evangelicals had failed to exercise the influence they ought to have had in the church, and the High Church party had consequently gained an inordinate amount of power over its organizations and meetings. 'Many of their ministers are active, useful, influential men; but as a party they fail to exercise that influence upon the Church which their numbers, at least among the laity, would entitle them to claim. Not only in Church Congresses and in Diocesan Conferences, but in the whole working and organization of the Church, the High Church party have, if not an absolute supremacy, at least a dominant and overpowering influence.' Bartlett, 'Church of England and the Evangelical Party,' *Contemporary Review*, pp. 66-67.

113 J. C. Ryle published a study of the English church in the Reformation and post-Reformation era in 1882. In the preface he defended the Evangelical party against its High Church critics. Ryle argued that true 'Anglican churchmanship' had to be measured in relation to the Reformers and suggested that the Evangelicals were their true successors. Ryle, *Facts and Men*, pp. vii-x.

CHAPTER 6

The Public Worship Regulation Act: Context and Reactions

The 1870s marked the high-water line of the anti-Ritualist campaign. The earlier litigation against Ritualists, such as the Mackonochie and Purchas cases, dealt only with ceremonial innovations. But with the prosecution of William Bennett, the CA challenged Ritualist doctrine. It was the one attempt by anti-Ritualists to have their opponents' beliefs legally declared to be beyond the limits of the national church's comprehension. The Evangelical view of Anglican doctrine was largely vindicated in the appeal before the Judicial Committee of the Privy Council, but that court also acquitted Bennett and allowed a broad degree of toleration. The verdict had far-reaching implications. It gave further impetus to the Ritualists and encouraged the expansion of their innovations and teaching. The judgment also delivered a blow to the anti-Ritualist cause and led some to raise fundamental questions about their place in the Anglican church. For the first time during the controversy, some Evangelicals talked of secession. Those who were determined to remain within the established church, however, voiced concerns about further litigation and forced the CA to justify its policies.

One alternative to prosecution was to leave matters in the hands of the episcopacy. It was evident, however, that their authority was limited, and the Ritualists, especially following the Bennett judgment, were unlikely to submit to episcopal admonitions that carried little or no threat. An unexpected result of the Ritualists' defiance was episcopal support for a legislative response. Their advocacy, combined with the general public outcry, resulted in the Public Worship Regulation Act of 1874. Despite all evidence to the contrary, anti-Ritualists still believed that if the legal process were simplified, and the Ritualists could be challenged in court on a broader basis and with fewer appeals, their resolve would be worn down. In fact, however, their optimism was unwarranted.

The terms of the Public Worship Regulation Act were first applied in 1876, when charges were brought against Charles Ridsdale. The divided results of the verdict once again led many Evangelicals to question the effectiveness of litigation. But the response of Ridsdale was even more significant and gave evidence of a fundamental problem for anti-Ritualist policy – the Ritualists were resolute in their refusal to acknowledge the authority of any negative judgments, either episcopal or judicial. For a time, their obstinacy would turn public opinion against their cause. But the anti-Ritualists were unable to capture broad popular support, and they were provoked by Ridsdale and others to adopt a stance that was increasingly strident in tone and severe in method. The controversy would continue for years to come, with a corresponding expansion of partisan tensions. But by the late-1870s, it was evident that the methods of the anti-Ritualists had failed to attain their goals and had created sharp divisions within the Evangelical party.

The Bennett Judgment and Its Impact

The anti-Ritualist campaign entered a new phase with the prosecution of William Bennett, Vicar of Frome, who had gained a reputation as a leading proponent of the extreme section of the Ritualist movement.[1] The early prosecutions had been concerned with ceremonial and liturgical innovations, but with the Bennett case the CA took up the question of doctrine using, as the basis of its case, Bennett's own publications and his recorded testimony before the Ritual Commission.[2] The Bishop of London initially vetoed the proceeding, hoping that the controversy might be limited to questions of ceremony without becoming entangled in doctrinal issues; but a writ was obtained by the prosecution, which compelled him to allow the case to proceed.[3] The CA targeted Bennett because he had affirmed, both in print and before the commission, 'the real objective presence of our blessed Lord, the sacrifice offered by the priest, and the adoration due to the presence of our blessed Lord.' He also used lighted candles on the altar, burned incense, wore eucharistic vestments and elevated the sacramental elements – all, he readily avowed, because he adored the presence of Christ there and taught his people 'to adore the consecrated elements, believing Christ to be in them.'[4]

For a time there were rumors of division within the CA over the wisdom of proceeding into the realm of doctrine. And when Bennett published a modest retraction of his more extreme statements in the *Church Times* (the leading Ritualist paper), the *Record* accused him of attempting to avoid prosecution. It urged the CA to proceed with the case as 'honourable men and true Protestants' and to disregard 'the counsels of timidity or self-interest.'[5] When the association decided to proceed with the case, Sir Robert Phillimore, of the Court of Arches, refused to hear it.[6] The debate within the CA apparently continued for some time. Although the case was returned to the Court of Arches on appeal, no petitions were filed for almost a year, and Phillimore threatened to dismiss it altogether if the prosecutors did not come forward immediately.[7] The case was finally heard in June 1870.[8] The charges involved three disputed points – the presence of Christ in the eucharistic elements, the repetition of sacrifice in the celebration, and the adoration of Christ in the elements.[9] In July, Phillimore issued a sweeping acquittal of Bennett on all the charges. He found Bennett guilty only of 'careless language' and, in his ruling, sought to legitimize the basic principles underlying the Ritualist position.[10] Anti-Ritualists were shocked by the ruling and the precedent it established.[11]

The CA immediately appealed to the Judicial Committee of the Privy Council. When their judgment was delayed, it became apparent that the judges in that court were divided, a sign the *Record* interpreted as an evil portent. Its fears were justified when Bennett was again acquitted. The judges concluded that his language had been unclear and 'rash,' but they were willing to give him 'the benefit of any doubt that may exist.'[12] The ruling, however, went on to censure the 'the extra-judicial statements' made by Phillimore in the Court of Arches. The Judicial Committee, no doubt attempting to define its role in response to the Ritualists' charge of erastianism, clearly intended to set aside Phillimore's logic and to place strict limits on the authority of any court to interpret doctrine:

> The Learned Judge has endeavoured to settle by a mass of authorities what is the doctrine of the Church of England on the subject of the Holy Communion. It is not the part of the Court of Arches nor of this Committee to usurp the function of a Synod or Council. Happily their duties are much more circumscribed – namely, to ascertain whether certain statements are so far repugnant to, or contradictory of the language of the articles and formularies construed in their plain meaning, that they should receive judicial condemnation.[13]

The ruling left the anti-Ritualist movement in a state of turmoil. On the one hand, Bennett's acquittal meant that a moderate form of sacramentalism must be tolerated. On the other hand, the judges had, in their response to Phillimore, elaborated a doctrinal position that was quite acceptable to Evangelicals. In many ways a parallel could be drawn to the Gorham case, only with the positions of the protagonists reversed. In both instances, the Judicial Committee adopted a position of broad toleration.[14] In the prior judgment, Evangelicals had rejoiced to have their position legitimated, and the court's decision fractured the Oxford Movement, resulting in a number of secessions to Rome. In the Bennett case, however, it was the High Church position that was allowed, leaving the Evangelical party in a state of disarray. The immediate impact of the ruling was to exacerbate divisions within the anti-Ritualist movement. For the first time during the controversy, some Evangelicals, albeit a very small minority, advocated secession.

The *Record* did not often open its pages to their protests and published only a few of their letters. But it was clear from the space it devoted to their refutation, both in its own editorials and in correspondence opposing secession, that the Evangelical party faced a serious internal challenge. In general, the paper and most of its correspondents argued that the ruling had changed nothing. T. P. Boultbee summarized their position:

> What is the real result of the Bennett case? The Court has decided the doctrine of the Church of England to be what we have always believed it to be. It has said that the defendant was quite wrong if he meant what everybody believes he meant, and probably did mean. But it said that as it was not quite sure what he meant, it would pronounce the case not proven and dismiss the suit.
>
> In other grounds our own position is quite secured, but one whom we believe to be heretical has narrowly escaped the condemnation we think he ought to have suffered.
>
> That this is a dangerous precedent to the peace and purity of the Church is painfully manifest; but, in the name of common sense, is it a reason for leaving our Church to go one knows not whither, or to add to the scandalous amount of petty sectional divisions already existing?[15]

The debate continued for some months, but the movement for secession gathered little support, and only a few Evangelicals of any prominence left the established church. The most important of them was Capel Molyneux, Vicar of St. Paul's, South Kensington, who published a pamphlet defending his decision. He adapted the logic used by conservatives against Evangelical participation in church congresses and argued that those who remained in the Church of England were guilty by association of the doctrinal errors of the Ritualists.[16] His secession was particularly troubling because he had been a member of the CA's council. But despite a great deal of concern on the part of many Evangelical leaders, few chose to follow his example. Still, it was feared that the threat of secession would raise doubts about the loyalty of the Evangelical party and would only make the anti-Ritualist campaign all the more difficult.[17]

The defeat in the Bennett case also brought the CA's policy of litigation under increased scrutiny. Even though the Mackonochie and Purchas cases had resulted in anti-Ritualist judgments, they had proved ineffective and difficult to enforce. And the loss of the Bennett case only cast further doubt on the association's program of prosecution. The council called a special meeting in April 1873, and asked its local branches to send representatives to London to consider the organization's future course of action.[18] It was later reported that 'the idea of a total and absolute withdrawal on the part of the Association from all legal action in the future found no favour' with the representatives who attended the confidential meeting. Even if litigation had not succeeded in completely repressing the Ritualists, its proponents claimed that they had at least been able to force the innovators to adopt a defensive position and to curtail their activities.[19] The meeting affirmed, however, that it was the obligation of the CA to see that the bishops fulfilled their duty in administering the law.[20] In effect, that conclusion meant that the organization would attempt, for the immediate future, to refocus its emphasis on efforts other than prosecution. But the fact that the discussion was necessary at all indicated that substantial opposition had arisen within the organization. In the end, the council left open the possibility that they would intervene if the bishops refused to act.[21]

The anti-Ritualist hope that Parliament might be compelled to act put further pressure on the CA to forego litigation for the immediate future. In late 1873, E. V. Bligh suggested there was little more to be gained through 'doubtful appeals to the courts.' Having ascertained the state of the law, and having also discovered that the bishops were doing little to enforce it, what should the CA do next, asked Bligh? In his view, it should work for the reform of the church and 'promote it by all possible means in the next session of Parliament.'[22] The CA's supporters also continued to promote the organization as the best hope for uniting the various sections of the Evangelical party.[23] Others, however, thought that work could be better accomplished by a new organization – one entirely distinct from the CA, that might draw members from a broader base if it did not have to bear the burden of a negative reputation linked to the prosecutions.[24]

The Limits of Episcopal Authority

A less immediate and more ambiguous result of the Bennett decision was the encouragement it gave to the Ritualists. But their more extreme innovations, as well as their attitude toward those in authority, only provoked new opposition. In particular, there was a general sense of dismay that clergy would be unwilling to pay due regard either to the admonitions of the episcopacy or to the judgments of the courts.[25] At least some of the bishops had grown weary of the unauthorized alterations to the services and of the disdainful attitude with which the Ritualists received their advice. The problem was illustrated by Bishop Magee of Peterborough in a speech during the second reading of the Public Worship Regulation Act in the House of Lords. Magee complained that the Ritualists demanded fatherly admonitions from the bishops rather than judicial declarations but were unwilling to reciprocate with filial obedience. Magee continued, 'When a monition is to be flung back in my face, and I am to be told that I am "neither a gentleman nor a divine," and that "my conversion is to be prayed for," I for one must say that I should like to see a little filialness on the part of those who are demanding this fatherliness.'[26] Anti-Ritualists, however, often complained that the bishops themselves were responsible for the expansion of the controversy. When the Ritualists openly defied episcopal admonitions, it was suggested that the bishops were merely reaping the results of their own misplaced lenience.[27] Unwilling to recognize that the bishops had but limited authority to put down the innovations, and equally unwilling to allow that they might use their discretion in cases where the congregations actually approved of and supported the ceremonial innovations, the anti-Ritualists continued to criticize the episcopacy and to campaign for the immediate and complete suppression of their opponents.[28]

In spite of the call for episcopal intervention, however, the fact remained that the bishops had little power to exert any direct control over the activities of the parish clergy unless specific charges were brought against them. And when charges were made, at least some of the bishops refused to forward the cases to the ecclesiastical courts, fearing that they would only exacerbate partisan tensions and expand the controversy.[29] By the early 1870s, however, some were beginning to take steps against the more recalcitrant and outspoken clergy. If they could not directly intervene in a parish, there were various indirect ways of applying pressure, such as refusing to license the appointment of curates and deacons to serve under Ritualists.[30] In criticizing the episcopacy's inactivity, the *Times* suggested other similar responses. If the bishops were opposed to prosecution, said the paper, there were many alternatives to doing nothing. They could, for example, refuse to consecrate new Ritualist churches or to license curates to incumbents of who refused to compromise. The real issue, concluded the paper, was whether or not they were determined to halt the innovations.[31]

The Public Worship Regulation Act of 1874

The early judgments handed down, culminating with the Bennett case, only compounded the difficulties faced by the leaders of the Church of England, as the Ritualists made it clear that they would not be bound by judicial rulings. Lord Shaftesbury had on several occasions attempted legislation for the reform of the courts and simplification of the legal process, but his bills found little support. They were, of course, opposed by Ritualists who condemned any ecclesiastical legislation proposed by lay members of Parliament as erastian, but many High Church moderates as well would not support any reforms that were not proposed by the bishops (or at least had their strong support).[32] The bishops were also concerned that legislation such as Shaftesbury's, by making litigation easier and less expensive, would only expand the controversy by provoking a flood of new lawsuits. But faced with the intransigence of the Ritualists and the resulting public dissatisfaction with the appearance of 'lawlessness' among the clergy, it was evident that some alternative proposal was necessary.[33] The immediate 'public incentive' that led to the Public Worship Regulation Act was a lay memorial presented to the archbishops in May 1873.[34] It was sponsored by the CA and gained the signatures of 60,200 'noblemen, baronets, members of Parliament, magistrates, and other lay members of the Church of England.' The protest called on the episcopacy to stand firm against the Ritualists in spite of the Bennett judgment.[35]

The archbishops cautiously acknowledged their concern with aspects of the Ritualist position, especially regarding the introduction of confession, and reaffirmed the necessity of clerical obedience to the law.[36] In considering the issues raised by the memorial, however, they confessed their belief that the bishops had fulfilled their duties. They argued, in response to the anti-Ritualists' complaints, that the central concern of the episcopacy could not be the enforcement of the law under threat of prosecution:

> Obviously it cannot be desirable that the Church should be harassed by the bishops being dragged into an unlimited number of judicial investigations founded upon charges and counter-charges

made by contending theological parties against their opponents, on the ground of alleged excess or defect in conforming to the ritual and preaching the doctrine of the Church. Episcopal government exists among us, charged with the grave responsibility of seeing that the undoubted law of the Church is observed, and, at the same time, of saving the Church, by the exercise of a wise discretion, from being plunged into endless unseemly contests. It will be generally admitted by Churchmen that a prosecution respecting doctrine or ritual is in itself an evil, even where it is necessary; and the bishops are bound in each case to consider the whole of the circumstances before they resort to their courts to procure obedience to the law.[37]

Finally, the archbishops concluded by expressing the view that the laity had to share a portion of the blame for the current state of affairs as well as the responsibility for bringing about its resolution.[38]

In an ill-fated response, the Ritualists presented a petition of their own to the Upper House of Convocation in May 1873, protesting any changes to the rubrics and calling on that body to sanction their innovations, particularly the use of confession.[39] The petition, however, did little to aid their cause – the practice of confession, more than any of their other innovations, was despised by the general public.[40] Anti-Ritualists strongly condemned the petition.[41] Although it represented only a small minority of the clergy, and that the most extreme section of the High Church party, anti-Ritualists thought it indicated the audacity of their opponents. The Ritualists apparently believed they were strong enough to gain the 'recognition and approval' of the bishops. The *Record* feared their attitude was symptomatic of the progress they had made. 'The disease,' concluded the paper, 'must have eaten deeply into the heart of the church.'[42] The bishops refused to legitimize a sacramental view of confession and referred the matter to a committee of the Upper House of Convocation, which concluded in its report that, despite exceptions made for those who were sick or particularly troubled in conscience, the framers of the rubrics had intended that those seeking peace of mind should find it in 'the forms of confession and absolution' that were 'set forth in her public services.'[43]

Beyond the religious concerns of Evangelical anti-Ritualists, many took a more secular view of the threat they presented. Those concerned with the stability of society, especially in light of unrest in Ireland and Wales, were disturbed by the appearance of lawlessness among the clergy of the established church. The Ritualists were increasingly viewed as a obstinate and rebellious group of conspirators, unwilling to be bound by either the judgments of courts or the admonitions of bishops.[44] Anti-confessional meetings were held across the country during the summer and fall of 1873 and on into 1874, and numerous counter-memorials were published calling on the bishops to take a firm stand against the Ritualists.[45] In January 1874, the CA issued a circular calling on Protestant voters to make the cause a prominent issue in the coming election.[46] With public pressure growing for some effective response, Tait notified Queen Victoria that the episcopacy was nearly unanimous in its support for some legislation that would enable them to exert greater control over the clergy.[47] The queen had suggested amending the rubrics of the church, but Tait did not think it prudent at that time. 'Probably,' he wrote, 'it would be found that the evils now complained of would disappear under a proper and vigorous administration of the law in the manner proposed. The proposal to alter rubrics, in the Archbishop's judgment, should be kept carefully distinct from an improvement in the mode of procedure.'[48]

The 'Act for the Better Administration of the Laws respecting the Regulation of Public Worship' was initially drafted by Tait himself, and with a legislative vacuum during the early days of Disraeli's government, Parliament devoted almost the whole session to 'the condition of the established Church.'[49] The measure did not attempt to change the substance of any existing laws with regard to the church or doctrine but sought only to simplify the legal process and give the bishops greater authority to enforce the rulings of the courts.[50] According to the *Times*, through whose editorial pages the bill was introduced to the public, the bishops had been unable to control the innovators for want of coercive power, and Tait proposed that the provision of such power ought to be supplied by legislative act. His bill would give the bishops broad powers of discretion, both in deciding whether the cases could go forward and in compelling the clergy to comply.[51]

But the original bill was subject to alteration in committee, and Lord Shaftesbury was concerned to limit the discretionary power of the bishops. He offered an amendment calling for the appointment of a single lay judge by the two archbishops, with a final appeal to the Judicial Committee.[52] The secular court of final appeal was thus allowed to remain, which became the focus of the Ritualists' protest and the basis for their rejection of any decisions handed down thereafter.[53] Tait was able, however, to secure an episcopal veto which allowed the bishop to prohibit legal proceedings in his diocese as long as he justified his decision in writing.[54] This would later become an important factor as the Ritualist controversy dragged on, both as a means of bringing the era of lawsuits to an end and in the resulting growth of episcopal influence in the church and society. As it became clear that litigation and court judgments could provide neither lasting consensus nor peace, the bishops began to exercise a more definitive influence, especially through the exercise of their veto.[55] The bill easily passed in August 1874, with Shaftesbury's alterations, but its implementation was delayed until 1 July 1875.[56]

Reactions to the Public Worship Regulation Act

The Ritualists immediately expressed their opposition to the bill.[57] In May 1874, the ECU held protest meetings in London, and a petition was adopted repudiating the new act.[58] The Ritualists condemned the bill as an instance of the erastian intervention of the state in sacred matters and proclaimed their intention of ignoring it.[59] It was argued that Parliament had no right to enact legislation for the church without the approval of Convocation or a general synod, and any court thereby created was secular in nature and could have no authority concerning spiritual matters.[60] A number of others in the High Church party apparently took a similar view – there was an immediate increase in the membership of the ECU.[61]

The vehement protests of the Ritualists provoked an interesting exchange of letters in the *Record*, which gave some indication of a division among Evangelicals over how best to proceed. Reginald Smith, Rector of Stafford, Dorchester, wrote to express his regret over the tone of the Ritualist meetings. He was sorry that 'there was nothing in the spirit of the meeting to conciliate the respect of those Evangelicals who earnestly desire to bear and forbear with Ritualism as long as it is possible to do so with a good conscience.'[62] Francis Close, however, sharply criticized Smith's moderation. In his view, the 'individual piety, sincerity, zeal, and even soundness of doctrine' of some of the Ritualists could have no bearing in the discussion concerning how best to oppose their innovations. While acknowledging the soundness of Smith's Evangelical faith, Close expressed astonishment that he could even consider the idea of desiring 'peace with such men.' In his estimation, compromise could obtain unity only at the cost of doctrinal truth.[63]

In his reply, Smith tried to make it clear that he was himself opposed to Ritualist teaching and thought it ought to be strongly protested against. But he was disturbed by the spirit of the controversy and differed 'from some Evangelical brethren' in his view of how that opposition ought to be expressed. He believed that, 'notwithstanding their very serious errors, many of the Ritualists 'really love Christ, and are living to promote his glory and the salvation of souls.' This being the case, they should be treated 'as erring brethren, and not as enemies of the Lord.'[64] Smith made, at this point in his argument, a distinction that was beyond the grasp of most anti-Ritualists. He believed that their opponents desired to 'Catholicize' the Church of England but not to 'Romanize' it. The distinction was, for him, an important one. The Ritualists might be intent on replacing the Reformation with the catholic church system of an earlier age, but he thought they had little interest in submitting the English church to the pope. All Protestants were opposed to their goal and thought it 'a sad perversion of the Gospel,' but they could nevertheless affirm that the Ritualists were 'true Christians.' Smith concluded:

> I believe the only right and Christian way of dealing with them, as well as the only way that can possibly deliver them and bring them into the glorious liberty of the Gospel, is by giving them credit for honesty of purpose and by carrying on our controversy with them in a kind, respectful, and conciliatory tone. I am not at all surprised that others should feel it necessary to use stern denunciation in dealing with them, but I think it better and wiser to listen to the voice of inspiration, which says, 'Yet show I unto you a more excellent way.'[65]

By the mid-1870s, many moderates who had initially supported the anti-Ritualist campaign, were weary of the controversy – a result related both to the program of litigation and to the negative and partisan tone in which the whole dispute was carried out.[66]

In the months following the passage of the bill, the bishops sought to ascertain the feelings of the clergy and laity concerning the two issues that had become the focus of the dispute – eucharistic vestments and the eastward position.[67] Archbishop Tait submitted questions in a circular to the clergy of each rural deanery:

> 1. Is it in your opinion expedient that the rubrics prefixed to the order of Morning and Evening Prayer, so far as it relates to the ornaments of the minister, should be dealt with by the provincial Convocations of Canterbury and York, with the view of seeking the sanction of Parliament for an alteration in the Acts of Uniformity on this particular point?
> 2. Is it in your opinion expedient that the rubric relating to the position of the minister at the Holy Table at the time of the celebration of the Holy Communion, should be dealt with by the provincial Convocations of Canterbury and York, with the view of seeking the sanction of Parliament for an alteration of the Acts of Uniformity on this particular point?
> 3. If you think it desirable that any concessions should be made

to those who wish to introduce the chasuble or other unusual vestment, at the celebration of Holy Communion, how do you propose that the demand should be met for corresponding concessions on the other side in matters at present equally illegal?

In the late debates in Parliament it was proposed that the concession of what is called the eastward position should be balanced by allowing liberty to omit the Athanasian Creed and the Commination Service.

4. What do you suppose to be the general opinion of the laity in your rural deanery on these subjects?[68]

A majority of the respondents adopted rather moderate positions. While some opposition to the use of eucharistic vestments remained, the eastward position was broadly approved and viewed by many as the legal position for the celebrant. And in most cases, it was agreed that there ought to be a degree of toleration so long as both the bishop and a majority of the parishioners supported any alterations. The Bishop of Lincoln, Christopher Wordsworth, summarized the conclusions in a pastoral letter to his diocese. A 'considerable majority' favored the eastward position, and Wordsworth declared his concurrence, suggesting that 'the position of the celebrant in saying the Prayer of Consecration' ought to be regarded as 'an open question.'[69] Opinions were somewhat more divided concerning the eucharistic vestments, and Wordsworth thought opposition 'had been increased by the lawless extravagance prevailing in some churches, where new-fangled and gaudy dresses have been introduced, at any time, and on any occasion, however incongruous.' Nevertheless, it was generally felt that they ought not to be prohibited where they were introduced with the approval of both the parishioners and the diocesan.[70]

In March 1875, the bishops issued a joint pastoral letter in an effort to diffuse the situation prior to the Public Worship Regulation Act taking effect in July. The statement, signed by all but two of the bishops, took a moderate and conciliatory position. The bishops suggested both parties were responsible for the bitterness of the controversy, but most of their criticism was directed toward the Ritualists. After considering signs that indicated great spiritual growth in the church, the bishops went on to acknowledge the 'serious evils' that disturbed its peace and threatened its future. They continued:

> One of these evils is the interruption of the sympathy and mutual confidence which ought to exist between the clergy and laity. Changes in the mode of performing Divine service, in themselves

sometimes of small importance, introduced without authority, and often without due regard to the feelings of parishioners, have excited apprehensions that greater changes are to follow; distrust has been engendered, and the edification which ought to result from united worship has been impeded. The suspicions thus aroused, often, no doubt, unreasonable, have in some cases produced serious alienation.

The refusal to obey legitimate authority is another evil in the Church at the present time. Not only has it frequently occurred that clergymen fail to render to episcopal authority that submission which is involved in the idea of episcopacy, but obedience has been avowedly refused to the highest judicial interpretations of the law of the Church and Realm. Even the authority which our Church claims, as inherent in every particular or national Church, to ordain and change rites and ceremonies has been questioned and denied.

We also observe with increasing anxiety and alarm the dissemination of doctrines and encouragement of practices repugnant to the teaching of Holy Scripture and to the principles of the Church, as derived from Apostolic times and as authoritatively set forth at the Reformation. More especially we call serious attention to the multiplication and assiduous circulation among the young and susceptible of manuals of doctrine and private devotion, of which it is not too much to say that many of the doctrines and practices they inculcate are wholly incompatible with the teaching and principles of our Reformed Church.

Further we feel it our duty to call attention to the growing tendency to associate doctrinal significance with rites and ceremonies which do not necessarily involve it. For example, the position to be occupied by the minister during the Prayer of Consecration in the Holy Communion, though it has varied in different ages and different countries and has never been formally declared by the Church to have any doctrinal significance, is now regarded by many persons of very opposite opinions as a symbol of distinctive doctrine, and, as such, has become the subject of embittered controversy.

We would seriously remind our brethren of the clergy of the solemn obligation which binds us all to be ready to yield a willing obedience to the law of the Church of England, of which we are ordained ministers, and to recognise the necessity of submitting our own interpretations of any points in that law which may be considered doubtful to the judicial decisions of lawfully constituted Courts.... We are convinced that the number of those who would refuse such reasonable obedience is small, and that the vast majority of the clergy and laity of the Church of England are thoroughly loyal to its doctrine and discipline. We fully recognise the difference between unity and an overstrained uniformity, and are well aware that our Church is rightly tolerant of diversity, within certain limits, both in opinions and practices. We would not narrow in the least this wise comprehensiveness; but liberty must not degenerate into license and self-will; as fundamental truths must not be explained away so neither must those clear lines be obliterated which separate the doctrines and practices of our Reformed Church from the novelties and corruptions of the Church of Rome....

Under these grave circumstances, we solemnly charge you all, brethren beloved in the Lord, to cultivate a spirit of charity and mutual forbearance.... We exhort the clergy not to disquiet their congregations by novel practices and unauthorized ceremonies, and to discountenance those who seek to introduce them. We entreat the laity not to give way to suspicions in regard of honest efforts to promote the more reverent worship of Almighty God in loyal conformity with the rules of the Book of Common Prayer.[71]

Conservative Evangelicals were generally critical of the letter. They were pleased the bishops had finally addressed the controversy but thought they were too willing to make compromises, particularly with regard to the eastward position.[72]

Memorials continued to circulate on the subject and a broadly based protest was drawn up when it became evident that Convocation would consider the use of vestments and the eastward position in its next session. In a letter to the *Times*, W. A. Scott Robertson, an Honorary Canon of Canterbury and a moderate High Churchman, noted that the memorial had been signed by 5,300 clergy, including a large number of High Church moderates as well as 'the main body of the Evangelical clergy.' According to Robertson, they did not desire to narrow the limits of toleration in the church, but deprecated 'any fresh legislation for giving authoritative sanction to the use of the eastward position or of Eucharistic vestments.'[73] When Convocation met, the CA presented another memorial to the Upper House outlining their objections on the two disputed questions and protesting against any alteration of the rubrics.[74] The memorial gathered a total 75,110 signatures – 3,860 clergy (including 2 bishops, 4 deans, 6 archdeacons, 39 canons, 15 prebendaries and 87 rural deans) and 71,250 lay members of the Church of England. The resolution under consideration was approved by the Lower House of Convocation but rejected by the Upper House.[75] In effect, the High Church majority in the Lower House, which included numerous prominent

Ritualists, concluded that the eastward position ought to be allowed even if some did not approve of the doctrinal affirmations associated with it.[76] Having failed to gain toleration for their position through Convocation, the Ritualists continued to protest against the Public Worship Regulation Act and, in a statement read by a number of them to their congregations on the last Sunday in June 1875, rejected the legitimacy of the legislation itself as well as the spiritual authority of the court it created.[77]

The Ridsdale Judgment

In the early years of the controversy, Ritualists experimented with a number of different practices and took a variety of positions regarding their relative importance. At its annual meeting in June 1875, with the Public Worship Regulation Act poised to take effect on the 1st of July, the ECU settled on 'six points' concerning which there could be no compromise: the eastward position, eucharistic vestments, the mixed chalice, wafer bread, altar candles, and incense.[78] Several of those points were brought before the courts again in the case of Charles J. Ridsdale, Vicar of St. Peter's, Folkestone. Ridsdale had been the subject of several earlier attempts at prosecution but had managed to evade them on technicalities. In 1876, however, he became the first Ritualist to be charged under the Public Worship Regulation Act.[79] Lord Penzance of the Court of Arches delivered his judgment in February 1876 and ruled against Ridsdale on all but one of the counts (the candles around the crucifix were not judged to be illegal).[80] Penzance noted the risk of an extreme reaction and rejected any wholesale condemnation of art in the church through 'Puritan excess.' But at the same time, he ruled that Ridsdale had crossed the boundary between the 'mere decoration which is free from harm, and the superstitious reverence which is full of peril.'[81]

Following the example of other Ritualists, Ridsdale refused to acknowledge the jurisdiction of the court or to be bound by its decisions.[82] Unlike those before him, however, Ridsdale decided to appeal four of the points to the Judicial Committee of the Privy Council.[83] The appeal reconsidered four issues: the legality of the vestments, the eastward position, the use of wafer bread, and the hanging of a crucifix on the chancel screen.[84] The importance of the case was widely recognized and the Judicial Committee was expanded to eleven judges, with Archbishop Tait and the Bishops of Chichester, St. David's, and St. Asaph serving as assessors.[85] The judges handed down their ruling in May 1877. The *Record* thought it a decision guaranteed to satisfy neither party and noted the conspicuous absence of Sir Robert Phillimore and Lord Chief Baron Kelly, both of whom had High Church leanings, when the judgment was read.[86] The use of the crucifix, eucharistic vestments, and wafer bread were condemned as illegal, but with regard to the latter, the judges found the evidence insufficient. The eastward position, however, was allowed so long as the actions of the clergy could be seen by the congregation:

> The words of the Rubric, in the opinion of their Lordships, as the Tables are now usually, and in their opinion lawfully, placed, authorize him to do those acts standing on the west side, and looking towards the east. Beyond this, and after this, there is no specific direction that, during this prayer (of consecration), he is to stand on the west side, or that he is to stand on the north side.... He must, in the opinion of their Lordships, stand so that he may, in good faith, enable the communicants present, or the bulk of them, being properly placed, to see, if they wish it, the breaking of the bread and the performance of the other manual acts mentioned. He must not interpose his body so as intentionally to defeat the object of the Rubric and to prevent this result.[87]

Evangelical reaction was mixed. There was some talk of secession, reminiscent of the response to the Bennett case, but few were willing to consider such an extreme step. Many, however, feared the judgment would cast doubt on the Protestant nature of the Church of England and give new impetus to the Ritualists.[88]

The bishops hoped the judgment would help calm the controversy and ease partisan tensions. Bishop Ellicott, writing from a moderate High Church position, thought it was a wise decision that would satisfy all reasonable clergy, particularly in its reversal of earlier rulings regarding the eastward position.[89] Ellicott thought the Ritualists had excited unnecessary opposition by linking their innovations to doctrinal concerns, 'talking nonsense about "sacrificial vestments," and so forth.' Many improvements in ritual would have been widely accepted, he thought, if they had not been linked to Romish doctrines widely opposed by the 'great body of the laity.'[90] In a letter to the clergy of the diocese of Carlisle, Bishop Goodwin took a similar perspective. He was quite satisfied with the court's approval of the eastward position because there were many High Church moderates for whom it was a long established tradition with no partisan intent.[91] Goodwin was optimistic that one less controversial issue would help calm the situation. Still, he recognized that both sides would need to compromise for any lasting peace:

If on the one side we could put a stop to vexatious prosecutions, and on the other side could secure such an agreement between practice and that which is understood to be the meaning of difficult rubrics as would take away much of the temptation to prosecute, we might hope for a season of peace such as we have not lately enjoyed. If, however, clergymen will persist in asserting the infallibility of their own interpretations, and their determination to be in no way guided by interpretations having such claims as I have endeavoured to vindicate or those contained in the 'Ridsdale' judgment, then I fear that peace is no nearer than it was before.[92]

On May 27th, Ridsdale presided at his church, St. Peter's, Folkestone, with a large congregation present expecting that he would disobey the judgment. Communion was celebrated twice that day, with Ridsdale wearing an alb, chasuble, stole and maniple. In addition, the mixed chalice and wafer bread were used, and two lighted candles were on the altar. In the evening service, Ridsdale justified his refusal to yield in the use of the vestments, lights, and the mixed chalice.[93] Other Ritualists were quick to voice their support.[94] Ridsdale, however, was convinced to relent when Archbishop Tait intervened and assured him that his conscience could rest at ease if he would obey Tait's admonition and abstain from further use of the vestments, candles, and mixed chalice.[95]

The adoption and implementation of the Public Worship Regulation Act had at least one unforeseen impact – the Ritualists following Ridsdale repudiated the authority of the Court of Arches, even though it was constituted as the Archbishop's court and, at least during the days when Sir Robert Phillimore presided, they had recognized its authority in ecclesiastical matters. In theory, they rejected the Court of Arches on the ground that it had been fundamentally altered by the new legislation. Having been given new powers by an Act of Parliament, it was now considered a secular court with no authority in ecclesiastical matters.[96] Penzance's rulings were also rejected because they accepted as final the judgments previously made by the secular Judicial Committee. The Ritualists had previously rejected the authority of the Judicial Committee as a final court of appeal, and they now broadened that position to include the Court of Arches as well.[97] After the Ridsdale judgment, they would refuse to appear in the court, to participate in its proceedings by way of defense counsel, or to acknowledge the authority of its rulings and admonitions. Their denial of the court's validity, whatever its theoretical basis, often appeared to be related to the fact that Lord Penzance frequently ruled in favor of their opponents, whereas Phillimore had attempted to moderate his judgments in favor of the

Ritualists whenever possible. At a popular level, the effect was to strengthen support for the arguments of their opponents – the Ritualists were increasingly viewed as a body of extremists, who were willing to submit to neither bishop nor judge, recognizing only the authority of their own private judgment.[98]

The Ritualist cause was further damaged by the exposure their views of confession received when Lord Redesdale read portions of *The Priest in Absolution* in the House of Lords.[99] The public discussion of the book, which professed to be a manual for the clergy on hearing confession and probing the hearts of the penitent, raised a tremendous protest. Most of the bishops, both in the House of Lords and later in the Upper House of Convocation, suggested that the threat came only from a small body of extremists, but they were quick to reiterate their opposition to the renewal of a practice clearly rejected by the Reformers.[100] The reaction in the general public was much stronger, both among Evangelicals as well as other anti-Ritualists. The *Record* used the occasion once again to suggest that the bishops were largely responsible for allowing the Ritualists to carry their innovations to such an extreme.[101] The *Times* was more temperate in its comments on the episcopacy, but no less harsh in its view of clergy who would attempt to force confession on a nation of Protestants. It suggested that disestablishment would be the final result if there was any attempt to expand the comprehensiveness of the national church to include that practice.[102] The public furor continued for several months, and the CA began gathering signatures for a memorial to the queen.[103] The protests over the confessional continued for several months; little was actually accomplished in terms of suppressing the movement, but the controversy provided fresh material for the anti-Ritualists.[104]

The 1870s began with a significant setback for the CA and the anti-Ritualist movement. By the waning years of the decade, however, their campaign had achieved a degree of success. The more extreme innovations introduced by the Ritualists, particularly the use of auricular confession, and their unwillingness to hear the voice of any existing ecclesiastical authority had alienated most of the moderates in the Church of England. By 1874, the bishops were convinced to lend their support to legislation. It was by then clear that their own limited authority would never suffice to settle the controversy, and the public outcry was such that some governmental intervention was necessary. It was assumed, although some of the bishops clearly had their doubts, that a few test cases would suffice to establish the legitimate limits of the church's ritual and that the clergy would abide by the rulings of the courts. In fact, however, the prosecutions under the Public Worship Regulation Act only strengthened the resolve of the Ritualists to resist any compromise.

Their obstinacy, however, created a backlash of support for their opponents. But despite having the sympathy of many bishops and sufficient public support to obtain an act of Parliament, the ultimate goal of the anti-Ritualists remained elusive. In the years to come, it became evident that a policy of prosecution and repression could not bring the Ritualists to submission. The aggressive program of the CA had disastrous results. It drove the Ritualists to ever greater extremes which in turn led to numerous bitter court battles and several imprisonments. It also dashed any continuing hope for a moderate coalition and, at the same time, made it more difficult for the bishops to intervene without the appearance of a partisan bias.[105] And finally, it drove a wedge through the Evangelical party, dividing moderates from those who valued, above all else, the absolute suppression of the Ritualist movement.

Notes

1   A survey of Bennett's career and involvement in the controversy can be found in the obituary for him in the *Times*. The paper reported that he was the first to illustrate the doctrines of the Tractarians 'by means of a revival of ritual.' *Times*, 18 Aug. 1886.

2   The *Times* wrote in an editorial as the trial began: 'As to the substantial question involved, it is of the highest importance, and in some way or other it is most desirable that it should be legally considered. The questions relating to vestments and ornaments are perfectly insignificant in comparison. The Ritualists constantly profess that their characteristic ceremonies are only important as symbolizing doctrine. So long, therefore, as the doctrine is left untouched, very little is gained by repressing vestments and incense; while, on the other hand, if the doctrine be pronounced illegal, there will be no place or occasion for the symbolical practices. In Mr. Bennett the prosecutors have selected one of the most pronounced and most courageous representatives of the extreme school. He does not hesitate to declare his belief in 'the real, actual, and visible presence of Our Lord upon the altars of our churches.' It is certainly desirable that it should be definitely ascertained whether a clergyman of the Church of England is justified in using such language.' *Times*, 18 April 1868.

E. H. Plumptre, a Broad Church moderate who opposed litigation, predicted that the matter could not be limited to ritual. 'It profits but little,' he wrote, 'to drive in the external, eruptive symptoms of disease, while the disease itself remains unhealed. You may restrain, by pains and penalties, those who find in vestments, lights, incense, gestures, the witnesses to what they hold as the truth of the Real Presence, but if you leave the doctrine itself unquestioned, you do but tempt them to a more explicit assertion of it in words, and a more subtle inventiveness in the art of evasive interpretation.... And if you make your assault upon the doctrine itself, then, over and above all the evils which attend the discussion of such a question in the hands of paid advocates, you are risking, on the one hand, failure, and, on the other, the disruption of the Church of England.' Plumptre, 'Church Parties,' *Contemporary Review*, pp. 337-38.

Charles Bury, in surveying the work of the CA, wrote, 'The cases of Messrs. Mackonochie and Purchas were merely Ritual cases: in them practices only were brought to the test of the law. It was important to establish the illegality of these practices, because innovation of no kind is allowable; and, further, because these innovated rites and ceremonies were said to symbolize doctrine.... But Mr. Bennett was prosecuted for teaching and publishing erroneous doctrines.' Bury, *Church Association*, p. 25.

3   The case was presented in London because the CA believed Bennett's diocesan in Bath and Wells was too sympathetic to the Ritualist movement. It was allowed to proceed in London because that was where Bennett had published his work and testified before the commission. *Record*, April 17, 1868.

The *Times* also supported the prosecution but sympathized with the dilemma faced by Bishop Tait. Since most clergy published with London booksellers, it would virtually make the bishop the censor for all of England, 'doomed to the perpetual perusal of novel heresies.' *Times*, 18 April 1868.

4   Bennett's testimony before the Ritual Commission, cited in the *Record*, 20 April 1868. The *Times* thought his language was 'probably the most extravagant language ever used in the English Church on the subject. Even Dr. Pusey was startled.... The cardinal doctrine of his school is well known as that of the Real Presence in the Elements in the Holy Communion. As corollaries from this doctrine, he taught the duty of paying adoration to such a Presence, and alleged that the Priest, in the celebration of the rite, offers a real sacrifice and exercises true Sacerdotal functions.' *Times*, 10 June 1872.

5   *Record*, 22 May 1868.

6   The *Record* immediately accused Phillimore of allowing his High Church sympathies to bias his judgment: 'He maintains that he has in himself a discretion to overrule and supersede the Bishop's discretion; and meanwhile the suitors are remitted either back to the Diocesan Court of Wells or onward to the Privy Council, on the question, not of the merits of the cause, but as to whose duty it is to hear it. Assuredly the state of our Ecclesiastical Courts is a scandal not only to the Church but to the nation.' *Record*, 30 April 1869.

7   It was rumored, according to the *Record*, that the legal committee was confident of the merits of the case but that the general council was receiving bad advice. The paper also reiterated the claim that the purpose of litigation was not to punish individual Ritualists and argued that prosecution ought not to be given up simply because some critics raised the cry of persecution. The purpose was simply to ascertain 'the state of the law' and to establish 'the Reformed faith of the Church of England.' *Record*, 30 May 1870.

8   Detailed reports of the legal arguments presented in court were printed in the *Record*, 17 and 30 June 1870.

9   Evangelicals were not alone in their opposition to the Eucharistic teaching

of the Ritualists. An essayist in the *Quarterly Review*, while questioning the usefulness of prosecution as a means of halting Ritualist innovations, repudiated their doctrine. He doubted that any clergy of the Church of England, forty years prior, 'would have affirmed that the consecration of the elements in the Holy Eucharist was the means of bringing before us, on the altar, an object of worship.' Yet this novel doctrine had become 'the very cornerstone of the Ritualistic edifice in doctrine and practice.' It was a view, he thought, that could 'not be found in Scripture, in ancient liturgies, in the liturgy of the English Church, or in the works of the Anglican fathers. A generation back, no one would have doubted for an instant that a man who held the doctrine that the presence of Christ in the elements was such as to be adored, must at once leave the Church of England and join that of Rome.' Anon., 'Church and the Age,' *Quarterly Review*, pp. 55-56.

10 Phillimore concluded: 'I have not to try Mr. Bennett for careless language, for feeble reasoning or superficial knowledge. It is my duty to decide whether the words in which he now expresses himself, and which he professes to have since borrowed from a profound theologian [Pusey], occupying one of the highest positions in the University of Oxford, do or do not contravene the formularies of our faith. If I were to pronounce that they did so I should be passing sentence, in my opinion, upon a long roll of illustrious divines who have adorned our Universities and fought the good fight of our Church – from Ridley to Keble, from the divines whose martyrdom the cross at Oxford commemorates to the divine in whose honour that University has just founded her last college.... Now, I have shown that no mode of the presence is defined by the formularies, and by a large induction of instances that the present opinions for which Mr. Bennett is articled are not, however loosely expressed, distinguishable in substance from those which have been maintained for many years by many great divines of our Church and by many learned men. The conclusions of law at which I have arrived are the following: – With respect to the first and uncorrected edition of his pamphlet, I pronounce that Mr. Bennett in his language respecting the visible presence of our Lord and the adoration of the consecrated elements has contravened the law of the Church. If Mr. Bennett had not renounced this language and substituted other for it I must have considered whether I ought not to pass a sentence of suspension upon him, accompanied by a monition to abstain for the future from such language.... With respect to the second and corrected edition of his pamphlet and the other work for which he is articled, I say that the objective, actual and real presence of the spiritual, a presence external to the act of the communicant, appears to me to be the doctrine which the formularies of our Church, duly considered and construed so as to be harmonious, intended to maintain. But I do not lay down this as a position of law, nor do I say that what is called the receptionist doctrine is inadmissible; nor do I pronounce on any other teaching with respect to the mode of presence. I mean to do no such thing by this judgment. I mean by it to pronounce only that to describe the mode of the presence as objective, real, actual, and spiritual is certainly not contrary to the law.' Judgment of the Court of Arches, cited in the *Times*, 25 July 1870.

11 The *Record* condemned the judgment and suggested it was beyond anything that had been expected, even from a judge who tended to support the Ritualists. *Record*, 25 July 1870.

12 Judgment of the Judicial Committee of the Privy Council cited in the *Times*, 10 June 1872. According to Charles Bury, Bennett was saved by altering his language regarding the presence of Christ in the Eucharist, changing the word 'visible' to 'objective' in the second edition of his pamphlet *A Plea for Toleration*. The Judicial Committee, wrote Bury, 'put the most favourable construction possible on the words in dispute, and showed an amiable ingenuity in finding a meaning for them which would allow of the acquittal of the accused; or rather, perhaps, they declined to see the meaning that would oblige them to condemn him.... But who does not know – will Mr. Bennett himself deny? – that the language of the first edition of his pamphlet expressed his real opinions and the doctrines he and his followers continue to preach so far as they understand their own meaning?' Bury, *Church Association*, pp. 15-16.

The *Pall Mall Gazette* satirized the ruling and the concessions of the judges. Stripped of 'decorous and reverential form' the judgment amounted to: 'The Church of England forbids you to say "hocus pocus," and you shall not say it; but if you like to say "ocus pocus" we have no objection at all. Nay, if you can show that, though you did actually say "hocus pocus," you meant to say "ocus pocus," but inserted the "h" by a natural or acquired infirmity about aspirates, you are within that broad liberty which the Church of England permits to her ministry, and "hocus pocus" is incomprehensible, or very imperfectly comprehensible, by the human understanding. The province of reasoning applicable to it is very limited, and the terms have not, cannot have, the precision of meaning which the character of the argument requires.' Cited in the *Record*, 14 June 1872.

13 The ruling went on to discuss the three points. With regard to the presence of Christ in the elements, it concluded that the church affirmed a presence 'to the soul of the worthy recipient.' It was a real presence 'after a heavenly and spiritual manner,' but the court rejected any narrower or strictly objective definition of that presence. The judges ruled that it was unlawful for clergy 'to teach that the sacrifice or offering of Christ upon the cross, or the redemption, propitiation, or satisfaction wrought by it, is or can be repeated in the ordinance of the Lord's Supper.' And finally, the court rejected the idea of adoration. Referring to its ruling in the Mackonochie case, it concluded 'that the Church of England has forbidden all acts of adoration to the sacrament, understanding by that the consecrated elements.' Judgment of the Judicial Committee of the Privy Council, cited in the *Times*, 10 June 1872.

Bennett nevertheless repudiated the court in a speech before the English Church Union: 'It was not a judgment, it was simply an opinion; if they called it a judgment, it inferred that there was a judge, but there was no judge there qualified to decide the question.... Their friend, Archdeacon Denison, spoke correctly when he said there were but two sentences in the judgment which were of any value – first, "that the subject matter is beyond the grasp of human intellect;" and secondly, "that the appeal was dismissed".' Report of *John Bull*, cited in the *Record*, 15 June 1872. The ECU also reiterated its condemnation of the court in a resolution; cf. *Record*, 24 June 1872.

14 The *Times* viewed the ruling as 'substantially, if not actually, the conclusion of a long series of experiments on the elasticity of the Formularies of the Church.' The Gorham case had stretched the limits of Anglican doctrine in one direction, and the authors of *Essays and Reviews* had taken it in another. Now, the extreme wing of the High Church demanded a similar liberty of opinion. The paper thought the final result, for good or evil, would 'depend on the use made by the Clergy of the extreme liberty of opinion now allowed them.... Unless such a license be very cautiously used, the question can hardly fail to be asked whether it is just to appropriate national property to the use of a Church of which the doctrines cannot be defined within any tangible limits.' *Times*, 10 June 1872.

According to Peter Marsh, the Judicial Committee made every effort, especially in doctrinal cases, 'to interpret the Church's formularies as broadly as possible.' That principle was evident in the earlier cases involving first Gorham and then the contributors to *Essays and Reviews*. Marsh, *Victorian Church in Decline*, p. 121.

15 Letter to the *Record*, 10 July 1872. Similarly, cf. letter of J. C. Ryle, *Record*, 28 June 1872.

16 Having discussed the other options, disestablishment or revision of the Prayer-book, neither of which was likely, Molyneux concluded that secession was the only other course of action. In his opinion, 'complicity with evil' or secession were the only alternatives. He concluded, 'I will secede! I will not, directly or indirectly, by consent, or complicity, sanction, or, in any wise be a party to, the idolatrous worship which, the Judicial Committee of the Privy Council, have, by their acquittal of Mr. Bennett, and legal recognition of his doctrine, permitted to exist, and to all intents and purposes, to be set up, in the Church of God, as by law established in these realms.' Capel Molyneux, *The Bennett Judgment. Our Duty: What is it?* (London: W. Hunt & Co., 1872), pp. 39-40.

J. Guinness Rogers, writing from a Nonconformist perspective, took a similar position. He suggested that clergy of widely differing views were bound together by the establishment in an 'unnatural alliance,' despite the fact that they regarded each other 'with mingled dread and aversion as teachers of error.' The Anglican Church for many years had been viewed by Nonconformists as the 'highway to Rome,' he wrote. But now 'it has made the journey unnecessary by bringing Rome here, and installing the worst errors and superstitions of Rome in the boasted citadel of Protestantism.' In Rogers's view, Evangelicals held an untenable position and ought simply to leave the Church of England. Rogers, *Bennett Judgment and Recent Episcopal Charges*, p. 8.

17 *Record*, 27 Sept. 1872.

18 Reprinted in the *Record*, 10 March 1873; cf. Appendix F. The final point seemed to indicate that the attempt to form a union of lay and clerical associations as an independent branch of the CA had been unsuccessful. After reporting on the union's initial formation, the *Record* took little note of the

organization in its pages during the following years. In a defense of the CA, written in 1873, Charles Bury still promoted the organization as the great hope for uniting the Evangelical party. He wrote, with something less than complete candidness, 'But there is one branch of its operations to which the Association may now devote its attention more directly than hitherto. It has been shown that without any marked efforts in that direction its influence has operated favourably in drawing into closer union the Evangelical body.' Bury cited the annual report of the CA's council for 1871, which touched upon the subject of Evangelical unity, but without noting the failure of the Lay and Clerical Union: 'The necessity of some measure for the promotion of greater unity of feeling and action among Churchmen attached to the principles of the Reformation has long forced itself upon their attention. It has for some time been their desire to take up this branch of work which from temporary circumstances had been suspended.' Bury, *Church Association*, pp. 34-35.

19 *Record*, 4 April 1873. Charles Bury claimed that the CA was the only effective force restraining the Ritualists: 'If no such Society had existed, who shall say whereunto these things might by this time have grown? There is no other efficient check to their proceedings. Therefore, great as are their extravagances, many and flagrant as are their breaches of the laws ecclesiastical, bold, boastful, and defiant as is the language of the leaders and public organs, how much worse, who can say, might have been the state of things but for the wholesome dread of the powerful interference of the Church Association!' Bury, *Church Association*, p. 27.

20 Bury thought it was impossible 'not to regret most deeply the present inactivity of the Bishops, and to dread its consequences to themselves and to the Church. We have to do only with the fact that the Episcopal Bench does not act with the decision which is essential and seems to be comparatively easy. And that fact establishes an additional necessity for the continued existence of the Church Association.' Ibid., p. 31.

The *Times* also thought the decision put a great responsibility on the bishops. While it might be difficult to prosecute concerning 'the subtle and incomprehensible distinctions of theological doctrine,' the courts had clearly marked out the limits of the law with regard to ceremony. And the Judicial Committee had noted that Bennett, had he been charged, was liable to the same condemnation as Mackonochie in that regard. The paper concluded that the result of the whole series of Ritualist judgments was 'to leave the clergy free to teach their peculiar opinions, but to prohibit them from using the Common Prayer and public ceremonies as instruments for inculcating such opinions. The service must always be such as not to exclude from participation those who differ from the Clergyman's views. The ceremonies must be national, though the doctrine may be sacerdotal. It remains to be seen whether this compromise will prove practicable. But it certainly imposes on the Bishops and all other responsible persons an additional obligation to enforce by all means in their power the previous Judgments of the Judicial Committee with respect to the posture and conduct of the officiating minister. Those Judgments have been most flagrantly and audaciously disobeyed; but now that they remain the sole protection of the

Protestant laity against the assumptions of a Romanizing clergy, it will be impossible that they should be allowed to continue in abeyance.' *Times*, 10 June 1872.

21 With regard to future action, the council later issued an address to its branches which concluded:

'1st. – As regards further legal proceedings, the Council express their decided conviction, which they believe to be the opinion of their friends, that while it would be most unwise for them to take up the position of prosecutors general of all Ritualists, they should at the same time reserve to themselves the power of again appealing to the law, if the continued inaction of some of those in authority, – the lawlessness of Ritualistic clergy, – the poverty of aggrieved parishioners, – or the rise of some new form of offence, should make it necessary.

'The Council, having succeeded in obtaining a declaration of the law of the Church, are determined to spare no efforts until imitations of the mass and other Romanizing practices of the Ritualists are banished from the Church of England.

'2ndly. – In accordance with the original aim of the Church Association, and sustained by the expressed wish of the Conference, the Council will use every effort to make this Association the great centre of union to all those faithful and earnest Churchmen who are contending with the superstitious or rationalistic tendencies of the age, and in carrying out such efforts they fully intend in the future to devote more time and attention to other than legal operations, and to take up any course of action that may seem desirable to secure the continuance of scriptural teaching and the promotion of Evangelical religion.' Cited in the *Record*, 30 April 1873.

22 Letter to the *Record*, 3 Sept. 1873.

23 Charles Bury wrote of the council's policy statement: 'This is so manifestly a work in the very spirit of the Gospel, that they who doubted or disliked the course of legal proceedings into which the Council were driven can hardly fail to acknowledge that, now at least the Church Association has got before it true and proper work. If any loyal member of the Church has doubted of the means hitherto employed "to uphold the Doctrines, Principles, and Order" of his Church, or of the wisdom and soundness of the course followed by the Council, surely he can doubt no more.' Bury, *Church Association*, p. 37.

24 The Ritualists had long charged the CA with persecution. The Bishop of Manchester, James Fraser, similarly referred to it as 'having notoriously become the instrument of party' as well as 'a persecuting association.' The language was challenged by T. R. Andrews, Chairman of the council of the CA. He claimed that the association had only become involved in litigation because the bishops, in dealing with the early Ritualist innovations, had claimed the state of the law was uncertain. 'It was under these circumstances,' he wrote, 'that it became necessary for some public body to undertake the duty of bringing the subject before the Courts of Law, as the Bishops declined the responsibility.... Is this persecution? If it be, then, my Lord, it seems that we must be content to be trampled on, and deprived of our privileges without presuming to resort to law for our vindication, lest in

compliance with the spurious charity of the day we should be stigmatized as oppressors and persecutors!'

Bishop Fraser, in response, refused to modify or retract his language, although he did note that he had referred in similar terms to the ECU as well. He wrote, 'The spirit of an associated body can only be ascertained by the language which it uses.' He then proceeded to cite several instances when CA speakers had used particularly violent language. Fraser continued, 'When I spoke of "persecution" I was not thinking of certain suits which have been conducted under the auspices and with the funds of the Church Association, which, if they have not done much to restrain the excesses at which they were aimed, have at least helped to ascertain the law; but I had in my mind the temper which such Associations appear to have a natural tendency to form, and which seems to me to be essentially intolerant and persecuting.' Fraser went on to suggest that in many cases, Ritualist excesses were 'largely provoked and intensified by partisan organizations, and the violent and uncharitable language of partisan (so-called) "religious" newspapers.' Correspondence cited in the *Record*, 4 Jan. 1875.

25 In 1870, the *Quarterly Review* published a review of two collections of essays written by moderates of the High Church and Evangelical sections. According to the reviewer, the Ritualists had 'awakened the keenest animosity' in both schools. No one doubted the earnestness and devotion of the movement's adherents, 'but it is felt that its characteristic tenets and practice have no support in Scripture or in the authorized formularies of the English Church, while they undoubtedly tend to alienate the great mass of lay Englishmen... And this appearance of unfaithfulness to engagements is so abhorred by Englishmen, that we cannot wonder at the opposition which has arisen against Ritualism, not only among vestry-orators, but among men of learning, candour, and ability.' Anon., 'Church and the Age,' *Quarterly Review*, pp. 54-55.

In 1876, Nevison Loraine, a non-partisan, took note of the many episcopal denunciations of Ritualist teaching over the years. He wrote, 'And not only has the Bench of Bishops spoken with marked unanimity, and reiterated condemnation of the teachings and tendencies of the Ritualist school, but from the *Times* down to the humblest provincial journal, and from the *Quarterly* through the whole range of serial publications, the entire public press of England has occupied itself with this extreme Ritualist movement; and, recognizing it as the ally and auxiliary of that Roman Communion which is the historic foe of civil and religious freedom, they have urgently condemned it as disloyalty to the genius and constitution of the English Church, and a source of mischief and danger to the rights and privileges of the English people.' Loraine, *Church and Liberties of England*, pp. 4-6.

26 MacDonnell, *Life of Magee*, vol. 2, pp. 1-2.

27 The *Record* published the correspondence between Bishop Wilberforce and Rev. Richard Wilkins, who had been a visiting preacher at St. Michael's, Southampton. Wilberforce prohibited Wilkins from presiding in his diocese after reading that Wilkins had worn a colored stole during the service and 'ostentatiously' kissed it prior to the sermon. Wilkins replied that he had no intention of obeying Wilberforce's demands and considered his inhibition

'null and void in the sight of God.' The *Record* thought it ironic that the Ritualists were now turning against even a High Church bishop such as Wilberforce. And although the paper had long been critical of Wilberforce, it applauded him for his response in that instance. *Record*, 15 and 19 July 1872.

The moderate Bishop Magee similarly thought that the state of the controversy was the result of 'the halting and undecided policy of some twenty years on the part of the bench.' But he noted the difficulty of the position in which the bishops found themselves. They did not have the power to intervene directly, and any attempt to gain further authority would be viewed by one party as 'a concession to popular clamour,' and by the other as 'an insidious attempt at increasing our powers, with the exercise of which already they are dissatisfied and suspicious.' MacDonnell, *Life of Magee, vol. 1*, p. 289.

28   The *Record* frequently reiterated the view that the bishops were to blame for the state of the controversy. It wrote in October 1872: 'In the abstract the duty of a Bishop to maintain firmly the administration of the Church's law cannot be denied. If he take it upon himself to choose in what cases he shall maintain it, and in what admit of its violation, he practically assumes the right to make the law, instead of discharging the duty of administering it. Shall it be said that the law has been doubtful? Why, then, the hue and cry against the Church Association for ascertaining it? Shall it be said that the only mode of procedure is tedious and expensive? Why, then, such a resolute episcopal opposition to all attempts to simplify it? The truth is that the Bishops are not disposed, some from excess of caution, some from mere timidity, some from a mistaken expediency, some from secret partiality to Ritualism, to discharge that office which the Primate of all England has publicly declared to be their bounden duty. Such an attitude is equally perilous to the Church and to themselves, and only serves to aggravate perplexities which a clear purpose and a firm courage would soon dissipate to the winds.' *Record*, 21 Oct. 1872.

A. O. J. Cockshut noted in his study of Victorian doctrinal controversies that there was much confusion during the period regarding ecclesiastical authority. There were conflicts between the High Church view of episcopal authority, the Protestant emphasis on the right of private judgment, and the erastian notion of the state's supremacy. All were in conflict during the period, and further confusion was introduced when court decisions on ecclesiastical matters were overruled on appeal. Cockshut, *Anglican Attitudes*, pp. 16-20.

29   The Bishop of Oxford presented the view of at least some of the bishops, who were opposed to ritual litigation, in his Charge of 1872: 'Looking back on the series of ecclesiastical trials which have occupied the attention of this generation, I cannot but see that they have exasperated party feeling, and supplied topics for mutual recrimination which else had not existed, or, if it had existed, had sooner died away. They have stimulated the creation of aggressive combinations among men of an uncharitable temper, which they mistook – the mistake had been repeated in the history of intolerance in every age – for zeal in behalf of Gospel truth. The decisions in these cases

have not, as far as I know, made a solitary convert, nor inspired a single controversialist with the sense of loyal obedience to their authority as oracles of the truth.' Cited in the *Record*, 19 April 1872.

30 The *Record* reported on a number of such cases during the early 1870s; cf. the correspondence between Bishop Baring of Durham and Thomas Brutton, Vicar of Tynemouth, reprinted in the *Record*, 2 Sept. 1872. Archbishop Thomson took a similar approach with R. Henning Parr, Vicar of St. Martin's, Scarborough in 1878. Thomson refused to license a curate if Parr would not moderate his Ritualism. Thomson, *Life of Thomson*, pp. 193-94.

31 The *Times* concluded, 'Moreover, lists of clergymen of extreme opinions have now become public, and a large number of names are notorious. Why should the Bishops accept the services of such men when applying for admission into their diocese? It is true these would be strong measures; but the evil is grave and the danger imminent. The question is whether the Bishops do or do not believe that the doctrines and practices of the Ritualists are utterly incompatible with the principles of the English Church. If they do, they are bound to discountenance such men by every means in their power.' *Times*, 26 June 1873.

In November 1873, however, the *Times* took an even more critical position in response to Bishop Ellicott's charge, in which he outlined a similar plan. He had denounced the activities of the Ritualists, but the paper thought his position weak when he went on to say that he thought they were best dealt with through 'moral influence and quiet persuasive moral force.' Rather than proceeding to enforce the law, when clergy disobeyed his admonitions, he placed a copy of his letter in the diocesan registry and refused to provide such clergy with episcopal testimonials so long as they refused compliance. The paper thought this a weak response and assumed it meant only that the Ritualists would be unable to obtain a transfer to another parish or to other positions in the church. *Times*, 3 Nov. 1873. Ellicott clarified his position in a letter, indicating that he intended a good deal more than the paper understood to be the case: 'The course I have been forced to decide on following does not refer to withholding testimonials. It means that I shall not be able to license curates or to ordain candidates on the nomination of such incumbents as may have refused to attend to my solemn request that they should obey the final decisions of the Court of their Metropolitan.' Letter to the *Times*, 8 Nov. 1873.

32 Cf. Carpenter, *Church and People*, vol. 2, p. 234.

33 Archbishop Tait's biographers noted that pressure had mounted as a result of Shaftesbury's frequent legislative efforts. With each successive year, they wrote, 'the conviction had grown upon the authorities, both lay and clerical, that legislation with reference to the Ecclesiastical Courts was absolutely necessary, and could no longer be postponed.' Davidson, *Life of Tait*, vol 1, p. 114.

34 A. J. B. Beresford-Hope, 'Peace in the Church,' *Nineteenth Century* 9 (1881): p. 759. According to G. I. T. Machin, the declaration of papal infallibility at the Vatican Council in July 1870 also gave new impetus to the anti-Ritualist movement, 'by defining more clearly the "Romanism" to which Ritualism was supposed to lead.' G. I. T. Machin, *Politics and the Churches in Great*

Britain, 1869-1921 (Oxford: Oxford University Press, 1987), p. 20.
35 Reprinted in the *Times*, 6 May 1873; cf. Appendix G. The *Times* also summarized the speech of T. R. Andrews, Chairman of the CA's council: 'Although, through the agency of the Church Association, the law was clearly set forth, obedience to the same was not enforced. The decision in the Mackonochie case was given in December, 1868, and that of the Purchas case in February, 1871, and he thought the faithful laity could not be charged with impatience if they now asked how long those decisions were to remain a dead letter.' Ibid. For a report of the CA meeting at which the memorial was discussed and debated, cf. *Times*, 25 July 1872.
36 They responded, 'There can be no doubt that the danger you apprehend of a considerable minority both of clergy and laity among us desiring to subvert the principles of the Reformation is real; and it is not unnatural that you should appeal to us for counsel and support. Since we had the honour of receiving your deputation our attention has been directed to a petition presented by upwards of 400 clergymen to the Convocation of the Province of Canterbury in favour of what they designate as Sacramental Confession. We believe that through the system of the Confessional great evil has been wrought in the Church of Rome, and that our Reformers acted wisely in allowing it no place in our Reformed Church, and we take this opportunity of expressing our entire disapproval of any such innovation, and our firm determination to do all in our power to discourage it. We feel justified in appealing to all reasonable men to consider whether the very existence of our national institutions for the maintenance of religion is not imperiled by the evils of which you complain.' Cited in the *Times*, 21 June 1873. On the archbishops' cautious approach, cf. Marsh, *Victorian Church in Decline*, p. 133.

The *Quarterly Review* thought the archbishops' reply set the stage for legislation by admitting 'the existence of the evil.' That admission, the journal wrote, was 'echoed from every side in the recent debates in Parliament, even by those who were most opposed to legislation. The reply of the Archbishops was probably the origin of the Public Worship Regulation Bill, which was an attempt on the part of the Bishops themselves to remove a wrong and a danger admitted on all hands to exist.' Anonymous, 'The Ritual of the English Church,' *Quarterly Review* 137 (1874): 566.
37 Cited in the *Times*, 21 June 1873. The concern to prevent an escalation of the controversy was widespread among the episcopacy. The Bishop of Ely raised the topic at a diocesan conference. 'Bishops,' he said, 'ought to be paternal governors and impartial judges, not public prosecutors.... I also believe that if I had adopted the plan of prosecuting any small departure from the strictest legal standard, I should have shut myself off from all hope of influencing by friendly and fatherly remonstrance, should have driven some into extremes who are now acting with moderation and wisdom, and should have lighted a flame of discord, which would have burned fiercely, long after I had been called to my account.' Cited in the *Record*, 11 July 1873.

Peter Marsh noted, however, that the appeal to the bishops' discretionary power only served to weaken the authority of the courts' judgments and increase the likelihood that the Ritualists would refuse to be bound by them. Marsh, *Victorian Church in Decline*, p. 128.

38 'With regard to the particular matters of ceremonial and doctrine to which you direct our attention, we wish we saw a readiness everywhere manifested on the part of the laity to use all the legitimate authority which is vested in them, through the election of churchwardens, and all their personal influence to check the growth of Romanizing tendencies... it is far more by kindly personal influence in our several families and neighbourhoods, by sound arguments, and appeals to the loyalty of those who are in danger of falling into error, rather than by judicial acts of authoritative interference, that the tendencies of which you justly complain can be met.' *Times*, 21 June 1873.

Evangelicals were dissatisfied with the archbishops' reply, but so also was the *Times*. In an editorial, the paper wrote, 'As is usual with indecisive answers, the reply has pleased no one. While the Ritualists are charged with disloyalty, the Memorialists receive no definite assurance of any more vigorous exercise of authority than that which has hitherto proved so ineffectual.... The Archbishops are in effect appealing to Churchwardens, or the general influence of the laity, or to Providence, to save them from the disagreeable task of authoritatively repressing Ritualism.' *Times*, 26 June 1873.

39 The petition was signed by 483 'priests of the Church of England,' who sought approval for their ritual innovations, a high view of the sacraments, and the use of confession (especially seeking the licensing of qualified confessors). While allowing for the use of confession in extreme and voluntary cases, most of the bishops who joined in the discussion condemned 'habitual or sacramental confession.' After touching upon a number of the Ritualists' teachings, Archbishop Tait concluded 'that if the House took these matters into consideration, it would be to distinctly condemn them.' Cited in the *Times*, 12 May 1873.

The *Record* thought the petition itself indicated the degree of responsibility the bishops bore for the growth of the movement. The Ritualists, it wrote, 'rest their plea for the authorized restoration of mediaeval doctrines and practices on the plea that a large number of unauthorized services and ceremonies are "extensively promoted by, or used under episcopal countenance and sanction."... What will the Bishops say, or how defend themselves from the gross inconsistency of which they are convicted?' *Record*, 4 June 1873.

John Kent suggested that by reintroducing the confessional, some of the clergy 'hoped to retrieve some of the professional status' they had lost during the course of the century. 'The authority of the confession, the expertise of spiritual direction, were to be set against the greatly increased professional prestige of other walks of life.' In Kent's view, that helps explain the emphasis put on it by the Ritualists in the early 1870s, 'when it was clear that the parson was about to lose the privileged position in popular education that he had retained so long.' Kent, *Holding the Fort*, pp. 283-84.

40 An essayist in the *Quarterly Review* concluded, 'We have contented ourselves with proving that private confession, as taught and practised by the Ritualists, is opposed alike to the teaching and the spirit of the Church of

England. But we should be wanting in our duty if we concluded without warning the Church of the danger to which this party is exposing her dearest interests. Of all the errors of the Church of Rome, that of auricular confession is most hateful to the people of England.' Anon., 'Private Confession,' *Quarterly Review*, p. 115.

By 1874, that journal thought the problem had only grown worse. 'Since that time nothing has occurred to change or even modify the opinions thus stated. On the contrary, the extravagances of the party that goes by the name of Ritualist have been multiplied rather than diminished, and their distinctly romanising tone has become so clear that it is impossible to mistake its true significance.' The writer went on to warn that the confessional was a far greater danger than the brightly colored vestments and other ornaments which were 'mischievous and absurd, but yet unreal.' In contrast to them, the exercise of 'spiritual tyranny' by priests, through the requirement of confession, was a form of "spiritual terrorism, which requires to be met by every species of serious argument, because it is a thing which cannot be touched by laws and by decisions of courts of justice." Anon., 'Sacerdotalism,' *Quarterly Review*, pp. 104-05.

In his 1876 critique of Ritualism, Nevison Loraine devoted a lengthy section to the subject of confession and absolution, citing a number of prominent Ritualists on the subject and then rejecting their doctrine as being outside the limits of toleration in the national church; cf. Loraine, *Church and Liberties*, pp. 30-44.

According to Peter Marsh, Tait and many of the other bishops would have liked to have condemned the use of confession even more strongly, but they restrained themselves 'in order not to appear to impede seeking of spiritual counsel' by those who were particularly disturbed; cf. Marsh, *Victorian Church in Decline*, p.132.

41 A large protest meeting was held at Exeter Hall on June 30th, led by Lord Shaftesbury. In his speech, he criticized the bishops for their refusal to respond immediately. For a report of Shaftesbury's speech and Tait's more moderate view of the events, cf. Davidson, *Life of Tait*, vol. 2, pp. 163-70.

42 *Record*, 4 June 1873. The *Quarterly Review* thought the petition was an act of 'simple-minded audacity.' 'Their only hope,' the writer concluded, 'was to get the bishops into a difficulty, and to induce the clergy and laity to imagine that the practice of confession was becoming actually common in the Church.' Anon., 'Sacerdotalism,' *Quarterly Review*, p. 107.

According to Walter Walsh, the memorial was the work of the secretive Society of the Holy Cross, which represented the extreme wing of the Ritualist movement; cf. Walsh, *Secret History of the Oxford Movement*, pp. 70-73. John Shelton Reed thought the Ritualists, unlike their Tractarian predecessors, were quite naive and actually thought their memorial was a prudent move. In fact, however, it alienated High Church moderates as well as further aggravating the episcopacy and the anti-Ritualists. Reed, *Glorious Battle*, p. 87.

43 Thus, they concluded, it was clearly intentional that the forms of private absolution included in the first Prayer-book of 1549, 'had been withdrawn from all subsequent editions of the said book.' Report of the Committee of

the Upper House of Convocation on Confession, cited in the *Record*, 25 July 1873. The paper was quite pleased with the report which went much further in its rejection of confession than the paper had expected; cf. *Record*, 28 July 1873.

When Bishop Ellicott referred to the statement and affirmed publicly his willingness to use all means necessary to repress those extreme practices that undermined the Reformation, G. A. Denison responded defiantly in the *Daily News*: 'Well, if the Bishop of Gloucester and Bristol, or any other bishop or bishops, will have open war, let it come. If they like to "snub" every Catholic and "pat on the back" every ultra-Protestant, let them follow their inclination. If they elect to stimulate popular ignorance and passion by calling us "dishonest," "disloyal," "plotters," "traitors," so be it. If they prefer to administer their dioceses inequitably, let them so administer; as some are doing now. If they propose to repeat the policy which drove out Wesley a century ago, let them try its effect upon us. If they think it will promote God's truth and the good of souls to see what can be done towards procuring persecuting Acts of Parliament, let them try their hand. We are quite ready; and we should fear nothing if they should succeed. But they will not succeed.' Letter to the *Daily News*, cited in the *Record*, 25 Aug. 1873.

The *Daily News* responded, 'If anybody is going to do battle in this country for habitual private confession, we are sorry for them and for the religious communion whose name and interests they thus compromise. Our countrymen know enough of that system to hold it in abomination. They reject it as fatal to the unity and peace of that domestic life which is the distinguishing happiness of this land.' Cited in the *Record*, 27 Aug. 1873.

Denison spoke at the Bath Church Congress in October 1873, and after making several 'provocative remarks' that were widely cheered by 'the Ritualist element,' he proclaimed the duty of the clergy to be the administration of the sacraments and the hearing of confession. At that point, indignant Protestants in the audience drowned out Denison and his supporters. The scene was repeated the next day when Denison attempted to speak on another topic and was again 'howled down.' *Record*, 10 Oct. 1873.

44 Peter Marsh, in his study of Tait's episcopacy, provided a thorough study of the Public Worship Regulation Act; cf. Marsh, *Victorian Church in Decline*, pp. 158-59. Cf. Davidson, *Life of Tait, vol. 2*, pp. 186-235.

Queen Victoria wrote to Gladstone, then Prime Minister, on the 20th of Jan. 1874: 'The process of these alarming Romanising tendencies has become *so serious of late*, the young clergy seem so tainted with these totally anti-Protestant doctrines, and are so self-willed and defiant, that the Queen thinks it absolutely necessary to point out the importance of avoiding any important appointments and preferments in the Church, which *have any* leaning that way.' *The Letters of Queen Victoria, Second Series, vol. 2*, ed. George E. Buckle (London: John Murray, 1926), p. 302 (her italics).

The *Quarterly Review* wrote, 'The condition of things in the Church has become such as to fill the boldest with astonishment and bravest with alarm. The Ritualistic party asserted their right to disobey alike the admonitions of the Bishops and the decisions of the courts in favor of "the voice of the Catholic Church." The voice of the Catholic Church, being interpreted by each clergyman for himself, is equivalent to the fancy of each clergyman.' Anon., 'Ritual of the English Church,' *Quarterly Review*, p. 565.

45 In response to a memorial from the rector and churchwardens of St. George's, Hanover Square, Bishop Jackson of London took a strict view of the illegality of clergy advocating 'habitual' or 'sacramental' confession. Nevertheless, he doubted that either episcopal admonitions or litigation would be particularly useful since evidence in such cases was nearly impossible to obtain. Ultimately, he thought, the matter would be decided by the laity: 'In the present day developments of ritual and matters of Church discipline and practice are governed less by law than by public opinion.... There would be few confessors if there were not many ready to confess.' The bishop argued that both the obligation and means of preventing the expansion of the confessional was in the hands of the laity, by which he meant the head of the house, who should instill the Protestant faith in his family. Correspondence cited in the *Times*, 6 Aug. 1873. He responded similarly to a memorial adopted by an anti-Ritualists in Chelsea; cf. *Record*, 6 Feb. 1874.

The *Quarterly Review* took a similar view: 'For this reason we cannot sympathise with the vehement appeals which are sometimes made to the bishops for their authoritative interference, or for some vaguely defined legislation against the Confessional. In the first place, you cannot put an end to the practice by any such means. If men and women are so mistaken as to imagine that any alteration in their relationship towards the Deity is effected by the utterance of the absolving words, no bishops and no Acts of Parliament can prevent their having recourse to some "priest" for his help. You might as well legislate against people swallowing patent medicines, or believing in this or that favourite doctor. As for the excited meetings, by which some zealous people attempt, as they say, to "put down the Confessional," their sole effect must be to irritate a mob of town roughs, who would prove the purity of their Protestantism by smashing the windows of Ritualist churches, and dragging Ritualist clergymen through the mud, while the persons who practice confession and absolution are only all the more confirmed in their convictions by the agitations against them.... Sacerdotalism did not grow spontaneously among us; as it did not grow spontaneously out of the teaching of the Divine Founder of our religion. A certain section of Church people were talked into accepting it by tracts, and sermons, and essays, and books, and private conversation. By similar means we shall get rid of it.' Anon., 'Sacerdotalism,' *Quarterly Review*, pp. 132-33.

46 'To the Protestant electors of the United Kingdom: –

'You are earnestly requested by the Council of the Church Association to obtain pledges from candidates for seats in Parliament, that they will support the Protestant principles of our Established Church, and for that purpose to put to them the question on the other side, and to forward the answer to the Secretary, Church Association, 14 Buckingham-street, Strand:

'Will you support efficient legislation for the repression of auricular and sacramental confession and priestly absolution, and the expulsion of other Romish doctrines and practices from the Church of England?' Cited in the *Record*, 30 Jan. 1874.

G. I. T. Machin noted that Nonconformists also raised the issue of Ritualism in the election campaign, although they went on to use it as an argument for disestablishment; cf. Machin, *Politics and the Churches, 1869-1921*, pp. 62-63.

47 The *Record* thought the bill differed little from Lord Shaftesbury's earlier attempts to reform the Ecclesiastical Courts. In effect, the bishops, motivated by continued Ritualist disobedience and the threat of anarchy, realized the necessity of a bill similar to those they had previously opposed. The paper reported that the Archbishop of York, in the House of Lords, 'concluded a vigorous speech by stating, amidst the cheers of the House, that the time had come when we must set limits to clerical disobedience, 'or else see the Church of England, which has been so active in the past and has never been more active and useful than it now is, deposed from her high position and the national trust withdrawn from her, simply because it is impossible to determine who or what she is.' *Record*, 22 April 1874.

48 Archbishop Tait to Queen Victoria, 16 Jan., 1874, in *The Letters of Queen Victoria, Second Series*, vol. 2, pp. 300-01. According to Peter Marsh, it was likely that the queen pushed Tait to introduce legislation to protect the Protestant nature of the church. Victoria was, thought Marsh, every bit as much a 'militant Protestant' as Shaftesbury, although not an Evangelical. Marsh, *Victorian Church in Decline*, pp. 159-60.

Some were pessimistic about the success of legislation. E. H. Plumptre, in an 1868 article, suggested that the Ritualists would find a way around any new restrictions imposed by law. It would be difficult, said Plumptre, 'for the most accomplished jurist to draw up an anti-Ritualist Act of Parliament through which a Ritualist pleader will be unable to drive his proverbial "coach and six".' Plumptre, 'Church Parties,' *Contemporary Review*, p. 337.

49 Marsh, *Victorian Church in Decline*, p. 158. According to Marsh, it was the last time Parliament's attention would be so thoroughly given over to the church. And for five months, Archbishop Tait would exercise a degree of influence not wielded since the time of Laud.

Tait explained the motive for the act, given his reputation for toleration, in his 1876 charge. He noted the growing sense of alarm throughout the country regarding the position of the Anglican church. At great expense, suits had been undertaken to defend the traditional view of the church's rubrics, but the innovators, had adopted a position of resistance, both with regard to the courts and the bishops. Tait continued, 'You cannot be surprised that this state of things was felt to be unendurable, and that the authorities of the Church, after long forbearance, and with an earnest desire to treat every one with the utmost amount of tenderness, at last resolved that some process must be found by which, when the law was once decided, the decision should be obeyed. Hence the introduction of the Public Worship Bill of 1874.' Cited in Anon., 'Archbishop Tait,' *Quarterly Review*, p. 22. For a brief summary of Tait's original intentions for the bill, cf. Davidson, *Life of Tait*, vol. 2, pp. 190-91; and Edwards, *Leaders of the Church of England*, pp. 116-20.

Interestingly, the non-partisan Bishop Magee of Peterborough claimed in his private letters that Tait was the wrong man for the times and failed to lead the church with a strong hand. In 1880, he complained about a controversy instigated by the Ritualists that involved the SPG. He felt a stronger stand against the Ritualists should have been taken, and he blamed Tait. 'When will the Archbishop of Canterbury give up driving and take to leading the Church? More and more am I convinced that the episcopate under his government is letting the Church drift on the breakers, when a strong hand on the helm might have saved her.' MacDonnell, *Life of Magee*, vol. 2, p. 127.

Tait's motivation was given a balanced treatment in the *Edinburgh Review*. The writer suggested that his whole life had been dedicated to establishing the church on 'a broad, comprehensive, national basis,' and he did not view the act as an attempt to narrow the toleration of the church. Anonymous, 'The Life of Archbishop Tait,' *Edinburgh Review* 174 (1891): 488-91.

50   The *Quarterly Review* suggested that Disraeli 'was wrong in saying that the measure was one to put down Ritualism,' because it would be equally applicable to those who failed to comply fully with the rubrics. 'But,' the reviewer continued, 'he was right in his interpretation of the will of the House of Commons, which accepted so eagerly, as a remedy against sacerdotal pretension and attempts which have sickened the heart of the constituencies, a measure of procedure neutral in itself and capable of other and wider applications.' Anon., 'Ritual of the English Church,' *Quarterly Review*, p. 543.

A decade later, the *Quarterly Review* still maintained that view: 'The Public Worship Act was not an attempt to alter the existing standards of doctrine or practice, or to narrow existing liberty in any single respect, but simply to render it more practicable to enforce the law as it existed.... The Ritualists, alone among English Churchmen, claimed to hold their position in the Church while repudiating all constituted authority within it; and the authorities did but accept the challenge with which they were thus defied.' Anon., 'Archbishop Tait,' *Quarterly Review*, pp. 22-23.

51   The paper complained that the process of determining the law was too complicated and expensive. But worse still, once determined, the law could only be put into effect with great difficulty. 'Practically, notwithstanding the decisions of the Courts, a self-willed Incumbent who chooses to defy the law and who disregards the authority of his Bishop and Metropolitan is irresponsible. However alien his proceedings may be from the letter and spirit of the Prayer Book, he can safely pursue his own course, provided only he is supported with sufficient funds by persons who sympathize with him.' It was now proposed, the paper continued, to give the bishops in reality that 'executive and discretionary power' that the Prayer Book had intended. In order to prevent abuses, however, it would be 'exercised on the advice of, and in co-operation with, a Diocesan Board composed in equal proportions of Clergy and Laymen.' *Times*, 10 and 13 March 1874.

According to Peter Marsh, the real strength of the bill came from Tait's speech introducing it. In that speech, Tait recalled the Purchas case and distinctly linked the bill to the suppression of Ritualism. Cf. Marsh, *Victorian Church in Decline*, p. 172. For an extensive discussion of the parliamentary debate, cf. Machin, *Politics and the Churches, 1869-1921*, pp. 70-78; and

Davidson, *Life of Tait*, vol. 2, pp. 190-217.
52 On Shaftesbury's views and involvement in the process, cf. Hodder, *Life of Shaftesbury*, pp. 681-84. A. J. B. Beresford-Hope, a Ritualist supporter, complained of Shaftesbury's entrance into the process, 'In the meanwhile a real demagogic power was at work.' Through his amendments, a civil judge was given authority to rule over the church such as no spiritual judge had ever had in the history of the Anglican church. And, 'for reasons which I cannot pretend to fathom, our metropolitans made sacrifice of their prerogatives at the bidding of Lord Shaftesbury.' Beresford-Hope, 'Peace in the Church,' *Nineteenth Century*, pp. 760-61.

There were numerous amendments offered after the second reading of the bill. The *Times*, in an editorial, summarized the more important issues involved. Lord Selborne suggested alterations to enlarge the bishops' discretionary power, while Lord Shaftesbury's amendments would have made the bishop 'a mere executive officer of the law,' with little discretion whatever and no power to veto proceedings. The *Times* favored a more moderate approach. *Times*, 30 May 1874.
53 Archbishop Tait was disturbed by this aspect of the amendment, which substituted judicial for episcopal authority, and he rightly foresaw that the Ritualists would refuse to be bound by the court's rulings. But Shaftesbury had the support of the government, and Tait had little choice but to support the bill with the amendments. Tait did, however, support another of Shaftesbury's amendments. 'It provided that, if both parties to a dispute agreed, the diocesan bishop could adjudicate it and pronounce a final sentence from which there would be no appeal. His decision would not, however, be regarded as a judicial clarification of the law.' Marsh, *Victorian Church in Decline*, p. 178-79.
54 Shaftesbury would have restricted prosecutions only by requiring the complainant to provide security for court costs in advance. Ibid.; cf. Elliott-Binns, *Evangelical Movement*, p. 58. The *Quarterly Review* thought the power to veto would eventually be very important. 'Whether a persistent refusal to allow a statute to operate would be protected by law we do not know; but a power almost without parallel has been entrusted to the Bishops, and there is no reason to doubt that it will be used so as to bring about a settlement of disputes without resort to the Courts.' Anonymous, 'Church Law and Church Prospects,' *Quarterly Review* 139 (1875): 274.
55 The bishop came to serve 'as the guide of the clergy amid disagreements, as the maintainer of a reasonable measure of agreement in modes of worship, and as the safeguard for a reasonable liberty in liturgical experiment.' Chadwick, *Victorian Church, Part Two*, p. 325.
56 The *Edinburgh Review* was pleasantly surprised by 'the eager unanimity' with which the bill was taken up in the House of Commons. The writer thought it reaffirmed the Protestantism of the nation, not in a purely negative sense, but as a matter of common public concern. It expressed 'the determination that the Church shall be not in name but in reality national, and that the clergy shall obey the law framed by the will of the whole nation.' Parliament was the only body, in the essayist's opinion, that could maintain the national character of the church 'as opposed to the clerical organiza-

tion.' The essayist hoped the act would reinvigorate the laity and encourage ecclesiastical reform. The article went on to argue that Convocation could not be trusted with that task. It had always represented the clerical party, and throughout English history, it was Parliament that defended the rights of the laity. Anon., 'Convocation,' *Edinburgh Review*, pp. 427-28.

An anonymous writer, surveying the strength of the church parties at the time, suggested that the bill's ease of passage was indicative of the Ritualists' lack of influence and a 'convincing proof that the nation as a body was entirely opposed to this Romanizing section of the Church.' Anonymous, *Church Parties, by a Queen's Counsel* (London: Houlston & Sons, 1874), p. 9.

The act is reproduced in full in the Appendix of Bentley, *Ritualism and Politics*, pp. 129-42.

57 Even the more moderate version originally proposed found little favor. E. B. Pusey wrote three lengthy letters to the *Times* criticizing the proposed legislation shortly after it was first announced. The *Times* responded to each letter with an editorial reiterating its support for the legislation; cf. *Times*, 19, 24 March and 1 April 1874. The paper was particularly disturbed when Pusey claimed that the legislation would be widely opposed by the laity; for it was 'acknowledged,' he wrote, 'that the so-called Ritual movement has come mainly from the people, not from the Clergy.' The *Times* suggested that such a fact would be acknowledged only by a few Ritualists. 'A more complete contradiction of the facts can hardly be conceived. Is it probable that a new school of theological thought and ritual observance would be originated by any other class than those whose ordinary studies lead them in such directions? Dr. Pusey will be refuted by the general experience of his readers. What has provoked all the bitterness of recent quarrels in parishes except that the Clergyman has introduced practices distasteful to his parishioners?' *Times*, 19 March 1874.

The *Quarterly Review* complained of the general High Church reaction, 'All the fountains of abuse in that strange portion of the press, the Ritualistic papers, poured forth their black streams anew. Nobody seemed to study the measure itself; every one viewed it through some distorting lens. What was less to be expected and more to be deplored was, that the High Church party, who would not come under the scope of the measure at all, joined their voices with the rest in indignant protest against legislation. They, too, refused to view the measure in its real nature.' Anon, 'Ritual of the English Church,' *Quarterly Review*, p. 567.

G. A. Denison complained in the Lower House of Convocation that the clergy had not been consulted, and that a bill passed by Parliament without their approval would have no authority. In fact, he said it might more properly have been titled, 'A Bill for the better Subjugation of the Clergy.' If approved, he suggested it would amount to 'a revival of the Inquisition.' *Times*, 1 May 1874.

Denison's complaint would be repeated for years to come as Ritualists repeatedly asserted that Parliament had no authority to enact ecclesiastical legislation without the approval of the church (either in Convocation or by some other 'ideal' but non-existent synod). Their argument was somewhat ironic in that the bill was drawn up and presented to Parliament by the

Archbishop of Canterbury himself. The *Times*, in an editorial, rejected the claim: 'Convocation, it should have been obvious from the outset, is not a body before which such a measure as that now proposed by the Archbishop should be laid. When legislation is required on matters involving professional learning, or when an alteration is to be made in the formularies to which the Clergy have subscribed, it is both reasonable and just that their supposed representatives should be formally consulted. But it is very different when the only question is how to enforce, in the interests of the whole Church, and particularly in the interests of the laity, obligations which already exist.' Ibid.

58 The petition read, in part, 'Your petitioners beg respectfully to say that the statements and explanations which accompanied the introduction of the Bill into our Lordships' House were not consistent with a measure having for its simple object improvement in the mode of conducting suits in courts ecclesiastical; and, in the second place, your petitioners are convinced that, whatever be the technical designation of the object of the Bill, the practical result of it would be to work a substantial change in the existing status of the Church of England; and that it is this conviction which has created so intense a feeling throughout the country.' Cited in the *Record*, 29 May 1874.

A. J. B. Beresford-Hope blamed the act for an increase of party strife in the church. He thought it made a Ritualist reaction inevitable: 'This measure, which began so badly, resulted in creating the judicature of partisanship – an enactment which, in professing to deal indulgently with ritual irregularities, really left them under a harsher *regime* than moral offences; while the spiritual democracy, organised as the Church Association, to whose existence and powers of mischief the authors of the Act had perversely shut their eyes, made themselves masters of its machinery.' A. J. B. Beresford-Hope, 'An Ecclesiastical Olive Branch,' *Nineteenth Century*, 15 (1884): 307.

The *Quarterly Review* thought it a moderate bill that simply demonstrated the Protestantism of the nation. The Ritualists had, thought the writer, 'a small but active following, who, like the supernumeraries at a theatre, create an impression of multitude by entering at many points in divers dresses. They are the same voices that shout at St. James's Hall, respond at St. Alban's, and demonstrate at Church Congresses. The present movement has furnished the first test as to the progress made by the Ritualist party in its ambitious programme of obliterating the Reformation and bringing back the nation to the position of past ages and of other nations. They have had unusual advantages, supporters in the present cabinet and in the last. But when the question was fairly before the House of Commons whether it was not high time to check their proceedings, the answer was unanimous, and their friends were unable even to divide. This is the really important point, far more so than the measure which was produced.' Anon., 'Ritual in the English Church,' *Quarterly Review*, pp. 580-82.

59 In November 1874, the ECU passed a resolution that it would not recognize the judgments of the new court; cf. Bentley, *Ritualism and Politics*, pp. 81-82. The Ritualist position was later summarized by Canon George Perry. The church, he said, was 'a divinely constituted society in the world.' It had 'di-

vinely appointed officers to govern it,' as well as duties and privileges that were 'divinely granted' to it. 'What churchmen want is that these privileges should not be interfered with, and one of these privileges they hold to be the right of this society to judge and decide by its officers all questions of the divine law, and all matters which may be properly described as spiritual or ecclesiastical.' George G. Perry, 'The Grievances of High Churchmen,' *Nineteenth Century* 26 (1889): 501.

The issue continued to divide the church throughout the rest of the century; cf. George Arthur, 'The "Lawless" Clergy of "this Church and Realm",' *Nineteenth Century* 45 (1899): 558-69. On the creation of a plan for passive resistance, cf. Reed, *Glorious Battle*, pp. 240-41.

60 Evangelicals were quick to reject the Ritualists' arguments, but they were not alone in that regard. The *Edinburgh Review* was encouraged by the intervention of Parliament, and hoped it would stifle 'the sacerdotal spirit' that gave 'undue prominence' to the clergy. The essayist distinguished between cases involving morals or doctrine and those of ritual, which should be treated 'as administrative details.' For that purpose, the reforms of the Public Worship Regulation Act were imperative. While not desiring 'to enforce a rigid uniformity in every detail,' the writer thought it was important that the courts should define the limits of the law for the national church. Anon., 'Convocation,' *Edinburgh Review*, pp. 427-28.

The *Quarterly Review* published an article on ecclesiastical law in the course of which it recounted the long history of Parliamentary legislation in which the church's courts and legal system were amended without the approval of Convocation. Anon., 'Church Law and Church Prospects,' *Quarterly Review*, pp. 268-70.

61 It jumped from 10,517 in 1874, to 12,602 in 1875. Cf. Marsh, *Victorian Church in Decline*, p. 219; and Reed, *Glorious Battle*, pp. 238-39.
62 Letter to the *Record*, 24 June 1874.
63 Letter to the *Record*, 1 July 1874.
64 Letter to the *Record*, 10 July 1874.
65 Smith was supported by an anonymous correspondent who wrote, 'As a moderate Churchman, with no sympathy with such a meeting of the E.C.U. as the one referred to, I may say that I believe nothing lowers the respect felt for the Evangelical body by all moderate men, as the bitter tone in which such men as Dean Close writes about all who differ from him in opinion. And I feel that such a man as Mr. Smith, who comes forward in the cause of peace, is a bright example to all parties of Christian love and hope, whose example may we all follow more.' Ibid.
66 At the annual meeting of the CA in 1876, T. R. Andrews, expressed the fear 'that there may be a growing disinclination in some minds to controversy and to keeping in the forefront the distinctive features of this Association, and in the general idea of resisting Rome, which is the bounden duty of every Protestant man, to merge the special duty of resisting Romanism in the Church of England. Applications have lately been made from the country for lecturers, with this reservation. They say we want lecturers against Romanism, but we want no allusion to be made to Romanism in the Church of England.... What has brought the Church Association together? What has

maintained its position? What but a determination to put our fingers on Romanism in the Church of England and every means in our power to seek to eject it from its wrong position? (Cheers.) We do not say that our opponents have not the right to maintain their views. But we say to them, "You have no right to entertain Romish views in the Church of England, and with God's help we will never abate one jot of effort or exertion until we have rendered it impossible for any man openly to teach Romish principles in the Church of England".' Cited in the *Record*, 12 May 1876.

67 An extended description of the eucharistic vestments, their symbolism, and their place in the controversy can be found in the article on 'Vestments,' in Cutts, *Dictionary of the Church of England*, pp. 605-14.

The *Quarterly Review* considered both points at some length and took issue with the idea of compromise. In particular, the essayist rejected the argument that they could be considered harmless aesthetic innovations apart from their doctrinal symbolism. Anon., 'Church Innovations,' *Quarterly Review*, pp. 526-68.

68 Cited in the *Record*, 21 Oct. 1874. Throughout the following months, the *Record* reported on the responses from the rural deaneries, which took a variety of forms. In response to a circular from the Bishop of Lichfield, the Rural Deanery of Cheadle, Staffordshire, voted on several questions: 'That the ornaments' rubric be retained without any alteration whatever – Ayes, 6; Noes, 5; Neutral, 2. That the Elizabethan advertisements be made the authoritative rule – Ayes, 5; Noes, 7. That exceptions be permitted by authority – Ayes, 10; No, 1. That the conditions of such exceptions be the being legalised by Convocation and Parliament and desired by a majority of the communicants – Ayes, 7; Noes, 5; Neutral, 1. That the north side means the north end – Ayes, 7; Noes 5; Neutral, 1. That "standing before the table" means standing at the north end – Ayes, 5; Noes, 7. That the eastward position is the law – Ayes, 7; Noes, 6. That deviations from the Purchas Judgment should be permitted – Ayes, 2; Noes, 3; Neutral, 7.'

The Rural Deanery of Birkenhead adopted a series of resolutions: '1. That the limits of permitted ritual should be plainly and clearly set down in the Book of Common Prayer and canons of the Church, and that excesses and defects beyond the legal limits should be promptly and effectively restrained by the proper authority. 2. That in particular churches no changes in the manner of conducting Divine service should be made without the licence of the Bishop and the concurrence of the congregation. 3. That it is not expedient to prohibit by new rubrics any ornaments or ceremonies which may be permitted by the present rubrics as interpreted by courts of law. A Resolution protesting against the eastward position and the use of Eucharistic vestments in parish churches was rejected by a majority both of clergy and laity.' Cited in the *Record*, 23 Oct. 1874.

69 Cited in the *Record*, 20 Jan. 1875. There were many, however, who remained convinced opponents, and not only among the Evangelical party. For a thorough study of the subject from a non-Evangelical, anti-Ritualist perspective, cf. Howson, *Before the Table*. His work received a favorable response in the *Quarterly Review* which reconsidered the whole issue and rejected the use of the eastward position. Anonymous, 'Church Innovations,'

Quarterly Review 141 (1876): 526-68.
70 Cited in the *Record*, 20 Jan. 1875.
71 Pastoral Letter of the Bishops, reprinted in Davidson, *Life of Tait, vol.* 2, pp. 271-75.
72 Bishop Baring of Durham refused to sign the document because of its tone of compromise, writing to Archbishop Tait, 'It is a perilous experiment when a patient is suffering from a dangerous fever to treat it as a slight cold, and administer only a little weak milk and water.' The High Church Bishop Moberly of Salisbury refused to sign for the opposite reason. Cf. Davidson, *Life of Tait, vol.* 2, p. 271.

The *Times* took a generally positive view and suggested that it was 'as clear and as grave a declaration' as the bishops could have issued to 'the contending parties in the Church.' It was, continued the paper, 'an announcement beforehand that the Public Worship Act will be administered.' Although the paper was willing to allow that the bishops might have taken action earlier, it was satisfied that they were at largely united in expressing the view 'that a certain party among the Clergy have now passed all tolerable bounds in their reactionary and disorderly innovations.' *Times*, 8 March 1875.

In contrast, Evangelical anti-Ritualists took a critical view. Later, the *Record* sharply criticized Bishop Browne of Winchester for adopting a similarly moderate tone. Browne suggested in his own pastoral letter that there was room in the church for both of the parties. He wrote, 'True Catholic piety and true Evangelical purity are, I am sure, compatible with each other.' The paper complained that he and the other bishops were simply trying to nullify the provisions of the Public Worship Regulation Act and prevent further litigation. According to the paper, Browne was guilty of two errors. First, he elevated the interests of the Church over those of the truth; and second, he equated the Ritualists with the High Church party in general. 'The Bishop regards Ritualism as a mere casual and unimportant accident of High Churchism, and occupies his Pastoral by placing High Churchmen and Evangelicals into comparison, and pleading for peace between them. By all means. With orthodox High Churchmen we hold no conflict, save that of legitimate argument.' With the Ritualists, however, the paper was unwilling to consider any compromise. *Record*, 22 Dec. 1875.

73 The memorial was reprinted in the *Times*, 18 Jan. 1875; cf. Appendix H.
74 Reprinted in the *Record*, 16 April 1875; cf. Appendix I. The whole controversy, in a sense, could be reduced to the issue of whether or not the clergy acted as sacrificial priests. Aesthetically pleasing ceremonial innovations might be adopted, although there was certainly no small debate generated even over such relatively minor issues; but those innovations introduced by the Ritualists that seemed to emphasize the separation of the priest from the congregation, elevating him to the role of mediator between God and the laity, were entirely rejected. The Evangelical view of the ministry was considered, along with a critique of the concept of 'priest,' by James Bardsley in an 1872 lecture presented under the auspices of the Church Association. James Bardsley, *The Christian Ministry: What it is and What it is Not* (London: Hatchards, 1872).

75 The resolution, as adopted, read: 'That this House having regard to the fact of the existing widespread diversity of practice with regard to the position of the celebrant at the administration of the Holy Communion, is convinced that it will be most for the welfare of the Church that such diversity be not disturbed, provided that in cases where changes are made and disputes arise it be left to the Ordinary to determine which practice shall be adopted. And, further, that by this Resolution no sanction is intended to be given by this House to any doctrines other than what are set forth in the Prayer-book and Articles of the Church of England.' Cited in the *Record*, 21 April 1875.

76 In an editorial published on 30 June 1875, the day before the Public Worship Regulation Act took effect, the *Times* criticized the Lower House. There was much they could have done as 'a body of adult ecclesiastics' to calm the situation and exercise a moderating influence in the controversy. But instead, said the paper, they had adopted resolutions certain 'to foster and aggravate the existing discontent.... The Legislature in the Public Worship Act has in reality provided for the enforcement of an impartial arbitration, which, when determined in one instance, would everywhere be applicable. But Convocation would refer each particular dispute to the judgment of the Bishop who would thus, in addition to his other work, be made a party to every local controversy.... These resolutions suggest a kind of Permissive Bill for Ritualistic ceremonial in every parish in England, and the country is to be exposed to all this incessant worry because Convocation cannot make up its mind to say plainly what we are confident a majority of its members individually feel, that the excitement raised on behalf of these innovations is utterly unworthy of the subject. It is significant that nearly every speaker deprecates the general introduction of the disputed practices, while he nevertheless proposes to legalize them. It is enough to say that these resolutions amount to nothing less than a proposal to undo the work which was done by the passsing of the Public Worship Regulation Act.' *Times*, 30 June 1875.

Some bishops and moderates hoped the controversy could be settled by allowing the innovations while denying the doctrinal interpretation imposed upon them by the Ritualists. Such was the view later expressed by Archbishop Benson in the Lincoln judgment. But Evangelicals were generally critical of such a compromise as were some other non-partisans. Dean Howson suggested it was no accident that the controversy had come to focus on the vestments and the eastward position. It was there that they were 'brought in contact with the great question whether a proper sacrificial priesthood is or is not a part of the religious system established by Christ on earth.' And on that question the two sides were fundamentally divided. Howson, *Before the Table*, p. 3.

77 The essayist rejected the Ritualists' argument that Parliament had no right to enact legislation for the church. Parliament had acted on numerous other occasions and lay judges had always sat in courts that ruled over ecclesiastical matters. 'Any clergyman who has taken holy orders or preferment since 1840 [when the Clergy Discipline Act established the existing legal process for ecclesiastical cases, with final appeal to the Judicial Committee of the Privy Council] has accepted his position knowing that he must rest

for the ultimate vindication of his rights upon a Court established not by Convocation but by Parliament.' Anon., 'Church Law and Church Prospects,' *Quarterly Review*, p. 268. The Ritualist protest was reprinted within this article on pp. 270-71.

78 T. T. Carter, of Clewer, moved a resolution: 'That without intending to put all the following points on the same ground, nor wishing to go beyond what recognised Anglican authorities warrant as to their use, the English Church Union is of opinion that in order to bring about a generally satisfactory settlement of the present Ritual controversy in the Church of England there should be no prohibition of the following usages when desired by clergy and congregations.' Cited in the *Record*, 28 June 1875.

According to John Shelton Reed, the adoption of the six points was part of the maturation process of the movement. In particular, they represented the increasing focus of the Ritualists on the doctrine of the real presence and those practices that emphasized it. Reed, *Glorious Battle*, pp. 68-70; cf. 'Six Points,' in *The Oxford Dictionary of the Christian Church, Second Edition*, ed. F. L. Cross and E. A. Livingston (Oxford: Oxford University Press, 1974), p. 1281.

79 Twelve charges were made, eight of which had previously been declared illegal. They were: the use of lighted candles on the altar, wearing the alb and chasuble, mixing water with the sacramental wine, using wafer bread, the eastward position, kneeling during the prayer of consecration, singing the *Agnus Dei*, and having processions. The four new charges were: celebrating Holy Communion with only one other person, erecting a crucifix on the chancel screen, burning candles around the crucifix, and erecting pictures illustrating the 'Stations of the Cross' without authorization. *Record*, 10 Jan. 1876. For a general discussion of the Ridsdale case, particularly in relation to the workings of the Public Worship Regulation Act, cf. Bentley, *Ritualism and Politics*, pp. 97-100.

80 With regard to the fabric of the church, Penzance agreed with the prosecution that the innovations could easily become, if they were not already, objects of 'superstitious reverence.' He concluded, 'When the Court was dealing with a well-known sacred object [the crucifix] – an object enjoined and put up by authority in all the churches of England before the Reformation, in a particular part of the church, and for the particular purpose of "adoration;" when the Court found that the same object, both in the Church and out of it, was still worshipped by those who adhered to the unreformed Romish faith, and when it was told that, now, after a lapse of 300 years, it was suddenly proposed to set up again this same object in the same part of the church as an architectural ornament only, it was hard not to distrust the uses to which it might come to be put, or escape the apprehension that what begins in 'decoration' may end in "idolatry".' Judgment of the Court of Arches, cited in the *Times*, 4 Feb. 1876.

81 Penzance concluded that 'there remained the obvious reflection that a false step in one direction was likely to be fraught with evils far greater than any that could ensue from an error committed in the other. If sculptured figures or pictures were once set up in our churches and sustained by the law; to which (whether from the natural tendencies and weaknesses of the human

mind on this subject, or from the teachings of books, or the promptings of individuals) adoration or superstitious reverence should, contrary to expectation, come to be paid, an irreparable step towards idolatry might prove to have been taken; for the outward object once sanctioned, the inward devotion was beyond the reach of the laws. In the opposite direction he could discern no evil comparable to that.' Ibid.

82 After the verdict, the *Times* published a letter Ridsdale sent to Archbishop Tait prior to the trial, in which he rejected the court's authority in spiritual maters. It had, he wrote, 'only a civil jurisdiction, capable, indeed, of commanding compliance under pains and penalties, but not of interpreting the law of the Church so as to bind the consciences of Churchmen.... In default of any authoritative fixing by the Church of the meaning of certain of her regulations respecting public worship, I feel not only at liberty, but morally and ecclesiastically bound to stand by the most obvious sense of the words of those regulations, notwithstanding any contrary decision of a Court not recognized by the Church as a regulator of her worship.' Correspondence cited in the *Times*, 4 Feb. 1876.

The *Record* noted that there was no change in the services at St. Peter's after the judgment. In his sermon, Ridsdale repudiated the court's ruling. At issue were not merely ceremonies but doctrine; 'it is the doctrine of the Creed, "I believe in the Holy Catholic Church." It is this doctrine that is attacked when we are called lawless and brought to trial for not having complied with the judgment called the Purchas Judgment – i.e., a judgment delivered about five years ago by a Court that had no authority from the Church to say what was right or wrong. This judgment of the Court, has been persistently called law, as if it was the only law on the subject, and we have been persistently called breakers of the law, because we have not complied with that judgment.... Yes, it has been and is the law of the land; but, my brethren, does that make it the law of God and the Church?' Cited in the *Record*, 14 Feb. 1876.

83 His appeal put the ECU in an awkward situation since it had already denied the authority of the court. C. L. Wood explained the decision at the ECU annual meeting: 'Mr. Ridsdale expresses our desire to do all that in us lies as loyal subjects of the Crown to avoid collision with the civil courts, and to obtain peace for the Church; Mr. Tooth, the determination in purely spiritual matters, if the question is forced upon us, to recognise no authority or power except that which is exercised according to the provisions made by our Lord Jesus Christ for the government of his Church on earth. We go with Mr. Ridsdale before the courts, not to ascertain the law of the Church, but to defend it. And with Mr. Tooth we shall be, please God, prepared, if need be, to suffer for it.... Churchmen, in my opinion, may even acquiesce for the moment in the judgments of civil courts in spiritual matters if those judgments are, as a matter of fact, equitable, and respect the Church of England's historical claims and position; but there is a limit to that acquiescence, and that limit will have been reached if certain recent judgments, whether of Lord Penzance or the Privy Council, are reaffirmed and attempted to be enforced.' Cited in the *Record*, 19 April 1876.

The Ritualists would soon move beyond Wood's limited acknowledgment of the court's authority. After the Ridsdale judgment, they were unwilling to recognize that it had any authority whatsoever in spiritual matters. Cf. Anonymous, *The Position of the Ritualists, by One of the Rank and File* (London: G. J. Palmer, 1881), pp. 6-9.

84 The proceedings before the Judicial Committee, with the arguments presented on both sides of the case, were fully reported in each issue of the *Times*, 24 Jan. to 2 Feb. 1877.

85 In an editorial, the *Times* complained that the case had effectively brought the whole justice system to a halt, with over one hundred cases backed up in the other courts, because so many judges had been added to the Judicial Committee. In the paper's view, four or five judges would have been plenty, along with the episcopal assessors. And for what was this auspicious group gathered, asked the paper? To hear 'arguments on such questions as whether a table not standing at a wall can be said to have any front or back to it; whether, as Sir James Stephen thinks, two persons who are at opposite sides of such a table can both be said to be before it; what is the definition of a wafer, as distinguished from ordinary bread....' For this purpose, 'two Lord Chancellors, three Lords Justices, a Lord Chief Baron, five other Judges, an Archbishop, and three Bishops are giving up time incalculable to listen to hair-splitting on these points, and that for this purpose, and this only, the whole judicial business of the country is obstructed.' In the view of the *Times*, the absurdity of the situation reflected badly on those responsible and was almost certain 'to bring discredit and almost to provoke contempt for the subject with which such disputes are identified.' The paper thought the importance of the Ritualist innovations had been greatly exaggerated by their opponents, but it nevertheless concluded that 'those are most to blame who make a difficulty of submitting to the law when once decided on such matters, by whomsoever it may be determined or whatever it may be. It is really intolerable, and a scandal to religion itself, that the business of the country should be brought to a standstill by such nonsense.' *Times*, 27 Jan. 1877.

86 *Record*, 14 May 1877. More optimistically, the *Times* hoped the result was 'such as may be accepted by all but extreme partisans on either side.' *Times*, 14 May 1877.

87 Judgment of the Judicial Committee of the Privy Council, cited in the *Times*, 14 May 1877. The *Record's* correspondent thought the judgment reflected the moderation of Archbishop Tait. The judgment on the use of vestments was thorough and persuasive, but when the judges considered the eastward position and wafer bread, 'all was slight, cloudy, and inconclusive. It partook of the nature of an *excuse*; it seemed to say, 'We must give these people something, and we must find some sort of a reason for doing so. The reason given was that the case was "not proven." It follows that if hereafter a stronger case shall be presented the result may be different.' *Record*, 16 May 1877 (their italics).

The Ritualists' arguments regarding the issues considered by the court, along with a moderate refutation of their position, was published the next year in the *Quarterly Review*. Anonymous, 'The Ritualists and the Law,' *Quarterly Review* 151 (1881): 219-26.

According to John Shelton Reed, the attempt to have the eastward position judged illegal was a tactical error on the part of the anti-Ritualists, as it had been widely used by moderates within the High Church party for many years. In his view, it was no accident that the judgment handed down in the Purchas case regarding the eastward position was reversed by the appeals court in the Ridsdale case. Following the view of several contemporaries, including Archdeacon Denison and the *Spectator*, Reed suggested it was a 'politically motivated' decision. Reed, *Glorious Battle*, pp. 117-18.

88 Cf. Letter of E. V. Bligh to the *Record*, 16 May 1877. But others, such as Hugh McNeile, thought the eastward position a minor point in comparison to the eucharistic vestments, and one on which there was room for compromise. In contrast to the vestments, he wrote, 'the Eastward Position teaches nothing, but the private judgment, or personal convenience, or both, of the individual celebrant. In this, there is no sanction of false doctrine; on the contrary, all sacrificial vestments and all postures of adoration being strictly forbidden, the false doctrine referred to is tacitly but most expressively condemned.

'Those extreme Ritualists, who have proclaimed the vestments and postures to be matters of conscience, have now no other resource than a violation of the law. Meanwhile, to stand with their back to the communicants as they have always done while reading the Prayer of Consecration, will prove a satisfaction to be enjoyed without controversy by the large body of old-fashioned High Churchmen.' Letter to the *Record*, 16 May 1877.

89 C. J. Ellicott, 'The Ridsdale Judgment and Its Results,' *Nineteenth Century* 1 (1877): 757. The *Times* took a similar position. The paper thought the use of wafers and a crucifix 'were of secondary importance, and involved no vital consequences to the peace of the Church.' The vestments and eastward position, however, were of central importance. The vestments were used by only a few Ritualists and had few other proponents, but the Eastward position was 'generally adopted, and a large number of High Churchmen who abstain from going the whole way with the Ritualists have been awaiting the decision with grave anxiety.' *Times*, 14 May 1877.

90 Ellicott, 'Ridsdale Judgment,' *Nineteenth Century*, pp. 767-8. In attempting to find a compromise between the parties involved in the controversy, mediators would repeatedly attempt to find a way around the doctrinal beliefs signified in the innovations. The final attempt would come in the Lincoln judgment, when Archbishop Benson ruled against the prosecution but rejected the supposed doctrinal symbolism of the ceremonies.

91 Correspondence cited in the *Record*, 13 June 1877.

92 Ibid. The *Quarterly Review* complained that the bishops, and particularly Archbishop Tait, had naively attempted to minimize the controversy for the sake of peace. The essayist, however, thought there was a genuine urgency to the crisis on two counts. First, it represented 'an unqualified revolt against the existing law, and against all authority which rests upon it.' And second, it was 'a persistent attempt,' through devotional manuals and the 'systematic imitations of Roman Catholic ceremonies, to transform the whole aspect and character of the English Church.' Anon., 'Ridsdale Judgment,' *Quarterly Review*, pp. 244-45.

93 Ridsdale concluded, 'You will see that I yield those things for which there is no rubrical direction, and do not yield those things for which some rubric can be alleged, on which (that is) the Church has spoken, and therefore ought to be consulted.' Cited in the *Record*, 28 May 1877.

94 T. T. Carter presided over a meeting of about three hundred clergy, 'including many of the leading incumbents of London,' at the Westminster Palace Hotel. Those present expressed their determination 'to disregard the recent decision of the Judicial Committee, as being clearly contrary to the plain meaning of the Rubrics of the Prayer Book.' *Times*, 1 June 1877.

The *Times* condemned the Ritualists' attacks on the Judicial Committee: 'If anything would provoke the public at large to be hard upon them, it would be the unmannerly way, to say no more, in which they deal with the decision of the Privy Council. It argues extraordinary self-confidence that they should coolly assert, like Dr. Pusey, that the judgment is a palpable misinterpretation of the law. But lawyers may err, and even the Judicial Committee are not infallible. Those who differ from them have a right to maintain their own opinion. But they have no right to insinuate, still less to assert loudly, that the Judgment is unfair and prompted by prejudice.' *Times*, 14 June 1877.

The *Quarterly Review* similarly complained that the Ritualists had a right to protest and defend their position, but then it was their duty to submit. Instead, they refused their obedience and 'set an example, never before, we believe, seen in this country, of flagrant and gross insult, on the part of those who should be gentlemen as well as clergymen, to the highest judicial authorities, together with a passionate determination to have their own way at all hazards, and to force their favourite practices upon the Church in defiance of the law.' The insulting language, the writer concluded, was inconsistent with 'the ordinary obligations of gentlemen.' Anon., 'Ridsdale Judgment,' *Quarterly Review*, pp. 247, 253.

95 The correspondence between Tait and Ridsdale provided a revealing look at the Ritualist mindset. Tait wrote, 'Making full allowance, therefore, for your scruples of conscience, I am quite willing to take upon myself the whole responsibility entrusted with the spiritual supervision of the diocese in which you serve.... I feel confident that, by paying a ready obedience to this my Episcopal admonition, you will place yourself in a much more satisfactory position in the sight of the whole Church, that your own people will appreciate your dutiful obedience.'

Ridsdale could hardly refuse obedience to the archbishop, but he refused to yield his position. Any compromise, he claimed, would require that Tait free him 'from the obligation of the Ornaments Rubric.' Finally, he desired assurance that Tait was 'not merely enforcing the late decision of the Privy Council' but delivering his own 'Episcopal judgment to the effect that the Ornaments Rubric does not prescribe the use of alb, chasuble, and the lighted candles at Holy Communion and the mixed chalice, and that, therefore, my obligation to use those things has been only a supposed one.'

Tait, in his reply, indicated that Ridsdale's difficulties of conscience were largely the product of his own imagination: 'I gather that, while you consider yourself as being under a sacred obligation to act upon what you conceive to be the literal meaning of the Ornaments Rubric in the Prayer-book, you yet acknowledge a general dispensing power in this matter to reside in me as your Bishop, and that you are ready under such dispensation to abstain from the use of the alb and the chasuble, and lighted candles at the time of the Holy Communion, and the mixed chalice. I am quite ready to satisfy your conscience in this matter, and do hereby grant you a complete dispensation from the obligation under which you believe yourself to lie.'

Ridsdale agreed to obey Tait only insofar as he spoke as the archbishop and not as a matter of compliance with the court's decision. He was also willing to obey only until the issue was addressed by Convocation, which he believed had final authority in the matter. Correspondence reprinted in Davidson, *Life of Tait*, vol. 2, pp. 241-45.

96 C. L. Wood, President of the ECU, made the argument following the suspension of a Ritualist by the Court of Arches in 1878: 'Lord Penzance has pronounced a sentence of suspension against the Rev. J. Edwards, of Prestbury – that is to say, a judge deriving whatever authority he possesses solely from Parliament decides how and in what way a priest shall administer the Sacraments, and for non-compliance with his orders requires him to abstain altogether from the exercise of his sacred functions. There can be but one answer to such an usurpation from those who believe the Church to be something more than a department of the Civil Service, and that is a decided *non possumus*. We cannot recognise in Parliament or the Crown the final arbiter of the spiritual destinies of the Church of England. It is not a question of ritual, important as ritual from its connection with doctrine necessarily is. It is a question of the Headship of Christ over his own Church, and as such one of which the ultimate issue, whatever suffering resistance may entail for the moment, cannot be doubted.' Letter to the *Guardian*, cited in the *Record*, 1 April 1878.

97 Having cited several of the protests adopted by the Ritualists, the *Quarterly Review* concluded, 'Now since every Ecclesiastical Court in the kingdom is 'bound to frame its decisions' in accordance with the judgments of the Judicial Committee of the Privy Council, it follows that the Ritualists have thus repudiated allegiance, in ecclesiastical affairs, to any coercive authority whatever now existing.... It must be evident, after this, that what we have to deal with is nothing less than an organised revolt against all established authority in Church affairs.' Anon., 'Ridsdale Judgment,' *Quarterly Review*, p. 254.

98 The *Quarterly Review* rejected the ritualists' arguments. 'What constitutes a secular judge? Here is an eminent lawyer, appointed to administer ecclesiastical law in two ecclesiastical Courts, and appointed by the two highest ecclesiastical officers. The only secular quality about him is that he is a layman. But in what respect is he more "secular" than all the Deans of the Arches since 1840?' Anon., 'Church Law and Church Prospects,' *Quarterly Review*, p. 274.

99 A report of the discussion in the House of Lords can be found in the *Times*, 15 June 1877.

100 In the Upper House of Convocation, the bishops unanimously voted in favor of a resolution reaffirming the 1873 declaration they had issued con-

demning the renewal of the confessional. *Record*, 4 July 1877.

101 It was greatly to be regretted, the paper suggested, that the issue had to be raised by a layman. 'We have in the Church of England Prelates; their functions are not those of lords over God's heritage; but, as the strict meaning of their designation implies, they are overseers, inspectors of their dioceses; they profess to be acquainted with what their clergy are doing. When evil exists, they have the right of public remonstrance, and, if need be, of appeal to public opinion in cases where the laws might not reach.' Instead, the paper complained, the bishops had attempted to find a moderate position. As a result, no decisive action had been taken to suppress the Ritualists. *Record*, 22 June 1877.

The *Quarterly Review* cited a number of better known, if somewhat less offensive, Ritualist works to suggest that the teaching was widespread and ought to have been repressed: 'We cannot but observe that from these common manuals alone the Bishops might well have been warned of the extent to which this practice was being introduced, and they ought long ago to have been aroused to take more stringent measures to repress it. They have dallied with the danger until their attention has been forcibly called to it.' Anon., 'Ridsdale Judgment,' *Quarterly Review*, pp. 261-62.

102 The English people, wrote the paper, would have none of that system repudiated during the Reformation. 'They will have it at no price; and there is no institution they would not sacrifice, no system they would not repudiate, if it became the home and the protection of such practices. If this Society [the Society of the Holy Cross which was responsible for the publication] cannot be suppressed among the clergy, rough times may be expected for the Church of England. The public take a comparatively languid and contemptuous interest in the disputes raised by the Ritualists on points of ceremonial. But if, as now appears, Ritualism means the inculcation of habitual confession, with all its consequences, Mr. Mackonochie and his friends must go, or the Established Church must go with them.' *Times*, 25 June 1877. The paper published a second, equally strident editorial on 7 July 1877.

The *Quarterly Review* expected a similar result and proclaimed that the priests of the Society of the Holy Cross had 'no rightful place in the Church of England.' And unless it was 'purged of such corruptions, the great edifice of the Establishment will either be shaken to its foundations by public indignation, or be left to fall unsupported amidst public indifference.' Anon., 'Ridsdale Judgment,' *Quarterly Review*, p. 274.

103 The protest was couched in language emphasizing the royal supremacy, no doubt in response to the growing opposition of the Ritualists to the secular courts: 'Your Memorialists, as sincerely attached to the National Church of their Fathers, view with deep alarm the efforts now openly made by a considerable number of the Clergy to introduce in the Church of England the teaching and practice of Auricular Confession, which they regard as contrary to the teaching of the Word of God, alien to the Doctrine, Principles, and Order of the Church, fraught with peril to its existence as an Establishment, and subversive of the principles of Morality, Social Order, and Civil and Religious Liberty. Your Memorialists therefore humbly pray that your

Majesty, unto whom the chief Government of all Estates of the Realm, whether they be Ecclesiastical or Civil, in all causes doth appertain, will be graciously pleased to use all the influence at your Majesty's command to repress the practice of Auricular Confession which is so repugnant to the conscience and feelings of this Protestant Country. And your Majesty's humble Memorialists, as in duty bound, will every pray.' Reprinted in the *Record*, 13 Aug. 1877.

104 In 1880, the *Edinburgh Review* published a lengthy critical article condemning the principle teachings of the Ritualists. It devoted almost ten pages to confession and absolution but proclaimed at the start, concerning *The Priest in Absolution*, 'We shall not pollute our pages with citations from a work which of late has acquired an unenviable notoriety.' The essayist complained that the Ritualists had gained a large degree of toleration, and the 'bishops no longer think of suspending the licenses of curate confessors, as in the case of Mr. Poole, or even of issuing commissions of enquiry, as in the case of Mr. West.' This despite the fact that their doctrine and practice were 'diametrically opposed to the authorised formularies of the English Church, and to the teaching of her great divines; in the eyes of a plain member of the Church of England those who adhere to these practices are schismatics and dissenters.' Anonymous, 'Ritualistic Literature,' *Edinburgh Review* 151 (1880): 304-11.

105 Bishop Magee complained that the bishops were caught between the two extremes, 'In this bitter strife of parties both distrust and hate the bishops, mainly, I do believe, because they honestly endeavour to be just to both in turn.' In Magee's view, it was hopeless 'for any bishop, who will not be a party man, to attempt to moderate or restrain any party.... Church parties are now so embittered, so committed to internecine strife, that they will listen to no voice save that which calls to war.' MacDonnell, *Life of Magee, vol. 2*, p. 57.

CHAPTER 7

The Impact of the Early Imprisonments

The late 1870s and early 1880s saw numerous prosecutions, three of which ended in the imprisonment of Ritualist priests for contempt of court. Despite the protests of the Ritualists and the scandal of an imprisoned priest, the first case, had little negative impact on the anti-Ritualist movement. The popular press took the view that Arthur Tooth had broken the law and deserved his punishment. Still, the results of the case led a few Evangelicals to question the wisdom of further litigation, if only because it had become evident that the courts could not compel the Ritualist clergy to obey. The next two cases, which resulted in the imprisonment of T. P. Dale and R. W. Enraght, had only a slightly more significant effect. In terms of public opinion, the Ritualists gained little. There was some criticism of the severity of the punishment, but the cases did little to advance sympathy for their cause. The bishops, however were concerned to limit the divisive effects of the controversy on the church and prevent further damage to its image at a time when the threat of disestablishment loomed. Some adopted new means of expressing their opposition to the Ritualists, such as refusing to license curates to assist suspect incumbents. A few, without directly expressing their support for the Ritualists, argued for a broader toleration. But almost all opposed further litigation, and the episcopal veto came to be invoked on an almost universal scale.

The CA and its supporters responded to their opponents and a cautious episcopacy by pressing their case for more aggressive prosecution. But moderate Evangelicals were increasingly alienated by the partisan tone and the litigious policy of the conservative section. By the early 1880s, division within the party was evident. Moderates advocated a less controversial position and suggested that the bishops could better resolve the crisis if Evangelicals would give them some positive form of assistance. Following the Dale and Enraght cases, prominent Evangelicals publicly challenged the CA's policies for the first time. The depth of separation between conservatives and moderates, made evident by the divisions over anti-Ritualist methods, once again led to the expression of concerns for the unity of the party. And as a result, moderates formed a new union of the regional clerical and lay associations in an attempt to gather a non-polemical center.

The First Ritualist in Prison: Arthur Tooth

Arthur Tooth, Vicar of St. James's, Hatcham, was the second Ritualist to be prosecuted under the provisions of the Public Worship Regulation Act and the first to be imprisoned for contumacy.[1] The case was heard undefended by Lord Penzance in the Court of Arches in July 1876.[2] Tooth was found guilty of all the charges made against him except for two that were under appeal from a prior case – the eastward position and eucharistic vestments.[3] When he refused to give up the condemned practices, he was suspended from office by Penzance for three months. Having received the official notice of his inhibition, however, Tooth conducted the services the following Sunday. The *Record* suggested, quite correctly in light of later events, that his blatant act of defiance represented a new phase in the controversy. In previous cases, Ritualists such as A. H. Mackonochie had obeyed under protest or at least submitted to the letter of the law while trying to evade its spirit. For a time, Charles Ridsdale had refused to comply with the court's ruling, but he was ultimately persuaded to relent by Archbishop Tait. Tooth, however, insisted on pursuing a course that the *Record* thought could only be construed as 'a willful and intentional act of defiance of the law.' Nor was Tooth alone in his defiance; he was encouraged in it by most of the prominent leaders of 'the Sacerdotal movement' who were present in the congregation to lend their support.[4]

Even during the early stages of the proceedings, long before Tooth or any of the other Ritualists received their sentences, the anti-Ritualists recognized that the imprisonment of a priest would have a negative impact on the popularity of their cause.[5] But Tooth openly courted a judicial response and continued to preside in his parish, undeterred by public protest or criticism.[6] The services at St. James's were frequently disrupted by anti-Ritualist protesters outside.[7] Citing the threat of continued disturbances, Bishop Thorold of Rochester intervened in January 1877, and prohibited further services.[8] Tooth was returned to the court and found guilty of contumacy. In his judgment, Lord Penzance defended the integrity of his court and rejected the argument that the church was not subject to the authority of a secular court. In terms quite similar to those used by anti-Ritualists, Penzance also refuted the notion that the Public Worship Regulation Act had somehow fundamentally altered the ecclesiastical courts.[9]

Penzance's defense of his court was immediately rejected by the ECU.[10] A protest meeting at the Freemasons' Tavern, Great Queen-Street, was chaired by C. L. Wood, President of the ECU, who in no uncertain terms repudiated the authority of the Court of Arches.[11] Those present at the meeting adopted two resolutions – one rejecting the authority of the courts to decide the matter, and the other giving their support to all who adopted a path of resistance.[12] Tooth was arrested on January 22nd, and taken to the Horsemonger-lane Gaol.[13] He was released after less than a month, when he allowed the curate appointed by the bishop to take charge of the parish.[14] Nevertheless, during the time he was in prison and for several months following his release, the parish remained in an uproar.[15] Tooth's conviction was later overturned on a technicality, but the judges of the appeals' court made it clear that their ruling had no bearing on the merits of the earlier judgment.[16]

Following Tooth's imprisonment, the Ritualists were briefly able to challenge the legitimacy of the Court of Arches in 1878. A. H. Mackonochie was once again charged with disobeying the admonitions of the court.[17] Lord Penzance, however, refused to take any action since a number of years had elapsed and the original promoter of the case was no longer involved in it.[18] He agreed, however, to issue another monition if the promoters could produce new affidavits giving evidence of Mackonochie's continued non-compliance.[19] When the case was returned to Lord Penzance, he recounted Mackonochie's long history before the courts. Having noted his own lenience and the opportunity he had given Mackonochie to reconsider his position, Penzance concluded:

> With this experience of the past before me, I can entertain no reasonable hope for the future that Mr. Mackonochie will be induced by any short suspension from his office to relinquish the determination which he has hitherto evinced to act as he thinks right, whether forbidden by law or not. The necessities of the case, therefore, require the Court to take more stringent measures, and I must pronounce Mr. Mackonochie to have disobeyed and contravened the monition of this Court, and decree that he be suspended for a period of three years *ab officio et beneficio*, and that he be condemned in the costs of this application.[20]

The ECU challenged the suspension on Mackonochie's behalf before the Queen's Bench Division of the High Court of Justice.[21] In August, the justices ruled in favor of Mackonochie, by a majority of two to one, and prohibited the Court of Arches from suspending him.[22] The *Record* predicted the Ritualists would be jubilant over the case, but sought to limit the damage by suggesting that the ruling involved only procedural issues, having no effect on matters of substance or the future judgments of the Court of Arches.[23] Lord Penzance immediately challenged the reversal, and his judgment was upheld by a majority of three to two in the Court of Appeal of the Supreme Court of Judicature.[24] When the promoter later requested that the suspension be enforced, Penzance once again defended his court and rejected the Ritualists' claim that they were being persecuted.[25]

The proceedings against Tooth and Mackonochie had a negative effect no doubt in terms of enlarging the controversy and partisan animosities, but they did little to dampen the fervor of anti-Ritualists or to create a backlash of sympathy for their opponents. Nor did the imprisonment of Tooth have any particularly significant consequences. Anti-Ritualists often acknowledged that imprisonment was an unsuitable punishment for clerical contumacy, but the law allowed no alternative, and the negative reaction was minimal. While regretting the embarrassing scene of a priest in prison, the opinions in the general press, for the most part, expressed concern as much with Tooth's flagrant disobedience of the law as with the ensuing result.

Questioning the Future of the Church Association

By the summer of 1877, following the conclusion of the Ridsdale and Tooth prosecutions, it was evident that the Ritualists would not submit to the declarations of the courts, even when urged to do so by their bishops.[26] A few Evangelicals expressed their doubts regarding the wisdom of further litigation. Charles Holland, Rector of Petworth, raised the issue shortly before the CA's annual meeting. Although the CA had been labeled a 'persecuting society' by its opponents, he thought the charge easily refuted. The group had, he wrote, contended for Evangelical principles with neither 'bitterness of tone' nor personal attacks; it only sought to ascertain the legitimate interpretation of the rubrics and to defend the Protestant character of the church. But it appeared that nothing short of coercive measures invoked on a national scale would bring the Ritualists to submit, and such a program, Holland feared, would only damage the reputation of the whole Evangelical party. He then made a distinction that would later be widely adopted – prosecutions undertaken for the purpose of clarifying the law and defining the limits of the rubrics had been a just cause, but 'the vindication of the law in bringing offenders under the penal consequences of a continued breach of its enactments and decisions is surely not the office of the Association.' Enforcement, he concluded, ought to be viewed as belonging to the domain of the ecclesiastical authorities.[27]

It was clear that the topic had become an important and potentially contentious one when T. R. Andrews devoted his opening speech to the subject at the CA's annual meeting. He first responded to the question, 'What is the Church Association to do?' in the negative; there were three things it would not do. First, having obtained judgments clarifying the law, it would not withdraw from the controversy and leave 'long-suffering and aggrieved members of our Church' to protect themselves. Second, it would not become a public prosecutor and seek out all offenders. That responsibility, he admitted, belonged to aggrieved parishioners and their bishops. In that regard, Andrews intimated that the CA might suspend its litigious activities for a time to determine if others would take appropriate action against the Ritualists. Finally, he suggested that the association would not disclose too much to its opponents about its future work, but he refused to rule out the possibility that they would undertake new prosecutions. 'If driven to seek the protection of the courts of law,' said Andrews, 'the Church Association may again have the duty imposed upon them of affording such assistance as in the circumstances of each case may seem needful and expedient.'[28]

The dwindling of support for further litigation was partly a result of the controversy and divisions in the church that ensued, but it was also driven by the general lack of result. For all of the lawsuits undertaken and judgments obtained by the CA, their program had little practical effect in suppressing the Ritualists. In an editorial defending the CA's policy, the *Record* suggested that the problem of lawlessness would be much worse were it not for the restraining influence of the courts. While acknowledging that many 'earnest Christians were repelled and shocked at the idea of making matters of religious ceremonial the subject of hostile litigation,' it thought the enforcement of the law was necessary for the defense of the church. The *Record* would have none of the argument that the prosecutions threatened the peace of the church. Returning to a common theme among anti-Ritualists, it suggested that fundamental principles could not be sacrificed for the sake of peaceful coexistence. The threat of scandalous divisions, concluded the paper, 'must not paralyze our efforts for the defence of the truth; and regarding these ecclesiastical suits as we do, as needful for the preservation of the work of the Reformation, we think that this part of its operations alone entitles the Church Association to the support of all Protestant Churchmen.'[29]

In addition, supporters of the CA thought it had an important role to play in keeping the issue before Parliament. In this regard, the association attempted, albeit with little success, to make its influence felt in the 1878 parliamentary elections. The council issued a policy paper under the heading, 'The Need for Electoral Effort,' which attempted to make anti-Ritualism a prominent campaign issue:

> To preserve our country the blessing of the Reformation is surely, at the present crisis, of all questions the most urgent, and this not merely in regard to the Protestant Church of England – against which the efforts of our adversaries are now more especially directed – but as vitally affecting the welfare of the nation at large. By this time the laity must be fully convinced of the need of the most strenuous exertions to defend their religious liberties against the flood-tide of superstitious error sweeping over the land through the agency of unscrupulous men claiming all the overbearing powers of that very sacerdotal system which our forefathers renounced and cast aside. Efforts have indeed been made in Parliament and in the Law Courts with undoubted success up to a certain point, but it is plain that a still more momentous conflict yet lies before us – imminent, and inevitable. The Council of the Church Association are convinced that the struggle will soon be transferred to the field of legislation; indeed the initiative has been already taken by the sacerdotalists, who – in preparation for a Parliamentary campaign – have repeatedly attempted to exact pledges from members or candidates whom they had any hopes of influencing. The Council therefore, while disclaiming any intention to become a centre of political organization, deem it advisable to declare their conviction that, in self-defence, the constituencies are bound to use every Constitutional effort to secure the return to the next Parliament of candidates as shall – as a primary qualification and irrespective of party politics – be found to be true and staunch Protestants, and who will distinctly pledge themselves to do their utmost to stem the torrent of sacerdotal pretension within the Church of England, as well as to secure full obedience to the law on the part of the rebellious clergy.[30]

The CA returned to the subject during the 1880 election as well, arguing that the electorate should vote on the basis of how the candidates responded to the Ritualist threat.[31]

Still, divisions were evident among Evangelicals, and several attempts were made to organize an alternate society that might elicit broader support. Even conservatives admitted that the CA was unable to unite the anti-Ritualist movement. While still supporting the work of the CA, G. T. Fox suggested that it could not be compared to the ECU as an organizational body. In contrast to the Ritualists, who were united in their cause and worked together to accomplish their goals, Fox thought Evangelicals lacked any real sense of solidarity. To that end, he believed the party needed an organization that could formulate a cohesive Evangelical position on the important issues of the day. In his opinion, Evangelicals should 'stand entirely aloof' from the Ritualists, avoiding any cooperation in missions, never attending church congresses, and uniting only with those of a common interest.[32] Fox did not intend for the new organization to supplant the CA, of which he remained a strong supporter. But he hoped that a new society, free from the negative reputation connected with the CA's appeal to the courts, might be more successful in unifying the entire party. The Evangelical Protestant Union, however, found little success. Two years later, J. B. Waddington, Vicar of Low Moor, Lancashire, was still attempting to attract new members. The union, he wrote, was for 'thoroughly decided men only,' who would not compromise with 'the fashion of the world,' but were willing 'to make a decided stand' in defending the principles of the Reformation.[33]

Moderates, however, were not attracted to the new union's reactionary program and countered that a policy of separation would only diminish Evangelical influence in the church. Robert Kennion, Rector of Acle, suggested that Evangelicals could do much good in combined meetings, whereas their absence would give the whole over to their opponents. He continued, 'Again, in Missions and Church Congresses, what is the abstention policy but an abandonment of influence, and therefore of duty – a tacit confession that it is not we who are the true Church of England, but our enemies – a pulling up of the wheat, while we leave the tares undisputed possessors of the soil?'[34] The position adopted by the union was too extreme even for some conservatives. Francis Close could find no distinctive purpose for supporting yet another society and thought its leaders appeared to require agreement on matters that were 'eminently trivial.'[35] The organization continued to hold annual meetings for several years but never attracted much support, and other than the fact that it sponsored no litigation, its aims and supporters appear to have been identical to those of the CA.[36]

The Imprisonment of Dale and Enraght

The Tooth case created a minor scandal and a general sense of concern among the bishops regarding any further prosecutions that might end in imprisonment, but at least some of them were willing to allow proceedings under certain circumstances. In November

1876, Thomas Pelham Dale, Rector of St. Vedast, Foster-lane, Cheapside, was brought before the Court of Arches for a second time. He was charged with refusing to comply with an earlier monition regarding numerous innovations, and was suspended for three months.[37] Two years later Dale was charged with continuing in the use of thirteen illegal observances, and in February 1880, he was found guilty on eleven counts.[38] Lord Penzance concluded his judgment with a lecture to the absent Dale concerning the absurdity of his behavior as he attempted to avoid being served any of the court's notices.[39] In March 1880, affidavits were filed to show that Dale had continued in all of the practices condemned, and Penzance inhibited him.[40] The following Sunday, the Rev. C. T. Acland, who had been licensed by Bishop Jackson to serve the parish during the suspension, presented himself at St. Vedast, accompanied by Mr. Lee, the bishop's secretary, but Dale refused to yield.[41]

When Dale was charged with contempt, Penzance again sought to distance his court from any accusation of partisanship and claimed no knowledge as to whether or not prosecution was the best means of dealing with clergy who continued to use ceremonies and decorations that had been declared illegal. Having recited the facts of the case, he announced that he had no choice but to find the defendant guilty and to sentence him to prison.[42] At the same time, the case of R. W. Enraght also came before his court. Lord Penzance noted that there were 'associations and societies' behind both cases, exercising a certain degree of influence with the individuals involved. He could not view them, therefore, as isolated cases and postponed judgment in the second case 'in order to see what course Mr. Enraght might feel disposed to pursue.'[43] Meanwhile, Dale was arrested on October 30th, and taken to the City Prison at Holloway.[44]

Charges were first brought against R. W. Enraght, Vicar of Holy Trinity Church, Bordesley, in 1878.[45] The unique element involved in the charges against Enraght involved the use of wafer bread, a charge that had been dismissed in several prior prosecutions for lack of evidence. In this case, however, the prosecution produced one of the wafers, which led to charges of sacrilege from Ritualists and created a degree of embarrassment for the anti-Ritualist movement.[46] On the first Sunday after receiving the monition to discontinue the illegal practices, Enraght continued to lead the services at Holy Trinity with no change in the ceremony.[47] In February 1880, Enraght was found guilty of contumacy and suspended until he agreed to comply with the judgment.[48] When it became clear that Enraght would not relent despite the result in the Dale case, he was also found guilty of contumacy and a warrant was issued for his arrest.[49] Enraght was arrested on the 27th of November in Birmingham.

An appeal was made by the ECU on behalf of both Dale and Enraght, on the grounds that the inhibition issued under the Public Worship Regulation Act had been improperly executed, but the judgment of the Court of Arches was upheld.[50] Both men were offered a Christmas parole, on the stipulation that they would not contravene the original inhibition during their leave. As it turned out, Dale would not return to prison. Enraght, however, refused to accept the limitations imposed by the offer and remained in prison for the holidays.[51] Shortly thereafter, a new appeal was filed by the ECU, and the Court of Appeal reversed the decision of the Queen's Bench Division. An editorial in the *Times* indicated that their imprisonment had done little to gain any sympathy for the Ritualists in the general population. The paper was no supporter of the CA, but it had even less regard for clergy who displayed their contempt for the law of the land.[52] Dale retired from his parish soon thereafter, but Enraght, after his release, returned to Holy Trinity and resumed his ministry with the same manner of ritual. A CA report, issued at its annual spring meeting, noted that Mr. Perkins, the churchwarden, had made a 'just and reasonable appeal' to Bishop Philpott, but the bishop had vetoed any further proceedings.[53]

Episcopal Influence and Opinion

The imprisonments of Dale and Enraght did only slightly more damage to the anti-Ritualist cause than had been the case with the Tooth judgment.[54] Many who voiced their displeasure had little sympathy for the Ritualists themselves; they only regretted that a sentence of deprivation was not an alternative under the Public Worship Regulation Act.[55] The *Times* continued to take a dim view of the innovations, and while it doubted that they were actually significant enough to warrant prosecution (suggesting that broader exposure only gave the Ritualists an opportunity to gain popular support), its greatest regret was that cases involving ecclesiastical discipline should end with the imprisonment of clergy. It was, thought the paper, 'a very roundabout way of arriving at a simple result,' when the goal of prosecution ought to be 'the restoration of simplicity of worship.' The editorial called for the reform of the ecclesiastical courts and a more straightforward means of dealing with the Ritualists: 'If the transgressors do not submit immediately to the doctrine as expounded by the proper tribunal, suspension, to allow time for tempers and vanities to abate, followed by deprivation of obstinate recusants, is the manifest and reasonable process.'[56]

More significant, for the anti-Ritualist movement, was the impact the cases had on episcopal opinion. The bishops could take slight satisfaction in the spectacle of clergy being committed to prison.[57] In spite of the fact that most of them still strongly opposed extreme innovations that often disturbed the laity and disrupted the peace of the church, it was clear, by the end of the 1870s, that the bishops were opposed to further litigation. As the emphasis of the CA's appeals to the courts turned from the clarification of the law to its enforcement, and particularly as those cases began to conclude with the imprisonment of Ritualists, the organization's efforts were defeated by the episcopal veto.[58] But while the bishops were driven to oppose further litigation, many continued to express the view that Dale and Enraght had only themselves to blame for their incarceration; it was the natural result of their determined defiance.[59]

That perspective was evident in Bishop Jackson's response to resolutions that were drawn up, according to Henry A. Browne, at a crowded parish meeting during Dale's imprisonment. The bishop suggested that Dale had only himself to blame for the outcome of his case. In the course of the letter, he also expressed his doubts regarding the popularity of the Ritualist movement. He questioned who the parishioners were that supported Dale since the numbers present at communion had steadily declined during the course of his ministry. Further, he noted that most of the communicants, excluding Dale's own family, were non-parishioners, and that many of those who signed the memorial were actually from other parishes with pastors of their own whom 'they had deserted.' Jackson continued, with a degree of sarcasm, 'All this put together appears to furnish slender material for a "crowded meeting".'[60] While acknowledging his great regret that any clergy should be imprisoned, Jackson concluded with a stinging rebuke of the Ritualists and the defiant attitude they adopted:

> An incumbent, at his institution to a benefice, has solemnly committed to him the cure of the souls of the parishioners of the parish. For them he is responsible to God and the Church; and here his direct responsibility stops. It is now some years since the parishioners of St. Vedast complained that they were driven away from their parish church by the introduction of ritual to which they were unaccustomed, and which they believed to be illegal, and their belief has been sustained since by the decision of one of the strongest Courts, both in number and character, which has ever sat. We honour the clergyman who, finding his own parishioners too few to exhaust or employ all his time and energy, endeavours to extend his usefulness to others who are not directly under his charge; but it must be rather a cause of regret when an incumbent who has dispersed his own flock, for whom he is responsible to

God, endeavours to supply their place with others towards whom he has no such solemn obligations.

While ready, therefore, to acknowledge your letter and its enclosure, I cannot admit them as coming from parishioners of St. Vedast, or from those (excepting, I believe, the chairman of the meeting) who have any proper right to call Mr. Dale '*their* Rector.' I reply, however, that I disapprove and greatly deplore the imprisonment of Mr. Dale on public as well as on personal grounds, for his sake as well as that of the Church.[61]

But after the imprisonment of Dale and Enraght, most of the cases involving matters of decoration and ceremony were vetoed.

At least some of the bishops had come to the conclusion that further proceedings would be senseless as the prosecutions had failed to obtain the desired effect. While regretting the appearance of lawlessness, Bishop Jackson of London, acknowledged in his 1879 charge that the Public Worship Regulation Act had been a failure. Given the nature of the Ritualist challenge, he doubted that the appeal to the courts could ever be truly effective. In his view, the best means of opposing the Ritualists was through moral persuasion and pastoral work.[62] Still, he had little sympathy for the Ritualist cause and refused to intervene when parishioners of St. Alban's, Holborn, requested that he prevent further proceedings against A. H. Mackonochie.[63] In addition to the argument from practical results, many of the bishops viewed the CA's activities as a case of partisan interference in their respective dioceses. The organization was often accused of provoking prosecutions where the participants might have otherwise been willing to consider episcopal arbitration or other more peaceful means of settling the dispute.[64] They were especially disinclined to allow proceedings when the innovations in question were relatively moderate, a majority of the congregation was satisfied with the services, or the clergy exhibited a willingness to heed their admonitions.[65]

In February 1878, the Bishop of Rochester rejected a presentation made against Rev. G. W. Berkeley of All Hallows, Southwark. The case was significant because the bishop was A. W. Thorold, himself an Evangelical. Thorold was particularly inclined to defend Berkeley, as he had declared himself open to the bishop's admonitions regarding those practices that were deemed illegal, particularly mixing water with the wine and making the sign of the cross.[66] Further, Thorold considered several of the innovations, such as Berkeley's wearing of a stole, insignificant.[67] Finally, and perhaps most importantly, Thorold expressed his impatience with the continuing appeals of the protesters and noted that clergy who conducted the services within the broad limits allowed by the church's formularies had every right to expect the support and protection of their bishop.[68]

In other instances, the bishops exhibited a more overt willingness to stretch the limits of toleration, either from sympathy with the Ritualist cause or simply out of concern to avoid the further development of partisan strife in their dioceses. In 1879, Bishop Mackarness of Oxford vetoed proceedings against T. T. Carter of Clewer, on the grounds that litigation had failed to produce the desired results and that Carter was an elderly incumbent who was widely respected and loved in his parish.[69] The CA appealed to the Queen's Bench Division of the High Court of Justice which issued a writ requiring Mackarness to allow the case to proceed.[70] That decision, however, was overturned by the Court of Appeal of the Supreme Court of Judicature. The judges there ruled that a bishop, in fact, had a broad discretionary power that could not to be limited by a secular court.[71]

At the height of the Dale and Enraght cases, Piers Claughton, Archdeacon of London and the former colonial Bishop of Colombo, attacked the policy of the CA in a letter to the *Times*. While condemning the apparent lawlessness of the Ritualists and their disregard for episcopal admonitions, Claughton repudiated the methods of the CA and its use of prosecution.[72] In a second letter, Claughton, suggested that the CA's policies had only created popular sympathy for the Ritualists.[73] Their object, he thought, was 'to multiply prosecutions' in order to compel 'the Bishops to take legal action against their clergy if so much as suspected of ritualistic practices.' In his view, the CA had no right to enforce the law and ought to leave the supervision of the church to the bishops whose work was only hindered by heightened partisan tensions. Claughton concluded, 'I would say to them, "Leave the task of driving away error to those on whom the responsibility is laid," whose action at present they are hindering, yet who share, most undeservedly, the odium which their conduct has incurred.'[74]

Claughton's second letter elicited a response from W. C. Palmer, Secretary of the Council of the CA. Palmer summarized the history of the CA's involvement in the controversy and defended its motives:

> Bishop Claughton's description of the objects, principles, and action of the Church Association is so different from the views entertained by the Council that they think it right to ask you to insert this letter, in order to disabuse the mind of the Episcopal Bench and to prevent the public from being misled by erroneous statements regarding their action.

Bishop Claughton admits that the errors from which the Church Association desires to free the Church 'have a real existence,' to which he says 'he has not been blind,' but that in his opinion they 'required great discrimination and patience to treat with success,' and that 'the intervention of the Church Association destroyed all hope of forbearance and caution being exercised.' To this the Council would reply that so long ago as the year 1851 the two Archbishops and 22 Bishops issued an address in which they said: –

'We long indulged the hope that under the influence of charity, forbearance, and a calm estimate of the small importance of such external forms, compared with the blessing of united action in the great spiritual work which is before our Church, these heats and jealousies might by mutual concessions be allayed. But since the evil still exists, and in one most important feature has assumed a new and more dangerous character, we feel that it is our duty to try whether an earnest and a united address on our part may tend, under the blessing of God, to promote the restoration of peace and harmony in the Church.'

The Episcopal remedy of a 'united address' had but little effect in grappling with the evil, and surely the number of years that passed between 1851 and 1865 (when the Church Association was formed), during which the laity acted in accordance with Bishop Claughton's advice, 'to leave the task of driving away error to those on whom the responsibility was laid,' will show there was no lack of patience or forbearance on their part.

The Bishops have frequently asserted their powerlessness to deal effectively with the evil; and, to give one instance, the Bishop of London, in his charges of 1875 and 1879, thus wrote: –

'The Bishops' authority in their Courts, no less than in their character as Ordinaries, has proved practically inefficient to check or regulate the illegal or obnoxious alterations in ritual of which complaints have been made to them. The cost, too, of such proceedings is great, ruinous to Bishops if they undertake them, and prohibitory for the most part to churchwardens or individual complainants, and the formation of a society [the ECU] many years back which advised and assisted clergymen to resist their Bishops or defend themselves against charges relating to ritual naturally caused the establishment of another to enable parishioners to seek the relief which the law professes to afford.'

In corroboration of this view of the all but insuperable difficulties which obstructed the path of our ecclesiastical rulers in the matter of legal redress against the party of innovation we have the equally recent and candid admission of the Bishop of Peterborough. His Lordship says, 'Before now' – that is, previous to the introduction of the Public Worship Regulation Act – 'a clergyman could do as he thought proper, and there was no power to compel his obedience. The result was that the Church was fast passing away from the paralyzed hands of her legitimate rulers.'

The Church Association have, after a considerable expenditure of time and money, obtained a definition of the law on most controverted points (60 in number), including those which in the aggregate tend to form the whole ceremony of the Romish Mass, which is now legally declared to have no standing in the Church of England, and for doing this Bishop Claughton writes, 'I utterly repudiate the action of the Church Association in resorting to prosecution at law,' thereby censuring us for giving most valuable aid to the Episcopal Bench at a cost of upwards of £30,000.

Bishop Claughton asserts that the object of the Church Association was to 'multiply prosecutions,' but that is far from the fact. In every case of complaint from aggrieved parishioners the Council have advised first a resort to the offending clergyman, then an appeal to the Bishops, and only after failure of obtaining redress from the Bishops have they advised a resort to legal proceedings, and every case that has been brought before the Court has received the sanction of the Bishop, who had power to refuse it if he thought fit.

In regard to Bishop Claughton's assertion that the object of the Church Association 'is to stimulate the Bishops to take legal action against their clergy if so much as suspected of ritualistic practices,' the council challenge his Lordship to produce a single instance in which any action whatever has been taken by them except where the illegal acts complained of had been repeatedly and defiantly committed.

The Council of the Church Association entirely agree with Bishop Claughton that the duty and responsibility of opposing what the Archbishop of Canterbury has termed 'a conspiracy in our body against the doctrine, the discipline, and the practice of our Reformed Church' rests with the Bishops, and they will be delighted to be relieved from the disagreeable task so soon as a general determination on the part of their Lordships to require and insure obedience to the law has been manifested.

They rejoice to find that there is good reason to hope that their Lordships are aware of the importance and urgency of the crisis, and Bishop Claughton has a good opportunity of showing that he, at least, is in earnest, for there are more extreme ritualistic churches in his archeaconry than in any other in the kingdom, and the Council have yet to learn that any effectual steps have been taken by him to check the spread of ritualism, which a leading organ of the Roman Catholic Church has lately stated to be 'indirectly the most powerful propaganda of the Church of Rome which England has yet seen.'

The Council of the Church Association are not aware of any 'dead-lock,' and are under no uncertainty as to their future course of action.

In the face of the efforts the Council have already made and are making for securing an alteration in the law, it is needless to reaffirm that they deeply deplore the necessity for resorting to imprisonment.[75]

While the CA regretted that the law required imprisonment in cases involving contempt of court, the society was committed to the suppression of Ritualism and the legal system offered them their only hope for success. Under the circumstances, they rightly viewed the episcopal veto as a threat to their program. In their opinion, the bishops were allowing the Ritualists to defy the law without consequence and preventing disturbed parishioners from their right of appeal to the courts. In the years to come, the use of the episcopal veto would lead the CA to shift its criticism and focus to the bishops themselves.[76]

Interestingly, the *Quarterly Review*, which had long since expressed the view that prosecution was not the best means of dealing with the Ritualists, defended the CA and the appeal to the courts the following year. The journal refused to judge either of the societies that financed the legal investigation of the church's rubrics, which, given the unreformed state of the courts, cost thousands of pounds.[77] The writer also questioned the legitimacy of the claims that the Ritualists were being persecuted; the cases were not really personal attacks on individuals, but concerned all clergy on both sides of the debate. A wit had referred to the prosecutors as a 'Joint Stock Persecution Society,' but the defendants were not without their own equally determined association. The review concluded that an alternative course was not readily apparent; how else was 'the Church of England to be defended against a kind of Trades' Union for keeping hold of the pulpits and wages of the English Church while doing the work of the Roman one, against which certain bulwarks were erected at the Reformation which the Ritualist boldly avow that they hate and mean to destroy if they can?'[78]

If most of the bishops were unwilling to allow further litigation, they were still concerned to bring a sense of order to their dioceses and sought to impose limits on the Ritualists.[79] Bishop Thorold announced a new method for dealing with Ritualists in a pastoral letter in 1878. Although he preferred to avoid the bitterness engendered by an appeal to the courts, he affirmed that he would not shirk his responsibilities if that course became necessary.[80] In cases where no formal complaint had been made, however, he advocated a policy of isolation:

> 'A house divided against itself cannot stand.' A Church with a foreign body inside it, such as the Ritual polity declares itself to be, must very soon either absorb, modify, or expel it. It comes to this, that what in the army would be mutiny and in the State outlawry in the Church is schism.... My individual method of personally and officially dealing with those of the clergy who feel conscientiously unable either to obey the courts of the realm or to accept the private monition of the Bishop, is that of isolation. These brethren of ours are outside the law, and it is their own act that has placed them there. Where I find them, I leave them; and what they have made themselves, that I must recognise them to be. Consequently I am compelled to decline either to confirm, or preach, or perform any official act in churches adopting an illegal Ritual, on the simple ground that, as one of the Church's rulers, I cannot even appear to condone by my presence and ministration a distinct violation of the Church's order.[81]

Evangelical reactions to Thorold's temperate but firm statement of policy were divided and served to illustrate the growing separation between moderates and conservatives in the party. W. W. Phelps, a fervent supporter of the CA, criticized Thorold for his weakness and suggested that the Ritualists would surely 'laugh at the shaking of such a spear as this.' The episcopacy, he believed, had the power to put down the innovators if they so desired, but it was evident that they were willing to sacrifice the truth of the gospel for the sake of peace in the church. According to Phelps, the Ritualists ought not to be ignored but expelled.[82] The *Record*, however, was loathe to criticize one of its own bishops and took a more positive tone. Thorold had, said the paper, taken a firm stance 'towards the Ritualistic party and their extravagances which leaves nothing to be desired. While the Bishop refuses to narrow the comprehension enacted by the law, he equally refuses to extend it.... This course is wise, faithful, and consistent.'[83] The paper only regretted that the rest of the episcopacy had not taken a similarly decisive stance.[84]

The Five Deans' Memorial

The imprisonments soon led to a reconsideration of the issue of how broad the church ought to be and what degree of toleration could be allowed for deviations in the worship service. Shortly before the release of Dale and Enraght, Archbishop Tait addressed the rural deanery of Westbere, Kent, and challenged the Ritualists to state precisely what changes they desired in the constitution of the ecclesiastical courts.[85] The response came in the 'Five Deans' Memorial,' which advocated the toleration of 'divergent ritual practice and an end to all ecclesiastical prosecutions involving matters of worship.[86] The memorialists' demands, however, were immediately challenged by anti-Ritualists.[87] Evangelicals, both moderate and conservative, drew up a counter-memorial protesting the notion of a broad toleration for Ritualists' innovations.[88] A lay memorial to the archbishop expressing similar concerns gathered 24,000 signatures by the end of May 1881.[89]

Nor were Evangelicals alone in their objections. Archbishop Tait, in a letter to Dean Church, indicated that he had little sympathy for Ritualists; however much they felt compelled to protest against the courts, they had no right to refuse their obedience to episcopal admonitions.[90] The *Times* was also sharply critical of the document. The paper acknowledged that theirs was an era of broad toleration and that absolute uniformity of ritual was neither expected nor desired. Clergy were given a great deal of freedom with regard to the specifics of the worship service and often introduced changes when they arrived at a new parish. But, concluded the paper, there was a vast difference between toleration for minor innovations and allowing new ceremonies to be introduced that implied doctrines unacceptable to a majority of the laity.[91] Relying on an argument often used by anti-Ritualists, the paper suggested that the 'sins of commission' involved in the conscious alteration of the service could not be equated with minor acts of 'omission.' The general public was 'not impaired by the common neglect of unimportant rubrics which have long fallen into abeyance' in the same way that it was scandalized by 'the revival of practices long discarded and beyond all question repugnant to the general feeling of Churchmen.' The Ritualists were, in fact, being singled out, because they were 'the chief disturbers of the recognized and long-established order of public worship.'[92]

The reaction to the memorial, particularly the *Times*' own editorial, elicited a letter from E. B. Pusey in defense of the Ritualists. In his letter, Pusey touched upon a number of the central topics of the dispute and concluded with an apologetic statement on the popularity of the movement.[93] Pusey then defended the doctrine symbolized by the ritual and claimed it was the same ritual that had been 'introduced by Cranmer under Edward VI and the Bishops at the restoration of Charles II.' It represented, said Pusey, the true doctrine of the church, 'sanctioned in the case of "Sheppard v. Bennett," both in the Court of Arches and by the Privy Council, in an undefended suit.' That case, he claimed, had involved nothing more than Bennett's endorsement of his own teaching, but when he dared the CA to prosecute him, they declined. Finally, he suggested that the Ritualists only wanted that degree of toleration that was granted to the other parties in the church. 'The Ritualists,' he concluded, 'do not ask to interfere with the devotions of others – only to be allowed, in their worship of God, to use a Ritual which a few years ago no one disputed, and that only when their congregations wish it.'[94]

Pusey's letter drew a storm of protest in the correspondence pages of the *Times* that continued for several weeks. Although the paper published only a few responses in his defense, almost every issue through the end of January contained one or more letters responding to his various arguments. The central point of debate was the popularity of the Ritualists, which was challenged on several levels. The *Times* itself had pointed out on several occasions that there was an important difference between attracting a congregation and having a church full of parishioners, and J. Llewelyn Davies suggested that it was legitimate to inquire who 'the people' were to whom Pusey referred. Still more questionable, he thought, was Pusey's specific claim with regard to the popularity of St. Alban's. 'If this claim could be substantiated,' a fact he obviously doubted, 'it would be a stronger argument in favour of Ritualism than any which can be drawn from the Ornaments Rubric.'[95]

Taking an entirely different approach, J. J. S. Perowne, a moderate Evangelical who later became the Bishop of Worcester, allowed, for the sake of argument, all of Pusey's claims concerning the popularity of Ritualism and the leading role the laity played in many parishes (although he questioned who it was, if not the priest, that first instilled "Catholic principles" in their minds). But having admitted all that, Perowne asked whether it was wise for the clergy to follow blindly after the desires of the people. He drew a parallel to the Israelites making idols during their sojourn in the desert, when the priests gave in to all of their demands rather than exercising a role of leadership. Perowne concluded that it was somewhat ironic to find Pusey, of all people, advocating 'a naked congregationalism' in which the desires of the laity determined the priest's direction; 'it is certainly a strange surrender of his solemn responsibility as a religious teacher and a disgraceful admission that popular clamour, not principle or truth, is to govern the worship of the Church.'[96]

Several correspondents also challenged Pusey's claim that the Ritualist view of the Eucharist had been sanctioned by the courts. Charles Bell, Rector of Cheltenham and Honorary Canon of Carlisle, argued that nothing had been so conceded in the Bennett judgment.[97] With regard to doctrine, Llewelyn Davies reiterated a point that was often made by anti-Ritualists of all sections. He noted that the church traditionally allowed the clergy a great breadth of discretion in the expression of their positions but that such toleration could not be legitimately expanded to include ritual innovations. It was commonly understood, said Davies, that the sermon represented the thoughts of the preacher and did not, as such, require the affirmation of the congregation. But, while they were free to proclaim from the pulpit his own particular doctrines, the clergy did not have the right to alter the ritual at will; it was the possession of the whole church. If the priest introduced ceremonial innovations simply to suit his doctrine, he 'trespassed' on the rights of the congregation and overstepped the legitimate boundaries of his discretion.[98]

Finally, the correspondence degenerated into a war of words over the facts regarding the prosecutions. W. C. Palmer suggested that Pusey had conveniently altered the facts to suit his purposes. With regard to Charles Lowder and the parish of St. Peter's, London Docks, Palmer claimed that the CA had never engaged any agents there. The association had been approached by three aggrieved parishioners who desired to bring charges against Lowder. Bishop Jackson of London attempted to mediate the dispute, but Lowder was unwilling to make any concessions. When a representation was then made to Archbishop Tait, he vetoed the proceedings. Finally, Palmer suggested that Pusey was well aware of the reasons for which his writings had not been 'submitted to a judicial consideration.'[99] Neither Pusey nor any prominent Ritualists responded to his many critics (assuming, of course, that the *Times* did not simply suppress their replies). When he did write again, it was only to respond to the last sentence of Palmer's letter, claiming that he had no idea what Palmer meant.[100]

In his response, Palmer implied that Pusey was being less than honest in his reply and suggested the correspondence should be ended if it could not 'be conducted with Christian courtesy and candour.' He went on to note that Pusey had acknowledged in a letter to H. P. Liddon, in December 1878, that he could not easily be prosecuted since his canonry was attached to his Oxford professorship and thereby endowed with a degree of immunity.[101] Ultimately, the only result of the debate was to offer further evidence of the level of animosity between the two sides.

The Growing Division among Evangelicals over Litigation

The reaction to the Five Deans' Memorial and Pusey's correspondence can be seen as an indication of the abiding depth of anti-Ritualist sentiment in the Evangelical party, among conservatives and moderates alike. But by the beginning of the 1880s, support for further prosecution was beginning to wane. Francis Close, whose conservatism was beyond question, suggested even prior to the imprisonments of Dale and Enraght, that further litigation was pointless – the Ritualists had demonstrated that they could evidently defy them with impunity. Close, for his part, thought it was time for the Evangelical party to pursue other means:

> My persuasion is that preaching more faithfully, pointedly, lovingly, and by using all and every means in our power, with unions for prayer, now so numerous in the land – in a word, by measures purely spiritual and intellectual – we shall win the hearts of men to God's truth. May we not be acting too much on secular lines? Do we forget where our great strength lies? It is pretty certain that as yet we have been little if at all successful in impeding the progress of Ritualism and infidelity. Controversy is a painful necessity, legal proceedings are still more vexatious to a Christian mind. Such may and probably must under some circumstances be used; but the true armoury of God, the faithful weapons of our warfare, are the Word of God and prayer! The best way to put down error is to preach Christ in all his fullness and sufficiency, and then men will not heed the sinister offers of the priest's absolution, or the 'Real Presence' in the Holy Communion.[102]

Close gave voice to the growing doubts among Evangelicals concerning both the effectiveness of litigation and its negative consequences.

By 1880, conservatives and moderates were divided over fundamental principles with regard to the conduct of the controversy. The conservative section of the party was disturbed by the growing influence of the Ritualists, even among Evangelical congregations. Equally troublesome for them, was the apparent decline of interest among moderates in the pursuit of an aggressive anti-Ritualist policy.[103] Moderates were, in general, more willing to consider compromise and less defensive about the state of the party and the church. Influenced by their willingness to make concessions to the spirit of the age, and perhaps by their personal interaction with their High Church counterparts at church congresses and diocesan synods (much as the conservative element had fearfully predicted), moderates were increasingly opposed to prosecution and concerned to frame the debate in less controversial terms.

As the imprisonments began to take their toll in the court of public opinion and the depth of the division within the Evangelical party was made more evident, even the *Record* began to question the wisdom of further prosecutions. The paper affirmed that the CA had done invaluable work on two fronts. First, it had undertaken expensive litigation in order to clarify the actual intent of somewhat ambiguous articles and rubrics. Second, its work had resulted in the repression or prevention of Ritualism in a great many parishes where 'the pressure of actual or apprehended proceedings' had restrained the clergy. Nevertheless, the paper concluded that litigation had failed to accomplish its most basic goal – the suppression of Ritualism. It thought the participants at the CA's autumn conference were obligated to consider a harsh fact: 'While the Association has been conspicuously successful in ascertaining the law, it has failed in enforcing it.'[104] The paper concluded that the fundamental problem was the need for legal reform and suggested that the CA should focus in the future on legislation rather than litigation.[105] Still, the *Record* held a hard line in opposition to the Ritualists. After the meeting, it reiterated its support for the CA. While expressing its regret that the law mandated imprisonment for a priest found guilty of contumacy, the paper rejected the notion that the Ritualists should therefore be allowed to go unpunished. If the only alternative to imprisonment was 'the triumph of wrong-doing,' the paper was willing to support the former. But it was evident that anti-Ritualists were increasingly concerned about the effect of the imprisonments on public opinion.[106]

For its part, the CA showed no inclination to moderate its policy. At its annual meeting in May 1880, during the midst of the proceedings against Dale and Enraght, the council made public its proposals for the future work of the association. It was clear from its policy statement that the leaders of the organization were determined to pursue an aggressive policy.[107] During the discussion afterward, it was evident that the voices calling for moderation were in a distinct minority at the meeting.[108] The moderates who remained in the CA had, from this period, to do without one of their strongest voices. Shortly before the meeting, J. C. Ryle was elevated to the bishopric of the newly created diocese of Liverpool, and he withdrew from the association.[109] The loss of his influence, at once anti-Ritualist yet inclined toward a moderate disposition, was one more factor in the growing separation of the extreme section associated with the CA. Increasingly, the control of the society lay in the hands of determined anti-Ritualists who, emphasizing above all else the controversial and defensive role of the party, were unable to gain the support of moderates.

At the 1880 meeting, the council of the CA also proposed a new fund to finance future prosecutions. T. R. Andrews affirmed that they were determined 'to shrink from no proceedings or consequence that may be forced upon the Association for the attainment of the ends which it has for so many years steadfastly set itself to accomplish.' They were resolute, he said, in their determination 'to continue the existing suits and to enforce the judgments by all means that the law permits.' They were also determined to seek the revocation of the episcopal veto, and many of the speakers sharply criticized the bishops for not taking a stronger position in opposition to the Ritualists.[110] Only one speaker at the conference opposed further litigation. Rev. Alfred Kennion, Vicar of Gerrard's Cross, was disturbed by the bitterness of the attacks upon the episcopacy and suggested that the bishops were in a most difficult position. Furthermore, he thought any continuation of the divisive appeal to the courts 'could only have the effect of alienating a large portion of the young Evangelical life of the country from them.'[111]

If Kennion was the only critic present at the meeting, the report of the proceedings called forth others. One of the most important was Samuel Garratt, Vicar of St. Margaret's, Ipswich, a prominent Evangelical whose commitment to the anti-Ritualist cause was beyond question. Garrett's letter to the *Record* represented the first significant public repudiation of the CA's policy from within the movement. He suggested that the policy had been doomed to failure from the very beginning and condemned it on both spiritual and practical grounds. The anti-Ritualists had resorted, wrote Garrett, to 'carnal weapons' in matters of spiritual import, and they could not expect God to bless their cause. Furthermore, their opponents were bound to view the campaign as an unholy persecution and to refuse to their compliance.[112] What would be the next step, asked Garrett? Would they next resort to the extremes of the inquisition?[113] In conclusion, he lamented the misguided severity of the CA's program and suggested that it would ultimately be self-defeating:

> There are numbers of Evangelical clergymen and laymen who have no sympathy whatever with the Church Association policy, and no means whatever of making their objections known. Its existence cripples the force of their opposition to sacerdotalism. They cannot reason with a man while their friends are knocking him down. The sword of the Spirit and the sword of human law will not well act side by side. I wish I could persuade my brethren to believe more in the power of truth and the mighty influence of the Holy Ghost, to cast away their dependence on human courts, laws, and judges, and to trust, in contending for the faith, only in the living God. Then I doubt not we should prevail, though, perhaps, ours then might be the prison and the death which in former ages

has been the frequent and honourable reward of faithful resistance to sacerdotal error.[114]

In the weeks that followed, the *Record* published numerous responses to Garratt's letter, the majority of which supported the CA's policies, although a few sided with Garratt.[115]

In 1881, Garratt elaborated on his argument in a pamphlet *entitled What Shall We Do? Or, True Evangelical Policy*. He argued there that the appeal to the courts had been an unmitigated disaster for the Evangelical party. Litigation had done nothing to settle the controversy and much to damage the reputation of the Evangelical party.[116] The many favorable decisions had been 'approved by the daily press, and by those who have above all things any troublesome conscientious convictions,' but they had also 'alienated the minds of numbers whom we would gladly see in our ranks, but whom this unfortunate policy has driven from us.' Furthermore, said Garratt, it was 'a policy which can claim no example in apostolic days.'[117] He concluded, 'Let us make up our minds, once for all, that compulsion there cannot be, that compromise there cannot be, that uniformity there cannot be, that the battle must be fought, and fought out; but that the weapons must be spiritual, not carnal – sound doctrine, fair reasoning, the comparison of fruits, the appeal to Scripture....' Ultimately, he said, Evangelicals must have faith in God that the truth would win out.[118]

Still, the CA maintained a hard line. At the association's next annual conference, T. R. Andrews reiterated the organization's commitment to its program and rejected the idea of an ecclesiastical courts' commission (the appointment of which was being considered by the government). Andrews concluded, 'We are still prosecuting, and we intend to prosecute. (Loud cheers.)... But as long as the law remains as it is now, so long we shall say that the law must take its course. (Applause.) We did not make the law, but we will enforce it.'[119] The council did, however, note that it intended to pursue other methods as well, including a new program of education and publishing. The *Record*, in an editorial on the subject, emphasized the need for a positive approach: 'We shall accomplish far more by teaching what is right than by exposing what is wrong. The latter is often necessary, but a grievous mistake is made when controversy is allowed to exclude all other methods of instruction.' The paper went out of its way to avoid controversy with the CA and refused to acknowledge the existence of any division within the party, claiming that the organization retained almost universal support. Still, it had to recognize the growing opposition and suggested that any future prosecutions that were likely to end in imprisonment would be self-defeating and find little support.[120]

In January 1881, after the imprisonment and release of Dale and Enraght, there was a new attempt to organize the independent clerical and lay associations. The CA had tried unsuccessfully to unite those groups under its own auspices several years earlier. Moderates who were gathered in London for the Islington Clerical Conference, were loathe to start a new organization, but they 'thought it useless to regard the Church Association as a common centre round which Evangelical men would be ready to rally in times of distress.'[121] According to the *Record*, the idea of a union had been circulating for some time and had the support of party leaders such as J. C. Ryle, Edward Garbett, Edward Hoare, C. S. Money, and William Cadman. It was proposed that a central committee would be formed, made up of representatives elected by the various regional associations, this time entirely separate from the CA. It was also noted that a resolution to that effect had been agreed upon at a private meeting held following the church congress the previous fall (which would indicate the presence of mostly moderate Evangelicals since the conservative section generally opposed participation in mixed meetings such as congresses). In May 1880, a preliminary meeting was held in London under the chairmanship of Charles Perry, at which representatives from a number of the associations formally agreed to the plan and the establishment of a central committee. That was followed by the January meeting of the Union of Clerical and Lay Associations (hereafter abbreviated UCLA), held at the Cannon-street Hotel. According to the *Record*, the meeting was well-attended by influential supporters of the movement and several papers were read calling for a renewed Evangelical unity. The paper concluded that there had been 'quietly launched an organization which, under the blessing of God, may command untold influence in the future for the Evangelical body.'[122]

The late 1870s and early 1880s saw the beginning of a fundamental shift in the support for the anti-Ritualist movement. The early imprisonments did not immediately turn public favor against the anti-Ritualists to any measurable degree, nor did they create a surge of support for their opponents. Many in influential positions, both in the ecclesiastical hierarchy and in the popular press, continued to oppose the ceremony and doctrine of the Ritualists as well as their defiant attitude toward those in authority. But there was a definite shift of opinion. While continuing to voice their disapproval of the Ritualist movement, the bishops were less inclined to allow litigation. Most were deeply concerned about the impact of the controversy on the unity of the church and simply desired a non-partisan and less divisive means of settling the matter. Convinced anti-Ritualists, however, interpreted their opposition to prosecution as a sign of weakness, or, worse still, as an indication of their sympathetic view of the innovations. Consequently, the bishops were made the target of an increasingly bitter polemic.

Still more disturbing for conservatives was evidence of a shift of opinion among moderate Evangelicals. Moderates were increasingly convinced that the Ritualists could not be contained through the compulsion of the courts. Mounting evidence indicated that the only significant impact of the imprisonment of clergy was its negative effect on their own cause, allowing their opponents to play on the sympathies of the general public. Above all, moderates had simply grown tired of the controversy and its bitter partisanship. Beginning in the early 1880s, their opposition to the methods of the CA was increasingly vocal and renewed interest was shown in the organization of a non-polemical body that might unite the whole party. In 1881, Samuel Garratt condemned the use of prosecution (implying that he and a few others had privately opposed such methods all along) as an illegitimate attempt to use worldly means for spiritual goals, suggesting that it could never accomplish the desired goal and that it would ultimately destroy the Evangelical spirit itself. In the wake of the imprisonment of Dale and Enraght, his was the voice of conscience representing a small minority. Over the course of the next few years, however, it would become the dominant view in the party.

Notes

1 For a general summary of the Tooth case and its context in the history of proceedings under the Public Worship Regulation Act, cf. Bentley, *Ritualism and Politics*, pp. 100-02.
2 Lord Penzance observed that it was little wonder that Tooth did not appear, 'as the acts were beyond dispute, and the law, under the existing discussion, beyond question.' Judgment of the Court of Arches cited in the *Times*, 19 July 1876.
3 Penzance summarized the service in his judgment: 'The service was preceded by a procession moving from the vestry to the Communion-table, upon which, or the ledge immediately above which, candles had just been lighted. That procession consisted of boys in cassocks carrying incense, lighted candles, and a crucifix on a pole, and was attended by Mr. Tooth himself or his curate in an alb, girdle, amice, stole, and chasuble, with a cap called a biretta on his head. Having arrived at the Communion-table the service proceeded. The different vessels were censed, the biretta was taken off the head and laid with ceremony on the table; water was mixed with the wine; the prayer of consecration was said with the back of the celebrant turned to the congregation; the celebrant knelt at certain parts of it, and af-

terwards elevated the sacred elements above his head. He made a sign of the cross in the air towards the congregation; the "Agnus Dei" was sung; the great bell of the church was tolled; two boys held up lighted candles high in the air, then retired, and the Holy Communion was then received either by the celebrant himself alone or by himself and one other person. All this was not casual, but apparently habitual.' Ibid.

4   The paper suggested that it was 'a well considered and deliberate policy' adopted by the Ritualists to discover how the bishops and courts would respond to 'open disobedience.' *Record*, 20 Dec. 1876.

The *Quarterly Review* also complained that the country had long been patient with the Ritualists and was willing to overlook a multitude of innovations if there was any indication they would obey either the bishops or the courts. But their protests, following the Ridsdale and Tooth judgments, made it evident that they would not. They were intent on 'nothing less than an organised revolt against all established authority in Church affairs.' Anon., 'Ridsdale Judgment,' *Quarterly Review*, pp. 253-54.

5   The *Record* expressed its hope that the court would levy a fine, perhaps followed by deprivation for a second offence, rather than resorting to imprisonment: 'Our reason for deprecating it is no tenderness for the lawbreaker, but only a reluctance to see him invested by the fact of personal suffering in the cause he has espoused with an importance and dignity which are not deserved and which are disproportional to the position of the individual. Who does not remember the imprisonment in Chelmsford gaol of John Thoroughgood, "the Church-rate martyr," some thirty years ago, and the handsome subscriptions paid to him during his incarceration?' Ibid.

6   The *Record* cited editorials from most of the leading London papers condemning Tooth's defiance. The *Daily Telegraph*, for instance, cited the many ecclesiastical statutes enacted by Parliament since the Reformation and rejected the Ritualist claim that the Public Worship Regulation Act was somehow unique. 'The Public Worship Regulation Act was only one in this succession of Acts of Parliament, and it made no change whatever in the law – it merely simplified procedure.' The paper was amused by the 'the spectacle of Mr. Tooth, who spurns "the secular arm," being protected in his revolt by the not very spiritual agency of "twenty stout constables of the P division," shielding him from the assaults of offenders who, brutal as they may be, are not more lawless than himself.' Cited in the *Record*, 10 Jan. 1877.

7   On January 7th, the mob was kept outside by the police, and admittance to the church was gained only by those with tickets. During the service, the crowd outside loudly sang 'God Save the Queen.' As Tooth was preparing the sacraments, there was a great uproar as the barrier surrounding the church gave way, and the mob began banging on the doors. Order was finally restored when constables arrived, but the mob could be heard singing the national anthem and 'Hold the Fort,' with the worshippers effectively held prisoner within the sanctuary for some time. When the doors were finally opened, the congregation had to leave down a walkway lined by the protesters and was greeted with cries of 'Change here for Rome – all tickets ready!' and 'No Popery,' or 'Down with the Pope!' The report continued, 'Every gentleman who appeared with a low-crowned and broad-brimmed

hat of Ritualist fashion was saluted with the cry, "Here's another hat!" followed by hisses, groans, and derisive laughter.... Shortly before one o'clock the Rev. Gentleman left the church, and was met with a perfect torrent of hisses and groans. Following him went several of the clergy, and it was with difficulty the police could restrain the mob from entering the vicarage garden after them.' Report from the *Daily Telegraph*, cited in the *Record*, 8 Jan. 1877.

According to the *Times*, 'the crowd for the most part was composed of well-dressed persons, there being very few of what is known as the "rough element" present. One man was taken into custody by the police for disorderly conduct.... Handbills were industriously circulated among the rioters, addressed to the "Men of England," and calling upon them to put down popery and priestcraft.' *Times*, 8 Jan. 1877.

8   The bishop's delegation posted the notice on the church doors following an early matins service: 'Thomas Legh, by Divine permission Bishop of Rochester. – To the churchwardens of the parish of St. James's, Hatcham, in the counties of Kent and Surrey, within our diocese of Rochester, greeting. Whereas there appears to us to be reason to apprehend that the opening of the church of St. James's, Hatcham, aforesaid, on Sunday, the 14th of January inst., will be an occasion for riotous conduct and breaches of the peace within and around the said church. Now we do hereby strictly enjoin you , the churchwardens aforesaid, to prevent the opening of the said church during the whole of Sunday, the 14th day of January inst., and the admission thereto of any person or persons and the ringing of any bell belonging thereto. And take heed that ye fail not herein.' Cited in the *Times*, 15 Jan. 1877.

The *Times* strongly supported the bishop's action in an editorial. The paper thought it was disgraceful that an obstinate priest should 'render it necessary to employ force in order to dispossess him, and, as Mr. Tooth did the other day, to allow himself to be surrounded by a bodyguard of partisans for the purpose of offering physical resistance to the Clergyman who the Bishop, in pursuance of what he deemed his duty, had commissioned to conduct the services of the Church. It is well it should have been shown, even at the last moment, that the legitimate authority of a Clergyman's Ecclesiastical superior cannot be thus set at defiance; and that if any Ritualistic Clergymen should in future behave like ill-conditioned children, the Bishop can at least prevent them from desecrating their churches by such a display of bad manners.' Ibid.

9   'It would be well if those who maintain these propositions were to read the statutes authorizing and establishing the two successive Prayer-books of King Edward VI. and the Prayer-book of Queen Elizabeth, which regulated the ritual of the Reformed Church for the first hundred years after its establishment. They would there find that a clergyman departing in the performance of Divine service from the ritual prescribed in the Prayer-book was liable to be tried at the Assizes by a Judge and jury – the Bishop, if he pleased, assisting the Judge – and, if convicted three times, was liable to be imprisoned for life. The intervention, therefore, of a temporal Court, if any such were in question, to enforce obedience in matters of ritual would at

least be no novelty. The novelty, if any, is in the claim to be exempt from it. But suppose this claim, for the sake of argument, to be admitted, what, I ask, are the Ecclesiastical Courts to whose judgment Mr. Tooth and those who act and think with him would be willing to defer?... What is the Court which has the jurisdiction to which he is ready to render obedience? Is it the Court of his Bishop? If so, he must surely be aware that by the Ecclesiastical law of this country, as well before the Reformation as since, an appeal from the Bishop's Court lies, and has always lain, to the Court of the Archbishop – this Court of Arches, whose jurisdiction he now denies.... Has, then, the Public Worship Act robbed this Court of its claim to obedience in matters ecclesiastical? All that the Act has done is to arm it with new powers, and these only in the way of procedure.... Mr. Tooth, therefore, denies the authority of the only existing Courts in the kingdom which, subject to appeal, have any power to review and correct his proceedings; and I cannot, consequently, regard his claim to immunity from the judgments and orders of this Court as anything short of a claim to be himself the judge of the ritual which the Prayer-book has prescribed. If so, there is nothing that I know of to prevent him from a still further approach to the ritual of the unreformed Church of Rome, if he can persuade himself that the language of the Prayer-book admits of it.' Judgment of the Court of Arches, cited in the *Times*, 15 Jan. 1877.

10   Even before the court's decision, the Newark and Southwell Branch of the ECU declared in a resolution to Bishop Wordsworth of Lincoln that any judgment of suspension would be considered 'spiritually null and void' and that the clergy would be strongly encouraged to ignore such judgments.

Wordsworth, in a stinging rebuke, defended the royal supremacy and the validity of the crown's courts to render verdicts in ecclesiastical cases. He wrote, 'When also a clergyman, who has solemnly promised at his ordination to obey his Ordinary (i.e., the Bishop of the diocese), is commanded by his Bishop, in the exercise of his episcopal authority, to submit to the decisions of the Court of Arches, as now constituted, I confess that I cannot understand how in such a case the decisions of the Court have no spiritual validity; but, on the contrary, a clergyman who sets them at defiance appears to be openly despising and resisting both spiritual and temporal authority.

'It may, indeed, be alleged by some well-meaning persons that such clergymen are suffering persecution, and have claims to sympathy and support. But the fact is, such clergymen are not martyrs but persecutors. They are persecuting the Church of which they are ministers, by disturbing its peace, and by stirring up strife, and by spreading confusion and anarchy, and by marring its efficacy and imperiling its safety.'

Wordsworth concluded that there had never been a time when there were not difficulties in the relations between church and state. But bad legislation or judicial decisions could never be corrected 'by disobeying God in resistance to lawful authority.' Cited in the *Times*, 13 Jan. 1877.

11   Wood declared, 'I take my stand on the broad principle that the decisions of all Courts, past and present, in so far as they profess to be governed by the

decisions of the Final Court of Appeal, not only do not and cannot exercise spiritual power, but are themselves founded upon an authority whose existence is in direct violation of the terms upon which the Church of England made her submission to the Crown.' Cited in the *Times*, 17 Jan. 1877.

12   The first resolution read: 'That the English Church Union, while it distinctly and expressly acknowledges the authority of all Courts legally constituted in regard to all matters temporal, denies that the secular power has any authority in matters purely spiritual.' The second read: 'That any Court which is bound to frame its decisions in accordance with the judgments of the Judicial Committee of the Privy Council, or any other secular Court, does not possess any spiritual authority with respect to such decisions. That suspension *a sacris* being a purely spiritual act, the English Church Union is prepared to support any priest not guilty of a moral or canonical offence who refuses to recognise a suspension issued by such a Court.' Cited in Ibid.

The *Times* sharply criticized the protesters: 'It must be presumed these gentlemen were aware that every Ecclesiastical Court in this country is bound to frame its decisions in accordance with the judgments of the Judicial Committee.... No interpretation can be placed on a single Rubric or other formulary which is not liable, upon appeal, to be reviewed by that Court. It follows, therefore, that what we have in this Resolution is simply a repudiation of allegiance to every Ecclesiastical Court in existence, and a claim to complete emancipation from all existing authority.... The Ritualists have once for all declared that they hold themselves emancipated from all authority to which they were understood to pledge themselves by their ordination vows, and by their declarations on appointment to their benefices.' *Times*, 18 Jan. 1877.

Bishop Ellicott complained that when a group of clergy could offer prayer for those who defied the law and when 'a so-called Church society denies to any court which is bound to frame its decision in accordance with the highest court in the land the possession of any spiritual authority, whatever, we must acknowledge with sorrow and humiliation not only that party spirit of the worst kind is now prevailing in the Church, but that good sense and even sanity itself are taking leave of the minds of many of our clergy under the pressure of present excitement.' C. J. Ellicott, 'The Church of England, Present and Future,' *Nineteenth Century* 1 (1877): 63.

13   The *Record* reprinted an article from the *Standard*, which suggested that Tooth was leading a rather comfortable existence in the jail. He was allowed 'to receive friends in the common room attached to the debtors' portion of the prison, where one of the "sisters of mercy"... is in constant attendance upon him between nine and three o'clock, the hours in which strangers are admitted. In the furniture of his own room, to which no visitor has access, the Reverend Gentleman has made some slight additions, including a table and easy chair.... Here he has his books and papers, and conducts his correspondence, which is of a somewhat voluminous character. Mr. Tooth is not called upon to do any menial work himself, having taken advantage of the regulation of the gaol by which he has been able to engage one of the "poor" debtors to make his bed, clean his room, and do the other necessary

work, inclusive of cooking such portion of his food as is brought from outside in an uncooked state, the rules permitting a prisoner committed for contempt of court to provide any edibles he may think proper.' Cited in the *Record*, 26 Jan. 1877.

14 The counsel for the promoters, Benjamin Shaw, said his 'clients had no object in view but the vindication of public justice and public order,' and once the Bishop's nominee was admitted to the church, "they had no desire that Mr. Tooth should be detained in custody." Cited in the *Times*, 19 Feb. 1877.

15 Richard Chambers was licensed to serve as curate in charge by the bishop, but he was unable even to gain entrance to the church. The churchwardens, who supported Tooth, refused to unlock the doors. Chambers resigned after several weeks without ever holding a service. *Record*, 22, 29 Jan. and 5 Feb. 1877. Benjamin Dale was then appointed curate in charge. When he met with similar resistance, he hired men to break into the church. The illegal ornaments in the church were removed, and services were finally held on February 11th. *Times*, 12 Feb. 1877.

It was feared that Tooth, after his release, would immediately return to his church, but he did not. His 'supporters and friends,' however, protested by leaving in the middle of the service the following Sunday. At the door, they were confronted by members of the Protestant League who blocked their path, and 'a most unseemly disturbance followed.' Most of the protesters were able to press their way out, but a number were 'forcibly detained inside the building.' In his sermon, Dale condemned all who disrupted the services of the church. *Times*, 26 Feb. 1877.

16 The appeal argued that Penzance's judgment was invalid because the case had been heard at Lambeth Palace, whereas the Public Worship Regulation Act required that the hearings take place either in London or Westminster. The Lord Chief Justice said, 'I have arrived at the conclusion that there must be a prohibition, but I arrive at that conclusion with extreme regret; for it is clear that it is an objection of the most technical character, and which has nothing to do with the merits of the case, which are of essential importance as regards the functions of the clergy and the administration of the worship of the Church of England.' Cited in the *Times*, 20 Nov. 1877.

The *Times* thought it 'a ridiculous conclusion' to 'the long and troublesome proceedings,' which it feared might further erode the authority of the ecclesiastical courts. With regard to the basis of the appeal, the paper noted sarcastically, 'some person given to ecclesiastical and legal antiquities discovered the other day that Lambeth is not in London.' Ibid.

17 Mackonochie, if not before the courts, had by no means been far from the controversy. In November 1877, the *Times* published correspondence that had passed between Mackonochie and Bishop Jackson regarding a crucifix and a picture of Mary, surrounded by flowers and candles, that he had erected in his church. Jackson argued not that they were strictly illegal, but rather that they had been put in the church without the authorization required by law. Without reference to the courts, he issued an admonishment as Mackonochie's bishop and reminded him of the oath of 'canonical obedience' taken by all clergy at their ordination. Mackonochie, however refused to yield. Correspondence cited in the *Times*, 26 Nov. 1877.

The paper followed with an editorial condemning the obstinance of Tooth and Mackonochie. The Ritualists generally claimed that they could never obey a secular court that had no authority in spiritual matters, but ultimately, they would allow no judge but themselves. *Times,* 27 Nov. 1877. Even T. T. Carter, who had himself been the subject of attempted prosecution, recognized the contradiction in Mackonochie's logic and urged him to submit to the bishop. Correspondence cited in the *Times,* 5 Dec. 1877.

18 It was later revealed that the original promoter refused to allow his name to be associated with further appeals against Mackonochie that might end in imprisonment. According to the *Record*'s obituary for John Martin, he was for many years a member of the council of the CA. But he would not consent to any further prosecution and withdrew from the council 'some years before his death.' *Record,* 22 May 1885.

19 *Times,* 25 March 1878. The *Times* viewed the Mackonochie case with no small degree of sarcasm: 'Mr. Mackonochie finds the glories of martyrdom hard of attainment. Sir Robert Phillimore, the Dean of the Arches, issued, as the result of suits some of which had been commenced ten years ago, a monition against him in June, 1875; he duly disobeyed with all the marks of quiet contempt that could be desired; and now in March, 1878, he is still at large, and apparently likely to continue so. Mr. Tooth at Hatcham was crowned and decorated for half-a-dozen months or so of genuflexions and processions. Mr. Alexander Heriot Mackonochie has paraded for years his magnanimous scorn of Bishops and Deans of Arches, even when so un-Erastian a Judge as Sir Robert Phillimore has held the office; and, after all, he has to content himself with a monition. He will doubtless be as persistently intractable as before. Our readers will have seen by the account we published of the St. Alban's services of Sunday last what is Mr. Mackonochie's view of Church of England rites and ceremonies. But it is difficult to lash a Dean of Arches into fury.' *Times,* 27 March 1878.

20 Judgment of the Court of Arches, cited in the *Times,* 3 June 1878.

21 It was argued that the case should not have proceeded because it was based on a ruling of the Court of Arches made prior to the Public Worship Regulation Act. The Court of Arches had then no authority to suspend for charges of contempt at that time, and consequently, claimed the defendant, that sentence could not be handed down. Further, it was claimed that the court had no authority to suspend clergy from their benefice, which was a 'freehold,' or personal property.

The arguments made before the Queen's Bench Division were reported at length in the *Times,* 28 and 29 June 1878. In an editorial a year later, when the case was under appeal before the Court of Appeal of the Supreme Court of Judicature, the *Times* published a lengthy editorial explaining the intricacies both of the case at hand and of the appeals process in English law. It noted that the Queen's Bench Division could rule only on technical aspects of the judgment and had no authority to reconsider the substance of the case. *Times,* 12 March 1879.

22 *Times,* 9 August 1878.

23 The *Record* cited Lord Chief Justice Cockburn who, despite the ruling in favor of Mackonochie, had sharply criticized his activities: 'It is clear that a

man cannot be allowed to remain a minister of the Church of England and enjoy the material benefits of the Church of England, and yet in his practices upset the doctrines of the Church of England and set the ordinances of the Church of England at defiance. I can understand a man becoming a martyr for the sake of his opinions, but I cannot understand a man remaining in the Church setting the ordinances of the Church at defiance, and taking the benefits of the Church, and yet be beyond the reach of proceedings of this kind, supposing them to be legal.' Cited in the *Record*, 12 Aug. 1878.

The *Times* thought the decision was more serious that did the *Record* and suggested that the difficulties involved pointed to the obvious need for reform of ecclesiastical law: 'In the present instance the victory over Lord Penzance is more complete and more galling than it was in Mr. Tooth's case. There the error which vitiated the proceedings of the Court was obviously a trivial and technical error. But the revocation of the sentence passed upon Mr. Mackonochie implies that Lord Penzance was mistaken as to the powers of his office, and that the Judicial Committee of the Privy Council shared in the responsibility for his mistake.' *Times*, 9 Aug. 1878.

24 *Times*, 30 June 1879.

25 Penzance noted, with regret, the many technical appeals that had delayed the proceedings unnecessarily. It was unfortunate, he concluded, 'that the assertion and exercise by a temporal Court of a jurisdiction over the proceedings of this Court which it now turns out was not warranted by law should have occurred in a case like the present, and have added upwards of another year to the long immunity of the respondent. It is, perhaps, still more to be regretted that the respondent has not on this occasion, of which he has had full notice, appeared before the Court and offered some assurance that the illegal practices complained of shall be discontinued in future. Any assurance of that kind would have been welcomed by the Court, and would have made it practicable to defer or even withhold all further proceedings against him; for, although the action of the Court takes the form of a punishment for contumacy in not obeying its previous monition, the substantial object which underlies the whole proceedings is not punishment for what is past, but obedience to the law in the future.' Judgment of the Court of Arches, cited in the *Times*, 17 Nov. 1879.

26 The obstinance of the Ritualists was evident in a correspondence between Tooth and Archbishop Tait during the summer of 1877. Tooth refused to be influenced by Tait's personal admonitions or his arguments regarding the position adopted earlier in Convocation. After a number of letters, Tait concluded that further correspondence would be pointless; 'I can no longer hope that anything I can say will induce you to act as you ought.' Davidson, *Life of Tait, vol.* 2, pp. 246-53.

27 Letter to the *Record*, 11 June 1877. An anonymous correspondent suggested a suspension of prosecutions, for a period of six months, to give the bishops time to use their personal influence with the Ritualists. Letter (signed 'A Rural Dean') to the *Record*, June 18, 1877. The *Record* itself adopted Holland's distinction a few years later when it finally concluded that prosecution was no longer viable.

G. T. Fox rejected Holland's argument and suggested that an end of litigation would only be playing into the Ritualists' hands. He did not believe the CA would have to take up 'wholesale prosecutions,' and countered that allowing law breakers to go unpunished would negate the good work already done in ascertaining the precise meaning of the law. Fox assumed that once a few Ritualists were made examples in the courts, the rest would soon comply. Letter to the *Record*, 18 June 1877.

28 Cited in the *Record*, 15 June 1877. Andrews later defended the work of the CA in an exchange with Bishop Mackarness. The bishop had criticized both the ECU and the CA, suggesting that there would be no peace in the church until both organizations were dissolved. Andrews claimed that the CA desired to assist the bishops and had appealed to the courts only because the bishops had declared the law to be obscure. As a result of their litigation, fifty-nine separate practices had been judged illegal. Mackarness was unconvinced. He replied, 'You tell me that it is the glory of your Association to have obtained sentences of illegality against fifty-nine ceremonial practices. If they were a hundred and fifty-nine I should not be moved. I have no sympathy with your appetite for condemnations. Too often they do but provoke men to revolt.... In things really objectionable, as ministering to superstition, we might have trusted the good sense and sound feeling of Churchmen to prevail if polemical confederacies had not almost banished reason and charity from the sphere of their discussion.' Correspondence cited in the *Record*, 17 and 24 Jan. 1879.

The *Times*, in an editorial following the CA meeting, expressed its hope that the Ridsdale judgment would be conclusive. On the whole, the paper thought the CA's prosecution of the Ritualists, up to that point, had been necessary and successful. 'The most significant innovations have been decisively condemned, and principles of interpretation have been established which will prevent any similar innovations for the future. But this result having been attained, the Association will not assume the part of a public prosecutor, and is not prepared to open a general crusade against Ritualistic clergymen. It will leave it to the Bishops and to congregations to put the law in force, and, for the present at all events, seems disposed to trust to the assertion by the law of its moral influence. Such a course will be at once fair and prudent. It would be unlike our usual method of controversy to press hardly upon defeated antagonists, and it would tend to transform error or perversity into obstinacy. The law is henceforth positive and clear, and no clergyman can escape being confronted with its directions. Should it be persistently disobeyed, it will of course have to be enforced; but there is good reason to hope that if time be allowed such extreme measures may be unnecessary.' *Times*, 14 June 1877.

29 *Record*, 5 March 1880. The distinction was a common one in Evangelical circles. In an address published in *Knots Untied* (1877), J. C. Ryle suggested that religious controversy was a disturbing matter. But, he continued, it would be still worse to have 'false doctrine tolerated, allowed, and permitted without protest or molestation.' Ryle warned that the age valued compromise over truth, and those who did not disturb the peace were called 'good Churchmen.' In his view, however, 'the truest friends of the Church

of England' were those who did the most 'for the preservation of the truth' and defended the church's true principles. Reprinted in J. C. Ryle, *Warnings to the Churches* (Edinburgh: The Banner of Truth Trust, 1967), pp. 110-12.

In contrast, R. E. Bartlett, writing from a moderately Broad Church perspective, suggested that the English laity were little inclined to support further bitter controversy and had recovered from 'the Protestant panic, which caused them to smell "Puseyism" in every proposal for the restoration or embellishment of a church, for the introduction of an improved hymnal, or for a more aesthetic form of service.' But, Bartlett suggested, they would not allow the extreme section of the High Church unlimited toleration; 'if their object is to persuade English people to accept what are technically known as "Catholic" or "Church" principles, and to bring back the ages of faith *minus* the corruptions of Rome, they will find that they have to deal with a somewhat stiff-necked generation, and that their breath would be more usefully employed in cooling their porridge than in trying to blow up the flame of Catholic zeal in the green and hissing wood of English Protestantism.' [R.E.B.], 'The Past and Future of the High Church Party,' *Fraser's Magazine* New Series 17 (1878): 247.

30 The notice went on to suggest activities that local branches could undertake in order to make their voice heard in the elections. It claimed that the CA had been forced into the political arena by the actions of the 'Catholic revivalists,' who intended to agitate for repeal of the Public Worship Regulation Act and possibly even disestablishment. Cited in the *Record*, 4 March 1878.

31 The Council of the CA requested the members of its 358 branches to pose the following questions to all candidates: 'Will you, irrespective of party politics, do your utmost to support the principles of the Reformation, and to oppose any legislation tending to undermine or weaken the Protestant character of the British Constitution? Will you do your utmost, by legislation if needful, to secure full obedience to the law on the part of the clergy, and to expel those Romish doctrines and practices which a section of them have been introducing into the Church of England?' *Record*, 12 March 1880.

32 Letter to the *Record*, 31 Jan. 1877. Several correspondents quickly wrote to express their strong support for the idea of a new Evangelical organization that would move beyond what they thought were the 'defensive' goals and methods of the CA. Cf. Letters of Arthur Roberts, S. A. Walker, and Samuel Fenton to the *Record*, 7 Feb. 1877.

33 The founders were apparently concerned about the drift of Evangelical moderates. Waddington declared that the party's position was 'becoming more and more critical.' He continued, 'Decided Evangelical Protestants who have resolved with the help of God to keep to the old paths, and to remain in the old Reformation moorings, each year find themselves more isolated and in an increasingly difficult position.

'This is owing partly to the attitude of the avowed foes of the Reformation becoming more aggressive as they increase in numbers and audacity, but more so to the time-serving policy of many who still profess to be loyal to Evangelical principles, but who are gradually slipping into the ways of High Churchmen, in which worldly-wise course they are often encouraged by Episcopal smiles and commendations.' Letter to the *Record*,

16 May 1879.

A month later, the union announced its goals in an advertisement: 'To unite decided Evangelical Protestant Congregations and Members of the Church of England and Ireland, who have determined, with the help of God, to use all their influence to maintain the truth in its integrity, and to oppose the progress of error, resolving to make no compromise with it, and to make no surrender of the sound Scriptural principles and practices of the Reformation.' The council of the union was listed as J. Bennett, G. T. Fox, Charles Guest, Alfred Hewlett, S. A. Walker, J. T. Waller, and J. B. Waddington. Advertisement in the *Record*, 25 June 1879.

34 Letter to the *Record*, 16 Feb. 1877. Similarly, cf. the letter of P. F. Eliot, Vicar of Holy Trinity, Bournemouth, *Record*, 23 Feb. 1877.

35 Close continued, 'The hoisting of gown and surplice as tests of brotherhood and flags of distinctive soundness on Protestant principles indicated so great a want of judgment and such misapprehension of the needs of our times as did at once deter me from joining such a body.' Letter to the *Record*, 25 June 1879.

36 At its sixth annual conference in 1884, the *Record* reported that 'there were barely one hundred' present, even though the union claimed a membership of one thousand. The paper also noted that 'there was a conspicuous absence of any fair proportion of younger people.' G. T. Fox, who was unable to attend, prepared a paper on the state of the Evangelical party compared to its past. The *Record*'s correspondent thought it gave evidence of 'the old warrior' spirit, but regretted to report that it lacked 'the tenderness one might have hoped for in him whose eyes are near the golden sunset.' Fox lamented the influence of the Ritualist and Broad Church parties among Evangelical moderates. They now called themselves 'Neo-Evangelicals,' but Fox thought it more accurate if 'they would omit the first vowel.' He concluded that there had been a serious decay during the recent past 'in the thoroughness and decision both of doctrine and action, amongst those who claim to be Evangelical.' Cited in the *Record*, 24 Oct. 1884.

J. B. Waddington, Honorary Secretary of the EPU, disputed the facts of the story and claimed that there were many more present than reported by the paper. According to Waddington, only the morning sessions were sparsely attended; by the afternoon there were some two hundred present, and about three hundred came to the evening session. Waddington also complained about the 'unfriendly spirit' of the article. Letter to the *Record*, 7 Nov. 1884.

37 Penzance concluded his judgment with a stinging rebuke of clergy who set an 'evil example of willful disobedience to the law.' If there were faults in the law, said Penzance, they needed to be corrected by lawful means. For a clergyman to refuse to obey, 'was nothing else than a claim on his part to be bound by no law at all, or to submit only to his own interpretation of it.' Judgment of the Court of Arches, cited in the *Times*, 4 Nov. 1876.

38 The charges were lighted candles on the altar, wearing eucharistic vestments and a cap called a biretta, adopting the eastward position, prostration before the altar, using wafer bread, mixing water with the wine, elevating the elements, making the sign of the cross, ringing a bell during the

prayer of consecration, elevating the offerings, singing the *agnus dei*, and putting a cross on a table behind the altar. *Times*, 22 Aug. 1878.

The charge concerning the cross behind the altar was dropped, and the charge of using wafer bread was judged 'not proven' on the ground of insufficient evidence. In addition to the two charges dropped, the eastward position was allowed so long as the priest's manual acts were not obscured from the congregation. But, Penzance ruled that Dale 'did interpose his body so as intentionally to defeat the object of the rubrics and prevent this result.' Judgment of the Court of Arches, cited in the *Times*, 10 Feb. 1879.

39 Noting that the Ritualists refused to appear in court, Penzance went on to criticize the extremes to which Dale had taken that policy: 'But, in addition to this, he has adopted the very novel and curious method of writing letters to the Registrar of the Court complaining of technical defects in the proceedings, and warning the Court that if the proceedings are continued against him he shall "take such steps as he may be advised for the protection of his just rights." Meanwhile, he has endeavoured in every possible way to avoid being served with any of the notices or other papers connected with the proceedings, and having refused to take out of the postman's hand a registered letter containing one of the most important of them, he has had the courage to write and complain that he never received it. As a climax to this line of conduct he has afforded the not very dignified spectacle portrayed to the Court by the witness this morning of a gentleman and clergyman of the Church of England running down a narrow flight of stairs into the basement of his house as soon as he caught sight of the officer of this Court with a paper in his hand. He can hardly have understood that the dreaded paper was nothing more than a notice to him that this cause would be proceeded with to-day, and he might safely have preserved his dignity without compromising "his just rights".' Ibid.

40 Judgment of the Court of Arches, cited in the *Times*, 15 March 1880.

41 The two spoke with Dale in the vestry and informed him that his benefice 'would be declared void in two years' if he continued to ignore the inhibition. Dale replied that he would neither comply with the decree of the Court of Arches nor allow anyone else to minister in his place. He was, he declared, 'a priest of the Church of God, and no earthly power could deprive him of his office.' An officer of the Court of Arches attached a copy of the inhibition to the door of the church, but it was torn down shortly thereafter, and Dale went on to celebrate the Eucharist in two services without deviating from his usual manner of worship. *Times*, 23 March 1880.

42 He concluded, 'I have no alternative, therefore, but to grant the present application. With the policy of these proceedings I have nothing to do. Whether they form the only or the best means of combating the evil against which they are directed or not is a matter beyond my province. But if appeal is made to the law, it is not only within the province, but it is the plain duty of this Court to see that the law is upheld; and, when called upon in a proper case, to enforce its own decree. On the other hand, the respondent has, I presume, some purpose in view in thus openly defying the law and forcing the promoters of the suit to the final resort of coercion. When this purpose, whatever it may be, has been attained (or, indeed, before then if he

should change his mind) the respondent can at once regain his liberty by announcing that he is ready to render obedience to the Court's decree. His imprisonment is of his own seeking, and his release will lie within his own reach.' Judgment of the Court of Arches, cited in the *Times*, 29 Oct. 1880.
43 Ibid.
44 *Times*, 1 Nov. 1880. The *Times* noted with some irony that Dale's brother 'was for many years legal adviser to the Church Association.' And his father, who had been Rector of St. Brides, Fleet-street, and later Dean of Rochester, was 'a well-known leader of the Evangelical Party.' *Times*, 5 Nov. 1880.

At the end of Dale's first week in prison, the *Times* took issue with several of those who had written the paper in his defense and particularly his son, who suggested that the churchwardens of St. Vedast's had been harassing his father for seven years. The paper wrote, 'What a son's piety cannot understand, but what it is bare justice to the churchwardens whose "rancour" he assails to remember, is that congregationalism is not, as Mr. Arthur Murray Dale appears to suppose, the theory of English Church government. Within very liberal limits church worship in the Establishment must obey the rule of the Establishment, not of a collection of persons who happen to use a particular edifice. It is not necessary to feel any more admiration for the temper of the Church Association than for that of the English Church Union in order to excuse the churchwardens of St. Vedast's from the charge of wanton hostility.... But it was their bounden duty not to look on without protest while the church in their charge was being applied to purposes they conscientiously considered infractions of Church of England law.' *Times*, 6 Nov. 1880.
45 The *Record* reported that the parishioners largely objected to Enraght's innovations and had elected a member of the CA, John Perkins, to be the people's churchwarden at the Easter vestry meeting. *Record*, 5 June 1878.

In his correspondence with the Bishop of Worcester, Henry Philpott, Enraght maintained that the majority of the parish supported him and that the protests were raised by only a few extremists of the 'Puritan party.' The correspondence was reprinted by Enraght in his pamphlet, *My Ordination Oaths and Other Declarations: Am I Keeping Them?* (London: Simpkin, Marshall, & Co., 1880).
46 It also resulted in a somewhat humorous exchange in the Court of Arches: Mr. Jeune, the lawyer for the prosecution produced the wafer and 'said he was prepared to prove the wafer was not bread as is usually eaten.

"Lord Penzance: That is perfectly obvious to the eye; but do not let me stop you proving it.

"Mr. John Perkins was called.

"Lord Penzance: Is this gentleman an expert in such matters?

"Mr. Jeune: Yes, my Lord, he is a baker.

"Mr. Perkins proved that the wafer was unleavened and was not 'bread such as is usual to be eaten".'

Proceedings of the Court of Arches, cited in the *Times*, 11 Aug. 1879.

C. L. Wood, President of the ECU, asked the CA join with his group 'in an indignant protest against the insult that has been offered to Our Lord, in the Sacrament of his love, by one who has ventured, at the time of Communion, to steal from the Church of the Holy Trinity, at Birmingham, the consecrated Elements for the purpose of producing them in a court of justice.' Despite their differences, proclaimed Wood, he could not believe the council of the CA could be 'so indifferent to the honour and reverence due to Our Blessed Lord' as to approve of such an act. W. C. Palmer, Secretary for the Council of the CA, disclaimed any prior knowledge of the evidence in the case. He suggested that the way to avoid further controversy 'would be for all the ministers of our Church frankly to acknowledge their actual practices and to conform in rites and ceremonies to the plain direction of the Book of Common Prayer, as interpreted by the usages of three centuries, and confirmed by judicial decisions on points which seemed of doubtful construction.'

In December 1879, Archbishop Tait wrote to Bishop Philpott of Worcester, in whose diocese Enraght served, to notify him that the proctors for the prosecution had released the evidence to him, and the wafer had been 'reverently consumed.' Correspondence cited in the *Record*, 19 Dec. 1879.

47 After the recitation of the Nicene Creed, Enraght read his own 'solemn declaration, protest, and warning' concerning the confiscated eucharistic wafer which had been 'secretly carried out of this church under the pretence of communicating, and carried about a public law court in London, exposed to common gaze and disparaging remarks.' He condemned the action as 'an outrage against God, his Church, and Christianity' and concluded, 'I warn all concerned of the sore judgment hanging over the heads of those who knowingly profane the Holy Sacrament, counting it a common thing, not discerning the Lord's body, and guilty of the body and blood of the Lord.' Cited in the *Record*, 3 Sept. 1879.

48 Judgment of the Court of Arches, cited in the *Times*, 1 March 1880.

49 In his judgment, Penzance went to some length to make it clear that the imprisonment involved neither the ritual nor the doctrine of Enraght, but resulted rather from his contempt for the court. Lord Penzance said, in concluding his ruling, 'A clergyman, like all others of Her Majesty's subjects, is free to practise what forms of worship he pleases, but as long as he retains a place in the ministry of the Established Church he is bound to conform to its laws and ordinances. He has, therefore, been admonished by this Court to desist from his illegal practices, and, as he failed to pay obedience to this monition, he has been suspended from all exercise of his office for a limited period. He took no heed of this order of suspension, and the promoters of the suit now claim the right to have it enforced.... I must, therefore, pronounce Mr. Enraght contumacious and in contempt in this – that, having been suspended from his office, he has wholly disregarded that suspension and continued to officiate in his church.' Judgment of the Court of Arches, cited in the *Times*, 22 Nov. 1880.

Anti-Ritualists, concerned about the impact of the imprisonments on public opinion, frequently refuted their opponents' claims of persecution and martyrdom. The *Times* turned to sarcasm. It was now apparent, said the paper, that Dale was 'not to enjoy the distinction of testifying alone to the persecuting spirit of Lord Penzance and the Church Association.... Mr.

Enraght and Mr. Green are probably much vexed that Lord Penzance's inopportune clemency has allowed a rival a start. On all sides they see competitors eager for such duress as is not incompatible with the receiving of panegyrical addresses and the diversions of an elegant leisure. They are conscious there can be only a limited number of apartments in Her Majesty's gaols at the disposal of condemned Ritualists, and they assert a prior title to their tenancy. Lord Penzance has reluctantly seen no way of gainsaying their right. As he explained on Saturday, he possesses no discretion to leave his own judgments a dead letter. Accordingly, as soon as the formalities are completed of instructing the proper department in Chancery of their defiance, Mr. Green and Mr. Enraght will, we presume, be lodged in Lancaster Castle and the county gaol of Worcestershire. They have invited their fate. Indeed, the only immediate sufferer by the catastrophe would appear to be the perpetual curate of St. Margaret, Liverpool, who, when his own offence is in its turn ripe for judgment, may find preoccupied the cell he boasts is in preparation for him, and upon which he has been confidently reckoning.' *Times*, 22 Nov. 1880.

50   The arguments presented to the court were reported in detail in the *Times*, 30 Nov. to 14 Dec. 1880. The judges concluded that all of the objections raised by the defense 'were not only "highly technical" (with one exception) but utterly untenable.' Judgment of the Queen's Bench Division, cited in the *Times*, 14 Dec. 1880.

The *Times* suggested that the nature of the technical appeals undercut the Ritualists' claims regarding the authority of the secular courts. Dale had 'a perfect right to avail himself of any flaw in the procedure, however minute and obscure it might be.' But, the paper concluded, he should not 'make too much of his position as a martyr' after he had been 'worsted in a war of quibbles and technicalities. If ingenious fallacies could have saved him, he would not be to-day in Holloway Gaol.' *Times*, 14 Dec. 1880.

51   Correspondence cited in the *Times*, 22 Dec. 1880.

52   The *Times* suggested that the verdict was no vindication. 'Not a point has been decided in their favour which has the remotest bearing on the doctrines for which or against which they have been striving.... If the success they have gained in the struggle on technicalities proves anything to the public mind, it is not that justice has been vindicated by the immunity for a day or a week of two recalcitrant clergymen from a penalty they have incurred, but that the threats and injunctions, of which they have shown how difficult it is to chastise the contempt, ought to be changed for sharper and swifter penalties.' *Times*, 17 Jan. 1881.

53   In light of the results of the two cases and fearing that the imprisonments would foster sympathy for the Ritualists, the CA announced that its legal counsel was drawing up new legislation to be presented to Parliament, that would replace imprisonment with deprivation as the penalty for contumacious clergy. The bill would also abolish the episcopal veto, which was being increasingly invoked, 'in cases where a Queen's Counsel certifies that the matters complained of have been judiciously decided to be unlawful.' *Record*, 11 March 1881. Such legislation, however, had little chance for serious consideration or passage.

54 Canon F. W. Farrar preached on the topic at Westminster Abbey in January 1881. Although he thought Dale and Enraght mistaken in their disobedience to the law, he concluded that the punishment was 'provocative' rather than 'corrective.' He continued, 'So far from checking, it strengthens the cause it is intended to suppress. Every day that they remain in prison they enlist on their side the sympathies of thousands.... False ideas can only really be vanquished by the substitution of true ones. "You cannot," as Luther said, "smite a spirit with the sword." When you put excellent clergymen in prison you naturally enlist men's sympathy not only with them but even with their cause.' Cited in the *Record*, 10 Jan. 1881.

During the debate over the appointment of a Royal Commission on Ecclesiastical Courts, Bishop Magee reacted to Lord Oranmore and Brown's defense of the CA and complained that their prosecutions had been 'odious, spiteful, and fatuous.' Furthermore, he thought they could not have done a better service for the Ritualists if the ECU had paid them: 'the persecutions... had simply ended in greatly increasing the number and zeal and success of the party which the Church Association were endeavouring to suppress.' Cited in the *Times*, 8 March 1881.

55 The *Times* published a lengthy letter from an anonymous diocesan chancellor who suggested that the Public Worship Regulation Act was faulty only insofar as it allowed contumacious clergy three years before they were subject to deprivation. In his view, they ought to have three weeks or three days in which to reconsider their position. He concluded, 'Instant deprivation is the proper and only real remedy for refusal to obey the law. And then if the deprivee invades the church and makes a disturbance, he can be dealt with summarily by the criminal law as the disturber of a congregation, without the interference of Lord Penzance or the Privy Council.... But, at any rate, the public ought to understand the real reason of these imprisonments – viz., because the Act was spoilt by not allowing simple deprivation, and also because of the timidity of the Privy Council in not enforcing it in one of the early cases for contempt – i.e., for repeated disobedience to the law.' Letter (signed 'A Diocesan Chancellor') to the *Times*, 22 Nov. 1880.

56 *Times*, 6 Nov. 1880.

57 The *Times*, in an editorial on Mackonochie's case, suggested that the Ritualists used that feeling to their own advantage: 'A street preacher who was causing an obstruction' would have been quickly dealt with, but the Ritualists were allowed endless appeals or were not pursued lest a scandal be created. 'If Mr. Mackonochie is secure against this sort of interference, if he is not forcibly removed from the pulpit he usurps, and is not thus compelled to give place to a legally appointed substitute, he owes his safety to nothing else but the desire which is felt to avoid a scandalous scene. In other words, he relies on reverential feelings, which he nevertheless persists in outraging. The public, he well knows, would be shocked to hear of a scuffle in a church, and he can venture, therefore, to provoke a scuffle. No one will be found to tread upon the tail of his chasuble, however temptingly it may be trailed.' *Times*, 19 Jan. 1880.

58 In 1878, for example, the CA initiated eight lawsuits, and seven of them were vetoed; cf. Bentley, *Ritualism and Politics*, p. 103.

Addressing the annual meeting of the Church Pastoral-Aid Society in 1876, Lord Shaftesbury admitted that he expected little to come from the Public Worship Regulation Act because of the episcopal veto. He said, 'Notwithstanding the new court of law, Ritualism is more rife, more active, and more insolent than ever it was before. (Hear, hear.) I never thought that Court would produce much effect, partly because, owing to the restrictions which are imposed, I did not believe many causes would be brought before it. (Hear, hear.)' Cited in the *Record*, 8 May 1876.

According to Owen Chadwick, the increasing use of the episcopal veto had two results. The first was an expansion of the limits of toleration allowed for ritual innovation. There was an immediate correlation between the halt of prosecution and the expansion of liberty. Second, there was a growth of the discretionary power of the episcopacy, or at least an expanded use of the power the bishops already had, with a corresponding increase in their authority and influence throughout the church; cf. Chadwick, *Victorian Church, Part Two*, pp. 348-50.

59 Archbishop Tait responded with scant sympathy to a protest from the parishioners of St. Vedast's during the imprisonment of Dale. He did express his regret that the complainants felt compelled to enforce the judgment immediately, arguing that it would have been better to let Dale continue in his defiance for three years and then be deprived of his benefice. But, he concluded, Dale was ultimately responsible; regardless of the court's decisions, he owed his obedience to his bishop: 'Have Mr. Dale and his supporters forgotten that the Convocation of the province of Canterbury has distinctly pronounced, in full accordance with the advice tendered by the hundred bishops of the Anglican communion assembled at Lambeth from all parts of the world, that the Bishop of each diocese is to be obeyed by his presbyters when he forbids the introduction of changes from established ritual, and that the changes Mr. Dale has of late years introduced in St. Vedast's Church are distinctly forbidden by the Bishop to whom he sworn canonical obedience? Unless, therefore, Mr. Dale claims to be entirely a law to himself, and that there is no authority to the decisions of which he will bow, he ought to have no hesitation in dropping the usages which his Bishop has condemned.' Correspondence cited in the *Times*, 13 Nov. 1880.

Bishops Woodford and Magee applauded Tait's letter and took a similar view of the rush to imprison Dale. Like Tait, they thought Lord Penzance had the authority not to punish him with an immediate sentence but to wait three years and then deprive him of his benefice. Correspondence reprinted in MacDonnell, *Life of Magee, vol. 2*, pp. 144-45.

60 Correspondence cited in the *Times*, 29 Nov. 1880.
61 Jackson concluded that the crime did not warrant imprisonment and thought the harshness of the sentence would only encourage public sympathy for the Ritualists. Further, he doubted that any of those who supported the Public Worship Regulation Act had such a penalty in mind. Ibid. (their italics).
62 'The real danger of our times lies,' said the Bishop, 'not in ritual but in doctrine, and is to be met, therefore, not in law courts or by Acts of Parliament, but in our catechizings, our confirmation and Bible classes, by the Press,

and especially in our pulpits; not by controversy, however, nor by denunciations either of error or of those who teach it, but by the plain, patient, systematic, and persevering inculcation of the truth.' The *Times* viewed Bishop Jackson's charge as a moderate and sensible review of the problem. In an editorial the paper wrote, 'The Bishop reiterates previous warnings against the excesses of the Ritualistic school, and a considerable part of his charge is devoted to this purpose. His warnings are, however, both gentle and hopeful, and he concludes his retrospect in language of encouragement and confidence.' Cited in the *Times*, 1 Nov. 1879.

63   The protesters argued, in their memorial, that the promoter of the suit, John Martin, was not even a parishioner and that some consideration ought to be given to the fact that Mackonochie was a man of great devotion and zeal. Bishop Jackson replied that Martin had been a leader of the parish, a devout Sunday School teacher, and helper of the poor for over thirty years. 'That he has not attended worship in your church may be reasonably accounted for by his knowledge that it was conducted in a manner and with ceremonies different from the usage of the Church of England for 300 years.' With regard to Mackonochie's zeal, the bishop admitted that he too appreciated his work and effort. But, he wrote, 'I only regret the more that all this was not done, as I believe it might have been done just as well, without the disregard of the laws and customs of the Church of England and disobedience to lawful authority, which have caused so much disquiet and disunion in the Church, so much trouble to yourselves, and to me so much anxiety and sorrow.'

Jackson concluded that Mackonochie's logic, if applied across the church, could be used by a heretic to defend his own personal doctrine and to refuse to obey either bishop or court. 'You must not be surprised, then,' he concluded, 'if I should hesitate to interfere if it should appear needful to take further proceedings in the case of Mr. Mackonochie; much and heartily as I should rejoice if he himself should render any such step unnecessary by abstaining from a line of conduct which seems to offer impunity to the teaching of errors which he abhors, and which he himself would expect the Bishops to do their utmost to "banish and drive away".' Correspondence cited in the *Times*, 7 Jan. 1880.

64   Bishop Selwyn refused to allow proceedings when the Wolverhampton Working Men's Branch of the CA complained about Charles Bodington, Vicar of St. Andrew's, Wolverhampton. He wrote, 'I have no sympathy with the proceedings of the Church Association.... You cannot expect me to take any part in this strife. My office is that of mediator. You have carefully studied the Public Worship Regulation Act, but you have hitherto kept out of sight that provision of the Act which is most in accordance with the spirit of the Gospel and the Book of Common Prayer. You have not, so far as I know, offered to the Rev. C. Bodington to refer the whole question to the Bishop, who may decide it without appeal. I have reason to think that by so doing you may restore peace to two parishes which will otherwise be hopelessly divided.' Correspondence cited in the *Record*, 21 March 1877. Selwyn's decision was supported by Archbishop Tait. In his view, Bodington had shown himself willing to make some concessions and to give heed

to his bishop's admonitions. For correspondence between Bodington and the two bishops, cf. Davidson, *Life of Tait, vol. 2*, pp. 254-60.

In late 1878, Selwyn's successor similarly refused to allow proceedings against Bodington and two others. Bishop William Maclagan justified his decision by saying that he would not "interfere with an arrangement which was come to between the Rev. Gentleman and the late Bishop of Lichfield." Correspondence cited in the *Record*, 23 Dec. 1878.

Bishop Fraser of Manchester, who had demonstrated his fervent anti-Ritualism in the Green case, responded negatively to the local branch of the CA, which had complained concerning the ritual introduced by Rev. J. Knox Little, Incumbent of St. Alban's, Strangeways, and Canon of Worcester. Fraser wrote, 'I cannot recognise the right of an external body such as the Manchester branch of the Church Association to interfere in matters of ecclesiastical order and discipline between a Bishop and his clergy.' Correspondence cited in the *Record*, 24 Oct. 1881.

65 In 1877, Bishop Magee of Peterborough had vetoed a case against the Rev. A. H. Winter of Weedon Beck, Northamptonshire. Many of the charges were deemed insignificant by the bishop and unworthy of controversy. But the most important factor in his decision was the fact that 'the incumbent had declared himself ready and willing to obey the Bishop's directions in each and all of the said matters.' Cited in the *Record*, 29 March 1877.

66 With regard to several other undefined allegations, Thorold chose to take the word of Berkeley who had pledged to abstain rather than that of the complainants who charged him with continued disobedience. 'Though I observe that two of your number are prepared, if needful, to verify on oath all the statements in your memorial, I prefer, out of two inevitable alternatives, to conjecture that there must have been some error of vision on your part rather than suppose that a young clergyman, for whose private character and diligent ministrations I have a sincere and kindly respect, can be capable of willfully deceiving me.' Correspondence cited in the *Times*, 18 Feb. 1878.

67 Thorold also defended Berkeley for administering communion to women 'dressed in the garb of nuns.' On that point, he wrote, 'I have simply to observe that if clergymen of the Church of England were to refuse to administer the Communion to pious women merely on the ground of some eccentricity of dress, or even extravagance in religious opinion, they would not only be guilty of grave personal injustice, but they would make themselves liable to proceedings at civil law.' Ibid.

68 He concluded, somewhat optimistically, 'You will probably agree with me in thinking that now that Mr. Berkeley's ministrations are quite divested of these irregularities, further interference with him or complaint against him, would assume a complexion and a character which I would regret to find it my duty to describe. English Churchmen, of whatever school, when fairly inside the lines of English formularies and ceremonial are entitled to claim from their fellow Churchmen toleration and from their Bishop protection.' Ibid.

The unsatisfied parishioners continued to complain about Berkeley, but Thorold's patience had been exhausted. He concluded, 'While a severe and unrelenting opposition must goad him eventually into a bitter and irreclaimable isolation, a wise and kind charity may win him yet further back within the lines of the English Church. It is certain that the future of our communion depends very much on the kindly wisdom with which the younger clergy are treated by their brethren. Where argument fails, kindness often touches. If we fail, it is better to try and fail than fail but not try. My duty, at any rate, is clear. Mr. Berkeley claims my protection, and while he deserves it he shall have it. Knowing what I should like another Bishop to be to any son of mine under similar circumstances, I have assured him that just so far as I can find a son in him shall he find a father in me.' Correspondence cited in the *Record*, 22 April 1878.

In 1881, Archbishop Tait noted, in response to the Five Deans' Memorial calling for toleration of the Ritualists and an end to all prosecution, that even if they did not respect the decisions of the courts, the clergy owed their obedience to their bishops. He pointed out to the memorialists that 'no case of prosecution for ritual has (at least for many years past) been allowed to proceed in the case of any clergyman who was willing to comply with such admonition.' Correspondence cited in the *Times*, 17 Jan. 1881.

69 The *Record* thought it a display of 'arbitrary and uncontrolled discretion' on the part of the bishop. *Record*, 10 March 1879. The *Times* initially adopted a similar view. In an editorial, the paper suggested that the importance of the case lay in the public concern for 'uniformity of ritual.... We might have adoration in one diocese, and in another a revival of the Puritan custom of sitting round a table in the middle of the chancel. It is not easy to see how a great public institution could be governed by such lax methods – if, indeed, it could be said, in such a case, to be governed at all. The pleas urged by the Bishop of Oxford why a Commission should not issue to inquire into the charges against Mr. Carter were obviously beside the mark. He may be an elderly and venerated clergyman, but he is accused of practices which have been condemned as unlawful.' *Times*, 10 March 1879.

70 Lord Chief Justice Cockburn, in his judgment, took a narrow view of episcopal discretion and suggested that 'extraneous circumstances or expedience were not legitimate reasons for the veto of prosecutions. Now, not only do we think that, on the construction of the statute, the Bishop had no discretion in this matter, but we are further of opinion that, the purpose of this legislation being to maintain uniformity of doctrine and ritual, and it being the right of the parishioners to have the services of the Church performed according to the law of the Church, even if the Bishop had discretionary authority in such a case, he ought, having here a judicial, or, at all events, a *quasi*-judicial duty to discharge, to have used it to allow an inquiry to take place.' Judgment of the Queen's Bench Division, cited in the *Times*, 10 March 1879.

71 The *Record* was quick to note that although the judgment was unanimous, one of the judges, Lord Justice Bramwell, had harsh words for both Carter and Mackarness: 'I have no doubt that the Right Rev. Prelate and the Rev. Gentleman who are appellants have been perfectly conscientious in their conduct in this matter. But it is admitted that Mr. Carter has committed and is willfully persisting in several breaches of the law of the land. By what

means he has persuaded himself that he can receive the wages of the State to do a certain duty and not do it, but do that which is opposed to it, I cannot conceive; and, with all submission, I feel nearly equal difficulty in understanding, how it can seem right to the Right Rev. Prelate not to bring him to justice.' Judgment of the Court of Appeal, cited in the *Record*, 2 June 1879.

In its editorial on the verdict, the *Times* reversed its earlier position and sided with Bishop Mackarness. The effect of the first judgment, the paper wrote, would have been 'to substitute for the arbitrament of the Bishop that of the Queen's Bench.' With regard to Bramwell's lecture, the *Times* thought he was in error. In fact, said the paper, 'Lord Justice Bramwell proposed to withdraw with one hand a good deal of what he had granted with the other. What would be the value of the Bishop's discretion if he is to be punished when he does not exercise it as some secular Court thinks that he ought?' While the paper sympathized with the promoters of the case, and suggested that Mackarness' application of his discretion had perhaps been too broad, it defended a larger view of episcopal authority. *Times*, 31 May 1879.

Almost a decade later, when Mackarness retired in failing health, the paper returned to the topic: 'The effect of this decision has been largely to check litigation in the matter of alleged Ritualistic practices, though whether the Bishop of Oxford has in all cases exercised his discretion with sound and impartial judgment is a question on which wide differences of opinion are likely to prevail, according to the ecclesiastical bias of those who entertain them.' *Times*, 23 June 1888.

72 Letter to the *Times*, 23 Dec. 1880. James Maden Holt, a member of the CA, immediately challenged Claughton's logic: 'What, in his opinion, ought laymen and clergymen to have done in the past, or what ought they to do now, to maintain the Protestant character which the Church of England has borne for 300 years, in the presence of a design, repeatedly and publicly avowed, to destroy that character?' Letter to the *Times*, 25 Dec. 1880.

73 They had, said Claughton, 'enabled certain sincere though misguided clergymen to pose as martyrs on grounds, doubtless, most unreal, but nevertheless misleading to the large number of persons who do not care to look closely into such things. Again, every day that the imprisonment of these gentlemen continues, the hands of a certain rival society are strengthened, a society already occupying in Church affairs a position similar to that of the Land League in Ireland.' Letter to the *Times*, 5 Jan. 1881.

74 Ibid.

75 Letter to the *Times*, 11 Jan. 1881. Claughton responded that he did not intend to question the motives the CA and fully agreed with their concerns but thought their appeal to the courts had been unsuccessful. It was evident that they had only made the situation more difficult for the bishops. While acknowledging the essentially lawless position of the Ritualists and affirming the necessity of a firm response, he warned that 'an indiscriminate attack upon ritual (I mean an attempt to enforce unduly one uniform rule without consideration of cases) may lead to an amount of resistance which it will be impossible to subdue without a disruption of the Church's unity;

and it is at such time to those who are the real authorities in such matters that we must look for the power to quiet the perturbed and angry spirit which has arisen.' Letter to the *Times*, 17 Jan. 1881.

76 During the controversy involving Bishop Mackarness in Oxford, the non-partisan Bishop Magee, who was generally opposed to prosecution, wrote in a letter, 'The nation will never tolerate absolute impunity for the clergy. Now, the bishops, since I have known them, have taken up – most mistakenly, as I think – the position that they will not prosecute. Well and good; that is an intelligible position, though a false one. But if they add to this Oxford's position, that they will stop any one else prosecuting, they will raise a storm that may blow down the Church.... The bishops abdicated when they assumed the non-prosecuting position. They must take the consequences now.' MacDonnell, *Life of Magee*, vol. 2, p. 109.

The *Quarterly Review* thought the Public Worship Regulation Act had been a failure but nevertheless complained that the bishops had no right to veto prosecutions simply to prevent imprisonments: 'Nothing can be more unreasonable or unfair. Can they not see that the moment it is understood that legal sentences will not be enforced, rebels and defendants of all kinds, clerical and lay, will simply laugh at all legal proceedings? People do not go to law for abstract declarations, but for practical results.' Anon., 'Ritualists and the Law,' *Quarterly Review*, p. 238.

77 The writer suggested that the Ritualists were determined to make the litigation as expensive as possible by appealing 'to every technicality which has nothing at all to do with the merits, and to the very courts which they profess to abhor most – the civil ones.' Anon., 'Ritualists and the Law,' *Quarterly Review*, p. 203.

78 Ibid.

79 Bishop Magee often complained in his private correspondence that the episcopacy was caught in the middle between the warring factions. He wrote to a Ritualist supporter in 1878, 'We may at least plead as proof of our wish to be fair that while the Ritualists complain of our tyranny and one-sidedness, the *Rock* and the *Record* never cease to abuse us for our treacherous connivance with Ritualism. As we cannot be at once the treacherous allies and the cruel oppressors of the same party in the Church, may it not after all be the case that we are striving under cruelly difficult circumstances to deal fairly by all?' MacDonnell, *Life of Magee*, vol. 2, p. 101. Later, after several of the imprisonments, he wrote to a friend, 'I cannot advocate unlimited concession to the Ritualists, and nothing less will satisfy them; while, on the other hand, I would be prepared to offer just enough of concession to enrage the Puritans.... It seems to me that the man in the middle is "safe" for nothing but a kicking from both sides.' Ibid., p. 150.

80 'It is certain that, in the event of the circumstances of the case compelling me to let it proceed, it would be with real and sorrowful slowness that I should use force, where a thousand times rather I would win by charity. Still in my own view of my function, for me to decline to administer the law, when such administration was on sufficient grounds proposed to me, would be to incur the risk, in the eyes of my countrymen, of being a lawbreaker myself.' Pastoral Letter of A. W. Thorold, cited in the *Record*, 22

Nov. 1878.
81 Pastoral Letter of A. W. Thorold, cited in the *Times*, 18 Nov. 1878.
82 Letter to the *Record*, 20 Nov. 1878.
83 *Record*, 22 Nov. 1878. Similarly, J. C. Miller, a widely respected moderate, hoped the pastoral would have a broad influence. In a sermon, he suggested that its position, 'if pondered by every bishop, clergyman, and Church layman, would go far to heal our difficulties and to promote unity so far as that be practicable in the present state of our Church.' Cited in the *Record*, 18 Nov. 1878.
84 The *Times* responded somewhat ambiguously to Thorold's pastoral, but in general, took a negative view. Unlike the *Record*, the *Times* feared that other bishops would follow Thorold's example, leading to what was, effectively, a congregational form of church government with no uniformity of worship. In adopting a program of isolation, wrote the paper, the 'Bishops, it can hardly be denied, accept a view of the Church of England which is scarcely the view of a State Church. It has hitherto been supposed that the benefices of the Church of England were the inheritance of the parishioners, and not the property of congregations. A certain discipline was presumed to prevail in edifices which Bishops had consecrated; and Bishops were presumed to be its guardian. Henceforth, at any rate in the diocese of Rochester, the clergy are to say what ritual is to be observed in their churches.... Be it so; but the ninety-eighth Bishop of Rochester must be prepared to find that in the new policy of isolation many persons will discover an argument for a yet more logical system of Voluntaryism.' *Times*, 18 Nov. 1878.
85 Tait said, 'What I would wish to urge on the attention of all of you is this – the absolute necessity, if you are dissatisfied with the present state of matters, of gravely and calmly considering the side issues raised in this controversy about ritual: I mean those which refer to the highest Court of Appeal, and the constitution of the Inferior Courts, and the rights of Convocation, and the authority of the Bishops. You will readily allow that these questions, which have reference, on the one hand, to the independence of the Church and the Christian conscience, and, on the other, to the controlling power which every well-ordered State must exercise over all bodies, ecclesiastical or other, which exist within its dominions, are extremely grave.... What I wish to commend to all who are agitated by recent events is this – that they should calmly ask themselves definitely what they want. The answer cannot be the short and easy one that they desire all intricate questions of law and procedure to be decided according to their personal wishes. If they are anxious for certain important changes in our existing constitution, let them state explicitly what they are, and they may rest assured that their suggestions will be respectfully and calmly considered.' Cited in the *Times*, 18 Dec. 1880.
86 The memorial was signed by R. W. Church, Dean of St. Paul's, and four other deans, W. C. Lake (Durham), B. M. Cowie (Manchester), Alwyne Compton (Worcester), and A. P. Purey (York), along with numerous other prominent High Church clergy. Reprinted in the *Times*, 12 Jan. 1881; cf. Appendix J.
87 Dean Church also complained about the courts in a letter to the *Times*. In re-

sponse to Tait's speech, he suggested that 'the short and easy method' of dealing with the Ritualists, had been for their critics to demand that they 'submit to all that Parliament orders as any other public functionaries – to submit or to resign; and by an established Church, as used in this argument, is sometimes expressly signified in words, but always implied, whether people see what they mean or not, a State Church, deriving all its rights, duties, and powers from Parliament.' In Church's opinion, the concept of the church as a divinely instituted body was given up entirely and the state was elevated to a false position. Letter to the *Times*, 16 Dec. 1880.

Church's argument was challenged by a number of correspondents and the *Times* itself in an editorial. W. R. Fremantle, Rector of St. Mary's, Bryanston-square, and a prominent Evangelical, suggested that Church had attacked a false and extreme position held by no one, in order to refute it with a rhetorical flourish. But, Fremantle concluded, Church had avoided the central point. 'The only question before the public now is whether the law, as defined by Parliament, is to be obeyed by Churchmen. I need not quote at length authorities such as Hooker, who closes his investigation of the matter with the words, "To define of our own Church's regiment the Parliament of England hath competent authority." If the Dean does not agree in this, let him say so and give the reason. If he does, let him use his great authority in the Church, not to charge the supporters of law with theories which they would probably repudiate, but to induce those whose theories contravene the law to obey it.' Letter to the *Times*, 18 Dec. 1880.

The *Times* challenged Church's portrayal of a simplistic erastianism. If anyone had stated the matter in such terms, Church owed it to his audience to give specifics. The paper continued, 'Tones are fair matters for criticism, but not of argument, and the present is an argumentative appeal. When prelates, or statesmen, or judges, or public writers are insisting on obedience to the laws of the realm, especially the laws constituting conditions and safeguards for the due exercise of spiritual authority, they may as easily say a word too much as too little, too strong as not strong enough. But nobody who can be fairly quoted in this matter has said that a Church in a position to be called a State Church derives all its duties, rights, and powers from Parliament. The whole argument falls to the ground from the failure of the alleged fact.' *Times*, 18 Dec. 1880.

W. H. Milman, Rector of St. Augustine's and St. Faith's, London, challenged Church to explain how it was, given his position on the state's authority, that he had himself 'very recently and in a perfectly gratuitous way... invoked the aid of the State' with regard to his own cathedral? Dean Church had apparently obtained an Act of Parliament to do away with an old order of minor canons 'who discharged many spiritual functions and administered sacraments' at the cathedral in order to replace them with a newly constituted body that owed its existence entirely 'to a recent Act of Parliament,' discharging its spiritual duties entirely as a result of the Act of Parliament and an Order in Council, both of which were 'obtained by the earnest solicitation, not to say importunity, of the Dean and Chapter.' Milman concluded, "I have my own solution of the apparent inconsistency, but it would be interesting, and perhaps amusing, to hear the Dean's.' Ibid.

88 Reprinted in the *Times*, 2 Feb. 1881; cf. Appendix K. The signatures on the anti-Ritualist memorial were headed by two former colonial bishops, Charles Perry, Canon of Llandaff, and V. W. Ryan, Archdeacon of Craven. In addition it was signed by seven Evangelical Deans: A. Boyd of Exeter, Francis Close of Carlisle, W. R. Fremantle of Ripon, J. S. Howson of Chester, H. Law of Gloucester, J. J. S. Perowne of Peterborough, and R. Payne Smith of Canterbury.

The *Record* published frequent updates on the signatures added. By the end of February, the memorial had been signed by 3,230 clergy, including three colonial bishops, ten deans, ten archdeacons, four masters of colleges, five principals, twenty-two canons, and eighty-seven prebendaries and honorary canons. *Record*, 23 Feb. 1881.

89 'We, the undersigned, lay members of the Church of England, beg leave hereby most respectfully to express to your Grace our firm attachment to the doctrines and ceremonial, established in the Church of England at the Reformation, and set forth in the Book of Common Prayer. We desire to represent to your Grace that whilst we are most anxious to maintain such reasonable latitude of opinion and practice as is not inconsistent with the teaching of the Formularies, Articles, and Homilies of the Church of England, taken in their plain grammatical sense, or with a faithful adherence to the rubrics of the Book of Common Prayer, as interpreted by the custom of three hundred years, we, nevertheless, feel ourselves constrained to enter our solemn and emphatic protest against the toleration, within the Church of England, of any doctrines or practices which favour the restoration of the Romish Mass, or any colourable imitation thereof, – any reintroduction of the Confessional, – or any assumption of sacerdotal pretensions on the part of the clergy, in the ministration of the Word and Sacraments.' Cited in the *Record*, 20 May 1881.

90 Tait referred to a letter he had written to Canon Wilkinson, in which he had elaborated his position. He continued, 'It certainly may fairly be taken to show that there must be some exceptional difficulty in present arrangements when clergymen of otherwise unimpeachable character think it their duty to run the risk of having their usefulness in their parishes rudely interrupted by the authority of the law rather than yield to those set over them in the Lord that degree of willing obedience which seems to most men to be enjoined alike by the traditions of their Church and by the written words of the Prayer-book (in the Preface 'concerning the service of the Church') as well as by their promise of canonical obedience.' Correspondence cited in the *Times*, 17 Jan. 1881.

The *Edinburgh Review* complained that, however much they spoke of 'the living voice of the Church,' the Ritualists had little respect for it 'so far as it has been expressed by her duly appointed rulers.' In that respect, wrote the essayist, they had little in common with their Oxford Movement predecessors. While still proclaiming the importance of apostolic succession, the Ritualists had little respect for the bishops, and the general tone adopted 'towards the most distinguished members of the Episcopal Bench is that of contempt, and not infrequently of abuse. The funds of the English Church Union are avowedly raised and expended in enabling clergymen to resist the so-called "unreasonable and illegal demands" of their bishops.' Anonymous, 'Ritualistic Literature,' *Edinburgh Review* 151 (1880): 320.

91 The Ritualists were not interested merely in obtaining '"a tolerant recognition of divergent ritual practice." To do the Ritualists justice, they and their recognized leaders are perfectly frank in the matter. The colour of a vestment or the fashion of a ceremony are nothing to them save as they represent a definite Eucharistic doctrine. Of that doctrine it is sufficient to say that it is deeply repugnant to the vast majority of English Churchmen, and therefore, it is idle to ask for toleration of the ritual which represents it, unless a like toleration is claimed for the doctrine itself. But to ask for a toleration of the eucharistic doctrine involved in the service of the Mass, or in anything at all closely resembling it, is virtually to ask that the work of the Reformation in England should be undone.' *Times*, 12 Jan. 1881.

J. S. Howson, the non-partisan Dean of Chester, strongly rejected the idea that the clergy ought to be free to express doctrine through ritual. There was a great deal of difference between the liberty they had in their preaching and the ordering of the worship service. In this regard he cited both Bishop Wilberforce and the Judicial Committee in its judgment in the Bennett case. While the clergy were given great freedom in their preaching, the ritual of the church belonged to all and variations were to be kept within strictly defined limits. Letter to the *Times*, 27 Jan. 1881.

92 The paper suggested that the effect of the Ritualist innovations was particularly troublesome in country parishes. In the cities, it was a simple matter for a worshipper to go a few blocks and find another church. 'But the country worshipper has no choice but to be content with the service provided for him. A new incumbent may introduce practices unfamiliar and distasteful. There is nothing for parishioners but to submit and grumble, and the temper thus engendered becomes the source of discord and ill-feeling in a once peaceful parish.' Ibid.

J. C. Ryle rejected any comparison between sins of commission and those of omission. In his first charge to the clergy of Liverpool, he refused to compare 'the conduct of the man who, in administering the Lord's Supper, introduces novelties of most serious doctrinal significance, and the conduct of the man who does not observe some petty obsolete direction, of no doctrinal significance at all.' Ryle, *No Uncertain Sound*, p. 24.

93 Pusey wrote, 'Whatever mistakes any of the Ritualists made formerly, no Ritualist would now, I believe, wish to make any change without the hearty goodwill of the people. But all along those who have closely observed the Ritualist movement have seen that it has been especially the work of the laity. While the clergyman has been hesitating, his parishioners have often presented him with the vestment which they wished him to wear. Mr. Enraght and Mr. Mackonochie have not been struggling for themselves, but for their people. St. Alban's was built by a pious High Church layman in what was one of the worst localities in London. It is now full of a religious population, who join intelligently in the service provided for them and love it. Agents of the Church Association tried in vain for years to find a third parishioner in the mission at the London Docks to disturb the Ritual of the priest who had won them to God, and whom, with the Ritual which he had

taught them, they loved – Mr. Lowder.' Letter to the *Times*, 14 Jan. 1881.
94 Ibid.
95 Letter to the *Times*, 15 Jan. 1881. W. C. Palmer, Secretary of the Council of the CA, noted that the 'pious High Church layman' to whom Pusey referred was Mr. Hubbard. In 1874, however, Hubbard had spoken of the ceremonial innovations at St. Alban's as 'the one great grief of his whole life.' Letter to the *Times*, 19 Jan. 1881.

In fact, Hubbard had been disturbed by Mackonochie's innovations almost from the very opening of the church. Hubbard was opposed to prosecution, although Bishop Tait offered him that option. His hope for episcopal intervention can be found in his correspondence with Tait. Cf. Davidson, *Life of Tait, vol. 1*, pp. 423-36.

A writer in the *Quarterly Review* complained that it was 'absurd' to suggest that a congregation should be allowed to decide if the clergy could go on breaking the law. But one also had to ask who composed the congregation? Often, complained the author, it contained few of the parishioners, who had likely been driven away by the innovations. The essayist was particularly concerned for country parishes and suggested that the Ritualists were the oppressors of the laity there. The 'Church of England may be practically extinguished' in a country parish 'by the willfulness of a parson who has the art of driving away his proper congregation.' Anon., 'Ritualists and the Law,' *Quarterly Review*, pp. 210-11.
96 Letter to the *Times*, 19 Jan. 1881.
97 He wrote, 'The reasoning of the Bennett judgment went one way, the sentence went the other. What the Evangelical party affirm is that the doctrine of Scripture and of our Reformed Church was most distinctly enunciated by "The Court of Final Appeal" on the three points brought before them – the Real Presence, the Doctrine of Sacrifice, and the Subject of Adoration. The language used by Mr. Bennett was declared to be "rash, ill-judged, and perilously near a violation of the law," and Mr. Bennett, being given the benefit of a doubt that his words did not mean all that they seemed to mean, escaped, so to speak, by the skin of his teeth. His language was tolerated, but his doctrine was condemned. It is, therefore, contrary to fact to say that in this judgment the Ritualist doctrine of the Eucharist was "fully conceded to the Ritualist party".' Letter to the *Times*, 20 Jan. 1881.
98 Davies also challenged the historical accuracy of Pusey's claims. He wrote, 'Cranmer did not introduce the ritual; he consented to its continuance for a short time, and then he abolished it. From the time of the second Prayer Book of Edward VI., "the ritual" has never been "introduced" into English parish churches except by Queen Mary and the Ritualists of today.' Letter to the *Times*, 15 Jan. 1881.

The *Quarterly Review* had argued the point in an 1876 essay. The claim for the liberty of the clergy to enact ritual, said the author, was not as broad as the liberty enjoyed in preaching. And it could not be elevated over the respect due to 'the consciences of the congregation.' It was called 'common prayer' precisely because the laity had the right to expect a particular form of service in the national church. 'If the minister be allowed to introduce at his own will variations in the rites and ceremonies that seem to him to interpret the doctrine of the service in a particular direction, the service ceases to be what it was meant to be, common ground on which all Church people may meet, though they differ about some doctrines.' Anon., 'Church Innovations,' *Quarterly Review*, pp. 563-65.

99 Letter to the *Times*, 19 Jan. 1881.
100 Pusey offered as evidence the letters he had written challenging the CA to prosecute him rather than Bennett. Bennett, adopted the traditional Ritualist position, which denied the legitimacy of the Privy Council to rule in spiritual affairs, and let the suit proceed undefended. Pusey, however, promised to argue the case in full on its own merits (without appeal to technicalities) and to abide by the decision of the court. The CA, however, without noting any particular reason, other than the fact that the Bennett case was already underway, declined his offer. Letter to the *Times*, 26 Jan. 1881.
101 Palmer wrote, 'The Council were advised that although Dr. Pusey offered to impose no legal hindrances to proceedings being taken against him, such an offer would not have been recognized or acted on by the authorities, and the Council would have incurred serious expenses to no purpose.' Letter to the *Times*, 31 Jan. 1881.

Pusey's credibility was defended by H. P. Liddon, who claimed that Pusey had only discovered his immunity long after the Bennett trial and the issuing of his challenge to the CA. Letter to the *Times*, 2 Feb. 1881.
102 Letter to the *Record*, 25 June 1879.
103 At a meeting of the Evangelical Protestant Union, H. Hely Smith, Vicar of Market Rasen, spoke of the need to convince others that theirs was no 'factious' party movement. He continued, 'One of the great obstacles to the spread of the Protestant truth was the apathy of the great bulk of the Evangelical party.' By Smith's account, there were seven thousand clergy in the Church of England who believed the doctrines of the Reformation, but too few 'were willing to come forward as the pronounced defenders of the Protestant faith," fearing that they might be labeled "controversialists.' *Record*, 20 Oct. 1880.

The CA, by this time, was apparently concerned about a decline of membership and influence. It advertised in the *Record* that a consultative meeting would be held the day before its fall meeting, for 'framing such resolutions as... should aim at effecting such changes in the organization of the Association as it is hoped would tend to increase its efficiency, and enlarge its influence.' Advertisement in the *Record*, 27 Oct. 1880.
104 *Record*, 3 Nov. 1880.
105 'We doubt not that ardent spirits exist who... will even accuse the Council of a change of front if they forsake it. At first sight there may appear to be justice in the accusation, but we think we have said enough to show that such is not the true view of the case. The past prosecutions were to ascertain our position and to vindicate great principles; but fresh prosecutions would be useless for these purposes, and would simply be directed against the individuals concerned. We are bound to confess that, having regard to this, and to the fact that such proceedings can only terminate either in failure or in the imprisonment of offending clergymen, we very seriously doubt whether

fresh funds expended in this mode would benefit the objects for which the Church Association exists.... It certainly appears to us that before attempting to bring fresh offenders before the Ecclesiastical Courts, it is most desirable that those Courts should be clothed with power to inflict punishments which, while effective and sufficient, shall yet bear a due relation to the character of the offences committed, and be in harmony with the feelings of modern days.' Ibid.

106 'Mr. Dale and his party are trading on the sympathy which they hope to excite in the public mind. At present there are no symptoms of its existence, and certainly if the facts are remembered it is difficult to conceive on what it could be founded. Mr. Dale can at any moment regain his liberty by obedience to the law.' *Record*, 5 Nov. 1880.

107 The proposals read:

'To draw up a statement vindicating the position of the Association, setting forth the work it has hitherto effected, and that which remained to be done, with a distinct and emphatic declaration that the Council were profoundly impressed with the importance of the crisis, and would continue to the utmost of their ability to carry out all measures that may be found necessary for the purpose of effecting the object they have in view – the elimination of Romanism from the Church of England;

'To continue the existing suits and to enforce the judgments by all means that the law permitted;

'To advise the Branches to recommend parishioners to submit to the Bishops in proper form every case where illegal practices were carried on, with a view to the exercise of their episcopal authority to suppress the illegalities;

'To proceed with all possible speed and care in the preparation of a Bill for securing amendments in Ecclesiastical procedure, in order that it might be introduced during the present session of Parliament;

'To seek an opportunity of approaching the Archbishops and Bishops, and urging them to increased efforts to stay the plague of Ritualism, particularly at a time when the support of all true members of the Church will be especially required;

'To keep a vigilant watch on all departures from Protestant principles on the part of those in authority, whether in Church or state, and to expose the same through the press and otherwise;

'To convene as soon as may be convenient a meeting of Protestant Churchmen at which an outspoken declaration of policy should be made, and an appeal addressed to the country for a new Guarantee Fund in support of the vigorous policy contemplated by the Council.' Cited in the *Times*, 13 May 1880.

108 Two speakers thought prosecution ought to be used only sparingly, but they were strongly opposed by numerous respondents. In addition, there was continuing discussion of the propriety of attendance at official church meetings, such as congresses or diocesan conferences, where Ritualists would be present. Moderates had long since settled on a policy of participation, and that view was expressed at the CA meeting by at least one lay member, Major General Burrows. He was opposed by several others, how-

ever, including W. W. Phelps, who thought 'it very undesirable for Evangelical men to give the sanction of their presence to members of the Society of the Holy Cross and other lawbreakers.' *Record*, 14 May 1880.

109 Ryle felt compelled to withdraw as a Bishop-elect, but affirmed that he had altered none of his opinions with regard to Ritualism, and had 'nothing to regret' with regard to his participation in the CA. Correspondence cited in the *Record*, 26 April 1880.

110 Cited in the *Record*, 5 Nov. 1880. Apparently fearing that they had begun to lose some support, the council drew up a position paper, which traced the history of some of the more important cases and their results, before elaborating the organization's future policy. 'The Church Association: Its Past Action and Future Policy,' reprinted in its entirety in Ibid.; cf. Appendix L.

111 A Capt. Frobisher, representing the Woolwich and Plumstead Branch read a list of resolutions, the second of which declared 'that until an alteration in the existing law has been secured, this Branch is opposed to the institution of any fresh legal proceedings, such as might necessitate the formation of a new Guarantee Fund.' He did not, however, appear to oppose further litigation as a matter of principle. Ibid.

112 'I did not believe that "friendly suits," as some wished to regard the early prosecutions, would carry any weight as such, when so regarded only on one side. I did not believe that prosecutions, even though resulting in imprisonment and loss of goods, would lead any sincere men, however unsound their doctrine, to do that which I should be ashamed to think of any whose doctrine is sound being led to do, – obey man's law in opposition to what they think, however erroneously, to be God's law. I did not believe that men who look upon the Church of England as, by means of apostolic succession, organically a party of what they consider as the Holy Catholic Church, would leave it because the decisions of courts of law were against them, any more than we should leave our country if there were bad laws and bad judges. And I did not believe that judgments dealing with matters of conscience could be enforced without processes resulting in imprisonment.' Letter to the *Record*, 10 Nov. 1880.

113 'If imprisonment fails, what will the Church Association do next? In opposition to Mr. Kennion's noble protest against the use of such means of coercion as imprisonment, Mr. Lovell referred to the command in Deuteronomy, "As to what should be done by a father to his son if he departed from the ordained worship," adding that "death was the punishment of those who contravened the Jewish system. Of course," he continued, "Christianity, in the days of the apostles, had no power." (I quote from the *Press*, having lost the part of the *Record* containing Mr. Lovell's speech) [in fact, the *Record* had not printed Lovell's extreme speech]. The Church of Rome, by inflicting death, when it had the power, on those whom they branded as heretics, extinguished Protestantism in Spain and elsewhere, and such a defence of the Inquisition by a Roman Catholic would be consistent. I am deeply pained at its adoption in an assembly of Protestants by a member of the Council of the Church Association. But it is, as I have often said, the legitimate result of what has preceded, and I think Mr. Lovell's incautious words must open the eyes of some Christian men to the nature of the policy

for which such a defence is needed.' Ibid.
114 Ibid. One anonymous writer wrote to support Garratt's protest. He thought the 'two prominent characteristics' of the discussion at the recent CA conference were, 'first, a consciousness that the litigation had not produced any diminution in the illegal practices, and secondly, a remarkable recklessness as to what would follow from a perseverance in the same course.' He went on to express his fears, somewhat prophetically, with regard to the results of a continuation of the policy: the bishops would be driven to protect the offenders, moderate Evangelicals would be driven away, and the general public would be driven to sympathize with the Ritualists. Letter (signed 'A Lawyer') to the *Record*, 12 Nov. 1880.
115 Kennion responded that he had supported prosecution originally, but thought the Dale case ought to be the end of it. 'Let the one case suffice for an example. We shall lose nothing, but gain everything, by remembering that "the quality of mercy is not strained." We shall retain the measure of public sympathy we now possess, and win over a good deal more. We shall throw the whole burden on the bishops, to whom it properly belongs, for they are the true executive; and public opinion will not only support them in taking much more stringent measures than heretofore, but will scarcely, after this great storm, allow them to neglect such measures.

'But if, on the other hand, further imprisonments are insisted upon, I warn my friends that they are playing with a very dangerous weapon. We do not mean to persecute. We deny that we have persecuted. But it will be out of our power to prevent a large number of persons from regarding our action as persecution, and we should not "let our good be evil spoken of." We are bound to consider in such matters the public conscience as well as our own. We cannot afford to go dead against the feeling of the community at large, the Bishops, and many of the most spiritually minded of Evangelical men, in the employment of a method which is without precedent in the New Testament, and against which the tenor of all Church history is a protest." Letter to the *Record*, 17 Nov. 1880.
116 'The Church Association set vigorously to work fifteen years ago with ample funds and untiring energy and the best legal advice, and the result is, as some not listened to foretold it would be, that, fifteen years after the commencement of prosecutions, Ritualism is stronger than ever.' Garratt, *What Shall We Do?*, p. 13.
117 Ibid., p. 15.
118 Ibid., p. 23. Garratt was also disturbed by the tone adopted by Evangelical controversialists. The party's message had only been hindered, he said, 'by the use of carnal weapons in our contention with error, – by want of fairness in controversy, as shown by an apparent inability to see the real meaning, and own the moral honesty of those from whom we differ, – by taking into alliance ungodly men, whose objections are not ours, and who would equally oppose whatever was troublesome, – and by the admixture of worldly methods in our Christian work.' Ibid., p. 24. He went on to note that many of the Ritualists were men of conscience who had suffered much for their beliefs and deserved a fair debate. 'I have,' he concluded, 'no sympathy whatever with the cynical tone of the daily press, or the mean jests of little

minds who laugh at consciences, having none of their own.' Ibid., p. 29.
119 Cited in the *Record*, 11 March 1881.
120 'The Council of the Church Association have need of very great judgment in directing the future policy of that body with reference to the vexed question of prosecution. While it is quite plain that the objects of the Association are in full harmony with the views of the whole Evangelical party, and of not a few outside it, it is not less plain that the Church Association has not by its operations acquired the entire support of all who might have been expected to belong to it. We may add that a conceivable line of policy, if adopted, would go far to alienate a large number, perhaps the majority, of its clerical members.' *Record*, 11 March 1881.
121 *Record*, 17 Jan. 1881.
122 Ibid. During the summer of 1883, the *Record* reported on the work of Rev. J. W. Marshall, Vicar of St. John's, Blackheath, who spoke to several of the regional lay and clerical meetings as the Secretary of the Central Committee. He encouraged the formation of committees in each diocese and the election of representatives to the Central Committee. That body proposed topics for discussion at the various regional meetings. Chief among them, during the summer of 1883, was the question of Evangelical participation in church congresses and diocesan conferences. A majority of the speakers, representing the increasingly influential opinion of the moderate section of the party, took a positive view of the meetings, arguing that their participation was necessary both to give voice to the positions of their own party and to exercise a restraining influence on the extremist section of the High Church party. Cf. *Record*, 8 and 15 June 1883.

In its obituary for Edward Garbett, published in October 1887, the paper noted that he had been greatly concerned for the unity of the Evangelical party and was a particularly important figure in the movement: 'He spared no time, no labour, and no expense, and if now that result has been obtained in the formation of the Evangelical Union of Clerical and Lay Associations throughout the country, it has been in large measure owing to his foresight, energy, and influence.' *Record*, 14 Oct. 1887.

CHAPTER 8

The Decline of the Anti-Ritualist Movement

By the early 1880s, the cracks forming within the Evangelical party over the tone and direction of the anti-Ritualist movement had developed into an open rift. The concern of conservatives was evident in their strident reaction to the perceived compromises that moderates were willing to make in accommodation to the sensitivities of the age. Their change of heart was disturbing for convinced anti-Ritualists on two counts. First, moderates were willing to adopt ceremonial innovations that were popular with their parishioners; but what they viewed as harmless concessions to aesthetic taste, conservatives condemned as evidence of the spreading influence of Ritualism. Second, it was clear that moderate support for the Church Association was waning. The early imprisonments had damaged the anti-Ritualist movement to a certain degree, but criticism was largely limited to a few scattered voices. With the case of Sidney Green, however, the sound of the opposition swelled to that of a massive (and probably surpliced) choir.

The scandal of Green's lengthy imprisonment also resulted in the appointment of a second government commission. The first attempted to deal with the controverted elements of ceremonial innovation. The second sought to find a way to reform the ecclesiastical courts system that was acceptable to both sides. Neither was successful. It was left for the bishops to find a peaceful settlement to the continuing controversy. Their efforts, usually enforced by their veto, were condemned by anti-Ritualists as one-sided compromise. J. C. Ryle, the Evangelical Bishop of Liverpool, allowed one final case to proceed. James Bell Cox was briefly imprisoned in the mid-1880s, but the case had little impact. The vast majority of Evangelicals had voiced their opposition to the prosecution and were chiefly concerned to distance the party as a whole from the case. Bell Cox was soon released on appeal, and the anti-Ritualists, with their reputation already in decline and their influence on the wane, were only further damaged by the ineffective results.

Evangelical Reactions to the Growing Influence of Ritualism

The spreading influence of the Ritualists remained a sore point for conservative Evangelicals throughout the later years of the century. Despite years of controversial polemic and the numerous legal judgments obtained by the CA, the popularity of many innovations continued to spread, and Evangelicals were divided in their response. Conservatives, such as G. T. Fox, viewed the growth of aesthetic elements in the worship service as evidence of the Ritualists' influence. Like Francis Close some years before, Fox noted its impact on church architecture and renovation, much of which was financially supported by the Ritualists, and complained that the 'fashion of the age' was linked to a 'sensuous, unspiritual, superstitious creed.' According to Fox, moderates, and the laity in particular, were not sufficiently aware of 'the danger to spiritual religion and to the principles of our Protestant Church,' and they had not set themselves to oppose it as firmly as they ought.[1] Fox feared Evangelicals were continually compromising and allowing the Ritualist influence to work its way into their own churches. Inevitably, he concluded, the changes were all in one direction – they were part of the movement toward 'a more sensuous service, a more ornate ritual, never in the opposite direction.'[2]

In contrast, A. W. Thorold, who later became the Bishop of Rochester, addressed the Islington Clerical Conference in 1875, on 'the duty of the Evangelical clergy in their ministrations in relation to the aestheticism and taste for ritual spreading so extensively among those not connected with the ritualistic party.' Thorold, who adopted a more moderate position than other speakers at the conference, suggested that the spread of aestheticism was a matter of fact that had to be acknowledged.[3] He argued for a broad degree of toleration, allowing for differences of opinion, styles of worship, and the desires of the congregation. In conclusion, he suggested that Evangelicals, while maintaining their distinctive beliefs and simple style of worship, 'need not be guilty of the narrowness of vision that measured all mankind by their own measuring line, nor lose the sympathies of the young, the educated, the devout, whether among clergy or laity, by a sourness of isolation or an obstinate refusal to read the signs of the times.'[4]

In 1877, the *Record* attempted to measure more precisely the spread of Ritualism by tabulating statistical information drawn from *Mackeson's Guide to the Churches of London and its Suburbs*.[5] It was evident from the results that many innovations first introduced by the Ritualists had, in fact, achieved widespread popularity during the 1870s:

The Decline of the Anti-Ritualist Movement

	1870	1871	1872	1873	1874	1875	1876	1877
Churches	651	677	719	742	759	786	802	848
Corrected Number	630	651	705	730	745	775	792	838
Weekly Communion	169	184	228	250	270	296	320	362
Early Communion	159	210	258	295	310	386	390	440
Evening Communion	97	130	153	178	179	187	205	219
Saints' Day Services	193	190	287	310	316	320	359	400
Choral Service	128	146	163	189	196	190	194	228
Partly Choral Service	115	170	189	196	203	209	244	245
Surpliced Choir	135	151	183	226	265	280	307	340
Surplice in Pulpit	83	180	274	337	370	388	428	465
Floral Decorations	–	–	–	–	153	194	213	269
Eastward Position	–	–	–	–	74	119	139	152

In contrast either to the Ritualists' claims concerning their own popularity or to the rather pessimistic expectations of conservative Evangelicals, it was evident that innovations closely identified with the Ritualist party found little acceptance:

	1870	1871	1872	1873	1874	1875	1876	1877
Daily Communion	20	23	23	25	26	29	35	39
Gregorian Tones	40	44	76	95	124	152	143	127
Eucharistic Vestments	20	22	23	25	30	36	37	35
Incense	7	7	6	8	14	17	18	16
Altar Lights	–	–	–	–	36	53	56	58

Those innovations representing the advanced position of the most extreme Ritualists could be found in only a small number of parishes.[6] The *Record* thought the numbers were a distinct indication of the limits imposed by the Protestant laity. About the same time, R. E. Bartlett suggested that it was an indication of the ultimate failure of the extreme High Church movement. Tracing its principle claims regarding the sacramental system, he concluded that despite its many beneficial results (including a brighter and more aesthetic service) its more extreme practices and the doctrines underlying them had found few disciples.⁷ Despite the figures, the conservative section of the Evangelical party remained defensive regarding the growth of Ritualism.

The debate over the assimilation of new ceremonial continued for years, with moderates arguing that the adoption of popular usages did not necessitate any compromise of fundamental principles. At the Islington meetings in 1877, J. C. Miller returned to the subject. Echoing Thorold's sentiments, he suggested that Evangelical narrowness disheartened many of the younger clergy who were less bound by tradition and more open to the spirit of the age. While denying that he meant to promote a form of latitudinarianism, Miller made the case for a broad degree of toleration:

> There is the narrowness of shibboleths, of making men offenders for a word, of branding, or at least suspecting, all who venture to claim liberty in things indifferent. For example, many of us know that the subject of Church music is a very serious practical difficulty. It is a fact (whether we like it or no) that very many of our people prefer a somewhat more florid service than we have hitherto given them. The young are actually driven away to Ritualistic churches – I speak from good information – because in many Evangelical congregations the service is cold. No man can well be more jealous than I am of the aesthetic element in worship. But we need great wisdom, much prayer for guidance, and a discerning consideration of the circumstances for our own case. We need firm faithfulness to know where to stop, and to stop there. (Hear, hear.) And this is my point. We need brotherly charity, not to insinuate, nor to suspect that a brother is 'getting high,' and is not a safe man, because (however mistakenly in our judgment) he thinks it duty to chant the psalms rather than to drive young people away to hear them chanted in other churches, and withal to hear false doctrine. I have counted the cost of saying even this much. But I will be honest.⁸

In spite of the statistical evidence and calls for moderation from prominent Evangelicals, conservatives grew increasingly defensive about the spread of Ritualism, and the more extreme polemicists were quick to condemn moderates on the slightest evidence. Their attitude can be illustrated in two incidents from the period. The first was an exchange of letters published in the *Rock*, the whole of which J. C. Ryle forwarded to the *Record*. The *Record* reprinted the correspondence without comment, obviously siding with Ryle in the matter.⁹ The original letter to the *Rock*, signed 'Three Protestant Tourists,' was an anonymous attack on Ryle, who was the visiting minister at a church they happened upon during their vacation in the Lake District. They were deeply disturbed when Ryle entered the pulpit wearing a surplice and stole. Still worse, however, was the approval with which he spoke of the church's elaborate musical service:

> He might have avoided casting a slur on those churches (alas! now but too few) where the services are conducted in the truly simple style to which our forefathers have been so long accustomed. We were also pained to be obliged to join in some of the pernicious *Hymns Ancient and Modern* which you so justly reprobate; and one of our number saw distinctly several of the congregation cross themselves at various parts of the service. But all this is as nothing compared to the fact, lamentable as it undoubtedly is, that one to whom we have so long looked up as a champion of Evangelical truth should stand up and defend an elaborate musical service. You, Sir, may be able to explain this, though we cannot.[10]

Ryle was willing to concede nothing to his anonymous critics and sharply protested their narrow and intolerant perspective:

Your correspondents are undoubtedly correct in their statement of facts. I did preach in a surplice, and I did wear a long black silk scarf over my shoulders. I did so deliberately, and I should not hesitate to do so again. And I will give my reasons. In the first place, I had not my own black gown with me at Keswick, and I am entirely dependent on the vestries of the churches in which I preach. In the second place, the vicar and clergy of Crosthwaite Church always preach in the surplice. I thought it would have been very scant courtesy on my part to require them to provide me with a preaching dress which they do not wear themselves. In the third place, it cannot be shown that the surplice is an unlawful preaching dress, although for my own part I very much prefer the black gown. If your correspondents mean to insinuate that I am departing from my long-cherished opinions about the Ritualistic controversy, I beg to inform them that they are utterly, entirely, and completely mistaken. But if they mean to take up this ground, that an Evangelical clergyman absent from home on a holiday is to refuse to preach in any church where the surplice is worn in the pulpit, the Psalms chanted, and *Hymns Ancient and Modern* used, I can only say that I totally disagree with them. I think it my duty and privilege to preach the Gospel in any church where the services are not contrary to the law, and where freedom of speech is allowed to me. The sermon is the grand point after all. If I were a hearer, I would far rather listen to a lively, searching, ringing Gospel sermon from a man in a surplice than to a dull, dreary, mumbling, stupid homily from a man in a black gown.... As to the 'stole,' I can only say that I have worn a black silk scarf over my surplice for thirty-five years, ever since I was ordained, and never regarded it as possessing any doctrinal significance. I like it because without it a clergyman looks like a surpliced adult chorister in a cathedral or college chapel. But I do not care a jot about it; and if my bishop tells me it is illegal, and requests me to lay it aside, I am quite ready to do so.[11]

Francis Close, whose own conservative credentials were beyond dispute, supported Ryle and suggested that the letter criticizing him had not been worthy of publication.[12]

A second incident illustrating the divisions within the party came in 1880, when W. W. Phelps complained about the use of *Hymns Ancient and Modern* in a church supported by a grant from the Church Pastoral-Aid Society, an Evangelical society that provided funds for curates and other parish help. Phelps had written to the general committee concerning the hymnal's adoption by Rev. J. A. McMullen, Vicar of Cobridge, Stoke-on-Trent, but received an unsatisfactory response.[13] He suggested that many long-time supporters of the society would be greatly disturbed by its 'departure from the strict uncompromising rule which has hitherto governed its proceedings.'[14] The responses to Phelps's letter undoubtedly did little to calm the fears of conservatives. Numerous correspondents questioned whether it was appropriate to judge a church or its pastor by the hymnal they used.[15] Many more were disturbed by the tone adopted by Phelps. One correspondent suggested that it was unwise, especially during the current troubled times, to be 'awakening distrust' with regard to 'our cherished Evangelical institutions' and those who directed them.[16]

These episodes illustrated two important points regarding the changing nature of the controversy and the growing tensions among Evangelicals. First, it was evident that perceptions had changed regarding minor innovations such as the wearing of the surplice in the pulpit or the use of a 'suspect' hymnal. The surplice, which had once been anathema to Evangelicals and had been the central issue during the earliest debates over ritual in London, was now considered by many to be a matter of indifference.[17] Still, there was an extreme section of the party that was opposed to the adoption of even seemingly insignificant changes.[18] Second, the incidents illustrated the degree to which internal divisions strained the unity of the Evangelical party, especially between those who were willing to make allowance for popular fashion (even if encouraged by Ritualists) and those who were opposed to any compromise.[19]

The Case of Sidney Green and Its Repercussions

In June 1879, Sidney F. Green, Incumbent of St. John's, Miles Platting, was found guilty of ceremonial usages previously condemned by the courts and ordered to refrain in the future.[20] In August, Green was found guilty of disobeying the monition and suspended for three months.[21] Green continued to ignore the ruling and he was brought before Lord Penzance again in November 1880. Along with R. W. Enraght, Green was found guilty of contumacy, but no immediate application was made for his arrest.[22] In March, that application was made, and Green was taken to the Lancaster Castle jail. An appeal was immediately made by the ECU, but it was rejected both by the Queen's Bench Division of the High Court of Justice and the Court of Appeal of the Supreme Court of Judicature.[23] The case was later rejected by the House of Lords as well.[24]

Green's case became a matter of concern as it stretched on into the summer of 1881, and many suggested that the prolonged imprisonment was having a negative impact on the reputation of the entire church. In July, the subject was taken up by the Convocation of Canterbury, and a protest was adopted by the Lower House, which was dominated by High Church clergy.[25] The bishops expressed their opposition to the imprisonment of clergy but recognized there was little they could do under the circumstances. While avoiding any partisan endorsement of the anti-Ritualist position, they continued to express the view that defiance of the law could not go unpunished. With regard to the supposed 'injurious effect' of the case on the Established Church, Tait thought 'it was difficult to understand how a man being imprisoned for breaking the law could injure the Church.'[26] Ultimately, the bishops adopted a rather innocuous statement of general concern, in which they deplored the imprisonment of the clergy but also noted the sanctity of the law and the need for clergy to obey the admonitions of their bishops.[27]

In August 1881, the House of Lords considered legislation proposed by Earl Beauchamp, a Ritualist supporter, similar to that enacted to free the Quaker, John Thorogood, who had been imprisoned for refusing to pay his church rates. Beauchamp's bill would have limited sentences for contumacy to six months. The bill, however, gained little support and was criticized in the debate by Archbishop Tait, who complained that it left unconsidered the likely prospect that those freed from jail would immediately return to the illegal practices that had led to their conviction. How, he asked, was a gentleman such as Mr. Green, 'with these conscientious convictions.... to be kept out of prison after he is released? How is he to be prevented from getting into prison again? (Laughter.)'[28]

In January 1882, Archbishop Tait met with members of the council of the CA to see if some means might be found to obtain the release of Green.[29] He suggested that they might use their influence with the promoters of the case to petition for his release, without any sacrifice of principle, 'if sufficient guarantees could be obtained from the Bishop of Manchester or from Mr. Green that the illegal ceremonial should cease at St. John's Church, Miles Platting.' After the meeting, the council adopted several resolutions and thanked the archbishop for his concern, but respectfully declined to intercede.[30] They forwarded their resolutions to the archbishop, together with copies of their earlier correspondence with Bishop Fraser.[31] The *Record*, while regretting the continued imprisonment of Green, thought an important principle was at stake in the discussion of his release:

> Meetings, petitions, deputations, remonstrances have been set on foot by the dozen, and all with one object – *the liberation of Mr. Green without his submission*. No doubt his friends have rightly discerned the point to aim at. The law is against them, but if they can once say, 'We have tested the strength of the law, we have borne its heaviest blows, and the result is that the law has been compelled to let go its hold of us without our letting go our hold of that for which the law punished us,' – if, we say, the Ritualistic party are ever able to make this boast, it is obvious that the law will have been vanquished and the question of toleration of Ritualism virtually settled.[32]

The paper was, in fact, quite accurate in its assessment of the dilemma, and prophetic in its recognition that the Ritualists would ultimately gain their victory over the established interpretations of the rubrics and the limits imposed by the law, if they were able to nullify its penalties without concessions on their own part.[33]

By August 1882, three years had passed since Green's initial suspension, and, under the terms of the Public Worship Regulation Act, he was liable to deprivation. His supporters called for his immediate release, but since the patron of the living, Percival Heywood, had not nominated a successor, it was suggested by anti-Ritualists that their protest was something less than honest.[34] At the beginning of November, however, Bishop Fraser decided to apply for Green's release himself on the grounds of his deprivation.[35] Heywood, upon learning of Green's deprivation, vowed to continue his defiance in a speech to ECU members at the Derby Church Congress.[36] Fraser then appointed a curate to oversee the parish in the interim, and Green was finally released on November 5, 1882.[37]

Although he had been the target of the CA's ire, Bishop Fraser was praised by moderate Evangelicals when he adopted a high view of the episcopacy's discretionary power in dealing with the parish after Green's deprivation. When Sir Percival Heywood finally nominated Green's replacement, he chose Harry Cowgill, who had served as a curate under Green and was an equally devoted Ritualist.[38] Fraser, however, refused to institute Cowgill, unless he promised to obey the law, a concession Cowgill was unwilling to make.[39] Fraser explained his position in response to a memorial offering him the support of the congregation of St. Edmund's Church, Manchester. While disavowing any partisan interests, Fraser avowed that, so long as the courts were legally constituted, the clergy and all citizens owed their obedience to the decisions of those courts regardless of their own private opinions.[40] Throughout the controversy anti-Ritualists often complained of the bishops ineffectiveness, and the more vocal section had often accused them of complicity. But moderates, at least, were quick to praise Fraser for his handling of the Miles Platting case and congratulated him for having taken a decisive stand with regard to the new appointment.[41]

During the controversy over Green's lengthy imprisonment, Bishop Fraser took an innovative step to prevent further cases that might lead to a similar result. In November 1881, he called a diocesan 'synod' in order to present the clergy of Manchester with an 'episcopal admonition.' Many of the bishops had attempted, with mixed results at best, to exercise their personal pastoral influence with the Ritualists. But Fraser's was the first such attempt presented in a public forum and bearing the symbolic weight of an episcopal declaration. In support of his position, he noted that the document had been drawn up with the assistance of 'the chief presbyters' of the diocese. A large number of the laity had been greatly troubled, said Fraser, by the introduction of 'questionable ornaments' into the services of the church and 'the continued and increasing growth of new and strange ceremonies which accompany their use.'[42] Further, the bishop doubted that the evidence was sufficient to prove that these innovations had the spiritual effect among the congregation that the 'earnest clergy' introducing them desired. He had, therefore, decided to issue an episcopal admonition to his clergy and to require the 'canonical obedience' they pledged at their ordination. Fraser avoided any reference to either ecclesiastical or secular courts that might 'complicate or endanger that claim,' and presented it solely as the decision of a bishop to his clergy, setting forth a 'maximum standard of ritual.'[43] He continued:

> It being a recognised principle among Churchmen that the voice of the bishop, speaking authoritatively, with the aid of his proper diocesan advisers, should be regarded by all the clergy of his diocese as sufficient to secure from them that "due and canonical obedience" to which every clergyman is bound by the oath which he takes when licensed to the cure of souls or admitted to a benefice; and whereas divers usages and ceremonies which, if ever generally observed at all in this Church of England, had certainly been in abeyance for at least 200 years, have recently been revived or introduced in certain congregations without any proper ecclesiastical sanction or authority, whereby the minds of many Christian people have been disquieted, and consequences have ensued much to be deplored by all who have the true welfare of the Church at heart,
>
> Now, I, James, by Divine permission Lord Bishop of Manchester, having called into counsel and deliberation the Dean and Chapter of my Cathedral Church and the Honorary Canons of the same, and the Chancellor, archdeacons, and rural deans of the diocese, and having duly considered with them the dangers that threaten our Church from the longer continuance of the present distracting controversies in matters of ceremonial, do hereby make it known to the clergy of my diocese that it is my admonition to them, as their Bishop, that, until it shall be otherwise ordered by lawful authority, in public worship in their churches, and especially in the administration of the Holy Communion, they do not exceed the limits of the ritual now practised and allowed, or which may hereafter be allowed, in the Cathedral Church of the diocese; and, inasmuch as it cannot be pretended that any essential truth or fundamental article of the faith is involved therein, I admonish and charge all who in their conduct of Divine service have gone beyond these limits to reduce their ritual accordingly; and, furthermore, I direct that no alteration in or addition to the existing or accustomed ritual of any church be made (except so far as may be necessary to bring such ritual within the limits prescribed by this admonition) unless and until the consent and sanction of the bishop has been obtained for the same. To all which admonition and direction I require my clergy to conform themselves with a 'glad mind and will' for the sake of the peace and unity of the Church, and in the interests of that charity which is the true 'fulfilling of the law,' and 'without which whosoever liveth is counted dead before God.'[44]

The *Record*, in an editorial that indicated just how far the paper had moved toward a moderate position, was quick to praise Fraser. While expressing some doubt as to whether the Ritualists would comply, the paper thought he had wisely avoided the issue of 'lay courts or Erastian Acts of Parliament' by requesting the clergy's obedience, not as 'the mouthpiece of the Privy Council,' but as their pastoral father. 'Surely here,' concluded the paper, 'is a combination of purely ecclesiastical procedure and obsolete ecclesiastical expressions which even Ritualists will feel it hard to ignore.' Still, the paper regretted to note that C. L. Wood, the president of the ECU, had already published 'an intemperate letter' condemning the admonition.[45]

The Green case marked the decisive turning point in the controversy with regard to support for the prosecution of Ritualists. Green's long imprisonment wore down popular support and turned moderates from all parties against the activities of the CA. It became obvious, as the months wore on, that the most important result was to make a martyr of Green and further the Ritualist cause in the court of public opinion.[46] The decisive shift, however, resulted less from Green's imprisonment, than from the CA's questionable decision to impound his household goods – auctioning first Green's possessions and then those of T. P. Dale – in order to pay the complainants' court costs.[47] The *Record* thought that action would end in the 'extraordinary spectacle' of a clergyman being turned out of his home and finally turned the weight of its editorial page against the CA. While allowing that clergy who obstinately broke the law and disobeyed the courts ought to be held responsible for the consequences of their actions, the paper condemned the severity of a policy that exposed 'many innocent persons to the severest trouble and inconvenience.'[48]

The paper suggested that the ultimate results of the policy had to be considered. Was the 'repression of the evil' in a particular case worth the risk of turning popular opinion in favor of their opponents? There had been, thought the paper, a fair and legitimate difference of opinion among Evangelicals with regard to the imprisonment of Ritualist clergy. But there could be no such debate with regard to the policy now adopted by the CA's council; its action was neither right nor wise:

> No one can pretend that the sale of Mr. Green's furniture will in the slightest degree repress Ritualism at Miles Platting. Mr. Green is already in prison, and any result likely to occur from the coercion of his person is already secured. The seizure of his goods, while it must add to his trouble of mind most painfully, is in the

highest degree unlikely to convince him of his errors. The privations of his wife and little children, and the loss of his property voluntarily inflicted by the Church Association, will certainly not strike him as powerful arguments in favour of the principles of the Association. Still less has the seizure of Mr. Dale's goods to do with his late irregularities of ritual. They are over and done with, and however much on other grounds we may regret his recent preferment, it has had one good result – namely, the final stoppage of ritual extravagance at St. Vedast. In his present position Mr. Dale has pledged himself to obey his Bishop, and we have as yet heard nothing to suggest that this engagement is not being fulfilled. The application to Lord Penzance last Friday has therefore nothing even remotely to do with the repression of Ritualism. As we have said, it is a simple question of debtor and creditor. Mr. Dale owes the Church Association £136. He says he has no money, and therefore cannot pay. The Church Association, a Christian Society, formed for the purpose of defending the purity of the Faith, proposes to enforce its claim, follow him to Sausthorpe, seize his furniture, and, if necessary, sell it, and so procure 'payment to be made.' Viewed in this light we cannot understand how any doubt can be felt. This is not a course which a Christian man could consistently take in the conduct of his own affairs, and its propriety is not increased by the fact that the loss of money would not fall on any individual, but on a Society supported by public subscription. Surely St. Paul's words apply, 'Why do ye not rather take wrong? Why do ye not rather suffer yourselves to be defrauded?'

After what we have said, the policy or impolicy of these new proceedings becomes a matter of comparative unimportance. Yet here again, we feel bound to say, we entertain a strong opinion. We are not in the secrets of the Church Association, and we therefore do not know whether the energetic policy of the last six or eight months has had much result in increasing the number of clerical and lay members of the Association, but we are very sure that this latest phase of that policy is viewed with extreme repugnance by the vast majority of those who agree with the Church Association in its opposition to Ritualism. It is no answer to the objection we have raised to say that the English Church Union is really prepared to indemnify the sufferers and to pay the costs. It very likely may be so, and no doubt the suffering and scandal of these executions and forced sales might be avoided if the condemned clergy chose to accept the help that is within their reach. But they do not choose, and the result is that the Church Association has to assume the deplorable position of a relentless creditor harassing his debtor and extorting his money with cruelty. This may very probably be the object at which the other side are aiming, and if so it would seem that the Council have shown but little wisdom in so readily falling into the snare laid for them. It is not without great reluctance that we write thus. The Church Association has done good work in the past, and, under wise guidance, it may do good work in the future. Its present position is one of considerable difficulty, which we should be very sorry to increase. Against the undeserved obloquy from which it has frequently suffered we have done our best to defend it, but this makes it the more necessary to speak out now. We have a duty to perform both to ourselves and to the public, and we feel that we should not discharge that duty if we did not express plainly and emphatically our disapproval of the proceedings to which we have referred. We regard them as not worthy of the character of a Christian Society, cruel and oppressive in themselves towards the condemned clergy and their families, and tending inevitably to prejudice the public mind against the cause which it is the object of the Church Association to defend.[49]

The response to the paper's editorial was mixed. Several moderates applauded the position the paper had taken.[50] But at least one member of the CA's council defended their policy, arguing that the case had little to do with Green and really involved the ECU and its 'policy of aggression.' The council was determined to force the ECU to pay the costs of the Green case and to pursue all pending cases to their respective conclusions. If nothing else was accomplished, they believed such action would prove 'to half-hearted bishops and a distracted laity' that they were determined 'to vindicate the right of the English people to the maintenance of the Reformed order of the National Church.' They had, he concluded, 'counted the cost' and were willing to proceed whatever the opinion of their 'less courageous friends' among the Evangelical clergy and laity, who were willing to compromise on truth for the sake of peace.[51] A few moderates continued to speak of the CA in terms of respect and to defend the value of the earlier prosecutions. But most refused to support any future action so long as there was no alternative to imprisonment for those convicted of contumacy.[52]

The Mackonochie Case Revisited

A. H. Mackonochie was the most prominent of the Ritualist clergy to be charged, and his prosecution, which dragged on for a number of years, was one of the most important although it did not end in imprisonment. After his initial suspension was upheld on appeal,

Mackonochie continued his parish duties in defiance of the court's ruling.[53] It was rumored that he would be charged with contumacy along with Dale and Enraght, but the promoter, John Martin, made it clear that he would not participate in the imprisonment of clergy. In effect, he left the CA with no alternative but to adopt a new course. Still, the decision not to pursue Mackonochie all the way to jail was unpopular with the extreme section.[54] In January 1880, Bishop Jackson of London agreed to allow a new prosecution under the Church Discipline Act.[55] The *Times* had little sympathy for Mackonochie and suggested that it was only by virtue of the antiquated and unreformed system of church discipline that he had been allowed to defy all authority for so long. But it clearly took a less controversial and less negative view than did the more strident anti-Ritualists. Unlike them, the *Times* had little genuine concern that the ceremonial innovations would spread beyond a limited number of parishes. Still, the paper thought the matter ought to be pursued rather than allowing seditious clergy to continue without restraint.[56] The new suit was dismissed when Mackonochie appealed his prior conviction to the House of Lords, and the conclusion of the case was delayed for a number of years.

About the time the Green case was ending, Mackonochie's case and those of several other prominent Ritualists were coming to their inevitable conclusions. In November 1882, R. W. Enraght was deprived of his benefice, since three years had passed without his compliance.[57] Shortly thereafter, Mackonochie would also have been deprived, but he was convinced to resign his benefice by Archbishop Tait, who lay on his deathbed.[58] The anti-Ritualists, however, had only a brief time to celebrate the apparently successful conclusion of the long running prosecution. In January 1883, it was announced that Bishop Jackson had given Mackonochie the parish of St. Peter's, London Docks, which had previously been served by another prominent Ritualist, Charles Lowder.

The Council of the CA immediately protested the appointment of one who had 'persistently deprived the parishioners of their Church rights, and set at defiance both the secular and ecclesiastical courts of the realm and his own diocesan.' They were similarly disturbed by his successor who 'had been instituted to St. Alban's, with the undisguised intention of continuing the illegal ritual for which his predecessor has been repeatedly condemned.'[59] The bishop refused to be swayed by the protest and responded that he only desired to promote peace in the church. He made an emotional allusion to the efforts of the dying Archbishop Tait and concluded that he had no authority to refuse 'a duly-qualified clergyman' regardless of the extenuating circumstances.[60] The *Record* rejected Jackson's appeal to the memory of Tait. In the paper's view, the intervention of the episcopacy in putting down Ritualism was absolutely necessary if further litigation was to be prevented.[61] The *Quarterly Review*, while praising Tait's moderate spirit and concern for the breadth of the national church, similarly suggested that it was a grave error to interpret Tait's actions as 'a complete surrender to the Ritualists.' Rather than capitulation to their demands for the sake of peace in the church, he really desired, 'a truce until the whole question of ecclesiastical procedure could be reconsidered,' expecting that the newly appointed commission to investigate the ecclesiastical courts would arrive at some concrete recommendations.[62]

In June 1883, Mackonochie was brought before the Court of Arches for a final time. It was argued that his previous deprivation disqualified him from receiving another benefice in the province of Canterbury.[63] In July, Lord Penzance ruled that, unlike a sentence of inhibition or suspension, deprivation was not attached to a particular living or preferment. It applied to the offender in 'all his ecclesiastical promotions,' and Mackonochie was therefore prohibited from obtaining another benefice.[64] Bishop Jackson initially refused to enforce the ruling, arguing that it was invalid since Martin was not a parishioner of St. Peter's, but he conceded when Martin threatened to appeal to the Queen's Bench.[65] Mackonochie was finally induced to withdraw from the living at the end of the year, bringing to an end a case that had spanned almost the entire length of the dispute. The *Times* surveyed the history of the case and suggested that the general public would be greatly relieved by the conclusion of the 'long and painful controversy.' Many, the paper thought, probably regretted that the case had been pursued to the bitter end by the CA and would have preferred to see it end when Mackonochie resigned from St. Alban's. But at the same time, the paper had little sympathy for a spirit of defiance among the clergy. If many were now 'disposed to tolerate a good deal of Ritualistic practice,' the paper hoped as well that the Ritualists would be forced 'to recognize the existence of law and to bow to its authority when duly invoked.'[66] The *Record*, however, held out little hope that it was a particularly significant decision, concluding that it was 'useless to deny that the party in favour of toleration of ritual extravagance is a large and even a growing party.' Theirs was an age, said the paper, marked by an 'indifferentism' and compromise; a latitudinarian spirit prevailed that tended 'to smile at the absurdity rather than to frown at the superstition of the modern mummeries.'[67]

The Moderation of Evangelical Opinions

Having come to oppose the use of prosecution and the whole tone of the controversy, most Evangelicals were nevertheless convinced that the principles of the Church of England could not be stretched to include the extreme Ritualists.[68] Still, it was impossible to ignore the fact that the attitude of a significant number of Evangelicals had moderated their views. In 1883, E. H. Bickersteth, who later became the Bishop of Exeter, published a pamphlet on the subject. He acknowledged that there were two competing principles in the party concerning 'churchmanship' and 'eclecticism.' All were agreed that there could be no change with regard to fundamental principles, but the two groups held contrasting views concerning 'the aids to spiritual life and external arrangements of public worship.' Bickersteth wrote:

> Is Evangelical Churchmanship changing its front? If by this it is meant to ask, Are Evangelical Churchmen willing to surrender one foothold of that great platform of Catholic and Protestant truth which we have received from our fathers? I for one am confident that thousands of the clergy of our Church and ten times ten thousands of the laity would answer, God forbid. But if it is meant, Are Evangelical Churchmen in non-essential matters of ritual – ritual which symbolizes no false doctrine – willing to use for the furtherance of the Gospel the prevalent aesthetic tastes of the age? Facts answer, Yes.[69]

Despite numerous negative responses to Bickersteth's vision for the future of the Evangelical party, the *Record* supported his conclusions with regard to the assimilation of moderate elements of ritual.[70]

The Islington Clerical Conference in January 1883 marked a decisive turning point for Evangelical moderates. Philip F. Eliot declared to the assembled clergy that the time had come for them to disavow prosecution and the party's reliance on a purely negative, defensive policy. In focusing on their opposition to the Ritualists, they had failed to emphasize the positive aspects of their own doctrine, particularly with regard to the church and the sacraments. Eliot believed that many Evangelicals were afraid to place due emphasis on the sacraments lest conservatives turn against them and question their commitment. In his view, however, they needed to reemphasize the positive statement of their own doctrine.[71]

Having outlined the need for a more positive presentation of the Evangelical position, Eliot went on to consider the negative impact of the anti-Ritualist movement:

> I have ventured to make these few suggestions as to our teaching under the strong conviction that a merely negative position in theology, as in politics or anything else, becomes in due course of time untenable. If Evangelical teaching is mainly, or gives the impression of being mainly, the denial of Ritualism and Broad Churchism, it must eventually lose its power. It was the positive teaching of the first Evangelical leaders which took the Church by storm. We want more of that positive teaching now. Let us be more sparing in our denunciations and condemnations, and more diligent than ever in our positive teaching of truth. Let us have done with the huge mistake of bringing our artillery to the front, and wasting our powder and shot against such mere trifles as surplices and choirboys and the like. Above all, let all Evangelicals have done with what many of them repudiated from the first – the disastrous policy of attempting to stay error by prosecutions and imprisonments. (Cries of 'No, no.') We have a battle, it is true, with what we believe to be error; but these are not the right weapons to use. If we are to stay Ritualism, or any other form of error, it will not be by the sharpness of our tongues, and still less by the terror of the law. How, then, shall we carry on the battle, and how shall we contend with our brethren who differ from us? I answer – Out-teach them, out-preach them, out-pray them, out-shine them in holiness of life and charity of spirit! (Cheers.)[72]

Eliot's reception was not entirely positive, but it was of great significance that the policy of prosecution was challenged from the platform of the Islington conference, the most prominent Evangelical clerical meeting in the country. In the weeks that followed, the *Record* published numerous letters from conservatives who defended the work of the CA while sharply criticizing Eliot and other moderates who had spoken at the conference.[73] But the paper, in its editorials, continued to support the moderate position.[74]

The Council of the CA, however, would not be swayed, and at the annual meeting in May 1883, J. Maden Holt, affirmed that the organization was determined to defend, by all necessary means, the Protestantism of the national church.[75] He went on to consider the difficulties hindering the CA's efforts to enforce the law. He was chiefly concerned by the attitude of the bishops and their use of the veto. But he was also disturbed by the 'apathy and indifference and, he must say, the selfishness and divisions in the Evangelical body.'[76] Several other speakers reiterated Holt's message. Rev. Charles Mason noted the association's declining membership, which he attributed to popular opposition to litigation. But while regretting the loss of many 'old supporters of the Association,' who had apparently tired of the controversy, he thought 'a great and noble work' still lay ahead for the CA.[77] Several speakers also complained of the treatment the organization received at the hands of the press. Little sympathy was expected from the secular press, but they were particularly disturbed by the new position of the *Record*.[78] Rev. W. Adamson, who claimed to be a long-time subscriber, lamented the recent changes. He challenged the editors to state publicly that the paper was not now 'the authorized organ of the new departure section of the Evangelical party.' Similarly, Rev. Dr. Wainwright complained that 'the truth was sold and bought by the press of the country. The *Record* in relation to Romanists and Romanism was mealy-mouthed. The *Record* of to-day was a new departure.'[79]

In its editorial response, the *Record* suggested that 'a certain air of discouragement' prevailed at the CA meeting. The paper, however, took a high road in the debate and refused to react to the criticism of its editorial policy; it simply stated its regret that the CA faced a difficult future while acknowledging that the organization deserved great respect for its earlier work. But the fact of the matter, said the paper, was that there had been a shift of opinion within the Evangelical party:

> It is useless to conceal the fact that the methods adopted by the Council during the last few years have been exceedingly distasteful to a vast number of Evangelical Churchmen. The policy of the imprisonments was obviously a very doubtful one. The principle of the matter seemed to us to be easily defensible, and we never heard any argument, impugning it, which demanded any great effort for its demolition. But the policy of putting men in prison, whose great desire was to be put in prison in order to obtain popular sympathy, was seriously open to question. If we look to results for its justification it must be admitted we shall look in vain. Whatever else has been the consequence of the imprisonments they have tended to separate the Evangelical clergy from the Association.[80]

The *Record* believed that if a less contentious course was pursued in the controversy, Evangelicals would find that they were not 'without support from those in authority.' And while acknowledging that the Ritualists still posed a grave threat to the church, the paper concluded that it took 'a more hopeful view of the future than was prevalent on the Church Association platform.'[81]

The paper also suggested that anti-Ritualists were mistaken in their willingness to criticize other Evangelicals for adopting popular trends. To bolster its argument, it returned to the figures gathered in *Mackeson's Guide to the Churches of London*.[82] It was clear that, since the paper's earlier survey, the more moderate elements of ceremonial innovation had continued to spread throughout the city. The popularity of a number of ceremonies first introduced by the Ritualists had grown substantially since the early 1870s. Early communion, choral services, and the surplice in the pulpit had been in use in roughly one third of the churches, but by the early 1880s they had been adopted in over one half of the London parishes. Other innovations had similarly grown in use:

	1878	1879	1881	1882	1883	1884
Churches	864	872	887	907	928	953
Corrected Number	854	864	877	903	920	940
Weekly Communion	390	409	454	488	525	546
Early Communion	458	478	533	588	627	662
Evening Communion	246	262	267	285	289	282
Saints' Day Services	415	417	433	470	482	488
Choral Service	261	275	303	350	379	399
Partly Choral Service	240	267	283	315	316	333
Surpliced Choir	355	375	397	476	502	538
Surplice in Pulpit	463	470	581	676	686	706
Floral Decorations	214	215	219	242	258	268
Eastward Position	179	214	234	270	304	335

The more extreme innovations, however, continued to find little support. Those ceremonies which remained distinctive symbols of Ritualist beliefs and party affiliation still found acceptance in relatively few parishes:

	1878	1879	1881	1882	1883	1884
Daily Communion	42	43	43	46	47	50
Gregorian Tones	115	120	124	123	133	117
Eucharistic Vestments	35	33	35	37	37	40
Incense	14	13	11	10	10	14
Altar Lights	58	56	54	59	64	95

The paper thought those who opposed 'the fashions of the day,' under the mistaken opinion that they were contending for fundamental principles, were wasting their strength and needlessly dividing the party over secondary matters. And, as the figures proved, Ritualism had gained little ground, relative to the overall number of churches, in the years following the Ridsdale judgment in 1876.[83]

Canon Tebbutt, Vicar of St. Andrew's, Nottingham, addressing the Midland Clerical and Lay Conference, reiterated the same point and spoke of the divisions created within the party by those who desired to delineate narrow boundaries. He acknowledged that conservatives who attempted 'to enforce a dull uniformity' were motivated by 'a holy jealousy for Gospel truth' and deserved a 'tender respect.' But he thought they unfairly narrowed the ranks of the party and weakened its influence when they attempted to enforce their view of the essence of Evangelical teaching. He suggested that Evangelical clergy ought to be allowed a broad range of toleration, without having to face questions regarding their orthodoxy:

> In things secondary the question is one of individual taste, wisdom, tact, and fitness. Amongst these are the use of surplice or gown – surpliced choirs, chanting the Psalms, weekly and early Communion, observance of holy-days. No one can reasonably contend that these practices concern fundamentals, or that they are inconsistent either with Gospel teaching or with personal godliness. Such matters, however, have in actual fact now passed out of the region of debate. None of us can desire 'distinctiveness' for mere 'distinctiveness' sake. Nor are these days when Churchmen can afford to stand aloof from one another. These changes in things indifferent are nothing more than the ripplings of a lake's surface under the passing wind. The solemn depths beneath remain unchanged.... In brief, then, I limit 'distinctiveness in ritual' to the refusal of all dress, gesture, and ceremony, which are by common

consent expressive (1) of a sacrificial, rather than a teaching priesthood; (2) of an objective presence in the elements, rather than a spiritual presence in the Eucharist to the believing soul. These appear to me to be the points at issue.... Only be faithful to the Reformation, and use whatever ritual you and your congregation desire.[84]

The debate following Tebbutt's speech indicated that opinions remained divided, but moderates were increasingly willing to take a stand for the heart of the party.[85]

The Ecclesiastical Courts Commission

An important result of the Ritualist imprisonments was the doubt created concerning the viability of the ecclesiastical legal process as revised by the Public Worship Regulation Act.[86] Claiming that the Court of Arches had no spiritual authority, the Ritualists refused to comply with the judgments of Lord Penzance. Their unexpected defiance left the anti-Ritualists in a difficult position; either they must leave the legal judgments unenforced, trusting that the bishops would somehow bring their influence to bear upon the Ritualists, or they must promote litigation that could only culminate in the imprisonment of the recalcitrant clergy. The spirit of the age, however, would no longer tolerate the latter alternative, and the ultimate effect was to accomplish that which the Ritualists had been unable to achieve on their own – the effective annulment of the Public Worship Regulation Act.[87] The bishops were almost unanimous in their opposition to further prosecution, and the search for an alternative soon led to the appointment of a royal commission.[88] Many anti-Ritualists were not opposed, in principle, to continued prosecution, but they believed deprivation was a more appropriate sentence than imprisonment. Bishop Ryle frequently repeated the view that the imprisonment of clergy for contumacy was 'a disgrace to ecclesiastical law' that demanded reform. Further, he suggested that it aroused popular sympathy and turned disobedient clergy into martyrs. In his view, clergy ought to be punished by suspension first, and then deprivation in cases of continued violations.[89]

The announcement of the Ecclesiastical Courts' Commission in May 1881 was opposed by fervent anti-Ritualists, who feared that it would only delay further prosecutions under the existing legislation while allowing the Ritualists to further establish their position. In contrast to the earlier Ritual Commission, however, there was little protest, an indication, perhaps, of how slight the expectations were with regard to any results that might follow.[90] Little excitement or anticipation was shown by moderate Evangelicals, who seem to have expected from the beginning that little would come of it.[91] For the *Record*, the most troubling fact was the inclusion of the Earl of Devon, who was a prominent member of the ECU. The paper thought it ill-advised for the government to have included him on the committee, but believed that a fair result could nevertheless be obtained, even though the earl's presence was not balanced by the appointment of any prominent Evangelicals.[92]

It would be two years before the commission concluded its work and issued its report. Moderate Evangelicals were largely satisfied with the result, at least insofar as it reaffirmed two fundamental principles: the right of Parliament to legislate for the Church of England with or without the approval of Convocation, and the legitimacy of an independent final court of appeal that protected the principle of royal supremacy (in the sense that every citizen who felt wronged had a right to appeal to the Crown), a right that would be negated if an exclusively ecclesiastical court was established.[93] The *Record* thought the latter point particularly important and cited two Ritualists who had testified before the commission, both of whom were adamant that, when matters of ceremonial or doctrine were involved, only a final court of appeal made of clergy would be acceptable in their view.[94] In response, the paper wrote:

> These statements are based upon an assumption regarding the rights and qualifications of the clergy which underlies the whole sacerdotal system, and is as un-Protestant as we venture to think it is unscriptural. The layman is as truly a member of the Church of Christ as is his clerical brother; there is nothing in Scripture which assigns to the clergyman the exclusive right of judging whether certain opinions are in conflict with the formularies of his Church or not; and if by reason of his professional training the layman is better qualified to decide such questions than the clergyman, common sense, to say nothing of justice, points to but one conclusion. We hold it, therefore, to be the policy of the Evangelical party to give a zealous and ungrudging support to what we regard as the leading principle of the Report, the establishment of a lay court of Final Appeal. We should not, indeed, be unwilling to see a certain number of Bishops included amongst the Judges, but the principle for which we earnestly contend is the controlling presence in such Court of a trained lay element.[95]

Interestingly, the *Edinburgh Review*, which generally adopted a Broad Church view of the toleration necessary in a national church, was decidedly more negative in its view of the commission's report.

In its view, the report attempted 'to reduce the Royal Supremacy over the Church, in legal matters, to a shadow, if not to repudiate it altogether.'[96]

In contrast to the moderates, the supporters of the CA were strongly opposed to the recommendations of the commissioners and condemned it as 'a most ignominious surrender and capitulation to the demands of the Ritualist party.'[97] The Central Committee of the UCLA, in an effort to express the opinion of moderates, issued a lengthy memorandum on the report.[98] In December 1883, the Central Committee of the union sponsored a memorial addressed to the archbishops. With two limitations, the memorial praised the work of the commissioners and urged that a measure would soon be brought before Parliament based upon their recommendations.[99] Ultimately, however, given the lack of unanimity among the commissioners and the fervent opposition of the Ritualists, none of the recommendations were acted upon by Parliament, and the Public Worship Regulation Act remained in effect.[100]

The Last Ritualist in Prison: James Bell Cox

Following the scandal of the Green case, and with the failure of the Ecclesiastical Courts Commission to agree upon any substantive alterations to the judicial process, the bishops were almost entirely determined to veto further prosecutions.[101] In general, they were simply concerned to reestablish a measure of peace in the church by any means available. The authority of the episcopal veto was unchallenged after the successful appeal of Bishop Mackarness in the case of T. T. Carter, and thereafter the decisions of bishops who refused to allow prosecutions were effectively the final word in the matter.[102] While moderates adopted a tolerant view and were willing to allow for the difficulties faced by the episcopacy, anti-Ritualists became increasingly combative and blamed the bishops for the growth of Ritualism. At the 1884 annual meeting of the CA, Capt. Alexander Cobham, condemned the episcopal policy. Not only had they prevented others from suppressing the Ritualists by vetoing prosecution, they had also promoted the movement by continuing to license and ordain suspect clergy.[103] At the autumn conference that year, the speakers returned to the offensive. In considering the future work of the CA, J. Maden Holt proclaimed that the council was determined not to back away from the appeal to the courts. Despite any hesitation on the part of moderates, Holt affirmed that the association was determined to force the bishops to fulfill their responsibilities, and, if necessary, 'to ascertain how far the law can be brought to bear upon an offending bishop.'[104]

Anti-Ritualists attempted one last clerical prosecution before focusing their attention on the bishops. When the case of James Bell Cox, Vicar of St. Margaret's, Liverpool, came before J. C. Ryle, the most fervent anti-Ritualist on the episcopal bench, he allowed it to proceed.[105] He had often expressed the view that further prosecution would not serve the best interests of the church. Still, he thought the Ritualist position untenable and, in his charges to the diocese, frequently returned to the point that it was the duty of the clergy to abide by the law, whether or not they believed it to be a good one.[106] Ryle was also opposed, as a matter of principle, to episcopal intervention through the use of the veto, viewing it as an unfair circumvention of every citizen's right of appeal to the courts.[107] As early as 1883, anti-Ritualists had pressured Ryle to suppress the innovations of Bell Cox or to allow his prosecution.[108] It was not until February 1885, however, that charges were formally brought by James Hakes, and the vicar was issued a citation to appear before Ryle to respond to the charges.[109] Shortly thereafter, Ryle notified Cox that the prosecution would be allowed to proceed.[110]

The *Record* used the occasion to condemn the litigation but also to vindicate Ryle. In an editorial, the paper gave a detailed account of its change of heart. It defended the earlier suits on the grounds that the results were not obvious, and there was a self-evident need for clarification of ecclesiastical law. But the progress of the controversy had clearly altered the circumstances by the 1880s, and the paper suggested that anyone beginning a suit must know that it would end either in 'an absurd failure' or the imprisonment of the defendant. 'We confess,' the editorial continued, 'that it seems to us the individual or society that, notwithstanding this knowledge, embarks on litigation, incurs a very heavy responsibility.'[111] Having condemned the prosecutors, however, the *Record* sought to exonerate Bishop Ryle from any charge of complicity.[112] The episcopacy, said the paper, had often abused the discretionary power the veto allowed them. Adopting the position taken by Ryle himself, the *Record* argued that the bishops' duty was neither more nor less than to satisfy themselves 'that the judgment of the court was being honestly invoked, and that there was nothing grossly inequitable in the continuance of the suit.' Having done that much, it was not within their power to act as judges and prevent the charges from being heard by the proper court. Given the difficulties of the situation, the paper thought it unfair 'to confuse the official action of the Bishop in permitting the new prosecution with the voluntary action of Dr. Hakes in promoting it.'[113]

The *Record*'s editorial provoked a great flurry of correspondence debating the continued use of litigation. One important letter, signed by three of the elder statesmen of the party – William Cadman, Emilius Bayley, and F. F. Goe – rejected the suggestion that the promoters of the case represented a majority of the Evangelical party:

> We have seen the report contained in your columns of what is called the Liverpool prosecution, and the correspondence to which it has given rise. We should be sorry if it were assumed that this fresh action carries with it the approval of the whole Evangelical body in the Church of England. We speak only for ourselves, but we have good reason for believing that we substantially express the opinion of a very large number of our Evangelical brethren.
>
> We do not question either the faithfulness or the good intentions of those who differ from us in their judgment as to the best way of dealing with Ritualistic excesses. But we have a strong conviction that prosecutions of individuals for Ritualism at the present time are neither politic nor wise. If the desire be to suppress Ritualism, experience shows that prosecutions will not do this. If the desire be to preserve or advance the interests of Evangelical truth, we are of opinion that those interests are likely rather to be injured than promoted by an appeal to the Law Courts. The apostle enjoins us to serve one another in love. How that service can be rendered to Ritualistic brethren whom we believe to be exceeding the wise limits of our own Reformed Church, may be a difficult question. But the duty remains; and we cannot forget with what force Archbishop Sumner once reminded some zealous remonstrants – 'You must remember that, after all, "the end of the commandment is charity".'[114]

In response to the letters of those who continued to support the CA, the *Record* published several editorials elaborating its position. In one, the paper recounted the growth of opposition to the CA, noting that many early supporters turned against the organization when it took upon itself the responsibility of enforcing the interpretative judgments.[115] Later, the paper responded to the CA's supporters who claimed that the principles at stake demanded the enforcement of the law. Experience, in the view of the paper, had proved the failure of the appeal to the courts, and principles, however worthy, could not be maintained by faulty methods. The *Record*, echoing the thoughts Samuel Garrett had voiced several years earlier, countered: 'To the inquiry what would you have us do, if we are not to invoke the law, we would answer – Have you lost all faith in the force of truth? Have you forgotten that in Apostolic days truth won its way, in spite of legalized opposition, by appealing to the understanding, the conscience, and the heart?' Similarly the paper cited the example of the early Evangelical movement, which had prospered in the face of extreme opposition during the eighteenth century. The movement's success came only through its positive work, 'the faithful preaching of the Gospel of the grace of God' proclaimed with 'untiring zeal.'[116] Still, the division between moderates and conservatives remained, and the controversy over the Bell Cox case only served to illuminate the fractured state of the Evangelical party.[117]

In December 1885, having already been found guilty of illegal innovations, Bell Cox was returned to Lord Penzance's court on charges of contempt. He was found guilty and suspended for six months, beginning the following January.[118] In the interim, he appointed A. H. Paine as curate in charge of the parish, and Paine continued the services with no alteration. Hakes attempted to institute proceedings against the curate as well, but Ryle would have no part of any further litigation. When Bell Cox returned to the church, the services continued as before and Hakes's lawyer proceeded to enforce the law through imprisonment.[119] The ECU immediately appealed to the Queen's Bench Division on his behalf, and a temporary restraining order was issued, postponing the enforcement of the judgment. But the appeal was dismissed, and on May 5, 1887 Bell Cox was arrested and taken to Lancaster Castle. The *Record* immediately expressed its regret that the case had been pursued to its logical extreme and sought to limit the negative impact. It noted that the vast majority of Evangelicals opposed the prosecution, and the actions of the individual or society that promoted it in no way represented the moderate section of the party. By then, however, the damage had been done to the Evangelical party's reputation, and the Ritualists could claim another martyred priest who had been willing to sacrifice his freedom for the faith.[120]

An appeal was immediately made on Bell Cox's behalf to the Queen's Bench Division on the grounds that the original suspension against him had expired and that his imprisonment was therefore illegal.[121] The judges of the court were compelled to agree with the logic of the argument, and they issued an injunction releasing him from prison.[122] When they published their final decision in July 1887, Hakes immediately announced his attention to renew the case and to bring charges against Bell Cox's curate as well.[123] Ryle, however, was satisfied that the prosecution had been given its day in court, and he refused to allow further proceedings.

The anti-Ritualists would continue their campaign for many years after the scandal of the Green case, but they had long since passed their peak years of influence, when they might have harbored some realistic hope of affecting the outcome of the controversy. Green's long imprisonment was sufficiently distressing to encourage the bishops to adopt the only means available of insuring that another case did not obtain a similar result. Their use of the episcopal veto allowed a breadth of toleration that was perhaps greater than some of them desired, but it was part of the price to be paid for avoiding further strife. Still more troubling, for moderate Evangelicals, was the seizure of Green's personal property. It was the climax of a bitter, partisan campaign to which they could, in good conscience, no longer give their support. James Bell Cox's imprisonment a few years later was almost an afterthought. His prosecution could gain nothing, and it could have no result except to further isolate the anti-Ritualist movement.

Conservative and moderate Evangelicals were fundamentally divided in their views of the controversy and their expectations for the church. Conservatives were largely pessimistic.[124] They feared the Ritualists were gaining influence, they resented the bishops for having refused to take decisive action, and they suspected that many moderates had been affected by the spirit of compromise that seemed to dominate the age. In contrast, moderates took a far more hopeful view. They were indeed willing to compromise, at least on minor points that they thought were non-essential. But still more, they had grown tired of the bitter and negative controversy. And by the mid-1880s, they were largely willing to leave the matter in the hands of the bishops.[125] Anti-Ritualists had long argued that the unity of the church was not worth the compromise of fundamental Protestant truths. Moderates agreed, but after several decades of fruitless debate they were willing to allow that previously disputed points might not be essential after all. But the controversy was by no means over. Anti-Ritualists, more isolated and defensive than ever, were determined to pursue their cause, even if it required taking the bishops to court.

Notes

1   In addition to ceremonial and architectural innovations, Fox was also disturbed by the introduction of new services such as 'harvest thanksgiving' festivals. He continued, 'That the Ritualistic clergy should have introduced such practices is natural – it is part of their system; but that men professing Gospel principles should show themselves so insensible to the dangers of the age as to lend their countenance to them is most lamentable.' Letter to the *Record*, 1 Nov. 1875.

2   Ibid. In an 1877 letter to a friend, Bishop Magee of Peterborough complained about the attitude of Evangelicals and the constant controversy. Why, he asked, did they 'prove themselves everywhere and always so impracticable and irreconcilable? I suppose that they feel themselves an expiring party, and are hair-sore and jealous accordingly.' Magee, however, thought their reactionary position was self-defeating. He confessed he was

no partisan, but the Evangelicals were driving him, little by little, 'into the arms of the High Churchmen.' MacDonnell, *Life of Magee, vol. 2*, pp. 71-72.

3   Thorold said, 'It would be unpardonable to omit and uncandid to deny – that the aesthetic movement had in its entire range done good as well as harm; that it had in some places introduced obnoxious novelties, in others it had removed serious scandals; that since some of them were boys the entire level of Divine worship throughout the kingdom had been appreciably and beneficially raised; and that much of the credit, if not of monopolizing, of initiating this movement, was fairly due to those who now, at least in their judgment, were in danger of pushing it to an extreme.' Cited in the *Record*, 22 Jan. 1875.

Similarly, E. H. Bickersteth thought Evangelicals ought to 'gratefully acknowledge the debt we owe to the High Church school for restoring and beautifying so many of the Houses of Prayer in our land. We can hardly over-estimate the costly toil during the last fifty years they have thus consecrated to God's service.' Bickersteth, *Evangelical Churchmanship and Evangelical Eclecticism*, pp. 24-25.

4   Cited in the *Record*, 22 Jan. 1875. Some moderates, while allowing for a degree of toleration, remained concerned about the influence of other parties on Evangelicals. David Stewart suggested that the early Evangelicals had learned 'the principle of separation.' If they were excessive in some of their concerns, they were intent on maintaining the distinctiveness of the Gospel. While willing to allow for the differing views of the High and Broad Church parties, Stewart maintained Evangelicals could be tolerant while still retaining their distinctiveness, and without 'being trammeled by any undue uplifting either of ritual or of free thought.' David D. Stewart, *Evangelical Opinion in the Nineteenth Century* (London: Hatchards, 1879), pp. 34-35.

In 1874, an anonymous writer suggested that the moderates represented the largest percentage of the Evangelical party. In contrast to the 'noisy' section of narrow-minded extremists, they were devoted but quiet, largely avoiding controversial issues. He thought they were being 'gradually absorbed into the Middle Church,' that growing body of moderates from all sections of the church. The middle church, he thought, was numerous but often overlooked. Anon., *Church Parties*, p. 16.

5   Cited in the *Record*, 23 July 1877. The 'Corrected Number of Churches' in the table represented those for which there was complete information with regard to ceremonial usages.

6   The next year, the *Record* noted that some innovations had grown rapidly, such as the use of the surplice, which had expanded from about one-eighth of the churches in 1870, to over one-half by 1878. 'Shortly,' the paper concluded, 'it will be used almost everywhere.' The percentages were similar with surpliced choirs, the observance of saints' days, and the increased frequency of the celebration of the Eucharist.

The facts were otherwise, however, with regard to innovations more exclusively identified with the Ritualists – those that were 'distinctive party signs' or were 'adopted as the outward expression of definite dogmas.' The paper found little evidence of growth with regard to the use of eucharistic vestments, incense, and altar lights. It noted that there had been a relative decrease (as a percentage of the total number of churches) in all three usages for the previous three years. That decrease, it suggested, was even more important when compared to the relative growth of the only usage that might be considered a distinctively Evangelical practice – the celebration of evening communion. The figures for that usage were:

in 1869 – 154 out of 588 churches (12.8%)
in 1875 – 187 out of 755 churches (24.12%)
in 1878 – 246 out of 884 churches (28.8%)

The paper concluded, 'In the face of these figures it is abundantly evident that Ritualism has not made the triumphant progress which its advocates have been pleased to claim for it; nor has Evangelicalism lost the ground which the too despondent temper of Evangelical Churchmen has led them to suppose. We have frequently called attention to the contrast presented by the two schools in this respect, and the result of the present inquiry should point the moral. The Ritualists and their organs habitually make the best of everything, and are jubilant over very small mercies indeed. Our friends, on the other hand, are depressed without a cause, and are blind to every encouraging circumstance of their position, while they are keen-eyed to their losses.' *Record*, 28 Aug. 1878.

In evening communion, Evangelicals found a practice common in the early church that they could emphasize in contrast to the Ritualists. The practice commended itself to them on two counts. First, it was widely proclaimed as a means of drawing the working classes into the church and to participate in communion during a less formal service. The logic of their argument was similar to that used for the evening theatre services. Second, it was a clear response to the Ritualists who favored an early morning celebration preceded by a fast. It was, they argued, a desecration of the eucharistic elements to have them mingled with food in the stomach. As a result, the Ritualists were strongly opposed to the celebration of evening communion. For a sampling of Ritualist opposition, cf. Walsh, *Oxford Movement*, pp. 215-16.

7   Bartlett continued, 'It has had the advantage of conspicuous intellectual ability and great saintliness of life among its promoters and adherents; it has had the command of the press and of the pulpit; it has not shrunk from publicity, but has striven and cried and let its voice be heard in the streets; and yet it has made no real impression upon the lay mind of England. How are we to account for this? There can be but one reason. The cause of its failure is the cause of the failure of Archbishop Laud, of King James II, of the Nonjurors – the invincible Protestantism of the religious mind of England. That Protestantism has often been very absurd, very wrong-headed, very fanatical: it has protested against chanting the Psalms, against preaching in the surplice, against the abolition of pews, against painted windows; but it has done so because it believed that these things were part of a system of sacerdotalism to which it was irreconcilably hostile.' [R.E.B.], 'Past and Future of the High Church Party,' *Fraser's Magazine*, p. 247.

In an editorial on the prosecution of A. H. Mackonochie, the *Times* challenged the Ritualists' claims of their own popularity. The paper acknowledged a 'general moderation and reasonableness' among the laity who were willing to make allowance for clerical eccentricities. But nowhere, claimed the paper, could supporters 'point to a case where the parish agrees with extreme Ritualist practices. Certainly, the Church of St. Alban the Martyr is no such case. Parishioners and congregations are there very distinct things. Its congregation is made up of two elements. There are the idlers who come to see its albs and its copes, and all the other strange and wondrous garments, of which the list reads like that of Darius's instruments of music in the Book of Daniel; and there are the disciples who come from remote quarters to admire and adore the idols of ecclesiastical tailoring. Outside in the dark are the actual parishioners, a vast Irish camp which stares bewildered or mocking at the mimicry by the eccentric English colony of their hereditary religious observances.

'These clergymen may minister in crowded churches; but they minister not to parishes, but to congregations. Whether they know it or not, with their rebelliousness against their Bishops and the wishes of their parishioners, they are rushing headlong into Congregationalism.' *Times*, 27 March 1878.

Owen Chadwick thought that a growing congregationalism was indicative of the period and a natural encouragement to Ritualism, especially in the cities. Chadwick, *Victorian Church, Part Two*, pp. 312-15.

8 Cited in the *Record*, 19 Jan. 1877. G. T. Fox criticized Miller's moderation. In his view, while compromise might gain a few adherents, many more were lost, 'and those the most valuable, experienced, and spiritually-minded of our people... [who] loath and abhor what our friend euphemistically terms "a more florid service," and can hardly now find a place of worship where the simplicity of the old Evangelical ritual is maintained.' Letter to the *Record*, 26 Jan. 1877.

The *Times* had kind words for Miller when he died three years later. The paper reported that he was a highly regarded preacher who had 'frequently occupied the pulpit in churches served by High Churchmen.' He had also played a prominent role in Evangelical meetings, but always, along with William Cadman and J. C. Ryle, 'on the side of moderation.' *Times*, 12 July 1880.

E. H. Bickersteth reiterated the moderate point of view several years later. He suggested that 'in matters of ritual or practice, which do not countenance error,' they should not question the commitment of those who introduced modest innovations. 'I fear we have lost many young men, both lay and clerical, and more young women still from our Evangelical ranks, because some of us have set ourselves against certain tastes of the age, although these tastes are free from doctrinal error, instead of using them to the utmost in our Master's service.' Bickersteth, *Evangelical Churchmanship*, p. 11.

9 D. W. Bebbington cited this incident but mistakenly concluded that the *Record* had censured Ryle for preaching in the surplice. By 1876, however, the *Record*, in contrast to the *Rock* (a penny paper that supported the extreme anti-Ritualist movement), was supportive of moderates such as Ryle, who no longer viewed the use of the surplice in the pulpit as an important point

in the controversy. Furthermore, it was Ryle himself who forwarded the correspondence to the *Record*. Cf. Bebbington, *Evangelicalism in Modern Britain*, p. 149.
10 The *Rock* added its comment, 'No, we cannot explain these things. All we can do is to heave a sigh and hold up our hands in utter amazement.' Correspondence cited in the *Record*, 18 Sept. 1876.
11 Ibid. Ryle himself was not unconcerned with some of the innovations. In his charge to the clergy of Liverpool in 1884, after he became bishop, he lamented the fact that many of the laity seemed to believe the disputed questions of 'ornaments, dresses, music, and decorations' involved merely petty disputes rather than 'attempts to subvert the Protestant principles of the Church, and to reintroduce some of the most dangerous doctrines of Romanism.' In Ryle's view, the issues involved were immensely important and not 'mere questions of taste.' Ryle, *No Uncertain Sound*, p. 83.
12 Close claimed that the Vicar of Crosthwaite, whom he counted a friend, was 'an old-fashioned High Churchman' and not a Ritualist. The surplice, unlike eucharistic vestments, involved no doctrinal system. Close concluded it was 'a false and an impolitic action' to make 'gown and surplice badges of party, or tests of orthodoxy.' Close concluded, 'I have some right to speak, for I preached for thirty-six years in a black gown, and for the last twenty years in a surplice, and I confess my preference for the latter; believing, especially in the morning service, that it is the legal, correct, and by far the most convenient dress for the pulpit.' Letter to the *Record*, 27 Sept. 1876.
13 Edward J. Speck, Secretary of the CP-AS, assured Phelps that the society had not deviated from its Evangelical principles. He concluded: 'I gather from your letter that you desire the Committee never to give a grant where *Hymns Ancient and Modern* are used. I am not aware that any parish aided by the Society uses this particular book; but, if it were so, the Committee, who are sound and faithful men, unanimously felt that, having carefully approved of an applicant for aid, they could not take upon themselves to say what book he should use.' Phelps was disturbed that the committee was unwilling to give some assurance that they would, in the future, withdraw their assistance from recipients who showed Ritualist tendencies. Correspondence cited in the *Record*, 18 Feb. 1880.
14 Ibid.
15 R. J. Crothwaite, Vicar of Brayton, Selby, gave an example from his own experience. He greatly differed from his High Church predecessor, but he thought it unwise when he arrived in the parish to begin his work by 'disturbing the minds of his parishioners' and condemning the hymnal which had long been in use there. While he did not himself receive CP-AS funds, he questioned whether it would have been fair to refuse funds to someone like himself simply because he refused to replace *Hymns Ancient and Modern* in his church. Letter to the *Record*, 20 Feb. 1880.
16 He concluded by suggesting that it was not 'a Christian course to seek to arouse suspicion and create division between those whose common desire is, as much as his own can possibly be, to uphold and to propagate the great principles of the Gospel of the grace of God.' Letter (signed 'An Evangelical Incumbent of Twenty-Four Years' Standing') to the *Record*, 20 Feb. 1880.

Evangelicals were by no means alone in their concern over Ritualistic hymns, although other anti-Ritualists wrote without the same degree of bitterness. The *Edinburgh Review*, in an essay published the same year, suggested that 'the distinctive tenets of Ritualism' were often spread through their hymns. 'The volume entitled *Hymns Ancient and Modern*, one of the most popular hymnals of the present day, and, as regards the greater portion of its contents, deservedly so, contains some hymns which – whatever the original design of their composers – are calculated to instill into the minds of unwary worshippers doctrine which are diametrically opposed to the formularies of the English Church.' Anon., 'Ritualistic Literature,' *Edinburgh Review*, p. 317.

17 In an 1874 defense of Ritualism, after the Public Worship Regulation Act was passed, W. E. Gladstone noted that in the years since the agitations in London and Exeter, the surplice in the pulpit had become widely accepted. In Gladstone's view, however, there was a basic inconsistency in the thought of those who viewed the surplice as a badge of Romanism. It was, thought Gladstone, 'rather Protestant than Popish;' for Popery, with its emphasis on the sacraments, 'would have led to the use of a different and lower garb in preaching, not to the use of the same vestment which was also to be used for the celebration of the Eucharist.' Gladstone, 'Ritualism and Ritual,' *Contemporary Review*, p. 670.

18 The surplice in the pulpit was still a divisive issue for some as late as 1890. Richard Glover, Vicar of St. Luke's, West Holloway, complained of the lack of unity among Evangelicals. He cited a recent meeting of the Union of Clerical and Lay Associations. Following a plea for unity by H. W. Webb-Peploe, Hugh M'Sorley, Vicar of St. Paul's, Tottenham, had immediately attacked 'in a fiery speech some of the very brethren that sat with him as virtual betrayers of Evangelical truth because, forsooth, they preach in a surplice!' Glover continued, 'Mr. M'Sorley talked of the surplice as though it were some quite illegal and suspicious "vestment." Does he not know that now-a-days it confessedly has no doctrinal significance? (The "vestments" so called have.) Does he not know that some of those men who preach Evangelical truth most faithfully – such as Canon Cadman, Prebendary Calthrop, and a hundred others – now preach in the surplice?' Letter to the *Record*, 18 July 1890.

M'Sorley replied that E. B. Pusey had made the surplice in the pulpit a party badge and that all Evangelicals who adopted it were compromising. 'If Canon Cadman represents the sentiments of the members of the Clerical and Lay Union, and if they represent the Protestantism of England, then Protestantism is dead, and the sooner it is buried the better.' Letter to the *Record*, 1 Aug. 1890.

As late as the 1930s, some conservatives were still disturbed by the spread of Anglo-Catholic influence through music and the adoption of *Hymns Ancient and Modern* in Evangelical parishes. Cf. Thomas Houghton, *The Oxford Movement Exposed* (London: Thynne & Co., 1932), pp. 52-55.

19 In 1878, a correspondent contrasted the way Ritualists treated each other to the self-defeating attitude of Evangelicals. He complained that they were 'always finding fault' with their friends. It was, he concluded, a disastrous

policy that alienated many. Regarding the criticism of J. C. Ryle, he wrote, 'This party drives many men to the Ritualists by its want of tact; and until its tactics are altered, and it can cheer and support its friends, instead of anxiously finding fault with them, it must not feel surprised if it loses ground on all sides, and if it finds men whose support it most requires shrinking from it.' Letter (signed 'A Layman') to the *Record*, 3 July 1878.

20 For an extensive survey of the Green case, with particular attention to Bishop Fraser's involvement, cf. Bentley, *Ritualism and Politics*, pp. 105-12.

21 Judgment of the Chancery Court of York, cited in the *Times*, 11 Aug. 1879.

22 Judgment of the Chancery Court of York, cited in the *Times*, 22 Nov. 1880.

23 The arguments presented before the Queen's Bench Division can be found in the *Times*, 7 April 1881. The *Record* thought it ironic that the Ritualists would appeal to a secular court in order to challenge the judgment of the Court of Arches: 'Mr. Green has appealed to the secular Courts to relieve him from the consequences of his obstinate disobedience of Lord Penzance's monition and inhibition. As in former cases, the grounds on which the application was made were minute points of absolute technicality.... There is indeed an extraordinary contrast between the tragic tone in which the imprisonment of Ritualistic clergymen is referred to by those who sympathise with them, and the ludicrously trivial technicalities by which they struggle to escape from "martyrdom".' *Record*, 8 April 1881.

The judges unanimously upheld Lord Penzance's ruling, and reiterated their position, first set down in the appeals of Dale and Enraght, that the Public Worship Regulation Act had not substantially altered the constitution of the Court of Arches as an ecclesiastical court. It had merely instituted new procedures and given the court new powers. Judgment of the Queen's Bench Division of the Court of Appeal, cited in the *Times*, 13 April 1881.

The Ritualists had long since condemned Lord Penzance as a secular judge who had no authority in spiritual matters. Regardless of the bishops' involvement, the power given to the Court of Arches and the Judicial Committee came from 'so-called Church legislation' that was '*secular* in its origin, a violation of the Constitutional settlement of the nation, dishonest and unjust in its aim and application.' Without the approval of the church through Convocation or general synod, argued the author, the clergy were bound to obey the laws of God rather than Parliament. Cf. Anon., *Position of the Ritualists*, pp. 6-7 (his italics).

24 After two days of arguments on behalf of Green, the judges ruled against him without even hearing the arguments of the promoters' lawyers. *Record*, 3 Aug. 1881.

25 It read: 'That the prolonged imprisonment of the Rev. S. F. Green, of Miles Platting, is producing an effect that perplexes the public mind, and fails to maintain the dignity of the law, and is calculated to affect injuriously the position of the Established Church in the eyes of the nation. *Reformandum*, that his Grace the President and the Bishops of the Upper House be respectfully requested to consider whether any and what steps can with propriety be taken to procure the release of the Rev. Mr. Green from imprisonment.' Cited in the *Times*, 22 July 1881.

26 Tait remained unsympathetic, noting that Green could effect his own release at any time: 'A man of common sense and common modesty would have been ready to defer to the authority of the Courts, to the authority of the Church, and to the authority of his own Bishop, to say nothing of the deference due to the law of the land.' He concluded, that 'it was difficult to keep a man out of prison if he were determined to get in, and it was as difficult to obtain the release of a man from prison when he appeared determined to keep there.' Cited in the *Times*, 22 July 1881.

Bishop Fraser, in a letter to the *Times*, similarly suggested that Green had only himself to blame for his continued imprisonment. Green had refused to consider any concession despite the bishop's affirmation that his beliefs and teaching would not be challenged. Letter to the *Times*, 23 July 1881.

In an editorial, the *Times* applauded the position taken by Tait and Fraser. The paper argued that Green's sympathizers were misguided: 'A cause is not good merely because a champion of it goes to prison, and we must not allow spurious or misguided commiseration to obscure the rights and wrongs of a very simple matter.... We may be sorry for the incumbent of Miles Platting, and yet think with the Primate that it would not do to release him only to enable him to exhibit himself before the people of Manchester as having successfully defied the law.' *Times*, 23 July 1881.

The *Quarterly Review* noted that the imprisoned Ritualists had been humorously dubbed 'the Martyrs of Penzance.' Anon., 'Ritualists and the Law,' *Quarterly Review*, p. 201.

27 Their complete response was reprinted in the *Times*, 23 July 1881; cf. Appendix M.

28 In its editorial, the *Times* sympathized with the effort to obtain Green's release but had no patience for the effort to crown him a martyr. He was in prison for contempt of court, and the duration of the penalty was the result of his own 'singularly stubborn conscience.' The paper echoed Tait's complaint. Reform was necessary and an effective penalty, such as deprivation for a second offence, was required to prevent any recurrence of the same events. *Times*, 10 Aug. 1881.

Beauchamp's bill was amended in light of Tait's criticism and sent to committee as 'A Bill for the Discharge of Contumacious Prisoners.' The amendment, which was offered by the Lord Chancellor, put the responsibility on the bishop with regard to the question of whether or not further charges might be brought against a repeat offender. The complete bill, with amendments, was reprinted in the *Record*, 15 Aug. 1881. It ultimately failed in the House of Commons.

By April 1882, with Green still languishing in prison, the bishops considered a similar bill of their own that would have allowed Green's release by substituting the consent of the archbishop for that of the promoters. But like the previous bill, it was defeated in the House of Commons. Cf. Davidson, *Life of Tait*, vol. 2, p. 468. The *Record* continued to oppose the bill because the offender would still be free 'to repeat with impunity the very acts which led to his imprisonment. It is because the Bishops' Bill makes no provision whatever against this evil, an evil clearly perceived and acknowledged by their Lordships last year when Lord Beauchamp's Bill was before Parlia-

ment, that we are bound to oppose it strenuously.' *Record*, 19 May 1882.
29 Tait also carried on, through his chaplain, a correspondence with Green himself to see if a compromise could be obtained that would allow him to maintain his own personal view of the rubrics or to submit under protest. Having repeatedly asked Green what authority he would recognize with regard to the interpretation of the rubrics, Tait's chaplain finally concluded that he would 'repudiate the direction, however given, of his own Bishop. of the Bishops of his Province, or of the United Episcopate of England.' Cf. Davidson, *Life of Tait*, vol. 2, pp. 457-64.
30 The resolutions read: '1. That the thanks of the Council be given to his Grace the Archbishop of Canterbury for his communication of the 10th instant. 2. That though the Council are most anxious to manifest the respect which they entertain for the opinion of the Archbishop and to comply with his wishes, they feel considerable hesitation in addressing the Bishop of Manchester with reference to Mr. Green's case, as from the decided terms in which his Lordship rejected a former communication from the promoters of the suit they cannot but entertain very grave doubts as to the probability of any sufficient guarantees being obtained for the future conduct of Divine service in St. John's Church, Miles Platting. The Council accordingly beg leave to represent to the Archbishop their strong convictions that a proposal for the release of Mr. Green involving conditions on his part ought to originate with his friends, and that it is scarcely within the province of the Council to advise the promoters of the suit to impose conditions upon Mr. Green, in order to secure his release from a penalty incurred by his persistent disobedience of the lawful commands of a competent tribunal.' Cited in the *Record*, 2 Feb. 1882.
31 The CA was annoyed that Fraser had refused to take steps against the curate in charge, who maintained Green's innovations while he was in prison. Bishop Fraser responded to their protest: 'I do not see any power given to you as "parties complainant" under the Public Worship Regulation Act to call upon me to exercise the powers given to me under Section 13 of the statute, with reference to making the due provision for the services of the church and the cure of souls in the parish of St. John's, Miles Platting, during the inhibition of the Incumbent thereof, and for what seem to me good and sufficient reasons I am not disposed to exercise those powers.' Correspondence cited in the *Record*, 3 Feb. 1882.
32 The editorial concluded, 'We believe that no scheme will be accepted by Mr. Green and his friends which does not either directly or indirectly leave him at liberty to indulge in the superstitious irregularities which have involved him in trouble. On the other hand, those who feel deeply the injury which Mr. Green's party are inflicting upon the purity of our Protestant Church cannot, as it seems to us, consent to Mr. Green's release on any other terms than that either willingly or by compulsion he should not renew his former course of illegal innovation. We fail, therefore, to see the basis of any compromise or agreement.' *Record*, 3 Feb. 1882 (their italics).
33 The *Times* noted in an editorial that the results had been largely the opposite of what the CA had intended, and Green's lengthy imprisonment 'provoked an outburst of the very thing it has specially set itself to prevent.' On

the anniversary of his arrest, Ritualists all over the country held elaborate services for him, all of which went well beyond those practices for which he was put in jail. Each act, thought the paper, was a declaration of war and 'a fresh breach of the law.' And ironically, they would all go unpunished. The CA had Green in prison, but all of his allies were virtually free to introduce whatever practices they desired because the bishops would not risk a similar result. Green's crimes were repeated by 'a thousand clerical offenders and done with a comfortable consciousness on the part of the performers that they were in no danger of sharing Mr. Green's fate.' *Times*, 20 March 1882.

34 The *Record* thought the Ritualists were attempting to find a way to circumvent the deprivation. It wrote, 'It is noting short of pitiable cant for Sir T. Percival Heywood to come whining before the public begging them to do what is wholly beyond their power, when he knows well enough that he himself is the only man who at this moment can liberate Mr. Green from his prison without sacrifice of principle. Let him fill up the preferment which for three months has been in his hands, or, if this would violate any conscientious scruple, let him tell the Bishop of Manchester frankly that he does not mean to exercise his right, and allow the Bishop to present to the living. This would be open and straightforward. It would at any rate entitle Sir T. Percival Heywood to a measure of respect which he will look for in vain so long as he strives to excite public sympathy by insincere appeals, while by underhand intrigue he is plotting how he may compass his own ends and evade the law.... So soon, then as Mr. Green's connexion with Miles Platting is effectually severed, so soon may the promoters properly and reasonably consent to his discharge. Until that connexion is effectually severed they have no choice but to remain passive.' *Record*, 8 Sept. 1882.

The *Times* published an interesting letter on the history of St. John's parish, from B. A. Heywood (without indicating whether or not he was related to T. Percival Heywood). He wrote: 'Some 27 years ago the late Sir Benjamin Heywood, of Manchester, informed the local secretary of the Church Pastoral-Aid Society that if the society would supply a clergyman to work at Miles Platting he would pay the salary. The offer was readily accepted, and if the rector of the parish had consented the clergyman would have been set to work. The opposition of the rector induced Sir Benjamin Heywood to build the church of St. John, which in due course was consecrated. The patronage was vested in the founder, and, by Order of Her Majesty, in her Privy Council, dated June 24, 1856, in pursuance of the Parish of Manchester Division Act, 1850, a district was taken away from the mother church and assigned to the new church. The first rector was an Evangelical. In 1865 Sir Benjamin died, and in 1869 the rector resigned, whereupon the present patron appointed the Rev. S. F. Green.

'The important point is this, that the rector of St. John's, Miles Platting, is the mere creature of an Act of Parliament, which was never submitted to Convocation, and save by virtue of such Act, he can neither officiate, preach, administer the Sacraments, nor visit the sick as parish priest at Miles Platting. Cancel the Act of Parliament and the rector is, by the ancient laws of the Church, merely an intruder. Surely those who live in glass houses should not throw stones; and Mr. Green, who is merely an Act of Parliament parish priest, is not consistent in decrying the Judicial Committee of the Privy Council as being like himself a mere creature of Parliament.' Letter to the *Times*, 25 Oct. 1881.

35 Green upon hearing of the deprivation attempted to resign. The *Times* suggested it was a meaningless gesture undertaken only to prevent Bishop Fraser's representative from appearing before Lord Penzance and lending credibility to his court. But, the paper wrote that Green himself, through his 'persistent disobedience to his Bishop and to every other authority,' was solely responsible for the intervention of the Court of Arches. 'He seeks now, by resigning a living he no longer holds, to prevent the mischief from spreading further. That the Bishop should appear before Lord Penzance on Saturday next is shocking to him. He would have done well if he had been equally scrupulous some years ago, before the office of the Judge had been promoted in his case.' *Times*, 3 Nov. 1882.

36 'I do not mean,' said Heywood, 'to accept that notice. (Loud and continued cheering.) I say that Lord Penzance has no power to deprive a clergyman of the Church of England. (Renewed cheering.) The English Church has fought Mr. Green's battle bravely and generously. (Cheers.) My turn comes now. (Loud and prolonged cheering, amidst which the entire audience rose.)' Cited in the *Record*, 6 Oct. 1882.

37 Bishop Fraser's letter to Percival Heywood, declaring the benefice to be void, was reprinted in the *Times*, 6 Oct. 1882. Notice of his intention to apply for Green's release and the appointment of Rev. Ruthven Pym as curate in charge was published in the *Times*, 2 Nov. 1882. The appointment of Pym was rejected by the parish, following a private meeting of the churchwardens, which was led by the former curate. The protesters signed a declaration regarding the new curate as 'an intruder' and refused him their fellowship. *Times*, 8 Nov. 1882.

38 *Record*, 24 Nov. 1882.

39 *Times*, 6 Jan. 1883. Fraser was determined to prevent any recurrence of the Ritualist activities of Green; cf. his letter to Archbishop Thomson, in Thomson, *Life of Thomson*, p. 203.

40 Fraser wrote, 'People are, of course, at liberty to say that they do not like the present constitution of the courts, or that their decisions do not carry conviction to their minds; but this only means that people are at liberty by lawful means to reconstitute the tribunals and to get the unpalatable decisions reversed. It cannot mean, unless anarchy is to be substituted for order, that the courts themselves, as existing, are to be ignored and their most solemn decisions trampled under foot.

'The President of the English Church Union has indeed proclaimed that the party with which he acts will not be satisfied till they have destroyed the appellate jurisdiction of the Privy Council in matters ecclesiastical; but till he has destroyed it by substituting for it a more perfect system he must bear his present burden with as much patience as he can command. The Church of England cannot afford to be deprived at once of the protection and authority of all law; for if you destroy the authority, you destroy at the same time the protection.

'If there is to be "a truce" at all, the only ground upon which it can be reasonably offered or accepted is that both parties should keep within the limits of defined law as it stands, existing provocations being withdrawn and no fresh ones being introduced. Is it unnatural or an improper thing to ask – 'Till the law is altered, keep within the limits of the law?

'I neither am nor ever was a party man. I am not seeking now popularity with a party, or to win a triumph for one; and I deeply deplore that I have been forced into a position which is unwelcome to all my natural inclinations and impulses. But there are principles which I feel found by every sentiment of fealty to my Church and to my office to endeavour to maintain.' Correspondence cited in the *Times*, 12 Jan. 1883.

41   Canon Blakeney, Rural Dean of Sheffield, forwarded to Fraser a memorial signed by fifty-two clergy of the deanery, expressing their respect and support for his wise use of his 'episcopal authority.' They concluded by voicing their hope that the strong direction of the episcopacy, following the example set by Fraser, would roll back 'the tide of clerical insubordination' and vindicate 'the character and interests of the National Church.' Fraser, in thanking them for their support, sought to maintain his non-partisan position and made a point of noting that he had no factional motive. He was only concerned, he avowed, to properly discharge his duties and 'to maintain the supreme authority of law in the regulation of public worship, as the only effective guarantee for the protection of the right of Churchmen.' Unlawful innovations, he concluded, threatened to loosen 'principles of anarchy' that would undermine the position of the church. 'The extreme party refuses alike to recognize the admonitions of the bishop and the decisions of the Court of Final Appeal; and it is time that Churchmen generally should consider whether such a spirit can be tolerated in the Church.' Cited in the *Times*, 19 Jan. 1883.

The *Record* wrote, 'Now, at any rate, we have no right to complain of the supineness of the Bishops. The Bishop of Manchester and the Archbishop of York, probably in concert with other prelates of the Northern Province, have decided on a policy which effectively vindicates the Protestant character of our Reformed Church. There is an opportunity now for union amongst loyal Churchmen of all parties which has never been furnished before, and it will be our own fault, if those who have come forward, at the very moment when everything seemed on the point of being lost, are not adequately supported.' *Record*, 12 Jan. 1883.

Percival Heywood appealed Fraser's veto to the Queen's Bench Division. After a year's delay, the judges rejected the appeal. It was announced shortly thereafter that there would be no further appeals, as a candidate had been found who was acceptable to both Heywood and Fraser. The *Record* concluded, with a note of sarcasm, 'He must be a very remarkable man.' *Record*, 25 Jan. 1884.

42   Fraser continued, 'It is not merely that a chasuble is worn at the celebration of the Holy Eucharist, but that it is put on and taken off at a peculiar time and in a peculiar manner, and with divers ceremonial accompaniments. Sundry ministrants and sub-ministrants and servers, variously clothed and variously employed – sometimes to swing the censer, sometimes to light the

altar candles, sometimes to "receive the priest's biretta and place it on the credence," sometimes tolling the sanctus bell – all help introduce a ceremonial which is, as I have said, new and strange to English Churchmen.' Cited in the *Record*, 28 Nov. 1881.

43 Fraser also thought his admonition would provide Evangelicals with the opportunity to raise their level of compliance if they were guilty of omitting anything: 'I by no means call upon you all, or all at once, to rise to that standard of the maximum. In many parishes it may not be expedient even to attempt to rise to it. But in all parishes it is not only expedient but right that there should be no neglect or even careless observance of plain, unambiguous, and important rubrics; and, further yet, that every attention should be paid to the decorous, orderly and reverent conduct of Divine service in all churches.... Because I would reduce excesses of ritual, it must not be supposed that I sanction, or am even indifferent to, slovenly, irregular, irreverent ways.' Ibid.

44 Ibid. Three years later, Bishop Fraser thought his approach had been successful. In his 1884 charge to the clergy of Manchester, he said it had been almost unanimously accepted, and several churches had reduced their ritual in compromise. But many more, said Fraser, had taken the 'opportunity to raise their services from the level of blandness, if not slovenliness, to something more akin to decency and order; and I believe that the general result has been a considerable increase of the spirit of reverence and devotion, so far as these can be influenced by external things, in the congregations of the diocese. And although I see it still pleases hostile critics in newspapers to describe the experiment as a complete failure, to those who know the actual results it will seem to have been a success far beyond what I dared to expect or even hope for.' Cited in the *Record*, 14 Nov. 1884.

Looking back at the end of the century, H. C. Corrance, a Ritualist turned Roman Catholic, noted the irony of the Ritualist position: 'They lost the habit of episcopal obedience, on which Newman so strongly insisted, at the time when the bishops were endeavouring to crush the ritualistic movement, and, although the bishops are either more favourable or less actively hostile to the movement than they were, they have not yet regained that habit.' H. C. Corrance, 'The Development of Ritualism,' *Contemporary Review* 74 (1898): 100.

45 C. L. Wood rejected Bishop Fraser's declaration as an attempt to enforce, 'under ecclesiastical disguise,' the erastian authority of Lord Penzance and the Judicial Committee. The Ritualists, he declared, would never submit to any bishop who issued admonitions based on judicial decisions. 'We intend,' he concluded, 'God helping us, to destroy it, and we shall not be cajoled into surrendering up the rights and liberties of the Church of England, her sacred ceremonies, and her prescribed ritual, into the hands of the Privy Council, at the bidding, not of a synod, for that is no synod in which presbyters are forbidden to speak, but of a bishop.' Letter to the *Times*, 28 Nov. 1881.

The Ritualists generally refused to acknowledge the authority of bishops as individuals, claiming that they would only be bound by the authority of the voice of the church, expressed either through Convocation or a general synod. Drawing an analogy to the situation faced by the early apostles when confronted by the leaders of the Jewish community, the Ritualists argued that, in all good conscience, they must obey the laws of God rather than those of human authorities. Cf. Anon., *Position of the Ritualists*, pp. 7-9.

The *Record*, along with the CA, had often blamed the bishops for having allowed Ritualism to develop unchecked. The more temperate tone adopted by the paper can be seen in its positive response to Fraser's admonition. One could easily imagine the paper, in the earlier years of the controversy, condemning his action for its moderation. But, the paper concluded, 'We refrain from saying one single word by way of prejudgment, and we await the result with considerable interest. Meanwhile it is but just to recognise the effort which by holding this Synod the Bishop of Manchester has made to abate the wretched condition of anarchy into which the Ritual struggle has plunged the Church of England. Whether successful or not, the Bishop has done what he can to put a stop to this state of things. We daresay that exception will be taken on the one hand to the method he has chosen, and on the other to the limited extent of his directions; but we confess we are in no humour to scrutinize too minutely any effort honestly and earnestly made to terminate the most dangerous crisis to which the Church of England has been exposed for the last two hundred years.' *Record*, 28 Nov. 1881.

Bishop Goodwin of Carlisle, in a pastoral letter to his diocese, viewed Fraser's admonition as an attempt to find 'an honourable retreat' for Green through which he might be released from prison by honoring his bishop's request without having to acknowledge the validity of the courts. Goodwin expressed great regret that Wood should have interfered to prevent such a result and accused him of 'Popery in a new form.' The clergy of Manchester were hardly allowed time to consider the appeal 'before a Bull issues from London denouncing the whole proceeding, and declaring authoritatively what *we* do or do not intend to do. I deplore this unauthorized interference of the President of the English Church Union between a Bishop and his clergy.' Cited in the *Record*, 13 Jan. 1882 (their italics).

46 The spectacle of Green's long imprisonment led most to oppose prosecution, but it did not engender sympathy for the Ritualists. The *Times* warned them not to make too much of their apparent victory: 'They may be free henceforth to gesticulate in any way they please, to light forbidden candles, to prostrate themselves at forbidden times, and generally to perform the various antics of devotion which their own rules order and which the law of the Church prohibits. But granting that they have got their own way, what do they imagine they have gained by it? Among men of sense and education what adherents can they claim, and what converts do they seem likely to make?... They will do very wrong if they suppose that the success they have gained by the defects of the law and its apparatus can be of any real value to them. Do what they will, they have no chance whatever of exercising a permanent grasp over the nation or the Church.' *Times*, 3 Nov. 1882.

At the end of the century, Eugene Stock wrote, 'For probably no one event in the history of the past half-century has done so much to foster the Romanizing movement, and to injure the Evangelical cause, as the imprisonment of Mr. Green; for – however important – it transferred to his side the sympathies of vast numbers of good and moderate men.' Stock, *Church Missionary Society*, vol. 3, p. 7.

47 Green refused to pay the court costs, as ordered, and his property was seized by a sheriff's officer. *Times*, 1 March 1881. In the end, Dale's costs were paid by several supporters and the sequestration on his property was removed. *Times*, 8 Dec. 1881.

James Bentley noted that the cumulative effect of the four priests in prison had been to alter public opinion with regard to the prosecution of the Ritualists. But the forced sale of Green's goods to pay legal costs, he concluded, was 'particularly horrifying.' Bentley, *Ritualism and Politics*, p. 112.

48 *Record*, 10 Aug. 1881.
49 Ibid.
50 H. Marshall thought the CA's policy would have a decidedly negative effect: 'I write under very serious feelings. The son of Evangelical parents, I desire to see my own children grow up in the faith of their fathers; but I see with pain and sorrow that the young and ardent, who have always a warm sympathy for whatever appears like injustice, are repelled everywhere from Evangelicalism by such cases as these. Rightly or wrongly they learn to associate Evangelicals with persecutors, and their Ritualistic friends make the most of this. It is difficult to defend the Church Association in the present case, or the Evangelical party.' Letter to the *Record*, 17 Aug. 1881.
51 Letter from 'A Member of the Council' to the *Record*, 24 Aug. 1881.
52 Bishop Ryle defended the appeal to the courts in his first charge to the clergy of Liverpool in 1881. The law could not be defended by the bishops until its meaning was ascertained by 'competent judges.' And he thought it unlikely that the innovators would give any credence to episcopal admonitions without that legal clarification. He rejected the charge of persecution. Rather, he said, 'those who break the law and refuse to obey their bishop are the real persecutors of the Church.' Ryle, *No Uncertain Sound*, pp. 21-22.

In an editorial on Ryle's charge, the *Record* took up a similar position: 'It is now the fashion to discredit and decry these efforts (which, on the whole, have been exceedingly successful) to ascertain the law of the Church of England as to questions of ritual. It is difficult to conceive how anyone who knows the facts can question the utility of this litigation. It must be remembered that in the early days of Ritualism it was the custom of its votaries to claim for themselves the credit of a scrupulous regard for the law. It was the Low Church clergy who were denounced as lawbreakers, and with so much confidence and persistence that many who had no sympathy with Ritualism yet felt doubtful as to the course they ought to pursue. If we compare that state of things with the present, and inquire what it is that has turned the Ritualists into acknowledged lawbreakers and anarchists whose contempt for authority has made them a byword among all classes of the nation, undoubtedly the change is due to the Church Association prosecutions, which have exposed the real nature of Ritualism and have stripped from it its mask of pretended adherence to Church law. Whatever view we may take of its more recent policy, it seems to us that the Church of England owes to the Church Association a deep debt of gratitude for this result of its doings.' *Record*, 21 Oct. 1881.

53 When Bishop Jackson sent his secretary, Mr. Lee, along with one of his chaplains, Rev. Sinclair, to take charge of the parish, Mackonochie read a letter of protest repudiating the authority of the court and of the bishop insofar as he acted as an officer of the state: 'I regard, as in duty bound, with very great deference and respect the document from his Lordship the Bishop of the diocese which has just been read to me. Notwithstanding this, however, it is my duty to God to refuse to recognize you, or any other priest not sanctioned by me, as entitled to supersede me, even for a time, in the cure of souls in this parish. The charge of souls in this parish was duly and canonically committed to me by his Lordship's predecessor on the 3d day of January, 1862. It is a charge as so given to me by the Bishop, of a purely spiritual character, conferred by him, not in his private capacity, or as a State officer, but as the successor of the Apostles, and through them, of Christ Our Lord.... Now, I have not been suspended from the office thus conferred upon me by any Court which has like authority from God to deprive me of what He has given, or thereby to release me from the responsibility of holding it and using it for Him to the best of my powers.... Therefore, I hereby declare that no priest has or can have any right or power to minister in this church save myself and any others whom I may authorize to officiate in my stead.' Cited in the *Times*, 24 Nov. 1879.

The argument became a common one among Ritualists. R. W. Enraght similarly refused to acknowledge the admonitions of Bishop Philpott, suggesting that his directions were dependent on the decisions handed down by the Judicial Committee. In the face of such 'unlawful and uncanonical "admonitions' and 'judgments",' wrote Enraght, it was his duty to refuse obedience. He was bound by 'a higher authority, the Rules and Orders, Constitutions, and Directions of the Church.' Furthermore, he suggested that the bishop's opinions expressed in the admonition, insofar as they contradicted Enraght's view of the true claims of the church, were only an expression of Philpott's 'private judgment and individual opinion.' As such, his ordination oath could not be invoked, and he was not bound to obey. Enraght, *My Ordination Oaths*, pp. 8-9.

W. J. S. Simpson, in his history of Anglo-Catholicism, attempted to justify the distinction. The bishops, he claimed, had no spiritual authority to compel obedience from Ritualist clergy. When they acted as 'agents of the State,' they forfeited their spiritual office and 'were enforcing the intrusive jurisdiction claimed by the Crown.' Sparrow Simpson, *The History of the Anglo-Catholic Revival*, p. 214.

54 To a degree, it was recognized that the popularity of the priest was a factor in any negative reactions to imprisonment. The *Record* thought the jailing of Mackonochie would be a grave mistake, given his prominence. He openly courted 'the martyrdom of a gaol,' said the paper, and the CA would be wise to undertake a new proceeding under the Church Discipline Act. That bill, unlike the Public Worship Regulation Act, allowed for deprivation rather than imprisonment. *Record*, 26 Nov. 1879.

At the CA's spring meeting, Lord Oranmore and Browne resigned his

Vice-Presidency in protest. The *Record* summarized his speech, 'The Association had for twelve years been carrying on a law suit at an expense, he supposed, of more that £12,000., and at last obtained a decree of suspension against Mr. Mackonochie. But notwithstanding that, he continued to officiate at St. Alban's in defiance of the order of the Archbishop's Court. Now it seemed to him (Lord Oranmore and Browne) that the simple course was to apply to the Court to enforce its decree. But the Council did not think fit to take that course, and he entirely dissented from the course which they had adopted. (Hear, hear.)' *Record*, 5 March 1880.

55 Lord Penzance acknowledged the logic of the proceeding, but thought it a frivolous use of the court that cast doubt on its authority in the prior case. He also questioned whether his court had the power to deprive in a case concerning matters of ritual. Judgment of the Court of Arches, cited in the *Times*, 19 Jan. 1880. The *Times* wrote that Penzance was willing to allow it to proceed since the case had the support of Bishop Jackson, but it was clear to him that it would only take more time, create further expense, and provide no insurance regarding the suppression of Mackonochie's activities. *Times*, 19 Jan. 1880.

Martin explained his position in a letter to the Bishop of London: 'It is due to Christian friends with whom I have been associated in this matter to state publicly that I did not leave them free to act on their own opinion as to enforcing submission by imprisonment to the judgments of the Court in the former suit; but positively refused to allow my name to be used in any measures which might have that end in view. In my own defence I can only say that when proceedings were originally taken, it was understood that their object was simply to ascertain authoritatively the law of the Church on certain points, which, when ascertained, would be acquiesced in on both sides, and obeyed. It never occurred to me, nor, I suppose, to anyone else, that the judgments of the Courts of Law would be set at defiance, and that obedience could only be enforced by imprisonment. Had such a result been foreseen, I should not have allowed my name to be used as the Promoter. In submitting to the severe rebuke of the Dean of Arches for not proceeding to imprison the Rev. Mr. Mackonochie, it is some consolation to me to know that the course I have taken has been in accordance with the views of your Lordship, and of many of those who hold positions of high authority in the Church of England.' Correspondence cited in the *Record*, 21 June 1880.

In its obituary for Martin, the *Record* praised his conscientious stand. It also noted that he had 'but little part in the later episodes of the Mackonochie litigation, and for some years before his death had withdrawn from the Council of the Church Association.' *Record*, 22 May 1885.

56 'If it were not for the bad precedent it would create, we should have been very glad if Mr. Mackonochie had been suffered to go on with his proceedings at St. Alban's without even the nominal interruption he has been subject to.... But what Mr. Mackonochie has been doing in an obscure street of Holborn might be repeated in other quarters if no interference were offered. It is not likely that so extreme an example will be copied at all points. Others might be willing to break the law, but scarcely anybody else could be found to defy the law and its terrors after Mr. Mackonochie's fashion. Mr.

Martin's success, however partial it may be, may thus avail to check the kind of proceedings against which the suit has been directed. There will be fewer unnecessary candles, fewer unlawful prostrations, fewer unlawful vestments than there might have been if Mr. Mackonochie had passed his off unchallenged.' *Times*, 19 Jan. 1880.

57 For a time, the parish was the scene of no small uproar. As Enraght's replacement, Rev. Alan H. Watts, attempted to read the articles before the church on his first Sunday there, about one hundred of Enraght's supporters disrupted the service and walked out in protest. The *Record* interpreted their disgraceful behavior as evidence of the natural outcome of 'Ritual lawlessness.' *Record*, 16 March 1883.

Enraght attended the spring vestry meeting, during which he 'made a violent speech subversive of all authority, and boldly avowed that he came there to create a disturbance.' One of his supporters was elected churchwarden and proposed a resolution declaring Enraght's deprivation illegal. He called on Rev. Watts 'to resign a position to which he has no ecclesiastical right.' Watts refused to allow the resolution and declared the meeting closed, at which point a general riot broke out. *Record*, 30 March 1883. The *Times* condemned Enraght's behavior in an editorial that would suggest that the imprisonments had not altered public opinion with regard to the Ritualists. The paper thought Enraght had 'forfeited once for all not only the sympathy, but even the respect of all right-thinking men.' *Times*, 30 March 1883.

Interestingly, the Evangelical Simeon Trust obtained the benefice and held the right of appointment following the deprivation of Enraght. At a protest meeting held shortly thereafter, Enraght acknowledged the inevitability of the final result and told those gathered that the church would pass into the hands of the 'bitter enemies of their cause.' *Times*, 7 Nov. 1882.

58 For the complete correspondence, cf. Davidson, *Life of Tait*, vol. 2, pp. 475-80. The *Record*, looking back on the turn of events, viewed it as Tait's final attempt to prevent further divisive litigation. 'It had become plain that whatever good was to be derived from the Law Courts had been attained in the judgments which settled the law, and that the prolongation of suits for the purpose of enforcing the law in special cases was doing harm. The late Archbishop, with his usual sagacity, perceived this, and on his deathbed strove to put an end to the Mackonochie litigation in the only possible way. His touching appeal to Mr. Mackonochie to resign his benefice and retire from further conflict with the Courts was the result.' The paper denied, however, that Tait had altered his view of the Ritualists or intended a broader toleration: 'His whole career bore witness to a keen realization of its errors, and of the peril in which its upholders have involved our Church. It would be in the highest degree unreasonable and unjust to assume that in the weakness of his last days he threw aside the settled convictions of a lifetime.' *Record*, 12 Jan. 1883.

59 In their protest to Bishop Jackson, they complained that his actions were an implicit approval of Mackonochie's innovations. They concluded with a 'solemn protest against a transaction which they look upon as a reproach to the episcopal bench, a betrayal of the Protestant Reformed religion estab-

lished by law, and a dishonour to the Gospel of the grace of God.' Cited in the *Times*, 3 Jan. 1883.

A similar memorial, signed by Evangelical clergy, was sent to Jackson. They regretted that Mackonochie had been given a new benefice 'without any securities as to his future good conduct' and expressed their belief that the bishop's action would 'appear to the public to be inconsistent with law and order,' implying that he tacitly approved of 'the illegalities of Romish ceremony.' The signatures were headed by: Charles D. Bell, Honorary Canon of Carlisle; H. B. Tristram, Canon of Durham; C. Clayton, Canon of Ripon; and Henry Pratt, Canon of Peterborough. Cited in the *Times*, 16 Jan. 1883.

60 Jackson's conclusion was particularly irritating for anti-Ritualists, suggesting as it did that the Ritualists ought to be left alone on account of their conscientiousness and zeal: 'If there are those who, knowing, as I do, the good and self-denying work done among the poor and ignorant by such men as Mr. Mackonochie and the late Mr. Lowder, are yet, on account of differences in discipline and doctrine (the seriousness of which I do not wish to extenuate), unable to appreciate or afraid to acknowledge it, I cannot sympathise with them; I can only pity them.' Correspondence cited in the *Times*, 6 Jan. 1883.

James Maden Holt responded on behalf of the CA: 'My Lord, I have read that paragraph in your letter with dismay.... Its sentiments would justify the promotion of Francis Xavier or of Ignatius Loyola, were they now living, to a benefice in your gift. I am deeply grieved to think that your Lordship is willing to entrust the care of the souls of the "poor and ignorant" to any clergyman, regardless of the doctrine he may teach, provided he be self-denying in his ministrations, and earnest in his erroneous convictions.' Correspondence cited in the *Record*, 19 Jan. 1883.

The argument was apparently a common defense of the Ritualists. Two years prior, following the imprisonments of Dale and Enraght, the *Quarterly Review* had rejected the idea that the Ritualists somehow deserved toleration because they were zealous and pious. Every society had to have some rules and regulations, and the journal thought it absurd that the clergy should not be held to 'certain doctrines, rites, and ceremonies' simply because they were fervent and devoted. Such broad toleration, the writer concluded, would never be allowed in any other denomination and could be used to justify the entrance of Dissenters and Papists into Anglican pulpits. Anon., 'Ritualists and the Law,' *Quarterly Review*, pp. 208-09.

61 The paper also thought the appeal to Tait was mistaken: 'We can only repeat what we have already said, that the late Archbishop's action was aimed at getting rid of a particular method of fighting Ritualism – viz., litigation, and had not for its object the encouragement of Ritualism itself. But, after all, what the late Archbishop meant, or did not mean, does not settle the question. If the toleration of the Mass is right it must be so independently of any desire for peace of the late Primate. And this is just where the Bishop of London's defence utterly fails.' *Record*, 12 Jan. 1883.

According to James Bentley, Tait had favored greater toleration, particularly in cases where the parishioners were satisfied with the services, even if the practices exceeded the exact limits of the law. He also vetoed the prosecution of C. F. Lowder, Vicar of St. Peter's, London Docks, on the basis of his conscientious work there; cf. Bentley, *Ritualism and Politics*, p. 113. Similarly, David L. Edwards suggested that Tait greatly regretted the unforeseen and disastrous results of the Public Worship Regulation Act he had sponsored. Edwards, *Leaders of the Church of England*, pp. 119-20.

In contrast, however, Archbishop Thomson and Bishop Fraser took a different view. In correspondence with Frederick Hanbury, a member of the ECU council, during the time of Green's imprisonment, Thomson and Fraser questioned his claim that Tait had sanctioned innovations similar to those of Green in another parish. Cf. Thomson, *Life of Thomson*, pp. 203-11.

The *Record* copied an extensive report of Mackonochie's first service at St. Peter's from the *Daily Telegraph*, which indicated that he had modified none of his ritual. *Record*, 2 Feb. 1883.

62 The article, written shortly after Tait's death, suggested that the new archbishop would do well to bear in mind that there were 'other persons and parties' to be considered besides the Ritualists. 'Neither the Evangelical party, nor the strong Protestant feeling which exists among a large proportion of the laity of all parties, can either with justice or safety be disregarded; and a compromise is the utmost that can reasonably be expected of them on this subject.' Anon., 'Archbishop Tait,' *Quarterly Review*, pp. 24-25.

63 The court proceedings were reported in the *Record*, 15 June 1883.

64 Judgment of the Court of Arches, cited in the *Record*, 27 July 1883.

65 According to the *Record*, Bishop Jackson intimated that he feared riots would break out among Mackonochie's supporters if the sentence was enforced. *Record*, 2 Nov. 1883.

66 Having expressed a certain sympathy for Mackonochie, the paper continued, 'If a man chooses to resist he is liable to the penalties attached to disobedience, and has only himself to blame if they are enforced against him. We may doubt the expediency of enforcing them in any particular case, or we may withhold our sympathy from the motives which have led to their enforcement, but it is impossible to deny the abstract obligation of obedience to the law when the law has been invoked, and when its decision has been declared.... The law may be harsh in its provisions, cumbrous in its procedure, inappropriate in its penalties. But the remedy is not disobedience, nor can the true interests of the Church be promoted by the spectacle of continued contumacy in its ministers.' *Times*, 1 Jan. 1884.

67 *Record*, 4 Jan. 1884. Anti-Ritualist concerns were reinforced when the Bishop of London immediately agreed to license Rev. Lincoln S. Wainwright, who had served as curate at St. Peter's for the past decade under both Lowder and Mackonochie. To their further dismay, Jackson also gave Mackonochie a 'general licence' to officiate in the diocese. Since it was unattached to a particular living, that licence was beyond the reach of the ruling of the Court of Arches. *Times*, 17 Jan. 1884.

J. B. de la Bere, who had also been deprived, was similarly licensed to assist in Brighton, by Bishop Durnford of Chichester. When the local Working Men's Branch of the CA protested, Durnford responded that de la Bere was a man 'of blameless character and exemplary diligence in his ministerial office,' who had been quite sufficiently punished for the nature of his offence. The protesters replied, with no effect, that the law could not possibly have intended to allow 'the immediate re-installation in office of the offender.' Correspondence cited in the *Record*, 12 Sept. 1884.

68 In April 1882, E. H. Plumptre, the non-partisan Dean of Wells, published a compromise he intended to offer in the Lower House of Convocation. He suggested that the Ornaments Rubric should be altered to legitimate the use of either the black gown or the surplice in the pulpit as well as eucharistic vestments in the communion service. The *Record* thought the proposal only concealed 'vital differences' through the use of 'reversible rubrics and ingeniously ambiguous expressions.' The paper continued, 'What are the facts? A section of clergy, full of earnestness and zeal... have brought back amongst us a system which may without injustice be called Popery without the Pope. They disapprove of the modern Roman dogmas, and they, as a rule, renounce the Papal supremacy, but they adhere tenaciously to the doctrine and the ritual of the Mass; they exalt the sacraments as highly as the Romish system does; and they practise and insist more and more on Auricular Confession. In short, they would restore the Church to the religious position it occupied at the close of Henry VIII.'s reign. Backed by a small but extremely earnest body of laity the Ritualistic clergy are steadfastly and immovably bent on carrying their point.... On the other hand, there are a large body of Churchmen (we trust the majority) to whom the principles of Popery, whether in the Church of Rome or outside of it, are the principles of Antichrist, men who standing in the place of the Reformers and reaping the benefit of their work feel bound to carry it on. To them unless the Church of England is a Reformed Church it is no Church at all. They dare not falter, they cannot hesitate, they can accept no compromise of principle, no "give and take" in this matter.' *Record*, 14 April 1882.

Samuel Garratt, who had previously expressed his opposition to further litigation, supported the *Record*'s position against compromise. 'The real point to be considered,' he wrote, 'is not how to make the appearance of agreement where there can and ought to be no compromise, but where and how the conflict is to be carried on – in books, in pamphlets, in sermons, in fair controversy, in which the Word of God is to be judged and the consciences of Christian men the executioners; or in courts of law, in which lawyers are the judges and jailers the executioners? In the one case the doctrines may themselves be examined and discussed, and we ought to have faith enough to believe that the truth will prevail; in the other case, the public vindication of God's truth is made to depend primarily on the judgment of lawyers, and ultimately, on overcoming a man's convictions, sincere though erroneous, by keeping him in prison till he yields, if he yields at all.' Letter to the *Record*, 21 April 1882.

69 Bickersteth, *Evangelical Churchmanship and Evangelical Eclecticism*, p. 3.

70 'Evangelical Churchmen as a body are clearly entering upon a new phase of their history. New circumstances entail, whether we will or not, new conditions, and to a certain extent a new policy. We cannot, however much we may wish to do so, simply imitate our fathers. Our effort must be, to be guided by their principles, to seek the same heavenly aid, and to trust in

humble faith that our acts and words may bear witness to the same zeal, the same love, and the same wisdom as they were permitted to show in the trying and difficult days of what is now generally known as the great "Evangelical revival".' *Record*, 12 Jan. 1883.

The *Guardian*, a High Church paper, also viewed Bickersteth's pamphlet favorably. 'It is certainly evident that some of the points which Mr. Bickersteth most rightly urges, go beyond mere externals, and indicate more than simple growth of aestheticism. They represent, in fact, not abandonment of any positive Evangelical principles, but undoubtedly an enlargement of the basis on which those who profess these principles have hitherto been content to stand.... Looking at them in connection with the adoption on the other side of much which would there have once been refused or depreciated, in regard to preaching of conversion and assurance of faith, we cannot but see in them signs of a certain mutual instruction of the two great parties of the Church, in which each learns from the other positive lessons, and unlearns certain negations, on which it once laid stress. Such interpenetration of ideas we regard as profoundly significant; and, we may add, of good promise, not only for the cause of unity but for the cause of truth.' Cited in the *Record*, 9 Feb. 1883.

In contrast, M. J. Bickerstaff, Vicar of Cookley, near Kidderminster, took a negative view of compromise. He did not believe aestheticism really promoted 'spiritual religion,' and suggested that there was 'a forgetfulness of the sublime truth that "God is a Spirit, and they that worship him must worship him in spirit and in truth".' Bickerstaff questioned whether the young would really be drawn to their churches simply by imitating the Ritualists, or if the proponents of assimilation were not merely 'sacrificing the feelings of the old and middle-aged to the fancies of the young.' Finally, he questioned whether the 'hearty service' often advised was really 'of the heart' simply because it was full of music, chanting and other aspects that appealed to the senses. In all these thing, the proponents of change suggested the 'leveling-up' of Evangelical churches. In Bickerstaff's view, 'all the changes made and advocated are in the one direction, of bringing us nearer in assimilation to the apostate Church of Rome.' Letter to the *Record*, 2 March 1883.

71 'Let us be plain and emphatic in our teaching in this matter. Let us not leave the impression on anyone's mind that we do not attach very much importance to Holy Baptism, or that we hold the erroneous idea of Zwingli that the Holy Communion is nothing more than a bare memorial of the death of Christ. I feel persuaded that the hazy and hesitating and negative teaching of many Evangelicals with respect to the sacraments has given an enormous advantage to the plain dogmatic teaching of extreme High Churchmen.... We must give people the positive truth on these matters, which they can lay hold of and make their own; and this will be a better preservative against error than any amount of warning, and condemnation, or any number of prosecutions in the law courts. (Expressions of dissent.)' Cited in the *Record*, 19 Jan. 1883.

72 Ibid. A similar opinion was expressed by the Broad Church Dean of Westminster, A. P. Stanley, in a collection of essays first published in 1880. Stan-

ley, while critical of the Ritualists, thought their innovations of little real significance. They displayed, he wrote, 'a morbid dependence on the priesthood; a vehement antagonism to the law; excessive value attached to technical forms of theology and ritual; a revival of a scholastic phraseology which has lost its meaning;' but all of those 'evils' were 'beyond the reach of legal or ecclesiastical tribunals.' In Stanley's view, they could only be countered 'first by fearless and dispassionate argument, secondly and chiefly by the encouragement of a healthier tone in the public mind and clerical opinion, as at once a corrective and a counterpoise.... Let us be firmly persuaded that error is most easily eradicated by establishing truth, and darkness most permanently displaced by diffusing light; and then whilst the best parts of the High Church party will be preserved to the Church by their own intrinsic excellence, the worst parts will be put down, not by the irritating and often futile process of repression, but by the pacific and far more effectual process of enforcing the opposite truths.' Stanley, *Essays on Ecclesiastical Subjects*, pp. 218-21.

73 Charles D. Bell, Rector of Cheltenham, wrote, 'I and many more felt pained and saddened by the tone of some of the addresses. We of the Evangelical body seem to be departing from the old lines. If we are to believe and receive all that we heard, what have we now distinctive.... I heard much from the speakers of the expediency of following the aesthetic tastes of the age, but nothing, as far as I remember, of this increased ritual being more for the glory of God or the edification of the worshippers. It is very true that the adoption of the surplice in the pulpit and putting surplices on our choirs may be matters indifferent in themselves, but do they not break the uniformity that has prevailed so generally among the Evangelical body? And if so, is not this to be deplored?' Letter to the *Record*, 26 Jan. 1883.

In his survey of the Evangelical movement, G. R. Balleine briefly mentioned the importance of the 1883 Islington meeting, but he mistakenly interpreted the *Record*'s report to imply that the participants of the meeting, in general, called for an end to prosecutions. In fact, the divisions ran deeper than Balleine suggested. Cf. Balleine, *Evangelical Party*, p. 231.

74 The *Record* noted that the differing opinions expressed at the meeting indicated the existence of two sections within the Evangelical party, hinting that it was somewhat unfair of conservatives to question the commitment of those who took a different view. 'Let these two, and possibly other more or less well-marked varieties of Evangelical opinion, be frankly recognised. If either section holds aloof from the other (or others) our united strength is gone. Let there be more cordial acknowledgment on all sides of the loyalty to principle and the purity of motive that animate, as we trust, all alike.' *Record*, 19 Jan. 1883.

An anonymous letter from an older Evangelical, suggested that conservatives were deluding themselves if they thought they were holding strictly to old principles while avoiding all outside influence. 'Look at our churches, look at the greater attention to outward appearance, the character of the singing, the very terms and things used. Why, in earlier days to speak of the "Holy Communion" instead of the "Lord's Supper," to use a lectern, or preach without bands, were considered high offences. And look at the clergy assembled at a conference or large clerical meeting; see how rare it is to find the old-fashioned tie and turndown collared coat. The stiff collar, the clerical coat, are well nigh universal, and so in other things.... Canon Bell deprecates aestheticism, but let him compare his own beautiful church of St. Matthew's, with its grand brass lectern and studied ecclesiastical appearance, with the old parish church where Francis Close preached for so many years, with its high pews and three decker, and say is there no advance in aestheticism there? I do not deprecate it; far from it. I only want to show that we have changed, and I believe rightly. We have, and I am not ashamed to own it, borrowed much from the High Church party, and they have borrowed much from us. There are as many shades of difference in the High Church party as there are amongst ourselves. The difference is they do not parade them as we do. Who can doubt the good work that Canon Eliot is carrying on at Bournemouth, and yet because he differs on some one point or two he is to be cried down. He must be more than mortal if these attacks can make him more affectionately disposed towards those who thus decry him....

'I have no desire to minimize the danger we are in from the Romanizing party in our Church, but to confound all High Churchmen with them, and to wrangle amongst ourselves, is surely playing into their hands and rendering our own work more difficult.' Letter (signed 'A Sexagenarian') to the *Record*, 9 Feb. 1883.

Another correspondent, viewed it in terms of a generational division. 'If those leaders of the Evangelical party in the south of England will persist in entertaining suspicions of those (generally) younger men who have surpliced choirs and preach in the surplice, I fear that they will not long be looked up to as leaders.' He thought the innovations found broader acceptance in the north and estimated that four-fifths of the members of the Craven Evangelical Union had adopted the surplice, 'without in any degree forfeiting their claim to be considered as Evangelical as Canon Bell.' Further, he thought that there was little difference in this regard between Evangelical churches and Dissenting chapels. At the same time, the distinctiveness of the Ritualistic parishes was diminished and fewer young people were drawn to them. Letter (signed 'A young West Riding Vicar') to the *Record*, 16 Feb. 1883.

75 'It was the opinion of the Council,' said Holt, 'that they must not for one moment think of abandoning the work in which they had been engaged, and they must not suffer the advantages already gained to be rendered nugatory; but it was their duty to follow them up by measures calculated to secure obedience to the law. (Hear, hear.)' Cited in the *Record*, 11 May 1883.
76 Ibid.
77 Ibid. Still there were some within the CA who questioned the policy. J. H. B. Gapper, a lay member, affirmed his support of the original prosecutions, but he believed the organization's money would be better spent on educational efforts. Letter to the *Record*, 29 June 1883.

An anonymous respondent claimed the CA had spent some £50,000. in their efforts to determine the meaning of the law and enforce it. Having clarified some sixty disputed points, he asked, were they to allow the Ritualists 'to defy the law with impunity?' The threat of the law was the only thing they feared. 'Argument is certainly as a principle better than law, but it is not so with the lawless and illogical. Christian men must not shrink from the opprobrium of going to law; the law is to protect the right.' Letter (signed 'A Member of the Council of the Church Association') to the *Record*, 6 July 1883.

78 J. Maden Holt complained that 'the London press was closed against them to a great extent.' Several letters had been sent to the *Times*, vindicating the position of the Association after it had been attacked in the paper's columns, but the letters were refused publication. In other ways as well, Holt suggested that the organization found it increasingly difficult to get its message to the public through the press. Ibid.

79 Ibid. According to G. R. Balleine, the Evangelical penny paper, the *Rock*, which had been known for its vituperation, following the lead of the *Record*, soon adopted a more moderate tone as well. The extreme anti-Ritualists were left without a journalistic organ until they purchased the *English Churchman* in 1884. Cf. Balleine, *Evangelical Party*, p. 232.

80 *Record*, 18 May 1883.

81 Ibid. In November 1889, in the course of an exchange of letters in the *Record* with Henry Miller, Secretary of the CA, R. Payne Smith, Dean of Canterbury, mentioned a private meeting that took place in December 1884, which was never reported in the paper. In arguing that the CA's policy of prosecution had only exacerbated the controversy, created sympathy for the Ritualists, and put the Evangelical party in a bad light, Payne Smith suggested that Miller, in an earlier letter, had conveniently ignored the meeting. He continued, 'I was one of a deputation which had an interview with the leaders of the Church Association in the library of the National Club. We thought that we had made you thoroughly understand that your prosecutions were disapproved of by a large number of Evangelical men, as being unspiritual weapons, without warrant in Holy Scripture, and for which you have no commission, being a private Society, in no way appointed or authorized to take upon you the maintenance of discipline in our Church. I feel bound now to say publicly what I then said privately.' Letter to the *Record*, 1 Nov. 1889.

Miller responded by suggesting that Payne Smith had broken a bond of confidentiality by detailing the events of the meeting, noting that all of the participants had 'pledged beforehand to regard its proceedings as private.' Letter to the *Record*, 15 Nov. 1889.

82 *Record*, 11 May 1883 and 31 Oct. 1884.

83 It was little wonder, concluded the paper, that anti-Ritualists were despondent when they considered even the use of the surplice in the pulpit as a sign of Ritualist influence. 'Great harm' the paper continued, 'is done by allowing the enemy to claim as fresh triumphs what are really nothing of the kind, and great injustice is done to brethren who, while true as ever to Reformation principles, yet think it wise to give in to the whims of the age on these minor matters. We are aware that in doing so we are laying ourselves open to fresh rebukes from critics like the gentleman who at the Church Association Conference challenged us to say whether the *Record*

had not become "the authorized organ" of this policy of yielding in matters of fashion.... We confess that we have no great relish for the modern taste in these matters, and rather prefer the old-fashioned ways which contented our fathers, but we see no use in attempting, and we feel no desire, to conflict with the spirit of the age.' *Record*, 18 May 1883.

In an editorial surveying the history of the Mackonochie prosecutions, the *Times* also noted the results of thirty years of controversy. 'Evangelical Protestantism,' said the paper, 'has lost something of its asperity, and Ritualism of the less irreconcilable type has secured a larger and more generous measure of toleration.' Aestheticism, it noted, had 'more or less affected all parties in the Church, and even some communions beyond its pale. Nonconformity itself and even Presbyterian Scotland have yielded somewhat to the influence of Ritualism, which may, in one aspect, at any rate, be regarded as little more than the ecclesiastical counterpart of the modern aesthetic movement.... Evangelicals are certainly more tolerant of practices which a generation ago they would have denounced as rank Ritualism, and Ritualists themselves, perhaps, are now less tempted to indulge in further aggressive innovations.' *Times*, 1 Jan. 1884.

The innovations continued to disturb conservative anti-Ritualists for years to come. At an 1890 meeting of the CA, Rev. Talbot Greaves bemoaned the state of the Evangelical party: 'It had been the folly of the past,' he said, 'to give up one point after another, till services which thirty years ago would have been regarded as decidedly Ritualistic were now looked upon as mildly Evangelical.' Cited in the *Record*, 14 Nov. 1890. In response to the planning of celebrations for the one hundredth anniversary of the beginning of the Oxford Movement, Thomas Houghton complained about its influence among Evangelical congregations. He was willing to allow that the movement's influence had spread throughout the whole Church of England, and even beyond, but he was unwilling 'to give God thanks' for that fact. He concluded with the lament, 'We feel that the Oxford Movement and the devil are at the bottom of the formalism, worldliness and the flesh-pleasing services of many Evangelical Churches.' Houghton, *Oxford Movement Exposed*, pp. 38-44.

84 Cited in the *Record*, 8 June 1883.
85 In May 1884, the *Record* noted with satisfaction the appointment of Boyd Carpenter as the successor to Bickersteth as Bishop of Ripon. The paper thought he held similar views and would continue the work begun by his Evangelical predecessor. *Record*, 23 May 1884. In the next issue, an anonymous writer suggested that men such as Boyd Carpenter ought to be rightfully claimed by the Evangelical party, but the conservative section was too often offended by such things as a surpliced choir, early communion, and the use of the High Church hymnal, *Hymns Ancient and Modern*. The correspondent continued, 'On matters of doctrine he probably differs little from the commonly received Evangelical views, though the frequent communions would appear to point to rather high sacramentarian opinions respecting the Lord's Supper. Now, will these things be admitted by the older members of the Evangelical body to be consistent with fidelity to the party (I use the word in no invidious sense) to which they themselves belong?

Would a man like Canon Carpenter be accepted as an Associate Secretary by the C.M.S., or receive a grant from the Pastoral Aid Society? I hardly dare hope so. There has been a feeling displayed in meetings, conferences, committees, and gatherings of all sorts during the last twelve months on the part of some of those who adhere to the older form of ritual, which has repelled and frozen up the sympathies of some who would gladly have united with them in those works which lie near their hearts. Is not this unwise?... Why should it be thought an impossibility by so many that a man whose use resembles that at Christ Church, Bayswater, should preach Christ faithfully? I hail with much pleasure, Sir, your recognition of the bishop-designate as a sympathizer with the views of your journal, and trust that no suspicion of disloyalty may attach to one who shall hereafter describe himself as an Evangelical like the Bishop of Ripon.' Letter (signed 'Neo-Evangelical') to the *Record*, 30 May 1884.

86   Bishop Jackson thought the unexpected imprisonment of clergy was the 'death-blow' of the Public Worship Regulation Act. Public sympathies almost immediately shifted to the imprisoned clergy who were viewed as martyrs. Jackson concluded that the act, at least with regard to its use in litigation concerning matters of ritual, was 'crippled if not dead.' Cited in the *Record*, 14 Nov. 1884.

87   The *Record* suggested it was time for the CA 'to look facts in the face and to draw from them those conclusions which we believe a little consideration will show to be inevitable.' After fifteen years of litigation, they were no closer to suppressing Ritualism. Given the intransigence of the Ritualists, 'two courses were open to the promoters of suits against offending clergymen. They could, like Mr. Martin, refuse to enforce the disregarded sentence by imprisonment, and allow the proceedings to fall into abeyance. This is of course a result which, after years of expense and labour, cannot be regarded as satisfactory. Or they might, as in the Dale case, pursue the remedy the law has provided, and procure the commitment of the offenders for contempt of Court. This again is felt to be a result to bring about which it would be altogether unfitting to initiate proceedings, though perhaps inevitable as to suits already commenced. The existence of this dilemma, while it causes infinite satisfaction to our opponents, is a matter to which in arranging our future policy, we must have due regard.' *Record*, 2 March 1881.

The result was, no doubt, that which the imprisoned Ritualists desired, even to the point of courting such a fate. As the Archbishop of Canterbury noted during the debate in the House of Lords, 'it was not easy to keep people out of prison who desired to be there. He felt great sympathy with what was said on a similar occasion by William III. – "That gentleman has made up his mind to be a martyr, and I have made up my mind to disappoint him".' Cited in the *Times*, 8 March 1881.

88   Even the Evangelical bishops were generally opposed to prosecution. In his 1885 charge to the clergy of Rochester, Bishop A. W. Thorold expressed the view that prosecution had been futile since the decision in the Bennett case. Even if Ritualists were forced to give up their ceremonies, the court had refused to prevent them from proclaiming their doctrine in their sermons.

Thorold reaffirmed his opposition and adopted a policy intended to isolate any Ritualist clergy who refused his advice, but he refused to allow legal proceedings. Cited in the *Record*, 30 Oct. 1885.

E. H. Bickersteth, the new Evangelical Bishop of Exeter, expressed a similar view in 1886: 'I cannot say that no infringement of the lawful usages of our Church, however offensive and persistent, would justify an appeal to the Court when the congregation are offended (for the laity have their rights as well as the clergy), but I am sure that it should be the very last resort. So long as the only ultimate penalty which the law courts can impose upon a recusant clerk is imprisonment (instead of suspension, and, if still refractory, deprivation of his benefice), prosecutions seem to me to aggravate the evil they are meant to suppress. I shall feel therefore bound, except in extreme cases, to exercise that right of veto which the Public Worship Regulation Act confers upon me. But I am sure this resolve gives me the strongest claim upon my clergy for their submission to my judgment and admonition as their Father in God.' Cited in the *Record*, 18 June 1886.

In a journal entry from January 1881, Archbishop Tait wrote approvingly of a recommendation made by Bishop Magee of Peterborough, 'if a Royal Commission be now issued, the Bishops would be justified in maintaining the *status quo* till it had reported, allowing meanwhile no fresh prosecutions for past changes, and insisting no new changes be allowed.' Cited in Davidson, *Life of Tait*, vol. 2, p. 432.

89 Ryle, *No Uncertain Sound*, p. 197. The *Times* complained about the imprisonment of clergy and expressed the hope that the Ecclesiastical Courts Commission would urge legislation that would prevent the Ritualists from claiming 'the martyrdom of a prison cell," and result instead in their deprivation. The editorialist concluded, "Mr. Green's friends say that Lancaster Castle is not the place for him; but neither is the rectory of Miles Platting, and the sooner he and conscientious opponents of the law as declared by the Privy Council recognize this, the better will it be.' *Times*, 23 July 1881.

90 J. C. Ryle, the new Bishop of Liverpool, held out little hope that the commission could resolve the controversy. He thought it doubtful that any legislation, satisfactory to both sides, would be able to pass through Parliament. The church's best hope, thought Ryle, was for clergy on all sides to agree to obey the law while, if necessary, working to amend it. Ryle, *No Uncertain Sound*, pp. 86-88.

91 Bishop Magee of Peterborough was one of the early proponents of a commission. His correspondence from this period reflected some of the conflicts that arose in raising support for it and the opposition of extreme Ritualists to any compromise. Cf. MacDonnell, *Life of Magee*, vol. 2, pp. 153-57. For correspondence regarding the political work involved in obtaining government assent to the idea of a new commission, cf., pp. 437-50.

92 In addition to the two Archbishops, it included Bishops Browne (Winchester), Mackarness (Oxford), and Benson (Truro). A complete list of the committee was published in the *Times* on 12 May 1881.

Interestingly, the *Edinburgh Review* was much more critical of the one-sidedness of the appointments: 'No one pretends, or could pretend, that the Commission was framed to represent with fairness the various parties of the Church of England.' The essayist went on to describe the members. In addition to the archbishops, the three bishops were all decidedly from the High Church party. The Diocesan Chancellor of Canterbury, who was a moderate, was included, but the Chancellor of York, Lord Grimthorpe, who was decidedly anti-Ritualist, was not. An editor of the *Guardian* was present, but there was no one from the *Record*. Similarly, the ECU was represented but not the CA. Of the lay members, the president of the CMS was on the commission, but the other members were 'High Churchmen of different shades of opinion.... The general good sense of the laity could hardly find expression through such a Commission. A statesman like Mr. Gladstone would hardly pretend that such a Commission was calculated for that end. It has no doubt given as well as it could the views of the High Church party in its various shades; and the most general result which readers will gather from it, is that the demands of the High Church party have very much extended during the last few years.' Anonymous, 'Ecclesiastical Jurisdiction,' *Edinburgh Review* 159 (1884): 213-14.

The *Times* was sceptical with regard to any results that might follow. It thought there might be a respite in the controversy but questioned whether the commission could agree on legislation that would satisfy either of the parties. 'There are clearly two distinct objects aimed at by the Bishops in proposing the inquiry. One is reasonable toleration and latitude of practice in matters not essential the other is a simple, certain, and accepted procedure in cases of dispute. It is difficult to say which of the two will be found to be the more difficult of attainment when the time comes for fresh legislation on the subject.' *Times*, 8 March 1881.

93 For an extensive summary of the recommendations made by the commission, cf. *Times*, 13 Aug. 1883. Under the recommended legislative changes, clerical contumacy would have resulted in suspension and, if repeated, in deprivation rather than imprisonment. The anti-Ritualists had long argued that imprisonment should be replaced by deprivation. The courts would remain largely unchanged, but the episcopacy would have greater authority. The *Times* thought the least alteration possible would be the best policy. It was chiefly concerned that disobedient clergy would no longer be sent to prison and allowed 'to set themselves above the law and to go on for a term of years doing what a series of tribunals have agreed in forbidding them to do.' Ibid. Similarly, cf. Ryle, 'The Church Courts Commission,' *Contemporary Review* 45 (1884): 170.

The *Quarterly Review*, prior to the publication of the commission's report, suggested that however the Public Worship Regulation Act was modified or amended, nothing could 'alter the fact, that in the last resort a State Court of some kind or other, whether the Queen in Council or the Queen in Chancery, must be supreme. If the Church of England were disestablished, this difficulty would still remain; and no device can evade it.' Anon., 'Archbishop Tait,' *Quarterly Review*, p. 25.

94 Canon Liddon said, '"What Churchmen who are of my mind have seriously and deeply at heart is this: That there should not be a lay Final Court of Appeal dealing with not merely ceremonial but Christian doctrine, and able to impose their decisions upon the Ecclesiastical Courts below." And in an-

swer to the question of the Dean of Durham – "You think a lay Court so objectionable as a Final Court of Appeal, that you do not see any mitigating circumstances to make it good?" – he says – "Certainly, I do not see that any body of laymen have authority from Christ our Lord to decide for the Church of Christ such questions as were decided in the Gorham case, or in the Essays and Reviews case".' The paper reported a similar response from C. L. Wood, the president of the ECU. Cited in the *Record*, 5 Oct. 1883.

Archbishop Benson recognized the central issue early on. In a letter to his wife, as the commission began its work, he wrote that he had dinner with Wood and several other Ritualists. Despite his own High Church leanings, he could not agree with their demands regarding the courts. He concluded, 'But without wishing to take any coloured view it does seem to me that the result of the E.C.U. determinations would be to re-constitute an appeal to an external See. There is no hope or help for it, if they will have no appeal to the Crown in any form. This will be our final crux.' Benson, *Life of Benson*, vol. 2, p. 245.

95 Ibid. The *Times*, in reporting on the discussion of ecclesiastical courts at the Reading Church Congress, similarly criticized the extreme Ritualists for their unwillingness to compromise. 'The ultimate supremacy of the temporal power,' wrote the paper, was 'a fact which cannot be got rid of, and would never be surrendered to the High Church party.' Many concessions had been made to 'the advocates of unrestrained spiritual authority,' but they had to realize that royal supremacy was non-negotiable. *Times*, 6 Oct. 1883.

The *Quarterly Review* optimistically suggested that Archbishop Benson might have a better chance of obtaining some compromise from that Ritualists, who had largely distrusted Tait. Nevertheless, the journal thought it would be 'a grievous mistake, far more serious than any yet committed, if it were to be understood that by some means or other the pretensions of the Ritualists were to be unreservedly admitted.' Anon., 'Archbishop Tait,' *Quarterly Review*, pp. 25-26.

96 'But whatever else this Report may be, it is certainly not, what some have termed it, a compromise. It is a reawakening of the clerical spirit, lifting its head and looking round on a world – how changed! There is scarcely a clerical claim urged in the time of Henry VIII. but finds its revival here. Nay, Canon Stubbs would take us back to the pretensions of the mediaeval Church. This Report might be called an epitome of the claims of sacerdotalism.' Anon., 'Ecclesiastical Jurisdiction,' *Edinburgh Review*, pp. 252-53.

97 The words were those of Canon Taylor at the fall meeting of the Liverpool Branch of the CA. Taylor noted that the report had received the support of the *Record*, and that the paper had claimed the Evangelical party was largely supportive, but he complained that it made too many concessions to the Ritualists. According to the *Record*, those at the conference applauded Taylor's condemnation. *Record*, 19 Oct. 1883.

The *Record*, which even when disagreeing with the CA usually couched its differences in temperate language, was sharply critical. It suggested that the complaints were ill-conceived and calculated to appeal only to 'an uneducated audience.' The paper continued, 'We look in vain for any capacity to grasp the present conditions of the conflict in which it has heretofore played so leading a part,' although it still held out hope that the CA might in the future 'still exert a great and salutary influence.' *Record*, 2 Nov. 1883.

98 The *Record* suggested that it deserved the careful consideration of all Evangelicals. The central committee took a generally positive view of the report, but would have preferred a stronger statement with regard to royal supremacy. It was also concerned that the commissioners were divided on the subject of the episcopal veto, although eight of them had indicated their opposition. Finally, it was disturbed by the fact that the previous judgments would be left open for the new court to reconsider. And the judgments of the new court would not be binding and could be reconsidered in each new case. The central committee feared that such an alteration of the courts would leave the Ritualists largely unrestrained, since previous rulings would not be considered binding in later cases. Cited in the *Record*, 5 Oct. 1883.

J. C. Ryle was strongly opposed to the episcopal veto even after he became Bishop of Liverpool. He argued that it undermined the right of appeal and gave the bishops a power better reserved for the judiciary. Ryle, 'Church Courts,' *Contemporary Review*, p. 172.

99 The two limitations urged in the memorial were: '(1) The necessity of guarding the rights of the laity from real, or apparent, infringement by the uncontrolled exercise of the episcopal veto. (2) The necessity of preventing questions fully argued in, and determined by, the Court of Final Appeal from being reconsidered whenever they happen to arise in subsequent cases.' The signatures were headed by R. Payne-Smith, Dean of Canterbury. It was signed by a number of prominent Evangelicals. Cited in the *Times*, 7 Dec. 1883.

The *Record* immediately supported the memorial: 'It gives us no little satisfaction to record our complete accord with the views expressed in the Memorial, the terms of which have evidently been carefully chosen.' The paper rejected the charge that the commissioners had compromised too much for the sake of peace. 'It is just because the Commissioners have declined to listen to those who advocated such a course that we are able to echo the hope of the memorialists that the Recommendations will be brought before Parliament at an early date with a view to their legislative adoption.' *Record*, 7 Dec. 1883.

The Council of the CA, however, adopted a resolution criticizing the report and the UCLA's memorial. Reprinted in the *Record*, 14 Dec. 1883; cf. Appendix N.

100 In an 1889 letter to the *Times*, Randall Davidson, then the Dean of Windsor, challenged the Ritualists to state publicly what sort of court they would be willing to obey. In reciting the history of the controversy, he wrote of the commission: 'During the autumn and winter the report was everywhere discussed, and it is an open secret that a Bill to give effect to its recommendations would have been introduced in 1884 but for the certainty that it would be opposed both inside and outside Parliament by the disaffected section of High Churchmen, and that the well-meant endeavour would thus prove worse than useless.' Letter to the *Times*, 2 April 1889.

James Bentley suggested that the lack of unity among the commissioners would not have encouraged Parliament to act. Only nine of the members signed the final report without reservations, and Lord Penzance issued a separate report altogether. Cf. Bentley, *Ritualism and Politics*, p. 114.

The division over what would constitute an acceptable court remained a point of controversy for years to come. In 1889, Canon George Perry published an article detailing 'the grievances' of the High Church party (largely from the Ritualist's perspective). He argued that the church was 'a divinely constituted society' with certain privileges. The most important of which was 'the right of this society to judge and decide by its officers [by which he meant the ordained clergy] all questions of the divine law, and all matters which may be properly described as spiritual or ecclesiastical.' Perry, 'Grievances of High Churchmen,' *Nineteenth Century*, p. 501. Augustus Jessopp, a moderate non-partisan, responded with a scathing critique of Perry's demands. He argued, in the first place, that the divine society never existed apart from and in relation to another society, the state. And in the second place, the society did not only consist of officers but of the laity as well. In Jessopp's opinion, the High Church 'officers... had gone on brooding so long over their own supposed wrongs that they had lost all power of conceiving that any one had any rights except themselves.' He further suggested that there was, across the nation, 'the sullen roar of a great people steadily getting louder, more distinct, more articulate, and struggling to shape itself into menacing self-assertion,' representing the voice of the laity who would never 'surrender the Royal supremacy into the hands of the clergy.' Augustus Jessopp, 'Are They Grievances?' *Nineteenth Century* 26 (1889): 831-32. The dispute would continue through the end of the century. Cf. George Arthur, 'The "Lawless" Clergy of the '"This Church and Realm",' *Nineteenth Century* 45 (1899): 558-69.

101 In his 1884 charge to the clergy, Bishop Fraser denied what was apparently a widely held view – that the bishops had decided together to veto all cases. Fraser said, 'I have several times seen it publicly stated that the bishops have come to an agreement among themselves, in the exercise of their discretion, not to allow any more ecclesiastical litigation till the constitution of the ecclesiastical courts has been revised. I do not believe that any such agreement has been either suggested or arrived at. I can only say that such a proposal, from whomsoever emanating, has never reached me.' Cited in the *Record*, 14 Nov. 1884.

Bishop Ryle argued in his 1887 charge that legislation was the only solution. The earlier acts had to be either amended or improved, and courts must be established that required the obedience of all. Ryle feared that legislation would probably lead to some secession, but he saw no alternative. 'No doubt the danger of legislation is very great. But in my opinion the danger of doing nothing at all is greater still.' He did not, however, think Parliament would ever approve two demands of the Ritualists – they would never approve of a purely clerical final court of appeal, nor would they again grant an episcopal veto. Ryle, *No Uncertain Sound*, pp. 163-65.

The *Edinburgh Review*, in its article on the report of the Ecclesiastical Courts Commission, suggested that Parliament was unlikely 'to renew a

power which has been used to an unexpected extent and capriciously.' Anon., 'Ecclesiastical Jurisdiction,' *Edinburgh Review*, pp. 239-41.
102 According to James Bentley, thirty-three proceedings were vetoed by the bishops between 1874 and 1906. Bentley, *Ritualism and Politics*, p. 121.
103 Cobham claimed they had vetoed seven out of eighteen representations made under the Public Worship Regulation Act. Speakers following Cobham took a similarly critical point of view. Rev. C. H. Wainwright proclaimed, somewhat optimistically, that the whole country would rally behind the CA when the defendant in a proceeding was 'not the Rev. Mr. So-and-so, but the Right Rev. the Bishop of So-and-so.' Cited in the *Record*, 30 May 1884.
104 Holt claimed that the CA desired, before proceeding, to have a mandate from the Evangelical party supporting their attempt to prosecute a bishop. 'We desire,' he said, 'in anything that we do in this matter to act as the agent for the Evangelical body in the Church of England, at any rate for that section of it which is dissatisfied with the existing state of things.' Cited in the *Record*, 14 Nov. 1884.

In an editorial, the *Record* made it clear that the CA represented only a small minority of Evangelicals and expressed its regret at the 'tone of exasperation towards the bishops' adopted at the meeting. While allowing that the bishops were partly to blame for the controversy, the paper sharply condemned the proposed policy: 'We profoundly regret the new scheme of bringing law suits against the bishops, because we believe that ecclesiastical litigation, whether against bishops or clergymen, is at the present time not only undesirable but extremely likely to do mischief to the cause of Protestant Evangelical truth in the Church of England.... We can hardly imagine any course more certain to prejudice public opinion against the party who pursue it, more inevitably doomed to failure so far as practical result is concerned, or more directly calculated to deaden spiritual vitality and promote a harsh un-Christian spirit.' *Record*, 14 Nov. 1884.
105 Ryle made no apologies for his determined opposition to the Ritualists, but he also claimed to deal fairly with all legitimate parties in the church. When he learned of his elevation to the episcopacy, he immediately withdrew from the CA. His concern to act strictly within the limits of the spirit of the law were evident in the position he adopted concerning the consecration of the parish of St. Agnes, which was endowed by a prominent Ritualist layman. Several Protestants protested when it was announced that a number of prominent Ritualists would preach at the service and requested that Ryle 'inhibit convicted violators of the law from preaching or officiating in the diocese.' Cited in the *Record*, 16 Jan. 1885.

Ryle replied that there were no legitimate grounds upon which he could comply with their request: 'Under these circumstances I am unable to see how I could refuse to consecrate St. Agnes' church on the ground of your suspicion that something may possibly be done there at some future time which the law has forbidden.' While acknowledging the reputation of the clergy invited, Ryle concluded that he had no legitimate right to prevent their participation: 'If I were to interfere with any one of them and forbid his preachings, I believe I should take up a position in which neither law, custom, nor public opinions would support me. My business is not to make laws, but to administer them.' Ryle spoke at the consecration of St. Agnes, but he indicated his personal protest at the Ritualist tendencies of the proceedings by not attending the luncheon held after the service. Correspondence cited in the *Record*, 23 Jan. 1885.

Interestingly, a 'clerical correspondent' suggested in the *Times*, when Ryle was nominated to the episcopacy, that no other Evangelical 'would be so acceptable to High Churchmen.' He suggested that Ryle had made many friends among the High Church party through his involvement in the church congresses and was known as a moderate. He noted that Ryle had offended many of the more conservative anti-Ritualists by his moderate tone and concluded, 'there can be no doubt that under his direction a higher tone of churchmanship will be realized than would have been possible under a Bishop of whom the Evangelical clergy would have been jealous.' *Times*, 16 April 1880.

106 Ryle continued, 'It is the plain duty of the Bishops to require obedience to the Queen's Courts, and it is not reasonable, just, fair, or kind, to expect them to sanction disobedience.... As for those clergymen who habitually persist in doing things which the Queen's Court have distinctly condemned, I fail to see how their conduct can be justified, and I wonder how any sensible layman can support them. They place their Bishop in a most painful and awkward dilemma. He must either sanction illegality, and pour contempt on his Sovereign's judicial advisers, or else he must sanction the prosecution of some popular clergyman, and at once be branded and denounced as a persecutor by a public which is always ready to support a defendant. What is a Bishop to do?' Ryle, *No Uncertain Sound*, pp. 89-90.

Ryle was not alone in his concern. The subject was also taken up by Bishop Mackarness in his charge to the clergy in July 1887, shortly after Bell Cox was released from prison. Mackarness, who was viewed by conservatives as a Ritualist sympathizer, nevertheless took a hard line on this point: 'I doubt whether it has been sufficiently noticed that the strategy of arraying public feeling against the enforcement of legal rights is widely extending itself, and with no promise of peace and quiet for our country in the future. The policy of the defendant in the Liverpool ritual case is not distinguishable from that of the persons who refuse to pay rent in Ireland or tithe in Wales. The attempt in all these cases is to make the law odious by a display of personal suffering.... It is not difficult to recall other cases in which resistance to unpopular statutes has been organized, and, if it has not wholly succeeded, has made itself felt sufficiently to weaken the general authority of law. Is this a result which Churchmen should seriously desire to promote?... It will, no doubt, be said that we ought to "obey God rather than men" – an obvious truth. But to obey man is sometimes the true way of obeying God. Disobedience to earthly authority is not, on the face of it, obedience to God; although in the heated atmosphere of controversy in which we now live too many persons act as if it were.' Cited in the *Record*, 1 July 1887.

107 Ryle explained his position in response to a lay memorial concerning the Bell Cox lawsuit: 'I do not enter into the merits of the case. I only say that to

interfere between a person who charges another with breaking the law and a court of justice is to take up a position which I decline to adopt. The law may be bad or good, but so long as it is the law I suppose every subject will admit that it ought to be respected.

'Let me add to this what I have already told the clerical memorialists, that I object strongly to what is commonly called "the Episcopal veto".... I consider that the "veto" places a bishop in a most invidious and difficult position, exposes him to the charge of partiality or undue severity, and invests him with an arbitrary power which I do not think should be reposed in a bishop's hands In this view of the "veto" I am supported by the high authority of eight members of the late Royal Commission on Ecclesiastical Courts, including, among others, the Archbishop of York and Lord Chief Justice Coleridge.' Correspondence cited in the *Record*, 13 March 1885.

108 The *Record* reported that Ryle had received a letter threatening to blow up the church with dynamite if something was not done to halt the Ritualist ceremonial practiced there. According to the paper, neither the bishop nor the vicar took the threat seriously, but a guard of police was directed to watch the church. *Record*, 27 April 1883.

109 The *Record* reprinted a report from the *Liverpool Courier*, which noted that since the church had opened in July 1869, 'the services had been conducted with what is commonly known as ritualistic ceremonial, the "six points" being uniformly adopted – namely, the eucharistic vestments, altar lights, incense, wafer bread, the mixed chalice, and the eastward position.' According to the report, similar charges had been brought some eleven years prior against Rev. Charles Parnell, the first vicar of the church. Those charges were abandoned when the promoter, Walter Roughton, withdrew from the suit. Parnell afterwards resigned, and in 1876, Bell Cox, 'who had been one of the assistant clergy for seven years previously, succeeded him as vicar.' The paper identified Hakes as 'a prominent local supporter of the Church Association.' Cited in the *Record*, 13 Feb. 1885.

110 The charges were the use of altar candles, elevation of the sacramental elements, the mixed chalice, prostration during the prayer of consecration, bowing before a crucifix, making the sign of the cross to communicants and at the absolution and benediction, eucharistic vestments, the eastward position, singing the *Agnus Dei*, concealing the elements during the prayer of consecration, the ceremonial washing of the cup after communion, and kissing the Bible after reading the gospel lessons. The *Times* reported on an exchange of letters between John Gamon, the bishop's legal secretary, and Bell Cox. Gamon noted that Ryle had refused to allow proceedings while the Ecclesiastical Courts Commission was meeting and afterward when there remained some hope for legislation amending judicial procedure. With no hope for immediate legislative intervention, Ryle felt bound to allow the case to proceed, but was willing to halt it if Bell Cox would make some concessions. Bell Cox, in his reply, rejected the idea of conceding anything and repudiated the authority of the courts. He also complained that the agitation came from outside his parish, raised largely by extremists who were disturbed by the consecration of St. Agnes. Correspondence cited in the *Times*, 17 Feb. 1885.

111 The paper continued, 'Has past experience, and we have certainly had plenty, proved the utility of such efforts? We venture to say it has not. The imprisonment of Messrs. Green, Dale, and Enraght did more to create a fictitious sympathy with Ritualism in the public mind than anything else which has occurred. It was, we cannot doubt, impolitic to procure the committal of these clergymen, but a repetition of the same mistake now would be unpardonable. At any rate, it should be clearly understood that the great body of Evangelical Churchmen look with neither favour nor acquiescence on the recommencement of ritual litigation at the present time. Let us oppose Ritualism with all our might, but let us do so with common sense.' *Record*, 20 Feb. 1885.

112 James Bentley cast Ryle in a more negative light, labelling him 'an anachronism.' He suggested that Ryle sought to keep the controversy alive. Disappointed with the failure of the Public Worship Regulation Act, what Ryle really wanted, according to Bentley, 'was a better instrument to hammer the Ritualists.' In a footnote, Bentley suggested that Peter Toon had put 'a favorable gloss' on Ryle's actions and attitudes. Bentley, *Ritualism and Politics*, pp. 114-15.

In the article to which Bentley referred, Toon merely suggested that Ryle sought to combine his Evangelical principles with a strong belief in the comprehensiveness of the Anglican church. He cited Ryle's speech to the Bishopric Committee of Liverpool, shortly after it was announced that he would be the first bishop of the newly created diocese. Ryle said, 'I come among you as a Protestant and Evangelical Bishop of the Church of England; but I do not come among you as the Bishop of one particular party. I come with the desire to hold out the right hand to all loyal churchmen, by whatever name they are known. I am sure you do not want me to come among you as a milk and water Bishop, a colourless Bishop without any opinions at all.' While not intending to narrow the comprehensiveness of the church, Ryle argued that there were nevertheless reasonable limits to toleration. Still, he acknowledged that there would always be differences of interpretation and suggested that the lines should not be unnecessarily sharpened. Toon noted, however, that Ryle thought the Ritualists stepped over the boundaries with their eucharistic doctrine, and still more, with their contempt for the court's rulings with regard to the interpretation of the rubrics Peter Toon, 'J. C. Ryle and Comprehensiveness,' *Churchman* 89 (1975): 277-81.

Archbishop Benson recorded his thoughts after discussing the matter with Ryle: 'He was very earnest and oppressed about it, seems to have tried honestly his best to avoid it. But these people like B[ell Cox] who are so excellent in theory of obedience, never obey a Bishop even when he speaks of his own authority.' Benson continued, referring to Ryle's dealings with the new Ritualist parish of St. Agnes, 'The Bishop had behaved magnanimously in consecrating a church for them. Without any sense of honour, the man immediately adopts all manner of illegal practice.' Benson, *Life of Benson*, vol. 2, p. 243.

There can be no doubt about Ryle's commitment to Evangelicalism and his opposition to the doctrines of the Ritualists, but he attempted for some time to keep the Bell Cox case out of the courts and was evidently motivated, in allowing it to proceed, by a strong sense of the need for upholding the law rather than a strictly partisan desire to pursue Ritualist clergy.

113 Ibid. Ryle defended his position in response to an article in the *Guardian*: 'My attention has been called to a paragraph at the end of your leading article last week, in which you say, "The peace of the Church has been broken by the determination of the Bishop of Liverpool not to use the discretion with which he is invested by law." This is a heavy charge, and I am not disposed to submit to it in silence....

'Let me then ask a plain question? Would it not have been more accurate, and much more fair, if you had made the following statement? – "The peace of the Church has been broken by an incumbent in the diocese of Liverpool, who refused to obey the friendly admonition of his Bishop to abstain from practices in the administration of the Lord's Supper which have been declared illegal by the Queen's courts. To the lawsuit against this incumbent which has been instituted, the Bishop is no party, though he has not prohibited it."

'I fail to see the justice of your language about a Bishop who upholds the law, and declines to prohibit enforcement, while you cannot find a single word of disapproval for an incumbent who has habitually disobeyed the law, and has twice within five years refused to listen to his Bishop's fatherly admonition about things which are certainly not essential to the administration of the Lord's Supper. Which of the two "has broken the peace of the Church;" the Bishop or the incumbent?

'If you tell me that it has been formally settled that the judgments of the Queen's courts about matters of ritual are not law, and therefore are not binding on the clergy and need not be obeyed, I ask you to inform me when and how and by whom that formal settlement has been made. At present I cannot learn that these judgments have been reversed, or declared null and void by any competent authority. Under these circumstances I think that a Bishop who considers it his duty to maintain the authority of the Queen's courts, as representing the Royal supremacy, has a just right to complain when an influential paper like the *Guardian* speaks of him as one whose "determination has broken the peace of the Church" in 1885.' Correspondence cited in the *Record*, 8 Jan. 1886.

114 Letter to the *Record*, 13 March 1885.

115 The paper suggested that a few Evangelicals, 'some of the wisest and most respected of our leaders,' had opposed litigation from the very beginning. The great majority, however, supported the CA as long as the suits aimed to ascertain the precise limits of ritual allowed by the church's articles and formularies. The paper concluded, 'Our own view, which has been consistently maintained from the commencement of these disputes, is that the suits to ascertain the law and to vindicate the Protestant character of our public worship were right and wise. When they were started it was assumed by everybody that whichever side was declared to be in the wrong would bow to the decision of the Church Courts. When, however, it appeared that the suits begun in this belief would, so far as the actual defendants were concerned, be abortive unless imprisonment were resorted to, it

became, in our view, a question of expediency rather than of principle whether it was wise to enforce the law or not. We pointed out again and again the great distinction between the completion of litigation begun without any thought or intention to imprison the offender, and fresh litigation begun with the knowledge that, practically, imprisonment must be its issue. Although there was much difference of opinion as to the wisdom of enforcing the sentences in the existing suits by committal to prison, no one, so far as we remember, ventured to defend the initiation of fresh litigation. The opinions which we then expressed not only hold good now, but have acquired double force by what has happened in the interval. The imprisonments, the wisdom or unwisdom of which was five years ago an open question, are now seen clearly enough to have been a serious blunder, honestly made, but which has, notwithstanding, produced very unfortunate results. Facts, therefore, seem to us to have themselves condemned in advance the new prosecution which has been instituted at Liverpool.' *Record*, 27 Feb. 1885.

116 *Record*, 27 March 1885. In June 1885, the paper gave a lengthy report of a lecture given by Rev. C. F. Newell at the Western Clerical and Lay Association meeting at Clifton. According to Newell, there was a general feeling of 'repugnance' created by the imprisonment of clergy which he attributed to three factors: 'First, that the selection of persons to be prosecuted seemed to be arbitrary, and the punishment personal, whilst others indulging in the same practices were allowed to go scot free; secondly, that the prosecutions were not for the most part promoted by persons who might justly complain as parishioners, but by outsiders; thirdly, that the Ecclesiastical Courts before which these cases were brought had not general confidence, as shown by the issue of a Commission of Inquiry, and the largely divergent opinions which that Commission had elicited.' But on a still deeper level, thought Newell, prosecutions ought to be objected to on fundamental Christian principles. 'He thought they would indeed do well more earnestly to cultivate a spirit of brotherly love – marking more eagerly points of agreement than matters on which they were constrained to differ. When they saw, as indeed he thought they might see increasingly, a deep spirit of devotion and a longing after holiness, surely they saw a man walking with God, and should it be said "that he shan't walk with me?" They might think him mistaken upon some points, and they might be right and he might be wrong, but did they not think they would convince him or anybody else by putting him into gaol?... As to uniformity in externals, he owned he did not value it highly, and would not enforce it at too high a cost, and would prefer to leave all enforcement to those in authority. He would regard external matters of mere ritual, as he thought men not heated by controversy were increasingly inclined to regard them. He argued that against error the grand weapon was not the sword of the magistrate, but the sword of the Spirit – the Word of God.' Cited in the *Record*, 12 June 1885.

117 Stevenson Blackwood, a prominent lay Evangelical, repudiated the anti-litigation position adopted in the letter of the three clergy and by the *Record* in its editorials. He was also disturbed by the paper's claim that those who relied on the courts lacked faith in the truth. 'This is a taunt,' wrote Black-

wood, 'unworthy of the ability and fairness of spirit in which the *Record* has now for some time been conducted, and makes me, for one, feel that it is gradually departing from the thoroughly Protestant lines which have hitherto characterized it.' Letter to the *Record*, 10 April 1885.

118 *Record*, 18 Dec. 1885.

119 In January 1886, Hakes attempted to extort Ryle's suppression of the curate, suggesting that he would not proceed with the case against Bell Cox if the bishop would take over the services at St. Margaret's or appoint a law-abiding curate. Ryle, through his lawyers, refused to have any part in the matter, and said Bell Cox had the right to appoint the curate during his suspension. When Hakes complained about the activities of Paine, Ryle refused to allow further proceedings. He had hoped, Ryle's lawyer concluded, 'that the promoter would have been satisfied with the decision in his favour without proceeding to enforce personal penalties against Mr. Cox as to the result of a position taken up by him which must, his Lordship thinks, in the course of events prove quite untenable.' Hakes threatened to publish the correspondence to show how Ryle himself was responsible for Bell Cox's imprisonment and the encouragement of Ritualism in Liverpool, but Ryle refused to even respond. Correspondence cited in the *Times*, 26 Jan. 1886.

120 The *Times* suggested that the time had long since passed when the church ought to be disturbed by 'vexatious or vindictive prosecutions for trifling irregularities of ritual.' But the paper had little sympathy for Bell Cox and suggested that he was only 'the victim of an inappropriate penalty.... He has preferred to let the law take its course, and though the penalty he has incurred is not in our judgment a good one, we cannot admit that a clergyman of the Church of England is entitled to set the law at defiance.' Imprisonment, thought the paper, only defeated the real intent of the law: 'It stimulates sympathy with disobedience and invests the contumacious clergyman with the dignity of a victim and martyr. This is derogatory to the authority of the law and injurious to the welfare of the Church.' Instead, the paper suggested that disobedient clergy should be suspended and deprived if necessary. *Times*, 6 May 1887.

In his charge to the clergy of Oxford, shortly after Bell Cox was released, Bishop Mackarness repudiated the imprisonment of clergy and described the Public Worship Regulation Act as 'a bungling piece of legislation.' Nevertheless, he challenged the Ritualist critique of the courts: 'If the decisions of the Judicial Committee of the Privy Council have been thought by some critics to be dictated by policy, it must be remembered that there are good men and wise who agree with the reasoning of the courts, and who strongly deny that there has been any miscarriage of justice, or any thought of wrong-doing in the Judges' minds. It is a great misfortune (if it be so) that the Church should be "in bondage to the secular courts;" it would be a worse misfortune that spiritual courts should decide wrongly. Error does not become truth because it is spoken by the lips of ecclesiastical, but perhaps incapable, Judges. It is possible that Privy Councilors may, after all, be right, and their critics sometimes wrong. And it is possible, too, that a great zeal for religion and for the Church may not always produce clearness of thought or accurate legal knowledge in those who are animated by it.' Cited in the *Record*, 1 July 1887.

121 The writ for his arrest was not issued until May 1887, long after the original sentence of suspension had expired. Bell Cox's lawyers argued that he could not comply with an order that had already expired. The arguments before the Queen's Bench Division were reported in the *Times*, 17 and 21 May 1887.

122 While again repudiating the prosecution, the *Record* noted the absurdity of the case and the state of the law. The judges' ruling, in effect, meant that clergy who disobeyed the law and were suspended had only to protract any suits brought against them through various appeals and proceedings until the suspension had expired, and by that means they could evade the law with immunity. *Record*, 27 May 1887.

The *Times*, in its editorial on the case, had harsh words for both Hakes and Bell Cox, and suggested that both Ryle and Lord Penzance had only done their respective duties, however distasteful they found them. The paper called the case 'an ecclesiastical comedy of errors.' *Times*, 21 May 1887.

123 *Record*, 8 July 1887. Later, the lawyers for the two sides exchanged threats on behalf of their clients. The counsel for Hakes wrote to affirm that he was only interested in securing legal worship at St. Margaret's and had no interest in punishing Bell Cox for previous offenses. They continued: 'Mr. Hakes instructs us to make the following offer: – If your client will give his written undertaking that henceforth the services at St. Margaret's Church shall be conducted in strict accordance with the monition of June 7, 1886, then Mr. Hakes will undertake, in writing, that so long as the services are thus conducted he will not make any further application to enforce the existing *significavit*. This offer has no reference to the question of costs. If it is not acceptable to your client, then Mr. Hakes proposes to enforce the law in such manner as he may be advised.'

The lawyers for Bell Cox responded with a terse rejection: 'We do not accept your proposition that our client is liable to re-arrest. We do not believe that he is so liable, and we think your client very fortunate in having the decision which he has from the Court of Appeal, and that he would do wisely to rest content with it. If you will write us word that he will rest content with it, we will let the decision alone; otherwise our instructions are to appeal to the House of Lords. If we succeed there, your client would probably be condemned in costs in both Courts.' Correspondence cited in the *Record*, 1 Dec. 1887.

124 A parallel could be drawn between their generally negative outlook and that of fundamentalists of the twentieth century. In a recent work, Evangelicals defended their position in the church and drew a distinct line between themselves and fundamentalists. The latter was 'a counter-cultural movement' characterized by 'a siege mentality,' whereas Evangelicalism was more positive in its perspective and involved in culture. It is difficult, however, to locate a theological basis for their differences. The narrow doctrinal views that came to distinguish modern fundamentalism were only just beginning to develop and had not yet divided the movement. The most plausible explanation is the generational shift the party underwent. Older

Evangelicals were more thoroughly indoctrinated in the anti-Catholicism of the early nineteenth century and could still remember when Evangelicals were an oppressed minority in the national church. In contrast, the younger generation was less likely to have their perceptions molded by those ideas. They had come into their own when Evangelicals were being elevated to many prominent ecclesiastical offices and the Roman Catholic threat appeared remote. Cf. The editors' 'Introduction,' in *Evangelical Anglicans*, ed. R. T. France and A. E. McGrath, pp. 5-8.

125 The *Quarterly Review*, following the death of Archbishop Tait, indicated that moderates outside the Evangelical party, while opposed to further litigation, were still determined in their opposition to a broad policy of toleration. The journal expressed the hope that Archbishop Benson might gain some compromise from the extreme Ritualists, but cautioned that capitulation was not the answer. It defended Tait's role in the controversy and concluded that many in the church believed it was necessary to voice their opposition: 'For our part, it is in the name of the old High Church party that we have ever opposed the Ritualists.' Finally, the writer warned, any attempt 'on the part of the Ritualists to boast of a triumph over those who, in the exercise of their full rights, have conscientiously resisted them, would be the most likely of all means to exasperate the quarrel afresh.' Anon., 'Archbishop Tait,' *Quarterly Review*, p. 26.

CHAPTER 9

The End of Litigation

An important result of the almost universal application of the episcopal veto in the years following Green's imprisonment was the broad expansion of the limits of toleration. The threat of prosecution, however distasteful to society in general, had actually worked to restrain many Ritualist clergy. With that threat gone and no other punitive measures to fear, they quickly expanded their activities. In several prominent cases, they used their position in the church (largely gained during the sympathetic tenure of Gladstone) to their own advantage, much to the dismay of Evangelicals. It was clear from the reaction that the years of polemic and conflict had created partisan tensions that would not quickly subside. If moderate Evangelicals were divided from the conservative section of the party over the methods and the tone of the controversy, they remained united in their deep-seated opposition to the idea of a national church dominated by the Ritualists.

But by the late 1880s, there were distinct limits to the anti-Ritualism of the moderate section. They had long since withdrawn their support from the CA, and when that organization announced its intention to prosecute Bishop King of Lincoln, the first Ritualist on the episcopal bench, they quickly denounced the decision. The prosecution of King was assailed then and later as the extreme action of a party in decline. In fact, however, it was sponsored only by one section of the party, which was, in fact, a defensive minority. Moderates attempted, apparently with little success, to distance themselves from the activities of the CA. The division between the two sections, which had long been a source of great tension, was only exacerbated by the King prosecution and led to the formation of the Protestant Churchman's Alliance. The new organization was committed to an anti-Ritualist program, but it was equally opposed to the CA's appeal to the courts.

When Archbishop Benson ruled in favor of Bishop King, the CA immediately appealed the decision to the Judicial Committee of the Privy Council. Moderates reiterated their opposition to the case, although the *Record* and the chairman of the new PCA were willing to allow that there were good reasons for the appeal. Anti-Ritualists were committed to an all-or-nothing view of the proceedings – the judiciary was their last hope of compelling the bishops, and the King case was their last chance to obtain a sentence that might prevent a policy of toleration. The results were predictable. When the verdict went against them, conservatives were devastated, and there was some talk of secession, as had been the case following their only prior defeat in the Bennett judgment. Moderates, who had no stake in the case, were better able to deal with the results. Several even suggested that the defeat would have a positive impact on the party – it would force Evangelicals to return to their own positive spiritual message which, it was suggested, ought to have been their focus all along.

The Continuation of Partisan Tensions

The failure of the Bell Cox prosecution, did little to alter the determination of the CA. They blamed the bishops for the triumph of their opponents, knowing that they would not be allowed to bring any future cases before the courts. Their focus increasingly shifted to the episcopacy, and a general sense prevailed that the anti-Ritualist campaign was entering a new phase. In contrast, moderates were optimistic that a degree of peace might prevail in the church. The Ritualists had obtained 'a large measure of licence' in the years following the Green case, but the *Record* thought further expansion of the controversy was unlikely without the support of the moderate section. It feared the consequences, however, if the Ritualists made a sustained effort to expand their influence with 'fresh and more outrageous defiance of the law of the Church and more abject imitation of the superstition and puerility of Roman Catholic worship.' In that case, the paper could not avow that moderates would remain passive and leave the matter in the hands of the bishops.[1]

In addition to the general divisions and polemics that kept the partisan spirit alive, several events in the mid-1880s exacerbated anti-Ritualist feelings. One was a sermon preached by Canon H. P. Liddon at the consecration of Bishops Bickersteth and King in April 1885. King was the first Ritualist to be made a bishop, and Gladstone apparently felt compelled to balance the appointment with an Evangelical as well (Bickersteth was one of the few Evangelicals to receive preferment of any kind during Gladstone's tenure).[2] Given the fact that the two bishops represented opposing parties, it was expected that a neutral tone would be maintained in the consecration service. In his sermon, however, Liddon adopted an extreme position, presenting as 'the settled teaching of the Church of England' a High Church view of the episcopacy as the essence of the church.[3] Liddon went on to repudiate the Judicial Committee of the Privy Council, arguing that it had no spiritual authority and could never be a legitimate court of appeal in ecclesiastical cases.[4] Shortly after Liddon's sermon, Lord Halifax (C. L. Wood) further alarmed Protestant sensibilities with a speech at the ECU's annual meeting, in which he suggested that the restoration of the visible unity of the church was the most important goal of the ECU.[5] Evangelicals, both moderate and conservative, were deeply disturbed by Halifax's proclamation and called for the members of the ECU to demonstrate their loyalty to the Church of England by repudiating the speech.[6]

A third incident occurred when Bishop Fraser died and his funeral sermon was preached by John Oakley, the Ritualist Dean of the cathedral. In the course of his sermon, Oakley claimed that Fraser had later regretted his course of action in the Miles Platting case; and in his benediction, Oakley offered prayer for the dead bishop. The Evangelical clergy of Manchester immediately protested. They thought Oakley had conveniently revised the facts of the case, and they also resented his introduction of a partisan tone into a solemn service by questioning the late bishop's actions and by introducing prayers for the dead. Oakley, in response to a letter from Prebendary Macdonald, rejected their concerns in rather harsh language. He accused them of having adopted 'such a habit of fancying that the Church of England belongs to you, that you put forward most sectional opinions as those of the church and the nation.' Macdonald suggested that the case was otherwise. Evangelicals were simply loyal members of the established church, honestly attempting to obey its articles and formularies. He countered that, in fact, it was the extreme section of the High Church party, who claimed a monopoly for themselves as well as 'the right to teach what contradicts her Articles, and to make additions to her Prayer-book, unauthorized except by themselves.'[7]

Macdonald's letter only further annoyed Oakley, who responded with a threatening notice:

> You have got to acquiesce in, I do not say to share (that is for your own conscience), but to admit and accept the fact of a very widespread belief that the old Puritan theology of the 16th and 17th centuries is practically dead, that the old Erastian Protestant theory of the Church of England is dying too (though it is dying hard in places), and that the keys of the house have passed into other hands! We do not in the least wish to deny you house-room. You have a history, and an intelligible and useful place and function in

the English Church. But you must really be careful and considerate. We do not wish, and we might not be able just now, to *coerce* you, it is needless; but those who differ from you (it is not one school only) are quite strong enough, and *very much tempted* at times to pull our common house-roof down over your heads, and we shall most assuredly do it, rather than let the key pass into your hands again.[8]

Macdonald suggested that Oakley underestimated the true hold that 'the principles of the Reformation' held on 'the mind and heart' of the English laity.[9] He closed the correspondence by turning Oakley's charge against the Ritualists. His threat to pull down 'our common house' at least made it clear which group actually believed that they possessed 'the power of opening and shutting the door.' And further, claimed Macdonald, it was good for the public to know where the real peril to the established church lay, and who it was the Liberationists could count on as allies; 'for we know that there are Churchmen who are ready to assist them to disestablish the Church if they cannot succeed to establish their own "most sectional" innovations.'[10]

Partisan animosities were also intensified on several occasions during this period when Ritualist clergy were forced on Evangelical parishes at the insistence of patrons who had little regard for the feelings of the congregation. Perhaps the most troublesome case came in the parish of St. Pancras, for which the right of appointment resided with the Dean and Chapter of St. Paul's Cathedral. The influential church had been served by a long succession of prominent Evangelical clergy, including several who later became deans (notably W. W. Champneys and Thomas Dale, the father of the Ritualist, T. P. Dale) as well as A. W. Thorold, who had been elevated to the episcopacy. In July 1887, however, Rev. Henry L. Paget, whom the *Record* considered 'an extreme Ritualist,' was appointed to the living.[11] The incident was particularly troubling because the problem of incompatible appointments was already widely recognized (there was a Church Patronage Bill soon to be considered by Parliament that would obtain for congregations some influence in the appointment of clergy in order to prevent egregious appointments). The *Record* considered the case even more troubling since it was made not by a private citizen but by 'patrons of high ecclesiastical rank,' who ought to have been able to rise above partisan interests.[12]

Finally, Evangelicals were disturbed by the erection in St. Paul's Cathedral of an ornamental reredos that included scenes of the crucifixion and the virgin Mary. They complained that the illegal decoration was all the more irksome for having been erected in a church of national importance that ought to represent all parties.[13] Opinions were divided over how best to respond, and those divisions were exaggerated by the fact that the Church Missionary Society had already planned a service to be held at St. Paul's. Major-General F. T. Haig, a member of the General Committee, was disturbed when it became evident that most of the committee were determined to go forward with the service. There was a debate over various options (such as canceling the service or holding it while issuing a remonstrance), but the committee decided to go forward without any protest, and Haig voiced his complaints in a sharply critical letter.[14] At a later meeting, held the day before the service, the General Committee adopted a statement explaining its position. Haig's charges were rejected by other committee members who denied any weakening of the organization's commitment to its Evangelical principles. Furthermore, they argued that it was the duty of the CMS to maintain its focus on foreign missions work and to avoid entanglement in theological controversies at home.[15] The service was conducted as scheduled on Feb. 14, 1888, and the *Record* suggested that the great Evangelical congregation filling the cathedral was perhaps the best protest of the reredos that could have been mounted.[16]

Many conservatives joined Haig in condemning the committee's decision regarding the policy of the CMS.[17] For almost a year rumors circulated of an attempt to form a new missions organization on a more thoroughly Protestant platform. Fearing that it represented a general trend in the party, conservatives had been concerned for some time by the moderate leadership of the society. And the reredos controversy, in their opinion, was another indication of a declining commitment to Protestant principles.[18] Shortly thereafter, the *Record* obtained a copy of a private notice being circulated by several members of the CA. Rather than supporting the establishment of a new organization, the circular called for a conservative coup within the CMS in order to reestablish its Protestant principles.[19] The paper again lent its editorial support to the moderate position, suggesting that the only conspiracy involving the CMS was that of the men who sought to subvert the organization and reshape it on their own narrowly partisan lines.[20]

At the next meeting of the General Committee, F. T. Haig presented two resolutions which, if approved, would have fundamentally altered the character of the CMS. The first would have compelled the society to protest any Ritualist activities encountered during the course of its work, and the second would have prevented CMS meetings or services being held in churches linked to the Ritualist movement.[21] Both of Haig's proposals were soundly defeated in a vote that reflected the moderate perspective of the society's constituency.²² The *Record* concluded that the changes would have required that the CMS spend as much of its energies protesting 'against error at home' as it did evangelizing the world abroad; in effect, it would be required to 'assume the functions of the Christian Evidence Society and the Church Association' rather than focusing on its missions work.²³

The controversy over the St. Paul's reredos continued for some time. W. H. Webb-Peploe, an Evangelical clerical representative at the London Diocesan Conference, attempted to raise the subject, but Bishop Temple refused to allow any discussion of the divisive topic.²⁴ The CA circulated a protest memorial, signed by about 9,000 clergy and laity, in which it threatened an appeal to the courts if Temple refused to take action.²⁵ The *Record* thought the action represented an improvement in the association's policy and was willing to support a court challenge of the episcopal veto. Unlike other recent prosecutions, it argued that the St. Paul's case involved no individual clergy and there was no threat of imprisonment.²⁶ In June 1888, Bishop Temple vetoed the prosecution. While reaffirming his commitment to Reformation principles, he rejected litigation on the grounds that the subject had already been considered by the courts in a case involving Exeter cathedral and that the laity were unlikely to be encouraged toward idolatry by the artwork in question.²⁷ The *Record* rejected both the logic and the historical accuracy of Temple's argument. The ruling in the Exeter case, it claimed, clearly divided artistic representations into two categories – those that might provoke superstitious reverence and those that would not. Discretion was necessary in each case, and the paper cited an instance five years after the Exeter ruling, when the Chancellor of the Diocese of Durham had refused to allow a painted reredos to be installed at St. Lawrence, Pittington.²⁸ Temple's use of the veto in the St. Paul's case was condemned as an arbitrary use of his power that denied the laity their fundamental right of appeal. The paper, which had opposed the prosecution of clergy since the Green imprisonment, thought it could be safely argued before the courts on the principles involved, with no bitter partisanship, since there were no individual defendants.²⁹

Temple's veto was challenged before the Queen's Bench Division.³⁰ Almost a year later that court ruled by a two-to-one margin in favor of the prosecutors and ordered Temple to allow the proceedings.³¹ Anti-Ritualists had complained about the misuse of the episcopal veto since the victory of Bishop Mackarness in the Clewer case. They hoped the judgment would stand as a partial reversal of the idea that the episcopal veto was final and absolute.³² Temple appealed the ruling, however, and a year and a half later the Court of

Appeals, in a unanimous decision, reversed the verdict. In their judgment, the Public Worship Regulation Act gave the bishops a great deal of discretion, and so long as it was clear that due consideration had been given to the circumstances of the case, the courts could not interfere.[33]

The Prosecution of Bishop King and Evangelical Divisions

For several years, the CA had been increasingly strident in its criticism of the episcopacy.[34] Before undertaking the prosecution of Bishop King, however, they attempted to challenge the innovations he had allowed at Lincoln Cathedral. Knowing that King would veto any presentation made against the dean of the cathedral, the association decided to prosecute the canon precentor, Edmund Venables, with the appeal being made directly to the archbishop.[35] Archbishop Benson, however, vetoed the case and criticized the prosecutors for their attempt to circumvent the traditional process of appeal.[36] Having failed in their attempt to prosecute the cathedral staff, the CA decided to bring charges against Bishop King himself.[37] At the CA annual conference in May 1887, the council vaguely alluded to the intended prosecution although they did not elaborate on the particulars of the case.[38]

When King was elevated to the episcopacy by Gladstone in 1885, there was little initial reaction.[39] Evangelicals, however, soon took a rather negative view of his episcopacy. The *Record* complained when King posed for a photograph in 'his cope, and his mitre, and his pectoral cross, and his pastoral staff, and his chaplains, with their lesser delights of birettas and coloured stoles.'[40] In the paper's view, however, the real damage was that which could not be illustrated by a photograph:

> Under Dr. King's superintendence Christian worship and teaching are being corrupted. The sacred ordinance of the Lord's Supper is turned into a tawdry pageant in which the mummeries of the Mass are closely imitated. A fine contempt is displayed for the law and practice of the Reformed Church, and every relic of monkish folly and superstition is treasured as part of the precious heritage of the Catholic Church. Auricular confession, the surest of all poisons which can be administered to a nation, is openly encouraged, and in a hundred other ways the Church, instead of being a witness for the truth, is made to serve the purposes of the enemy.[41]

In June 1888, the CA decided to prosecute Bishop King, invoking 'the long-forgotten Court of Audience of the Archbishop of Canterbury.'[42] The decision immediately opened up a flood of correspondence that dominated the pages of the *Record* for several months and again illustrated the serious nature of the divisions within the Evangelical party.[43] Moderates expressed their dismay at the announcement and their doubt that the case, even if successful, could have any positive effect on the suppression of Ritualism.[44]

Initially, Archbishop Benson declined to hear the case, questioning whether the precedent cited by the prosecution was sufficient to prove his authority to sit in judgment over a bishop.[45] The CA, upon Benson's request for a judgment regarding the extent of his power, appealed to the Judicial Committee. The judges ruled that the archbishop did, in fact, have jurisdiction to consider complaints made against bishops.[46] The Ritualists responded with a declaration repudiating the appeal to the courts and calling for the toleration of divergent interpretations of the church's rubrics.[47] In a letter to the *Record*, G. A. Denison defended the document and suggested that the prosecutions were simply an attempt by one of 'the two primary sections of the Church of England' to suppress the other. The paper denied Denison's charges, claiming neutrality for itself and the Evangelical party as a whole. The CA and its supporters were solely responsible for the prosecution, said the paper; 'the Evangelical body, as a body, have had nothing to do with his prosecution, and they will do nothing to impede the regular course of justice. They stand aside.'[48]

In opposition to the Denison Memorial, supporters of the CA drew up a 'Protestant Declaration' apparently fearing that moderates might choose to side with the tolerant position of their opponents. Their statement, with a call for signatures, was reprinted in an advertisement calling for support of the King prosecution.[49] But even if moderate Evangelicals did not cross party boundaries to sign the Denison memorial, they found other ways they could express their opposition to the CA and its renewal of litigation. A counter-declaration was drawn up by a committee appointed by the council of the UCLA. That body, representing the moderate position, repudiated the suggestion that the peace of the church could be obtained by supporting those who broke the law, while it simultaneously refused to support any attempt to put down that lawlessness through prosecution.[50]

Archbishop Benson finally issued his citation in January 1889.[51] King responded by proclaiming that there were two great principles at stake in the case. The first was the right to use 'external ritual in our acts of worship,' since human beings needed both outward and inward helps in their approach to God. The second and more important principle, however, was the affirmation of 'the sacerdotal character of the Christian ministry.'[52] The *Record*, in commenting on King's statement, thought it an interesting admission since critics of the anti-Ritualist movement had long argued that the disputed points at the center of the controversy did not necessarily imply doctrinal beliefs. The paper thought King had touched on the fundamental issue dividing the two parties:

> The fashion has been to deprecate objections to vestments and ritual on the plea that they mean nothing, and that, since they edify or at least gratify those who adopt them, it is churlish and narrow on the part of others to raise difficulty. The answer has, of course, been that these outward things are of consequence because, instead of being meaningless trifles, they have a profound significance which history has stamped deeply upon them. They must be dealt with as the ensigns and tokens of what they symbolize. Now this is admitted, and Churchmen are exhorted to rally to the defence of the maniples and chasubles of Dr. King in the name and for the sake of the priesthood.[53]

The prosecution, however, left moderate Evangelicals in a difficult position. They had long since expressed their fervent opposition to further litigation involving matters of ritual and had no interest in supporting the failed policies of the past, despite the fact that there were mitigating circumstances in the King case (since the defendant was a bishop, there was little likelihood of imprisonment).[54] On the other hand, they did not want to appear, by way of condemning the prosecution, to suggest that they condoned the Ritualistic doctrines and practices of Bishop King.[55] Moderates found themselves caught between the two sides of the controversy – they could not support the litigation, but neither were they willing to compromise with the Ritualists and the other memorialists who attempted to brush aside fundamental differences.[56]

The controversy and the light it shed on the divisions among Evangelicals evoked a lengthy anonymous letter (signed 'Nemo') on the future of the party. The correspondent suggested that the King case should be seen as a call to union; a challenge for Evangelicals to move beyond a 'narrow partisanship' that was willing to condemn others 'for a word, a gesture, an ornament, a service.' Many moderates – both those within the party and those who were non-partisan but 'largely at one with Evangelical men in their aims and sympathies' – were driven away by a policy of intolerance.[57] The letter elicited a number of complaints from conservatives, most of whom took offense at his attack on the CA and accused him of fostering divisions in the party with his willingness to compromise.[58]

In a later letter, 'Nemo' refuted the charges of his critics. He questioned whether the party was really so fragile that it could be damaged by the consideration of honest differences. It was clear to all, he continued, that Evangelicals were divided on a number of issues. And many who had been driven away from any party affiliation by the bitterness of the controversy remained deeply attached to 'Evangelical truth.' Finally, he repudiated the notion that his position implied any compromise of fundamental principles. He only asked for the toleration of those who expressed 'the great truths of the Gospel in somewhat different language,' and were 'not insensible to the bearing of modern thought and recent discoveries upon Biblical and theological questions,' or of those who recognized the aesthetic tendencies of the age and adopted elements of ceremony that were different than those of earlier Evangelicals.[59]

A few moderates went still further in expressing their impatience with the continuing controversy. Rev. J. W. Milner of St. James's, Birkenhead suggested that it ought to be clear to all that the prosecutions had been without success. Legal judgments had failed to halt the disputed innovations, and in a state of heightened partisan tension, anti-Ritualists were unable to recognize that the revival of the High Church movement was by no means 'an unmixed evil.' Positive aspects of the movement, said Miller, ought to be acknowledged and adopted, and 'the follies and errors' associated with Ritualism, 'if not thus violently opposed,' would ultimately be discouraged by the common sense of the English laity.[60] In conclusion, Milner drew an analogy between the controversy and the rise of Wesleyanism, a parallel that the Ritualist, A. H. Mackonochie, had drawn many years earlier.[61]

The responses elicited by Milner's letter indicated that divisions existed even among moderates concerning how best to respond to the Ritualists. H. C. G. Moule thought it was a great error to admit any correlation between the case of the Methodists and that of the Ritualists. The former had attempted to revive 'those great outstanding truths of the New Testament,' such as conversion and justification by faith, that had long been forgotten by the leaders of the Church of England. In contrast, he suggested, the heart of the Ritualist message was alien to Protestantism.[62] While the Methodists had a valid claim to a place in the Protestant Church of England, no compromise ought to be allowed for the Ritualists. In his response, Milner allowed the distinction between the two movements but reiterated his basic point. Whatever its extremes, he concluded, 'it cannot be said that the awakening and activity, whether it be termed High Churchism or Ritualism, by which the Church has been stirred during the last fifty years or more, has not been for good.'[63]

The Protestant Churchmen's Alliance

One of the more important results of the CA's decision to prosecute Bishop King came in June 1889, when a conference was held on 'the state of ecclesiastical affairs, with a view to maintain the principles of the Reformation in the Church of England.' The meeting was another attempt by moderate Evangelicals to encourage moderates in the High Church party to unite in opposition to the Ritualists.[64] It attracted a broad spectrum of anti-Ritualists, including several who were not affiliated with the Evangelical party such as Lord Grimthorpe, Lord Hartington and the Duke of Westminster.[65] The meeting, attended by about a thousand clergy and laity, was presided over by Grimthorpe and resulted in the formation of the Protestant Churchmen's Alliance (hereafter abbreviated PCA). The new society was determined to maintain 'the principles of the Reformation, the present Prayer-book and Articles, and the Acts of Uniformity as standards of ritual and doctrine in the National Church.'[66] The discussion during the meeting, however, indicated that the audience was not necessarily of one mind on the subject. Three groups were represented at the meeting, each with its own interests in mind.[67]

Supporters of the CA were anxious to prevent the formation of a new society that might counteract their own activities or unite the moderate opposition to their policies. Evangelical moderates, who initiated the meeting and were in the majority, expressed the view that some means other than prosecution must be found to oppose the Ritualists.[68] Lord Grimthorpe and a few other non-Evangelicals hoped a new organization might attract the support of moderates from the High Church section, but to that end insisted that the membership be limited to Anglicans. An amendment was offered that would have expanded the alliance to include Nonconformists, but Grimthorpe refused to allow it despite the concerns of some that the new organization would suffer as a result of its narrowness.[69] The most fervent critics of the new PCA were the worried supporters of the CA.[70]

Although members of the CA were present, the meeting was clearly intended by moderates to organize an alternative to that society.[71] To obtain a broad range of support, the new union had to be free of the negative reputation associated with the CA's program of litigation. At a meeting of the London Clerical and Lay Union, J. W. Marshall elaborated the rationale for the PCA. A growing number of moderates, he said, were concerned that no existing Evangelical society could effectively counter the activities of the ECU and other Ritualist groups. Marshall acknowledged the past successes of the

CA and disavowed any divisive intent. But claiming that they must deal with 'the facts,' he argued that the CA could never unite the whole Evangelical party. He thought that 'many men who were looked up to by the Evangelical body as leaders had ceased to belong to the Church Association, and that rightly or wrongly there existed in all parts of the country a strong determination not to join its ranks.'[72] He also noted that the Protestant Alliance had done a great deal of work in support of true religion, but as an organization that included dissenters, it could not gain the support of High Church moderates and would never be able to counter the influence of those who sought to undermine the Church of England from within. Finally, Marshall acknowledged that he and other members of the UCLA had also come to the conclusion that their own organization suffered from implicit limitations as well.[73] Following on their assessment of the needs of the movement, and the various limitations of existing bodies, it was suggested that the formation of another society was necessary.

The *Record* hoped the establishment of the new organization would force the CA to acknowledge its limitations as a body representing only one section of the Evangelical party. The paper suggested that it would be far easier to work on friendly terms once the CA admitted its true position. It had done much good work and the early lawsuits had established the legitimate interpretation of the rubrics, but it was impossible to avoid conflict while the CA continued to pursue a policy of prosecution, in the name of the Evangelical party, when it was clear that the majority no longer supported it. The CA could pursue whatever policy it wanted so long as it was made clear that they did not represent all Evangelicals. 'If we do not always agree as to particular measures,' concluded the paper, 'it is of small consequence so long as we are not called on to answer for them.'[74]

But other supporters of the new organization took a sharper tone. When Robert Payne Smith, Dean of Canterbury, addressed the South-eastern Clerical and Lay Church Union on the importance of the new PCA, he expressed the hope that it would create a bond of union that had been lacking among Evangelicals. It had once appeared that the CA might fill that role, but there were many who would not support it. 'I cannot justify to myself,' he said, 'a private association undertaking the work of prosecuting for breaches of ritual, and therefore I have never been able to join the Church Association. Nor do I consider that the Law Courts are the proper places for our warfare. Our weapons ought to be spiritual, and our appeal should be to the consciences of men.'[75] Payne Smith went on to suggest that the activities of the CA had only exacerbated party feelings, created popular sympathy for the Ritualists, and limited the influence of Evangelicals.[76]

Henry Miller, Secretary of the CA's council, immediately challenged the criticism. He suggested that Payne Smith was being less than honest since, on occasion, he had himself spoken on behalf of the CA and presided over one of their lecture meetings in January 1887. Miller also rejected the argument that the CA was responsible for any negative reactions to anti-Ritualism. They had simply undertaken to discover and protect the legal interpretation of the rubrics.[77] Payne Smith responded by reiterating his original argument and noting that the leaders of the CA, in a private meeting of influential Evangelicals in December 1884, had been warned that there was a growing and substantial opposition to their policy.[78] In contrast to the CA, the PCA was determined to pursue a different course, although a list of their objects implied that litigation might be a viable alternative if defendants found guilty of contempt of court could be punished by deprivation rather than imprisonment.[79]

Evangelical opinions were still further divided when it was later announced that yet another organization had been formed. In July 1889, J. J. Stewart Perowne and T. Teignmouth Shore, along with several others, announced the formation of a group called Churchmen in Council. Some confusion existed, however, and the organizers found it necessary to note that their organization was not related to the PCA.[80] The Churchmen in Council desired to find a peaceful means to end the controversy, even if it involved compromise with the Ritualists.[81] It was clear, thought the organizers, that years of litigation had only worsened partisan feelings and reduced church discipline 'to a state of practical anarchy.' They were convinced that the best means of resolving the crisis was to present resolutions to Convocation seeking the revision of the rubrics in order to allow for a broader toleration. At their first public meeting in February 1890, they affirmed that the best hope for resolving the controversy 'regarding questions of ritual' would be 'obtained by the exercise of the constitutional powers of the Convocations of the Church, whose authority all Churchmen are bound loyally to recognize.'[82]

Many moderates were skeptical of the plan and opposed to the idea that fundamental Protestant beliefs should be compromised for the sake of peace. The *Record* thought the plan was supported only by a small section of liberal Evangelicals who were overly zealous for peace. To a large degree, the difference between moderates and liberals in the party came down to a question of how much ought to be given up to end the controversy. 'We venture to ask,' wrote the paper, 'whether the alternative of arresting the conflict by surrendering our principles is as right as it is undoubtedly tempting.'[83] The group, however, was unable to attract much support, and their proposals continued to be criticized as a fundamental compromise.[84] Nevertheless, the *Record* viewed the development of the new organizations, even with all the ensuing disputes, as a sign of a growing wave of Protestant concern. The paper thought the Ritualists and the secular press had long underestimated the depth and variety of Protestant feeling in the country. It was commonly assumed that anti-Ritualism could be equated with the CA, and too hastily inferred that the Protestantism of a small minority was consequently 'a safe object for derision.' In reality, however, their critics failed to recognize that 'the belligerent section of Protestants' had for a long time been 'a small minority of the whole mass.' They underestimated 'the Protestantism of Lord Grimthorpe' as well as that of 'the majority amongst Evangelical Churchmen.'[85] Now, said the paper, under the stress of current events, and particularly out of feelings aroused by the case involving the Bishop of Lincoln, there was 'a decided revival of strong Protestant feeling.' It amounted, the paper concluded, to the awakening of the long dormant Protestantism of the English laity, 'hitherto quiet and unobtrusive, but now goaded into prominence by the fatal policy of those who, wishing it dead, have acted as if it were.'[86]

The Lincoln Judgment and the Appeal

Archbishop Benson's court gathered at Lambeth Palace Library in February 1889, with Bishops Temple of London, Browne of Winchester, Stubbs of Oxford, and Wordsworth of Salisbury present as assessors.[87] Bishop King immediately protested, demanding the right to be tried before 'the whole body of Bishops of the Province.'[88] Benson, however, had already given much consideration to the subject and overruled the protest. In his view, the assessors were needed for their advice and council, but the judgment lay with the archbishop alone.[89] King admitted all of the practices with which he was charged but denied their illegality.[90] The actual trial began in February 1890 and lasted for about a month, but Archbishop Benson did not deliver his judgment until November.[91]

It took Benson almost four hours to read his closely argued verdict.[92] The use of the mixed chalice was allowed so long as the mixing of the water and the wine was done prior to the service. The charge regarding ablutions, or the cleansing of the ceremonial vessels, was dismissed since it was not technically a part of the service. The eastward position was held to be legal so long as there was no attempt on the part of the celebrating clergy to conceal the manual acts from the congregation (King was found guilty, however, of having obscured his actions). The singing of the *Agnus Dei* was also judged to be legal, as was the use of lighted candles on the altar. Finally, the practice of making the sign of the cross during absolution and the benediction was judged to be illegal. While his verdict largely favored the Ritualists, Benson sought to soften the edge of its impact by denying the doctrinal significance and sacerdotal implications that were often attached to the disputed points, especially the eastward position and the altar lights.[93] Although King was found guilty on two counts, each side was ordered to pay their own costs, and no mention was made of any punitive sentence following the guilty verdicts.[94]

The CA immediately announced that Benson's decision would be appealed to the Judicial Committee. The wisdom of that appeal was questioned by many moderates, although the *Record* took a middle ground and found several reasons that justified the appeal. First, the CA would make its own way regardless of what moderates thought. Second, the importance of the points that had been lost, especially the use of altar candles and the singing of the *Agnus Dei*, could not be overlooked.[95] And finally, despite the archbishop's 'scrupulously fair historical inquiry,' the paper thought the question of the proper application of legal principles and rules should ultimately be decided by appellate judges with an expertise in those areas. The *Record* concluded:

> What, then, ought Evangelical Churchmen to do? What ought they to ask for? It seems to us the answer is plain. By the action of others, and through no fault of theirs, the crisis of a generation ago has returned. The legality of practices and ornaments which they do and must hold to be profoundly dangerous is once more an open question. The lawyers have decided one way. The Archbishop, who is not a lawyer, has decided the other way. It is of the highest consequence to the Church itself that this doubt should be as speedily and thoroughly removed by one or other of these antagonistic opinions being definitely adopted by authority.... Let the legal Judges of the Privy Council review the work of the historical Judges of Lambeth, so that the Church of England may have the assistance of both. We are acutely alive to the disadvantages of further litigation; we do not quite share the robust confidence in the result which seems to inspire the Church Association; we have warned our readers from the outset that the Lincoln prosecution meant trouble for the Church of England, and the outlook is not clearing; but none the less it seems to us that loyalty to the truth, and justice to our children require that these grave questions – we

refer especially to Altar Lights and the singing of the *Agnus* – should not continue moot points, but should be sifted to the bottom. In other words, we regard an appeal to the Final Court as the inevitable sequel to the Archbishop's marked disagreement with the previous decisions of that tribunal.[96]

The correspondence pages of the *Record* were filled for some time with arguments for and against the appeal. The correspondents focused on a few central points involving the future of the anti-Ritualist movement. Reginald Smith, Rector of Stafford and Canon of Salisbury, questioned the spirit of the movement and its impact on Evangelicalism. He acknowledged that he had once been a supporter of the CA and who feared 'a general conspiracy' that could return the English Church 'into subjection to the Papal obedience.' His experience in Salisbury, however, had convinced him otherwise. In sixteen years, he had encountered only one Ritualist who was truly 'a Romanizer at heart, and he received a well-merited rebuke from the present Bishop of Salisbury for his disloyal foolishness.' No doubt the CA and its supporters were firm in their beliefs and 'sincerely religious men,' but he thought they misunderstood the nature of the threat and were overly pessimistic in their outlook. Smith condemned the proposed 'fresh litigation as unwise, un-Christian, and suicidal.'[97] Rev. Beauchamp Stannus, Rector of Arrow, near Alcester, among others, took issue with Smith. He claimed that anti-Ritualists were merely fulfilling St. Paul's commandment in 'earnestly contending for the faith.' In contrast to Smith, he claimed that the work of the CA bore 'the marks of the Spirit of Christ.... Assuredly it does; abhorrence of false doctrine is one of the most reliable tests of godliness. The ministry of Christ was controversial; so was that of His Apostles.'[98]

At an even more basic level, other critics questioned the final result. In a letter to the promoter of the case, J. Wagstaff, Vicar of Christ Church, Macclesfield, questioned the usefulness of further litigation. Even if they obtained a partial reversal from the Privy Council, he asked, what would be gained?[99] It would accomplish nothing in terms of the suppression of innovations, and the bishops would only be reinforced in their use of the veto by the creation of further popular sentiment favoring the Ritualists. In the process, the influence of Evangelicals would only be diminished and they would miss 'the golden opportunity now afforded by the Archbishop's Judgment.' While legitimating some controversial ceremonies, Benson had undermined the offensive doctrines that the Ritualists claimed they represented. In Wagstaff's view, Evangelicals should accept the decision and allow it time to filter down to the parishes.[100]

Finally, a number of letters addressed the subject of the archbishop's repudiation of the doctrinal significance of the innovations. Anti-Ritualists had long taken the view that what the Ritualists themselves intended must be the definitive meaning of the ceremonies. Others, however, questioned that perspective. P. V. Smith suggested that Benson had undermined the Ritualist position. Should the symbolic meaning that 'irresponsible individuals' attached to 'a particular ceremony,' he asked, be the determinative factor in its permissibility? If such were the case, he concluded, the sacraments themselves would have to be discarded since the Ritualists ascribed to them a character and significance that Evangelicals could never affirm. In Smith's view, none of the ceremonies 'declared lawful by the Archbishop's Judgment' could be proven 'contrary to the Word of God or necessarily symbolical of false doctrine.' They were under no compulsion to accept their opponents' view of the ceremonies, and if the archbishop's decision legalized those rites, it gave Evangelicals a broader liberty as well.[101] On a related note, a number of writers pointed out that the archbishop's decisions compelled Evangelicals to alter nothing in their services. If there was some compromise, and the Ritualists got a judgment from a 'spiritual Court' that they could conscientiously obey, it also set specific limits and Evangelicals were not obliged to adopt any of the innovations judged 'not illegal.' Since the practices were not 'the law of the Church,' and Benson had rejected their doctrinal significance, many moderates were prepared to give their assent.[102]

In response to the critics, Capt. Alexander Cobham defended the CA's decision to appeal the judgment. According to Cobham, the CA had fully considered the possibility of 'an adverse judgment,' and from the beginning had viewed the archbishop's court as a means to get the case before the Judicial Committee of the Privy Council. Apart from the merits of the case itself, he thought it was equally important to demonstrate the authority of the Royal Supremacy over the 'spiritual courts.'[103] Cobham acknowledged that there were some who took a different view of the matter, but he thought other Evangelicals owed them the justice of recognizing 'that we are acting consistently, and that we have all along determined at any sacrifice, however great, to bring to an issue the toleration of Popery within the Established Church.'[104] Interestingly, the Chairman of the PCA, Lord Grimthorpe, also defended the appeal of the verdict. Even though the alliance was formed to provide an alternative to the CA, Grimthorpe argued that it was necessary to defend the principle of royal supremacy. And that principle, he affirmed, was the only means of protecting the rights of the laity against the claims of the clerical party.[105]

Ultimately, the CA's prosecution of Bishop King and appeal of the judgment only further diminished episcopal support for the anti-Ritualists. Except for the prosecution of James Bell Cox, which Bishop Ryle had allowed, for almost a decade every presentation made by the CA was vetoed. By the early 1890s, it was evident that the bishops had grown impatient with the effort to force their hand. When the CA complained to Bishop Davidson of Rochester about a book on the immaculate conception written by the Rev. F. G. Lee, they received a sharp rebuff. Davidson refused to recognize the right of an outside body to interfere in his diocese and make demands with regard to his supervision of the clergy. Capt. Cobham defended the organization and claimed that it had been formed with the implicit approval of many of the bishops, who desired its assistance in ascertaining the state of the law with regard to matters of ritual. It was intended to be, and still was, declared Cobham, 'a Bishop's Aid Society.'[106]

Bishop Davidson would not allow Cobham's claims to stand unchallenged. He suggested that the CA had departed 'so widely from the lines originally laid down,' that it had 'forfeited the support, and even incurred the strongest reprobation, of not a few Evangelical Churchmen who were disposed a quarter of a century ago to regard such an Association as necessary, and perhaps even as desirable.' Davidson continued:

> It seems to me not quite ingenuous on the part of those who represent the association to claim support for its present action and policy on the plea that the society's object is now, as it was 26 years ago, to assist in ascertaining the law of the land in matters of ritual. What the association now professes to do is something quite different.... It is placed beyond question that the association now exists in order, so to speak, to force, if it can, the hands of the Bishops with reference to their executive action in matters belonging strictly to their own province – matters upon which the Church Association would be the last to affirm that technically speaking, the law is still uncertain. In other words, the association endeavours to take out of the hands of the constituted authorities the duty of enforcing technical points of law which have already been declared, but upon which, in the opinion, I had almost said, of every reasonable man, some discretion is intended to be vested in those upon whom is laid the solemn responsibility of episcopal office.[107]

Davidson noted that he expressed no opinion on the early work of the CA, but only questioned whether it could legitimately claim to be proceeding on the same path. It was, he thought, 'a matter of simple honesty' that the officers of the CA should distinguish between the organization's present work and that of its early years.

Cobham indignantly responded that the CA had no desire to overstep the boundaries of episcopal discretion. He complained that it was the 'apparent indifference and neglect' of the episcopacy that forced their intervention. The bishops' reticence to act, and still worse their sheltering of the Ritualists through the use of the veto, forced loyal Protestants to 'the reluctant continuance of legal proceedings after the law had been ascertained.'[108] Davidson offered no further response, but the exchange indicated the degree to which the episcopacy had grown weary of the CA's attempt to force them into a partisan position.

In June 1891, the appeal of the Lincoln Judgment came before the Judicial Committee of the Privy Council. In addition to the judges hearing the case, the Bishops of Chichester (Durnford), St. David's (Jones) and Lichfield (Maclagan) sat as assessors.[109] Following the hearings, the judges took the case under consideration, but it was over a year before their verdict was published. In the interim, the Ritualist controversy largely disappeared from the pages of the *Record*, although there were some indications of continuing tensions, such as the debate over a Clergy Discipline Bill in Parliament, which was supported by Evangelicals but widely opposed by Ritualists.[110] The paper continued to publish occasional anecdotal reports that gave evidence of the abiding division between the parties.[111] But, to a large degree, the interest of moderates in the anti-Ritualist campaign dwindled over the course of the year spent waiting for the decision of the Judicial Committee.[112] The CA, however, continued to stress the importance of the final verdict for the existence of the Protestant establishment.[113]

The Judicial Committee Verdict and Evangelical Reactions

The Judicial Committee finally handed down its decision on 2 August 1892. The verdict was apparently widely anticipated, and the *Record* suggested that there was very little interest taken in the proceedings. The audience in the Council Chamber, other than the lawyers and prosecutors of the suit, was extremely small, numbering not many more than twenty.[114] In the judgment of the paper, the logic of the ruling was chiefly important for the consequences it would have should any other litigation be undertaken – two central arguments made by the promoters were denied by the judges. The first involved the authority of Archbishop Benson's judgment, based as it was, on historical and theological evidence rather than on legal precedent. The CA's lawyers had suggested that historical and theological arguments were insufficient for the establishment of a legal verdict, but the Judicial Committee disagreed.[115] The second and related question involved the right of the archbishop, in effect, to overturn prior verdicts delivered on appeal by that court. The principle had been raised in the Ridsdale case, and the Judicial Committee had ruled in that instance, that although there might be exceptions, prior judgments in similar cases ought not to be reconsidered without the greatest possible hesitation. Again, however, the judges found that Benson had ruled correctly in response to 'fresh light' on the issues.[116] The judges concluded, as well, that contrary to the argument of the prosecutors, Archbishop Benson was under no obligation to issue a monition to Bishop King with regard to those practices which were found to be illegal. If the archbishop was satisfied that the offenses in question were not likely to be repeated, he was 'entitled to accept the assurance of future submission' without inflicting any penalty, even one such as a monition. Consequently, the judges were determined to 'humbly advise Her Majesty that this Appeal should be dismissed.'[117]

In reporting the judgment, the *Record* sampled the opinions expressed in a number of prominent papers around the country. In general, the reaction was positive, and the hope was widely expressed that the case would bring the bitter controversy to a close.[118] The *Record* itself published two important editorials that undoubtedly reflected the general concern of moderates to redirect the tone of the party's future course. In the first piece, the paper summarized exactly what the judgment meant and laid the blame for the reversal of earlier judgments squarely on the CA. The result, said the paper, was exactly the opposite of what the organization had desired and confidently expected:

> Instead of procuring the condemnation of the Bishop's practices, they have succeeded in undoing no inconsiderable part of the work of their earlier years. The former Privy Council Judgments must be read subject to this the latest of the series, and, so read, it is obvious that they are much more favourable to modern ritual innovations than before the Lincoln prosecution began. We consider it of importance to point out this fact with some emphasis, because it abundantly justifies the disapproval which for the last ten or twelve years we have expressed at all fresh ritual litigation. We have been severely taken to task by the militant section of Churchmen who direct the Church Association, and our advice to let litigation alone has been resented as an indication of lukewarmness. The Council of the Church Association have insisted on acting on their own view of what was right and sagacious, and in

complete independence of the great mass of Evangelical Churchmen. They have had their way; they have carried out their policy, and they are to-day in a position which it is kinder not to enlarge upon. They are entitled to the sympathy and forbearance of their Evangelical fellow-Churchmen, but it is well that it should be recognized that the disaster which has overtaken the Church Association is the direct result of their own action and their very determined rejection of the general feeling amongst Evangelical Churchmen.[119]

The paper attempted, however, to minimize the impact of the decision. The adoption of the eastward position prior to the prayer of consecration was viewed as relatively unimportant since it had been allowed by the judgment in the Ridsdale case during the consecration itself. Neither was the paper particularly disturbed by the mixed chalice or the ablutions. It regretted only the legalization of lighted candles on the altar and the singing of the *Agnus Dei*. It considered both to be 'alien to the spirit of simple worship' of the Church of England and 'tending to superstition.'[120] But in a paradoxical way, the *Record* was relieved that the court had upheld the archbishop's decision. 'The larger interests of the Church,' thought the paper, required an agreement between 'the Spiritual and Crown Courts.' The paper concluded that any disagreement between the courts would have had little effect in the 'discouragement of ritual practices,' but it might have resulted in 'very serious embarrassment and a considerable addition to the forces which make for Disestablishment.'[121]

In its second editorial a week later, the *Record* directed its attention to the future policy of the Evangelical party. The paper thought the most important result was the general agreement now expressed regarding 'the practical uselessness of litigation under present circumstances.' It was to be regretted that the more strident anti-Ritualists could not be convinced 'without the sharp experience of the recent Judgment.' But, the paper concluded, 'we take it that all sections of Evangelical Churchmen will henceforth be agreed in discouraging ritual litigation as a policy to be pursued.'[122] The *Record* suggested that the time had come for the party to come to an agreement on practical and positive goals, rather than being absorbed by the bitter controversies of the anti-Ritualist campaign:

> The wise course lies plainly before us. It is by doing good rather than by preventing evil that the Evangelical body exert a real influence in the Church of England. The repression of illegal and disloyal practices in parish churches is primarily the duty of the

authorities; their responsibility will, perhaps, be more readily recognized, and, to speak fairly, will be more easily discharged when it is not attempted to be shared by volunteers. But, on the other hand, Evangelical work – work which Evangelicals alone are likely, or indeed able, to perform – is heaped up around us, waiting to be done. It would, for instance, be a satisfactory and logical result of the Privy Council Judgment if the Church Pastoral-Aid Society were to find its resources suddenly reinforced by the energy and efforts of active Evangelicals. We mention the Church Pastoral-Aid Society because it stands for the whole vast field of Home Missions in an Evangelical aspect, and it is at this moment preparing for a special public effort or appeal. But there are, we need not say, numbers of other organizations framed on lines of Evangelical churchmanship which only fail to exert their proper influence because they lack due support.[123]

The *Record* also reiterated the point that the court's decision had in no way mandated the adoption of any 'dubious innovations.' The Ritualists might have gained toleration, but the ruling compelled Evangelicals to change nothing. The paper concluded that its significance ought not be exaggerated.[124] On the one hand it was to be regretted that objectionable practices had been deemed 'lawful within our Church.' But on the other hand, even cast in their worst light, the Ritualist innovations were 'insignificant compared with the bulk of the Reformed Liturgy and Ritual.' The paper could not agree with those who thought the situation was desperate. It concluded, 'Its first result will apparently be good, for it must, we imagine, lead to the final surrender of a policy which has become not only useless but mischievous. But it will be better still if it turns the united energies of the Evangelical body into the direction of a positive – we shall not be misunderstood if we say an aggressive – activity.'[125]

For the most part, the correspondence published in the paper, which allowed the letters debating the judgment and its implications to fill extra pages for two more months, followed a line similar to that of the *Record*'s own editorial position.[126] Some were even more optimistic than the paper with regard to the results.[127] There were, however, some notable exceptions. A few writers defended the CA and suggested that the paper had not dealt fairly with the organization.[128] Many more expressed a negative view of the judgment and were unwilling to concede the propriety of a shift in the emphasis of the party. A few suggested that disestablishment would be the likely result. W. F. Taylor, Archdeacon of Warrington, thought those who expected the judgment to bring peace to the church were only deluding themselves. It could no longer be affirmed that the Established Church was as exclusively Protestant as it had once been thought; and 'those who defended the Establishment solely on the ground of its exclusive Protestantism' could no longer do so.[129] Nor was Taylor convinced by the argument that Archbishop Benson had undermined the sacerdotal tendencies of the innovations by repudiating their doctrinal significance. The real meaning, he argued, was that which the Church of Rome gave them, the doctrines that had been rejected by the reformers of the Church of England, and which the Ritualists were attempting to reintroduce.[130] Despite his great pessimism, Taylor rejected the idea of secession as long as no doctrinal alterations were imposed. The *Record* did not publish any letters that openly advocated secession, but the frequency with which that alternative was refuted gave evidence of the concern within the party. Many who took a grim view of the judgment nevertheless affirmed that it was the duty of Evangelicals to stand by the established church.[131]

Charles Stirling, Vicar of New Malden, Surrey, was the only prominent Evangelical to withdraw from the church. Throughout the controversy, Evangelicals had complained that the Ritualists' defiance of the courts undermined the social order and respect for the law. When faced with their own difficult verdict, they generally attempted to avoid the appearance of disrespect for the courts, however much they might disagree with the decision. In most cases they concluded their protests by admitting that once the courts had spoken the judgment must be obeyed.[132] In contrast, Stirling questioned the integrity of the judges and claimed that the ruling had been politically motivated. In his view, it was 'abundantly evident that the Evangelical body, from the Bishop of Liverpool downwards,' had no intention of taking a stand, and consequently, the judges knew they need not worry about any anti-Ritualist reaction or public protest. They ruled, said Stirling, not on the merits of the case itself, but from a concern to placate the dominant party and to restore peace in the church.[133] In a later letter, Stirling noted that he had long since given up on the methods of the CA and left the organization to support the Prayer-book Revision Society. He argued that the reformation of the church would never be complete without a thorough revision of the Book of Common Prayer to delete the remaining vestiges of popery.[134] After resigning his benefice, Stirling went on to work on his revision and hoped to gather other seceders into a more thoroughly Protestant alternative to the Church of England.[135] But Stirling found little support for his views, and even the most extreme anti-Ritualists were generally unwilling to consider the idea of secession.[136]

The divisions among Evangelicals could also be seen in the way their bishops responded to the judgment. In November 1892, Bishop

Thorold issued a pastoral letter to the clergy of the diocese of Winchester. In discussing the case, Thorold defended the motives of the anti-Ritualists and noted their commitment to principles, while issuing a passionate plea for toleration and peace.[137] But, he continued, the positive aspects of the aesthetic movement could not be underestimated, including the encouragement of church music and a more dignified and reverent worship service, as well as the development of theological and historical studies. Whatever elements there were in that movement that might be objectionable to Evangelicals, Thorold suggested that they could no more prevent its 'subtle but growing influence.... by denouncing it as Popish,' than they could hold back the water of Niagara Falls 'by shaking a stick at it.' He concluded, 'If we cannot and will not accept any of it for ourselves, let us not be so unwise or so unfair as to grudge it to our neighbours. Our grudging it, indeed, will make no difference in their taking what they please, and what the law of the Church gives them, but it puts us utterly in the wrong and diminishes our influence for good.'[138]

In contrast, Bishop Ryle took a decidedly more negative view at the 1892 Liverpool Diocesan Conference. He questioned both the 'soundness' of the court's reasoning as well as the 'correctness' of its conclusions, although he admitted that he and all loyal clergy must submit to the judgment even if he could not 'approve or admire' it. Further, Ryle had little hope that the judgment would bring peace to the divided parties of the church.[139] In particular, he was concerned with two likely results. First, he feared that the Ritualists would view the decision as a license to expand their activities without the threat of further prosecution and suggested that such a response would only heighten tensions and further alienate the laity. Second, he was concerned that Evangelicals would be viewed as a defeated minority and treated with contempt in the church. Ultimately, Ryle thought any further worsening of the divisions would only weaken the church and lead eventually to disestablishment.[140]

The prosecution of Bishop King did not bring the Ritualist controversy to a close. Evangelicals would maintain their anti-Ritualism, to a greater or lesser degree, throughout the remaining years of the nineteenth century and for some time to come in the twentieth. But the verdicts of Archbishop Benson and the Judicial Committee in the case brought to an end the most important phase of the controversy. A few conservatives harbored a waning hope that the laws governing the ecclesiastical courts might be amended (especially to allow a final sentence of deprivation rather than imprisonment), but even the CA was forced to concede that new methods were required. Some moderates remained committed to an anti-Ritualist program of some sort, a fact that was evident in the formation of the PCA. But for some, even that degree of commitment was too much. Many had simply tired of the controversy and were convinced the future of the Evangelical party lay in a return to its purely spiritual roots. In their view, the defense of the Protestant position required a positive program rather than the continual protest against that to which they were opposed. Following the King judgment the CA attempted to refocus its programs and to reclaim its once prominent role in the party, but leadership of the party had passed over to the moderates. The two groups held many beliefs in common and shared a long heritage, but to a great degree, the animosities engendered by years of partisan controversy would continue to be a divisive factor within the Evangelical party as much as they would between the two parties involved in the conflict.

Notes

1   *Record*, 1 July 1887.
2   Owen Chadwick listed the Ritualists preferred by Gladstone and his successor, Salisbury. 'By 1885,' he wrote, 'the Oxford Movement was at last attaining the summit of its influence in the Church of England.' Chadwick, *Victorian Church, Part Two*, pp. 337-38. Chadwick was perhaps guilty of too easily equating the Ritualists with their predecessors. Much was made of Palmerston's elevation of a number of Evangelicals to the episcopacy (under the influence of Shaftesbury). But Gladstone's equally one-sided appointments have been scarcely noted.
3   According to the *Record*, Liddon thereby 'cut off from the body of Christ all the Lutheran and Presbyterian Churches on the Continent and in Scotland, as well as the English Nonconformist bodies.' The paper later noted that he softened his claims when his sermon was published. 'Thus the portentous assertion that the greater divines of our Church held the doctrine of *nullus episcopus nulla ecclesia* is silently, and without note or comment, changed into a tentative suggestion that there have been individuals willing, like Canon Liddon himself, to excommunicate the Protestant non-episcopal Churches. Further, it is a singular fact that, although many notes are appended on almost every page of the sermon, Canon Liddon has not thought it desirable to support his appeal to authority, even in its present attenuated shape, by a single reference to any English divine, either greater or less.' *Record*, 12 June 1885.
4   He complained that it could be defended only if one could imagine 'that St. Paul would have allowed the questions pending between himself and the Galatian Judaizers, or between himself and the Corinthian deniers of the Resurrection, to be settled by the nearest proconsul.' Cited in the *Times*, 27 April 1885.
    The *Record*, rejected Liddon's logic: 'The Queen is not Caesar, and her judges are not proconsuls. The attempt to obliterate the distinction between a Christian Prince and a heathen ruler, which has of late years become

fashionable among Ritualistic apologists, is utterly futile, and must remain so long as the Establishment lasts.... If the "proconsul" is an accurate correlative of the Queen and her advisers, it must be so in other matters besides ecclesiastical appeals. For example, Canon Liddon himself holds his canonry on the appointment of the Crown. Shall we say that he is indebted to "Caesar" or the "proconsul" for his position in the Church? Would St. Paul have consented to pray every Sunday for "our most religious and gracious proconsul," or would he have solemnly acknowledged Caesar to have been supreme governor "as well in spiritual things as temporal?" If not, where is Canon Liddon's analogy?' *Record*, 1 May 1885.

In contrast to the *Record*, the *Times* took a more favorable view of Liddon's attempt to elevate the episcopacy. But it recognized the irony of his position and noted that he would have 'to condemn a good deal more than Church Courts and the Public Worship Regulation Act' if he wanted to return to the truly primitive state of the early church. The paper also noted that the Ritualists had often 'magnified the episcopate in the abstract' while refusing their obedience in more practical matters. It concluded, 'May we venture to recommend to Canon Liddon's admirers and followers his sermon of last Saturday, and the sketch it gives of the origin and nature of the authority which they have very frequently and very daringly defied?' *Times*, 27 April 1885.

5   'East and West alike, but above all with the great Apostolic See of the West, with the holy Roman Church which has done so much to guard the true faith – these surely should be our objects and the objects nearest our hearts.' Cited in the *Record*, 12 June 1885.

J. C. Ryle, in an address to the Liverpool Diocesan Conference, used the incident to illustrate the depth of the division in the church. He argued that Halifax's speech far exceeded the just limits of the church's comprehensiveness and suggested that Protestants would rather risk disestablishment than consider any abdication of the church's Reformation principles. Ryle, *No Uncertain Sound*, pp. 111-12.

Halifax returned to the subject in an 1895 speech, when he advocated reunion with Rome. That speech again raised the opposition of anti-Ritualists; cf. Walsh, *Oxford Movement*, pp. 352-53. Halifax's efforts, however, only resulted in a papal bull (*Apostolicae Curae*), issued in September 1896, that condemned Anglican orders. Some of his correspondence can be found in Benson, *Life of Benson*, vol. 2, pp. 589-620.

6   The *Record* returned to the subject when Gladstone obtained a seat for Halifax on the Ecclesiastical Commission, which virtually held 'the purse strings of the church.' It was ironic, thought the paper, to give such an important position to one who would, if he had his way, subjugate the Church of England to the Bishop of Rome. *Record*, 11 June 1886.

7   Correspondence cited in the Manchester *Courier*, reprinted in the *Record*, 27 Nov. 1885.

8   Ibid. (their italics). The references to erastianism and the establishment should be taken in the context of the time. During the summer and fall of 1885, it was rumored (and feared by many Anglicans) that Parliament would take up the issue of disestablishment in the coming session.

9   Oakley's attitude was prevalent among Ritualists. In an 1878 editorial during one of A. H. Mackonochie's several appearances before the courts, the *Times* suggested that the Ritualists greatly exaggerated their own importance. 'Many of them fancy that Disestablishment might benefit them by emancipating them from parochial control. We think their imagination doest not enable them to conceive the difference which the change would make to themselves. Now, though they do not fulfill their duties to the State, the State fulfills all its duties to them. They may not value Church endowments, but how great the value is of the status and dignity arising from the fact that they are the only religious ministers recognized by law they will only discover when they have lost it. They may imagine the Church when disestablished and even disendowed would be the same to them, only with more freedom to proselytize and follow out their own fancies. They do not appear to understand that to attain this emancipation from control they might have to take a step further. They have come to believe they are a majority in the Church, and in a Church freed from the State would reign supreme. All appearances indicate an opposite result. One of the first measures taken by a free Church of England would probably be to offer the Ritualist section of the clergy the choice between conformity and expulsion. They now, while pretending to be Churchmen, act in the spirit of Congregationalists.' *Times,* 27 March 1878.

10 *Record,* 27 Nov. 1885. The Ritualists had long argued that they were being persecuted and desired only to obtain tolerance for their own beliefs with no intention of imposing their views on others. One of their number who had converted to Roman Catholicism, suggested that they were less than honest in that regard: 'Extreme "Protestants" try to exclude extreme "Ritualists" from its all embracing fold, and, though the Ritualists do not adopt such tactics, they claim in theory the whole Church as their own.... But the Ritualists having fought a good fight and won their niche in the Pantheon are not satisfied with mere toleration; they claim the whole Temple as their property, which is hardly fair. According to their own account, the object they set before themselves is the "Catholicising" of the Church of England.' Corrance, 'Development of Ritualism,' *Contemporary Review,* p. 95.

11 The paper wrote, 'The Dean and Chapter have, we believe, announced for some time past that they intended to select a man for St. Pancras who would "bring up" the services to the level of the Cathedral. Considering what some of these services are, especially those in the Crypt Chapel, far away from public view, there is a dreary prospect before St. Pancras people. The Dean is now and again forced to appeal to the Police Magistrate to help him keep order in St. Paul's, and unedifying reports of personal encounters between Reverend Canons and infuriated or crazy disturbers appear with unpleasing frequency in the newspapers. If, after fifteen years of leveling up, the Dean and Chapter cannot secure even passive acquiescence for their Ritual in the Cathedral itself, what chance is there of peace in St. Pancras when the feelings of the people and the customs of the parish are being deliberately ignored and outraged.' *Record,* 8 July 1887.

    In a later editorial, the paper suggested that the Dean and Chapter had purposely done 'irremediable' damage to an important Evangelical church.

'They have willfully brought confusion and discord into a great parish where there was peace, and have done their best to dissipate the largest congregation and to wreck the most extensive Church organization in the northern quarter of London.' *Record*, 29 July 1887.

12   This was the second prominent instance of a Ritualist being forced on a predominantly Evangelical parish. In June 1885, Gladstone had offered the living of Holy Trinity, Stroud Green, to Rev. Robert Linklater, who was a member of the Society of the Holy Cross and had served as a curate to both W. J. E. Bennett and Charles F. Lowder. Evangelicals were particularly incensed because the right of appointment fell to Gladstone only because the living became vacant before the new Bishop of London (Frederick Temple) had been consecrated. The churchwardens, on behalf of the congregation, wrote to Gladstone to request 'a pastor who would continue the teaching of their late Vicar, the Rev. John Robertson... a moderate and tolerant Evangelical.' Gladstone's response was to offer the parish to Rev. John Sheepshanks, a Ritualist. When he declined it, Gladstone hurriedly offered it, on his last day in office, to Linklater. *Record*, 19 and 26 June, 1885.

In a letter to the paper, P. V. Smith wrote that the events were still more troubling since it was the congregation itself which had built and subscribed the church under the guidance of the previous Evangelical pastor. Letter to the *Record*, 3 July 1885. The case of Holy Trinity helped foment Evangelical support for a Church Patronage Bill that would create church councils with some influence in the appointment of clergy. Evangelicals generally supported the formation of parochial councils. Lord Sandon had introduced bills for their establishment in the House of Commons as early as 1870. Cf. Machin, *Politics and the Churches, 1869-1921*, p. 49.

13   For a description of the dedication service and the elaborate artwork of the reredos, cf. *Times*, 26 Jan. 1888. In the *Record*'s view, the incident indicated the self-serving nature of the Ritualists' claim that they only desired toleration for their views. In fact, however, it was clear from their actions that they intended to impose their interests on the rest of the church wherever they obtained the power to do so. 'So utterly wanton an abuse of power by the legal guardians of the great national church of the metropolis might excite surprise if we had not already had long experience of the reckless perversity of self-will which dominates the Chapter's counsels and blinds its members to obvious considerations of duty and charity....

'It has been the fashion of late years to speak hopefully of the decline of party strife, and to impress upon Churchmen the necessity of mutual consideration. By putting up an admittedly Romish reredos in St. Paul's Cathedral, the Chapter have, in the most deliberate manner, gone out of their way to wound the consciences of tens of thousands of loyal Churchmen, and to stir up afresh the embers of a strife that seemed to be dying down.' *Record*, 10 Feb. 1888.

For a High Church account of the events, cf. G. L. Prestige, *St. Paul's in its Glory, 1831-1911* (London: SPCK, 1955). Prestige accused the protesters of 'intolerant and litigious Puritanism.' Ibid., pp. 211-14.

14   'As a member of the Committee... I must publicly disclaim all responsibility for the result, and protest in the strongest terms against this last and most

humiliating step in our long downward course of concession and compromise.... Where are we to stop? How much further will fidelity to God and His Truth permit one to go with a Society which appears to have become so seriously entangled with High Churchism throughout its operations, both at home and abroad, and which is so deplorably weak in its administration that it is incapable of taking a decided step even in so simple a matter as the service in St. Paul's?' Letter to the *Record*, 10 Feb. 1888.

15 The statement adopted by the committee read:

'(i.) That it is their duty to devote their whole attention to Foreign Missions, and while upholding at all times the standard of Protestant and Evangelical truth, to avoid as far as possible taking part in controversies at home.

'(ii.) That it is not their province to lay down any general principle respecting the use of the national cathedral, or of other churches, for the special worship of God, for the advocacy of Missions, or for the ordination of candidates for the ministry.

'As all arrangements for the Service were made before anything was known respecting the figures, the Committee repudiate the charge of having manifested indifference or indicated approval; on the contrary, they view with the deepest alarm the re-introduction into our churches of representations of figures calculated to encourage image-worship or mariolatry, remembering that at cost of their lives our fathers obtained deliverance from those perils in Reformation times, and believing the introduction of such representations to be wholly alien to the spirit and teaching of the Church of England, and likely greatly to retard the cause of Missions, which is so dear to them.' Cited in Stock, *Church Missionary Society*, vol. 3, p. 344.

As a result of its neutral position, the CMS was highly esteemed even outside the Evangelical party. When the non-partisan William Magee was asked to preach a CMS anniversary sermon, he described it as the '"blue ribbon" of the Evangelical pulpit,' and said he would gladly identify himself 'with the best of Evangelical Churchmanship.' He had to turn down the request, but accepted the offer for the next year. MacDonnell, *Life of Magee*, vol. 1, p. 108.

16 *Record*, 17 Feb. 1888.

17 At the annual meeting of the Bristol branch of the CA, James Inskip read the report of the council. In an apparent reference to the CMS committee, he noted that 'some Evangelical members of the Established Church shrank from the controversy, and excused themselves by suggestions that other work was more important. To such reasonings the Committee could only reply by pointing out that nothing could be more important than the preservation of pure doctrine and spiritual worship in our National Church.' Cited in the *Record*, 24 Feb. 1888.

18 The *Record* suggested, it was not an important enough issue to justify the creation of a schism within the most influential Evangelical organization in England. The paper complained that while direct assaults had always failed, conservative critics were doing the work of the party's opponents by attacking the CMS from within. *Record*, 16 March 1888.

19 The circular was signed by Lord Lichfield, A. T. Cotton, F. T. Haig, James

Maden Holt, and James Inskip. Reprinted in the *Record*, 23 March 1888; cf. Appendix O. On some of the controversies mentioned in the protest, cf. Stock, *Church Missionary Society, vol. 3*, pp. 336-43.

20   The paper wrote: 'The basis of the new party, which it is sought to organize at Salisbury-square, is at best a miserable misconception of matters which have been fully explained again and again. And, if suggestion of evil were not so far easier to spread than its antidote, this one consideration ought to prevent the circular from doing an harm whatever.

'But we look upon it with special distrust, because we do not know exactly what it means, or how the movement is being fomented. We do not want to call it a conspiracy, but at any rate, it is veiled in a suspicious secrecy. This circular is being sent hither and thither in "private".... It emanates from the same men who, a week or two ago, were said to be projecting a rival Missionary Society. The rumours are very far from having been disowned or contradicted. Has the scheme been exchanged for this of internal intrigue, or are the two to go on side by side?... Surely common honesty, to say nothing of Christian principle, will cry shame on a crooked, underground policy like that. The gentlemen who have combined in this remarkable manner would gain in public respect if they were more open.' *Record*, 23 March 1888.

Rev. C. Jex Blake wrote to defend the remonstrants and challenged the *Record*: 'I would ask what test do you apply to prove that this charge is untrue, that there has been a departure from distinctively Protestant and Evangelical principles in the C.M.S. Committee? Can there be any doubt that the Evangelical school as a body are declining from Protestant principles? A great deal of the correspondence in your paper of late respecting the service in St. Paul's Cathedral shows it. Besides, does not the increased circulation of your journal prove the same? Had the *Record* newspaper maintained the decidedly Protestant principles which it held thirty or forty years ago, it would not have the circulation it now enjoys. It is this feature in our Evangelical religion which causes much uneasiness in the minds of many of the sincere friends of the C.M.S.' Letter to the *Record*, 29 March 1888.

21   The first resolution acknowledged the CMS's missionary focus but continued, 'that... the Committee at the same time fully recognize the solemn obligation not only to bear clear and emphatic testimony in support of the great principles which they are thus pledged to uphold, but to discountenance and, when necessary, to protest both by word and action, against error whenever it may be encountered in the prosecution of the work of the Society, inasmuch as the extension of those very principles in heathen lands is the one great object for which the Society was formed and exists.'

With regard to meetings, the second resolution proclaimed that 'this Committee resolves that it be an instruction to the Secretaries and Staff generally to avoid all arrangements for the advocacy of the Society's claims in those Churches in which ritual and ornaments are allowed, which have been condemned by the Courts of this Church and Realm, or which, while evading a violation of the letter of the law, are plainly opposed to its spirit and intentions.' Cited in the *Record*, 13 April 1888.

22   Cf. Stock, *Church Missionary Society, vol. 3*, p. 345.

23 *Record*, 13 April 1888.
24 Webb-Peploe's resolution read: 'That this Conference, recognizing the fact that in the Metropolitan Cathedral, members of all schools of thought in the Church of England are accustomed to meet for worship, deplores the introduction there of a reredos the ornamentation of which is calculated to arouse (and has aroused) difference of opinion, and to hurt the consciences of many Churchmen.' Cited in the *Record*, 29 March 1888.
25 The CA memorial was reprinted in the *Times*, 12 April 1888; cf. Appendix P.
26 The paper thought the prosecution was a legitimate attempt 'to get the judgment of the proper Ecclesiastical Court upon the legality of the reredos. It is confidently asserted that it does not transgress established rules. If it does not, the prosecution will fail, and, little as Protestant Churchmen will like the result, they will loyally acquiesce. But if the reredos is declared illegal, it has no business to be retained in a position where it shocks and pains the feelings of a vast number of Churchmen. The first question is whether the Bishop of London will exercise his veto and stop the case at the start. We can hardly believe his Lordship will betray such extraordinary inconsistency.' *Record*, 20 April 1888.

At the same time, the UCLA, which was challenging the CA for prominence, presented its own memorial. Like the other protests, the union's memorial focused on the issue of idolatry and the negative effect the reredos would have being situated, as it was, in the most important cathedral in the country. It also suggested, in addition to the threat of idolatry and Roman influence, that the negative impact would carry over into the field of missions, creating a hindrance to the proselytization of Jews and Mohammedans, 'who entertain the strongest repugnance to the presence of images in places of worship.' Cited in the *Record*, 11 May 1888.
27 Temple argued that while litigation involving religious issues might occasionally be necessary, it was always an evil with negative consequences. 'It keeps up irritation and party strife, it embitters men's feelings, it inflicts mischief on the Church and on true religion; and it is only tolerable as a preventive of worse mischief that would otherwise follow.' Correspondence cited in the *Times*, 31 May 1888.
28 *Record*, 1 June 1888. Alexander Cobham, Chairman of the Council of the CA, made a similar point in his response to Temple's letter. He noted that the judges in the case of Phillpotts v. Boyd limited their decision 'to the special circumstances of that particular case' while noting that it involved 'no question of superstitious reverence.' Cobham claimed that four of the judges later participated in the Ridsdale judgment in which they ordered the removal of a crucifix. 'This was done on the express ground that a crucifix differs from other "sculptured representations of our Lord" in "having a history of its own" so that (it was held) "there does exist a danger and a likelihood that it may be an object of adoration and superstitious reverence".' Cobham concluded by lecturing the bishop on biblical history, 'May I suggest to your Lordship that the Commandment given by St. John, "Little children, keep yourselves from idols," has not lost all meaning for Christians in this country; and that the history of Jewish backslidings is expressly stated to have been "written for our learning." Human nature has not

The End of Litigation 435

changed in the interval.' Correspondence cited in the *Record*, 8 June 1888.

29 Far from raising partisan feelings, the *Record* thought a legal judgment would clarify the issues involved. 'The solemn litigation of the matter would clear the air and would remove the sense of grievance and injustice which now will inevitably rankle in the minds of all persons who disapprove of the Reredos. So far from the litigation keeping up irritation and embittering men's feelings, we believe that irritation and bitterness will be rather engendered by its suppression.' *Record*, 1 June 1888.

Bishop Goodwin took a similar view in his Christmas pastoral to the clergy of Carlisle, in which he discussed both the St. Paul's case and that of Bishop King. While denigrating the prosecution of King, Goodwin was undisturbed by the other litigation. He concluded, 'The question brought forward seems to be one which might be fairly argued before a Court of Law, and I do not know that evil need be anticipated from the argument or the decision whatever it may be.' Cited in the *Record*, 4 Jan. 1889.

30 The arguments before the court were reported in the *Times*, 19 and 21 Nov. 1888.

31 Lord Chief Justice Coleridge expressed his personal sympathy for the artwork but complained that it was 'very mischievous' that the complaints of the laity 'should be met with the simple will of a Bishop, who tells them that the matter shall not even be discussed, and that, like naughty schoolboys, they must learn to obey their spiritual pastors and masters.' Judgment of the Queen's Bench Division, cited in the *Times*, 3 June 1889.

32 Lord Grimthorpe, Diocesan Chancellor for the Province of York and an increasingly vehement High Church opponent of the Ritualists, responded negatively to Bishop Wordsworth's proclamation that the secular courts could have no authority in religious matters. Grimthorpe replied, 'Here at last we have the clerical supremacy cat let out of the bag without reserve. By their veto the Bishops have been most foolishly allowed to repeal every law of the Church as to doctrine or ritual, as declared by the only Courts that will ever declare it honestly according to the Prayer Book and the 39 Articles.' Letter to the *Times*, 2 May 1888.

33 Judgment of the Court of Appeal, cited in the *Times*, 16 Dec. 1889. In its editorial, the *Record* sought to downplay the importance of the decision, suggesting that it had been widely expected. More important, in the view of the paper, was the dean and chapter's misuse of their authority 'for the gratification of their own personal views and for the advancement of their own party ends.' *Record*, 20 Dec. 1889.

34 W. E. Shipton chaired the autumn meeting of the CA in 1887, and denied that the bishops could be trusted to enforce of the law. He complained that they desired to water down the Protestantism of the church, and questioned whether they could be trusted. 'Had they deserved,' Shipton continued, 'the confidence which had been asked for them, that they should be left to protect their interests in the future? (No.) How many Evangelical men had ever received episcopal patronage? Whatever confidence might be due to them in other respects, the Bishops at least had proved themselves to be no friends to the Protestant section of the Church of England. (Applause.)' Cited in the *Record*, 11 Nov. 1887.

The contrast in attitude between the conservatives and moderates could hardly be sharper. Rev. Sir Emilius Laurie, Rector of St. John's, Paddington, addressed the London Clerical and Lay Union meeting in July 1887, on 'The Present State of Evangelical Religion in the Church of England.' Of the twenty-eight bishops in the church, he thought more of them were sympathetic to the Evangelical cause than at any previous time during the church's history. He classified eight as Evangelical, nine as sympathetic, and eleven were 'out in the cold.' Furthermore, he believed that the number of Evangelical clergy in general had grown in influence since the early days of the century. In light of such indisputable facts, Laurie adopted an optimistic view of the progress and position of Evangelical religion. Cited in the *Record*, 1 July 1887.

Their complaints would continue for a number of years. At the turn of the century, John Kensit accused the bishops of 'masterly inactivity.' They continued to promote and ordain clergy who were 'pledged to promulgate doctrines entirely opposed to God's Truth and the principles of the blessed Reformation.' J. C. Wilcox, *Contending for the Faith: John Kensit, Reformer and Martyr* (London: Protestant Truth Society, 1902), p. 50.

35 The complaint, involving the use of the eastward position in the ante-Communion service, was made against the canon precentor rather than the dean, who had also adopted the innovation, because the canon's benefice was held by the bishop, and a complaint against him would therefore be made to the archbishop instead. *Times*, 30 Dec. 1886.

36 'The provision here resorted to was evidently designed simply to withdraw the defendant from the jurisdiction of his own patron. But in this complaint the proper defendant is not accused before the proper judge, but is passed over that another less responsible person may be accused before a merely provisional judge. Complainant can have no right to anticipate the judgment of the proper judge, and virtually to select his own judge in his own case. I must allow that this purpose is not disguised in the documents laid before me, but it is a contortion of the spirit of the law to which I cannot consent to be a party.' Cited in the *Times*, 30 Dec. 1886.

An anonymous diocesan chancellor protested Benson's decision in a letter to the *Times*. He contrasted Benson's approach to that of the Archbishop of York (Thomson), who several years before, had forbidden the minor canons of the cathedral to adopt illegal innovations. The correspondent complained that it was the Ritualist innovators and the Benson himself who were contorting 'the spirit of the law.' He concluded, 'It would be both more simple and more honest if these bishops would announce at once something of this kind: – 'The two Acts for enforcing the Act of Uniformity gave us, instead of the judge, a discretion to stop frivolous and vexatious suits. They gave it to us in a way which enables us to repeal all the Acts, and the Prayer Book and all its rubrics, and allow the service of the Church of England to be reconverted into the Mass if the clergy like, and to repeal every judgment of the Privy Council thereon; and we mean to do it. Therefore you need not come here with your complaints.' Letter (signed 'Another Chancellor') to the *Times*, 3 Jan. 1887.

37 C. H. Wainwright, told the autumn meeting of the CA, that 'as the bishops

stood out prominently in their open defiance of law, they should be the first people attacked – (applause) – and if the Council failed to take notice of a case so flagrant as that of the Bishop of Lincoln, it would require argument stronger than any he had heard to justify their existence as a society. He hoped that the Council would without delay take steps to show that Bishops were subject to authority, and were not allowed to sanction or to practise Romish ceremonies in a Protestant Church. (Applause.)' Cited in the *Record*, 5 Nov. 1886.

According to Owen Chadwick, they could not have selected a less likely target. King was 'the saintliest bishop on the bench' and beloved by his clergy, both Evangelical and Ritualist. Chadwick, *Victorian Church, Part Two*, p. 353.

38 The correspondent for the *Record*, thought the speeches of the meeting were of 'a very pessimistic character' and noted the diminished attendance from previous years; the audience was not even large enough to fill one of the smaller rooms at Exeter Hall. His report on the principal speech of the evening, given by Lord Robert Montagu, indicated just how divided the moderate Evangelicals were from the extreme anti-Ritualists and how far the paper's sympathies had shifted: 'Lord Robert Montagu spoke for close upon an hour. Had he chosen some new and stirring subject this might have been tolerated, but he did not. He harped away on his one string – viz., that there is to-day a regular conspiracy existing in England similar to that of 1687, to bring this country again under the dominion of Rome – and it must be confessed that even some of the audience grew a little weary of his alarmist statements. Here and there I occasionally noticed a person nodding in sleep, while an old lady in a corner was beguiling the time with an orange. He mentioned "five points in the conspiracy" of 1687, and he declared that the same things were being re-enacted in our own time. But he dwelt especially on two points, viz., the attempt to discredit the representative system, and the exercise of a "dispensing power" by those in authority. Many of his arguments were of an extravagant character. He endeavoured to prove his first point by showing that at Parliamentary elections local men now stood no chance; the candidates were sent down from London. Lord Salisbury and Mr. Gladstone, I understood him to say, are Romanizers, and the men chosen to stand by the leaders of the two great parties are those with the greatest Romanizing tendencies, so that whether the Tory or Liberal candidate be elected the result is the same – a Romanizing Member of Parliament. But what is more surprising than the statements themselves is that any body of persons could be found to cheer such remarkable theories as did that assembly of yesterday. As his Lordship sat down I did not feel at all inclined to re-echo the remarks of a lady who was sitting near me, that "We want a few more men like that".' *Record*, 20 May 1887.

39 The *Record* actually preferred King to some of the other candidates whose names had been mentioned. Although he was known to represent the 'extreme High Church section,' King had shown an appreciation for Evangelicals on several occasions. The paper concluded, 'To put the same thing in other words, it has always seemed to us that the truths on which Evangeli-

cal and High Churchmen are agreed, occupy a larger relative place in Canon King's teaching and writing than they do in those of other High Churchmen. In a well remembered speech of Canon Ryle's, delivered at the Islington Meeting in 1872, Canon King is mentioned as one of the twelve representative men of different "schools" amongst whom "a vast amount of unity" really subsisted.' *Record*, 6 Feb. 1885.

40 The reintroduction of the episcopal cope and mitre disturbed anti-Ritualists. In 1891, the *Record* campaigned against the ceremonial attire after Bishop Ellicott of Gloucester and Bristol wore them in public for the first time, joining the Bishops of Lincoln, Ely, Chester and Peterborough. Their adoption seemed curiously inconsistent, thought the paper, for 'a Bishop who a few years ago accused Ritual lawbreakers of "digging the grave of the Establishment".' While acknowledging that they were not strictly illegal, the paper suggested that the elaborate garments were indicative of a general outlook that would only encourage further Ritualist excesses. *Record*, 24 Dec. 1891.

In January 1892, the anti-Ritualist clergy and laity of Bristol addressed a memorial protest to Bishop Ellicott. In their view, 'it was beyond dispute' that those who organized the gift of cope, mitre and staff for Ellicott were ECU members who were intent upon undoing the Reformation. The protesters expressed their deep regret that Ellicott had 'accepted the gifts, and thus laid upon the consciences of your own people a burden heavy to be borne, and enabled the section before-mentioned again to cause divisions, as they have effectually done for many years.' It was their Protestant duty, they believed, to protest a manner of dress that was 'inconsistent with the history and teaching of the Reformed Church of England; and at the same time quite in harmony with the attempt of the English Church Union to reimpose an ecclesiastical system from which our country, after lengthened struggles, was mercifully delivered through the Reformation.' Cited in the *Times*, 8 Jan. 1892.

41 *Record*, 29 Jan. 1886.

42 The CA took out a large advertisement under the heading 'Special Appeal for Funds' detailing its position, the threat the Ritualists presented, and calling for new funds to finance the prosecution of Bishop King. Advertisement in the *Times*, 12 July 1888; cf. Appendix Q.

43 Samuel Garratt, whose eloquent letter several years earlier had set the tone for moderate opposition to further prosecutions, returned to the subject: 'That it is not by prosecutions and the bitter language of public meetings Ritualism is to be met, has been the deep conviction of my own mind for twenty-one years. And now it seems that this policy is to be renewed. That those who have prosecuted presbyters so vigorously should think it necessary to their consistency to prosecute a Bishop I can understand. But I confess I cannot understand their taking a step which must necessarily lead to a reconsideration of the Privy Council judgments, for a Bishop will hardly be put in prison without an appeal to the highest Court. Are they quite sure that a reconsideration may not result in a reversal?'

Garratt echoed the words of another anonymous correspondent (letter from 'Evangelical' to the *Record*, 22 June 1888) who had suggested that success in the controversy could hardly be obtained by the use of secular weapons, but would rather be won at a spiritual level through much prayer. 'As far as stopping Ritualism is concerned, the result, as a whole, of the prosecution has been hitherto failure – an additional proof, if any were wanted, to the experience of all ages, that "the cause of Christ," as "Evangelical" says, "can only be won by spiritual weapons".' Letter to the *Record*, 29 June 1888.

44 The four promoters of the case were Mr. Ernest de Lacy Read, a churchwarden in the parish of Cleethorpes, and Mr. William Brown, a solicitor, along with Mr. John Marshall and Mr. Felix Wilson, who were working men from Lincoln. Marshall and Wilson were the 'aggrieved parishioners' from St. Peter's, Gowts, where Bishop King had presided over a service. *Record*, 8 June 1888.

45 The lawyers for the CA could find only one case in the three hundred years since the Reformation. In his private correspondence during the course of the controversy, Archbishop Benson was critical of both sides for their unwillingness to compromise. For Archbishop Benson's thoughts on the extent of his authority and much of the correspondence with his advisors; cf. Benson, *Life of Benson*, vol. 2, pp. 320-36. To Bishop Magee he wrote, 'These are small matters, but anything is enough for either of the factions to fight about – God help us.' Ibid., p. 353. Cf. correspondence of his legal secretary, H. W. Lee, cited in the *Record*, 6 July 1888.

46 At the first sitting, the judges suddenly adjourned the court after determining they would need ecclesiastical assessors before ruling. A week later, with five bishops present, the judges ruled that the archbishop did have the authority to hear the case. The proceedings were reported in the *Times*, 30 July and 4 Aug. 1888.

47 The original declaration, made up of eight points, was reprinted in the *Record*, 14 Sept. 1888. A much shorter and less specific document (the changes apparently made to secure a broader acceptance) was adopted at a public meeting called by G. A. Denison in November 1888. The second document read: 'We, the undersigned priests, deacons, and lay members of the Church of England, being persuaded that, under the present condition of discipline in the Church, the promoting of a particular class of proceedings at law directed against certain manner or manners of worship of God in cathedrals, churches, and chapels thereof, is a scandal to religion, an injury and hindrance to the growth of the spiritual life, and cannot promote unity or even permit peace, do hereby, to and before the whole English people, make this our declaration and remonstrance against the promoting of such proceedings. And we do this irrespectively of, and apart from, any conclusions to which we may have come in connecting with the subject matter of any one or more of such proceedings, past or present.' Cited in the *Record*, 16 Nov. 1888.

48 *Record*, 19 Oct. 1888. A month later, the paper reiterated the point: 'The Evangelical position in this very grave business must not be misunderstood. They are not in any sense responsible for the prosecution. It has been launched without consultation, so far as we can ascertain, with any single Evangelical leader. Whatever else it is, it is not the work of the Low Church

party.' *Record*, 16 Nov. 1888.

The paper noted as well that moderates, in fact, had little influence with the extreme section of the party. It wrote, 'There is no Evangelical leader who possesses influence with those who have initiated the proceedings or with the Church Association itself. It is necessary and fair that this should be understood by those on the other side. The Evangelical party neither set the ball rolling nor can they stop it. It became obvious years ago that Evangelical Churchmen, as a body, were not in sympathy with the Church Association or its methods. As times goes on they do not get nearer together. The Church Association, it must be owned, has shown a robust determination to stand alone and maintain its own course. It has done so with consistency, and it would be wholly unreasonable for those who have stood deliberately aloof now to claim a voice in councils to which they have either never belonged or from which they long ago separated themselves.' *Record*, 1 Feb. 1889.

49 The Declaration was reprinted in an Advertisement in the *Record*, 4 Jan. 1889; cf. Appendix R.

50 'We, the undersigned Clergy and Laity of the Church of England, having read a Declaration accepted by a meeting held at the Westminster Palace Hotel, on November 13, 1888, in reference to "a particular class of proceedings at law directed against certain manner or manners of Worship of God," in which the Signatories deprecate "the promoting of such proceedings": – desire to state our conviction that the real "scandal to religion" and "injury and hindrance to the growth of the spiritual life" is the re-introduction into our places of worship of mediaeval doctrines and practices.

'We feel strongly that those who sign such a Declaration will thereby countenance these doctrines and practices, and encourage a condition of lawlessness which must be fatal alike to an ecclesiastical as to a civil polity.

'We, on our part, appeal to our fellow Churchmen to stand together on the basis of the Reformed Church of England, from a heartfelt love for the Person and cause and people of our Lord Jesus Christ, the true foundation of unity and peace.' Reprinted in the *Record*, 4 Jan. 1889.

51 The text of the citation, detailing the charges made against King, was reprinted in the *Times*, 10 Jan. 1889. The *Record* published a helpful survey of the charges made. It listed the ritual at issue, gave citations of the evidence for its usage in the early church, summarized the cases in which it had previously been brought before the courts, and cited prominent Ritualist writers with regard to their perspective on its symbolic meaning. The charges were: lighted candles on the altar, the mixed chalice (water mingled with the wine), use of the eastward position, singing of the *Agnus Dei*, making the sign of the cross to the communicants and at the benediction, and the public ablution of the vessels after which the remnants of the bread and wine were consumed by the celebrant. *Record*, 8 Feb. 1889.

For a summary of the events from King's perspective, cf. John A. Newton, *Search for a Saint: Edward King* (London: Epworth Press, 1977), pp. 93-103.

52 Cited in the *Record*, 11 Jan. 1889.
53 *Record*, 11 Jan. 1889.

54 The *Record* explained its opposition in an editorial, 'We have done so on the plain ground that litigation, having been fairly and fully tried, had conspicuously failed in suppressing illegal and superstitious ritual, while, from the unfortunate character of its processes, it had turned a very large and important section of public opinion into a channel of sympathy with the wrongdoers and acquiescence in their wrongdoing.' *Record*, 10 Aug. 1888.

Bishop Goodwin of Carlisle touched upon the failure of litigation in his Christmas pastoral. There was a time, he admitted, when he had 'fondly imagined that a legal decision upon disputed rubrics would be accepted by all parties.' It had become painfully evident, however, that the effort had failed. In Goodwin's view, 'well-informed thoughtful men' had come to fundamentally divergent views of the meaning of certain passages of the rubrics, and it was evident that further prosecutions would lead to no good result. 'I candidly confess,' he wrote, 'that the restoration of uniformity of practise with regard to certain points of ritual, which I need not specify, by process of law, even if it were desirable, seems to me to be, and to have been demonstrated to be, simply impossible.' Cited in the *Record*, 4 Jan. 1889.

55 The *Record* complained about King's partisan activities: 'Dr. King, having accepted the weighty task of presiding over an English diocese, should not have seen it his duty to place himself above party, but, on the contrary, should, alone amongst the English Bishops, have remained a member of the English Church Union, and by acts and words let it be clearly understood that he was as much a party man as ever. If, instead of constantly repeating all known Ritualistic innovations, even having a photograph of himself attired in unlawful vestments hawked about the streets of London, Dr. King had recognized that whatever his private views, his position in the National Church made acquiescence in the law of the Establishment a duty – we are putting the matter in a way that assumes no controversial point – there would have been no protest and certainly no prosecution. But Dr. King has invited litigation and made it very hard for those who would help him if they could, to do anything to arrest its progress.' *Record*, 10 Aug. 1888.

56 The paper continued, 'We should regret exceedingly if words of ours in any way hindered the cause of peace. But we should not be doing our duty if we seemed to falter or hesitate in this matter.... The Evangelical position always has been and always must be that the Mass is anti-Christian, that its doctrine and its ritual are subversive of a pure faith, that a system which finds in sacraments a substitute for conversion imperils the salvation of mankind, and that teaching which gives tradition a co-ordinate place with the Bible, or installs the Church as the authorized interpreter of the Bible without which it cannot be safely studied, willfully clouds the light of Divine Revelation with the fog of human opinion. We fail to see in any of these subjects room for compromise or a basis for negotiation.' Ibid.

57 The writer continued, 'Men attached to Evangelical principles will remain attached to them, no doubt, however the future may shape itself; but they will either become, especially the younger and more liberal among them, absorbed in that great middle body in the Church, which, without a name, is rapidly embracing the more moderate members of all schools of thought,

or else be isolated units with no cohesion or readiness for united action. Thus the Evangelical body, weak to-day, will be infinitely weaker ten years hence, to the incalculable loss of the Church of England at a time when, perhaps, more even than at the present she will need its voice and influence in her counsels.

'The Islington Clerical Meeting of 1889, with all the interest belonging to it, and the authority attaching to the names of the appointed speakers, despite the number of clergy who attended it, was not without its warning note; the absence of the younger brethren was conspicuous, the absence of certain well-known faces was suggestive.' The author believed that a 'comprehensive Evangelical Churchmanship' as distinguished from 'narrow partisanship' would ultimately prove beneficial 'and compensate to some extent for the mischief done through the Church Association by indeed a small and diminishing minority, but for which the Evangelical body as a whole has been held responsible.' Letter (signed 'Nemo') to the *Record*, 15 Feb. 1889.

According to Owen Chadwick, the prosecution of King did more to damage the reputation of the Evangelical party than any of the previous prosecutions, even those that ended in the imprisonment of clergy. Despite the opposition of most moderates, the CA 'proceeded in the name of Evangelical truth, and the Evangelicals suffered.' Chadwick, *Victorian Church, Part Two*, p. 354.

58 In particular, cf. the letters of Charles D. Bell and C. H. Waller. The latter was particularly vehement in his response and suggested that he had only noted the absence of many 'half-hearted men' at the Islington Conference. Letters to the *Record*, 22 Feb. 1889.

'Nemo' took particular exception to Waller's remark. It was, no doubt, a term to be attached to all who disagree with Waller; 'who, e.g., while regretting most deeply the spread of Ritualism and the position taken up by the Bishop of Lincoln, would discourage a prosecution which, issue as it may, must in their judgment lead only to disaster; who distinguish between Evangelical partisanship and fidelity to Evangelical principles; who recognize as brethren in Christ men belonging to other schools of thought. Mr. Waller is glad that such men absented themselves from Islington, and sees in their doing so much ground for encouragement. To my own mind, and I believe that many will agree with me, the absence of such men from the great representative gathering, half-hearted though they may be, as judged by Mr. Waller's standard, but whole-hearted in the cause of Christ and in their attachment to the Evangelical principles of the Church of England, is a thing to be deplored, and can only be regarded as most discouraging by all who have at heart the best interests of the Evangelical body.' Letter to the *Record*, 1 March 1889.

59 Letter (signed 'Nemo') to the *Record*, 29 March 1889.
60 Letter to the *Record*, 18 April 1889.
61 Milner wrote, 'Might not an opportune lesson be learnt from what occurred in England in the last century, when, if legal coercion was not resorted to, yet the attempt was made to laugh or frown down the great Wesleyan movement which then arose, and the consequence was the loss of that body

to the Church? Whereas, had the new life then manifested been sympathized with and welcomed, it would have been a source of incalculable blessing and strength to the Church in which it sprang up, and which unwisely cast it out.

'The case now is somewhat different, obviously, but yet there are points of essential correspondence. However we may disapprove of the proceedings of some now amongst us, yet it cannot be denied that they have done good. There is much earnestness and undoubted piety in very many of them, and if, instead of forbearance, a course is now pursued towards them which may eventually lead to their estrangement from us, we may ultimately lament this, as we now grieve that our forefathers did not hold out the right hand of fellowship and brotherhood to the followers of John Wesley.' Ibid.

62   Was not the essence of Ritualism, Moule asked, in 'the proper sacerdotal character of the Christian ministry, the sacrificial nature of the Eucharist, a practically *opus operatum* view of both (or of *all*) Sacraments, the vital necessity of episcopacy to a true Church, the autocracy (in a considerable sense) of the clergy over the laity and the Bishops over the clergy?' Letter to the *Record*, 26 April 1889 (his italics).

63   Milner continued, 'Are not the Sacraments more reverently administered, and more largely observed, than they used to be? Are not our Church services more solemn, more impressive, and less calculated to induce slumber than in bygone times? Is not the idea, which seemed to prevail, that the study after adornment or beauty was to be eliminated from the interior of our churches, and confined to secular or domestic edifices, being dissipated with the result that our churches offer an altered and, in various ways, a more attractive aspect? Are not a multitude of efforts, mainly religious, but partially moral and social, being made in our parishes, which are in some measure to be ascribed to the new impulse we are considering; and is not the outcome of all that the Church is a greater power in the land for good than it was?' In Milner's view, the church was stronger and better for the High Church movement, and whatever their errors, they did not warrant prosecution. Letter to the *Record*, 26 April 1889.

64   Throughout the course of the controversy, there had been a few moderates from the High Church who had strongly opposed the Ritualists, but, in general, the majority were not disposed to unite with Evangelicals, finding the extreme section of that party equally unattractive. Bishop Ellicott of Gloucester and Bristol attempted to encourage the coalition in his pastoral letter for 1883. He suggested that 'the old, historic and loyal High Church party' owed no support to the extremists. 'If this old and true party,' he concluded, 'recruited as, perhaps, it may be, by some members of the Evangelical party, could solidly re-form, disavow extreme men, rally round legitimate authority, and reassert those Anglican principles which it is now the fashion to sneer at – then verily we might avert the dangers that are now at our doors, and remain the true Church of the nation, a light and a blessing to our country, far, far into the future.' Cited in the *Times*, 15 Jan. 1883.

65   *Record*, 14 June 1889. The *Times* reported that it was attended by "a large

and influential body of clergy and laity from all parts of England. *Times*, 21 June 1889.

Lord Grimthorpe, Diocesan Chancellor for the Province of York and a vocal High Church opponent of the Ritualists, was invited by moderate Evangelicals to lead the new organization. According to Eugene Stock, however, the attempt to unite moderates across party lines proved to be too difficult. Stock, *Church Missionary Society, vol. 3*, p. 281.

66   The resolution establishing the alliance was reprinted in the *Times*, 21 June 1889; cf. Appendix S.

The secretary of the new organization was Rev. J. W. Marshall, who served in the same capacity for the UCLA. He indicated, in a report for the Central Committee of the union, that the idea for the PCA had actually arisen out of the union and that there was no conflict between the two bodies. The committee believed the two could be mutually beneficial; 'the Alliance could by its aggressive work stir up the latent Protestant feeling in the country,' which could assist the endeavors of the union, while the union could help with the local organization of meetings and lectures for the PCA. Cited in the *Record*, 17 Jan. 1890.

The issue of a conflict of interest was a matter of concern to some. Alexander Roberts, Rector of Kimberly, and Honorary Secretary of the Midlands Clerical and Lay Association, addressed the subject in a letter to the *Record*. He noted that the organizational structure had been borrowed from the UCLA and that many of their interests and concerns overlapped. 'This being so,' wrote Roberts, 'it follows that great care must be exercised to avoid friction, and waste of energy. The older associations will rejoice if the new Alliance is able to effect what they have not as yet effected – or to put it more correctly, to complete – what they have begun. On the other hand, the new Alliance must exercise every care that they do not interfere with and injure the work of the older and parent Society from which they have sprung.' Letter to the *Record*, 2 Aug. 1889.

67   'First, there was the Church Association; secondly, there was the majority of those present, consisting of Evangelical Churchmen who on the one hand desire to combine in defence of the Reformation, and on the other are unable to go with the Church Association. Thirdly, there was Lord Grimthorpe, who proclaimed himself a High and Dry Churchman, whose Protestantism is scarcely less staunch against Dissenters than against Rome and Ritualism' *Record*, 21 June 1889.

68   In a pamphlet supporting the new organization, Archdeacon Straton suggested that many had left the CA after the Ridsdale judgment, believing that the laws had been clearly defined and that they could rely on the bishops to protect the Protestant principles of the church. Moderates, said Straton, had hoped for a reduction of party strife. But the Ritualists had only grown stronger and were rewarded with prominent ecclesiastical appointments by the government. Consequently, they had become more audacious in their innovations, and threatened the peace of the church. Under the circumstances, many moderates believed a new union, organized on broadly Protestant lines, was necessary. N. D. J. Straton, *Why We Should Join the Protestant Churchmen's Alliance* (London: John Kensit, 1889), pp. 1-3.

69 The *Record* suggested that this was the single great limitation of the PCA, and it feared that the association would suffer from its lack of comprehensiveness. *Record*, 21 June 1889.

G. R. Balleine mistakenly reported that the PCA absorbed the Protestant Association. In fact, the latter group included Nonconformists, and it continued to maintain a separate identity. Balleine, *Evangelical Party*, p 232. G. I. T. Machin repeated his error; cf. Machin, *Politics and the Churches, 1869-1921*, p. 179.

70 Stevenson A. Blackwood, a prominent lay Evangelical, outlined his reasons for opposing the new body in a letter to the *Record*. He argued that it would gather its support at the expense of the CA: 'It cannot do otherwise than take the wind out of their sails and the money out of their pockets, just at the moment when they are needing it most in order to carry on the battle in which they are engaged. Our friends will be confused, our counsels and supporters divided, and the energies of the party dissipated instead of concentrated and strengthened. I therefore regard the formation of a new Society as distinctly dangerous.' He did affirm, however, that he would have supported the organization if it had been formed on a broader basis and attempted to unite all Protestants in the country. Letter to the *Record*, 28 June 1889.

71 Archdeacon Straton emphasized that the union's supporters were not interested in narrowing the comprehensiveness of the church; they only desired to gather together Protestants from all church parties who were opposed to include those sacerdotalists whose theology was 'intolerable.' What was needed was an organization capable of uniting all Protestants. The lay and clerical union focused only on spiritual concerns, and the CA was engaged in legal undertakings. That left two great spheres of activity for the PCA – educational and parliamentary. Straton, *Protestant Churchmen's Alliance*, pp. 10-11.

72 Cited in the *Record*, 14 Feb. 1890.

73 Marshall listed the major obstacles: '(1) that it was made up of several local associations, not one of which would alter a word of its constitution so as to meet wider needs; (2) that, with two exceptions, no attempt was made by them to organize Evangelicals as a whole; (3) that the associations had deliberately rejected the scheme of organization pressed upon them; (4) that by the constitution of the Union the co-operation of the working classes could not be solicited; (5) that it objected to public demonstrations; (6) that its aim was rather spiritual edification than aggressive work; and (7) that it was for Evangelical men only.' Ibid.

In 1891, an organizational meeting was held for the formation of a Ladies Branch of the PCA. The objects and rules of the group were read and explained by Marshall, who went on to note 'that he believed that Ritualism had been to a great degree spread through the influence of ladies, and he thought it was only right that they should try to band themselves together to undo the evil.' Marshall's interesting statement indicated, assuming his view was somewhat representative, that the perception remained that the Ritualists drew most of their adherents from women (and those chiefly from the upper class) who could be more readily influenced than men.

Record, 27 Nov. 1891.
74 *Record*, 5 July 1889. An anonymous letter expressed a similar view: 'The subject of the Church Association was sure to create some uncomfortableness. I have no hesitation in saying that the Church of England owes an immense debt to that body, and that without its operations we should at this moment know very little about the law of ritual. But its friends and members really must bear in mind that thousands of strong opponents of Ritualism will not work with them, and yet have the same objects in view. However much they may regret that they are apparently passed over, I think they ought to accept the position, and not look coolly on the new "Alliance," but let it wear its own uniform and fight in its own way.' Letter (signed 'An Old Soldier') to the *Record*, 5 July 1889.
75 Letter to the *Record*, 18 Oct. 1889.
76 He concluded, 'If we had followed the spirit of the advice given by St. Paul in 1 Cor. vi., and borne wrong and let our brethren alone, using no weapons but those of prayer and persuasion, I believe there would not have been the rapid ritual development which we have witnessed, and that our own growth in divine things would have been far greater than it has been. We often complain that the moderate men in our Church, and the young, are not with us. The reason they give is that we prosecute those who differ from us. And what will be the end if we lose the young?... Now, the object of the Protestant Churchmen's Alliance is not to oppose the Church Association, but to provide a wider basis on which they and we can work. They hold the same doctrine that we do, though we think that they must fail in attempting to exercise a disciplinary power in our Church.' Ibid.
77 Letter to the *Record*, 25 Oct. 1889.
78 Payne Smith admitted giving lectures for the CA but claimed never to have spoken in favor of prosecution. 'There is a speciousness about the plea that at a large cost you have obtained decisions in courts of law on disputed points of ritual; and I pleaded this for you at a small meeting in a schoolroom here. But it was upon the supposition that such suits were things of the past. For you ought to have mentioned that on Dec. 19, 1884, I was one of a deputation which had an interview with the leaders of the Church Association in the library of the National Club. We thought that we had made you thoroughly understand that your prosecutions were disapproved of by a large number of Evangelical men, as being unspiritual weapons, without warrant in Holy Scripture, and for which you have no commission, being a private Society, in no way appointed or authorized to take upon you the maintenance of discipline in our Church. I feel bound now to say publicly what I then said privately. And I add that in my humble opinion the prosecutions on which you so rashly enter, are detrimental to the best interests of us Evangelicals; that you have failed in abating any one ritual excess; and that by the reaction from your proceedings you have given vitality and strength to many extreme doctrines.' Letter to the *Record*, 1 Nov. 1889.

Miller briefly responded by questioning Payne Smith's honesty, since he had lectured for the CA and then turned against it. He also suggested that the meeting to which Payne Smith referred at the National Club was private and that he had broken a pledge of confidentiality by revealing the pro-

ceedings. Letter to the *Record*, 15 Nov. 1889.
79 The objects of the PCA were listed in an Advertisement in the *Record*, 20 Dec. 1889; cf. Appendix T.
80 A letter of C. R. Alford, former colonial Bishop of Victoria, gave evidence of the confusion and seemed to assume that the two groups were somehow related. He complained that both were inclined to compromise the truth for the sake of peace. Letter to the *Record*, 5 July 1889.
81 At the organization's first public meeting, Shore proposed two principles upon which it was established: '(1) a full recognition of the wide tolerance, both as regards doctrinal opinion and ritual, which is the historic and traditional characteristic of the English Church; and (2) loyalty to the Catholic principles on which the Church took her stand at the Reformation settlement when she recovered her rights as a National Church and reasserted her primitive doctrine and practice.' *Times*, 7 Feb. 1890.

In a letter to the *Guardian*, Perowne proclaimed the distinction between the two groups: 'As I find there is still an impression in some quarters that I am a member of the "Churchmen's Protestant Alliance," permit me to repeat my disclaimer of being in any way connected with it. My allegiance to the principles of the Reformation is just what it ever was; I do not swerve a hair's breadth from what I have always believed and taught; I have no sympathy with Ritualism. But Ritualism is, after all, the inevitable expression of certain forms of enthusiasm; and where the Church herself, as it seems to me, has given liberty, it is not for any party or school in the Church to curtail it.' Correspondence cited in the *Record*, 26 July 1889.
82 *Times*, 7 Feb. 1890.
83 Ibid. Perowne defended the proposal in another letter: 'I know that Ritualism means doctrine, and I am as much opposed as ever both to the statement of the doctrine and the manner of exhibiting it to the eye. But will any conceivable process get rid of the one or the other? Strip off the vestments if you can, put out the altar-lights, extinguish the incense, forbid the bowings and crossings and all the parody of Rome, unless you can shut the mouths of these men the doctrine will remain. And after all, it is the doctrine for which the most earnest among them are fighting. And that doctrine has been declared to be lawfully held and taught in the Church of England, both by the Bennett Judgment, on which a doctrine scarcely differing from Transubstantiation was allowed, and by the Ridsdale Judgment, which by permitting the Eastward position did much more than declare "that sacerdotalism is now an open question in the Church of England.

'It is my firm conviction that any attempt to put down Ritualism will be a disastrous failure. It is my no less firm conviction that the permission within such reasonable limits as the Ornaments Rubric allows, and for which Dr. Littedale contends, would do more than anything else, not only to allay the heats of the present controversy, but to destroy much of the glamour which now hangs about Ritualism.' Letter to the *Record*, 6 Sept. 1889.
84 In February 1890, Churchmen in Council sponsored a public meeting at which they detailed their plan for the alteration of the rubrics by Convocation. The *Record* was unimpressed, particularly with the power that the plan

assumed for Convocation. In the first place, the paper suggested that an unreformed Convocation did not truly represent the parish clergy and left the laity with no voice at all. Therefore it could not be trusted with any real power. And in the second place, it had already attempted to consider the rubrics in earlier debates and had been unable to arrive at any meaningful conclusion. *Record*, 7 Feb. 1890.

85 *Record*, 31 Jan. 1890. At the other end of the spectrum, and representing 'the belligerent section' the *Record* referred to, was John Kensit, who formed the Protestant Truth Society to lead protests and publish anti-Ritualist materials. Cf. Yates, *Oxford Movement*, p. 32.

86 The paper described the various groups: 'The time has come when they find silence no longer possible. Some, in almost panic-stricken alarm at the signs of confusion around, discuss the wisdom of secession from the Church. They find little support; but their suggestion is most eloquent as to the straits in which they believe the Church to be, and the gravity of the measures needful if affairs are to be set right. Others, like "Churchmen in Council," cherish the hope that some plan of compromise may be evolved which shall remove the more serious dangers born of the Ritual controversy. Others, again, conscious that a policy of prosecution has deprived the cause of Protestantism of much popularity, have united to form the Protestant Churchmen's Alliance. And, lastly, the forces which find a vent in the conduct of the Bishop of Lincoln's case have shown signs of increased vitality. The dwindling resources of the Church Association instantly recovered strength, and subscriptions poured in, directly it became apparent that the Council had real aggressive work in hand.' Ibid.

87 Bishop Thorold of Rochester was also to have been an assessor, but he was absent in Australia. The *Record*'s correspondent noted that 'when the Archbishop called for prayer,' at the beginning of the proceedings, 'a good many of those present seemed overcome with surprise, appropriate as this beginning was.' *Record*, 15 Feb. 1889. Bishop Browne later resigned due to ill health and was replaced by Bishop Atlay of Hereford. *Record*, 26 July 1889.

88 The Ritualists, who had rejected the validity of the ecclesiastical courts, applied their arguments to the archbishop's court as well, having assumed that he would follow the earlier decisions handed down by the Judicial Committee. In April 1889, the Dean of Windsor, Randall Davidson, challenged the Ritualists to declare publicly what court they would agree to obey. He noted that they had condemned all existing bodies as secular, but they had always set themselves to oppose any reforms and had never described what sort of court they would acknowledge. And in Davidson's view, it could not be demanded that the court would be purely clerical in nature, for such was a principle 'which Parliament after Parliament has refused to accept.' A continuation of the program of civil disobedience, he said, would soon end with disestablishment; so the onus was upon the protesters to declare their position. He was no proponent of a rigid uniformity, but he did not think they would be allowed to continue with every priest 'insisting on his right to interpret the rubrics exactly as he pleases.' The Ritualists, concluded Davidson, owed it to the nation to declare their position. Letter to the *Times*, 2 April 1889.

Davidson's letter evoked a storm of criticism from Ritualist correspondents, none of whom were impressed by his arguments. In August 1890, after the hearings had ended but before the verdict had been announced, a small meeting of some of the more extreme members of the ECU (attended by only 136 clergy) met to pass four resolutions condemning the proceedings. Their resolutions included the arguments commonly made against the Court of Arches and Privy Council, and extended them to include the Archbishop's Court. They indicated as well, that they would not be bound by his decision when announced. The resolutions were: 1. 'That his Grace the Archbishop has no spiritual authority to cite and try the Bishop of Lincoln otherwise than in, and by, the Synod of the Province; therefore, the judgment will be destitute of all spiritual authority.' 2. 'That his Grace having admitted the superior authority of the Privy Council in matters of spiritual concerning this cause, his judgment will not be possessed of spiritual authority, inasmuch as it is controlled and regulated by the principle of appeal to the Privy Council, a secular court, as the supreme ultimate authority in ecclesiastical matters.' 3. 'Certain matters, the legality of which have been impugned before his Grace, e.g., the use of artificial light at the Celebration of the Holy Eucharist, and the use of the Mixed Chalice being of Oecumenical authority, it is *ultra vires* even for a Provincial Synod, and, therefore, *a fortiori* for an Ecclesiastical Court, to pronounce either for or against their lawfulness.' 4. 'Any inquiry in an Ecclesiastical Court being directed only to the question of the guilt or the innocence of the accused person, the judgment of the Court is personal to and affects him only, and therefore is not binding on any other person or persons.' Cited in the *Record*, 1 Aug. 1890.

89 Cf. Benson, *Life of Benson*, vol. 2, pp. 339-47.
90 Bishop King's plea presented by his lawyers was reprinted in full in the *Times*, 14 Aug. 1889.
91 A complete account of the hearings and the arguments presented by both sides can be found throughout the month of February 1890, in the *Times*. While awaiting Archbishop Benson's decision, the *Record* published an extensive digest of the issues involved in the various charges made in the case and the arguments presented by the lawyers on both sides for each point. Cf. *Record*, 1 Oct. 1890.
92 The judgment was reprinted in the *Times*, 22 Nov. 1890. The *Record* summarized the judgment on each point and noted the instances where the archbishop had overturned earlier rulings. *Record*, 21 Nov. 1890. For a survey of the several points and Benson's view of the matter, cf. Benson, *Life of Benson*, vol. 2, pp. 359-64.
93 Without questioning the general position of the High Church party, said Benson's biographer, 'the High Sacramental doctrine which was, by the extremists of both sides, associated with these points, was found to be an unauthorised and unjustified interpretation of the ritual.' Benson, *Life of Benson*, vol. 2, p. 365.

The validity of Benson's argument was hotly debated. 'Broadly speaking,' wrote the *Times*, 'the judgment authorizes the characteristic practices of the Bishop of Lincoln and his friends, but declares most positively and learnedly that they have no meaning or import whatever.' The paper gave the archbishop great credit for his attempt to find a peaceful resolution but questioned the effectiveness of his argument. Their importance might be denied 'in the light of impartial common sense,' but their practical meaning was more troublesome; 'and it may be doubted whether any amount of learned exposition will explain away the associations of at least fifty years of controversy, and the practical evidence of men's eyes and of common knowledge.' While supporting a compromise between the two parties, the paper feared that Benson had given 'a distinct advantage to the innovating forces. Whatever the Ritualistic practices ought, or ought not, to mean, no plain man can doubt that they have the practical effect of assimilating the administration of the Holy Communion to the celebration of the Mass, and that they are, at the very least, intended as a repudiation of Protestant doctrine on the subject.' *Times*, 25 Nov. 1890.

94 The *Record* suggested that Benson's decision, in overturning the earlier rulings of the Court of Arches and the Privy Council, took a fundamentally different view of the proposition that 'omission' in the rubrics was equivalent to 'prohibition.' This had been 'the governing principle' for the courts in the earlier cases, and it had come under strong attack from King's lawyers. Archbishop Benson did not specifically address the issue, and it was nowhere either approved or denied, but throughout his judgment the proposition was set aside. *Record*, 21 Nov. 1890.

The *Times* noted that Benson had begun by affirming that his court had considered, 'with the utmost carefulness and respect,' the decisions handed down by the Court of Arches and the Judicial Committee on the issues at hand. His judgment went on, however, by proceeding 'on its own course, without attempting to come to an explanation or understanding with them.' *Times*, 25 Nov. 1890.

Archbishop Benson further elaborated on his judgment and its practical import in a pastoral letter to the clergy of Canterbury. His central concern was to bring the controversy to a conclusion for the sake of the peace, charity, and unity of the church. Reprinted in the *Times*, 20 Dec. 1890. For Bishop King's view of the judgment, cf. his letter to the archdeacons and rural deans of Lincoln, reprinted in the *Times*, 18 Dec. 1890.

95 For a general survey of the use of candles throughout church history, cf. D. R. Dendy, *The Use of Lights in Christian Worship*, Alcuin Club Collections, vol. 41 (London: SPCK, 1959). Dendy surveyed the role of lighted candles in the Ritualist controversy and the various court decisions involving them. He also noted that the Lincoln Judgment largely ended the debate concerning their use. Citing figures from the *Tourist's Church Guide*, Dendy showed the rapid growth in use throughout the country after 1892, until two candles became 'almost universal,' and six were 'not uncommon.' Ibid., pp. 167-74.

96 *Record*, 28 Nov. 1890.

97 'May we not ask of the present litigants whether legal prosecutions, carried on to the bitter end, are marks of the Spirit of Christ? Are mistakes concerning ritual and its symbolical meaning to be treated as unpardonable sins? Are they to be punished with excommunication and imprisonment?

Are such men as Canon Liddon, Bishop Hamilton, or the present Bishop of Lincoln to be looked upon as aliens from the family of Christ? Were they not eminent saints of God in whose brotherhood we ought to rejoice? The same is true of many hard-working Ritualists.' Letter to the *Record*, 12 Dec. 1890.

98 Letter to the *Record*, 24 Dec. 1890. Reginald Smith replied that St. Paul would have condemned the CA's actions. Referring to Romans 14-15, he argued that differences on minor points were 'not sufficient grounds for driving one another out of the Church.' He concluded, 'It is ignorance, sheer ignorance, which causes us to alienate ourselves from those who worship the one Eternal triune Jehovah as ourselves, who trust in the same Saviour, and are baptized by the same Spirit. If we would but seek for enlargement of heart instead of narrowness, and cultivate the personal acquaintance of those Ritualists, the mainspring of whose lives is the love of Christ, we should soon get to love them for His sake, Who loves them even as he has loved us and given Himself for us.' Letter to the *Record*, 24 Dec. 1890.

One anonymous correspondent drew a parallel to the Reformation and noted that 'the law, public opinion, the Government' had all been unable to halt its progress. 'The fires of Smithfield did more for the Reformation than all the Tudors, and,' in the view of the writer, 'the Church Association is likely to do for the Ritualists more than all its friends.... I reckon that the "fighting" character supposed (I believe wrongly) to accompany Evangelical religion has done more to keep Low Churchmen off the Bench than many think. I warn leaders that young men will not follow a party which seems to persecute, and men of the world will be repelled, and so will be those many souls who, having no liking for theological disputations, seek a life of reverent piety.' Letter (signed 'W.B.') to the *Record*, 9 Jan. 1891.

99 'You will, of course, obtain judgment against the Bishop of Lincoln, and compel him to conform, or else deprive him of his Bishopric. The latter is perhaps the more probable event; but in that case you can only reach your end by first imprisoning him. And I can conceive no course better calculated to discredit in the popular esteem the very truths for which you are contending. Popular sentiment is stronger than Acts of Parliament or decisions in a Court of Law. If you array it on the wrong side, you will have done more to undo the Reformation than all your adversaries could ever do.' Letter to the *Record*, 2 Jan. 1891.

100 Thus the Judgment,' he concluded, 'offered fair grounds for retreat from extreme and untenable positions, and I believe that in time – and that no long time – the tacit condemnation of the slow but sturdy common-sense of the English people would have caused these ritual extravagances to die a natural death. Your course, I fear, will tend to keep them artificially alive. To breathe the word "peace" is now almost dangerous. One is at once assailed as a traitor to truth and thought to have no regard to the Divine order – "first pure, then peaceable." But a disposition to peace is, after all, no small part of the "purity" it is said to succeed. And "purity" and litigations are not necessarily the same things. I believe you would more effectually promote both purity and peace, and that in the Divine order, by abandon-

ing your appeal.' Ibid.
101 'That liberty, among other gains, will have the advantage of counteracting all attempts to attach a spurious doctrinal significance to the disputed ceremonies. For, when it is finally settled that the Church regards these ceremonies as permissible but by no means imperative, those who practise them will be reduced to the dilemma either of admitting that the Church does not hold as essential the doctrines which it is contended that the ceremonies represent, or else of admitting that the ceremonies are not the necessary exponents of those doctrines.' Letter to the *Record*, 20 Feb. 1891.
102 Letter (signed 'A Churchman') to the *Record*, 6 March 1891.
103 Cobham was convinced the Judicial Committee would reverse at least some of Benson's judgment: 'I need not say that I do not believe that the Privy Council will consent to humiliate itself by adopting at the hands of six Bishops a reversal of its own formal pronouncements. It will be bound, for decency's sake, to bring its future judgment into some appearance of agreement with the older ones. I do not doubt that the Judgment of the Archbishop will be reversed.' Correspondence cited in the *Record*, 16 Jan. 1891.
104 Ibid. Supporters of the CA were capable of extreme hyperbole in defense of their position. At the organization's spring conference, E. C. Bovile, the vice-chairman, called for a united front in support of the CA's appeal to the Judicial Committee. The *Record* summarized his speech: 'Surely the time had come when they should show an undivided front against the enemy. It was no longer a question of candles and vestments, but of whether England should be Catholic or Protestant, whether it should be enslaved or whether it should be free. Behind it all was the Jesuitism of the Church of Rome. There was a vast conspiracy going on in this country to enslave us, and he was sorry to say that it came from the highest people in the realm, and that Jesuitism, which had caused more mischief in the world than any other influence, was at the bottom of it. If the appeal in the Bishop of Lincoln's case failed, they might say a long farewell to the maintenance of religious freedom and thought, to the privileges which the present settlement had conferred upon us, and which had fostered the growth of humanity and civilization everywhere. In lieu of that they would lose a free Gospel and an open Bible, and have the spirit and the letter of the Church of Rome dominant everywhere.' *Record*, 13 Feb. 1891.
105 Letter to the *Times*, 6 Dec. 1890.
106 Correspondence cited in the *Record*, 31 July 1891.
107 Correspondence cited in the *Times*, 30 July 1891.
108 Ibid.
109 Complete reports on the hearings before the court can be found in the *Times*, 11 June to 9 July 1891.
110 The *Record* published frequent articles and editorialized on the Clergy Discipline Bill during the spring of 1892, but since it dealt only with cases of immorality and excluded ritual prosecutions, it was a less dominant concern than might otherwise have been the case. A thorough description of the bill's intent can be found in Archbishop Benson's introduction before the second reading in the House of Lords; cf. *Times*, 4 March 1892.

111 In March 1892, the *Record* published a letter written by Bishop Perowne to a priest in his diocese who requested a dispensation from fasting during Lent since he and his family had been sick during the outbreak of influenza. Perowne responded to the request, somewhat incredulously, that he was unaware the church had prescribed a fast for Lent or laid down 'rules for its observance.' Consequently, he replied, 'I do not see how I am to grant a dispensation (even if I possess the dispensing power) from a law of the very existence of which I am ignorant.' Correspondence cited in the *Record*, 18 March 1892.

Shortly thereafter, the paper reported that Canon Knox Little had bitterly attacked Perowne in a sermon. He accused Perowne of denying fundamental doctrines such as the priesthood, confession, absolution, the real presence, and fasting in Lent and suggested that he had more respect for an 'honest Dissenter' than he did for the Bishop of Worcester. The *Record* concluded, 'Is this quite the language in which a Canon should talk of his Bishop?' *Record*, 8 April 1892.

112 Lord Grimthorpe suggested that the prospects for 'the Protestant cause were not very bright.' The Ritualists were going to excess throughout the country, and the laity had no means of protest or recourse. But he also feared that there was growing sense of indifference among the laity. *Times*, 6 May 1892.

113 Capt. Alexander Cobham addressed the annual meeting of the CA and noted that they anxiously awaited the decision which, he believed, would be 'the most momentous' judgment delivered by the 'Supreme Court for the past three centuries.' Upon the decision, said Cobham, 'depended very much more than was generally supposed – the fate of the Church of England and the liberties of the country.' Cited in the *Record*, 6 May 1892.

114 *Record*, 5 Aug. 1892.

115 Judgment of the Judicial Committee of the Privy Council, cited in the *Times*, 3 Aug. 1892. For Benson's view of the judgment, cf. Benson, *Life of Benson*, vol. 2, p. 375.

116 Ibid.

117 Ibid.

118 Only the *Daily News* responded with a largely negative article. It was concerned that the Judicial Committee had chosen such an important case to establish the disturbing principle that the court was 'not bound by its own previous rulings.' Still more troublesome, however, was the fact that the court had not commented 'upon the Bishop's ostentatious contempt for Her Majesty's Courts of justice.' Bishop King had only barely condescended to appear, objecting 'that an Archbishop is not a Synod, and that for a "Synodical declaration" his soul was yearning.' The paper continued, 'The Judicial Committee he has wholly ignored, and that not from the indifference or want of means, but because he desired to flaunt in the face of the world his defiance of the Queen's authority as Head of the Church, to whom he "did homage for the temporalities".... A greater man than the Bishop of Lincoln, whom the Bishop at least believes to have been Divinely inspired, said, "The powers that be are ordained of God." But St. Peter is obsolete, unless he happens to square with the nostrums of modern Sacerdotalism.' Cited in

the *Record*, 5 Aug. 1892

The *Times* expressed its hope that the judgment would bring to an end the long history of prosecutions that had only intensified party strife, dividing those within and alienating those without. While recognizing that the judgment was in part a political decision, the paper hoped that it would lead to compromise and end to the controversy. Still it suggested that peace could only be obtained if the extreme Ritualists did not 'abuse their victory' and attempt to expand on their position in utter 'disregard of the opinions of the majority of the Church.' *Times*, 3 Aug. 1892.

119 *Record*, 5 Aug. 1892. In considering the policy statement issued by the CA a few months later, the *Times* suggested that it was not surprising that they felt a sense of crisis. Having initiated many prosecutions and obtained many favorable judgments, the organization now found its work almost entirely overturned. They had learned 'that neither deprivation nor prison, nor even a monition or other form of censure, awaits people who do what the Bishop of Lincoln did; in other words, that the Ritualists may defy the Association and may practically do and teach what they please.' *Times*, 3 Nov. 1892.

120 Ibid. In November, a committee headed by the former colonial Bishop, C. R. Alford, addressed a memorial to the archbishops and bishops. The document, signed by about 1,000 clergy and laity, chose to protest only the decision regarding the use of the *Agnus Dei*. The memorial read: 'As loyal Churchmen we enter our respectful protest against any permissive use of the *Agnus Dei* before the consecrated elements on the Holy Table at the administration of the Lord's Supper in the Church of England. We regard its permissive use as presenting an "opportunity" to those who would make it such for "idolatrous adoration" of the Holy Sacrament in the Parish Churches of the land. As members of the Church of England, in accordance with the Reformation settlement, we express our sense of the extreme hardship felt by numerous Churchmen who are under the necessity of worshipping with their families in their Parish Church, perhaps the only church within their reach, where at the will of the incumbent a form of words which in pre-Reformation days was "abused" for the purpose of Eucharistic adoration, may be now, after an interval of 340 years, again introduced and maintained under the protection of a Judgment of the Judicial Committee of Her Majesty's Privy Council. As faithful and conscientious members of the Reformed Church of England we implore relief.' Cited in the *Record*, 25 Nov. 1892. In early December, the committee published a similar memorial to the Queen. Cf., *Record*, 9 Dec. 1892.

121 Ibid.

122 The paper regretted to hear of a rumored public conference to protest the decision and gather signatures for a memorial. 'There is little either of good or evil in such formal manifestoes. Their day is past. The signatories write their names unwillingly and the public read them with indifference. We venture to think that Evangelical Churchmen will consult their own self-respect no less than the welfare of their cause by refraining from any public demonstrations of the kind we have indicated.' *Record*, 12 Aug. 1892.

Although the CA acknowledged that further litigation would be useless

The End of Litigation 453

under the present circumstances, it was not willing to commit itself to a program of restraint beyond the immediate future. At a meeting in October, to discuss its future policy, Capt. Alexander Cobham, Chairman of the Council, suggested that 'circumstances might arise in the future when prosecutions might once more become necessary, and advance the cause of Christ.' Cited in the *Record*, 28 Oct. 1892.

123 Ibid.
124 'It seems to us,' continued the paper, 'that the necessity of a rigid adherence to a simple, as distinguished from a squalid, ritual on the part of Evangelical Churchmen is emphasized by recent events. Whatever may be the case for the moment, the future is not with the grotesque dresses and semi-civilized pomp of a high ritual.' Ibid.

Bishop Bickersteth of Exeter took a moderate perspective at his diocesan conference and expressed his hope that the judgment would lead to peace in the church. He believed it would establish both liberty and order if the extreme sections on both sides would restrain themselves. He appealed to the Ritualists not to abuse the 'permissive decisions' handed down by the courts, and urged their opponents 'not to condemn their brethren who availed themselves of them as if they were not true members of the one Reformed Church, and thus to break the law of charity.' Cited in the *Times*, 20 Oct. 1892.

125 Ibid. One correspondent suggested it was the best thing that could have happened to the Evangelical party; 'the prop has been taken away by a wise overruling Providence, and the carnal weapon has broken in their hands. The strength, the *raison d'etre* of that party is its spirituality, and there are not many things more harmful to spirituality than the conviction that the letter of the law is on one's own side and the determination to put it in force.... I rejoice that Evangelicals are now thrust back upon their true and proper weapons.' Letter (signed 'W.B.') to the *Record*, 12 Aug. 1892.

The PCA took a similarly moderate view. In its statement on the ruling it affirmed that while Protestants 'must deeply deplore the decision which permits any ritual intended to lead the thoughts of the worshippers towards doctrines which were repudiated at the Reformation, neither the Archbishop's judgment, nor its endorsement by the Privy Council, can be adduced in favour of those doctrines, or as in any way changing the doctrinal character of the Church of England.' In the PCA's opinion, the ruling, insofar as it represented a setback to the anti-Ritualist movement, was 'a distinct call to all Protestant Churchmen to band themselves more closely together and resist the attempt to undo the work of the Reformation.' *Times*, 2 Dec. 1892.

126 The paper published a lengthy letter (filling several columns of the page) from William Sinclair, Archdeacon of London. Sinclair argued that the judgment, however much they might dislike it, did nothing to alter their position. He suggested that Evangelicals, in refocusing on positive endeavors, should support more thoroughly their theological colleges, make better use of the press, and take a more active interest in the general life of the church and its clerical meetings. Letter to the *Record*, 12 Aug. 1892.

127 J. E. C. Welldon, Head Master of Harrow School, emphasized the fact that

Evangelicals were left to continue their work undisturbed, except that they could not 'impose the precise ritual which they think best upon other Churchmen who prefer a ritual of another kind.' The judgment offered, with a minimal compromise on their part, the best opportunity for peace in the church. 'High Churchmen, as represented by the Bishop of Lincoln, have shown a pacific temper in obeying the terms of the Judgment. If the Evangelical party adopts a tone of suspicion, aggressiveness, and intolerance; if it is on the look-out for the chance of fresh legal proceedings; if it will not put up with any ritual anywhere, or in any circumstances, except its own, is it not certain that it will lose the sympathy of the great body of Churchmen who care more for peace than for party, and is it not equally certain that the loss of that sympathy cannot be compensated by any possible, though improbable, victory in the Law Courts?' Letter to the *Record*, 12 Aug. 1892.

128 Charles Bell took that position, and suggested that it was better to have the final defeat of the anti-Ritualist cause come at the hands of the Privy Council than from 'a Spiritual Court' whose ruling satisfied no one. Letter to the *Record*, 12 Aug. 1892.

129 Taylor wrote, 'I must confess I am unable to entertain the rose-coloured views which some take of the Judgment, nor can I minimize its importance.... I regard it as the most serious blow and heavy discouragement which the Protestantism of the Church of England has received since the final settlement of our constitution in 1688.' Letter to the *Record*, 26 Aug. 1892.

130 Taylor concluded, 'One can fancy the smile with which the advocates of these observances hear such statements. They know perfectly well that it is not in the power of the Archbishop nor the Judicial Committee, nor both combined, to deprive these observances of any meaning which those who adopt them attach to them.' Ibid.

In contrast, Benjamin Clarke, Rector of Christ Church, Southport, and Archdeacon of Liverpool, defended the importance of the rulings. He wrote, 'Lambeth and Westminster have concurred in this, and we cast away our only shelter if we reject their ruling. Is it not possible for things that had a very serious meaning once to cease to have that meaning any longer? Who has not read of the Wars of the Roses? Did not the mere colour of the flower rend England into two great factions? Yet there came a day when that symbolism ceased to exist for ever, and England rejoiced in peace. Let the Church of England of to-day rejoice that, by the Judgment of the highest Court in the land and by the august sanction of the Sovereign, those symbols that distracted her have no more meaning now than the red rose of Lancaster and the white rose of York.' Letter to the *Record*, 16 Sept. 1892.

131 Taylor's position largely reflected the opinions expressed at the autumn meeting of the CA in November 1892. E. C. Bovile, Vice-Chairman of the Council, called it a 'crisis in the National Protestant Church.' The judgment, in his view, 'destroyed all former judgments of the Privy Council and destroyed all sense of finality. It had sent a thrill of strong disappointment and dismay throughout the Protestants of the country, because they saw nothing but the legalization of the Romish Mass.' He concluded, however, that it

was their duty to continue the struggle 'between Protestantism and Romanism.' Cited in the *Times*, 4 Nov. 1892.
132 Bishop Ryle in an address to the clergy at the Liverpool Diocesan Conference: 'In common with many others, I cannot admit the soundness of its reasonings and interpretation and the correctness of its conclusions. Nor am I able to believe that the famous ritual points in dispute have no doctrinal significance, when I know that their principal advocates never admit this for a moment. However, the judgment is the decision of the highest Court of the realm, and at present that decision cannot be reversed, though some future Judicial Committee may possibly reverse it. As a law-abiding Englishman and a believer in the Royal Supremacy, I submit, though I cannot approve or admire.' Ryle, *No Uncertain Sound*, p. 248.

In March 1893, the *Record* questioned the wisdom of fifty prominent moderates who issued a document protesting the decision: 'The signatories are anxious not to be seen "to approve" the Judgment. Elsewhere they very properly express their dutiful submission to it, and we confess there is something unsuitable in the notion of private persons, however respected and influential, expressing "approval," and still more disapproval, of binding judgments of Courts of law, the validity of which does not depend upon outside concurrence. We should be very sorry if Evangelical Churchmen were even remotely to imitate the undignified attitude of the Ritualistic clergy, who are accustomed, as a matter of conscience, to repudiate Courts which decide against them, and to cover the Judges with abuse and obloquy, while even the Privy Council has grown pleasant in the eyes of the extreme party since it formed an appetite to devour its former Judgments.' *Record*, 3 March 1893.
133 Letter to the *Record*, 9 Sept. 1892. Samuel Garratt, with an entirely different emphasis, similarly suggested that the judgment had been informed by other factors than the simple merits of the case. Such had also been the case with the Gorham decision, wrote Garratt, as well as the decisions against slavery. 'Throughout English history the decisions of the highest Courts have always, and rightly, in public matters, been decisions of policy.' But in Garratt's opinion, that was to be expected with any appeal to the courts, and no one was to blame except those who made the appeal. It was good that the verdict had finally forced on Evangelicals the conclusion 'that to hand over the controversy to lawyers, and to carry on the contest against error by means of Courts and Judgments and their necessary consequences, was to trust to carnal weapons instead of to the sword of the Spirit, and to render the Scriptural method of by sound doctrine convincing the gainsayers impossible.' Letter to the *Record*, 19 Aug. 1892.

Benjamin Clarke sharply criticized those who questioned the motives of the judges: 'I refuse to believe that such men as the Archbishop of Canterbury or the Lord Chancellor of England would ever have degraded themselves by setting aside the merits of the case and adopting an unworthy compromise. I decline to accept the statement that the two men who occupied the highest position in England under Royalty could from the seat of judgment pronounce certain things to be meaningless ceremonies unless they firmly believed what they said to be true, however different their view

may be from that of private individuals.' Letter to the *Record*, 16 Sept. 1892.
134 In the course of the letter, Stirling said he had been one of the founders and a long-time council member of the CA. He realized however, after the Bennett and Ridsdale decisions, that the courts could never suppress the Ritualists. What was needed was a revision of the Book of Common Prayer. Letter to the *Record*, 30 Sept. 1892.
135 The *Record* published his resignation letter, written to Bishop Davidson of Rochester, which began: 'It is my painful duty to state that I have to-day, with feelings of profound grief, executed the deed of resignation of this benefice. In placing my resignation in your Lordship's hands, I must be allowed to say that the recent judgment in the Lincoln Case has rendered it impossible for me to retain my connection with the Established Church as she now is, with Popery taught by her clergy on every hand, her Communion-tables turned into "altars," her ministers into "sacrificing priests," her churches into Mass-houses, and with auricular confession inculcated, practised, and where possible enforced. All this done under the eyes, with the knowledge, and under the protection of the Bishops, who first introduce the "wolves in sheep's clothing" into the fold, and then shield them when the flock remonstrates.' Correspondence cited in the *Record*, 2 Dec. 1892.

In August 1893, he informed the *Record* that his revised version of the Book of Common Prayer was ready to be published. He detailed the many changes that had been made in order to delete all vestiges of pre-Reformation language and doctrine. In addition to deleting saints days, the use of the word 'priest' and other minor details, his most fundamental alteration was the removal of infant baptism. In his view, the adoption of a truly Protestant Prayer-book was the only alternative to the existing state of the national church. 'The Established Church is now apostate, and is simply established Popery. Romanism is now dominant within her pale, and is fostered and protected by the Bishops.' There were, however, 'the faithful remnant' who were slowly separating themselves and Stirling believed they were the only hope for the defence of 'the Protestant religion and the liberties of England.' Letter to the *Record*, 11 Aug. 1893.
136 Eugene Stock reported that a total of three Evangelical clergy, including Stirling, seceded. Stock, *Church Missionary Society*, vol. 3, p. 282.
137 Thorold wrote, 'We all of us want more clear apprehension of doctrinal truth, more jealous love for it, more unflinching firmness in declaring it, more absolute refusal to condone the cheap and mischievous and paltry civilities that must end in no creeds at all; but we should not think to do our duty by hindering other men from doing theirs. If we expect toleration for ourselves, we must give it to our neighbours, who do not deserve to be called Roman because they light candles and mix the chalice and turn to the East.... There have always been at least two currents of religious thought in the Church, and there always will continue to be; and to try to drive out of the Church brethren who alarm or distress us, but who have a distinct right to be there, may provoke dangerous reprisals, and will but fatally retard the spiritual and vital duty which is the only sure way of maintaining the pure truth of God.' Cited in the *Times*, 1 Nov. 1892.
138 Ibid. The *Times* contrasted Thorold's pastoral with the CA's adoption of its

new program for combating the Ritualists outside of the courts. The paper wrote: 'It is no wonder that the Church Association should take up a desperate policy; for here is so Evangelical a prelate as the Bishop of Winchester boldly defending the Lincoln judgment and occupying a number of positions which 20 years ago would have been thought extremely High Church.' With a note of approval, the paper hoped that Thorold's position was representative of a new and peaceful perspective. *Times*, 3 Nov. 1892.

The *Record* supported Thorold's moderate tone but was somewhat more pessimistic concerning the future activities of the Ritualists. It thought many of the more extreme section had already moved far beyond the disputed elements considered in the Lincoln judgment and feared that they would feel no constraints in their activities. Still, the paper hoped a positive effect of the judgment would be to end 'the militant efforts of those who have promoted litigation in ritual matters.' *Record*, 11 Nov. 1892.

The paper's fears were, in fact, justified. Following the Lincoln judgment, the Ritualists quickly expanded their activities, knowing that little would be done to hold them in check. In his diary, Archbishop Benson lamented the effect after attending a service at St. Paul's: 'Alas! those minor canons are allowed their own way in everything, have introduced ablution since the Lincoln Judgment, and have turned the order on openness in consecration into a new bit Ritualism, lifting the cup high and breaking the bread and drawing the arms apart with the two pieces of broken bread. Thus, what was meant to give plainness is by these perverse folk turned to a far more ceremonious mode. Full tilt we go to alienate the laity all we can. If they were not so much wiser than the clergy they would be all gone to Dissent before this.' Benson, *Life of Benson, vol. 2*, pp. 244-45.

The moderate Alfred Barry complained in 1898 that there was a growing tendency among Ritualists, with no fear of consequences, 'to set aside the appointed order of our Church worship.' This was usually defended on the grounds that 'a parish priest and his congregation (who are not necessarily his parishioners) agree on a particular phase of worship and ritual.' In effect, said Barry, 'the "aggrieved parishioner" has passed into a proverb of scorn; the canonical authority of the Bishop is, to say the least, very narrowly limited by those who have promised to obey it,' and 'the principle of congregationalism' was established in the national church. Barry, 'Breach of Church Law,' *Nineteenth Century*, p. 944.

139 Ryle, *No Uncertain Sound*, pp. 248-49.
140 Ibid.

CHAPTER 10

The Division of the Evangelical Party

Challenges to the Policy and Position of the Church Association

After a period of relative silence, the CA finally addressed the issue of the Lincoln judgment at its autumn conference in November 1892. In the opinion of the council, the adverse decision was a crisis for the national church. Immediate reform was needed to protect the Protestant principles of the church, they warned, or the nation would be forced to face the "disastrous alternative" of disestablishment. The participants enumerated six points that required legislation to avert a disaster:

> (a) the granting of legal redress to the laity, without any hindrance of justice by the episcopal veto; (b) the fusion of the ecclesiastical Courts into the High Court of Justice, or the assimilation of their procedure to that of the civil Courts; (c) the substitution of deprivation for imprisonment in the case of contumacious clergymen who refuse obedience to the orders of the Courts; (d) an ecclesiastical franchise for lay members of the Church, secured, and capable of enforcement by law, as in the case of churchwardens; (e) the concession to the laity "as of right" of an effective share in the administration of Church matters; (f) the power being given to the incumbent or to any churchwarden of the parish to remove without a faculty any ornament or addition which may have been illegally introduced into a church.[1]

The meeting concluded by unanimously adopting a protest resolution.[2] The organization, however, had little hope either for the enactment of its proposals or of reclaiming its once prominent place in the Evangelical party. Even with the divisive issue of prosecution having been set aside, there was little in the spirit of the CA to attract the support of moderates.

In December, the association held a day of 'Meetings for Humiliation, Confession of Sin and earnest Prayer to Almighty God for pardoning and restoring grace, and for the revival of Scriptural Religion in the Church and Realm of England' at Exeter Hall, followed in the evening by a 'Great Protestant Demonstration.'[3] At the evening meeting, the CA unveiled its new policy, the general outline of which was later condensed in a full-page advertisement taken out in the *Record*.[4] Of particular interest was the first paragraph of the advertisement, in which the organization demanded reform with regard to the episcopal veto, the ecclesiastical courts, and the substitution of deprivation for imprisonment as the penalty for clergy convicted of contempt of court. The CA's interest in those reforms indicated its rather limited commitment to methods other than prosecution. Evidently the Council continued to believe that litigation could be effectively used against the Ritualists if only the proper reforms were enacted to make it more effective and precise.

With the end of the litigious period of the controversy, however, the CA's program was less appealing than ever to moderates who were concerned to redirect the focus of the party.[5] Toward that end, they continued to express their desire for some central organization that might unify the party.[6] Many believed that some new organization was needed to move the Evangelical party beyond the purely negative focus of the anti-Ritualist campaign and to articulate a positive message through which it could exercise a broader influence in the church and society. In the fall of 1892, there was talk of combining the three most prominent partisan organizations: the CA, the PCA and the UCLA.[7] The plan was supported by Bishops Ryle (Liverpool) and Straton (Sodor and Man), but it was unable to elicit the sympathy of 'the more ardent members of the Church Association.'[8] Given the depth of the divisions within the party, any organization that was capable of attracting moderates, was certain to be considered too compromising by anti-Ritualists. In contrast, an organization such as the CA, which focused solely on a polemical theme and was quick to condemn any who appeared to waver, could only gain the support of an increasingly isolated conservative minority.

In December 1892, a private meeting was held at the home of H. W. Webb Peploe, Vicar of St. Paul's, Onslow-square, and a leader in the UCLA. The discussions indicated that broad interest remained in an amalgamation of the three organizations. While the *Record* thought that there was some likelihood that the PCA and the UCLA would join forces, it suggested that the CA had received 'so much support for its "Scheme of Future Policy" that it would doubtless expect to dictate the terms of any comprehensive scheme.'[9] In February 1893, it was reported that the combination of the UCLA with the PCA had been largely settled, lacking only the approval of the two central committees.[10] Meetings of the respective committees of the two groups were scheduled for April. From the discussion of the proposal at the meeting of the London Clerical and Lay Union, it was apparent that confusion remained with regard to what exactly the proposal entailed. W. J. Smith explained that the PCA was a single society with branches across the country, whereas the UCLA represented 'a number of independent (though federated) Clerical and Lay Associations for different dioceses.' Those associations, represented by the UCLA, were now being asked to unite with the PCA. 'The federated associations,' said Smith, 'would be left intact, although the logical consequence of the fusion of the central bodies would be that the associations should become branches of it.'[11] After some discussion and debate over the future body, which was tentatively labeled the 'Protestant Churchmen's Union,' the members of the London Union approved the proposal.

In April 1893, the new union was approved at separate meetings of the central committees of the PCA and the UCLA, and the National Protestant Church Union (hereafter abbreviated NPCU) was formed.[12] The first meeting of the new body, held in early May, was chaired by Bishop Straton of Sodor and Man, who had been a prominent supporter of the PCA. Archdeacon Farrar, in a speech at the meeting, indicated that the NPCU's focus would continue to be opposition to the Ritualists and the defense of the Reformation. According to Farrar, there were elements of the Ritualistic movement concerning which they were 'supremely indifferent' and for which it was clear that toleration must be allowed. There were also, however, fundamental issues concerning which there could be no compromise; according to Farrar, those included the idea of a priestly sacerdotalism and the renewal of auricular confession. He concluded with an appeal to the laity for a concerted effort in defense of Protestantism; the Ritualists could never lead England back to Rome, but they might drive many out of the church and into infidelity.[13]

Apart from the tone in which their respective campaigns were to be conducted, it was evident that there was little else to distinguish the program of the NPCU from that of the CA. The new organization was clearly intended to offer Evangelicals an alternative body working for the defense of the Protestant tradition but distinct from the aggressive and confrontational reputation of the CA.[14] Still, some moderates was disturbed by the tone of the meeting. One anonymous correspondent, while welcoming the prospect of an organization that could unite Evangelicals, regretted the essentially negative emphasis of the conference. His letter is worth extensive quotation as an illustration of the continuing concerns felt by moderates:

> There is a positive and a negative to Protestantism, a protesting for as well as a protesting against. The latter is our modern usage, the former was the usage of those who first brought the word to birth; they protested the truth of the Gospel. Am I wrong in thinking that the old sense is the most important – that negative Protestantism should only be the handmaid of the positive?
>
> There is this great difference between the two, that while the negative is far the easier to talk about, it is far harder to effect anything thereby, and in general while it is far more easy to assail evil than to laud virtue, on the other hand, a minority of people who want something positive can maintain their position against a host who wish merely to deprive them of it....
>
> Teach a man to hate Romanism, and you have made a 'Protestant,' a fanatic, but you have not necessarily done anything to advance Christ's Kingdom; it may even be farther off than ever in his heart. Why, when was England most doggedly Protestant, when was the name of Papist most detested? I should say some 100 or 150 years ago – at the very time when England was darkest and wickedest. Are we not all familiar with the person who may be the most godless man in the parish and is never tired of denouncing the parson as a 'Roman?'... It seems to me, then, we ought to oppose the confessional not principally by 'exposing' it as by loving, living, and teaching the doctrine of 'Assurance.' We ought to oppose the Mass by experiencing and teaching the universal communion of the soul with Christ. We ought to oppose Sacerdotalism by becoming, and leading our people to become, soul-winners. We ought to oppose Sacramentalism by being full of the Holy Ghost, rubric worship by holiness and prayer, frigid ceremonials by meetings where the word is with power. If we have these we shall then have what the other party now have – something positive to fight for. We might as well try to stop the pilgrims to Mecca by denouncing them as the Ritualists. They are fighting for their altars as truly as ever the people of Latium; and if we are merely fighting against their altars, we shall go down before them as the armies of nations have ever gone down against the zealot of religious war.
>
> And suppose we succeed; suppose that to-morrow every altar, every candle, every priestling disappeared, what would be our victory? I know a church, I know many churches – who does not? – where the gown is as black as midnight, where the service is dull to perfection, where unconventionality reigns supreme, where services are long and infrequent, where no early Communion ever rouses vicar or verger. It is Protestant unmistakably, and empty.

Let not anyone think that the absence of the bad argues the presence of the good; spiritual life is a greater and a prior need to lack of Ritualism.[15]

Moderates who were concerned to reaffirm the positive aspects of Evangelicalism, a concern not entirely met by the NPCU, called for the renewal of support for the CP-AS. It was suggested that the Evangelical party needed a home missions organization, parallel to the CMS, to refocus its energies.[16] Arthur T. Robinson, Rector of Holy Trinity, Marylebone, supported the adoption of a new course by the party, suggesting that there were lessons to be learned from the long-term success of the CMS. Evangelicals had been successful in foreign missions because in that field, at least, they had avoided the controversies that otherwise divided the party.[17] In Robinson's opinion, a united effort behind a positive organization was the best means of reestablishing the place of the Evangelical party in the national church. The division that remained between moderates, such as Robinson, and the extreme anti-Ritualists who continued to promote the CA, was also evident in his appeal; Robinson concluded with the plea, 'Let me earnestly and with all respect urge the militant section amongst us to ask themselves whether the course I venture to recommend is not most in accordance with the mind of Christ.'[18]

In the months that followed, the *Record* lent its support to the effort to reinvigorate the CP-AS and to establish its position as the dominant home mission agency of the Evangelical party. In the fall of 1892, the paper published an extensive three-part series detailing the rise of the organization, the nature and extent of its work in its present condition, and the "paramount necessity" of Evangelicals coming to its support to insure its future success.[19] Shortly thereafter, several prominent Evangelicals published a letter outlining the moderate position and challenging the party to unite in support of the CP-AS:

We, the undersigned, clergy and laity of the Church of England, who are warmly attached to those Evangelical principles which the Church Pastoral-Aid Society has firmly and consistently maintained for more than half a century, are deeply impressed with the urgent necessity for immediate and increased effort in carrying on the pastoral and evangelistic work of the Church.

This necessity arises partly from the rapid increase in the population of our large towns, and partly from the adoption all around us of new plans and new agencies intended to meet the religious needs of a growing population.

We greatly regret that the income of the Church Pastoral-Aid Society has not enabled it to keep pace with these increasing demands upon it, and is no larger at the present time than it was twenty or even thirty years ago. The result is that pressing calls cannot be answered or new depths of work be entertained by the Committee.

We therefore believe that it is fully time that the absolute need of increased efforts, expanded operations, larger self-sacrifice, and more vigorous support of this Evangelical Home Mission Society should be earnestly pressed upon the Evangelical laity of the Church of England, so that the duty of the Church towards the great masses of the population may be more effectually discharged.

If this were done, and the crying needs of the day for fresh and improved organization were met, we believe that other important results, very urgently needed at the present crisis, would immediately follow.

In these we include: –

I. A closer union amongst those who hold the same great principles: The Church Pastoral-Aid Society becoming, like the Church Missionary Society, a very real bond of union and rallying-point for us all.

II. A clearer manifestation of the truth that Evangelical principles are still a living force in the work of the Church of England.

III. A full justification to our own friends, and to the Church at large, of the existence of the Church Pastoral-Aid Society.

The position which the Church Pastoral-Aid Society holds is unique. It ought to be, and it might easily become, for work at home, the great central agency of the Evangelical members of our Church.

We therefore address ourselves to the Committee of that Society, confident that they are anxious to carry out the great evangelistic and pastoral work so urgently needed, if only the funds were forthcoming.

In conference with the Committee we shall be able to point out more definitely the needs which require to be met; we shall be ready to do our utmost to strengthen their hands, and to secure such an increase of income as will enable them more effectually to grapple with the constantly increasing demands upon their funds.[20]

A New Direction for the Evangelical Party

The Lincoln judgment left the Evangelical party thoroughly divided. The party had also to face the additional pressure of being once again in a distinctly minority position, after many years of some influence and power. The Ritualists, while holding only one episcopal seat, had received numerous other prominent appointments in the church during the years of Gladstone's ministry. They were certainly the ascendant party of the era, and the judgment in the Lincoln case gave them new confidence. By the time of his 1893 charge to the clergy, Bishop Ryle of Liverpool thought those holding a sacrificial view of the Lord's Supper were a majority in the church. In contrast, he thought Evangelicals were a distinct minority and faced with new difficulties. While urging the Ritualists to restrain the extreme section of their movement and avoid any new innovations, he thought it necessary to urge Evangelicals to remain loyal to the church and to reject the temptation of secession.[21]

Without specifically addressing with the subject of the Lincoln Judgment, the Islington Clerical Conference took up the issue of the future policy of the Evangelical party at its meetings in January 1893. In introducing the lecturers, William H. Barlow, Vicar of Islington, indicated that those involved were clearly aligned with the moderate section.[22] The conference lectures were divided into four categories of concern. The first was the need for a renewal of religious education, both for laity and clergy. The second dealt with the need for expanded pastoral work throughout the country, but particularly in the urban centers. In particular, Barlow emphasized the need for increased support of the CP-AS. Third, the conference discussed the question of how best to spread the Evangelical view of the church in the press, through newspapers and cheap tracts, as well as in books directed at a more academic market. Finally, however, and in sharp contrast to the spirit of the undertakings sponsored by the CA, it was suggested that the success of their endeavours must ultimately rest with God. All of their activities, Barlow concluded, would be fruitless 'except as they are preceded, accompanied, and followed by the gifts of God's Holy Spirit.'[23]

The moderate position adopted at the Islington meetings was immediately criticized by Charles R. Alford, former colonial Bishop of Victoria, in a letter to the *Record*. Alford questioned how the speakers at the conference could have avoided direct reference to the Lincoln Judgment, which, with all of its implications, involved a 'new phase in the Ritualistic controversy.' He continued:

> Has nothing special occurred to call for direct remark and seasonable counsel and guidance? Was the Privy Council Judgment of last autumn a proscribed subject at the Islington Memorial-hall? Might not Evangelical brethren have been invited to some preliminary discussion, and a wider welcome given? The Meeting might have assumed a bolder aspect. The arrows fell all about and all

around, but did not hit the mark. What is the result? The judicial toleration of the idolatrous Mass at the Lord's Table in the Church of England is to all appearance accepted by silent assent as ruling ritual by the Islington Clerical Meeting. So it will be represented. Moreover, the Islington Clerical Meeting will be taken to represent the Evangelical and Protestant body in the Church. I think a disclaimer is due.[24]

In Alford's opinion, the Lincoln Judgment ought to have been sharply refuted, and every Evangelical society and conference should have issued a 'public protest against official toleration of the Mass in the Church of England.' He suggested that the whole party should align itself with the conservative anti-Ritualist position, supporting 'a bold and resolute stand in behalf of the distinctive truths of the Reformation.' Even missions organizations such as the CMS and the CP-AS, he claimed, ought to have made the anti-Ritualist campaign a prominent part of their respective programs. What was needed was a firm defense of Protestant principles, and Alford thought that work took precedence even over evangelization; the CA should be supported in advance of the CP-AS. While evangelization, at home and abroad, would always be important, 'there are times (and such is the present) when to desert the citadel and fly to fields, white though they be to the harvest, to the abandonment of our homes and altars, and to give place to the foe, within and from without, is strategy no wise soldier could applaud.'[25]

Alford's letter indicated the fundamentally different perspectives that separated moderates from conservatives. The essence of the moderate position, in contrast to the defensive and controversial posture adopted by Alford, was that the prosecutions and the polemics of the anti-Ritualist movement had failed. Moderates were opposed, not only to litigation, but to the negative tone of the controversy as well. While conservatives continued to view the suppression of their opponents as the fundamental concern of the Evangelical party, moderates were committed to pursue a more positive policy. In addition to the evangelistic and pastoral work supported by the CP-AS, they also emphasized the necessity of taking a more active role in the life of the church. Rev. G. Arthur Sowter, of St. Silas', Bristol, argued that the judgment would have a good result if moderates from all parties were drawn closer together. Instead of appealing to courts of law, he thought they should take their place as dedicated members of the church and present their opinions 'in Ruridecanal Chapters, in Diocesan Conferences, on Congress platforms, and in Convocation.' It was there, said Sowter, that 'Evangelicals are conspicuous by their absence, and where others are allowed to hold the field. The fault is our own if we are 'snubbed and cold-shouldered'.... We have shown too little interest in the welfare of the Church as a whole to deserve any other treatment.'[26]

In June 1893, the *Record* reprinted in its entirety a sermon of J. F. Kitto, Vicar of St. Martin-in-the-Fields, London, which he had preached at the Ipswich Clerical Conference. Kitto's address, entitled 'The Evangelical Position,' surveyed the results of the anti-Ritualist movement and its impact on the Evangelical party from a moderate perspective. The *Record* offered no editorial comment, but the fact that the paper chose to publish the sermon in its entirety would indicate a degree of sympathy with the perspective presented. Having surveyed the fundamental doctrines affirmed by Evangelicals, Kitto turned to the development of Ritualism. In contrast to the condemnations of the anti-Ritualists, he was willing to acknowledge the contributions of the High Church party, most notably their revival of 'reverence in all matters connected with Divine worship' and their reassertion of the fact that the church was 'a Divine Society.' With great perseverance, they had pressed their reforms until "every department of Church life" had been renewed by their energy. Kitto concluded that, when the history of the past fifty years was written, it would be a story of 'extraordinary vitality shown in the marvelous development of every kind of Mission work, and a rapid spread of Ritualistic influence.'[27]

Having said that, he went on to ask what Evangelicals had accomplished during the same period?

> Is it too much to say that they have allowed themselves to be identified with a policy of abstention, of defence, of repression, of prosecution, of despair? I am not unmindful indeed, of the magnificent work of the Church Missionary Society, or of the growing enthusiasm in the cause. Thank God for it. I do not forget how much has been done by the Church Pastoral-Aid Society during the last fifty years in enabling the Church to hold its own amongst the masses of the people. I thank God for it. I do not forget that in hundreds of parishes faithful and earnest men have maintained the principles which we hold so precious, and have been doing noble service for the Lord; but for the most part we have been content to teach each in his own sphere, and to work each in his own way, without recognizing the value of co-operation and the strength of comradeship. And towards all those changes, whether in Church work or in Divine worship, which have left so strong an impression upon the history of the past fifty years, we have been prone to regard everything that is new with suspicion and distrust. What has been our attitude at first towards – the Church Con-

gress? – Resolute abstention. To Diocesan Conferences? – Coldness and dislike. To Sisterhoods and Organized Women's Work? – Suspicion. To the maintenance of schools and colleges? – Complete indifference. To Parochial Missions? – Marked hostility. To Theological Colleges? – A feeble and irresolute support. To changes in details of Church worship, wearing the surplice, chanting canticles and psalms, flowers, harvest festivals, and midnight services? All these have been in turn resisted; the whole force of the Evangelical party has been hurled against them at first, though most of them are now universally adopted by us all. Can we wonder if, as the tide of human thought and life rises higher and higher, the dreary waste of an unvarying *non possumus* is covered over and lost?[28]

In Kitto's opinion, the results had been as negative as the policy itself. Every attempt to consolidate or unite Evangelicals had failed and, as a result of their internal divisions, the party was largely 'discredited and despised' in the church at large. 'We have been known,' said Kitto, 'only in opposition – we have been evident not so much in working as in impeding and hindering the work of other people, and that work has advanced, not by our aid, but in spite of our opposition.' Consequently, it was commonly suggested that the Evangelical party was 'dead or dying fast.'[29]

Kitto concluded his sermon by offering four suggestions for the revival of the Evangelical party, points that had been widely discussed by moderates since the King judgment. First, Evangelicals needed to abandon their suspicious outlook. A great deal of time and energy had been wasted arguing over trivialities and matters of secondary importance. More importantly, such debates had divided the party and alienated many among them.[30] Second, Kitto thought Evangelicals should use their influence in positive campaigns, both political and social, rather than in defensive measures. Third, they must be willing to work at home missions. In this regard, he suggested that they unite in support of the CP-AS in order to meet the growing needs of the country, especially among the masses in the urban centers. Finally, he affirmed that Evangelicals, whatever compromises might be made with regard to ritual and ceremony, must remain firm in their principles. The future of the party, he concluded, was in positive work and the maintenance of 'that which is committed to our trust.'[31]

Conclusion

Despite their crushing defeat in the Lincoln judgment and the clear opposition of moderate Evangelicals, the anti-Ritualists would continue their campaign well into the next century.[32] John Kensit, an anti-Ritualist bookseller, became the most visible figure of the opposition. At the end of the century, he led a series public protests, often interrupting the services at prominent Ritualist churches, and conducted rallies across the country.[33] The disturbances created no small controversy and once again brought the subject into public awareness. In an essay on the protests, the *Edinburgh Review* condemned Kensit's tactics but noted that there was much about the Ritualists that continued to disturb the lay members of the Church of England.[34] Many moderates were disturbed by the continuing innovations of the more extreme Ritualists, who had little to fear from either bishop or court following the judgment in the Lincoln case. But they had no inclination to support another divisive and bitter campaign that could only further weaken both the party and the church in general.[35] The heightened public concern eventually led to the establishment of a Royal Commission on Ecclesiastical Discipline (1904-06), but the last outburst of a fading perspective otherwise had little lasting effect, at least in regard to the suppression of Ritualism.[36]

It did, however, cap a half century of controversy that sealed the negative reputation of Evangelicalism for many years to come. When Leonard Elliott-Binns wrote a not unsympathetic history of the movement, shortly after the turn of the century, he noted that the label 'Evangelical,' had become burdensome. For many, he thought, 'and those not altogether ignorant or perverse,' the Evangelical party had become 'associated with the refusal to take the Eastward position in the Eucharist or with a morbid fear of "lights".'[37] From its earliest years, the movement has had its share of opponents and critics who made much of its shortcomings on several counts. High Church critics noted its emphasis on individual conversion and suggested that it lacked a valid understanding of the church. From at least Gladstone on, it has been argued that the strain of individualism latent in the Evangelical mindset was both the source of all its best work as well as its single greatest flaw.[38] Historians have continued to suggest ever since that Evangelicals had no adequate theological framework to ground the individual in a broader social setting, and consequently, they failed to develop a real understanding of the nature of the church or of the church's ministry in the world.[39] On a more general level, the Evangelical party has also been criticized for a general anti-intellectualism. In the nineteenth century, opponents often claimed that the best of the younger generation of Evangelicals had steadily moved in a High Church direction, driven away by the narrow-mindedness and intellectual shortcomings of their inherited tradition. And the charge has been often been repeated by historians of the present day.[40]

There is an element of truth to both charges, and they help explain what became of the Evangelical movement and its influence in the second half of the nineteenth century. Perhaps more important, however, are the matters that affected the reputation of the party at the popular level. Since its rise in the eighteenth century, the movement was known for its stern opposition to seemingly harmless but 'worldly' pleasures, a characteristic feature that roused the derisive contempt of many. The teetotaler and sabbatarian movements of the nineteenth century did nothing to alter those views, either among the literary classes or the working classes whose slight hope for a few hours distraction were most seriously imperiled. Those features of the Evangelical movement and their impact on its popularity have been well-covered.[41] What has been left largely unconsidered is the effect of the anti-Ritualist movement. It is the thesis of this dissertation that the bitter partisan controversy, spanning the entire second half of the century, played a fundamental role in the fragmentation of the Evangelical party and is a significant factor in explaining the decline of its influence.

It is evident in the history of the controversy traced here that the Ritualists aroused a broad spectrum of opposition that far exceeded the limits of the Evangelical party. Evangelicals clearly made up the majority of the anti-Ritualist movement, and they played the most active role in attempting to counter its expansion in the formation of the Church Association. But they were by no means alone in their campaign. Through the first two or three decades of the controversy, they had the support of many prominent secular journals such as the *Times*. It became evident, however, that there was a clear distinction of perspective between the two allies. For anti-Ritualists, the dispute was a religious one, involving the fundamental doctrinal affirmations of the Reformation and the very foundation of the national church. It was, for them, a spiritual battle for beliefs that could not be compromised. For the general press, however, the issues hinged more on the stability of the establishment and the belief that English citizens (and, above all, those who were gentlemen and held a prominent place in society) ought to obey the law. Quite simply, the clergy took an oath of allegiance and they should be required to honor it.

The two arguments were not mutually exclusive, but they were clearly distinct and evoked different levels of emotional involvement. Anti-Ritualists of the religious sort, reaching great heights of rhetorical symbolism, could fret about Jesuitical conspiracies and the attempt to subvert English freedom by returning the church and nation to the spiritual oppression of a Roman ruler. They could also justify, at least to their own satisfaction, the use of almost any means for the suppression of their opponents, including imprisonment. Secular anti-Ritualists, in contrast, were less deeply committed to the controversy. Most were members of the church and shared to a certain degree the religious concerns. But they were generally much less threatened than Evangelicals by the innovations themselves. Particularly as the debate continued, the *Times* suggested that the alterations were mostly harmless (although sometimes absurd) and noted that the more moderate forms were being adopted even in non-Ritualist parishes. They worried, however (particularly in the context of growing unrest in Ireland), about the example of passive resistance being set by clergy of the established church. They were less concerned about the Protestant foundations of the church than they were about the social stability of the nation. And as clergy were imprisoned, protests were raised, and a generally more tolerant attitude developed over the course of the century, that stability was more endangered by continuing the controversy than by compromise.

The anti-Ritualist movement, over the course of half a century, gradually lost its external support. In addition to the secular anti-Ritualists of the press, a section of moderates within the High Church party were equally opposed to the extremes to which the Ritualists were given. High Church moderates shared some of the Protestant concerns of Evangelicals, but with less fervor and vehemence. Sharing some basic presuppositions with the Ritualists concerning the sacramental nature of the church, they were less likely to allow a bitter tone to consume their polemics. And they were even less supportive of prosecution. In keeping with their own theological position, they were more likely to encourage the bishops to take an active role in the suppression of extremes. For many years, however, moderate Evangelicals hoped to establish a united opposition that would include a convincing majority of the clergy. Conservative Evangelicals were less concerned with gaining any support from the High Church and were often given to including the moderates in their wholesale condemnation of that tradition.

For a time, the policy of litigation held a certain attraction. It was widely admitted, even by some of the bishops, that ambiguities remained in the church's rubrics and formularies. It was also hoped by most that a few lawsuits, covering the most important issues of dispute, would lead to clarification and obedience. The early appeals to the court had the support of some of the bishops (particularly those who had already encountered the wrath of the Ritualist clergy towards their episcopal admonitions), most of the press, and almost the entire Evangelical party. And the cases were largely successful.

None of those involved, however, had counted on the Ritualist reaction. Their refusal to be bound by the rulings of the court escalated the controversy. In turn, the anti-Ritualists brought more suits and attempted to enforce the rulings of the courts. In the process, they multiplied many times over the bitterness of the dispute, made it impossible for the bishops to act without appearing to adopt a partisan position, and alienated the more tolerant secular anti-Ritualists.[42] Finally, they split the Evangelical party. Having won most of the battles, they ultimately lost the war.

Moderate Evangelicals had supported the anti-Ritualist movement from the beginning. There were apparently a few who were opposed to litigation in principle, but they were mostly a silent minority. One can trace, however, the steady growth of opposition as the appeal to the courts moved from the attempt to clarify the state of the law to its enforcement. It was particularly evident in the correspondence and editorial pages of the *Record* that moderates turned against the movement in the late 1870s and early 1880s, as the CA sought to compel obedience even if it required imprisonment. Sharing a common religious view of the Ritualist threat, moderates were the last to desert their conservative relatives. When they did, their logic remained the same, only turned on its head. The controversy itself had now become the spiritual threat, relying as it did on secular methods and strident polemics. It was time, they avowed, for Evangelicals to return to their roots and reemphasize the positive affirmations of their position instead of focusing upon that which they opposed. A few moderates began to suggest that the greater threat lay elsewhere. In an increasingly secular age, they argued, church parties needed to overcome their differences in order to maintain their influence on the nation.

Conservative anti-Ritualists were unconvinced. They continued their campaign, in the name of true Protestants and the Evangelical party, through the turn of the century, long after they had lost any hope of influence or success. Long after their defeat, the impact of their divisive crusade remained, but only in a negative sense.[43] In 1987, writing of a revitalized Evangelical movement in the Church of England, Michael Saward surveyed the several phases of the party's history. Comparing it to the ebb and flow of the tides, he suggested that the movement suffered for many years as a result of the conflicts of the later nineteenth century:

> The consequences of these legal battles were not, however, confined to the place and manner in which eucharistic liturgies were performed. Far more damaging to the Evangelical cause was the bitterness of spirit, on both sides, which lasted for well over half a

century afterwards. To the rest of the church, Evangelicals were legalistic, narrow-minded, hard-faced bigots who were prepared to put their brother clergy into prison for trivial liturgical and sartorial reasons. Enormous damage was done and the final vestiges of its impact are still with us in the 1980s.[44]

The anti-Ritualist movement engendered a partisan attitude and defensiveness among Evangelicals that did not serve them well. It divided the party as it did the church and left them with little influence beyond their own narrow circles. The sins of the fathers were visited upon their children for several generations to come.

Notes

1   Cited in the *Times*, 1 Nov. 1892.
2   The resolutions were reprinted in the *Record*; cf. Appendix U. E. C. Bovile, Vice-chairman of the Council, affirmed that they were determined to press forward with their struggle against Ritualism in spite of the fact that the appeal to the courts was no longer an option. In his view, there could be no thought of either secession or compromise; 'they would not abandon the Church in which they had been brought up, nor would they submit to the Romanizing practices of the Ritualists.' *Record*, 11 Nov. 1892.
3   Advertisement in the *Record*, 2 Dec. 1892. The *Record*, either from its own disinterest in furthering the cause of the CA, or as an indication of the general lack of support for the meeting, only briefly reported on the proceedings. *Record*, 9 Dec. 1892.
4   Advertisement in the *Record*, 23 Dec. 1892; cf. Appendix V. With regard to the relief of Evangelical laity who were forced to sit under Ritualist clergy, which the CA addressed under the section of 'Mission Work,' an apparently separate organization was formed in February 1893, with a similar goal. The *Record* reported that the CP-AS had been formed, with its object being 'to supply clergymen to congregations who are at present unable to worship and receive the Lord's Supper in their Parish Churches on account of the introduction of Romish doctrines and practices.' The intent was not to form a separate congregation or Dissenting body, except insofar as they dissent from the 'Romish' innovations 'introduced into their own Church which they cannot countenance, and are unable at present to remove.' According to the *Record*, the following ceremonial conditions were to be observed: 'The surplice to be used "in all ministrations of the Church" as defined by law, and therefore excluded from the pulpit and choir. The Communion-table to be a *bona fide* table. The following to be held as being distinctly contrary to the principles of the Reformation: – (a) The Eastward position at any part of the service. (b) All Romanizing practices, such as the congregation rising at the entrance or exit of the clergy, prostrations, crossings, processions, singing of the *Agnus Dei*, flowers, crosses, candles, on or above or behind the Communion-table, incense, mixed chalice, wafer bread, holy water, adoration of the elements, etc. The following doctrines to be also protested against, namely: Consubstantiation or any objective presence in the Lord's

The Division of the Evangelical Party 475

Supper – Auricular Confession – Requiem or Memorial Services – Mariolatry, Invocation of Saints, Purgatory, and all the other errors of the Church of Rome.' *Record*, 17 Feb. 1893.

Ritualist clergy had apparently evoked such reactions for quite some time. When Tait was the Bishop of London, he had to deal with a number of cases where disgruntled parishioners supported 'a rival place of worship, where the old-fashioned doctrine and ritual should be retained.' In effect, the parishioners opened a dissenting chapel. Tait suggested 'a quiet forbearance' with regard to the separatists and thought the vicar should not seek to enforce the law by compelling them to register their building as 'a dissenting meeting-house.' At any rate, he concluded, 'No clergyman of this diocese will think of officiating in the building in question.' Tait, in a subtle reprimand to the pastor, said there was no way of knowing 'how far it would have been possible for you by greater tact to avert the rupture which has ensued.' Davidson, *Life of Tait, vol. 1*, pp. 529-31.

5   The *Times* compared the CA's new policy statement to the much more moderate position adopted by Bishop Thorold in a pastoral letter to the clergy of Winchester, and concluded that the time for controversial dispute had passed. 'The Church Association is far less influential than it was; clerical prosecutions are less in favour; the aggrieved parishioner is less aggrieved, or people pay less attention to him; and persons who have not the least intention of becoming Roman Catholics look with equanimity upon 'objective and artistic' developments which, thirty years ago, would have been thought to lead straight to Rome. And in those who have little sympathy with these forms of worship there is a spirit of greater tolerance abroad, and a greater readiness to permit diversity of method in realizing the 'immense opportunities,' as the Bishop of Winchester calls them, of the Church of England.' *Times*, 3 Nov. 1892.

6   Even before the appeal of the Lincoln Judgment to the Judicial Committee, the *Record* noted that there were rumors of a new council gathering representatives from all the various societies. It was apparent, however, that the CMS desired to avoid any involvement in partisan strife and refused to participate. The paper supported the decision made by the council of the CMS and questioned the need for another society. 'We all desire to unite; we deplore the lack of cohesion which too often marks the policy and procedure of Evangelical men. But what hope is there that another consultative body would promote this end? Surely the scanty leisure of clergy is already sufficiently occupied by Societies, and Unions, and Alliances, and Committees, all more or less successful, yet all more or less disappointing to their promoters. The Clerical and Lay Associations were meant to do this work. The Protestant Churchmen's Alliance might, it was thought, assist the same end. If these have not succeeded to the full, would still another Committee supply what is lacking?' *Record*, 15 May 1891. Ultimately, nothing came of the plans.

7   An anonymous correspondent suggested that Evangelicals still lacked an organization that could compare to the influence of the ECU among their opponents. 'Will not the heads of the Evangelical section,' he asked, 'rouse themselves and do something to supply the evident want to form an orga-

nization on such sufficiently broad principles as to embrace as large a number as possible, e.g., drawing the line at the E[astward] P[osition]? Let little differences be laid aside, and a united effort be made to maintain the Protestant doctrine and worship of our beloved Reformed Church of England.' Letter (signed 'Vicar') to the *Record*, 22 July 1892. For a brief summary of various attempts to unite the separate organizations, cf. Balleine, *Evangelical Party*, pp. 232-33.

8   It was reported that Bishop Ryle had gathered a few clergy for a private meeting at his palace in September. A resolution had been passed suggesting that the three organizations be merged under the name 'The Church League.' Capt. Alexander Cobham, Chairman of the Council of the CA, said the question remained open for discussion. He also suggested that the organization was not entirely willing to allow that there would be no further litigation. Although they recognized the futility of further appeals for the present, 'circumstances might arise in the future when prosecutions might once more become necessary, and advance the cause of Christ.' *Record*, 28 Oct. 1892.

According to the *Times*, Bishop Ryle was largely responsible for the idea, but it thought the CA's new policy statement made the amalgamation of the three groups 'more remote than ever.' *Times*, 25 Nov. 1892. Several days later, the secretary of the CA denied that the council had made any negative decisions on the matter. 'They would gladly entertain any definite proposal for securing united action; but up to the present no definite proposal has been received. It is incorrect to say that the programme of "future policy" published by this association was put out as a 'reply' to the suggestion made by the Bishop of Liverpool.' Letter to the *Times*, 30 Nov. 1892.

9   *Record*, 23 Dec. 1892. In March 1893, at the meeting of the London Clerical and Lay Union, G. F. Whidborne described the events leading to discussion about unification. 'A private Meeting had been held at the instance of certain persons whom he named, at which it was decided to ask the Protestant Churchmen's Alliance, the Church Association, and the Union of Clerical and Lay Associations to appoint committees of nine each to meet a committee of three appointed by the private Meeting and discuss the question of amalgamation. The Church Association had not as yet fallen in with the suggestion; but the other two bodies had met, and the result was a scheme for amalgamation which had been issued to members of the country Clerical and Lay Associations for consideration.' Cited in the *Record*, 24 March 1893.

10 *Record*, 3 Feb. 1893. The *Record* thought the union would give new life to a body that it hoped would 'show more vitality than either of the organizations' from which it was formed. The new union's program was roughly parallel to that of the CA, although undertaken in a somewhat more moderate spirit. The union planned to defend the Protestantism of the Church of England through sermons, lectures, classes, education, and publications. It also desired to elect Protestant members of Parliament, broaden the Protestant influence in Convocation, Church Congresses, and other church bodies, and to establish the rights of the laity. *Record*, 3 March 1893.

11 Cited in the *Record*, 24 March 1893. There was apparently continued concern

The Division of the Evangelical Party 477

among the various local clerical and lay associations their own autonomy might be limited by the new union. That concern had been a point of contention when the original association was founded. At a meeting of the London Clerical and Lay Union in June 1893, H. W. Webb Peploe addressed the issue and suggested that the various local associations would in no way 'lose their individual identity' as a result of the union. They would continue as separate bodies 'in affiliation' with the new union, and would continue to send representatives to the council as had been the case with the previous UCLA. Cited in the *Record*, 16 June 1893.

12 *Record*, 28 April 1893. Cf. Machin, *Politics and the Churches, 1869-1921*, p. 208; although Machin failed to note that the new organization was formed by a combination of two existing bodies.

13 *Times*, 11 May 1893.

14 As such, it was opposed by CA supporters. One anonymous letter writer thought it was good to replace the former PCA, 'having all along held that there never was any *raison d'etre* for the existence of the Alliance.' But, he continued, anti-Ritualists could not approve 'of the policy which it is intended to pursue, or of the methods of pursuit.' In no way would it promote the unity of the party. 'We have not confidence in the chief members of the executive, and advise future federation with or fusion into the Church Association, as the chief centre of Protestant churchmanship for all Societies.' Letter (signed 'Protestant Minority') to the *Record*, 26 May 1893.

But the new union was able to do something the CA had never been able to accomplish, it obtained the public support of some of the Evangelical bishops. The CA had never had any episcopal members other than Charles R. Alford, the retired colonial Bishop of Victoria. J. C. Ryle had been a member of the CA, but he resigned upon being made the Bishop of Liverpool. The bishops, as a matter of general principle, avoided membership in partisan societies. King broke that tradition when he maintained his membership in the ECU after becoming the Bishop of Lincoln (a point that only served to annoy further the anti-Ritualists). In contrast to strictly partisan societies, however, the CMS was clearly viewed as a missionary organization that happened to be Evangelical. There were a number of bishops who were members, and all who agreed to join were made Honorary Vice-Presidents (even Bishop King of Lincoln held that position). But in October 1893, the *Record* announced that Bishop Ryle had agreed to become a Vice-President of the NPCU, joining Bishops Perowne (Worcester) and Straton (Sodor and Man). Despite its anti-Ritualist position, their membership and support would indicate that the new society was viewed in a fundamentally different light than the CA. *Record*, Oct. 20, 1893.

15 Letter (signed "W.B.") to the *Record*, May 19, 1893.

16 To a degree, the NPCU, in addition to challenging the position of the CA, was also a threat to the renewal of support for the CP-AS. The various groups were all seeking to establish their position and gather popular support. And their proliferation could only diffuse the support base that each group could drawn upon both in terms of membership and financial assistance.

17 Robinson continued: "Let us cease "biting and devouring one another" at

home. Let every Evangelical clergyman and layman throughout England throw all his strength, and energy, and money into Evangelical Church Societies only. For instance, let all support the CP-AS and the Church of England Scripture Readers' Society. People speak as if the Evangelical Church party were dead. The C.M.S. abundantly disproves that. But what is true is, that our want of cohesion, our suspicions of each other, our suicidal proceedings in supporting all sorts of Missions called "unsectarian," instead of acting with perfect loyalty in our own Church, divide us and make us a laughing-stock at home. In our work abroad we are united and succeed. In our work at home we divide our forces and are beaten in detail. As Evangelical Churchmen there is amongst us ample talent, wealth, and energy, but we fritter it about." Letter to the *Record*, Aug. 12, 1892.

In his history of the CMS, Eugene Stock noted the negative impact the Ritualist controversy had on the work of that society, particularly in the decade from the early 1860s to the early 1870s. The "combative spirit" of the anti-Ritualist movement did not, said Stock, "help forward definite spiritual work," and it often hindered missionary and evangelistic causes. Stock, *Church Missionary Society*, vol. 3, p. 700. Stock thought Robinson's letter was influential in altering moderate opinions and effecting a return to "true Evangelical policy." Ibid., p. 282.

Leonard Elliott-Binns noted that there was a renewed interest in missions from the early 1880s onward, although he did not link it to the decline of Evangelical interest in the anti-Ritualist movement. Elliott-Binns, *Evangelical Movement*, pp. 65-66.

18 Letter to the *Record*, Aug. 12, 1892. The divisions were evident as well in the view that conservatives expressed of moderates, often questioning their commitment to the Protestant cause. One correspondent wrote to express his gratitude to the *Record* for the position it had taken. Many of the younger clergy, he thought, viewed most of "the disputed points" as "matters of comparative indifference so long as they were not binding." And although they had no intention of adopting the innovations themselves, they were called "trimmers," "traitors," "neo-Evangelicals," and other names if they suggested that toleration ought to be granted to the Ritualists. He concluded, "Sir, we hope you have changed all that. Fidelity to Evangelical principles is not to be incompatible with a respect for English Church history, or sternly hostile to a broad and loving spirit of tolerance." Letter (signed "A Young Vicar") to the *Record*, Aug. 19, 1892.

19 *Record*, Oct. 21, Nov. 4, and 18, 1892.

20 Included among the signatories were: W. H. Barlow, Vicar of Islington; Gordon Calthrop, Vicar of St. Augustine's, Highbury and Prebendary of St. Paul's; J. F. Kitto, Vicar of St. Martin's; Arthur T. Robinson, Rector of Holy Trinity, Marylebone; and H. W. Webb Peploe, Vicar of St. Paul's, Onslow-square. Among the prominent laymen who signed the document were T. Fowell Buxton, Sydney Gedge, E. S. Hanbury, F. A. Bevan, and H. D. Ryder. Correspondence cited in the *Record*, Dec. 16, 1892.

21 Ryle concluded, "But stand firm so long as nothing new is required or forced on you, and your are allowed to work on your old lines." Ryle *No Uncertain Sound*, pp. 272-73.

In contrast to Ryle's negative perspective, G. R. Balleine presented a much brighter portrayal in retrospect. Based on the support of the CMS, he suggested that well over one quarter of all parishes were in the hands of Evangelical clergy. There were a little over 13,000 parishes in the church, and over 5,000 supported the CMS with funds. Balleine, *Evangelical Party*, p. 248.

22 Barlow said: "The programme of the day's proceedings has been specially prepared in reference to the requirements of the present time. Important events have occurred since we met last. Many minds have been filled with anxiety and alarm. Some have thought it their duty, under the present distress, to retire from the ministry of the Church of England altogether. Others, and these a large majority, having deemed it right rather to hold fast by the opportunities presented to them of ministering the Word of God and the Sacraments as before, however much they may regret the changed circumstances which a recent Judgment has brought about. It is not my purpose to enter into a discussion of controverted points of this nature, but rather to ask the question, What is to be done at this time to strengthen the hold upon the country which the teachings of the Reformed Church of England ought to possess, has possessed, and does still in a measure possess?" Cited in the *Record*, Jan. 13, 1893.

23 Ibid. One could argue that the increased emphasis Evangelical moderates put on the role of the Holy Spirit in the success of pastoral and spiritual work was an indication of the growing influence of the Keswick movement. That is not to say that the more strident anti-Ritualists did not use similar language with regard to God's involvement in their work, but there was a more direct connection between Keswick and the Islington conference. There were a number of speakers who often addressed both meetings, the most prominent being H. W. Webb Peploe and H. C. G. Moule, although at least one prominent anti-Ritualist, A. M. W. Christopher, was involved in both the Keswick movement and the CA. But, in general, the Keswick movement avoided controversial topics and seemed to engender a spirit that focused its concern on personal holiness and spiritual concerns over theological and ecclesiastical disputes.

24 Letter to the *Record*, Jan. 20, 1893. Strident anti-Ritualists would continue to charge that moderates were lukewarm in their commitment to the defense of Protestantism. At the turn of the century, John Kensit complained about the lack of support he had received for his protests: "The more I see and hear of some [Evangelical] clergy and their followers, the more contemptible do they appear; for although they know the Truth, they are kept back by the fear of man, and never speak out boldly for Protestantism." Cited in Wilcox, *John Kensit*, p. 51.

25 Having challenged the leaders of the Islington conference, Alford suggested that Evangelicals should not criticize one another. If they could not agree on "all that may be done or written, Evangelical Churchmen should respect one another's motives, and eschew discourtesy as unworthy of themselves and their cause." Letter to the *Record*, Jan. 20, 1893.

In March 1893, fifty prominent Evangelical clergy published a memorial defending the Protestant view of the church and listing their "convictions and apprehensions" resulting from the judgment in the King case. They avoided any direct criticism of the court's ruling, however, and sought to reassure other Evangelicals that their position in the church remained unchanged. The *Record* applauded the document's moderate tone, but suggested that the time had long passed for remonstrances. *Record*, March 3, 1893.

In contrast, C. R. Alford condemned the declaration. He suggested that "Protestant Churchmen" would read it "with great regret." Alford was disturbed that moderates had remained silent for so long, but he was still more irritated by the final result. There was no excuse, he thought, "for the absence in such a document of a plain and direct protest against the idolatry of what is called 'the Catholic Mass,' accompanied with Sacramental elevation and Eucharistic adoration, as now practised in many a parish church." Letter to the *Record*, March 17, 1893.

26 Letter to the *Record*, Aug. 19, 1892.
27 Cited in the *Record*, June 23, 1893.
28 Ibid.
29 Ibid.
30 Kitto continued, "Shall we make a man an offender for a word, a flower, a vestment, or a gesture? I know full well that in thus speaking I am exposing myself to the suspicions which I deprecate. But I plead for generous sympathy and cordial co-operation for Christ's sake. Surely it is possible for us to cast off our suspicions if men hold firmly to our grand Evangelical position, even though they may in some things act and speak as we ourselves should not." Ibid.
31 Ibid.
32 For a general survey of the continuing debate, cf. Machin, *Politics and the Churches, 1869-1921*, pp. 234-55.
33 He began with a protest of a service for "The Adoration of the Cross" at St. Cuthbert's, Kensington, on Good Friday, 1898. After creating a great sensation for several years, Kensit was attacked following a lecture in September 1902. He was hit on the head with a large metal file and languished in the hospital for several weeks before he died. His story is told in Wilcox, *Contending for the Faith: John Kensit, Reformer and Martyr*.

According to Owen Chadwick, the protests led by Kensit were the worst disturbances in churches since the anti-Popery riots of 1850-52; cf. Chadwick, *Victorian Church*, Part Two, p. 355.
34 The laity, said the reviewer, had a legitimate right to challenge the doctrine and practices of the clergy, thought the journal, without being charged with intolerance. While rejecting the strident rhetoric of the anti-Ritualists, the essayist suggested that the events had revealed a far greater "amount of extreme Ritualism among the clergy than was suspected." And if the age called for a broader degree of toleration in the church than might have been the case in the past, the ecclesiastical authorities ought to require due obedience from the clergy. And while the proper exercise of their non-coercive authority might be the best means of dealing with disobedient clergy, the reviewer suggested that there were still cases that deserved to be brought before the ecclesiastical courts. Anonymous, "The Unrest in the Church of

England," *Edinburgh Review* 189 (1899): 1-23.
35 In 1898, Alfred Barry noted that the issue have been forcibly raised by Kensit, but he acknowledged that there could be no return to the past and the attempts to enforce a narrow uniformity. Ritualist ceremonies could no longer rouse a popular "No Popery" cry except among "a few fanatics." But moderates, wrote Barry, despite having little sympathy with those of a "narrow and intolerant spirit," were disturbed by "the obvious disposition in many of our Churches to set aside Church Law in public worship, even where it is plain and unmistakable." Barry, "Breach of Church Law," *Nineteenth Century*, p. 943.

Writing in 1901, H. C. G. Moule closed his history of nineteenth-century Evangelicalism by referring to "the Crisis in the Church" occasioned by three years of vigorous advance among those propagating a "medieval, and often distinctively Roman, ritual and teaching." While mildly denigrating recent "incidents of agitation," Moule suggested that they were indicative of a spontaneous opposition among the Protestant laity that should not be underestimated. Moule, *Evangelical School*, pp. 108-09.
36 Cf. Chadwick, *Victorian Church*, Part Two, pp. 357-58. Geoffrey Bromiley, in his "Appendix" to Balleine, claimed that the report of the commissioners validated, in many respects, the complaints of the anti-Ritualists. It also urged the bishops to halt the more extreme innovations. But he also suggested that Evangelicals failed to press the advantage. In part, they did not have sufficient influence to do so, because they were under-represented in higher ecclesiastical positions. But they were also limited by their own failure. Bromiley concluded that they concentrated too much "upon the purely negative task of preventing the aberrations of others, and were blind both to their own lesser divergences and to the need for a constructive work of reform." G. W. Bromiley, "Appendix," in Balleine, *Evangelical Party*, pp. 253-54.
37 Elliott-Binns, *Evangelical Movement*, pp. ix-x.
38 Gladstone, "Evangelical Movement," *Quarterly Review*, p. 13.
39 It has often been suggested that Evangelicals, with their interest on conversion, focused only on the meaningfulness of the crucifixion of Christ, and failed to consider the importance of his life and work on earth. It was left to High Church theologians to develop a theology of the incarnation which was then expanded as a model for the church as the body of Christ in the world. Cf. Elliott-Binns, *Evangelical Movement*, pp. 77-80.
40 Cf. Bowen, *Victorian Church*, pp. 146-53. Owen Chadwick noted that "nothing is commoner that the charge that evangelicals were ignorant," but thought that it was not entirely fair. He suggested that several of their most prominent theologians deserved a better reputation. Chadwick, *Victorian Church*, Part One, p. 450.
41 Cf. Chadwick's section on Evangelicals, in *Victorian Church*, Part One, pp. 440-76.
42 The tone of their complaints often frayed their relations with their bishops. In establishing a Church Extension Society in Northampton, Bishop Magee of Peterborough noted that Evangelicals had raised disputes over the issue of patronage. They offered, he said, "a royal exhibition of the narrowness

and suspiciousness and bitterness of Evangelicalism" that "was really pitiful to see and vexatious to endure." MacDonnell, *Life of Magee*, pp. 13-14.

43 In 1950, the *Churchman*, which was the most prominent Evangelical quarterly of its time, published an editorial commenting on a recent statement made in the *Church of England Newspaper and Record*, the paper that succeeded the *Record* of the nineteenth century. In an editorial on the state of the party, the paper raised again many of the same issues that had faced the party during the years of debate over anti-Ritualism: "Evangelicalism today, by and large, is sadly adrift from its moorings. Instead of being strong and united in passionate concern for the Gospel it has become divided and disorganized within itself and has tended to adopt an apologetic and defensive attitude towards others. All too often it has attached an exaggerated importance to secondary matters of faith and practice and at the same time has lacked a definite sense of churchmanship. An Evangelicalism which is little more than a negative Protestantism on the one hand or a sentimental Pietism on the other is far removed from the great Evangelical tradition."

The *Churchman* continued, in support of the position taken by the paper: "If at the present time Evangelicalism is not the spiritual force in our Church that it used to be, the fault is due not only to numerical weakness – for in actual fact Evangelicals are still a comparatively numerous body – but to a departure from essential principles, resulting in a narrow outlook upon Church life in general and a negative attitude to certain current problems in particular.... Fresh hopes for the future of the Evangelical cause are stirring in many hearts through the formation of the "Church Society," amalgamating the two bodies formerly known as the Church Association and the National Church League. The united society has declared that its basic principle is "the furtherance and defence of the Christian Gospel, to be maintained by a definite and affective churchmanship through faithfulness to the Church's acknowledged standards of doctrine, worship, and order." In taking grateful note of that fact we express the hope that the Church Society will rapidly become a rallying centre for all loyal churchmen, and will also prove a means of promoting the spiritual life and forwarding the pastoral work in our Church." Anonymous, "Editorial," *Churchman* New Series 64 (1950): 1.

44 Michael Saward, *The Anglican Church Today: Evangelicals on the Move* (London: Mowbray, 1987), p. 24.

Chapter 11

Appendices

A. PROTEST OF THE CLERGY OF THE DIOCESE OF LONDON (1867)

'We the undersigned, being clergymen in the Diocese of London, desire to make our public and emphatic Protest against the introduction, under cover of an elaborate Ritualism, of some of the fundamental and most pernicious errors of the Church of Rome into the Protestant and Reformed Church of this realm.

'We are not insensible to the objections which may be urged against such voluntary declarations on the part of clergymen, who have already made the subscriptions legally imposed on them.

'But we are convinced in our consciences that the time is fully come, when, for the satisfaction of the great majority of the Lay Members of the Church of England, and for the vindication of our Church in the eyes of others, some authoritative check should be put to practices which are confessedly introduced and maintained as symbolical of doctrines against which our Reformers protested, and in protesting against which many of "the noble army of Martyrs loved not their lives unto death."

'Having waited anxiously for the effective application of any such check, by lawful authority, we now make public this our solemn Protest against the doctrine and ritual, the tendency of which is to assimilate the teaching and worship of the United Church of England and Ireland to the teaching and worship of a church which we have declared to be "idolatrous;" and whose "sacrifices of masses" we have been called on to renounce as "blasphemous fables and dangerous deceits."

'And We declare our conviction that the claim of our Church to be the Established Church of the realm, rest mainly upon her fidelity to the principles of the Reformation.'

30 Nov. 1866 (signed by 423 clergy). Reprinted in the *Record*, 4 Feb. 1867.

B. RITUALIST REMONSTRANCE TO THE PURCHAS JUDGMENT (1871)

'We, the undersigned clergy of the Church of England, hereby offer our solemn remonstrance against the decision of the Judicial Committee of the Privy Council in the case of "Hebbert v. Purchas."

'Without referring to all the points involved in this judgment, we respectfully submit the following considerations touching the position of the minister during the Prayer of Consecration at the Holy Communion: –

'1. That the rubrics affecting this particular question having been diversely observed ever since they were framed, the Judicial Committee has given to these rubrics a restrictive interpretation condemnatory of a usage which has continuously existed in the Church of England, and has for many years widely prevailed.

'2. That this decision is opposed to the comprehensive spirit of the Reformed Church of England, and thus tends to narrow the Church to the dimensions of a sect.

'3. That this restriction will press very unfairly upon a large body of clergy who have never attempted, by resort to law or otherwise, to abridge the liberty of those whose practice differs from their own.

'4. That the rigorous enforcement of a decision so painful as this to the consciences of those whom it affects might involve the gravest consequences to a large number of the clergy, and lead to results most disastrous to the Established Church.

'On these grounds, although many of us are not personally affected by the judgment, we earnestly trust that your Lordships will abstain from acting upon this decision, and thus preserve the ancient liberty of the Church of England.'

Signed by over 4,500 clergy. Reprinted in the *Times*, 13 April 1871.

C. LETTER OF THE EVANGELICAL UNION FOR CHURCH REFORM (1874)

'In consequence of the dissolution of Parliament, a new Convocation will speedily be summoned, and new Proctors to represent the clergy in every diocese in England and Wales must be elected.

'At this momentous crisis we believe the reform of Convocation to be in the foremost rank of questions calling for reform.

'The best qualified and competent authorities, both among clergy and laity, have for some time pronounced the constitution of Convocation to be very defective. It does not adequately represent the

Church of England, and it is not adapted to the requirements of the times, and recent changes in the Legislature have shown that Lay Churchmen are virtually excluded from the councils of the Church as a corporate body.

'It is not therefore unreasonable for Churchmen to require that Convocation shall be so organized that it may possess their confidence.

'Under these circumstances, we now venture to express an earnest hope that in the coming election of proctors for your diocese the great subject of Convocation Reform may be steadily pressed on the attention of all candidates for office, and that they may be requested, if elected, to give such reform their best consideration, and to support any well-devised measures by which it may be obtained.'

The letter was signed by the secretaries of the union who were all moderate Evangelicals: W. R. Fremantle, Edward Garbett and C. F. S. Money. Reprinted in the *Record*, 2 Feb. 1874.

D. REPORT OF THE COMMITTEE OF THE UPPER HOUSE OF CONVOCATION ON THE REVIVAL OF DIOCESAN SYNODS (1867)

'That, whereas the main object of diocesan synods was that the bishop should promulgate the decrees he thought needful for the good government of the diocese, and, whereas, though the presbyters present on being consulted by the bishop gave their advice, he was not compelled to follow it; and, whereas, the decrees so promulgated bound legally the diocese in all matters in which they did not contradict the decisions of the Provincial Synod; and, whereas, we deem that the action of such synods would be incompatible with the present condition of our Church: Resolved, – That we do not recommend their restoration. 2d. We have further considered whether, in the abeyance of such diocesan synods, we should recommend the adoption of any other and what diocesan gathering: Resolved, – That we believe that it would be of great use if the bishops and clergy and laity were from time to time to assemble and consider matters needful for the well-being of the diocese; that we believe it must be left to the several bishops of the province to judge of the urgency of the occasion, and to settle the time for calling and the mode of conducting such gatherings, subject to the following general suggestions: – 1. That they must be convened, presided over, and directed by the bishop; 2. that though, possible, all the clergy and a representation of the laity might in some of the small dioceses be convened, in the large dioceses the attendance both of the clergy and laity by representation would be generally most convenient; 3, that in case the bishop should think fit to put any question to a vote, the clergy and laity should have an equal voice; 4, that it be distinctly understood that the decisions of such gatherings do not claim any legal authority.'

Reprinted in the *Times*, 8 June 1867.

E. PROTEST OF RITUAL INNOVATIONS IN MISSIONS SERVICES (1874)

'We the undersigned householders or residents of the metropolitan district, finding to our great surprise and regret that there is an avowed intention in certain quarters of using the proposed Mission in London for the purpose of introducing and propagating the Confessionalist system, do hereby protest against such use being made of it, and against any permission or facilities being granted or allowed for that purpose by the bishops of the metropolitan district.

'We claim from the bishops every protection which it is in their power to give against such a use being made of the movement which their Lordships have inaugurated.

'We protest against clergymen who avow themselves to be uncompromising advocates of the Confessional; who have published or circulated the most advanced books in its favour – who are the avowed enemies of the Reformation – who ostentatiously refuse obedience to the laws – who are either openly or overtly in rebellion against the Bishops – being permitted to take any part in this Mission, at least, so far as the Bishops have power to inhibit them.

'We therefore earnestly request their Lordships to make use of the power which the law places in their hands, and beg to assure them of any sympathy or support which we may be able to give.'

Reprinted in the *Record*, 2 Feb. 1874. A week later the paper noted that some six hundred signatures had been collected. *Record*, 9 Feb. 1874.

F. QUESTIONS SUBMITTED BY THE COUNCIL OF THE CHURCH ASSOCIATION TO ITS LOCAL BRANCHES REGARDING ITS FUTURE POLICY (1873)

'1. Is it desirable that further legal proceedings in cases of breaches of known law should be undertaken by the Council at its discretion, or that assistance should be given in similar cases to aggrieved parishioners, and, if so, shall the Council ask the Guarantors for permission to apply the Guarantee Fund to such cases?

'2. What steps can be taken to allay the alarm that prevails in many minds, in consequence of the recent 'Bennett' Judgment?

'3. Shall the Council of the Association ascertain the power and duty of the Bishops, as the executive officers of the Church, to enforce the decisions of the Courts of Law on such questions as have been decided in the 'Mackonochie' and 'Purchas' cases?

'4. Shall the Council forthwith test the right of the laity to proceed in the Ecclesiastical Courts without the previous consent of the Bishop?

'5. What additional effort can be suggested to counteract the unscriptural teaching which prevails in the Church of England, and to oppose the efforts by which several organized bodies are seeking to subvert the principles of the Protestant Reformation?

'6. In what manner can greater unity of action between the Council and the Branches of the Association be secured in order to carry out the original objects of the Association as a centre of union, to represent Evangelical Churchmen combining their activities for the defence and dissemination of Evangelical religion?'

Reprinted in the *Record*, 10 March 1873.

G. MEMORIAL TO THE BISHOPS URGING THE SUPPRESSION OF THE RITUALISTS (1873)

'We do earnestly appeal to your Lordships, as bound by your solemn Consecration vows, to use "all faithful diligence to banish and drive away all erroneous and strange doctrine contrary to God's Word," [a commitment made by the bishop in his vows of office] and both privately and openly to call upon and encourage others to do the same, and a means thereto;

'1. To exercise all the authority vested in your Lordships, for the entire suppression of ceremonies and practices adjudged to be illegal, and in the event of that authority proving insufficient, to afford all other needful facilities for the due enforcement of the law.

'2. To take especial care that in the consecration of new and in the restoration of old churches, no architectural arrangements and no ornaments be allowed, that may facilitate the introduction of the superstitious practices and erroneous doctrines, which the Church at the Reformation did disown and reject.

'3. And, lastly, in the admission of candidates to Holy Orders, – in the licensing of curates, – and in the distribution of patronage, to protect us and our families from teaching, – which – though it may not subject the individual offender to judicial condemnation, – is, when taken in its plain and obvious meaning, subversive of those truths to which our Protestant Church, as keeper and witness of holy writ, has ever borne its faithful testimony.

'We feel bound in all faithfulness to assure your Lordships of our deliberate conviction, that any hesitation on the part of the rulers of our Church in the present crisis to take action on these points, will destroy the confidence and alienate the affection of a large portion of its lay members, and imperil its position as the Established Church of this Protestant kingdom.'

Signed by over 60,000 lay members of the Church of England. Reprinted in the *Times*, 6 May 1873.

H. CLERICAL MEMORIAL ON EUCHARISTIC VESTMENTS AND THE EASTWARD POSITION (1875)

'We, the undersigned Clergy of the Church of England, have learnt, with great concern, that the issuing of the Queen's Letters of Business to Convocation has led to a movement for obtaining authoritative sanction for the use of the eastward position, and of a distinctive Eucharistic dress, by the clergy when officiating at the administration of the Lord's Supper.

'This use is avowedly, by many persons, desired as typifying and implying such a sacrifice in the celebration of the Holy Communion, and such a sacrificial character in the Christian priesthood, as we believe are not in accordance with the teaching of the Liturgy and Articles of the Church of England.

'We beg leave to represent that such doctrines should not be inculcated by symbolical acts and things in a service which is intended to form a common ground whereon all Churchmen may meet "in perfect charity."

'We should, therefore, deeply deplore any fresh legislation whereby authoritative sanction might be given to such use of the eastward position, and of a distinctive Eucharistic dress.'

Signed by 5,300 clergy. Reprinted in the *Times*, 18 Jan. 1875.

I. MEMORIAL OF THE CHURCH ASSOCIATION TO THE UPPER HOUSE OF CONVOCATION ON EUCHARISTIC VESTMENTS AND THE EASTWARD POSITION (1875)

'Your memorialists regard with much concern and anxiety the proposal recently made in the Upper House of the Convocation of Canterbury to legalize the use of some "distinctive dress in ministering the Holy Communion," and the proposal also recently made in the Lower House of that Convocation to legalize the "Eastward Position" of the officiating clergyman at the time of the administration of the Lord's Supper.

'1. With respect to the proposed "distinctive dress in ministering the Holy Communion," the undersigned, while they fail to recognise any provision whatever for it in the Book of Common Prayer, would, on the contrary, refer to the Book of Advertisements of 1564, whereby it is directed that "every minister saying any public prayer, or ministering the sacraments, or other rites of the Church, shall wear a comely surplice with sleeves, to be provided at the charge of the parish;" and to the uninterrupted use in parish churches of the surplice in conformity with this direction for upwards of 300 years....

'2. With regard to what is termed "the Eastward Position," the undersigned are fully persuaded that there is no warrant for this position in the Book Common Prayer. In the first Prayer Book of Edward VI., the direction was as follows: "...the priest standing humbly afore the middes of the altar...." In the Second Prayer Book, this direction was changed to the following: "...the priest standing at the north side of the table...;" and this last direction continued through the successive books, and is found in our present Book of Common Prayer.

'The undersigned are unable to believe that it could have been the intention of the framers and reviewers of the Liturgy, by the rubrical change above noticed, simply to remove the officiating minister a very short distance to the left of his former position. On the contrary, they are persuaded that it was intended definitely to alter his position from "afore the middes of the altar," where his back would be to the people, to the "north side of the table"....

'Your memorialists would on this point refer to the decision of the Privy Council in Hebbert v. Purchas; by which the right position of the officiating minister during the Prayer of Consecration was decided to be at the north side of the table, so that he shall look south, and which stated that the words of the rubric, which directs that the priest shall stand before the table while ordering the bread and wine, could not be construed to justify the minister in standing with his back to the people, as this would frustrate the very object of the other portion of the same rubric which requires the priest to break the bread before the people.

'3. In view of both these proposed changes, your memorialists would also lay stress on the fact that the adoption of a "distinctive dress in ministering the Holy Communion" and of the "Eastward Position" is avowedly coupled, by many who contend for it, with sacerdotal functions on the part of the clergyman repugnant to the spirit of the Liturgy of the Established Church, which knows nothing of a priest being engaged in offering a propitiatory sacrifice for the remission of the sins of the people, or of a priest being engaged in an act of ministry before the Lord, in the presence and on behalf of the people, but only recognises a minister leading and joining in the devotions of the congregation.

'The undersigned, with all respect and deference, desire to record by this memorial their decided protest against both the above proposed changes, which are rightly associated in the minds of the great majority of the people of England with the doctrine of the Romish Mass, and to express their earnest hope that both of them will be strongly resisted by your Lordships. The attempt to authorise them excites considerable alarm, and, if successful, must prove highly dangerous to the Established Church.

'4. Your memorialists would take this opportunity of stating their views with respect to Convocation itself; the more so, in consequence of the recent issue of letters of business....

'Your memorialists do not venture to enter into the history of Convocation, nor to propose any measure for its reform. They are, however, constrained to say that, considering the existing constitution of Convocation, it cannot be recognised as a body properly representing the Church of England. Its voice can in no fit sense be called the voice of the Church. Its action, therefore, cannot be regarded as expressive of the mind of the great body of attached and loyal Churchmen.'

Signed by over 75,000 clergy and laity. Reprinted in the *Record*, 16 April 1875.

J. FIVE DEANS' MEMORIAL TO THE ARCHBISHOP OF CANTERBURY (1881)

'Your Grace has been pleased to invite those of the clergy who feel dissatisfied or alarmed at the present circumstances of the Church to state what they desire in the way of remedy. Encouraged by this invitation, we venture to submit to your Grace the following suggestions.

'First of all, and especially, we would respectfully express our desire for a distinctly avowed policy of toleration and forbearance on the part of our ecclesiastical superiors in dealing with questions of ritual. Such a policy appears to us to be demanded alike by justice and by the best interests of religion. For justice would seem to require that unless a rigid observance of the Rubrical Law of the Church or of recent interpretations of it be equally exacted from all the parties within her pale, it should no longer be exacted from one party alone and under circumstances which often increase the difficulty of complying with the demand. And, having regard to the uncertainties which have been widely thought to surround some recent interpretations of ecclesiastical law, as well as to the equitable claims of congregations placed in the most dissimilar religious circumstances, we cannot but think that the unrecognized toleration of even wide diversities of ceremonial is alone consistent with the interests of true religion and with the well-being of the English Church at the present time.

'The immediate need of our Church is, in our opinion, a tolerant recognition of divergent ritual practice; but we feel bound to submit to your Grace that our present troubles are likely to recur unless the Courts by which ecclesiastical causes are decided in the first instance and on appeal can be so constructed as to secure the conscientious obedience of clergymen who believe the constitution of the Church of Christ to be of Divine appointment, and who protest against the State's encroachment upon rights assured to the Church of England by solemn Acts of Parliament. We do not presume to enter into details upon a subject confessedly surrounded with great difficulties, but content ourselves with expressing an earnest hope that it may receive the attention of your Grace and of the Bishops of the Church of England.'

Reprinted in the *Times*, 12 Jan. 1881.

K. EVANGELICAL COUNTER-MEMORIAL TO THE FIVE DEANS (1881)

'We, the undersigned, have read the Memorial addressed to your Grace on January 10th, by certain dignitaries and other clergymen, in which they express their "desire for a distinctly avowed policy of toleration and forbearance on the part of our ecclesiastical superiors in dealing with questions of ritual."

'We have no desire to narrow the comprehensiveness of the National Church, or to abridge that reasonable liberty which has always been conceded to Churchmen in matters non-essential. We are, however, firmly convinced that neither in Public Prayer, nor in administration of the Sacraments, ought there to be granted any toleration of the use of vestments and symbols avowedly reintroduced as exponents of doctrines which we believe to be unscriptural, and which have been declared to be not in accordance with the plain intention of the Articles and Formularies of the Church of England.

'We therefore respectfully but firmly entreat your Grace to give no countenance to any attempt to procure toleration for ritual practices, which for more than 300 years, and until a very recent date, were almost unknown in the Church of England, and which, when submitted to the highest Courts, have been declared to be contrary to the laws of the Church and realm.

'We fully recognise the authority of the Bishops to exact a rigid observance of the rubrical law of the Church from all parties within her pale; but we cannot see how justice requires that such variations as have no symbolic meaning, and have never been condemned by authority, should be placed in the same category with the reintroduction of long discarded ceremonial, which symbolizes doctrines repudiated by our Church at the time of the Reformation, and which is therefore identified with the superstitious doctrines and practices of the Church of Rome.

'As regards the constitution of the Ecclesiastical Courts and the Judicial Committee of the Privy Council, we beg to assure your Grace, without expressing dissatisfaction with the existing arrangements, that any alterations really calculated to improve them will always receive our ready acquiescence.

'We cannot refrain from recording our deep conviction that the present circumstance of the Church constitutes a perilous crisis in her history, and we shall not cease to pray that your Grace and the Bishops of the Church of England may be guided by the Holy Spirit to such conclusions as shall be for the glory of God and the maintenance of true religion.'

Reprinted in the *Times*, 2 Feb. 1881.

L. THE CHURCH ASSOCIATION: ITS PAST ACTION AND FUTURE POLICY (1880)

'The Church of England has reached a crisis in its history which is of unprecedented magnitude and importance. No desire to make the best of things should be allowed to call off the attention of earnest Protestants from the gravity of this crisis, as it stands related to the moral and religious interests of the nation at large, as well as to the future of our ecclesiastical institutions.

'At such a juncture the Council of the Church Association cannot be surprised that their own position and policy have been discussed, have been by many much misunderstood, and by others gravely, not to say purposely, misrepresented.

'They deem it, therefore, a duty of paramount importance to refute the objections commonly raised to the proceedings of the Association, to set forth as distinctly as possible its purposes and its principles, with the magnitude and value of the great work it has hitherto been privileged by God's grace and guidance to achieve, and the nature and importance of the work upon which it is now engaged, and they ask for this statement the candid consideration of all parties concerned; whilst they especially claim for it the attention of loyal and God-fearing Churchmen.

Constitution and Policy.

'The Lord Bishop of Oxford has recently asserted that the Church of England will never enjoy peace so long as it is divided into two hostile camps by the Church Association and the English Church Union.

'As far as this charge refers to the Church Association, the Council answer: –

'(1). That if the association of men who think and feel alike on religious matters, and therefore naturally seek to give combined effect to their common views and sentiments, is in itself a just matter for deprecation, then it becomes altogether unintelligible on what grounds it is possible to justify the existence of the various religious Societies already doing useful work of various kinds within the Church, or even the existence of the Church itself, composed as it is assumed to be of members professedly animated by the same spirit, believing the same doctrines, and governed by the same laws.

'(2). If, however, such associations are only to be justly condemned when they aim, as their main object, at undermining the principles and perverting the doctrines of the very Church within which they exist, it is the fairest and most logical of inferences to assume that when such dangerous combinations exist it becomes the highest of all duties, for men who value God's truth, to associate for the purpose of resisting by every legitimate means in their power such an aggrieved conspiracy against the principles and constitution of their Church.

'(3). Those who deplore the existence of contention and strife within the body of the Church of England, should in all fairness blame those who are guilty of having initiated and provoked them, and not those who have had them forced upon them, and been driven to combine to defend principles against the conspirators.

'Six years before the formation of our Association, the English Church Union entered upon its crusade against the Protestant Church of this country; waging war, be it remembered, not so much against any party in the Church, as against the Church itself as a Protestant Reformed Church, as well as doctrines and practices which most distinctly mark her deliverance from the corruptions and degrading superstitions of mediaeval Popery. Whatever guilt attaches to the division of the Church of England into two hostile camps, and whatever may be the disastrous consequences, the blame must rest, in all justice, on the English Church Union, and on it alone, which, to re-establish the idolatrous service of the Popish Mass, raised the standard of rebellion against the Bishops, the guides and rulers of the Church , and against the law, tribunals, and judges of their Church and country.

'(4). The Church Association neither is nor professes to be a party combination; it is a society of Churchmen, founded on the broad basis of the Church of England. It is marked throughout by that comprehensive character contemplated by the framers of the Book of Common Prayer and the Articles; its single aim is to defend the Church against all who seek to narrow or broaden its teaching and principles, within or beyond the limits prescribed by authority; its purpose has been, and is, to defend against the whole body of Ritualists, those principles which animate the worship and permeate the doctrines of the Church.

'(5). For fourteen years the CA has been in active existence, and during the whole of this period in no single case has the law pronounced against the principles of the Association, nor has a single bishop on the bench ever condemned it as a "schism" or a "conspiracy" against the Church of England. On the other hand, in almost every case the law has condemned the Ritualists, while almost every member of the Episcopal Bench has denounced them, and some have branded them as "conspirators" and "schismatics" and "the enemies of the Church."

'The Archbishop of Canterbury, for example, has denounced the movement as "a conspiracy in our body against the doctrines, the discipline, and the practice of our Reformed Church." The late Archbishop Longley, the present Archbishop of York, the late Bishop of St. David's, and the present Bishops of London, Rochester, Gloucester and Bristol, and Bath and Wells have all spoken in the same strain of condemnation, while even the Episcopal representatives of the High Church party have been severe in their denunciation of this dangerous and widespread conspiracy.

'Nor is this the whole of the evidence that Ritualism is a treasonable conspiracy doing the work of the Church of Rome within the Church of England. Cardinal Manning, so far back as 1866, declared "the clergy of the Established Church have taken out of the hands of the Catholic (i.e. Roman) clergy the labour of contending for the doctrine of *Transubstantiation and Invocation of Saints*. The Catholics have been left the much more happy task of reaping the field." In the *Essays on the Reunion of Christendom*, edited by the Rev. Dr. F. G.

Lee, with a preface by the Rev. Dr. Pusey, their agreement with the view taken by the Romish Cardinal is thus expressed (p. 180): –

"Admitting that we are but a lay body with no pretensions to the name of the Church, we yet, in our belief (however mistaken) that we are one, are doing for England what they (i.e., the Papists) cannot do. *We are teaching men to believe that God is to be worshipped under the form of bread, and they are learning the lesson from us which they have refused to learn from the Roman teachers that have been among us for the last three hundred years.* We are teaching men to endure willingly the pain of confession, which is an intense trial to the reserved Anglo-Saxon nature, and to believe that a man's 'I absolve thee' is the voice of God. How many English Protestants have Roman priests brought to Confession compared with the Anglican clergy? Could they have overcome the English dislike to "mummery" as we are overcoming it? *On any hypothesis we are doing their work.*"

'Can there be a clearer demonstration of the treasonable aims of the Ritualists than such language, or a stronger proof of the lawless and defiant character of this self-confessed conspiracy than is furnished by the following proclamation of open rebellion against the law and the bishops?

'The Hon. C. L. Wood, the President of the English Church Union, in November, 1878, declared, amongst other objects of the Union, that "they must *resist* the civil tribunals, however much supported by Parliament or Royal pretensions, in spiritual matters, in things which touched upon the life of the Church." This language is altogether in harmony with the rebellious tone of the Annual Report of the English Church Union of 1867, which declares, in effect, that no bishop will be permitted to attempt to restrain any practices which find favour with the President and Council, without being opposed by the whole force of the Union, backed by funds derived from its 5,000 supporters.

'(6). If Ritualism then appears as a conspiracy in the eyes of the bishops of the Church of England, and of the nation at large, as represented in Parliament and in the press, as well as of the Roman Catholics who scornfully repudiate their fellowship and proffered help; if the more outspoken Ritualists have openly declared it to be their design "to bring our Church and country up to the full standard of Catholic faith and practice, and *eventually to plead for her reunion with Rome,*" what would now have been the position of the Church of England if during the last fourteen years there had been no organization to counteract that design, and detect and defeat these treacherous machinations? Was it for the Church of England to surrender at discretion the most distinctive and cherished doctrines of the Reformation at the demand of the English Church Union?

Was it for the Ritualists to organize for the Destruction of the Reformed Church, and for those who value it and love it as blood-bought gift to England, not to organize in its Defence? This question demands the attention of all Protestant Churchmen who have stood aloof from the Association on the ground of its alleged partisan and prosecuting character.

The Work Done

'The work done by the Church Association has been to assert and maintain the true principles and practices of the Reformed Church, and to expose and check the Romish practices and teachings of the Ritualistic conspirators.

'The most onerous, expensive, and painful part of their work – that of legal prosecution – has been *forced* on the Association, but it has always been conducted in a spirit of forbearance, and has resulted, in almost every case, in a legal vindication of its principles, and hence in a justification of its procedure.

'The Council cannot lay too great stress on the fact that the Church Association was established after the Bishops had repeatedly asserted that they were unable to cope with the evils presented by Ritualistic innovations The Bishops, while collectively and individually condemning these practices in Pastorals and Charges, as well as in Convocation, assigned as a reason for not taking legal action, that the law was not sufficiently clear on the points at issue, and that the expense of ascertaining it would be ruinous to themselves. They in effect said to the Protestant remonstrant, "We must allow all the novelties until you have proved them illegal." Thus the onus and odium of originating legal proceeding was thrown on the Church Association.

'The dilemma in which the Bishops found themselves in dealing with the Ritualists has been well stated by the Bishop of London in his Charges, as well as by the Bishop of Winchester, who in his justification of the Public Worship Bill (which was the result of the appeals made by the Association to the Bishops and to public opinion) wrote as follows: –

"It is said, no doubt, that if a judgment of this kind were given by a Synod of Bishops, and not by worldly lawyers, it would demand respect. May I remind you that clergymen of very high character some few years since were wont to say: – 'The law is on our side, and therefore, with all respect for our bishops, we cannot listen to them?' May I remind you again that on one occasion an unusually large body of bishops, sitting in Convocation, including Archbishop Longley, Bishop Wilberforce, and others, expressed themselves deliberately and unanimously on certain questions of ritual; and that not only did their words receive no attention or respect, but that the Church papers treated their utterances with unmitigated scorn? Again, when it has been urged that the Preface to the Prayer-book enjoins, when any doubts arise, that 'the parties that so doubt, or diversely take any thing, shall always resort to the bishop of the diocese,' the answer has always been 'We do not doubt; and therefore we do not resort.' Now I am by constitution and by principle most desirous to give fair play and full latitude to all schools in the Church; but I ask whether it can be right, first to reject all voice of the bishops, to appeal to law as superseding the authority of the bishops, and then, when lawyers not bishops expound the law in an adverse sense, to turn round and say, 'We would have obeyed the law if it had been expounded by the bishops, who are our legitimate rulers and judges'."

'The Bishop of Lincoln (Dr. Wordsworth), another High Church Prelate, thus disposes of the fallacy that the Ritualists are a persecuted body, martyrs deserving support and sympathy: –

"It may indeed be alleged by some well-meaning persons that such clergymen are suffering persecution, and have claims to sympathy and support. But the fact is such clergymen are not martyrs but persecutors. They are persecuting the Church of which they are ministers by disturbing its peace, and by stirring up strife, and by spreading confusion and anarchy, and by marring its efficacy, and imperiling its safety. As was observed long ago by St. Augustine, such persons are like Agar and Ishmael, who complained of persecution, but who persecuted Sarah and Isaac (Gal. iv. 29)."

'The Bishop of London in his Charge of 1875 thus admitted his utter powerlessness even in his own court to deal with the evil: –

"The bishops' authority in their courts no less than in their character as ordinaries has proved practically inefficient to check or regulate the illegal or obnoxious alterations in ritual of which complaints have been made to them."

'And in his recent Charge (1879) he explicitly vindicates the action of the Church Association, saying: –

"Reasons have been found sufficient to satisfy the consciences of those who are unwilling to obey, in disobeying the Bishop himself to whom obedience had been sworn, the Diocesan or Provincial Courts in which a learned layman alone presides, and the Crown itself, in last resort, advised by bishops and learned lay judges together in council. The cost, too, of such proceedings is great, ruinous to bishops if they undertake them, and prohibitory, for the most part, to churchwardens or individual complainants; and the formation of a Society many years back which advised and assisted clergymen to resist their bishops or defend themselves against charges relating to ritual, naturally caused the establishment of another to enable parishioners to seek the relief which the law professes to afford."

'In corroboration of this view of the all but insuperable difficulties which obstructed the path of our ecclesiastical rulers, in the matter of legal redress against the party of innovation, we have the equally recent and candid admission of the Bishop of Perterborough. His Lordship says, "Before now" – that is previous to the introduction of the Public Worship Regulation Act – "a clergyman could do as he thought proper, and there was no power to compel his obedience. The result was that the Church was fast passing away from the paralyzed hands of her legitimate rulers".'

'It is now universally admitted, and nowhere more fully than in the *Quarterly Review*, that it was owing to the action taken by the Church Association that this Bill became law.

'Are not the Council therefore fully warranted in stating that the past action of the Church Association has by the Divine aid materially contributed to defend the Church of England from dangers that at one time seemed altogether without remedy or redress?

'And yet the Association, assailed on the one side for that which it has done, is told on the other that it has done nothing.

'The Church Association has, at considerable outlay, obtained the condemnation by the Ecclesiastical Courts of sixty ceremonies and practices symbolical of Popish doctrines, and illegally introduced by the Ritualists into the services of the Reformed Church.

'This fact alone would be a sufficient justification of the action of the Association, though it is undoubtedly true that the work is far from complete, the delays have been wearisome, the difficulties great, and the cost enormous.

'In the following cases the Council have assisted parishioners in resisting illegal practices, and in each case the incumbent has left the parish; but unhappily in some cases Ritualistic practices are suffered to continue.

1. Teignmouth (Flamank v. Simpson)
2. Brighton (Hebbert v. Purchas, now deceased)
3. Liverpool, St. Margaret (Roughton v. Rev. C. Panell)
4. Barrow-in-Furness (Hurford v. Rev. T. Barrett)
5. Wolverhampton, St. Andrew (Howard v. Rev. C. Bodington)
6. Wolverhampton, Christ Church (Howard v. Rev. E. Glover)
7. Hatcham, St. James (Hudson v. Rev. A. Tooth)
8. Clewer, St. Andrew (Julius v. Rev. T. T. Carter)
9. Chiswick, St. Michael and All Angels (Rev. M. Ben Oliel)

'In the following cases the incumbents discontinued illegal practices complained of:-

10. Swanmore (Bishop Sumner v. Wix)
11. Manchester (Bishop Lee v. Sedgwick)
12. Folkestone Case (Clifton and others v. Rev. C. J. Ridsdale)
13. Donhead, St. Andrew (Grove v. Rev. H. E. Chapman)
14. Smethwick, St. Matthew (Fowler v. Rev. H. Gardner.

'In the following churches Ritualistic articles have been removed, by order of the Court: –

15. Hatcham, St. James (Bradford v. Fry)
16. St. Barnabas, Pimlico (Bowron v. Rev. G. C. White), where the erection of a baldacchino was declared illegal.
17. Lynton, Devonshire (Riddell v. Baker and another)

'In the following cases complaints were made to the bishops, and through their intervention the illegal practices have been discontinued: –

18. London Diocese – St. Ethelburga, Bishopsgate
19. London Diocese – St. Mary-the-Virgin, Primrose Hill
20. Gloucester and Bristol Diocese – St. Rahael's, Bristol
21. Rochester Diocese – All Hallows', Southwark

'In the following cases complaints were made by parishioners, but the Bishop refused to allow proceedings to be instituted; the illegal practices therefore are still being continued: –

22. London Diocese – St. Peter's, London Docks
23. Gloucester and Bristol Diocese – All Saints', Clifton

'The following cases are still in progress: –

24. St. Vedast, Foster-lane (Serjeant v. Rev. T. P. Dale)
25. St. John, Miles Platting (Dean v. Rev. S. F. Green)
26. Holy Trinity, Bordesley (Perkins v. Rev. W. Enraght)
27. St. Alban, Holborn (Martin v. Rev. A. H. Mackonochie)
28. Prestbury (Combe v. De la Bere)

'Further – in 1875 the Council obtained the signatures of 140,480 members of the Church of England to a Memorial to the Queen against the Vestments and the Eastward Position. It was presented to Her Majesty on the 30th June of that year.

'In 1878 a like Memorial praying Her Majesty to use all the influence at her command to repress the practice of Auricular Confession, signed by 40,702 members of the Church of England, was also presented.

'Three Hundred and Ninety Branch Associations have been formed; the number of members is Thirteen Thousand.

'There have been about Four Thousand Meetings and Lectures in London and the Provincial Towns, to further the objects of the Association.

'Three Millions of Sermons, Lectures, Pamphlets, and Tracts have been distributed.

'So much has been done. But apathy, indifference, and ignorance still prevail to an alarming extent. Much remains to be accomplished. Yet the value of the work done must not be underrated. It affords ground for hope, and ought to stimulate Protestant Churchmen to renewed effort.

Legal Proceedings

'Few cases have more taxed the patience, and called forth the energetic action of the council, than those of Messrs. Mackonochie and Bennett. The two former singularly illustrate the spirit and power of Ritualism to defy alike the bishop and the law.

'The case of Mr. Bennett at least rendered this signal service to the Church, that it proved beyond a doubt that the Sacerdotal system, which is at the basis of Ritualism, has no foundation in the formularies of the Church of England, as is shown by the judgment pronounced by the Court.

'The cases of Martin v. Mackonochie demand, from several points of view, more especial attention.

'It will be remembered that in its early stage this long pending case was regarded on both sides as a practical means of ascertaining authoritatively the law of the Church on the points at issue. Under this impression the Church Association entered upon the prosecution, and it was in seeming accordance with the same view that the English Church Union affected to declare that it only defended what the law of the Church of England ordered or permitted; adding, "of course there are points in which the law was not very clear, *but whatever the Courts of Law should decide, the Union of course would be bound by.*"

'The first suit against the Rev. A. H. Mackonochie for illegal Ritualistic practices was commenced in the year 1867, by letters of request from the Bishop of London to the Arches Court of Canterbury. From thence it was carried to the Judicial Committee of the Privy Council. The result was that all the practices complained of were declared to be illegal, and Mr. Mackonochie was admonished to discontinue them.

'Two subsequent applications were made to the Privy Council to enforce their monition, and in November, 1870, the Court suspended him from all clerical duties and offices for three calendar months. Mr. Mackonochie submitted to this suspension, and paid the costs awarded against him.

'In 1874 a second suit was commenced in a similar manner by letters of request from the Bishop of London, and the Dean of Arches passed on him a sentence of suspension for six weeks. Mr. Mackonochie submitted to the suspension and paid the costs.

'On the 23rd of March, 1878, a further application was made to the Court of Arches to stop the illegal practices continued by Mr. Mackonochie. The Court directed the issue of another monition, which was not obeyed, and on the 1st of June the Judge gave a sentence of suspension, *ab officio et beneficio*, for three years.

'Thereupon application was made to the Court of Queen's Bench for a writ of prohibition on a technical point, which was granted; but on appeal to the Lords Justices, the judgment of the Queen's Bench was reversed.

'On the 15th of November, 1879, the Dean of Arches ordered that the suspension for three years should take effect from the date of publication. This sentence was ignored, and Mr. Mackonochie officiated as before. A fresh suit was commenced with the sanction of the Bishop of London.

'The proceedings in the last suit were taken under the most distinct legal advice, that Mr. Mackonochie's persistent disobedience entitled the promoter to a judgment of deprivation. The Judge refused the application on the ground that the promoter, Mr. Martin, had not taken steps to enforce obedience to the previous sentence of suspension which could only have been by imprisonment.

'The Council carefully considered the question of an appeal to the Privy Council from this judgment, but were of opinion that in all probability such an appeal would only result in upholding the ruling of the Dean of Arches, whose object was to maintain the dignity and authority of his ancient Court, and under these circumstances they considered it inadvisable to incur the heavy expenditure consequent on a doubtful appeal to a higher tribunal.

'Many members of the Association not unnaturally regret that Mr. Martin could not see his way to resort to the serious step of imprisonment. There is no doubt, however, that he was entirely supported in his refusal to do so by the Archbishop of Canterbury and the Bishop of London. But with what result? Has the leniency of Mr. Martin produced a better state of feeling in Mr. Mackonochie? Certainly not. He offers the same determined opposition to the Bishop that he has lately done to the Courts of Law. It remains to be seen whether the Bishop can restore him to obedience by his Episcopal authority, or whether his Lordship may not after all be driven to legal proceedings.

'To those who doubt the policy of proceeding to the imprisonment of the offending clergy, it must be apparent that the Dean of Arches left no other course open to the complainants but imprisonment.

'In addition to these Ecclesiastical suits the Council have in many important cases materially assisted churchwardens and aggrieved parishioners with advice, and by procuring for them counsel's opinion on the points at issue with reference to ritual and otherwise, and redress has thereby frequently been obtained without the necessity of an appeal to the Courts of Law. The Council have also in very numerous instances advised parishioners with reference to the election of churchwardens, and in many cases, in consequence of the advice given and assistance rendered, Ritualistic churchwardens have been superseded and Protestants elected in their place.

The Work to be Done

'With the aid of the branches and members the Council have resolved to persevere in the work still before them, which may be specified as follows: –

'I. To continue the existing suits and to enforce the judgments obtained, by all the means that the law permits.

'II. To encourage the branches to take vigorous action on their own account, aided in all cases by the advice of the Council when required, and by pecuniary assistance in special cases when necessary.

'Nothing can be clearer than the right of the parishioners to have the services of their church performed according to the form prescribed by the law of the Church. The obvious duty of the clergyman towards his parishioners is violated, and the most sacred rights of the parishioners infringed when the clergyman introduces a form of ritual which is not only alien to the Church, but has been deliberately rejected by it, and condemned alike by the bishops and legal authority. In the words of Lord Chief Justice Cockburn, in the Clewer Case, March 8, 1879: –

"It is the undoubted right of every inhabitant of every parish in the kingdom, desirous of frequenting the parish church, to have the services of the Church performed according to the ritual of the Church, as established by law, without having his religious senses shocked and outraged by the introduction of innovations not sanctioned by law or usage, and which may appear to him to be inconsistent with the simplicity of the Protestant worship and to pertain to a religion which he believes to be erroneous, and the ritual of which is not that of the Church of England."

'This is a question of the utmost importance, to which the Council will devote their best energies and efforts in the interest not only of aggrieved parishioners, but of the Church itself, which is suffering by the continued absorption of some of its members by the "Free Church of England" to which they have been driven, solely by Popish practices in their parish churches.

'III. To bring public opinion to bear upon the Archbishops and Bishops, to urge them to enforce the judgments already obtained on ceremonial matters, now that the law in all disputed points has been clearly ascertained.

'IV. The Church Discipline Act, and the Public Worship Regulation Act, which govern the present state of the law against contumacious clergymen, require amendment in matters of procedure. The Council have prepared a Bill to be brought before Parliament, entitled "The Ecclesiastical Procedure Bill," which would enable *the judge* in lieu of imprisonment to suspend for contumacy a delinquent clergyman from office and benefice, either absolutely or for such term or terms, and either with or without such conditions as the judge may think fit. It also gives the judge power of passing an additional and definitive sentence of deprivation, in case of persistent contumacy. The Bill further provides that the bishop shall not have a discretionary power in deciding whether proceedings ought or ought not to be taken, if the acts charged against a clergyman be certified to have been judiciously decided to be an offence, and it provides that in the third section of the Public Worship Regulation Act, the words "one parishioner" shall be substituted for "three parishioners." This Bill they hope will be introduced in the House of Commons very early after the meeting of Parliament.

'V. An attempt will probably be made in the ensuing session of Parliament to legalize the Revised Rubrics and Canons Ecclesiastical which have been drawn up by Convocation, and now only await the sanction of Parliament. The Rites and Ceremonies Bill presented to Parliament aims at vesting in Convocation alone the absolute power of initiating all legislation affecting the rites and ceremonies of the

Church. It would virtually repeal and alter the 25 Hen. VIII., c. 19, to which it is diametrically opposed in aim and in spirit; the Draft Bill aiming at making the laity submit to the clergy as represented in Convocation. Its true character has been thus exposed by the *Times*. "The whole scheme looks engagingly simple and innocent. We can only say, once for all, of the whole scheme, it will not do. It is antiquated in purpose, inept in conception, and will be mischievous in execution." The Council will offer it a firm opposition.

'VI. The assailants of the Protestant Church are rigorously striving to overthrow the jurisdiction in ecclesiastical matters of the Judicial Committee of the Privy Council, and to procure the constitution of another Court of Appeal, in the expectation that thereby they will recover the ground they have lost, and get their lawlessness legalized. The Council will watch with the utmost vigilance any attempt to alter the constitution of the present Court of Appeal in ecclesiastical causes.

'VII. The principles of Rationalism being actively at work within the Church, unsettling, if not overturning, the faith of thousands, requires to be still combated. Hitherto the Council have been under the necessity of postponing this great work, in order to concentrate their efforts against Ritualism, because it was the more extensive, the more aggressive, and the more immediate of these two dangers, threatening the very existence of the Reformed Church, and having a distinct organization of its own, to execute it designs.

'VIII. With a view to the revival of Protestant feeling throughout the country, and the better education of the public mind on the grave questions which are at issue in this controversy, and for the advancement of spiritual religion amongst the people, the Council propose to secure the larger assistance of the clergy in Sermons and Courses of Sermons on the great doctrines of the Reformation; the arrangement of Bible Readings and other similar meetings of a devotional character, especially in parishes where the people suffer from a dearth of spiritual privileges through Ritualistic teaching; and, further, to promote closer fellowship among members of the Association in London and other large towns, by meetings for conference, prayer, and the study of God's Holy Word.

'IX. The organizing officers of the Association have been for some time engaged in consolidating the existing Branches of the Association, and in uniting small neighbouring Branches for common purposes. This work will be continued and fresh Branches formed.

'In order to carry out the important work detailed above, the Council urge their members to assist them by forming a new Guarantee Fund.

Conclusion

'To those who imagine that, having ascertained the law, the work of the Association is done, as well as to those who lament that more has not been accomplished in the way of suppressing the conspiracy with which they have had to combat, the Council suggest the inquiry – what would have been the state of things had the Church Association not existed, and what would probably happen should it pass out of existence? If these considerations are duly weighed, the Council have little doubt that all the support needed to continue this momentous conflict will be abundantly forthcoming.

'If mere questions of form and ceremony, of posture and of dress, were alone involved, the Council would have spared themselves the anxious labours of the past fourteen years; but the far-reaching importance of the great contention in which they are engaged arises out of its relation to the great truths of the Gospel and Church order.

'It is because the teaching and practices of the Sacerdotalists are contrary to the plain teaching of God's Holy Word; because they obscure the finished work and Divine glory of the Redeemer; because they interpose hindrances to the access and immediate communication between the sinner and his Saviour, that the Council feel bound to resist to the uttermost this unscriptural and soul-endangering movement.

'Hence also the urgent need for the exercise of diligent effort to instruct, build up, and guide the people of the land, with special reference to the dangers in which our common faith and our national Church are involved, and to lead our brethren in the faith to seek the protection and power of the Holy Spirit; to study and induce the study of God's Holy Word as the sure antidote to religious errors; and to draw near to the throne of grace in prayer and supplication for a blessing on our work, and thus also on our Church and nation.'

Reprinted in the *Record*, 5 Nov. 1880 (their italics)

M. RESPONSE OF THE UPPER HOUSE OF CONVOCATION TO A MEMORIAL ADOPTED BY THE LOWER HOUSE REGARDING THE IMPRISONMENT OF REV. S. F. GREEN (1881)

'The Upper House having received a representation from the Lower House on the prolonged imprisonment of the Rev. Mr. Green, of Miles Platting, with a request that the President and Bishops of the Upper House would consider whether any, and if so what, steps can be taken to procure his release, would observe that the matter primarily concerns the Convocation of the Northern Province, in which Mr. Green is beneficed, and, further, that an appeal upon the case is now pending before the House of Lords. At the same time, this House assures the Lower House that it cordially concurs with it in deploring that imprisonment, and in desiring to see it at an end. It is also of opinion that while it must be quite impossible to exempt either ministers of the Church or ministers of Nonconformist bodies from the usual method by which both alike are liable in the last resort to be prevented from disobeying the orders of the Court, it would nevertheless be desirable that some modification of the existing law might be provided, so that such a remedy as imprisonment under *significavit* should not be resorted to. And it looks with hope to the action of the Royal Commission recently appointed for some improvement in the procedure of the Ecclesiastical Courts in this respect. It would also be thankful to hear that the prosecutors in the present case had applied to the Court for the release of Mr. Green. But it does not appear that in this stage of the proceedings any action that would lead to the release could be taken either by the House or by the individual members of the House. This House, however, desires to impress on the members of the Lower House, and on the Church generally, its persuasion that for the allaying of the disquietude in the public mind, and for the maintenance of the dignity of the law, and for the peace and safety of the Church, it is essential that while the bishops of the Church endeavour to administer in a wise and fatherly spirit the discretionary authority with which they are invested by appeasing strife and for settling differences in matters ceremonial, the clergy of their dioceses should also be duly mindful of the solemn obligations by which they bound themselves at their ordinations and institutions, and should be willing to submit their dutiful and filial loyalty to the lawful authority and godly admonitions of their Lordships. And this House entertains little doubt that if this course were adopted by Mr. Green his release would speedily follow, to the general satisfaction of the Church.'

Reprinted in the *Times*, 23 July 1881.

N. MEMORIAL OF THE CHURCH ASSOCIATION PROTESTING THE REPORT OF THE ROYAL COMMISSION ON ECCLESIASTICAL COURTS (1884)

'That this Council hereby records its strong disapproval of the recommendations, as a whole, contained in the Report of the Ecclesiastical Courts Commission.

Appendices 507

'The Council also records the extreme regret with which it has seen the Address to the Archbishops, emanating from the Dean of Canterbury and others.

'The Council also resolves to prepare for signature by clergymen and laymen a memorial to Her Most Gracious Majesty the Queen, as Supreme Governor of the Church of England, deprecating the recommendations of the Ecclesiastical Courts Commission, which infringe the constitutional and time-honoured rights of the laity.

'The Council further resolves upon a manifesto to the country couched in the most decided language, setting forth the gravity of the crisis, and calling for united and unflinching action on the part of those who value Protestant truth.'

Reprinted in the *Record*, 14 Dec. 1883.

O. PRIVATE CIRCULAR ON THE CHURCH MISSIONARY SOCIETY (1888)

'Many of the best, oldest, and truest friends of the Church Missionary Society have for some years been pained and grieved at a tendency to depart from the old paths, and from distinctively Protestant and Evangelical principles.

'The questions arising out of the Ceylon, Japan, and Jerusalem Bishoprics, with the overture to the Bishop of Lincoln (Dr. King) to become a Vice-President, he not being a member of the Society; and now the Service recently held in St. Paul's Cathedral, notwithstanding the new, idolatrous Reredos – all these have deeply stirred the hearts of many, and have been the subjects of painful controversy at home, and of injury to the work abroad.

'While some have already left the society and others are leaving, this circular is to invite you to consider how best past mistakes may be rectified, present evils remedied, and future troubles averted.

'The battles have been fought in Committee and lost by decreasing minorities, because of the want of proper organization. Our friends have gone to Salisbury-square not knowing whether any, few or many, would be present to support them.

'It may not be generally known that every clergyman who subscribes 10s. 6d. is qualified to be on the Committee, and can have summonses and the agenda paper sent to him on application. We are now in the presence of a gigantic conspiracy, whose evil effects are seen in the Church at large, and it is therefore an urgent necessity that the true friends of the Society should unite in forming themselves into a compact body pledged to attend meetings of the General Committee, and to use their utmost influence in keeping the

Society in the old paths.

'It will be necessary that some arrangements should be made to send notices to those who co-operate in this movement, whenever important business requires their attendance.

'This and other details will be considered at a meeting called for this purpose, when replies to this circular have been received.

'Let us pray that the proposed action may receive such support, that it may be productive of the best results, in promoting the glory of God and the true interests of the Society.

'If you are willing to join in thus banding ourselves together, as those who love the Lord Jesus Christ better than we love any Church, or any Society, will you kindly sign the enclosed duplicate and post it, addressed C.M.S., 13 Buckingham-street, Strand, W.C.'

Reprinted in the *Record*, 23 March 1888.

P. CHURCH ASSOCIATION MEMORIAL PROTESTING THE ST. PAUL'S REREDOS (1888)

'The memorial of the undersigned members of the Church of England, resident within the Diocese of London, showeth: – That a large crucifix and an image of the Madonna has been set up recently over the table of the Lord in St. Paul's Cathedral. That such images so placed were worshipped by our English forefathers, but are denounced by the Homilies of the Church of England as being "lying images," and their worship as being distinctively "Romish" by the 22nd Article. That such images were at the Reformation removed by authority from our English churches, while quite recently faculties for their removal have been granted by the Ecclesiastical Courts, and faculties have been refused for their erection. That your Memorialists are advised that this particular erection at St. Paul's is illegal, while it is especially obnoxious as being erected in the mother church of a diocese in which the humblest worshipper may justly claim, as of right, that no graven image should be thrust upon his attention, more particularly in contrast and competition with that memorial of the sacrifice of the death of Christ, which Christ Himself ordained for its "remembrance." That the private discretion of a small body like the Dean and Chapter of St. Paul's should be subject to correction, when their privileged position has been abused for the purpose of introducing graven images into the noblest national temple of your diocese. Your Memorialists therefore pray that, as visitor, your Lordship will transmit to the Archbishop the representation made to you under the Public Worship Regulation Act, 1874, with a view to the obtaining of a judicial decision upon a matter affecting deeply every diocese, not only in this country, but in each of our colonies.'

Reprinted in the *Times*, 12 April 1888.

Q. CHURCH ASSOCIATION ADVERTISEMENT: 'SPECIAL APPEAL FOR FUNDS'

'The present very grave position of the Church of England calls for the serious and prayerful consideration of its members, and we therefore ask your special attention to the steps the Church Association is taking with the view of upholding Scriptural truth, and of arresting the wave of Sacerdotalism which threatens to overthrow that Church as an Establishment.

'The law has been authoritatively declared on no less than sixty points, and the Protestant character of the Church of England thereby vindicated; but the earnest hope once entertained by the Council, and by the general body of the Church Association, that Judicial decisions would be respected by the Clergy generally, has proved fallacious.

'The law has been deliberately defied, and the authority of the Queen's Courts, explicitly denied, while all action on the part of aggrieved laymen and the presentments of Churchwardens have alike been treated with studied and systematic neglect. The aggressive activity of the Ritualistic Clergy, carried on under the aegis of the English Church Union, the encouragement given to them not only by the Bishops, but even by successive Prime Ministers of the Crown, and inadequately resisted by the Protestant laity, has resulted in the rapid advance of practices which are alien to the spirit of the Church of England, and unless effectually repressed can have but one result, to wit, its disestablishment.

'Requiem Masses for the dead, celebrated on the Romish festival of All Souls, and at the funerals of Mr. Mackonochie and others, have failed to elicit any censure on the part of the Bishops; whereas any innovation in a Protestant direction, however harmless, is at once severely checked, thus showing unmistakably the strength of the Episcopal leaning towards Sacerdotalism.

'The Bishop of London's Veto of the St. Paul's Reredos Case, in the face of a Memorial bearing about 9,000 signatures readily obtained within the Diocese at very short notice, is only one amongst many instances of the substitution of the personal will of a Bishop for the administration of justice. Bishop Temple forbids any appeal to the Law Courts on the part of loyal members of the Church, though they honestly believe that the crucifix is illegal, and, being used in Roman Catholic Churches as a necessary adjunct to the service of the Mass, constitutes (with the accompanying images of the Madonna and Child) a direct and ever-present incentive to idolatry.

'These facts sufficiently prove that a "lying spirit" is at work within the National Church, threatening to transform all her agencies for good into a vast machinery for the destruction of those vital truths which our Reformers died to vindicate, and which will involve in their overthrow those civil and religious liberties and that social and material progress which have made England the mother of freed men throughout the world.

'The voice of the Church has been substituted for the authority of Holy Scripture, and an administration of the Lord's Supper has been illegally introduced, which is not merely at variance with the plain order of the Book of Common Prayer, but with the purpose of the original institution of our Saviour. These are not questions of mere ecclesiastical or antiquarian interest. While they are vital to the spurious claims of 'sacrificing priests,' they are equally of importance to ourselves as affecting the office and work of the Lord Jesus Christ as the one mediating Priest in His Church, the character and efficacy of His Atonement, and that covenant freedom of access to God which under the Gospel dispensation is the precious heritage of each individual sinner.

"The question, therefore, is forced upon us – Are the laity of England to be left without a remedy? Are the laws of England to be ostentatiously broken, and the authority of the Queen's Courts to be defied? Are the distinctive doctrines and practices of Rome to be reintroduced into the worship of a Church from which they were publicly cast out by the unanimous consent of the Sovereign, the Parliament, and the people of England? Shall the Mass with its obscuration of truth, it "blasphemous fables" and "dangerous deceits," be restored in our parish churches?

'The Council of the Church Association share the belief, strongly expressed in many quarters, that another appeal to the Courts of Law is imperatively demanded. Proceedings have accordingly been commenced against the Bishop of Lincoln for illegal practices in his own Cathedral and at St. Peter's-at-Gowts in the city of Lincoln. Action has also been taken to compel the Bishop of London to allow the case against the Reredos in his Cathedral to go forward.

'The Association is already committed to considerable outlay, and its success must depend on whether the means placed at the disposal of the Council are sufficient to enable them to carry out with vigour any proceedings which the progress of events may render necessary. A Guarantee Fund of at least £10,000. is required, to which contributions are earnestly invited. Payments to be distributed over five years, and made yearly in equal proportions.

'Increased activity in the ordinary work of the Association also calls for an increased income, and the Council trust that the necessities of the General Fund will be remembered, and additional means provided for the work, which is constantly growing.'

Advertisement in the *Times*, 12 July 1888.

R. PROTEST DECLARATION OF THE CHURCH ASSOCIATION (1889)

'We, the undersigned Clergy and Laity of the Church of England... desire: –

'I. To Protest that, in our humble judgment, those who sign such a Declaration thereby countenance doctrines and practices at variance with the Articles and Prayer Book of the Church of England – tending to a condition of lawlessness fraught with danger to morality and righteousness in our midst – and dishonouring to that God Who has blessed us with all spiritual blessings in heavenly things in Christ Jesus, and by Whose Holy Spirit alone can true unity and peace be maintained and preserved within the Church of God.

'II. To Vindicate the position and right of the Church Association, and of all those loyal and devout members of our Protestant Reformed Church, who have felt themselves called upon, in the Providence of God, to appeal to the Courts of our Realm against such erroneous doctrines and practices – conscientiously believing them to be destructive of the Civil and Religious liberties restored to us by our martyred fore-fathers, and to be contrary to the Word of the Living God, which plainly declares that other foundation can no man lay than that which is laid – even Jesus Christ: – And

'III. To Appeal to all Christian Brethren at home and abroad to accord their personal sympathy and prayerful support to those, who, in spite of obloquy and reproach, are so engaged in defending the Truth of God – maintaining the liberties of this our Church and State as secured by the Reformation and subsequent Protestant Settlements – and furthering the interests of the Gospel of the Grace of God, so that the kingdoms of this world may become the kingdoms of our God and of His Christ.'

Reprinted in an Advertisement in the *Record*, 4 Jan. 1889.

S. RESOLUTION OF THE PROTESTANT CHURCHMEN'S ALLIANCE (1889)

'That, while gratefully acknowledging the past efforts of existing Protestant organizations in vindicating the Reformation principles of the Established Church, and disclaiming all desire to interfere with their work, this Conference is of opinion that the present critical state of the Church of England demands that Churchmen, who desire to maintain the principles of the Reformation, the present Prayer-book and Articles, and the Acts of Uniformity as standards of ritual and doctrine in the National Church should further unite and organize; and that for this purpose a Union, under the name of the Protestant Churchmen's Alliance, be hereby formed, with branches in every diocese of England and Wales, for the furtherance of the following objects – viz.: –

'1. To afford a basis of union, and opportunities for consultation and concerted action, for all Churchmen who desire to maintain the principles of the Reformation, the present Prayer-book and Articles, and the Acts of Uniformity, as their standards of doctrine and ritual, and, especially, the non-sacerdotal character of the ministry of the Church of England.

'2. To adopt whatever means may, from time to time, seem desirable to inform and instruct the public as to the true history and principles of the Church of England, and the Book of Common Prayer, as based on the teaching of God's Holy Word, with a view to secure and maintain their attachment to the Established Church, and to prevent the alienation of the people by misrepresentations of her doctrine and discipline.

'3. To obtain by parliamentary action the abolition of the Episcopal veto on suits for the maintenance and enforcement of the law; and, in cases of contumacy, to provide for summary deprivation, with a view, as far as possible, to avoid imprisonment.

'4. To make better provision for the furtherance of the above objects in Parliament and the Press, and while recognizing the comprehensiveness of the National Church, within the limits of her authorized standards, to deprecate and discountenance, as inimical to her maintenance and defence, whatever is taught or practised in violation of the principles of the Reformation, the directions of those standards, and the decisions of the Queen's Courts thereon.'

Reprinted in the *Times*, 21 June 1889.

T. ADVERTISEMENT DECLARING THE OBJECTS OF THE PROTESTANT CHURCHMEN'S ALLIANCE (1889)

'(1) To afford a basis of union, and opportunities for consultation and concerted action for all Churchmen who desire to maintain the principles of the Reformation, the present Prayer-book and Articles, and the Acts of Uniformity as their standards of doctrine and ritual, and especially the non-sacerdotal character of the ministry of the Church of England.

'(2) To adopt whatever means may, from time to time, seem desirable to inform and instruct the public as to the true history and principles of the Church of England, and the Book of Common Prayer as based on the teaching of God's Holy Word, with a view to secure and maintain their attachment to the Established Church, and to prevent the alienation of the people by misrepresentations of her doctrine and discipline.

'(3) To obtain by Parliamentary action the abolition of the episcopal veto on suits for the maintenance and enforcement of the law; and in cases of contumacy to provide summary deprivation, with a view, as far as possible, to avoid imprisonment.

'(4) To make better provision for the furtherance of the above objects in Parliament and the Press, and, while recognizing the comprehensiveness of the National church, within the limits of her authorized standards, to deprecate and discountenance, as inimical to her maintenance and defence, whatever is taught or practised in violation of the principles of the Reformation, the directions of those standards, and the decisions of the Queen's Courts thereon.

'The Alliance will seek to accomplish the objects for which it is formed by the following means: –

'(1) By urging upon its Members the importance of regular prayer that the Lord would protect the Church from the assaults of its great spiritual enemy.

'(2) By seeking to secure the sympathy and co-operation of the Laity, especially the working men, by means of literature and oral teaching setting forth the true history, and the Primitive and Protestant principles of the Church of England and the Book of Common Prayer; and showing how the Mass, the Confessional, and Sacerdotalism in all its forms, were deliberately put aside at the time of the Reformation, and by using every possible means to explain to the people the Protestant character of the Church of England.

'(3) By presenting memorials on the present condition of the Church of England to the Queen, the Prime Minister, and the Bishops.

'(4) By securing adequate representation of Protestant principles in Parliament and the Press.'

Advertisement in the *Record*, 20 Dec. 1889.

U. CHURCH ASSOCIATION PROTEST REGARDING THE JUDGMENT OF THE JUDICIAL COMMITTEE OF THE PRIVY COUNCIL IN THE LINCOLN CASE (1892)

'That this Meeting deplores the recent Judgment of the Judicial Committee of the Privy Council because it has contravened the principle of interpretation previously applied to the rubrics of the Book of Common Prayer through a long course of years and a series of decisions; because it has introduced confusion, contradiction, and uncertainties into the ecclesiastical law; because it has sanctioned the unconstitutional proceeding of an inferior Court overruling the decision of the superior Court; and because it has tolerated parts of the distinctive ritual of the Mass in the services of the Established Church.

'In the opinion of the Meeting the Judgment has placed a more urgent duty upon all Protestants to aid the Church Association in its continued resistance of Romish or Sacerdotal teaching and practices by clergy of the Reformed Church of England.

'That the distinctly Evangelical character of the Liturgy, Articles, and Homilies of the Church of England, certified as this has been by so many Judgments of the superior Courts of law, justifies the Evangelical clergy and laity in a continued adherence to her communion, and that the Sacerdotal ritual now made permissible by the Lincoln Judgment should stimulate them to faithful and combined action for the maintenance and vindication of the pure and Scriptural doctrines of the Reformation of which she has hitherto been the exponent, and which alone justify her position as the Established Church of the nation.'

Cited in the *Record*, 11 Nov. 1892.

V. ADVERTISEMENT OF THE CHURCH ASSOCIATION (1892)

'In other matters, the Council recommend: –

Organization
'An increase in the Evangelical Members of Convocation, and of Diocesan and Ruri-Decanal Conferences.

'Free Election by Ballot, under Lay presidency, of representatives

Appendices 515

for the Laity to be regarded as an essential, precedent to the eliciting any true "voice of the Church."

'Clerical "Canon Law" to be resisted.

Education

'Additional efforts to increase the number of Protestant Candidates for Ordination.

'Increased support to Protestant Middle-Class Schools for Boys and Girls.

'Prizes annually for examinations on Reformation History.

'An increase in Protestant Classes, Children's Mission, Lectures (Illustrated or otherwise), Sermons, Meetings, Conferences, and Open-Air Demonstrations.

'The Colportage and Van Agency of the Association to be developed to educate the Rural Population.

'The training of experts in the Ritual Controversy, and of Lay Evangelists and Colporteurs.

'More extended use of the valuable Library at the Offices of the Association.

'Attention to be called to the teaching required by Diocesan Inspectors of Religious Education.

Mission Work

'In those parishes where "the Protestant Religion" has been disestablished by the occupation of the Church by Romanizing intruders, encouragement be afforded to establish centres for Divine Worship, for the instruction of children and others in the verities of the Bible, for philanthropic and educational objects, and for the dissemination of the Gospel for Christ our Lord.

'A systematic study of the first three centuries of Church History.

Parliamentary

'Petitions to Parliament from parishes affected by Ritualism to be repeated until redress is obtained.

'The return of Protestant Candidates to Parliament, and for this purpose the Lodges of the National Protestant League be largely increased and strengthened.

'A Parliamentary Party be formed in the House of Commons, and that the support of the Association be accorded to the Parliamentary Registration Committee of the National Club.

Press

'Better looking after the interests of the Protestant Cause in the Newspaper Press.

Individual Action

'No contributions whatever to be given for any purpose connected with a Romanizing Incumbent.

Publications

'Papers to be prepared showing the extent which Ritualism has attained in each Diocese.

'Regularly and systematically supplying the rank and file of the Ritualistic Party with Protestant literature.

'Flooding the country with literature to awaken Protestant Churchmen to the danger which is now threatening them.

'A careful watch be kept on the publications of the religious Societies.

'In order to carry out the above Programme, the Council suggests that Protestant Churchmen should be urged to join the Church Association, and to form Branches of the Association and Lodges of the National Protestant League in every town and village; and it recommends that an earnest appeal be made to the country for the necessary funds to enable the Council to bring to a practical issue these far-reaching schemes.

'The Council have given the most serious thought to the above scheme, and they consider the parts which most urgently press for immediate financial support are those which concern Education, including Schools, Meetings, Lectures, Classes, Colporteurs, and Vans; Mission Work in Ritualistic Parishes; and Publications.

'The Council estimate the cost for this at £11,000. a year for the first three years; and that at the end of that period, the first great outlay in training Colporteurs, Experts, and Mission Agents, the purchase of Vans, and the printing of special publications, etc., having been made, the work begun can be carried on for an outlay for £5,300. a year.'

Advertisement in the *Record*, Dec. 23, 1892.

Bibliography

Primary Sources

Aitken, Robert. *Truth Against Truth; or, the Battle of the Covenants* (London: W. M. Pardon, 1851).
Alford, Henry. 'The Next Step,' *Contemporary Review* 10 (1869), 1-9.
Anonymous. 'Amendment of the Anglican Rubric,' *Edinburgh Review*, 126 (1867), 499-523.
- 'Archbishop Tait and the Primacy,' *Quarterly Review* 155 (1883), 1-35.
- 'Archdeacon Hare,' *Quarterly Review* 97 (1855), 1-28.
- 'The Church and the Age,' *Quarterly Review* 129 (1870), 39-63.
- 'Church Extension,' *Quarterly Review* 103 (1858), 139-79.
- 'Church Innovations,' *Quarterly Review* 141 (1876), 526-68.
- 'Church Law and Church Prospects,' *Quarterly Review* 139 (1875), 248-90.
- 'Church of England and Her Bishops,' *Quarterly Review* 114 (1863), 538-80.
- *Church Parties, by a Queen's Counsel* (London: Houlston & Sons, 1874).
- 'Connop Thirlwall, Bishop of St. David's,' *Edinburgh Review* 143 (1876), 281-316.
- 'Convocation, Parliament and the Prayer Book,' *Edinburgh Review* 140 (1874), 427-61.
- 'Ecclesiastical Jurisdiction,' *Edinburgh Review* 159 (1884), 212-55.
- 'The English Evangelical Clergy,' *Macmillan's Magazine* 3 (1860-61), 113-121.
- *Facts and Documents showing the Alarming State of the Diocese of Oxford*, by a Senior Clergyman of the Diocese (London: Wertheim, Mackintosh & Hunt, 1859).
- 'The Haldanes,' *Quarterly Review* 98 (1856), 353-83.
- 'Is the Church of England Protestant?' *Quarterly Review* 146 (1878), 519-49.
- 'The Life of Archbishop Tait,' *Edinburgh Review* 174 (1891), 462-92.
- 'Memorial of the Life and Services of Vice-Admiral Sir Jahleel Brenton, Baronet, K.C.B. Edited by the Rev. Henry Raikes, Chancellor of the Diocese of Chester,' *Quarterly Review* 79 (1847), 27-310.
- 'Mr. Voysey and Mr. Purchas,' *Fraser's Magazine* New Series 3 (1871), 457-68.
- *The Position of the Ritualists, by One of the Rank and File* (London: G. J. Palmer, 1881).
- 'Private Confession in the Church of England,' *Quarterly Review* 124 (1868), 83-116.
- 'The Privy Council Judgment,' *Quarterly Review* 115 (1864), 529-80.
- 'Recent Movements in the Church of England,' *Fraser's Magazine* 74 (1866), 277- 96.
- 'The Ridsdale Judgment and "The Priest in Absolution",' *Quarterly Review* 144 (1877), 241-76.
- 'The Ritual of the English Church,' *Quarterly Review* 137 (1874), 542-86.
- 'Ritualism,' *Edinburgh Review* 125 (1867), 439-69.

- 'Ritualistic Literature,' *Edinburgh Review* 151 (1880), 281-320.
- 'The Ritualists and the Law,' *Quarterly Review* 151 (1881), 201-41.
- 'Rubic Versus Usage,' *Quarterly Review* 89 (1851), 203-56.
- 'Rubrics and Ritual of the Church of England,' *Quarterly Review* 72 (1843), 232-90.
- 'Sacerdotalism, Ancient and Modern,' *Quarterly Review* 136 (1874), 103-33.
- 'Ultra-Ritualism,' *Quarterly Review* 122 (1867), 162-212.
- 'Ultra-Ritualists,' *Quarterly Review* 126 (1869), 134-70.
- 'The Unrest in the Church of England,' *Edinburgh Review* 189 (1899), 1-23.
- *Women and Priests* (London: Haughton & Co., 1878).

Arthur, George. 'The "Lawless" Clergy of "this Church and Realm",' *Nineteenth Century* 45 (1899), 558-69.

Ashwell, A. R. and Wilberforce, Reginald G. *Life of the Right Reverend Samual Wilberforce, D.D.* Three Volumes (London: John Murray, 1880-82).

Bardsley, James. *The Christian Ministry: What it is and What it is Not* (London: Hatchards, 1872).

Barry, Alfred. 'Breach of Church Law: Its Danger and its Remedy,' *Nineteenth Century* 48 (1898), 943-56.

Bartlett, R. E. 'The Church of England and the Evangelical Party,' *Contemporary Review* 47(1885), 65-82.

_____ [R.E.B.]. 'On the Position of the Evangelical Party in the Church of England,' *Fraser's Magazine* New Series, 17 (1878), 22-31.

_____ [R.E.B.]. 'The Past and Future of the High Church Party,' *Fraser's Magazine* New Series, 17 (1878), 240-49.

Benson, Arthur Christopher. *The Life of Edward White Benson, Sometime Archbishop of Canterbury.* Two Volumes (London: Macmillan & Co., 1899).

Beresford-Hope, A. J. B. 'An Ecclesiastical Olive Branch,' *Nineteenth Century* 15 (1884), 305-16.

- 'Peace in the Church,' *Nineteenth Century* 9 (1881), 756-77.

Bickersteth, E. H. *Some Words of Counsel; A Charge Delivered at the Primary Visitation of the Archdeaconry of Exeter, 1886* (Exeter: H. Besley & Son, 1888).

- *Thoughts for Today, No. 1: Evangelical Churchmanship and Evangelical Eclecticism* (London: Sampson, Low, & Co., 1883).

Bird, C. S. *The Dangers Attending an Immediate Revival of Convocation, detailed in a letter to the Rev. G. Hutton, Rector of Gate Burton* (London: T. Hatchard, 1852).

Buckle, George E., Editor. *Letters of Queen Victoria.* Second Series. Two Volumes (London: John Murray, 1926).

Burgon, J. W. *The Oxford Diocesan Conference; and Romanizing within the Church of England: Two Sermons.* Second Edition (Oxford: James Parker & Co., 1873).

Bury, Charles A. *The Church Association* (London: William Macintosh, 1873).

Close, Francis. *An Apology for the Evangelical Party* (London: J. Hatchard & Son, 1846).

- *Auricular Confession and Priestly Absolution: Three Sermons* (London: Hatchard & Sons, 1873).
- *The Restoration of Churches is the Restoration of Popery* (London: Newman & Co., 1881 reprint).

Colley, James. *Evangelical Churchmanship: True Churchmanship* (London: William MacIntosh, 1869).

Colquhoun, J. C. *Shall Protestant Churchmen Take Part in Convocation and Diocesan Synods?* (London: Hatchards, 1869).

Conybeare, W. J. 'Church Parties,' in *Essays Ecclesiastical and Social*. Reprinted, with additions, from the *Edinburgh Review* (London: Longman, Brown, Green & Longman, 1855).

Corrance, H. C. 'The Development of Ritualism,' *Contemporary Review* 74 (1898), 91-106.

Cutts, Edward L. *Dictionary of the Church of England* (London: Society for Promoting Christian Knowledge, 1877?).

Davidson, Randall Thomas and Benham, William. *Life of Archibald Campbell Tait, Archbishop of Canterbury*. Two Volumes (London: Macmillan & Co., 1891).

Davies, J. Llewelyn. 'The Revivals of 1859,' *Macmillan's Magazine* 1 (1860), 363-73.

Ellicott, C. J. 'The Church of England, Present and Future,' *Nineteenth Century* 1 (1877), 50-71.

— 'The Ridsdale Judgment and Its Results,' *Nineteenth Century* 1 (1877), 753-73.

Enraght, R. W. *My Ordination Oaths and Other Declarations: Am I Keeping Them?* (London: Simpkin, Marshall, & Co., 1880).

Farrar, F. W. 'The Principles of the Reformation,' *Contemporary Review* 64 (1893), 351-61.

— 'Sacerdotalism,' *Contemporary Review* 62 (1892), 48-58.

— 'Undoing the Work of the Reformation,' *Contemporary Review* 64 (1893), 60-73.

Garbett, Edward. *Diocesan Synods* (London: William Hunt & Co., 1868).

Garratt, Samuel. *What Shall We Do? Or, True Evangelical Policy* (London: William Hunt & Co., 1881).

Girdlestone, Charles. *An Appeal to Evangelical Churchmen in Behalf of Liturgical Revision* (London: William Hunt & Co., 1864).

— *Gospel Christianity; or, the Religion of the Bible Compared with Sceptical Theology and Papal Superstition* (London: William Hunt & Co., 1866).

Girdlestone, W. Harding. *The Romanizing Tendency of Ultra-Ritualism* (London: Rivingtons, 1867).

Gladstone, W. E. 'The Evangelical Movement: Its Parentage, Progress and Issue,' *British Quarterly Review* 70 (1879), 1-14.

— 'Ritualism and Ritual,' *Contemporary Review* 24 (1874), 663-81.

Goode, William. *The Doctrine of the Church of England as to the Effects of Baptism in the Case of Infants* (London: Hatchard & Sons, 1849).

Gresley, W. *The Real Danger of the Church of England* (London: James Burns, 1846).

Halifax, Viscount. 'The Present Crisis in the Church of England,' *Nineteenth Century* 45 (1899), 173-97.

Hodder, Edwin. *The Life and Work of the Seventh Earl of Shaftesbury, K.G.* Popular Edition (London: Cassell & Co., 1890).

Howson, J. S. *Before the Table* (London: Macmillan & Co., 1875).

Jessopp, Augustus. 'Are They Grievances?' *Nineteenth Century* 26 (1889), 825-32.

Knox, E. A. *An Address Respecting Cuddesdon College, Intended to Have Been Delivered at the Oxford Diocesan Conference, 1878* (London: Simpkin, Marshall, & Co., 1878).

Knox Little, W. J. 'Archdeacon Farrar and the "Ritualists",' *Contemporary Review* 64 (1893), 182-97.
Lecky, William E. H. 'The History of the Evangelical Movement,' *Nineteenth Century* 6 (1879), 280-92.
Loraine, Nevison. *The Church and Liberties of England* (London: Smith, Elder & Co., 1876).
MacColl, Malcolm. 'The Rationale of Ritualism,' *Contemporary Review* 17 (1871), 176-91.
MacDonnell, John Cotter. *The Life and Correspondence of William Connor Magee.* Two Volumes (London: Isbister & Co., 1896).
Mant, Richard. *Horae Liturgicae: Containing, Liturgical Discrepancy; Its Extent, Evil, and Remedy... and Liturgical Harmony; Its Obligations, Means, and Security against Error...* (New York: Stanford & Swords, 1847).
Miller, John C. 'The Confessional,' in *Church Association Lectures, 1867* (London: Hatchards, 1867).
– *Special Services in the Church of England: A Letter to the Rt. Hon. the Earl of Shaftesbury* (London: Thomas Hatchard, 1858).
Molyneux, Capel. *The Bennett Judgment. Our Duty: What is it?* (London: W. Hunt & Co., 1872).
Moule, H. C. G. *The Evangelical School in the Church of England* (London: James Nisbet & Co., 1901).
Paddon, T. H. *Thoughts for the Christian Laity* (London: William Macintosh, 1873).
– *Thoughts on the Evangelical Preaching of the Present Day.* Fourth Edition (London: William Macintosh, 1872).
Pelham, John T. *A Charge delivered to the Clergy and Churchwardens of the Diocese of Norwich* (London: Rivingtons, 1872).
Perry, George G. 'The Grievances of High Churchmen,' *Nineteenth Century* 26 (1889), 500-08.
Plumptre, C. H. 'Church Parties, Past, Present and Future,' *Contemporary Review* 7 (1868), 321- 46.
Price, Aubrey. 'The Doctrines of Our Church Positive and Primitive; Ritualism Negative and Novel,' in *Church Association Lectures, 1869* (London: Hatchards, 1869).
Richardson, John. 'Ritualism, Too Late and Too Soon; Too Little and Too Much; Too Narrow and Too Wide,' in *Church Association Lectures, 1869* (London: Hatchards, 1869).
Rogers, J. Guinness. *The Bennett Judgment and Recent Episcopal Charges* (London: Hodder & Stoughton, 1872).
Ryle, J. C. 'Archbishop Laud and His Times,' in *Church Association Lectures, 1869* (London: Hatchards, 1869).
– *A Charge Delivered to the Clergy of the Diocese of Liverpool... October 27, 1887* (London: William Hunt & Co., 1887).
– *Church and State, a Paper Read at the Croydon Church Congress* (London: William Hunt & Co., 1877).
– 'The Church Courts Commission.' *Contemporary Review* 45 (1884), 168-74.
– *A Churchman's Duty about Diocesan Conferences* (London: William Hunt & Co., 1871).

- *Facts and Men. Being Pages from English Church History, between 1553 and 1683* (London: William Hunt & Co, 1882).
- *No Uncertain Sound: Charges and Address* (Edinburgh: The Banner of Truth Trust, 1978).
- *The Outlook: An Opening Address at the Liverpool Diocesan Conference, 1886* (London: William Hunt & Co., 1886).
- *Warnings to the Churches* (Edinburgh: The Banner of Truth Trust, 1967).
- *We Must Unite!* (London: William Hunt & Co., 1868).

Shore, T. Teignmouth. 'Auricular Confession,' *Nineteenth Century* 37 (1895), 71-85.

Stanley, Arthur P. *Christian Institutions: Essays on Ecclesiastical Subjects.* Fourth Edition (London: John Murray, 1884).
- 'How Shall We Deal with the Rubrics?' *Contemporary Review* 23 (1873-74), 485-96.

Stewart, David D. *Evangelical Opinion in the Nineteenth Century* (London: Hatchards, 1879).

Stock, Eugene. *The English Church in the Nineteenth Century* (London: Longmans, Green, & Co., 1910).
- *The History of the Church Missionary Society: Its Environment, its Men, and its Work.* Four Volumes (London: Church Missionary Society, 1899).

Straton, N. D. J. *Why We Should Join the Protestant Churchmen's Alliance* (London: John Kensit, 1889).

Sumner, George Henry. 'The Rationale of Anti-Ritualism,' *Contemporary Review* 17 (1871), 540-58.

Taylor, W. F. 'Ritualism, the Enemy of Domestic Peace, Doctrinal Purity, Social Progress, and National Independence,' in *Church Association Lectures, 1869* (London: Hatchards, 1869).

Thomson, Ethel H. *The Life and Letters of William Thomson, Archbishop of York* (London: John Lane, 1919).

Thorold, Anthony W. 'The Evangelical Clergy of 1868,' *Contemporary Review* 8 (1868), 569-96.
- *Parochial Missions* (London: W. Isbister & Co., 1873).

Tinling, J. F. B. *The Gospel in the Churches; a Plea for Special Evangelistic Services by the Regular Ministry* (London: Samuel Bagster & Sons, 1879).

Vaughan, Edward T. 'The Commission on Ritualism,' *Contemporary Review* 6 (1867), 62-81.

Waldegrave, Samuel. *The Christian Ministry not Sacerdotal but Evangelistic* (London: W. Hunt & Co., 1867).

Walsh, William. *The Secret History of the Oxford Movement* (London: Swan Sonnenschien & Co., 1897).

Wilcox, J. C. *Contending for the Faith: John Kensit, Reformer and Martyr* (London: Protestant Truth Society, 1902).

Secondary Sources

Alister, D. S. 'Anglican Evangelicalism in the Nineteenth Century,' in *The Evangelical Succession in the Church of England.* Edited by D. N. Samuel (Cambridge: James Clarke & Co., 1979).

Altholz, Josef L. 'Alexander Haldane, the *Record*, and Religious Journalism,' *Victorian Periodicals Review* 20 (1987), 23-31.

Balda, Wesley. 'Simeon's "Protestant Papists": A Sampling of Moderate Evangelicalism within the Church of England, 1839-1865,' *Fides et Historia* 16 (1983), 55-67.

Balleine, G. R. *A History of the Evangelical Party in the Church of England*. Revised edition with an Appendix by G. W. Bromiley (London: Church Book Room Press, 1951).

Bebbington, D. W. *Evangelicalism in Modern Britain: A History from the 1730s to the 1980s* (London: Unwin Hyman, 1989).

Bentley, James. *Ritualism and Politics in Victorian Britain* (Oxford: Oxford University Press, 1978).

Berwick, Geoffrey. 'Close of Cheltenham: Parish Pope, Parts One and Two,' *Theology* 39 (1939), 193-201, 276-85.

Best, G. F. A. 'Popular Protestantism in Victorian Britain,' in *Ideas and Institutions of Victorian Britain*. Edited by Robert Robson (New York: Barnes & Noble, 1967), 115-42.

Bowen, Desmond. *The Idea of the Victorian Church* (Montreal: McGill University Press, 1968).

Brilioth, Yngve. *Three Lectures on Evangelicalism and the Oxford Movement* (Oxford: Oxford University Press, 1934).

Carpenter, S. C. *Church and People, 1789-1889: A History of the Church of England from William Wilberforce to 'Lux Mundi'* Three Volumes (London: SPCK, 1959).

Chadwick, Owen. *The Victorian Church, Part One: 1829-1859*. Third Edition (London: A. & C. Black, 1971).

– *The Victorian Church, Part Two: 1860-1901*. Second Edition (London: A. & C. Black, 1972).

Coats, R. H. *Types of English Piety* (Edinburgh: T. & T. Clark, 1912).

Cockshut, A. O. J. *Anglican Attitudes* (London: Collins, 1959).

Cowie, Leonard W. 'Exeter Hall,' *History Today* 18 (1968), 390-97.

Crowther, M. A. *Church Embattled: Religious Controversy in Mid-Victorian England* (Hamden: Archon Books, 1970).

Cuming, G. J. *A History of Anglican Liturgy* (London: Macmillan & Co., 1969).

Davies, Horton. *Worship and Theology in England, Volume 4: From Newman to Martineau, 1850-1900* (Princeton: Princeton University Press, 1962).

Dendy, D. R. *The Use of Lights in Christian Worship*. Alcuin Club Collections, Volume 41 (London: SPCK, 1959).

Edwards, David L. *Leaders of the Church of England, 1828-1944* (Oxford: Oxford University Press, 1971).

Elliott-Binns, Leonard. *The Evangelical Movement in the English Church* (Garden City: Doubleday, Doran & Co., 1928).

France, R. T. *Women in the Church's Ministry* (Grand Rapids: William B. Eerdmans Publishing Co., 1997).

Heeney, Brian. *A Different Kind of Gentlemen: Parish Clergy as Professional Men in Early and Mid-Victorian England* (Hamden: Archon Books, 1976).

Hempton, David. *Religion and Political Culture in Britain and Ireland* (Cambridge: Cambridge University Press. 1996).

Houghton, Thomas. *The Oxford Movement Exposed* (London: Thynne & Co., 1932).

Hylson-Smith, Kenneth. *Evangelicals in the Church of England, 1734-1984* (Edinburgh: T. & T. Clark, 1988).
Johnson, Dale A. 'The Oxford Movement and English Nonconformity,' *Anglican and Episcopal History* 59 (1990), 76-98.
Kent, John. 'Anglican Evangelicalism in the West of England, 1858-1900,' in *Protestant Evangelicalism: Britain, Ireland, and America, c.1750-c.1950.* Studies in Church History, Subsida, Vol. 7. Edited by Keith Robbins (Oxford: Basil Blackwell, 1990).
— *Holding the Fort: Studies in Victorian Revivalism* (London: Epworth Press, 1978).
Klaus, Robert J. *The Pope, the Protestants and the Irish: Papal Aggression and Anti-Catholicism in Mid-Nineteenth Century England* (New York: Garland Publ., 1987).
Lewis, Donald M. *Lighten Their Darkness: The Evangelical Mission to Working-Class London, 1828-1860* (Westport: Greenwood Press, 1986).
Machin, G. I. T. *Politics and the Churches in Great Britain, 1832-1868* (Oxford: Oxford University Press, 1977).
— *Politics and the Churches in Great Britain, 1869-1921* (Oxford: Oxford University Press, 1987).
Marsh, Peter T. *The Victorian Church in Decline: Archbishop Tait and the Church of England, 1868-1882* (London: Routledge & Kegan Paul, 1969).
Mole, David E. H. 'John Cale Miller: A Victorian Rector of Birmingham,' *Journal of Ecclesiastical History* 17 (1966), 95-103.
Neill, Stephen. *Anglicanism.* Fourth Edition (London: Mowbray & Co., 1977).
Newsome, David. *The Wilberforces and Henry Manning* (Cambridge: Harvard University Press, 1966).
Newton, John A. *Search for a Saint: Edward King* (London: Epworth Press, 1977).
Nias, J. C. S.. *Gorham and the Bishop of Exeter* (London: SPCK, 1951).
Nikol, John. 'The Oxford Movement in Decline: Lord John Russell and the Tractarians, 1846-1852,' *Historical Magazine of the Protestant Episcopal Church* 43 (1974), 341-57.
Norman, E. R. *Anti-Catholicism in Victorian England* (New York: Barnes & Noble, 1968).
Paz, D. G. 'Popular Anti-Catholicism in England, 1850-1851.' *Albion* 11 (1979), 331-59.
Pollard, Arthur. 'Anglican Evangelical Views of the Bible, 1800-1850,' *Churchman* 74 (1960), 166-74.
Prestige, G. L. *St. Paul's in its Glory, 1831-1911* (London: SPCK, 1955).
Ralls, Walter. 'The Papal Aggression of 1850: A Study in Victorian Anti-Catholicism.' *Church History* 43 (1974), 242-56.
Reed, John Shelton. *Glorious Battle: The Cultural Politics of Victorian Anglo-Catholicism* (Nashville: Vanderbilt University Press, 1996).
Russell, George W. E. *A Short History of the Evangelical Movement* (London: A. R. Mowbray & Co., 1915).
Saward, Michael. *The Anglican Church Today: Evangelicals on the Move* (London: Mowbray, 1987)
Scotland, Nigel. *John Bird Sumner, Evangelical Archbishop* (London: Gracewing, 1995).

- 'John Bird Sumner in Parliament,' *Anvil* 7 (1990), 141-53.
Simpson, W. J. Sparrow. *The History of the Anglo-Catholic Revival from 1845* (London: George Allen & Unwin, 1932).
Smyth, Charles. 'The Evangelical Movement in Perspective,' *Cambridge Historical Journal* 7 (1943), 160-74.
Taylor, J. R. S. 'Gorham on Infant Baptism,' *Churchman* New Series 66 (1952), 141-47.
Toon, Peter. *Evangelical Theology, 1833-1856: A Response to Tractarianism* (London: Marshall, Morgan & Scott. 1979).
- 'J. C. Ryle and Comprehensiveness,' *Churchman* New Series 89 (1975), 276-283.
Voll, Dieter. *Catholic Evangelicalism* (London: Faith Press, 1963).
Welch, P. J. 'Bishop Blomfield and the Development of Tractarianism in London,' *Church Quarterly Review* 155 (1954), 332-44.
White, James F. *The Cambridge Movement* (Cambridge: Cambridge University Press, 1962).
Wolffe, John. 'Evangelicalism in mid-nineteenth-century England.' In *Patriotism: The Making and Unmaking of British National Identity*. Vol. 1. Edited by Raphael Samuel (London: Routledge, 1989).
Wood, M. A. P. 'The Vestments Canon,' *Churchman* New Series 72 (1958), 5-9.
Yates, Nigel. *The Oxford Movement and Anglican Ritualism* (London: The Historical Association, 1983).
Yates W. N. '"The Only True Friend": Ritualist Concepts of Priestly Vocation,' *in Religious Motivation: Biographical and Sociological Problems for the Church Historian*. Studies in Church History. Vol. 15. Edited by Derek Baker (Oxford: Basil Blackwell, 1978).

Index of Persons and Subjects

Aitken, Robert 59n73
Aitken, William Hay 224n90
Alford, Charles R. 447n80, 454n120, 477n14, 466f.
Alford, Henry 73n130, 93, 186
Allen, Hugh 28
Altar Candles 84, 86, 91, 115n54, 132, 245f., 356, 397n109, 418, 424, 440n51, 450n95
Andrews, T. R. 108n27, 255n24, 259n35, 269n66, 285, 301f.
Auricular Confession 30f., 199, 205n7, 238f., 248, 462, 486.
Auriol, Edward 175n87

Bardsley, James 271n74
Baring, Charles 90, 258n30, 271n72
Baring, Frederick 31
Barlow, William H. 466, 487n20
Barry, Alfred 208n22, 459n138, 481n35
Bartlett, R. E. 214n52, 226n100, 230n112, 314n29, 339f.
Battersby, T. D. Harford 152
Bayley, Emilius 361
Bell, Charles 381n59, 385n73, 442n58, 456n128
Bell Cox, James 359f., 398n112
Bennett, William J. E. 53n53, 55n56, 136, 190, 221n78, 232f., 297f., 332n100, 447n83, 500
Benson, Edward W. 218n63, 276n90, 390n92, 392n94, 398n112, 403n125, 410f., 417, 420, 422f., 449n93, 452n110, 459n138
Beresford-Hope, A. J. B. 266n52, 268n58
Berkeley, G. W. 291f.
Bickerstaff, M. J. 384n70
Bickersteth, Edward H. 102n7, 217n62, 219n75, 352, 364n3, 366n8, 390n88, 405f., 455n124
Bird, C. S. 54n55, 183f.
Blackwood, Stevenson 400n117, 445n70

Bligh, E. V. 235, 276n88
Blomfield, C. J. 17f., 22f., 62n83
Blunt, Walter 18
Bodington, Charles 322n64
Body, George 220n76
Boultbee, T. P. 234
Bovile, E. C. 456n131, 474n2
Browne, Edward H. 271n72, 390n92, 417
Burgon, J. W. 202f.
Bury, Charles 107n24, 178n97, 252n12, 254n19

Cadman, William 169n69, 304, 361, 366n8, 368n18
Calthrop, Gordon 487n20
Cambridge Camden Society 19
Carter, T. T. 273n78, 277n94, 292, 311n17, 359
Champneys, W. W. 65n88, 407
Christopher, A. M. W. 479n23
Church, R. W. 297, 327n86
Church Association 72n125, 81f., 85f., 88f., 95f., 132, 134, 136, 139, 142, 149f., 151f., 177n96, 200, 202, 232f., 235f., 237, 239, 244, 248, 269n66, 284f., 289f., 292f., 301f., 317n44, 330n93, 344, 347f., 350f., 353f., 359f., 405, 408f., 410f., 414f., 418f., 421f., 425f., 447n67, 454n122, 456n131, 458n138, 460f., 467, 486f., 488f., 492., 506f., 508f., 514f.
Church Congresses 187f., 336n122, 467f., 476n10,
Church Missionary Society 38, 59n67, 116n61, 128n116, 408f., 464, 475n6, 477n14, 479n21, 507f.
Church Pastoral-Aid Society 38, 321n58, 342, 425, 464f., 467
Churchmen in Council 416f., 447n84
Clarke, Benjamin S. 216n61, 456n130, 457n133
Claughton, Piers 292f.

Clerical and Lay Associations 89, 151f., 188, 253n18, 304, 475n6
Clifford, J. B. 200f.
Close, Francis 20, 47n22, 71n120, 145f., 170n70, 191f., 201, 240, 287, 300, 329n88, 342
Cobham, Alexander 359, 434n28, 420f., 453n113, 454n122, 476n8
Colenso, John W. 79f.
Coleridge, John 121n77, 123n88
Collette, C. H. 177n95
Colley, James 50n31, 106n22, 155n11
Colquhoun, J. C. 89, 96f., 149, 185, 190, 198, 210n30, 218n66
Compton, Alwyne 327n86
Convocation 83f., 93, 95, 98, 183f., 238, 240, 244f., 248, 267n56, 343, 358, 383n68, 416, 467f., 476n10, 484f., 488f., 505f.
Conybeare, W. J. 40
Court of Arches 22, 56n60, 112n40, 131f., 135, 143, 233, 245, 247, 282f., 288, 343, 351, 357, 449n88, 450n94
Courtenay, John 101n4
Cowie, B. M. 327n86

Dale, Thomas P. 288f., 290, 321n59, 347
Davidson, Randall 393n100, 421, 448n88, 458n135
Davies, J. Llewelyn 298f.
Denison, George A. 80, 127n114, 149, 192f., 262n43, 267n57, 411
Diocesan Synods 195f., 336n122, 467f., 476n10
Disestablishment 248, 264n46, 425n5, 460
Dobson, J. P. 38

Eastward Position (Eucharist) 115n54, 136, 140, 241f., 245f., 339, 355, 397n109, 417, 424, 440n51, 470, 484, 488f.
Ebury, Lord (Robert Grosvenor) 65n88, 111n39
Ecclesiastical Courts Commission 357f., 394n101, 506f.
Edouart, A. G. 26
Eliot, Philip F. 352f.

Ellicott, C. J. 118n68, 202, 246, 258n31, 262n43, 309n12, 438n40
English Church Union 66n93, 78, 84f., 96f., 107n24, 153, 240, 245f., 252n13, 274n83, 283, 287, 289, 309n12, 329n90, 343, 345, 348, 362, 376n45, 391n92, 406, 438n40, 441n55, 449n88, 477n14, 493f.
Enraght, R. W. 288f., 330n93, 350, 378n53,
Episcopal Authority 236f., 240, 242f., 285, 289f., 302, 329n90, 343f., 357, 359f., 374n41, 378n53, 396n106, 409, 421f., 461, 487f., 503
Evangelical Alliance 38
Evangelical Protestant Union 287, 332n103
Evangelical Union for Church Reform 186
Evening Communion 339, 355

Farrar, F. W. 72n122, 320n54, 462
Faulkner, R. R. 20
Five Deans Memorial 296f., 324n68, 490f.
Fox, G. T. 50n31, 286f., 313n27, 315n33, 338, 366n8
Fraser, James 108n27, 143, 255n24, 323n64, 344f., 370n26, 394n101, 406
Fremantle, W. R. 80n 186, 328n87, 485

Garbett, Edward 96, 101n6, 178n96, 194, 196, 304, 336n122, 485
Garratt, Samuel 44n10, 48n26, 53n52, 112n41, 199f., 302f., 383n68, 438n43, 457n133
Generational Division 191f., 302, 315n36, 340, 366n8, 377n50, 386n74, 402n124, 441n57, 478n18
Girdlestone, Charles 79, 105n21, 111n39
Girdlestone, Harding 106n22
Gladstone, William E. 97, 159n29, 170n72, 262n44, 368n17, 405, 431n12, 470
Glover, Richard 368n18
Goe, F. F. 361
Golightly, C. P. 35f., 75n133

Goode, William 22, 81
Goodwin, Harvey 120n73, 168n62, 246, 376n45, 435n29, 441n54
Gorham, George C. 4, 21f.
Green, Sidney F. 343f., 347f., 362f., 376n46, 390n89, 505f.
Gresley, William 40, 47n22, 51n38, 172n82
Grimthorpe, Lord 414, 417, 420, 435n32, 453n112
Gurney, J. H. 34, 65n88

Haig, F. T. 408f.
Hakes, James 360f.
Haldane, Alexander 101n6, 150
Hamilton, Walter K. 87
Hanbury, Culling 88
Hawksley, John 160n31
Heywood, Percival 344f.
Hoare, Edward 178n96, 304
Hoare, J. Gurney 65n88
Holland, Charles 284f.
Holt, James M. 325n72, 353f., 359, 381n60, 387n78
Hook, William F. 26, 71n119
Hope, A. J. Beresford 120n72
Hope-Scott, James 56n60
Howley, William 19
Howson, J. S. 229n110, 270n69, 272n76, 329n88
Hymns Ancient and Modern 145, 341f., 368n16

Incense 91, 132, 245f., 356
Islington Clerical Conference 88, 146f., 151, 304, 338, 340, 352f., 442n57, 466f.

Jackson, John 139f., 143f., 228n106, 263n45, 290f., 310n17, 350f., 378n53
Jessopp, Augustus 394n100
Jones, Harry 223n85
Judicial Committee of the Privy Council 22, 80, 97, 112n40, 132, 136f., 138f., 193, 233, 239, 245f., 277n94, 309n12, 347, 378n53, 401n120, 406, 411, 420, 422f., 449n88, 450n94, 453n118, 491f., 504, 514

Keble, John 55n56
Kennion, Alfred 302
Kennion, Robert 287
Kensit, John 436n34, 448n85, 470, 479n24
King, Bryan 28f.
King, Edward 405f., 410f., 417f., 423, 451n97, 453n118, 477n14
Kitto, J. F. 468f., 478n20
Knox, Edmund A. 76n142, 217n63
Knox Little, W. J. 72n122, 323n64, 453n111

Lake, W. C. 327n86
Laurie, Emilius 436n34
Lee, Frederick G. 28f., 421, 494f.
Legislation (Anti-Ritualist) 79, 82f., 88f., 92, 94, 134f., 267n57, 422
Liddell, Robert 31f., 112n40
Liddon, Henry P. 35, 299, 358, 405f., 451n97
Littledale, R. F. 180n105, 220n76, 447n83
Litton, Edward A. 103n16, 210n30
Lloyd, H. W. 37
London City Mission 100n4
London Clerical and Lay Union 169n69, 462, 477n11
London Diocesan Home Mission 26
Longley, Charles T. 84, 117n65, 132
Loraine, Nevison 256n25, 261n40
Lowder, Charles 299, 350
MacColl, Malcolm 173n83, 175n88
Mackarness, John F. 76n142, 141, 292, 313n28, 359, 390n92, 396n106, 401n120, 409
Mackonochie, Alexander H. 67n100, 87, 131f., 137f., 151, 190, 282f., 291, 320n57, 330n93, 349f., 365n7, 413, 500f.
Maclagan, William D. 221n78, 323n64
McMullen, J. A. 342
M'Neile (McNeile), Hugh 27, 61n78, 127n114, 191, 210n30, 276n88
Magee, William C. 75n132, 102n7, 107n24, 219n74, 226n101, 236, 257n27, 264n49, 280n105, 320n54, 323n65, 326n76, 363n2, 390n91, 432n15, 481n42

Manning, Henry E. 55n56, 73n126
Mansfield, George 220n77
Mant, Richard 42n6, 99
Marshall, J. W. 336n122, 414f., 444n66
Martin, John 132, 311n18, 322n63, 350, 501f.
Mason, Charles 353f.
Miller, Henry 387n81, 416
Miller, John C. 61n78, 63n86, 80, 108n26, 116n59, 133, 147f., 201, 210n30, 327n83, 340
Milman, W. H. 328n80
Milner, J. W. 413
Mixed Chalice (Eucharist) 115n54, 132, 136, 245f., 397n109, 417, 440n51
Molyneux, Capel 62n83, 234f.
Money, C. F. S. 199, 304, 485
Montagu, Robert 437n38
Morrison, W. Robert 209n28
Morse, Francis 192f.
Moule, H. C. G. 225n91, 413, 479n23, 481n35
Musgrave, Thomas 21, 184
Music 82, 144f., 340f., 384n70

National Protestant Church Union 462f.
Neo-Evangelical 315n36, 478n18
Newell, C. F. 400n116
Nightingale, Florence 33f.

Oakley, John 406f.
Osborne, Sydney G. 87f.

Paddon, T. H. 168n62, 208n24, 214n52
Page, A. S. 226n96
Palmer, W. C. 292f., 299, 318n46, 331n95,
Payne Smith, Robert 329n88, 387n81, 415f.
Pelham, John T. 185, 189
Penzance, Lord 245f., 247, 278n96, 282f., 284, 288, 318n49, 343, 351, 357, 362, 375n45, 379n55,
Perowne, J. J. S. 298f., 329n88, 416, 447n81, 453n111, 477n14
Perry, Charles 304, 329n88

Perry, George 268n59, 394n100
Perry, Thomas W. 114n54, 119n70
Phelps, W. W. 193, 296, 334n108, 342
Phillimore, Robert 100n4, 118n68, 120n73, 123n88, 132, 135f., 233, 246f.
Phillpotts, Henry 18f., 21, 23, 85
Plumptre, E. H. 125n96, 147, 155n12, 179n103, 249n2, 264n48, 383n68
Poole, Alfred 31f.
Prayer Book Revision 239, 426
Price, Aubrey 162n38
Protestant Churchmen's Alliance 414f., 447n81, 455n125, 461f., 475n6, 512f.
Protestant Truth Society 448n85
Public Worship Regulation Act (1874) 142, 237f., 245, 248, 282f., 289, 291, 326n76, 357, 369n23, 382n61, 395n103, 410, 503
Purchas, John 135f., 138f., 484
Purey, A. P. 327n86
Pusey, E. B. 55n56, 80, 97, 190, 251n10, 267n57, 297f.

Rationalism 79f., 96f.
Record 6, 19, 29, 33, 38f., 79f., 85, 88, 91f., 97, 104n20, 113n48, 135, 137, 139f., 144f., 149, 151f., 184, 186f., 189, 192, 198, 202f., 205n3, 223n87, 225n95, 232f., 238, 248, 257n28, 284f., 296, 300f., 303f., 306n5, 324n71, 338f., 344, 347f., 350f., 353f., 358, 360f., 372n34, 376n45, 377n52, 389n87, 391n92, 392n97, 393n99, 395n104, 405, 408f., 412, 415f., 418f., 422f., 424f., 429n6, 435n33, 437n39, 439n48, 441n54, 459n138, 464f., 473, 475n6, 476n10
Richards, Upton 157n15
Richardson, John 105n21, 189
Ridsdale, Charles J. 245f., 282, 447n83
Ritualist Popularity 143f., 286, 290, 298f., 314n29, 338f., 352, 355f., 413, 427, 468
Roberts Alexander 444n66
Robertson, W. A. Scott 244
Robinson, Arthur T. 464, 478n20

Rock 178n96, 340f., 387n79
Rogers, J. Guinness 178n98, 253n16
Royal Commission on Ritual (1867) 90f., 98, 142f.
Russell, John 23
Rust, Herbert J. 22
Ryle, J. C. 61n78, 70n112, 82, 95, 115n56, 122n80, 133, 146f., 149, 160n31, 169n69, 177n96, 185, 188, 190f., 196f., 201, 208n22, 215n60, 220n76, 230n113, 301, 304, 313n29, 330n92, 340f., 357, 360f., 366n9, 377n52, 393n98, 427, 429n5, 457n132, 461, 466, 477n14

St. George's-in-the-East 27f.
Sacramental Elements (Elevation) 84, 132
St. Paul's Mission College 65n88
Secession (Evangelical) 234f., 246, 426, 448n86, 466, 474n2
Seeley, Robert B. 150f.
Selwyn, George A. 169n66, 195, 322n64
Shaftesbury, Lord (Anthony Ashley Cooper) 4, 23, 25, 65n92, 70n113, 79, 89, 94, 97f., 103n12, 116n59, 119n69, 134f., 181n114, 186, 206n7, 212, 237, 239f., 261n41, 321n58
Sheppard, George W. 177n95
Shipton, W. E. 435n34
Shore, T. Teignmouth 416
Simpson, T. B. 85
Sinclair, William 455n126
Smith, H. Hely 332n103
Smith, P. V. 420
Smith, Reginald 240f., 419, 451n98
Smith, W. J. 462
Society of the Holy Cross 261n42, 279n102
Sowter, G. Arthur 467f.
Speck, Edward J. 367n13
Stanley, A. P. 41n1, 121n77, 168n61, 186, 384n72
Stannus, Beauchamp 419
Stephens, Archibald J. 153n3, 189
Stewart, David D. 364n4

Stirling, Charles 106n23, 426
Stowell, Hugh 210n30
Straton, N. D. J. 444n68, 445n71, 461f., 477n14
Sumner, Charles 124n93
Sumner, George H. 176n89, 210n30
Sumner, John B. 4, 22f., 25, 31, 184
Surplice (Choral) 106n22, 339, 355, 385n73
Surplice (Preaching) 17f., 117n63, 133, 135f., 143f., 339, 341, 355, 385n73

Tait, A. C. 26, 28f., 31f., 75n132, 84, 86, 93, 112n43, 117n64, 125n100, 132, 142, 161n35, 165n53, 239, 241f., 245, 250n3, 260n39, 274n82, 276n92, 297, 312n26, 321n59, 324n68, 331n95, 343f., 350f., 390n88, 403n125, 475n4
Taylor, W. F. 72n125, 174n86, 392n97, 425f.
Temple, Frederick 97, 227f., 409, 417
Thirlwall, Connop 156n12
Thomson, William 90, 96, 134, 258n30
Thorold, Anthony W. 116n61, 147, 169n69, 186, 199, 225n94, 282, 291f., 295f., 338, 389n88, 407, 427, 475n5
Times 7, 19f., 61n82, 67n102, 69n107, 71n119, 77n148, 87f., 109n30, 118n68, 121n74, 123n90, 127n114, 131f., 146, 153n1, 158n25, 161n34, 177n91, 209n27, 213n45, 221n78, 236f., 239, 248, 249n2, 253n14, 260n38, 267n57, 272n76, 275n85, 277n94, 289, 297f., 309n12, 312n23, 317n44, 319n52, 320n57, 325n71, 328n87, 350f., 370n26, 371n33, 376n46, 391n92, 392n95, 401n120, 429n4, 454n118, 458n138, 471f., 475n5
Tinling, J. F. B. 223n85
Titcomb, J. H. 191f.
Tooth, Arthur 140, 274n83, 282f., 312n26

Union of Clerical and Lay Associations 304, 359, 368n18, 411, 415, 434n26, 444n66, 461f.

Vaughan, Edward 118n66, 123n90
Venn, Henry 90, 103n15, 123n88, 225n91
Vestments (Eucharistic) 29, 84, 89f., 110n31, 115n54, 135f., 241f., 245f., 339, 355, 383n68, 397n110, 488f.
Villiers, Henry 26f.
Voysey, Charles 95f., 212n40

Waddington, J. b. 287, 315n36
Wafer Bread (Eucharistic) 115n54, 136, 245f., 288
Wagner, H. M. 158n24
Wagstaff, J. 419
Wainwright, C. H. 436n37
Waldegrave, Samuel 100n4
Walker, Samuel 210n34, 215n60
Waller, C. H. 442n58
Walsh, Walter 99n1, 261n42
Walter, John 19
Webb-Peploe, H. W. 368n18, 409, 461, 477n11, 478n20, 479n23

Welldon, J. E. C. 455n127
Westerton, Charles 221n78
Whiting, J. B. 116n61
Wickham, Edmund 194
Wilberforce, Henry 45n13, 53n53, 55n56
Wilberforce, Robert J. 55n56
Wilberforce, Samuel 25, 26, 35f., 55n56, 71n119, 80, 90, 117n64, 120n73, 143f., 209n26, 256n27, 496
Wilkins, Richard 256n27
Wilkinson, G. H. 220n76, 329n90
Wilson, Daniel 45n11, 65n88, 127n114, 146
Wood, C. L. (Second Viscount Halifax) 96, 274n83, 278n96, 283, 317n46, 347, 376n45, 406, 495
Wordsworth, Christopher 83, 242, 308n10, 417, 497
Worsfold, J. N. 218n66

Young, Edward 144f.

www.ingramcontent.com/pod-product-compliance
Lightning Source LLC
Chambersburg PA
CBHW071431300426
44114CB00013B/1384